GOVERNMENT AND POLITICS

AN INTRODUCTION TO POLITICAL SCIENCE

RANDOM HOUSE · NEW YORK

GOVERNMENT

 RANDOM HOUSE   NEW YORK

AND POLITICS

An Introduction to Political Science

Bernard E. Brown

Wilder W. Crane, Jr.

John T. Dorsey, Jr.

Alex N. Dragnich

Bernard K. Gordon

Daniel R. Grant

Avery Leiserson

John C. Wahlke

Under the editorship of

ALEX N. DRAGNICH VANDERBILT UNIVERSITY

JOHN C. WAHLKE UNIVERSITY OF IOWA

Preface

This book had its beginnings in a collective effort to teach the rudiments of political science. All the authors were at various times jointly involved in designing, teaching, and developing a beginning course in political science at Vanderbilt University. Our concern in that course, as in the writing of this book, was not to propound our various individual conceptions of the subject matter or to present seriatim the minutiae of our individual fields of specialization. It was rather to introduce students to knowledge which seemed to us the property and province of all political scientists, foundations on which students might build further by their own efforts.

It would be presumptuous to imply that this book, the result of our collective efforts toward that end, constitutes a unified, fully integrated, and totally comprehensive account of the fundamentals of political science. But we have sought to achieve considerable unity in both premises and outlook among the chapters we have individually written according to our own professional specializations. In so doing we have attempted to sketch broad outlines and to present illustrative discussions of key topics rather than to "cover" exhaustively every possible topic and subtopic. We hope, however, that the outlines are clear and commodious enough so that no teacher of political science feels we have altogether left out of the picture any topic important to the beginning student of political science.

Our concern in writing as in teaching introductory political science has been to help students understand the political world in which they must live. It was our uneasy sense that beginning students, even those who come to the study of the subject with seeming interest and concern for contemporary issues and events, often have inaccurate and quite inadequate factual information about the political realities around them. It was our conviction that undisciplined study of "current events," even if it were provocative of greater interest and concern in political affairs, would not add materially to students' understanding. What we intended to give them was some general knowledge about government and politics in human affairs generally, knowledge which they might themselves apply to whatever political issues and events become current in the future. This book, therefore, combines two different sorts of material which are usually offered separately in most political science curricula. To provide all students with some minimum common store of essentially factual awareness of the political world around them, we present country-by-country discussions of several political systems, after the fashion of many courses and many textbooks called "foreign political systems" or "comparative government." But this is a beginning only, and not the main part of the work. To help students understand more fully the factual material we have presented and to help them acquire the tools for interpreting political events around them, we offer more general, analytical discussions of the kind found in courses and books called by such names as "elements of politics" or "principles of political science."

As all authors know, credit for whatever merits this work may have is due far beyond the roster of authors and editors, numerically formidable as that roster is in this instance. All who were our colleagues in political science at Vanderbilt during the years the work was taking shape have our gratitude for their innumerable contributions and criticisms. In particular we should like to repeat our thanks to J. Leiper Freeman, Robert J. Harris, and Burton M. Sapin for their assistance during that time. Of course, as all teachers know, an especially great debt is due our students, who generously submitted to our trying out different formulations and approaches on them. By at least seeming to grow wiser over the years, even if it were not as a result of our pedagogical efforts, they have encouraged us to persevere. Anne Dyer Murphy, Random House editor, contributed greatly to the readability of the manuscript. Finally, we should acknowledge the unique contribution of Charles D. Lieber, who labored mightily to convince prospective authors that they should put pen to paper and equally mightily to make them keep it there.

JOHN C. WAHLKE
ALEX N. DRAGNICH

February, 1966

Contents

Part One

THE UNIVERSE
OF PUBLIC GOVERNMENTS

Part Two

POLITICAL RELATIONS
AMONG GOVERNMENTS

Part Three

POLITICAL BEHAVIOR
AND POLITICAL FUNCTIONS

Part Four

POLITICAL THEORY
AND POLITICAL ANALYSIS

GOVERNMENT AND POLITICS

AN INTRODUCTION TO POLITICAL SCIENCE

INTRODUCTION

On Political Science

A serious concern with the problems of government hardly needs elaborate justification today. Whoever is concerned for human values and purposes or for human survival itself must necessarily wrestle with these problems. But to deal with them intelligently men must mobilize knowledge and bring it to bear on them. This book for the beginning student of political science surveys and summarizes the political knowledge men have managed to accumulate to date, and introduces the student to the problem of adding to it by research and study. For the term "political science" refers both to a systematic body of existing knowledge and to a process for systematically expanding it.

What is the character of this "knowledge" which political science seeks and slowly accumulates—knowledge which can be found in treatises by Greek philosophers of the fifth century B.C., in commentaries by modern-day journalists, and in difficult statistical analyses by professional political science researchers, and which is at the same time relevant both to the clash of governments armed with nuclear weapons in the twentieth century A.D. and to the administration of an empire in the time of Christ? To whom is it accessible? In what form? By what means? To what uses can it be put, and by whom? These are essentially philosophical questions, and they are extremely difficult ones. The student will no doubt feel more competent to formulate his own answers after he has read and reflected on the entire book, particularly Chapter 18, where the practical implications of some of these questions are discussed more fully. But to comprehend the term "political science" and the knowledge it seeks, and to be able to analyze his own political knowledge, he must begin by grasping clearly a few basic distinctions.

Facts and Generalizations in Political Science

Public officials, average citizens, and students of government all need some familiarity with what may be called the basic "facts" of political life. A diplomat ignorant of the difference between Ghana and Guiana would be ill-equipped indeed; a voter unaware of who is incumbent in the office he votes on, of the party affiliation of candidates he chooses among, or of the duties of officials he helps elect is badly informed by any standards. A congressman or member of Parliament is universally expected to know the persons and groups he represents, what they want and do not want, as well as the established practices and procedures for dealing with them in his official capacity. Students of government are expected to know much the same sort of thing.

Most of us, for that matter, have at least an unsystematic fund of such information, gathered from a variety of sources. Journalists supply us with a stream of facts about who is who among political persons and groups, about changes in the constitution of this or that nation. Historians tell us what events preceded which in political history, how government was organized in the Roman Empire, and in what way the Roman system differed from governmental organization in ancient Greece. Anthropologists give us facts about the exotic customs and rituals of kingship in this or that primitive society.

Although it may well be desirable that one's political knowledge include all the information of this kind one can possibly digest, the most prodigious such accumulation can never in itself suffice as knowledge. We cannot use endless lists of facts by themselves to understand situations or to act in them. What we can legitimately call knowledge begins only when we make generalizations about the facts we know.

In particular, what we usually call knowledge comprises generalizations which "explain" facts. For example, in politics or government, as in physics and psychology, the questions we most want our knowledge to answer are "Why?" and "How?" Usually we already know the answers to such questions as "Who?" "What?" and "When?" Thus most of us know that there are two main political parties in the United States, two in Great Britain, one in the Soviet Union, three in West Germany, and at least six in France. But *why* is this so? Perhaps because different methods of electing legislative bodies encourage proliferation or elimination of parties. Perhaps because of the political attitudes and opinions of the respective electorates. Perhaps because of the different relations between legislature and executive in the various countries. Perhaps for all these reasons. In any case, the search for political knowledge usually begins with curiosity about why certain facts are as they are.

But by "explanation" we do not mean just the providing of simple answers to the question "Why?" "Explanation" can also lead to the discovery of new or unsuspected relationships among several sets of facts. To take a simple example, it is an easily observable fact that in countries with extensive suffrage, not everyone eligible to vote does so in any given election. It is also easy to observe that there are rich and poor, propertied and propertyless voters. The discovery that non-voting is substantially greater among poorer, propertyless voters than among richer, property-owning voters explains something about both the phenomenon of non-voting and the consequences of class differences. Non-voting can be further explained if we discover how it is related to the character of political issues in the elections, the type of political system, and to certain characteristics of voters, such as age, sex, and religious affiliation. Thus, the answer to the question, "*Why* do not all eligible voters exercise their franchise?" can take the form of a series of statements about *how* the facts of non-voting relate to various other facts.

It is not easy to satisfy curiosity about the why or how of certain facts. Once we get a satisfactory explanation for our initial inquiry, we tend at once to demand an explanation for that explanation. If it is true, for example, that election by a plurality in single-member districts promotes the two-party system in Britain, whereas proportional representation in multi-member districts has promoted a multi-party system in France, how does the electoral system bring such results about? And what difference does the number of parties make to the working of the respective governments anyway? Each answer tends to produce more questions.

To summarize this part of the discussion, we can say that whatever its particular content the knowledge political scientists seek has, to begin with, these characteristics:

1. It is embodied above all in generalizations intended to explain political facts. Although these generalizations are based on and refer to simple factual information, mere enumeration or description of the facts is not in itself knowledge for political science.

2. It aims at maximum generality. The more generally applicable an explanation, the more fundamental is the knowledge it contains. Thus we can say we know more about voting behavior if a generalization about it applies to voters in all Western democracies than if it applies only to American voters. If we could generalize accurately about voting behavior in any electoral system anywhere, we would know still more.

3. It is, as a body of knowledge, always open-ended and incomplete, never closed and final, since it inevitably includes more questions than answers. (The student should not be discouraged, therefore, if at times he finds that things appear increasingly complex instead of simpler,

or feels that the more he knows, the more there is yet to learn. On the
contrary, these are signs of increasing political wisdom.)

Facts and Values (Norms) in Political Science

There is another kind of question that we might hope to answer through
an explanation of political facts. Instead of inquiring about how something came to happen, or how one thing relates to another, we might
say, "Give me some justification why I should do thus and so," or "Of
what use is it to me to hold such-and-such a belief?" To grasp the
difference between this kind of concern and the one previously discussed, let us imagine three cases of people applying political knowledge
as we have so far described it.

Consider first a voter about to choose between candidates A and
B. Let us assume he knows the probable intentions of both candidates
and understands the processes of election and the workings of the
government in which the candidates seek office. Let us assume, indeed,
that he has perfect knowledge of all the facts about candidates and
government and of the explanations of these facts. But before he can
decide intelligently how to vote he must still know something else:
Will the state of affairs resulting from A's election be better or worse
than that which would follow B's? If he is a reasonable man, he will
vote for the candidate likely to produce the better state of affairs.

Or imagine a political leader fully educated in the causes and
conditions of revolution and perfectly informed about current political
opinion and alignments in his country. Suppose that on the basis of
this knowledge he is certain he can organize a successful revolution.
Before he can decide intelligently for or against such a course, he
must know whether the state of affairs after the revolution would be
better than what prevailed before.

Finally, consider the student who has mastered all the facts and
explanations concerning the structure and functioning of the American
system of government as compared with, say, that of Great Britain.
He cannot on the basis of this knowledge alone say which system is
better than the other. He must first ask, "Better for what?" and then
know why a system should be good for whatever that is.

Careful examination of certain features common to all three
hypothetical cases will further reveal the character of the knowledge
which political science seeks. Notice, first, that each case has to do
with making a *choice* of some kind, but in no case does the choice
involve deciding whether something is or is not factually true. Rather it
involves deciding whether something is better or worse than something
else, that is, determining the *value* of something. In two cases, the
problem is to evaluate alternative courses of action; in the third, it is
to evaluate the relative merits of two political systems.

Second, in all three cases, the knowledge we presumed for our chooser enables him to make reliable predictions about the *consequences* of the alternatives he evaluates—for example, taxes will be lower if A is elected; social burdens and benefits will be more widely shared if society is changed by revolution; the British system is better because it focuses political responsibility. The chooser in each case can say with some assurance what factual situations are associated with the different alternatives. In other words, his knowledge tells him which *means* will produce certain consequences or *ends*.

Last, and most important, the basic choice to be made in each case is the *choice among ends,* or consequences. If the chooser knows which end is better, then his knowledge enables him to choose the means of achieving it by applying simple logic. Of course in actuality the distinction between means and ends is never so simple or clear-cut. Furthermore, men frequently must choose between equally efficacious means to a given end. They may, for example, select their means on the grounds of aesthetic appeal, without regard to their actual efficacy. In any situation, means and ends act and react on each other so that the persons making choices cannot say which steps in the process concern means and which ends. Often means and ends are so bound together that choosing a given end necessarily entails choice of particular means to attain it; and any choice of means necessarily entails accepting even their unanticipated consequences. Nevertheless, the essential point for our purposes is that however simple or complicated the ends-means relationship in particular cases, there are many situations in which the decision-maker requires a kind of knowledge which we did not allot to the choosers in our three hypothetical situations above—knowledge of a *norm* or *standard of values* by which to judge the consequences of his decisions.

Everyone has the beginnings of such a standard in his unreasoned, unreflective preferences for one consequence over another. But the mere fact of subjective preference is not in itself ordinarily considered a norm or standard of values. We get norms or standards only when we begin to offer reasoned explanations why such-and-such is better than something else, when we begin to justify our belief that this is good and that is bad.

To think clearly, therefore, it is fundamentally necessary to distinguish between two classes of statements: *factual* statements, which include elementary assertions about simple facts, more abstract summarizing and descriptive generalizations about such facts, and complex explanations of them, and *normative* or *value* statements, which have to do with judgments of goodness or badness that we apply to various states of affairs or sets of facts. A factual statement asserts that something is or is not so according to observable evidence. A normative or value statement asserts that something is good or bad, worthwhile or not, better or worse. To be technically correct and to facilitate analysis of our beliefs, we should, in speaking of value statements, distinguish further between *value premises,* which assert or proclaim the standard (norm) by which one passes value judgment on something, and *evaluative statements,* which embody the actual value judgments arrived at by logical application of value premises to what is to be judged. But social scientists in general have been rather careless about such distinctions. To alert each other to the kind of intellectual problem presented by a given statement, they commonly use the shorthand terms "facts" and "values," by which they mean, respectively, any statement dealing exclusively with matters of observable fact and any statement which in any way includes either a value premise or an evaluation or both.

It is not always easy to distinguish between statements of value and factual statements. True, certain turns of speech often suggest strongly that one is making a value statement: "It would be a *good* thing if we had a change of administration"; "We *ought* to outlaw all testing of nuclear bombs"; "Every citizen *should* vote." But one must beware the many statements which appear to be factual assertions but which actually are not. From its grammatical form one might suppose the classic statement in the American Declaration of Independence that "All men *are* created equal" is quite factual. But from what we know of its authors' beliefs, we must infer that it is a disguised value statement meaning "It would be *good* if all men were treated as equals." A statement that "It *is not* a function of government to provide medical care for its citizens" usually means something like "By my scale of values it is a *bad* thing for a government to provide medical care for its citizens."

Political scientists, even more than natural scientists, must be alert to distinguish factual from value statements because, unlike natural scientists, they find value statements as part of the data they study. Moreover, the body of knowledge generally placed under the heading "political science" has traditionally included value statements as well as factual statements, although there is today a school of thought which would reserve the name "political science" for the factual parts of this knowledge and call the normative part something like "political ethics." In any case, the distinction between factual and value statements is crucially important, because words like "true" do not mean the same thing when applied to the two types of statements. Nor does to "explain" a belief about values mean the same thing as "explaining" a set of facts. In other words, the process of validation is significantly different in the two cases. Therefore, since political science deals with both "facts" and "values," the political scientists must pay special attention to the problem of validation.

Validation, Proof, and Truth in Matters of Fact

No matter how certain one feels that a statement is true, he must not confuse his merely subjective feeling of certainty with evidence or proof of truth. Political knowledge comprises statements about a real world around us, which is what it is, whatever we like to think about it at any given moment. The proof of factual statements lies not in *subjective* convictions about them but in what the distinguished scholar Arnold Brecht has called the *"inter*-subjective transmissibility" of the evidence and proof supporting them[1]—that is, the statement of reasons for believing a statement is true in terms which are communicable to others so that they, too, may test the statement.

In the effort to promote "inter-subjective transmissibility" of knowledge in many fields (including political science), scholars have developed over the years a complex body of rules of evidence and proof which have come to be called "scientific methods." In the intellectual community of mankind there is practically unanimous agreement first, on the proposition that these methods are the only ones appropriate for determining truth in matters of fact; and second, on the principal procedures and practices which make up "scientific methods."

Insofar as we are dealing with observable political facts and phenomena, the knowledge we seek is essentially scientific. Although the data it relates to and particular methods of acquiring it may differ considerably from those of the natural sciences, it shares four fundamental characteristics of all scientific knowledge. All four characteristics relate to the established rules for determining the truth or falsity of factual statements. Factual political knowledge, then, is: (1) empirical, (2) probabilistic, (3) hypothetical, and (4) theoretical.

Empirical Evidence. Any statement that something is or is not so in the political world must, if we are to accept it as true, be consistent with the observable facts. It must be consistent not just with such facts as a given observer sees or chooses to select but with all he can find or contemplate and all anyone else may point out to him. And the facts must be observable by others too, not secret facts forever unavailable to any but the person claiming to state the truth about them.

"Observing" facts is not always as easy as it may sound. There are very strict rules and very complex procedures for observing and reporting facts carefully and accurately so as to promote the "inter-subjective transmissibility" of statements about them. But this is not the place to examine those rules; here it is enough to grasp the essential requirement of empirical proof: that the terms in our state-

[1] Arnold Brecht, *Political Theory* (Princeton, N.J.: Princeton University Press, 1959), pp. 113–16.

ments ultimately have reference to observable facts and that the statements be fully consistent with what we or anyone else can and do observe.

Probabilistic Truth. Scientific political knowledge, like scientific knowledge in other fields, does not claim to embody absolute certainty. The reasons for this lie partly in the impossibility of ever bringing all the relevant facts under a single generalization and partly in the eternally questioning character of the search for knowledge we referred to earlier. *All* important propositions about politics and government are only more or less certain. All are tentative in lesser or greater degree; all are subject to continual revision; all are subject to total rejection on the basis of new evidence. No "truth" is so final that it may not in its turn be overridden by a "truer" truth. In fact, the logic of scientific research entails constant efforts to *dis*prove statements rather than to prove them. Political scientists believe the probability that their statements are true is greater in proportion to how often and how hard they have tried to prove them wrong and have failed to do so.

All this is by no means to say that one belief is as good as another. A cardinal rule of scientific method requires that we always choose the most probably correct among competing statements, however much it may upset our established beliefs. The point is that dogmatic or doctrinaire beliefs have no status as factual or scientific knowledge of government or politics. We must be satisfied with as nearly certain a probability as we can get, in the full knowledge that the odds are never 100 per cent that we are correct.

Hypothetical Knowledge. We first take the facts we know at any given moment and from a careful consideration of these facts make guesses about facts still unknown or about the meaning of those we do know. Then we methodically set out to observe as fully and accurately as possible all the facts referred to by our guess to see whether they are as we guessed they would be. If they are, then we accept the statement as probably true. The technical name for such a reasoned guess to be tested by empirical evidence is *hypothesis*.

Once we have tested and accepted a hypothesis the method of its genesis no longer interests us. Its status and character as knowledge are the same as those of the many accepted statements which preceded it into our body of knowledge. The truth of hypothetical statements, therefore, is only probable, never absolute. Hypotheses, moreover, are conditional in another sense: they usually include a specification of the circumstances or conditions under which they hold true. "In *American* elections, *if* there is a large voting turnout, *then* the odds favor the Democratic candidate." "*Where* great inequalities of wealth exist, political equality tends to polarize political alignments along class lines."

Another characteristic of hypotheses is that they generally state a *relationship* between two or more elements known as *variables*. They tell us how changes in one variable (Democratic electoral chances, political alignments) take place when changes occur in another (voting turnout, distribution of wealth). The less ambiguous the variables and the more precisely stated the relationship between them, the more useful and valid the hypothetical statement will be.

Political knowledge is therefore ideally stated in terms of clear and unambiguous concepts. Most propositions making up that knowledge are not universal, all-embracing assertions that such-and-such is true without qualification. They are rather statements which assert limited relationships among precisely defined variables and specify precisely the circumstances under which those relationships will occur.

Theoretical Knowledge. A mass of unorganized and undigested hypothetical propositions is no more adequate as knowledge, even if all the propositions are very probably true, than is a mass of disconnected facts. One function of theory is to tie together in a logically consistent fashion all our facts and hypotheses about a subject. Theoretical statements therefore use more abstract concepts than do factual or hypothetical statements, which describe more limited and particular ranges of phenomena. And since one goal of theoretical development is maximum generality, theoretical statements tend to be more universal, less conditional or qualified than those we have mentioned so far. But even though they are the most abstract and general of all statements making up our political knowledge, they are subject to all the scientific criteria discussed above.

It is wrong, therefore, to imagine that "theory" is a body of less probable and more fanciful statements than the rest of our knowledge. Theory properly so-called is the capstone on an integral structure of statements which begins with the simplest factual statement and ends with the most general and abstract. All our statements ultimately make sense, or constitute knowledge, only insofar as they fit coherently into this unified logical structure, which spans what has been called "the theory-data continuum."[2] Because of this logical connection among our statements at all levels of generality, we are able to proceed from a welter of miscellaneous facts to the simplifying summaries and explanations that are called theory. We are also able to deduce from theory new hypotheses which direct our attention to unexplored sets of facts.

Political knowledge, like other scientific knowledge, thus moves forward simultaneously along all points of the theory-data continuum, or it does not advance at all. Without the high-level abstract concepts

2 Avery Leiserson, "Problems of Methodology in Political Behavior Research," *Political Science Quarterly*, LXVIII (1953), 558–84. The term emphasizes the logical connections that make it possible to reason from miscellaneous facts (data) to high-level generalizations about large numbers of facts (theory) or from theory to facts; that is, the interconnectedness from one end to the other (continuum) of properly formulated, valid assertions about the subject matter.

of the theorist, we can know very little about political facts; but without the "grubby facts" of the empirically-minded researcher, the theorist has nothing to talk about and nothing to tell us.

Validation, Proof, and Truth in Value Problems

The hardest problems confronting statesmen, citizens, and students of government are often problems of conflicting values. One candidate says the present government policy concerning aid to education is abominable; his opponent finds many virtues in it. One set of diplomats and journalists insists their country go to war to achieve certain goals, while some of their compatriots say those goals are worthless. One person insists all "socialism" is bad; another demands immediate nationalization of all major industries.

We have seen that insofar as these opinions involve predicting what in fact will be the consequences of undertaking a given action or entertaining a given opinion, scientific knowledge may be of direct help in deciding what to do. But where the difference of opinion is narrowed to a dispute about what in essence is good and what is bad, how can we know which side is right? What knowledge can be applied to value judgments about government and politics?

Cultural Relativity and Normative Truth. We are forced at the outset to admit several perplexing difficulties. One has often been called "cultural relativity." It has always been apparent enough—and the work of modern anthropologists has made it more so—that men within a given culture may almost unanimously believe that something is good while men in another culture may be equally unanimous in thinking the same thing bad. For example, in European cultures most people would agree that trickery, brutality, and outright fraud are evil practices, in elections or any other activity. Some individuals might engage in such practices but they would be judged to be doing wrong, if not to be evil men. There are other cultures, however, where tricking, beating, and defrauding one's opponents—in political conflict, in marriage rivalries, or anywhere else—are respected and honorable practices which bring not shame but prestige and honor to the doer. Of course there are and have always been less dramatic instances of disagreement within as well as between cultures. But in a shrinking world where human relations daily mix together people of different cultures, such differences in basic value beliefs become all the more apparent. Who is to say which culture, or which competing belief within a culture, is right about what is good or bad? And how?

This brings us to a second difficulty. Not only is there a conflict about what is right or valuable, there is no agreement about the methods and standards appropriate for testing the validity of assertions about value. Some men have maintained that basic truth on these questions is set forth in an authoritative text, such as the Bible or the Koran, or pronounced unequivocally by an authoritative human voice—for example, the Pope's. But there has never been agreement among these men on who or what that authority is. Some men (not many in recent times) have thought that scientific research can reveal basic value truths, even though it has not yet succeeded in doing so. Still others have maintained that there is no such thing as basic truth in matters of values, that statements asserting something is good or bad merely report the fact that the one making the assertion likes something or doesn't, and that there can therefore never be any rational way to choose between the different preferences of different men, however violent a conflict those differences provoke. If any event, the basic requirement for "inter-subjective transmissibility" of accepted statements —practically universal philosophical agreement about the foundations of knowledge—which we found to underlie our knowledge in matters of fact is totally missing when it comes to matters of values.

Logical Analysis of Value Statements. But just because there are philosophic difficulties in demonstrating the truth of ultimate value propositions, we need not leap to the conclusion that value statements are trivial or meaningless. Whether we like it or not, they are part and parcel of the political world we want to study. Neither should we leap to the conclusion that any value belief in politics is as good as any other; that if men disagree about the values of policies, programs, or systems of government, there is no way to choose rationally between them; or that the only way to settle every value conflict is by having the stronger party impose its will on the weaker ones.

To begin with, careful analysis of the elements of statements involving values will often enable us to recognize more precisely the exact value judgment we are making. For example, in the 1930s some people frequently said that "fascism is good because it makes the trains run on time" (that is, it provides efficiency in material services). We could probably determine the factual validity of the clause asserting fascism "made the trains run on time." If that is factually true, then a person setting a high value on punctual trains (or efficiency in general, no matter what the function performed) should logically say, so far as our one original statement goes, that fascism is a good thing. And a person who for some strange reason might prefer trains never on schedule should logically conclude that fascism is a bad thing. Once we point up the precise value choice involved (not "fascism in general" but "trains running on time"), and once we investigate the factual question involved (does fascism promote punctuality or not?), then, *given* the value premises, we can assess the rationality of a value judgment on this particular point. But we still can't "prove," of course, who is "right" in his value premises.

But conflicting evaluations of something as undefined and complex as "fascism" are never so simple as this. A similar process of logical analysis, however, can clarify even complex value problems. Isolating the factual from the normative elements of statements may reveal to us an organization or hierarchy in our value beliefs of which we were unaware. For example, laymen and scholars alike have for years debated whether disciplined legislative voting of the type characteristic in the British Parliament is better or worse than the relatively undisciplined or "free" voting of American congressmen. Most of them have discovered such a question entails many essentially factual questions: Which system better promotes comprehensive and comprehensible debate? Which more readily permits powerful minority interests to obstruct debate and action? Which more effectively enables interested citizens and groups to express their opinions on pending measures? To make a value judgment between the two systems of legislative voting, one must somehow rank the values he puts on orderly and thorough debate, on quick and decisive legislative action, on full expression of views by lesser and greater interests, and on other consequences of each system. Rational evaluation of the two systems is thus promoted by knowing the consequences of each and by specifying as precisely as possible the scale of values by which one evaluates those consequences. But again, even though clarity about our value premises is of inestimable help in deciding what to believe, we are still unable to prove that those values are right.

Logical analysis can do more than help us in complex problems to differentiate issues of fact from issues of value, thereby clarifying and focusing the points at issue. It can also help us to differentiate between genuine issues of either fact or value and mere emotional reactions to words or symbols. For example, arguments between "socialists" and "free enterprisers" sometimes generate intense feeling, supposedly because each party to the dispute feels his basic values threatened by proposals stemming from the contradictory values of the other party. In many such cases, however, careful examination reveals that if there is any genuine disagreement underlying the emotional friction, it is not about values at all but about questions of fact. When the socialist inveighs against the damage to human dignity and welfare which unregulated business enterprises may inflict on numbers of wage-workers and the "free-enterpriser" extolls the capacity of a competitive and unregulated economy to provide more material goods and services for everyone and to permit the full development of every individual's potential abilities along lines each freely chooses, the ends both have in view appear fundamentally alike. The dispute, then, logically centers around the factual questions: Does the system called "free enterprise" produce results more like those expected by the socialist or the free-enterpriser? Does public ownership or other regulation of economic enterprise such as "socialists" advocate produce the kinds of results they foresee or not? And are the facts of economic life and economic relations in existing societies called "free enterprise economies" or "socialist economies" anything like the abstract "free enterprise" and "socialism" from which the disputants reason?

Many participants in this kind of doctrinal controversy may attach such emotional value to symbol-words like "capitalism," "free enterprise," and "socialism," that they in effect treat these systems as ends in themselves. Few would admit they are doing so. Most would maintain that what really matters is not the systems themselves, regardless of their consequences, but more basic human values or ends to which the systems are thought to be means.

Political Philosophy. Logic and science, then, can help us clarify and often simplify value problems. Indeed, they must be applied if these problems are to be understood and dealt with rationally. Still, they cannot supply us with certain proof or disproof of the truth of value premises. But this by no means justifies one's smugly trumpeting whatever value beliefs he happens to hold, casually accepting the rightness of whatever happens to exist, or feeling excused from thinking at all about questions of good or bad, right or wrong. Even though the validation process for value beliefs is different from that for factual matters, and even though we cannot expect universal agreement on fundamental value questions, the rational person is nonetheless obligated to strive as hard for sound value positions as for sound factual understanding.

Political study is therefore, to an important degree, philosophic study. The study of human values, or ethics, is an important branch of philosophy. Political values, like others, are properly studied by the modes of analysis devised and used by ethical philosophers. It is only when one comprehends the status of his own value beliefs and those of others in the context of ethical philosophy that he can claim in any degree to have "justified" them.

Philosophy is relevant to the understanding of politics in a still broader way. The ultimate or "essential" character of facts, particularly those about "political reality" and "human nature," is just as much a fundamental philosophic problem as is the nature of values. The character and meaning of such concepts as "truth," "knowledge," or "meaning" itself are equally fundamental philosophic problems. For example, the conception of political knowledge set forth in the preceding pages and the account of politics and government in those which follow both rest upon major philosophic assumptions which not all men share. Political understanding therefore entails philosophic analysis of all ranges and all aspects of our thinking about politics, factual or normative.

The names of great political philosophers who have wrestled with such problems—Plato, Aristotle, Aquinas, Hobbes, Locke, Rousseau, Marx, and others—loom large in the history of political science. Not only do the works of such men offer comprehensive explanations of what is true in human government and why, and comprehensive prescriptions of what they think ought to be true and why; they also attempt to relate both their accounts of actual political fact and their doctrines of political right and wrong to comprehensive and integral philosophic premises. From their works we gain both insight into political reality and understanding of political science itself.

To study political philosophy, however, is to do more than merely learn the names of several dead men and their works or a few words symbolizing their major ideas. The purpose of studying political philosophy is intellectual commitment—to learn where one ought to stand on the fundamental questions of political knowledge, and why. The study of political philosophy, therefore, means grappling with the problems treated by the philosophers in an effort to clarify or solve them, for others as well as for oneself. The same might be said for the utility of philosophy in any branch of knowledge, but the nature of the political world makes philosophy particularly germane to its study.

Science, Applied Science, and Art in Political Science

Most of us probably expect more from our political knowledge than just the satisfaction of possessing it and communicating it to others—we expect somehow to use it. Just as the pure science of physics is considered useful because men have built upon it applied sciences like engineering and electronics to solve their problems in the physical world, so the kind of "pure" knowledge of politics and government we have been describing is considered useful by many people only if it, too, can be applied to solving human problems. We should therefore consider what our political knowledge can and cannot do for us as an "applied science."

In general, there is much less agreement about what are "problems" in human relations than about what problems engineers should solve. And even where people agree that something is a problem they often disagree about a satisfactory solution to it. Where men disagree fundamentally, political knowledge cannot tell us whose definition of a problem or whose conception of a satisfactory solution is right, because it cannot tell us what political ends we ought to seek or to what particular goals our factual knowledge ought to be applied.

This means that political knowledge can often be used for purposes of which we thoroughly disapprove. The knowledge itself is neutral as far as the ends or purposes it can be put to are concerned. An often-cited illustration is Book V of Aristotle's *Politics,* which offers knowledge about the causes of revolution that can equally well serve a tyrant to protect his power against rebellious subjects, a democratic statesman to work for stability in a democratic society, a self-serving agitator to gratify his ego by commanding the forces of revolution, or a sincere reformer to work for revolution as a means to human progress.

The utilization of political knowledge, in other words, involves more than mechanical application of what is known. The choice of goals or ends to be served by it is something like the creative act by which an artist decides what kind of painting or statue he will make with his knowledge of art. Mere abstract knowledge of the mixing of paints or the structure of marble will not produce a picture or a statue. Similarly, neither "pure" knowledge of the principles of government nor more practical knowledge about campaign tactics will tell a politician whether to run for governor or mayor, or what to do in either office if he is elected.

This suggests a still more obvious way in which the application of political knowledge involves an element of "art." To be a political leader, to serve as head of an executive agency, or to write political columns for a newspaper all call for skills, talents, and knowledge beyond the "pure" understanding of politics and government. How well a person performs any of the numerous roles in society that can utilize political knowledge therefore depends on much more than the general state of that knowledge or his particular proficiency in it. Conversely, success in any of these political roles does not necessarily prove one possesses the kind of political knowledge we are discussing.

Thus there is a significant difference between the knowledge of the student of politics and government, whether professional or layman, and the art of the competent statesman, official, or intelligent citizen. The skilled political scientist may inform and enlighten men who practice the political arts. But he cannot tell them which political roles to play or where to aim their creative efforts as they play them.

Some Primitive Vocabulary

A number of words we use to express our knowledge are so basic that we should state clearly how we are using them. In some respects they come close to being what logicians call "primitive terms," terms which cannot be rigorously defined because they are elemental and used to define all other terms in a given universe of discourse. We shall therefore not attempt to give dictionary-type definitions of such words; we shall instead note carefully what assumptions about the world are embodied in our use of them.

We have used the word *government* itself, for example, as if everyone knows exactly what it means. Actually, the precise formulation of this concept is a theoretical problem of high order. Still, the term does imply several simple but basic beliefs about the world around us. Its common usage usually implies, for example, the belief that government is ubiquitous; that is, we expect to find the phenomena of government in whatever society we examine.

What is it we expect to see when we look for "government"? By anybody's definition, we look for certain people doing certain things. This simple formulation makes it perfectly clear that government is an aspect of human behavior. To understand how government works and why, we must understand how people behave and why. What we say about government must be consistent with what we observe and know of human behavior.

But we are not interested in behavior in general—only in certain things certain people do. Nor is it their physical activity as such which interests us; rather it is what their actions have to do with other men and with the whole society. We have in mind above all certain *functions* or services which we think the activities relate to. Although we may find it difficult to put into words exactly what we conceive these functions to be, still we operate on the assumption that there are certain essentially governmental functions which, human beings being what they are, must be performed wherever men live together.

The word government suggests still other assumptions about how men behave. We think of government as a *structure of institutions,* and we identify in any particular government *institutionalized groups* of men engaging in activities relevant to the performance of governmental functions. The italicized words all refer to regularities or uniformities in behavior—patterns which recur in the behavior of particular individuals over a period of time and which are seen when we compare the behavior of a series of individuals occupying an office or position. The conception of government as a structure of institutions within which men engage in activities relevant to the performance of governmental functions in society thus rests on the assumption that a distinguishable patterning of human behavior is normal and commonplace in every society. The patterns may differ from one society to another, but we expect to find patterned behavior in all of them.

Besides referring to such patterns and continuities in men's behavior, the word "government" also brings to mind the notion that things *happen* within the framework or structure of governmental institutions. We think of important actions which are not the product of the mere automatic performance by individuals of established or institutional rituals. Government is also, therefore, a process or set of processes involving choices and decisions among alternative goals and demands put forward by competing groups and individuals. We tend to use the terms *politics* or *political process* when our attention is focused on the dynamic elements which stimulate activity within the governmental structure, whereas terms like *governmental institutions* focus our attention on regularities and limitations that channel and confine activity.

Our most common political terms, therefore, reveal the fundamental assumption that it is natural and normal for human individuals and groups who live together to experience certain kinds of conflict and to use institutions of government to carry on and resolve them. There is nothing abnormal or strange about the existence of either "politics" or "government" in any society; indeed, the absence of either would be surprising.

The Contents of This Book

We can now summarize what has been said about the meaning of *political science* as an intellectual discipline. It is the study of government and politics, of human institutions and behavior concerned with the process of authoritative control of human societies. It focuses both on existing knowledge and on the means for acquiring new knowledge in these areas. Traditionally it has included study of both factual questions and ethical, or value, problems. Increasingly, however, men tend to restrict the term "science" to the study of basically factual questions by methods called scientific. In this book we have therefore reserved the term "political science" for knowledge about matters of political fact acquired by the methods of science.

But it should be clear from all we have said so far that we do not denigrate other aspects of political study. We have used broader terms like "political study" or "political knowledge" to refer to the wider field of which scientific study of government is a part. Despite the terminological ambiguity involved, we would accept the traditional view that the proper concern of the "political scientist" is with the larger field as a whole. Although the heaviest emphasis in the following chapters is on matters where we can have more or less certain knowledge, we have not hesitated to consider issues involving value choices. And though we have not especially attempted to eliminate or hide our own value preferences on any issue or problem, we have tried to distinguish clearly between these preferences and what is offered as substantial knowledge.

Part One, "The Universe of Public Governments" (Chapters 1 through 7, is essentially descriptive, presenting basic factual information about the structure of government and the actual political forces operating in a few selected contemporary governmental systems—those of Great Britain, the United States, France, Germany, the Soviet Union, and several "non-Western" countries. These systems have been selected partly because of the manifest importance of each in the political world today and partly with a view to later analytical discussion which will profit by comparison and contrast of the features they exhibit. The student will recall the admonition that factual information, even the most extensive, does not in itself constitute knowledge. Accordingly, the chapter which opens this section discusses the general framework which guides political scientists in their examination of political facts.

Part Two, "Political Relations Among Governments" (Chapters 8 through 10), presents some further basic descriptive information dealing with political relations among governments, both within nations and among them. But this section is more analytical than the first in that it begins with a general analysis of problems of intergovernmental relations and ends with an analysis of the relationship between decision-making structures and processes of domestic systems and the politics of international relations.

Part Three, "Political Behavior and Political Functions" (Chapters 11 through 17), is primarily analytical. Although additional descriptive information is offered in many cases, these chapters draw essentially on the facts presented in preceding chapters to examine the principal analytically distinguishable functions and processes of government— administration, adjudication, the formation of public opinion, interest expression, legitimate formulation of public policy, planning, and management. While the method of presentation and analysis is comparative, utilizing the major systems described earlier in the book, the aim is generalization about the institutions, functions, and processes of government, not simple comparison of descriptive facts about those systems.

Part Four, "Political Theory and Political Analysis" (Chapters 18 through 19), is devoted to problems of political theory. Here we look back at the knowledge presented in Parts One through Three and examine the key concepts used and the methods for accumulating them.

The careful reader will have noted the omission of one ingredient, political philosophy, which was mentioned earlier as part of our political knowledge. This omission results only from the complexity and seriousness of that subject. It signifies no intention to discourage the student from coming to grips with the great issues discussed by the political philosophers. Rather it reflects the belief that problems of political philosophy can most profitably be handled after the student has some political information to philosophize about.

SUGGESTIONS FOR ADDITIONAL READING

CHASE, STUART, The Proper Study of Mankind, 2nd edition (New York: Harper & Row, Publishers, 1962).

DAHL, ROBERT A., Modern Political Analysis (Englewood Cliffs, N.J.: Prentice-Hall, 1963).

HOSELITZ, BERT F. (ed.), A Reader's Guide to the Social Sciences (New York: The Free Press of Glencoe, 1959).

HYNEMAN, CHARLES S., The Study of Politics (Urbana, Ill.: University of Illinois Press, 1959).

KUHN, ALFRED, The Study of Society: A Unified Approach (Homewood, Ill.: The Dorsey Press, 1963).

LASSWELL, HAROLD D., *The Future of Political Science* (New York: Atherton Press, 1963).

LERNER, DANIEL (ed.), *The Human Meaning of the Social Sciences* (Cleveland: Meridian Books, 1959).

SOMIT, ALBERT, and JOSEPH TANENHAUS, *Profile of a Discipline* (New York: Atherton Press, 1964).

VAN DYKE, VERNON, *Political Science: A Philosophical Analysis* (Stanford, Calif.: Stanford University Press, 1960).

WALDO, DWIGHT, *Political Science in the United States* (Paris: UNESCO, 1956).

WHITE, LEONARD D. (ed.), *The State of the Social Sciences* (Chicago: University of Chicago Press, 1956).

Part One

THE UNIVERSE
OF PUBLIC
GOVERNMENTS

Chapter 1

POLITICAL SYSTEMS OF
THE WORLD

More than one hundred political entities, variously called countries, nations, or states, are displayed on a map of the world today.[1] Important as it might be to know their names and locations, however, such memory work alone would produce very little understanding of their politics. Knowledge of that sort follows from attempting to answer two basic and fairly difficult questions. The first is, *What is a political unit,* or, to put it another way, *What are the attributes of a viable political community*? The second is: *What kind or form of government does a given country have?*

These are not, of course, the only questions political scientists are concerned with. We have seen, for example, that they are interested in the purposes that are, or ought to be, sought through government: the *ends* of politics. Another line of inquiry examines what governments do: the *functions* of politics. Still another is concerned with how and by whom governments are managed—who has political power, how they exercise it, how they are controlled—the *process* of politics. All these questions are closely related and hard to disentangle. Taken together, they lead to the concept of *political systems*, the comparative analysis

[1] By "political entity" we mean a country that has relative independence and discretion in the determination of its foreign, military, fiscal and domestic policies. Within any such political unit there may be thousands of subordinate governmental units. For example, in 1957 the United States had over 100,000, consisting besides the national government and the 50 states, of some 3,000 counties, over 17,000 municipalities, more than 17,000 townships and towns, over 50,000 school districts, and 14,000 special utility or service districts. U.S. Department of Commerce, Bureau of the Census, *1957 Census of Governments* (Washington: Government Printing Office, 1957), Vol. I, p. 1.

of which is the oldest and most honorable tradition of political science,
going back to Aristotle over 2,000 years ago.

In this chapter, we shall be dealing with the first two questions
stated above. We shall see how they lead us to differentiate among political systems and to arrive at a classification whereby we can obtain
some sense of the total pattern of world political organization—or dis-
organization, depending upon whether we look at the world from the
standpoint of the unity and harmony, or diversity and conflict, of mankind.

The Unit of Political Community: A Panorama of Political Organization

The prevailing unit of political community today is the nation-state. It
has been defined as a body of people occupying a legally defined territory
and rendering habitual obedience to a politically determinate superior
authority which is at least formally independent of external control.
But this definition is not only extremely formal, artificial, and legalistic;
it is also, comparatively speaking, very modern. Both in conception and
in fact the nation-state probably does not date back further than the
sixteenth or seventeenth century. Furthermore, in our modern world
of revolutionary technological progress, cultural diffusion, economic
interdependence, and electronic communications, the nation-state as it
was known from 1500 to 1918 may well be a transitional unit of political organization.

Before the emergence of the modern state, the feudal system prevailed in most of Western Europe. This was a highly decentralized
structure of class relations, based upon the local manor or barony and
building up through a complex set of interpersonal duties and obligations, of both economic and military character, to a larger territorial
unit that might be as broad as a county, dukedom, principality, or even
a kingdom. At the higher levels in the feudal hierarchy, however, there
was usually considerable rivalry and conflict among feudal chieftains,
so that the political history of feudal systems emerges as a picture of
warring dukes and princes, each of them working through various sorts
of alliances and combinations to extend the boundaries of personal,
family domains.

The European feudal system grew out of the Roman Empire, one
of the large-scale territorial empires of ancient times. These empires
were based upon highly developed military organizations and civilian
bureaucracies, but either degenerated and decayed from within or were
broken down and conquered piecemeal by foreign "barbarians." Other
examples of the territorial empire are those of the Ottoman, Byzantine,
Macedonian, Persian, Babylonian, Assyrian, Egyptian, and Chinese

dynasties, whose rise and fall more or less cover the period from the beginnings of recorded history down through the first five hundred years of our era. The Egyptian Pharaoh and the Sumerian city-king were established institutions at the time of the earliest documents, dating from around 3000 B.C., unearthed by archaeologists. It is interesting that as one delves deeper into the past and the known facts about government become fewer, it becomes harder to distinguish the *unit* from the *form* of government. There is a considerable literature on "the origins of government," but it is much more concerned with the problems of how government arose and what form it took than with the area it covered. Did government originate spontaneously and naturally from the needs of men living in groups, or was it established through conquest and violence? Was the earliest form of government the traditional council of elders (gerontocracy), or was it perhaps the sacred and hereditary kingship that developed from the office of public magician (priest or shaman), and his control over the technique of irrigated agriculture (and consequently over the success or failure of crops)?

Despite the absence of conclusive evidence on such questions, some generalizations are warranted about the development of political units under which men have lived since the Stone Age. The Greek city-state was a highly developed unit of government whose forebears extend far back to the prehistoric village community we can still find today in India and Africa. The Bible and modern anthropology both teach us about the wandering tribes of shepherds and their nomadic unit of government, a mode of life and rule that contrasts with the settled existence of agricultural, rural communities. The latter were invariably primitive until associated with a central city or trading center. Studies of political organization among African and Australian tribes, as well as among the American Indians, have disclosed very sophisticated forms of rule, based upon extensive land areas ("hunting grounds") for hunting and fishing, but also including agriculture with copper and bronze implements. From the vantage point of the present, we may speak of a "primitive" period, in which the unit of government was the tribe or kinship group, or the isolated village community.

Either of these units of government could be welded, by conquest or agreement, into wider territorial units. By the beginning of recorded history, however, civilization seemed to be associated with two types of political unit: "country-states" or empires, and the less prevalent "city-states," composed of a commercial and financial center and a surrounding agricultural and animal-breeding area that served the double purpose of providing food and military protection. The city-states also sometimes formed maritime leagues or alliances for trading and mutual aid and protection. As a rule, however, the predominant unit of political organization in what we call ancient civilization was the land-based empire, created and ruled through military conquest by a dynastic ruler. Rome grew to greatness as a republican city-state, but in its later

flowering and widest hegemony it also followed the earlier models of
military and imperial despotism.

With the decline of the Roman Empire, political institutions in the
West evolved through the medieval patterns of feudalism, which were
eventually broken up and replaced by centralized monarchies based upon
national states—still the predominant form of rule in the eighteenth
century, when the American republic was established. Today all forms
of nation-states pride themselves upon being democracies. But notwithstanding the relatively rapid political development of the more advanced
areas, the majority of the peoples and places of the earth remained in
the earlier stages of tribal, village, and imperial-feudal class systems
that rested upon centuries of custom and tradition. (Several of these
systems surviving in modern times are discussed in Chapter 7.)

Contemporary Units of Political Community

DEMOGRAPHIC BASES OF POLITICAL UNITY

As might be expected from the foregoing sketch of human political
evolution, the members of the "world community" today are characterized by the greatest variety and inequality. The 117 government-members
of the United Nations in 1965, when compared on the basis of *territory*, included at one extreme the Soviet Union with 8,649,000 square
miles, and at the other Luxembourg with only 998. With respect to
population, it is estimated that the People's Republic of China (the Communist mainland) has over 600,000,000 people; Iceland has 170,000.
Eight countries have over a million square miles of territory; only 40
have over 100,000 square miles; three-fifths of the world's countries are
smaller than the state of Colorado. Ten countries have a population of
over 50 million; only 34 have over 10 million; two-thirds of the countries of the world have fewer people than the state of Illinois. *Natural
resources* contribute to a nation's strength as well as to its standard of
life, and here a similar range of inequality prevails among the nations,
whether we look at their energy resources (water power, coal, and
petroleum); their potential for the production of iron, steel, and machinery (iron ore, bauxite, manganese); or their grain- and food-producing
areas.

Technological and economic growth, or modernization, is an objective of national policy in almost all countries nowadays, and it is
common knowledge that the Western world and the Soviet bloc are
competing to demonstrate how their respective systems can facilitate the
industrial development of the so-called "backward" areas. A country's
level of modernization can be measured in various ways; for example,
by national income, by the proportion of the labor force engaged in
manufacturing or non-agricultural employment, or by a scale of rela-

tive economic capacity. It is significant that in 1960, out of 78 United Nations members assessed to pay the organization's expenses, only 17 countries taken together were considered able to pay over 85 per cent of the total, while the other 61 together were asked to pay less than 15 per cent.

But it takes more than people, territory, natural resources, technology, and economic capacity to make a viable unit of political organization. These factors are important, but certain other moral and emotional attributes of human association must also be taken into account, however difficult it may be to assign to any of them an exact significance. For example, politics and political organization are unquestionably influenced radically by certain effects of *geography* and *place*. Attachment to climate, topography, soil, and scenery—the sense of belonging *somewhere*, of having roots—is an important ingredient of political loyalty, though the symbol toward which such emotions are directed may be local, regional, national, or even global in scope. (We tend to think that pride of origin produces a local or narrowly circumscribed political identification, but reflect for a moment upon the incentives and qualities of the people who produced "the glory that was Rome," or "the empire upon which the sun never set"!)

Another factor that through history has powerfully influenced political unity is *race*, or nationality in a biological sense. The ancient concept of blood—the foundation of family and kinship—which we now, since the discovery of genes and chromosomes, know to be a myth, was for thousands of years the assumption upon which political organization was based. It still flourishes in areas where the tribe is the effective basis of political obligation, as in the areas settled by the Kurds in western Asia or in much of Africa, and in scattered cases like the Sicilian or Macedonian blood feuds. In such a view of politics, political jurisdiction is where the tribe is, regardless of the fixed formal boundaries of national states. Vestiges of this idea recur even in modern nations like Nazi Germany and Israel, where citizenship was explicitly derived from race and blood (*jus sanguinis*) rather than place of birth (*jus soli*).

Still another factor that influences political jurisdiction is shared *ideology*. An ideology may be defined as a relatively brief, consistent system of preferred ideas, beliefs, and values that explains the nature and destiny of man and provides a desirable course of conduct for political leaders and their followers. In earlier times ideologies were usually religious in form; since the seventeenth century, religion as a basis of political ideology has been largely displaced in the Western world by more secularized, intellectualist doctrine. Another possible basis of political community is a common stock of moral and religious beliefs: common ways of perceiving the world, typical reaction patterns to basic situations of life (marriage and the family, for example), similar ideas of right and wrong behavior among people. Sociologists call these bases of community *folkways* or *mores*.

A more popular, shorthand device for explaining political differences among peoples is the concept variously called *national character, cultural type* or *basic personality structure*.[2] It is quite persuasive to people interested in a sociological or psychological explanation of the origin of differences among national, racial, or cultural groups. But the idea of a dominant character type utterly fails to fit the facts of multi-national or multi-racial states, nor does it explain the fact that culture patterns or character types may be found over many different, and sometimes conflicting, political units, the Muslim-Arab configuration in the Middle East, for example. The strength of the idea of national character as an organizing concept lies in its emphasis upon the powerful evolutionary processes of selection, conformity, habit, and convention in producing similarities of outlook and behavior within such diverse (biologically speaking) racial or national groups as Hindus, Arabs, Jews, Frenchmen, Englishmen, Spaniards, or Americans.

THE FUNCTIONAL BASES OF POLITICAL UNITY

The viability of a political unit (as well as its size) is also related to its citizens' needs and the demands they make upon government, that is, the goods and services for which they are able and willing to pay taxes. We must not forget, however, that a political community is always more than a purveyor of services on a contractual basis that can be terminated at will by the fancy of the parties. Edmund Burke's description comes closer to the truth: "It is a partnership in all science; a partnership in all art . . . in every virtue and in all perfection."[3] Yet the performance of certain functions in response to the needs of their members undoubtedly affects the formation and persistence of political units.

Perhaps the most basic need is for *protection* from the forces of lawlessness and violence, domestic as well as foreign, so that some minimum standard of law, order, and justice prevails in the community. Many students of government believe that political organization originated in force, and that the police and military establishments perform the most basic governmental functions because they are so closely connected with the maintenance of order and political independence and the survival of the political community. A related view holds that political organization first came about naturally, but that institutionalized force quickly became necessary with the rise of social-class differentiation. Yet justice and personal liberties lie close to the center of what governments are supposed to secure for their citizens, and many would say that courts, or a judicial system for the orderly and equitable settlement of disputes between persons and of complaints against

---

[2] Walter Bagehot, *Physics and Politics* (London: 1869), chaps. 3–4; David Riesman, *The Lonely Crowd* (New Haven, Conn.: Yale University Press, 1950). For a critique, see Gabriel A. Almond, *The American People and Foreign Policy* (New York: Harcourt, Brace & World, 1950), chaps. 1–5.

[3] Edmund Burke, *Reflections on the Revolution in France* (London: J. M. Dent & Sons, 1945), p. 93.

governmental officials, are no less primary a governmental function than the provision of security by the police and the military. Regardless of such differences, note that both viewpoints agree that personal security (rights) and justice are functions of government so basic that they must be fulfilled before any question of economic functions or services arises.

Most modern communities nevertheless expect their governments to provide a wide range of *material* or *economic services.* Governments everywhere today are called upon to provide a water supply, dispose of sewage, build streets and transportation facilities, and educate children until they reach some arbitrarily decided age. In the United States, unlike most developed countries, the provision of electricity, gas, and other forms of power has commonly been left to private enterprise, but the merits of minimum housing and medical care are being increasingly debated as a proper charge upon the tax resources of the community at large. Support of a stable monetary and credit system, maintenance of reasonably full employment and prosperous conditions for business and agriculture, and provision for self-respecting conditions of old age and retirement have come to be considered "necessary" responsibilities of modern governments. The question of which *level* of government should undertake which responsibilities may of course be a subject of controversy, involving conflicts both of political values and of considerations of efficiency, as we shall see in Chapter 8. But there is no doubt today that a host of such material and economic services are among the "functions of *some* government" in all modern political systems.[4]

Governments exist, then, to secure for their people both material and nonmaterial ends, which may include political independence, security, order, justice, freedom, equality, and prosperity. Beyond such political values in all political communities, however, there is also a widespread expectation that government should pursue what is variously called public interest, the general welfare, or the common good. These phrases are, of course, symbolic, and politics in every system often revolves around different definitions of such terms, different demands made upon government in their name by contending persons, groups, and parties. The "public interest" can therefore never be defined objectively in terms of particular policies or services of government; but it is nonetheless real as a standard by which citizens evaluate their public officials, as a test of whether or not they have done their best to make the community a better place for all to live in. As one contemporary political theorist puts it, one of government's most important functions is "to make the community more of a community."[5]

4 For a functional list and classification of governmental services applicable to all political systems, see Alfred DeGrazia, *The Elements of Political Science* (New York: Alfred A. Knopf, 1951), chap. 2.
5 A. D. Lindsay, *The Modern Democratic State* (New York: Oxford University Press, 1947), Vol. I, p. 245; S. I. Benn and R. S. Peters, *The Principles of Political Thought: Social Foundations of the Democratic State* (New York: The Free Press of Glencoe, 1965).

The foregoing discussion of the specific functions and general purposes of government is not intended to introduce the question of what governments should and should not do. At this point the question that concerns us is, rather, how are the *political* functions of a society related to the area or jurisdiction of its government?

The problem is partly one of terminology, because the term "government" can refer to agencies charged with providing *technical services,* such as the post office, the sanitation department, or health and welfare departments; agencies which perform regulatory or *judicial services,* such as deciding disputes between persons or disputes involving collective entities like corporations and unions (the National Labor Relations Board in the United States, for example); agencies charged with *maintaining public order and safety,* such as the police, the courts, and the military; and the ultimate *policy-determining and coordinating authorities,* the political executive and lawmaking bodies. We most often use the term "political" with the last of these connotations. But the problem is more than one of definition, because both the manner of making political decisions and the limiting factors in such political judgments depend upon the way government is organized and staffed and upon conditional understandings in the community—sometimes explicit, sometimes traditional or customary—about the functional role and scope of governmental activity, the legal powers and privileges of groups or classes in the society and economy, and individual rights.

Thus the problem of the political unit involves not merely a country's geographical boundaries, but also the vital *functions* a political society must carry on. Normally these functions are performed in a routine, conventional way, but from time to time they inevitably become the basis of controversy between groups within the community. The conflict may be major or minor; it may raise a question of whether or not government should perform a given function, or of which level of government is the most appropriate to carry it out. If it is a major issue, some sort of political machinery must be utilized when the groups involved cannot themselves agree on a solution, if the conflict is to be settled without resort to physical force. Such machinery of authoritative political allocation and coordination (whether we call it the legitimate control of physical coercion or the organization of controversy) is as natural and necessary as any feature of social living. Whether it is used constructively or destructively depends upon the values, capacities, and skills of the people, of the leaders of their groups, and of their political representatives and governmental officials.

SUMMARY

We have seen that political units are arbitrary, conventional, and historical, whether we think of them in geographic, demographic, or functional terms. The political analyst's central concern, therefore, is to identify the conditions in any country under which there is sufficient political loyalty, cohesion, and sense of obligation among its citizens when the policies of their leaders are brought into question at times of stress and crisis. In this context, each of the factors we have discussed may be significant for that country's tendency toward unity or disunity, stability or instability, with respect to the survival of the existing governmental regime.

At one time, no doubt, a map or a table could have been constructed which would have accurately described the distribution of political systems on the basis of the racial or religious composition of their populations. To some extent this would still be a significant mode of procedure to describe the non-Western regions of the world. In most of Europe, the Western Hemisphere, and the new nations of Africa, however, the predominant form of political organization is the nation-state, the outstanding feature of which is the *multi-racial* composition of its population.

To conclude, we may state with reasonable certainty a few general principles about the problem of political units. First, political boundaries are rarely congruent with the cultural, technological, or economic bases of cohesion. Further, structures of political authority are likely to be based upon a combination of fear and force, habit and convention, identification and consent. Third, functional arrangements for securing governmental services vary among developed countries as well as between more and less modernized countries. Fourth, differences between political systems are real, as one could observe if he were to live for a time in a religious theocracy and then move to a military oligarchy, or if he were to live first in a constitutional republic and then move to a totalitarian bureaucracy. Finally, the values, perceptions, and behavior patterns of political loyalty, cohesion, and obligation held by citizens of different political systems may be objectively studied, compared, analyzed, and interpreted.

The Form of Political Organization

POLITICAL CULTURE AND POLITICAL ORGANIZATION

Varying and complex as are the geographic, economic, and cultural indices of nationhood, they seem like simplicity itself when compared with the political differences among countries. We may compare countries with respect to their type of *political system*, a complex concept that we shall use here in a composite sense. We can think of a political system as consisting of, first, *political culture*—attitudes toward and values concerning politics, political leaders, and governmental processes—and, second, *political organization*—the formal and effective power structures, including institutions for expressing public opinion

Table 1.1

Geographic Distribution of Countries of the World, by Type of Political System, 1960

	Continent and Number of Countries				
Political System	EUROPE, AUSTRALIA & NEW ZEALAND	ASIA	AFRICA	NORTH & SOUTH AMERICA	Total
1. Political democracy	17	8	—	5	30
2. Tutelary ("guided") democracy	—	4	3	4	11
3. Terminal colonial dominions	—	1	18	—	19
4. "Modernizing" oligarchy	—	4	2	—	6
5. Totalitarian or authoritarian oligarchy	13	1	—	10	24
6. Colonial, racial, or traditional oligarchy	1	7	12	3	23
Total	31	25	35	22	113

SOURCE: Classification adapted from G. A. Almond and J. S. Coleman, *The Politics of the Developing Areas* (Princeton, N.J.: Princeton University Press, 1960), pp. 559–67.

and political opposition, whereby government is controlled and authoritative decisions about public purpose and policy are expressed. On the basis of these elements, we can construct a rough classification which shows how widely the majority of the world's political systems diverge from what Westerners usually think of as the model of democratic self-government (Table 1.1).

The categories in Table 1.1 are ambiguous and controversial, but they do give us a basis for comparing the bewildering variety of political systems in the world. The student may wish to read into the table a tendency of countries to group themselves around two polar concepts—constitutional democracy and authoritarian oligarchy—toward or away from which the "intermediate" political societies may be considered as moving. Other interesting inferences can be drawn from the table; but one must be clear about the questions one is asking and reasonably sure that one's reasoning bears some verifiable and communicable relation to his observations, either about world political organization at a given point in time, or if his interest is historical, to basic trends over time.

The "classical" division of governmental forms according to the number participating in the process of governing (the one, the few, or the many) is not found in Table 1.1 because few governments, even the most centralized monarchies or dictatorships, are really run by one man, and none are "run," in the sense of their detailed, day-to-day operation, by "the many." This point raises one of the most fundamental problems in political analysis, namely, the distinction between formal (ceremonial or symbolic) rule and effective authority (the way decisions are actually made and work gets done). Both elements are important, but to make a realistic appraisal of political systems, one must understand the interworking of both. In this context, Table 1.1 follows the example of Aristotle, who in his *Politics*, based upon empirical study of the constitutions of over 150 Greek city-states, observed that most were either oligarchies or democracies, and that both types had "tyrants." In modern forms of government no less than in ancient, most decisions are made by "a few" politicians, administrators, and judges. The difference between oligarchies (authoritarian and totalitarian) and democracies rests upon the degree to which participation and responsibility for decisions are formally and effectively centralized or shared, and on the frequency with which responsible decision-makers are required to submit to a popular or legislative accounting. For short periods of time any form of government is susceptible to "one-man rule," symbolically speaking; but dictatorships are usually found to rest upon some form of oligarchical underpinning, and few democratic leaders are permitted, except sometimes in periods of national emergency, to assume the role of "indispensable man."

A no less fundamental distinction among political systems separates those with governments that are constitutionally limited and controlled by law from those that are restricted only by their leaders' estimates of what is politically good for the system (*raison d'état*). "Peoples' mass democracies," whether of the French Revolutionary or Russian Revolutionary type, no less than authoritarian oligarchies and absolute kings, are of the latter sort; conversely, constitutional monarchies, republics, and democracies are found in the former category.

Popular attitudes toward politics, political leaders, and government—that component of political systems we have called "political culture"—also powerfully affect the actual operation of government through their influence on the reverence and obedience people render to the symbols, rituals, and offices of political authority. For example, the United States is usually said to have a "presidential" as opposed to a congressional or parliamentary form of government. The term calls attention to the importance in the American political system of the President, who exercises as much power as did many hereditary kings and emperors—if not more—but only to the extent that he has public support. Popular attitudes toward politics thus includes both the *per-*

ceptions and *normative expectations* that citizens have as to the proper functioning of government. The fashionable term today is "the political culture," a term whose scope may include one or more of the following: the citizens' constitutionally protected rights and liberties to engage in political discussion and activity, the formal rules and unwritten understandings of the constitution, the formal and informal structure called the party system, the demands and behavior of those powerful political forces called pressure groups, and the interaction of the vast networks of mass communication with personal opinion formation and with the processes of executive, legislative, and judicial decision-making (the opinion process). These topics are discussed in detail in Chapters 13 and 14; here we point out only that political culture has as much to do with a people's form of government as the legal, formal, and symbolic structure of governmental offices and powers.

FORM OF GOVERNMENT AND TYPE OF ECONOMIC SYSTEM

We now turn to another important factor affecting political communities. To what extent is the influence and stability of a political system dependent upon economic and social conditions?

Not long ago, forms of government were thought to be *determined* by the socio-economic system, or more precisely by a society's level of economic development. Scholars constructed an evolutionary ladder with five steps: (1) the nomadic kinship or tribal group (pastoral tending of animals); (2) the fixed agricultural community; (3) the city-state, consisting of a limited geographical-agricultural area, surrounding and depending upon a central marketing and commercial center; (4) the multi-racial city or tribal empire; and (5) the modern national state. Stages 3 through 5 were thought to be associated with partly successive, partly overlapping forms of capitalism—commercial, industrial, or financial. According to this "evolutionary" theory, the original forms of wealth are primarily pastoral and agricultural; later the predominant forms become commercial, financial, and industrial, depending in great measure upon the development of communication and transportation. These later capitalistic forms of wealth make possible the accumulation of large personal or corporate fortunes, substantial portions of which need not be spent immediately for consumption or hoarded in useless ways but can be devoted to the creation of more wealth both through private investment and through taxation to pay for public services. Thus (so the theory goes) the forms of government change as socio-economic changes dictate new functions and new modes of operation for government.

One trouble with this "stage" theory was that it attempted to separate economic from political development in order to arrive at a purely "economic" explanation. Another was that the stages were not discrete, mutually exclusive steps, but overlapping steps in an evolutionary pattern; even today, for example, agriculture remains an important component of national production and political power in the most advanced industrial nations. Nevertheless, the "state" of the economy, by which we mean broadly the degree of industrial development and the pattern of distribution of wealth within the political system, is a primary factor affecting a country's status in the community of nations. The difference between the contemporary and the older perspective is that the latter sought primarily to place a country in one category or another (agricultural versus industrial, pastoral versus commercial), whereas the contemporary approach seeks to ascertain the blend or proportionate *mix* of political and economic elements.

But wealth is only one indicator of politico-economic growth and power. Others are the proportion of persons living in towns and cities (urbanization) or employed in manufacturing, finance, commerce, and service occupations (industrialization); literacy and school enrollment (educational level); newspaper readership, radio and TV ownership and exposure (mass media consumption); and patterns of voting and other political activities (political participation). Systematic research suggests that, chronologically, urbanization and literacy (including the growth of mass communication) precede industrialization upon any considerable scale, whereas the modernization of the political culture appears to depend upon the functional interconnection between each of these factors.

The politically interesting question is whether there is any necessary connection between form of government and these socio-economic variables. Philosophers of liberalism, constitutional government, and democracy have always argued that literacy and high educational achievement are positively correlated with preferences for democracy and with more or less stable democratic institutions; conversely, the more backward economies and the more dictatorial political systems have historically been associated with a higher degree of illiteracy and a lower level of education among the population as a whole. But the examples of Nazi Germany and Soviet Russia show that literacy and education are quite compatible with dictatorial political regimes if the political culture and the predominant political groups combine to maintain an economic system associated with non-democratic values and institutions. To the extent that industrialization, literacy and higher education, widespread exposure to mass communication, and increasing political participation are functionally interrelated, however, there is the possibility that the contradictions inherent in any political system will provoke inquiry and demands for institutions allowing greater freedom and equality for the great number of citizens.

Perhaps the most confusing problem is the changing nature and role of property, or the legal authority to control wealth and services. The issue is often presented in ideological terms as if it were an exclusive contest for survival between capitalism and some form of socialism or communism. But any comparative analysis of the composition of the gross national products of various countries shows how oversimplified such a notion is. So-called capitalist countries may actually produce a majority of their goods and services through a combination of public enterprise and governmental expenditure; by the same token, public bodies and corporations in so-called collectivist countries are constantly striving to achieve results in wages, productivity, and capital formation for the benefit of the state bureaucracy and new class system established under the banner of socialism.

What is often overlooked is that a radical change has taken place in the nature and forms of property under both modern capitalism and state socialism. Under both systems, property is *instrumental* to the achievement of other values, whether they be national or ideological aggrandizement, the accumulation of consumer goods, or personal freedom and self-realization. The real issue is not victory for the absolute right of either individuals or the state to own property, but the legal and constitutional conditions under which the *de facto* controllers of property— the private and public managers—are required to account for their acts and to behave responsibly for the welfare of the greatest number of people.[6] Any political system has certain amounts of both public and private property; the practical question is how much belongs in each category. This is not a matter of ultimate or absolute ends, but one over which individuals and groups disagree and which they may settle by political means.

POLITICAL STABILITY AND CHANGE

Any mid-twentieth-century discussion of the relation between society and the form of government must conclude by contradicting the assertion that there is a necessary progression of governmental forms from "lower" to "higher," with the highest constituting a final stage of political development (as Hegel is said to have believed of the Prussian monarchy in the first quarter of the nineteenth century). We may accept the assumption of change, however, because all societies seem to have conflicts between those groups that want to change society or the form of government and those that want to keep things as they are. In Communist countries, there are those who see advantages in an open class structure supported by a totalitarian, hierarchical party system which forecloses the institutions of free public opinion and political opposition. To such persons, a political system that allows open conflicts over the form and personnel of government and that settles conflicts of economic and group interest through democratic processes of agitation, pressure, public persuasion, and compromise will seem unstable and

6 E. S. Mason, *The Corporation in Modern Society* (Cambridge, Mass.: Harvard University Press, 1959), chaps. 1–5; J. M. Keynes, "The End of Laissez Faire" in *Essays in Persuasion* (New York: Harcourt, Brace & World, 1931); A. A. Berle, *The Twentieth-century Capitalist Revolution* (New York: Harcourt, Brace & World, 1954).

unsatisfactory. The traditional cultures now struggling toward modernization had been stabilized on a low level of economic and educational
achievement for centuries; in the third quarter of the twentieth century,
however, it is these political systems which show the greatest signs of
upheaval and instability. The oldest political systems today, outside of
the few totally isolated, aboriginal societies, are the democratic regimes
of Western Europe and their extensions in North America and Austral-
asia. But these countries too, having undergone tremendous changes in
the last hundred years, have their own internal conflicts and stabilizing
pressures, both from within and without, and may yet be forced to transform the forms as well as the processes of government to meet the demands of the nuclear-space age.

The relation between economic organization, the class system, and
governmental institutions can be observed most sharply in times of
revolutionary crisis, when consciously organized struggles for power
come out in the open between groups concerning the direction and
tempo of social and economic change. But even when overt overthrow of
the established regime is not imminent, both democratic and autocratic
systems base their ideological claims for superiority upon stability, potential for expansion, relative ability to achieve more equitable standards
of life for their people, and higher levels both of civilization and material
culture. The validation of democratic claims depends, in addition, upon
the continued effective operation of constitutional, procedural checks
upon majority decision, which provide their own built-in mechanisms of
social, political, and economic change without the necessity for violent
revolution. Other continuing conditions of democracy are an active and
informed citizenry, institutions of a free public opinion (with freedom of
press, speech, and association), a competitive party system in elections
and legislation, and steady extension of equality and individual rights
under the law.

The Classification of Political Systems

Why try to classify the more than one hundred organized political systems in the world today? Probably because we want to bring order out of
bewildering variety, to understand more precisely the characteristics in
which governments differ from or resemble one another, to have a sense
of the total pattern of world political organization and of the trends
within that picture.

There is no "natural" classification inherent in the systems themselves; rather, classifications are made by political analysts according
to their particular purpose or the object of their curiosity. Thus the
number of possible ways to classify governments is legion.[7] Several

7 Excellent discussions of the problem of classifying states and governments may
be found in J. W. Garner, *Political Science and Government* (New York: American
Book Company, 1928), chaps. 11–14; and Karl Loewenstein, *Political Power and the
Governmental Process* (Chicago: University of Chicago Press, 1957), chap. 2.

economic and demographic criteria were suggested in the preceding sections. Table 1.1 offers a classification based on the criterion of *approximation to political democracy*. Another basis of classification, most relevant to international law, is the *degree of sovereignty or independence*, which distinguishes between sovereign and partly sovereign states. Students of international politics interested in ranking or grouping countries on the basis of *national power* might use such indices as size of military establishment, annual military appropriations, and number and striking capacity of nuclear weapons, as well as the factors of population, geography, natural resources, economic capacity, and political organization.

Another classification may be based upon *formal features of the constitutional-legal system:* written versus unwritten or rigid versus flexible constitutions, and so on. The *degree of centralization* in governmental structure is indicated by the dichotomy between unitary and federal systems; the *relation between the executive and legislature* provides the categories of parliamentary and presidential governments. While all these criteria have considerable descriptive and pedagogical value, as general classifications of governments they all suffer from the defect of failing to penetrate to the real differences in the political process, namely, the *ways in which governing power is controlled*—a defect that applies also to the famous Aristotelian classification (monarchy, oligarchy, and democracy) which is based upon the presumed number of persons participating in the ruling authority. And, for a different reason but with the same result, classifications of so-called state-societal types—militaristic, theocratic, agricultural, feudalistic, capitalist-bourgeois, proletarian, or bureaucratic—are analytically defective. These categories pretend to explain political and governmental behavior by the assumption that a predominant form of social-class relation determines political structure, attitudes, and behavior. In fact these "ideal types" turn out to be not scientific principles of classification, but ideological labels to support preconceived ideas, preferences, or prejudices.

Modern political classifications, in contrast, start from the analytical relation of rulers and ruled. Every political system consists of a minority of public officials, representatives, and managers exercising coercive authority over the vast majority of citizens, who accept that authority as legitimate and lawful. This minority of rulers need not consist of a single, organic group or unified ruling class. It may be recruited from an official group constituted by law, from an unofficial stratum of society, or indeed from the mass of citizens at large. What is crucial is the processes whereby the authority of these ruling officials is exercised and controlled; that is, whether they occupy positions of official and formal responsibility or exercise informal authority based on personality or organizational or social prestige. This criterion of the control of ruling power leads to a classification of political systems in terms of the following:

I. Constitutional democracies (shared powers)
    A. Parliamentary
    B. Cabinet
    C. Presidential
II. Intermediate forms
    A. Tutelary or "guided" democracy
    B. Terminal colonial dominions (in preparation for self-government)
III. Autocratic oligarchies (concentrated power)
    A. Authoritarian (political despotism combined with cultural and economic pluralism)
    B. Totalitarian (compulsory coordination and integration of all areas of society and state)

Most political scientists agree that one cannot determine what kind of political system a country has from any single factor (its written constitution, its electoral system, and so on). In each case, empirical analysis of the power structure and the political process in the state and society is necessary, with consideration of such factors as the differentiated independence and institutional effectiveness of the courts, the press and public opinion media, voluntary group associations and communication, "opposition" political parties, and recognition of the distinction between "politics" and other forms of control over public administration.

From Nation-States to Political World Order

We return to our original question: What is the viable unit of government for the twentieth century, or the twenty-first? Here we face the ironic paradox of contemporary world politics: the number of "states" is increasing rapidly at the very time when military technology, conditions of economic prosperity and viability, and revolutionary developments in communications and transportation seem to be making the nation-state obsolete. Economic and cultural life, trade and commerce, news and information, scientific progress and communication, national survival, and the avoidance of wars all depend not on the self-sufficient, mutually exclusive sovereign state, but on those interdependent relationships among men and groups across national boundaries that lead to such concepts as world community, world federation, and the Parliament of Man.

In addition, the internal principles of patriotism and nationality may be as "inimical" to the sovereign state as factors such as economic welfare and military security. For example, in the period between World Wars I and II, the principle of national or racial self-determination, often called national "liberation," did not stop with liquidation of the Austro-Hungarian and Turkish empires, but continued to divide and disrupt such "new" states as Yugoslavia, Czechoslovakia, and Poland. In 1959–1960, when the Congo Republic emerged from Belgian rule, the Congolese province of Katanga then began to view the new central government as tyrannical. National self-determination thus may become a disruptive and anarchical force with respect to world order, a principle of Balkanization and barbarization, particularly when wedded to absolute ends and moral standards that are not shared by other nations. There are always racial and national minorities within every large national state which make a one-to-one correspondence between nationality and statehood a tragic illusion. Thus the principles of nationality and nationalism, projected onto the scale of world order, become self-defeating unless they provide a steppingstone to a larger and more inclusive basis of unity and order.

The Communist challenge accentuates the problem for the West. Soviet Russia offers the world "the age-old peace of empires"—along with the destruction of freedoms, the enslavement of cultures, and absolute subordination to Soviet-controlled bureaucracies. Against the utopian promise of present enslavement for the sake of a steadily receding future millennium ("the withering-away of the state"), can the West rely upon a political strategy of rational calculation and adjustment of national interests by means of armed diplomacy? Upon a deliberate effort to establish the conditions for equilibrium in a universal organization composed of independent national states? Upon chances for a steady expansion of the jurisdiction of agencies enforcing rules of international conduct upon nations? Upon the creation of intermediate, regional instruments of multi-national cooperation such as the Organization of American States, the European Coal and Steel Community, the North Atlantic Treaty Organization, or the European Common Market?[8]

The practical problem is complicated by those feelings of nationalistic separatism, aggravated by the historic factors of anti-imperialism and colonialism, found in so many areas in the world that are characterized by inequalities of education, economic development, and cultural opportunity. It is possible that some of the newer and developing nations may see a basis for self-help by entering into wider units of economic, scientific, and cultural cooperation, which in turn may provide the foundation for political integration.

But transformed institutions and citizen attitudes favorable to organized international cooperation are probably not sufficient for the

[8] Leslie Lipson, *The Great Issues of Politics* (Englewood Cliffs, N.J.: Prentice-Hall, 1960). Chapter 13 contains an excellent discussion of the historical and contemporary background of the problem of international order. See also Charles A. McClelland, *The United Nations: The Continuing Debate* (San Francisco: Chandler, 1960).

survival of civilization. And obviously more is needed than a religious symbol such as the Cross or the Crescent to transcend the pride, honor, and interest of national groups. What we need is hard to define but is certainly more than simply people who provide "ideological camouflage for existing structures of power"; what we are looking for is a group or stratum of political-administrative leaders who combine the universal, humane outlook with skills in technological development, economic organization, and urban(e) living. It is not necessary that political leaders and citizens always be super-patriots, corrupt self-seekers, or guardians of class interest and privilege. The motivation and techniques of political power are not incompatible with feelings of responsibility for mankind and of dedication to its welfare. Such men are not the exclusive possession of any country, any class, or any ideology. The men we describe are not self-serving cynics or do-gooders, martyrs or extremists; they are aware of the conflicts of power and interest inherently associated with all political action and organization. The criterion is that they are found in positions of responsibility in which they must act as representatives of both a narrower unit and a larger organizational aggregate, of both partial and universal groups. Such men are recognized by their skill in upholding the more inclusive policy against the more restrictive, the general against the particular, or perhaps more precisely, by their competence in perceiving and bringing about the realization of the common good out of the clash of special interests and powers. It is to such men that we must look for the forging of the instruments and the structural units of organization appropriate to the demands of the nuclear age.

SUGGESTIONS FOR ADDITIONAL READING

ARON, R., *The Opium of the Intellectuals* (New York: W. W. Norton and Company, 1962).

DAHL, R. A., *Modern Political Analysis* (Englewood Cliffs, N.J.: Prentice-Hall, Inc., 1963).

DE JOUVENEL, B., *Sovereignty* (Chicago: University of Chicago Press, 1957).

FRIEDRICH, C. J., and A. BRZEZINSKI, *Totalitarian Dictatorship and Autocracy* (Cambridge, Mass.: Harvard University Press, 1956).

MERRIAM, C. E., *Political Power* (New York: McGraw-Hill, Inc., 1934).

MOSCA, G., *The Ruling Class* (New York: McGraw-Hill, Inc., 1939).

NEUMANN, S., *Permanent Revolution* (New York: Harper & Row, Publishers, 1942).

PARKINSON, C. N., *The Evolution of Political Thought* (New York: The Viking Press, 1960).

TALMON, J. L., *The Origins of Totalitarian Democracy* (New York: Frederick A. Praeger, Inc., 1960).

WOLIN, S., *Politics and Vision* (Boston: Little, Brown and Company, 1960).

THE GOVERNMENT OF GREAT BRITAIN

Great Britain is a democracy in that it is governed by popularly elected representatives. But the institutional arrangements (the legislature, the executive, and so forth) of British democracy differ in significant respects from those found in the United States. On the other hand, Americans have inherited much from Britain, particularly their legal system, so we can expect to find in the British system important similarities to American institutions. Studying Great Britain, as well as other democracies, should help us reach some conclusions about (1) which institutional arrangements are necessary to a democracy and which are not, (2) why some institutional devices may be preferred over others, and (3) the degree of uniqueness in each democratic political order.

Constitutional Development

The British constitution is the result of a long process of slow growth rather than of deliberate creation at any one time. It is not, moreover, written down in one document. Rather, the constitutional rules by which Great Britain is governed are found in a series of documents (great charters, statutes of a constitutional nature, judicial decisions) and unwritten political usages or conventions that have gained general acceptance. These documents and conventions represent important milestones in Britain's constitutional development.

MONARCHY, CABINET, PARLIAMENT

Great Britain is a constitutional monarchy in which the monarch exercises only such limited powers as the constitution confers on him. Formally speaking, all acts of government are performed in His (or Her) Majesty's name, but real political power is exercised by persons responsible to popularly elected representatives assembled in Parliament. Nor may the king or queen veto any act of Parliament.

This state of affairs is the end result of the transition from a more or less absolute monarchy to parliamentary democracy, a transition accomplished over a period of several centuries. Initially Parliament was a gathering of non-elected feudal representatives who assembled to vote taxes required by the king. With the passage of time, the membership of Parliament became divided into three groups (lords, clergy, and commons), subsequently reduced to two, Lords and Commons, as they are now known. The power of Parliament evolved from successful efforts on the part of the Commons to present petitions to the king and to originate bills providing for expenditures and the raising of revenue. By the fifteenth century, Parliament had gained control over finance. But monarchs were slow in relinquishing power, with the result that there was a severe struggle over the relation of king to Parliament during most of the seventeenth century. In the course of this struggle the doctrine of the divine right of kings was proclaimed, the Stuarts were driven from the throne, civil war erupted, republicanism was tried, and monarchy restored. The whole process culminated in the so-called bloodless revolution of 1688, which brought to the throne William and Mary, who readily acknowledged the supremacy of Parliament. Since that time, the power and influence of the monarchy have steadily declined, and no king has challenged the supremacy of Parliament.

In practice parliamentary supremacy has meant that the monarch appoints the heads of the important government departments (ministries) from among men acceptable to Parliament. In other words, ministers must be selected from the political group or faction that can manage or has the confidence of Parliament, and more particularly of the House of Commons. Before the rise of political parties in the modern sense, there were times when the monarch could play one parliamentary faction off against another. In the end, however, he had to choose his advisers from the group which commanded a majority in the Commons.

Under these circumstances, the king's advisers (ministers) understandably began meeting without him to determine what advice they were going to give. In the end this meant that they would only give such advice as the political party they represented was willing to see translated into public policy. They could not do otherwise, or they might be removed from office by an adverse vote in Parliament. Thus the body of the king's advisers, who came to be known collectively as the cabinet, became in effect a committee of the majority party in Parliament.

A further development was the requirement that ministers resign whenever they met with an adverse vote, or a vote of no confidence, in the House of Commons. This phenomenon, known as *ministerial responsibility*, developed in the first part of the eighteenth century, although it was not until 1782 that responsibility became *collective*, in other words, that the defeat of one minister meant the defeat of the whole cabinet. Subsequently the cabinet acquired an alternative to resignation: the power to dissolve the House of Commons to ascertain, through new elections, whether or not the electorate's opinions were accurately represented by the House.

The source of political leadership in Britain, therefore, is the cabinet. It is chosen from Parliament, or, more precisely, from the political party having a majority in the House of Commons. The cabinet is the real executive; it formulates policy and is collectively responsible for it and the way it is administered.

During the time that Parliament was gaining ascendancy over the monarch, and subsequently when the principle of ministerial responsibility was being established, Parliament was anything but a democratic body. Even the members of the elected house, the Commons, were not democratically chosen. Each borough and each county, regardless of its population, was entitled to two members in the Commons. On the eve of the Reform Act of 1832, moreover, the eligible voters in a population of some 24 million numbered considerably under one million.

The democratization of Parliament, begun in 1832, culminated in the establishment of universal suffrage in 1928. The Reform Act of 1832 redistributed seats in the Commons to take into account the shift of population (occasioned by the industrial revolution) from the rural areas to the growing industrial towns. The act also extended the suffrage, nearly doubling the number of eligible voters. In 1867 a new reform act added nearly a million voters to the rolls and provided for a further redistribution of seats. In 1872 the secret ballot was introduced. In 1884 there was another redistribution of seats and a further extension of the suffrage, followed by an act designed to suppress corrupt practices. The process was completed with the extension of the franchise to all adult males in 1918 and to all adult women ten years later.

The broadening of the suffrage was perhaps the single most important constitutional development in nineteenth-century Britain. Its effect was to base political power on popular election, and thus to make political leadership accountable to a free electorate. Political power had passed from the monarch to Parliament and from Parliament to the party organizations that competed for a majority of seats in the House of Commons.

As Parliament became more democratic, the power and influence of the Commons increased, while that of the upper chamber, the House of Lords, declined. After 1850 no cabinet regarded an adverse vote in the upper house as requiring a confidence vote in the Commons. A test of power was precipitated, however, by the Lords' defeat of the budget in 1909. Following the election of 1910, in which the power of the Lords was the main issue, the struggle was resolved in favor of the Commons. The Parliament Act of 1911 stipulated that money bills must become law within thirty days whether the Lords act on them favorably or unfavorably or not at all; in the case of other bills, however, the Lords could delay action for as much as two years (reduced to one year by the Parliament Act of 1949). Although the House of Lords may still effect changes in legislation, it no longer is an equal partner with the Commons in the legislative process. In any test of wills the Commons must prevail.

THE CONSTITUTION TODAY

Modern democratic constitutions may be said to consist of the sum total of the basic rules, written and unwritten, that establish orderly political processes and provide for effective restraints on the exercise of political power. Constitutions allocate powers and in general define the spheres of governmental activity. They prescribe limitations on government, both in the form of certain prohibitions that safeguard basic freedoms from curtailment by government, and in the form of procedural safeguards that force the government to exercise its powers in conformity with certain rules or principles that are considered just and fair. Viewed in this light, modern democratic constitutions serve to limit political power and to channel its exercise.

The constitutions of modern democratic states consist of several elements, the most obvious of which is a written document actually called the constitution. Of nearly equal importance—in some countries even more so—are certain basic statutes, binding judicial interpretations, and customs or precedents that have become an integral part of a nation's political practices. Although, as we have seen, Great Britain does not possess one compact document called the constitution, the British system does offer numerous examples of the other elements. Usually, the elements of the British constitution are placed in two categories—the law of the constitution and the conventions of the constitution, only the former being written.

The *law of the constitution* is embodied in historic documents or charters, in statutes of a constitutional nature, and in the common law. The best known of the historic documents is Magna Carta (1215). Others are the Petition of Right (1628), the Bill of Rights (1689), and the Act of Settlement (1701). In one way or another these charters served to limit the authority of the monarch and to provide for an orderly redress of grievances. Other historic documents, such as the Reform Act of 1832 and the Parliament Act of 1911, altered the basic political structure. Although they are less important than the great charters, parliamentary enactments dealing with the suffrage, election methods, and the powers and duties of public officials are nevertheless a part of the constitutional system. British political institutions have also been shaped by the common law, that body of judge-made legal rules which grew up apart from any parliamentary action and in which are rooted most of the guarantees of civil rights. This body of rules, as well as the historic charters, has been altered by judicial decisions which from time to time have reinterpreted their meaning.

The *conventions of the constitution,* although less precisely formulated than the law of the constitution, are no less fundamental. Such important institutions as the cabinet and the office of prime minister stem from custom and usage, and not from legislative enactment. Moreover, the basic attribute of the parliamentary system, the responsibility of the cabinet to the House of Commons, was evolved through usage. The principle that the monarch cannot refuse his consent to acts of Parliament and that he must ask the leader of the majority party in the Commons to be prime minister is likewise rooted in convention.

What basic characteristics of the British political system can be deduced from a study of the British constitution? (1) *Democracy.* Political decisions are made by popularly elected leaders. The monarch acts only on the basis of their advice; he is politically neutral. (2) *Supremacy of Parliament.* Legally, Parliament can do anything it wants. There is no provision that any court can declare an act of Parliament unconstitutional. (3) *Unitary government.* All power is vested in one central government; whatever powers are exercised by local units of government are granted by the central authorities and may be revoked by them. (4) *Fusion of legislative and executive powers.* The leaders of the majority party constitute the executive (the cabinet) while retaining their seats in the legislature. There is no separation of executive and legislative powers in the American sense. (5) *Independence of the judiciary.* Although the political branches of government are fused, the judiciary is independent and free from political interference. Judges serve for life and have developed a tradition of impartiality in dispensing justice. (6) *Protection of civil rights.* Although the British have no neat enumeration of civil rights such as exists in the American Constitution, these rights are nevertheless protected. No people in the world are more determined to preserve civil liberties than are the British.

Social Forces and Ideological Trends

All societies are beset with contending social forces, and change is the law of life. But the factors—historical, technological, political, economic, and the like—that contribute to change can be impeded or facilitated by the social and political organization of a particular society.

Where change is impeded, violent revolution is the likely result. In Britain change has on the whole come about peacefully, although some of the transitions have not been without pain.

THE HISTORICAL ALIGNMENT OF SOCIAL FORCES

Great Britain, like other European countries, had its feudal period, with its manifold gradations of social rank. The descendants of the feudal lords, as the chief beneficiaries of the old system, wanted to preserve their vested interests. But by the late eighteenth and early nineteenth centuries, the industrial revolution could not be held back, and the struggle of those who stood to benefit from it was resolved in their favor. Subsequently the growth of trade, a consequence of the industrial revolution, resulted in a contest between those who stood to gain from free-trade policies and those who would lose. This contest was won at first by the free-trade advocates, but in this century the protectionists had their day.

In addition to setting the stage for these conflicts, the industrial revolution also brought into being a new class—the industrial workers—and a whole host of new problems associated with urban civilization. In the eighteenth century landed property owners had dominated politics; in the nineteenth, the interests of those involved in the development of large-scale industry and the growth of factory towns were gradually recognized in the system of parliamentary representation. By the beginning of the twentieth century the industrial workers had their own political party, the Labour party, which by mid-century had not only reached the status of a major party but had also come to power and achieved some of its basic objectives.

The existence of a system of democratic representation had enabled Labour to realize many of its goals more rapidly than did the bourgeoisie in the nineteenth century. Yet it is important to recognize that the Conservatives, the other major modern party, have accepted Labour's reforms. Just as a consensus had been reached between the landed and industrial classes in the previous century, a similar understanding was arrived at between Labourites and Conservatives in the twentieth, although certain disharmonies remain and the struggle to control public policy continues.

The political battle in Britain is waged according to certain agreed-upon rules. Those favored by the existing system are not inclined to give it up easily, but there is a tacit understanding among the British that their political system must take account of the forces, domestic and foreign, that make for change not only in the direction of British policy but also in the rules and personnel through which change is implemented. The significant thing to note is that the dominant social groups have repeatedly been able to devise political forms that eventually won their opponents' support. The social structure could change, and did.

The new social forces generated by industrialization were able to play an increased role while the influence of the farmers, the landed aristocracy, and the small shopkeepers waned. And the fact that the working classes were able to rise in influence may to a large degree explain the lack of Communist success among British workers.

A final word should be said, however, about the persistence in Britain of classes in the *social* sense. Apart from differences resulting from occupation and income, British society has been stratified also by differences in appearance, accent, and manner. Before the last century even a rudimentary primary education was unavailable to any substantial part of the population, a factor which contributed in no small measure to the perpetuation of social classes. The British social structure has been conducive to the creation of personal connections among those in established positions of power and prestige. Class consciousness is still prevalent in Britain, but the equalization of educational opportunities over the past two decades has gone a long way to open up the avenues to social as well as economic advancement for the children of most Britishers.

FACTORS SHAPING THE BRITISH CONSENSUS

What accounts for the capacity of the British system to accommodate without violence profound social change? One factor may be that though they are of mixed Celtic, Roman, Saxon, Danish, and Norman origins, the British have developed a strong sense of national identity, which has caused some observers to confuse agreement with homogeneity. While regionalism is evident in Scotland and Wales, it would be inaccurate in discussing British life to speak of minorities and diverse ethnic blocs.

Another factor contributing to the British consensus grew out of the general British respect for the ideas of freedom, dissent, and toleration. The result has been moderation and a minimum of violence. A third factor is the British moral sense. Politically civilized people are restrained people, but restraint must rest upon concepts of right and wrong. For the British, Christianity has been an important source of these concepts. To be sure, the British have had their differences over religion, but these very differences have contributed to political discussion and political debates and have given rise to tolerance for divergent views. And in a more concrete way, the Anglican Church and other Christian churches in Britain have contributed significantly to the abolition of the slave trade, to prison reform, to the elimination of child labor, and to factory reforms.

Education, too, has contributed to peaceful social transitions, although the British were slow to recognize a public responsibility to provide opportunities for the development of talent. Significant government financial support was not available for primary schools until after 1870 and not until 1900 for secondary schools, while the universities had to wait until after World War II. It is true that the government recognized the importance of education much earlier. It chose, however, to channel its support through grants to the church-supported schools. Since the Second World War the government has, in large measure, equalized educational opportunities, through specific legislation that provided for recognition of talent, financial aid, and the establishment of a number of new universities. While these measures have not reduced the demand for entrance into the independent schools, they have made it possible for children of all social classes to advance on the basis of ability and individual effort to a much greater degree than was heretofore the case.

Finally, peaceful social transitions have been aided to some extent by the enlightened self-interest of the propertied class. Class differences in Britain have been considerable, yet British capitalists have made important concessions to the workers, both in accepting their right to strike and in acquiescing to considerable government regulation of business. The result has been a more satisfied working class, one able to promote its interests politically through Parliament with no need to engage in violence and revolution.

THE WELFARE STATE

The ability of the major social classes to promote their interests politically has resulted in increased governmental activity in the social welfare field. This means, first, that the government assumes the responsibility of keeping the economy functioning at a high level and along certain lines and, second, that each member of society receives a certain minimum of the available goods and services. A high level of economic activity is achieved by public ownership of certain segments of the economy, by economic planning, and by government regulation. A minimum standard of welfare for the individual is achieved through such devices as minimum wages and the free provision of certain goods or services, such as medical care.

The British welfare state is often identified, erroneously in large part, with the postwar Labour government. Actually, a great deal of public economic control and considerable social security legislation existed long before Labour took over in 1945, much of it representing measures passed by Conservative governments. The first public health measures, for example, were enacted around the middle of the nineteenth century. Thus Labour, although desiring to go farther and faster, was in fact building on past accomplishments.

In the postwar period, moreover, the choices open to either party were limited. Britain's international economic position was unstable; for the country to survive it was imperative to expand the volume of exports. To do this, all sorts of controls were needed, particularly measures to curtail domestic consumption. In addition, Britain's economic plant needed rejuvenation. Its age created a domestic economic crisis that could only be met with a government-directed capital investment program. In short, had the Conservatives been victorious in 1945, they too would no doubt have been forced to engage in a great deal of economic planning and government enterprise.

The Labour program therefore had a broader popular consensus than is generally realized in the United States. This was made possible, in part, because the British have not been overly doctrinaire about free enterprise, but highly pragmatic and utilitarian in their approach. And the two major parties, although in apparent disagreement, seem constantly to be reaching new areas of agreement through a process of disagreeing.

This ability of the British political system to direct the forces of change along peaceful channels has resulted in the avoidance of severe stresses and strains, and hence the absence of divisive ideological struggles. Differences have been discussed and resolved on the basis of alternative pragmatic solutions rather than in terms of doctrinaire ideological positions. In an age of ideological struggles, this relative insignificance of ideology is perhaps of major interest and significance.

Political Groups

In a democracy people organize into various kinds of groups in order to realize some of their goals. Such groups take two major forms: political parties and interest groups. The former attempt to attain a variety of goals by seeking public office for their members and then assuming general responsibility for the conduct of public affairs; the latter seek the attainment of more limited goals by exerting direct or indirect pressure on government officials.

It would be difficult to visualize democratic government functioning without parties, for it is through them that the popular will is ascertained and ultimately translated into action. Parties develop the programs and bring forth the leaders to present to the electorate. And they also seek to influence the public between elections. Interest groups, on the other hand, function in terms of their own more limited interests. In some countries, such as France before the advent of De Gaulle, they tend to be dominant, with political parties relegated to a secondary role. In Great Britain, however, the emphasis is primarily on political parties, although interest groups also fulfill an important function.

THE NATURE OF BRITISH PARTIES

British political parties can be traced back to about 1700, when two groups in Parliament began calling themselves Whigs and Tories. They, along with other factions and cliques, were loose groupings; they did

Table 2.1

Popular Vote for British Political Parties in General Elections since World War I

Year	Conservative	Labour	Liberal
1922	38.2%	29.5%	29.1%
1923	38.1	30.5	29.6
1924	48.3	33.0	17.6
1929	38.2	37.1	23.4
1935	53.7	37.9	6.4
1945	39.8	47.8	9.0
1950	43.5	46.1	9.1
1951	48.0	48.8	2.5
1955	49.7	46.4	2.7
1959	49.4	43.8	5.9
1964	43.4	44.1	11.2

SOURCE: David Butler and Jennie Freeman, *British Political Facts 1900–1960* (London: Macmillan, 1963), pp. 123–24. The 1964 figures are from *Fact on File Yearbook 1964*, p. 361 E2.

not even call themselves political parties. There was no large-scale party organization outside Parliament, and in view of the fact that each member of the House of Commons prior to the Reform Act of 1832 represented on the average 330 voters, there was little need for one. Political parties in the modern sense date from early in the nineteenth century, when the Tories began to be known as the Conservative party and the Whigs assumed the name Liberal. Although they received no formal recognition in British constitutional documents, these parties, as they evolved, have played an increasingly vital role in the political processes of the nation.

One of the most striking characteristics of the British political system is its two-party character. Third parties have not endured. With the rise of the Labour party in the early twentieth century the Liberal party, which had been one of the two major parties in the nineteenth century, declined, although it was not finally eclipsed until the elections of 1945. Table 2.1 indicates the fortunes of British parties since World War I.

The high degree of governmental stability in Britain has caused some observers to wonder what conditions produced the two-party system that seems to be associated with it. Some have suggested that the system of plurality elections, which provides that the party polling the largest number of votes in a district wins that district's seat in the Commons, has served to force the electorate to line up on one of two sides. Others have concluded that the tradition of strong government, in which the cabinet is not buffeted about by an irresponsible legislature, has motivated voters to think in terms of getting a working majority in office. Whatever the reasons, the fact remains that British voters have preferred to vote for a party with a reasonable chance of forming a cabinet, even though in the process they might elect a Parliament that was a less perfect reflection of popular views than a multi-party assembly can sometimes be.

Another characteristic of British parties is their elaborate organization. This is a product of the past one hundred years, for when the electorate was relatively small there was no real need for extensive organization, and parties remained little more than groups of men within Parliament. But as more and more people won the right to vote, particularly after the Reform Act of 1867, the rudiments of party organization were found in the party-sponsored registration societies, which were devices to get prospective supporters on the electoral rolls. Subsequently local party organizations began to group together, until eventually there was a full-blown party organization on the national as well as the regional level.

THE CONSERVATIVE PARTY

In the eighteenth century the Conservatives were dominated by landed interests. In the nineteenth century, however, especially after the Reform Acts of 1832 and 1867, merchants and manufacturers gained in political influence, and the importance of the landed interests declined. The Conservative party came to be identified with the new sources of wealth. In the process, however, particularly in their passage of the Reform Act of 1867, the Conservatives gained a sizable middle-class following as well as a good deal of working-class support, much of which they retain to this day.

Organizationally the Conservative party has three important components: the leader, the members of the party in Parliament, and the party in the country (see Figure 1). Of the three, the leader is the most important in power and prestige. He is the actual or potential prime minister, and it is to him that party adherents look for day-to-day leadership. He may receive advice, but the formulation of policy is his responsibility alone. Moreover, he has control, through appointments of key personnel, of the national party organization.

The Conservatives, prior to 1965, had a singular method of choosing their leader. They staged no formal contests for the post: the leader emerged from a process of consultation involving important party stalwarts, although it was not always clear who was or was not consulted;

Figure 1
Organizational Structure of the Conservative Party

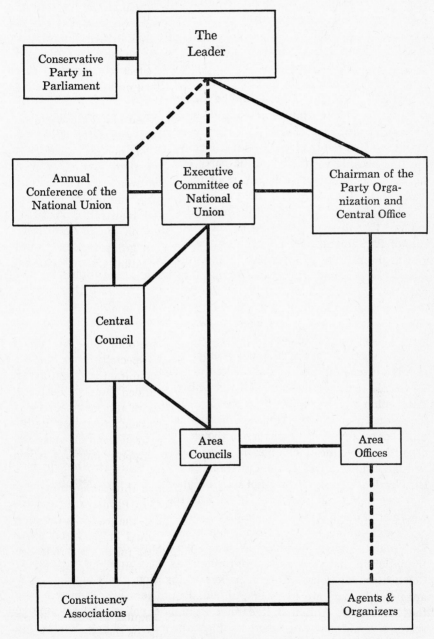

SOURCE: R. T. McKenzie, *British Political Parties,* 3rd edition (London: Oxford University Press, 1964).

some rank and file members of the House of Commons have sometimes complained that their opinion was not asked. This was true, for example, at the time of the Suez Crisis (1956–1957), when Anthony Eden stepped down as Prime Minister and Harold Macmillan succeeded him after brief consultations among an unknown number of Conservatives (some voluntarily conveyed their preferences to the party's chief whip). In 1963 Harold Macmillan's decision to retire precipitated similar informal consultations, but the selection of Sir Alec Douglas-Home was in the end the work of Macmillan alone. To cite an earlier example, years before Winston Churchill stepped down in 1955 everyone knew in advance that Anthony Eden would be the next party leader. But whether or not it was clear who would succeed to the leadership, the Conservatives have always preferred to have the man become prime minister first, then invariably electing him leader without opposition. When the position became vacant while the party was out of power, it remained vacant, the Conservative members of the Commons merely electing a leader in the Commons and those in the Lords doing likewise.

In selecting the leader by this method, influential Conservatives realized that their choice must be acceptable to the Conservative members of Parliament, to the party's prospective parliamentary candidates, and to the members of the party's executive committee. The leader attained his position after many years of intimate association with his party colleagues (a man usually serves *at least* 20 years in Parliament before becoming leader). At times there have been rivals for the leadership, but before 1965, the question was always resolved before any formal meeting took place.

By 1965, however, the old method of choosing the leader had clearly become outmoded. Consequently, a change was made providing for his election by the Conservative members of the House of Commons. This action was precipitated by the dissatisfaction which accompanied the selection of Douglas-Home, a dissatisfaction heightened by his failure to carry the party to victory in the election of 1964. Several months after the announced change in party rules, Douglas-Home resigned, and the Conservatives in the Commons elected Edward Heath as leader. His election was significant not only because it was the first under the new rules, but also because Heath was the first Conservative leader who had never attended an elite private school.

Next to the leader in importance is the Conservative group in Parliament, known popularly as the "1922 Committee" because of its formation in that year, and more formally as the Conservative Members Committee. All Conservative members of the House of Commons who are not ministers are members, although ministers may appear before the Committee. Although it cannot formulate policy, the Committee serves several important functions. First, the membership is divided into functional committees which correspond to the several ministries and which discuss and report to the full membership of the Committee the thinking of the functional committee members on important issues—a procedure which gives all Conservative members of the Commons a feeling of participation in decision-making. Second, the Committee conveys its views on various issues to the leader, enabling him to know the mood of his followers in the Commons. Finally, the existence of the Committee enables the leader to convey to the rank and file the views and attitudes of the leadership. When the party is out of power, the Committee serves as the place where leading issues are debated and the party's policy is crystallized.

The party outside Parliament, officially called the National Union of Conservative and Unionist Associations, is primarily an electoral machine. It also serves as a two-way channel of communication between the rank and file membership and the party in Parliament, and provides an opportunity for party supporters to become politically active and to play a limited role in selecting party leaders. It consists of two hierarchies, one professional and the other voluntary. At the base of the voluntary structure are the associations at the constituency or local level, and at the top is the Annual Conference of the National Union. The managers of this structure are the Central Council, the governing body of the National Union that also meets annually, and the Executive Committee of the National Union. The latter, made up of the leader, the principal officers of the party, and area representatives, meets once a month. One of its main functions is to decide what is to be discussed by the Central Council and the Conference. The Conference, powerless to formulate policy, is a large gathering, in the main consisting of the Central Council and delegates chosen by constituency associations, a noisy rally of the party faithful demonstrating party unity and support for the leaders. Although it passes resolutions, it rarely takes a position that the leadership opposes.

On the professional side, the National Union is epitomized by the Central Office, the personal instrument of the leader. It is run by a member of Parliament, known as the chairman, who, along with the other principal officers, is appointed by the leader. The Central Office, with a staff of about 200, is officially described as the headquarters of the party organization. Its role is said to be "to guide, inspire and coordinate the work of the party throughout the country . . . and to provide such services as can best be organized centrally." In fact, however, it controls such vital party matters as finance and candidacies. Party agents and organizers, although technically responsible to local party organizations, are selected and paid by the Central Office.

THE LABOUR PARTY

The Labour Party is relatively new. But it has grown rapidly, and forty years after its founding in 1905 it had a sizable majority in the House of Commons. It is basically a socialist party, although it has discarded many of the doctrinal precepts of traditional socialism. For example, it no longer espouses nationalization of land, and its advocacy of nationalization in the industrial sector of the economy has been tempered by a change in method; in the future it would have the government gain control of an industry by buying shares on the market. Its membership is based largely on trade unionism, although its appeal goes considerably beyond the trade unions.

Organizationally the Labour party, in and out of power, operates in fact if not in form much like the Conservative, although there are certain differences (see Figure 2). In power and influence, the leader is all-important. He is free to select his colleagues. Unlike the Conservative leader, however, he does not formulate policy; he is in theory obligated to seek the implementation of a program determined by the party organization and the Labour members of Parliament. Nor does he exercise personal control over the party's head office. Furthermore, the Labour leader is elected annually, so that the choice of a leader has proved to be more of a contest for the Labourites than for the Conservatives. Careful studies of British politics suggest, however, that even these differences are more apparent than real.

The Labour party organization in Parliament, known as the Parliamentary Labour Party (PLP), is like its Conservative counterpart in that it does not permit the party outside Parliament to control it. This has been a hard-won gain, for in the early years of the party Labour members were agents of an extra-parliamentary body, the Party's National Executive Committee. Now PLP leadership is not seriously challenged, although internal divisions have at times threatened the party's unity.

The PLP is similar to the Conservatives' 1922 Committee, although it is more tightly organized. Moreover, the party leader and his colleagues attend all meetings, because the PLP can make binding policy decisions. (This function is not so important when the party is in power, for then the cabinet is the real policy-maker.) The PLP has "subject groups" similar to the functional committees of the Conservatives, and with scarcely more influence on policy formulation.

Outside Parliament, the Labour party, like the Conservative, is primarily an electoral machine. Its composition is different, however, because the bulk of the membership comes from the party's affiliation with the trade unions. Unless a union member signs a statement that he does not wish to affiliate with the party ("contracts out"), his union will deduct and pay party dues for him. In this way over 5 million trade unionists are members of the Labour party. Individuals may also become members of constituency party organizations at the local level.

At the top of the voluntary side of the Labour organization outside Parliament is the annual Conference. In theory it is the ultimate authority for the party. In practice, however, its actions have been largely

Figure 2
Organizational Structure of the Labour Party

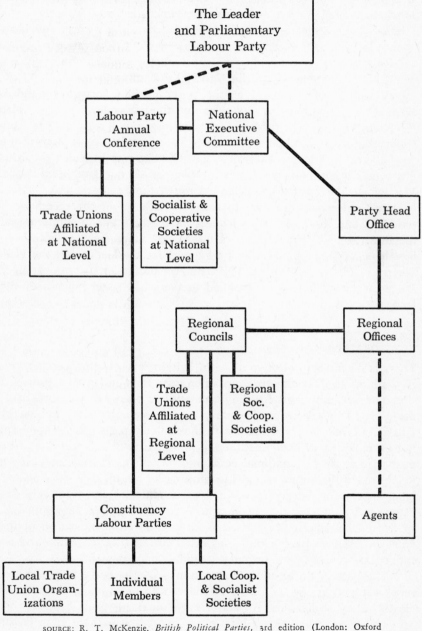

SOURCE: R. T. McKenzie, *British Political Parties,* 3rd edition (London: Oxford University Press, 1964).

advisory; the leaders have either been in control or they have been prepared to ignore the Conference's advice. In any event a two-thirds vote
of the Conference is required to include items in the party program,
and even then it is left to the PLP and the National Executive to decide
what goes into the election manifesto. Unlike the Conservative leader,
who merely comes to address the Conference after it concludes its work,
the Labour leader must report to the Conference on his stewardship.
Moreover, the professional organization of the party reports and is responsible to the Conference and not, as in the Conservative party, to
the leader.

The Conference selects the National Executive Committee (NEC),
which supervises the work of the party outside Parliament and is
responsible for enforcing party rules and the party constitution. It also
directs the work of the professional party organization through its control of the party's head office, popularly known as Transport House from
the building in London where it is located. The way in which the NEC
has been chosen, however, assures the leader of considerable influence.
First of all, the great trade unions, through their representation at the
Labour Conference, are able to select a majority of the members of
the NEC, and the trade union leaders have been staunch supporters of
the PLP. Second, in recent years most NEC members have also been
members of Parliament, assuring support for the leader and the PLP.
The net result has been that the NEC and the professional organization of
the party have generally responded to the wishes and policies of the
leader.

ELECTORAL PROCEDURES

There is no national elective office in Britain; even the prime minister,
as we have seen, is chosen from among the members of the House of
Commons. Nominations for the Commons are party affairs. Candidates
are selected by the respective party organizations at the constituency
(district) level, in consultation with the national party office; they need
not be residents of the constituency in which they run. There are no
primaries or state or national conventions. Only those nominated by a
party are entitled to use its label in running for office (although no party
label appears on the ballot). Frivolous candidacies are effectively discouraged by the rule that each candidate must deposit the equivalent
of $420. The deposit is returned if he polls at least one-eighth of the
votes cast. Minor party candidates often forfeit their deposits, and on
rare occasions even a major party candidate may have to do so.

The date of an election is determined by the party in power, or,
more particularly, by the prime minister, who presumably consults his
closest cabinet colleagues. An act of Parliament, however, specifies that
an election must be held at least every five years. In case of an acute
emergency, such as war, an election may be postponed for a year at a

time until the emergency comes to an end. Because it can choose the time for elections, the party in power has the advantage of selecting the time it thinks most propitious for victory, although its choice becomes increasingly limited as the end of the five-year term approaches.

British election campaigns are brief, for the election takes place within a month of the announcement that Parliament is dissolved. British campaigns are more limited than American campaigns in other respects, particularly in the amount of money that is spent. Television and radio time, for example, cannot be purchased, but each major party is provided an equal amount of free time. Commentators do not discuss the campaigns or the candidates. Even newscasters stay away from political news during the campaign, although the newspapers report freely what the candidates say.[1] It is illegal for anyone to spend money on behalf of a candidate unless authorized by the candidate or his election agent, and the total that can be spent by or on behalf of each candidate is severely limited.

INTEREST GROUPS

In a free society in which individuals may combine to promote their aspirations, organizations emerge into the political arena to advocate a variety of interests. This is natural, because where there is power pressure will be applied. Because of their activities these organizations are often referred to as pressure groups, but since the word "pressure" may imply a value judgment, it is perhaps preferable to call them interest groups. Among the better-known British interest groups are the National Farmers Union, the Federation of British Industries, the National Federation of Property Owners, the National Union of Manufacturers, and the various trade unions.

The pattern of interest group activity in Britain, as in other nations, is diverse and complex, although the channels that British interests utilize are less conspicuous than those employed by their American counterparts. In the United States we are familiar with interest group activity at the national as well as the state level. Lobbyists for special causes are freely at work, pleading their cases before legislative committees and individual legislators. The distribution of power in the American system practically forces interest groups to concentrate much of their activity on Congress and the various state legislatures.

In Great Britain, on the other hand, such activity seems absent. This is understandable, because British legislative committees are not powerful and cannot override the leaders of the government (a term roughly equivalent to our term "administration"). The cabinet's control over its majority is such that the votes of individual members cannot be

---

[1] During the 1959 and 1964 election campaigns, however, there was radio and television coverage of the activities of national party leaders and certain constituency campaigns, perhaps signifying a change in this respect.

changed by the actions of interest group representatives. Consequently lobbying of the type Americans are accustomed to is futile.

This does not mean that British interest groups are not effective, but that they act in different ways. Because power in Britain is concentrated, they must focus their attention on those who make decisions: the cabinet ministers and their advisers and associates. They must convince ministers that what they want is in the national interest, or at least that it can be so defended. Perhaps their most effective method is to work through the political parties—that is, by working for the nomination and election of candidates who will be sympathetic to their interests. In this way, interests come to be represented directly in Parliament.

The British have not generally speaking been suspicious of the political activity of interest groups. In a sense the Labour party is an association of pressure groups, and most business organizations are aligned with the Conservative party; contacts between lobbyists and decision-makers have therefore not seemed out of order. As a matter of fact interest groups are frequently consulted by the government. Consultative and advisory commissions, representing various interests, work closely with government committees and councils. Drafts of proposed laws are submitted to affected interests for their reaction, and whenever royal commissions are set up to study various problems outside interests are liberally represented.

Interests also have an opportunity to state their views when new administrative regulations are being written. And they continually try to influence administrative agencies in an effort to gain the most favorable interpretation of laws and regulations which affect them. This form of activity has been accelerated by the growth of welfare-state legislation, which has vested an increasing amount of decision-making in administrative agencies. It is here, by and large, that decisions are made on what prices will be guaranteed to farmers, what salaries are to be paid the doctors in the British Health Service, and what licenses (import, building, and so on) are to be granted or denied.

The influence of interest groups depends in part on their size, that is, on how many people who share the same interest or aspiration are organized for political action. It also rests on the ability of the group to supply the type of expert knowledge that ministers or administrators require. One of the most effective groups in this respect is the medical profession, whose expert knowledge shapes the policy of the British Health Service. Finally, the influence of an interest group is affected by the extent to which its cooperation is necessary to the government. It would be difficult, for example, to envision a workable farm program without the cooperation of the farmers.

Governmental Institutions

British political institutions center on the cabinet and Parliament. The former shapes policy and indeed governs the nation, but it must always have the confidence of the latter or it cannot stay in power. Parliament may pass or amend any law; there is no executive veto. And while there is an independent judiciary, there is no judicial review, that is, the courts cannot declare an act of Parliament invalid. When cabinet and Parliament are in agreement, they are invincible—except that both must concern themselves with the winds of public opinion.

THE CABINET

In the British system, as in other parliamentary systems, there is an essential fusion of legislative and executive powers. The cabinet, consisting of about eighteen members, including the most important ministers, is the executive. Its members are chosen from Parliament, or, more precisely, from members of the majority party in the House of Commons. Cabinet members retain their legislative seats while serving in the cabinet. Most, certainly the most important ones, come from the House of Commons although a few sit in the Lords. The leader of the majority party in the Commons[2] becomes the leader of the cabinet, the prime minister.

The prime minister is more than a first among equals. Before becoming prime minister he will have had some twenty years' experience in the Commons. He will not have achieved this position without having won the confidence and respect of his party colleagues, upon whose support he must depend. As the king's first minister, he appoints approximately one hundred high officials, including the ministers, the most important of whom will be his cabinet colleagues. He presides at meetings of the cabinet and has the leading voice in the determination of policy. There may be times, however, when his views are at variance with the prevailing mood of the cabinet, and he may not be able to have his way.

Collectively, the cabinet governs. It is in charge of administration, but it also decides what legislation is needed. Its measures have priority over other business, and in recent years have taken up most of the time of Parliament. Broad policy decisions are hammered out in cabinet meetings. Once a consensus has been reached, those who were in disagreement must be prepared to defend cabinet policies in public or resign. The cabinet is collectively responsible to the House of Commons for all

[2] The selection in 1963 of the Earl of Home, who had previously served many years in the Lords and who upon his designation as Prime Minister relinquished his peerage and became a member of the Commons in a special election, resulted from unusual circumstances which are not likely to be repeated in the near future.

of its political and administrative acts. An attack upon one minister is an attack upon all of them; they must stand or fall together.

If the cabinet meets defeat in the Commons, it must either resign or dissolve the House and set a date for new elections. The choice is determined by the prime minister after whatever consultation he chooses to make among his colleagues. Since resignation would result in the leader of the opposing political party being made prime minister, the more frequent decision is to hold new elections, giving the electorate an opportunity to pass on the issue or issues which precipitated the crisis. In view of the party solidarity which exists in Britain, however, a cabinet is not apt to meet defeat in the Commons so long as it has a majority there.[3] Members of the prime minister's party know that a majority vote against the leadership is tantamount to a vote for new elections, in which the dissidents might conceivably lose their party's nomination. A vote against one's party leaders, therefore, is politically suicidal, and is likely to occur only in case of a most serious split in party ranks.

Under these circumstances the cabinet has the upper hand, a situation that has led some political leaders to assert that British government has deteriorated into "Cabinet Dictatorship." This charge would be difficult to substantiate, because the cabinet is continually in touch with its supporters in Parliament, and thus able to gauge what will or will not be acceptable to them. After all, the cabinet's authority rests on its majority. The cabinet must always pay attention to what this majority thinks—for a new election is always in the offing. The cabinet must pay attention to public opinion, for without popular support it cannot exist for long.

While the majority party names the cabinet, the minority party has its "shadow cabinet," ready to assume the task of governing if political fortunes should provide the opportunity. The members of the shadow cabinet are the opposition-party members who, on the basis of experience and party standing, would assume ministerial posts if the cabinet resigned or if a new election gave the party a majority in the Commons.

PARLIAMENT

Parliament is made up of two houses, the House of Commons and the House of Lords. The latter is largely a hereditary body, although in recent years it has included a small number of "life peers," men and women of distinction whose peerages exist in their lifetimes only and are not passed on to their heirs. Once superior to the Commons in political influence, the power of the Lords has diminished so that today they merely have power to delay legislation, for one month in the case

[3] No government having a majority has been defeated in the House of Commons since 1895. Minority governments, such as Labour was in the twenties, have dissolved the House following a defeat and new elections have been held.

of finance bills and one year in other matters. Although the House of Lords still serves useful functions, such as providing more careful and deliberate consideration of bills by men of wide knowledge and great experience, its power has been so reduced that many observers speak of Parliament and the House of Commons as if the two were synonymous.

The House of Commons is made up of 630 popularly elected members. The chamber in which it meets is rectangular, with a wide aisle down the middle. The members of the two major political parties sit facing each other across the aisle on tiers of benches. At one end of the chamber is the Speaker's chair. On the benches to his right sit the members of the majority party and on those to his left the opposition. On the respective front benches sit the leaders of the two parties.

The presiding officer of the Commons, the Speaker, is elected from among its members. Once elected he withdraws from partisan politics and becomes completely impartial, unlike the speaker of the United States House of Representatives, who is an intense partisan. There has been, moreover, an unwritten understanding (violated by Labour in some recent elections) that the Speaker will be automatically re-elected to his post, and that he will not be opposed in his bid for re-election to the Commons.

All bills must be submitted to the House of Commons, although some may originate in the Lords. In the Commons they undergo consideration both by committee and by the whole House. The principal provisions of a bill are debated by the House before the bill is sent to committee; indeed, a bill is sent to committee only if the initial vote is favorable. Committees therefore know that every bill sent to them is assured of final passage, and must work to realize the aims and purposes of the bills under consideration. They cannot seek to change them radically. In the case of measures proposed by the cabinet, the appropriate minister or his deputy is in the committee, helping to shape and to guide the bill through. Bills introduced by ministers are known as government measures, while other bills concerning public policy are called private members' bills. Those of purely local concern, that is with a local or personal application, are called private bills.

It is interesting to note that House of Commons committees are not specialized (for foreign affairs, agriculture, and so on) but are simply designated by letters (Committees A, B, C, and so on). The membership of each committee changes to some extent with every new measure sent to it, so that a member of the Commons with special qualifications may be assigned to a particular committee which may be considering a measure in his area of competence. There is no seniority principle and no competition for committee membership. Committee chairmen, like the Speaker, are impartial. Bills do not carry the names of House of Commons members, nor are committees referred to by the chairmen's names.

As we have seen, cabinet measures have priority in Parliament, assuring the government that its proposals will be acted upon. The cabinet, moreover, has control of finance: it alone submits bills for the spending and raising of revenue. Standing orders—that is, the rules of the House—prohibit motions to increase expenditure, thus avoiding "pork-barrel" legislation. Motions to reduce expenditure are in order, but such motions would be regarded as expressing a want of confidence in the cabinet, and treated as such. Finally, the government has no problem in bringing a measure to a vote. Debate can be cut off by an ordinary majority vote.

Since the cabinet governs, the primary role of the House of Commons is criticism and control, a function the House exercises in several ways. Four times a week at the beginning of the day's session there is the Question Hour, a time when any member of the Commons may address questions to ministers about any matter within their province. Ministers generally reply fully and carefully, although on occasion (particularly when questions are in the realm of foreign affairs or defense) they may assert that it would not be in the national interest to answer. In addition to Question Hour, there are the debates on bills brought in by the cabinet. And from time to time, motions of censure may be introduced, forcing the ministers to defend their actions and policies. Conversely, the cabinet itself may propose a motion expressing confidence in the government, usually after criticism has been voiced by the opposition. Through these various means, the opposition can, on behalf of the public, extract information, ventilate its grievances, and voice its concerns about governmental measures and policies. The cabinet, for its part, has the opportunity to explain and defend its acts.

It is significant that a considerable amount of parliamentary time is set aside for the use of the opposition. The Speech from the Throne, delivered by the queen at the opening of each session of Parliament but actually written for her by the prime minister and his colleagues and presenting their program, is subject to considerable debate, following which a vote is taken on the Address, the House of Commons' general response to the Speech from the Throne. Moreover, the so-called "Supply Days," consuming about a month's time, are for the exclusive use of the opposition, which determines what items in the cabinet's budget are to be debated. Most of this debate concerns matters of policy rather than specific items in the appropriation bills. Finally, the opposition has little difficulty in getting two or three days set aside now and then to propose and debate a censure motion involving specific policies on such matters as foreign affairs, defense, or colonial policy. In brief, the opposition's rights in Parliament must not be underestimated.

ADMINISTRATION

The day-to-day operation of modern government requires a vast army of civil servants, a body of non-elective officials often referred to collectively as the bureaucracy or civil service. These people are engaged in public administration. Because modern governments have expanded their areas of concern, the administration of public affairs has had an increasing impact on the average citizen; indeed, his principal contact with government is at the administrative level.

In Great Britain most of the work of administration is carried out through some thirty ministries. Each is organized on a hierarchical basis. At the top of the hierarchy is the minister. A member of Parliament, he is the political head of the ministry, shaping policy. At the same time, he is the administrative chief, responsible for the day-to-day administrative work of his department. Assisting him are a handful of officials whom he appoints, principally his parliamentary secretary, who belongs to the same political party and is also a member of Parliament. If the minister sits in the Lords, the parliamentary secretary is always in the Commons, although the reverse is not necessarily true.

When political control of the House of Commons changes, therefore, only the minister and his few top aides change. For all practical purposes, each ministry remains intact. Its work is supervised by a permanent secretary and a number of assistant secretaries, all of whom are permanent civil servants. They and those below them are recruited on the basis of ability, not political preferment.

The recruitment and assignment of civil servants is under the Treasury, which in this respect exercises functions comparable to those of the United States Civil Service Commission and the Bureau of the Budget. In contrast with the American practice, the British is to recruit people for the civil service on the basis of their potential for growth rather than on the basis of training and preparation for a specific job. This is especially true of recruitment for the administrative class, the highest class in the civil service. The British attract the best university graduates, irrespective of their course of study, on the assumption that such people can easily be trained for specific jobs and that they are the most promising candidates for really important positions in the future. (Of course for certain special posts, such as those calling for scientists or technicians, specialized training is necessary.)

Administrative coordination is achieved through the cabinet, for it is the cabinet, of course, that lays down the basic guidelines of policy. Much of this coordination is actually performed, however, by the Treasury. Since the Treasury is responsible for the ways money is spent, other ministries must justify their requests for money and personnel. The Treasury has a further check on them in that it also exercises an accounting function, seeing to it that money is actually spent for the purposes for which it was authorized. In broader policy matters, however, the power of the Treasury is no greater than the influence of the Chancellor of the Exchequer in the cabinet.

As we have seen, a minister is responsible to Parliament for the way his department functions. And only he is responsible, because permanent civil servants cannot be summoned by the Commons or its committees to answer for their work. Consequently, civil servants can serve their ministers to the best of their abilities without fear that they may be called to account for advising courses of action which may be politically unpopular at the moment. If the Commons is not satisfied with the minister's answers to questions put to him about the conduct of his department, it can always vote to censure him, although that is not easy.

In recent years the matter of responsibility has been complicated, however, by at least two developments. The first concerns the operation of nationalized industries. Parliament decided to put each such industry under the jurisdiction of a ministry, thus making the minister responsible for it. At the same time it wanted each nationalized industry to have some autonomy. The result was a compromise, with the minister being empowered to appoint the governing board of a nationalized industry and to pass on its basic decisions, for example the borrowing of money. In these matters the minister can be held to account. But for the individual activities of the board, over which he does not have control, he cannot be held responsible.

The second development is that of delegated legislation. With the increasing complexity of social legislation Parliament found that it could foresee fewer and fewer eventualities. Consequently it began writing legislation in broad outline form, empowering the agency charged with its administration to draft such rules and regulations—called statutory instruments—as were necessary to give the legislation effect. These rules and regulations came to be known as delegated or subordinate legislation. Since ministers were overworked, civil servants far removed from Parliament were thus writing most of the subordinate legislation. To make ministers more truly responsible, Parliament requires such statutory instruments to be laid before it. Some require affirmative parliamentary action, but most go into effect if the House of Commons does not act adversely within forty days. It is the task of the Committee on Statutory Instruments to study subordinate legislation and to call to the attention of the Commons those statutory instruments that it believes the House should consider.

THE CROWN AS AN INSTITUTION

The British have a way of preserving the form of their institutions long after their substance has been completely altered. This tendency is well illustrated by the position of the Crown. At one time all power inhered in the person of the monarch. It was not conferred by Parliament or anyone else; and it was unlimited. Today the Crown retains full power to do anything and change anything—but only on the advice of ministers who possess the confidence of the House of Commons. Thus the powers of the Crown still exist nominally, and all political acts are done in the monarch's name; but these powers, as we have seen, are now in fact exercised by officials ultimately responsible to the people.

Consequently it is necessary to bear in mind the distinction between the terms "queen" and "crown," between the person of the monarch and the monarchy as an institution. The powers of the Crown have been transferred from the queen as a person to the Crown as an abstraction. Thus Queen Elizabeth's official acts are determined for her by her ministers. But the Crown is the agency through which these acts—the appointing of civil servants, the concluding of treaties, the calling and dissolving of Parliament—are given legal form.

Perhaps the familiar announcement: "The King is dead; long live the King!" should be changed. It might more appropriately read: "The King is dead; long live the Crown!" because it is the monarchy as an institution that never dies.

LAW AND THE JUDICIARY

Great Britain is the mother of one of the world's principal legal systems, the common law, which the United States has inherited. Common law is sometimes referred to as case law, because it developed from the application by the king's judges of local custom to individual cases that came before them. After a time, these judges were applying similar legal rules throughout England, hence the term common law—law common to the whole realm. The hallmark of case law is *stare decisis,* the principle that decisions in past cases decide future ones. Hence the importance of precedent in common law.

The common law has been modified over the years in two important ways, by equity and by statute law. Equity rules grew out of appeals to the king from cases in which under the application of the common law an injustice would result. In torts, for example, the common law provided for damages to the injured party, but there was no way to prevent wrongs before they occurred. With respect to contracts, moreover, the common law forbade threats against life or limb as a means of getting a signature, but did not provide against more subtle means, such as getting a man drunk. Out of these types of cases grew up a whole system of rules known as equity law or simply equity. The common law has also been modified by statute law, particularly in recent centuries. In case of conflict, statute law supersedes both the common law and equity.

The British judicial system is characterized by independence and the rule of law. British judges are appointed for life and serve during good behavior. Independence, however, does not mean judicial review, for as has been already mentioned, no British court has the power to nullify an act of Parliament. The principle of the rule of law means that no one is above the law and that individuals can be punished only for those things which the law forbids. The end result of the application of these principles has been a high degree of impartial justice.

The English court system (Scotland has a separate judicial system) is organized into two hierarchies, one civil and the other criminal. Civil cases involving less than $600 are tried in county courts. Other civil cases originate in the High Court of Justice, which has three divisions: Queen's Bench; Chancery; Probate, Divorce and Admiralty. Appeals from county courts and from the High Court of Justice may be taken to the Court of Appeal. On the criminal side, petty offenses are tried by justices of the peace—one or more depending on the nature of the case. Offenses like assault and robbery are tried in Quarter Sessions, the first instance where a jury is used (juries are also used in civil cases). More serious crimes, such as murder and treason, are brought to the Assize courts, made up of judges assigned by the Queen's Bench division (which also assigns judges to civil cases). An example of an Assize court is the Central Criminal Court in London, popularly known as the Old Bailey. Appeals from both Quarter Sessions and Assizes are taken to the Court of Criminal Appeal.

The final court of appeal for both civil and criminal cases is the House of Lords, or more precisely, those members of the House known as the law lords acting in the name of the whole House. These are not hereditary peers, but men with legal training who are appointed for life. In the main the law lords hear appeals from civil cases involving particularly difficult points of law. It should be noted that appeals in Great Britain are much more difficult than in the United States. In virtually all instances, permission of the higher court is required, and appeals are normally restricted to cases in which the lower court's interpretation of the law has been challenged.

LOCAL GOVERNMENT

Great Britain has a long tradition of local government (units of local government were in existence before there was a central government), but the areas of local discretion have been increasingly narrowed. Although they are organizationally independent, local authorities have been more and more engaged in the local administration of national programs. Certain services once provided locally, such as public assistance, gas, electricity, and hospital management, are now a national responsibility. On the other hand, local authorities still exercise wide discretion over sanitation, street lighting, recreational and cultural facilities, and child welfare. In the field of education, national authority has also been on the increase, although actual administration (the hiring and firing of teachers, for example) is a local responsibility. This trend toward national responsibility has been facilitated by the circumstance that there is no constitutional division of authority between national and local authorities.

The central government exercises three types of control over local authorities. The first is legal: Parliament can grant powers to local authorities and it can take them away. The second is financial: the national government provides over half the funds needed by local authorities and in large measure specifies the way they are to be spent. The third is supervisory: various national ministries, through statutory instruments, memoranda, inspectors and district auditors, and also through their power to approve or disapprove local proposals in many areas of activity, influence and control the work of local government. The Home Secretary, for example, has significant supervisory powers over the police, and the Minister of Education over the schools.

Although units of local government have been in existence a long time, the machinery of local government was radically overhauled and modernized by several acts of Parliament during the nineteenth century. Today the principal institutions of local government are the elected councils in the cities and counties and the appointed full-time officials who perform the day-to-day tasks of local government. The councilors are the unpaid amateurs, though they are responsible for local policy and administration. Most of the actual work of the council, however, is performed by committees and sub-committees. Although some party politics enters local government, rigid partisan attitudes are rare. The full-time appointed officials are paid, and because salary and other benefits have improved in recent years, local administration is looked upon as a worthwhile career. Similarly, service on the local council is considered advantageous to those who aspire to a parliamentary career.

The System in Action

The British system of government is a good example of a democratic system that has been able to adjust peacefully and well to changing circumstances. Since the peaceful revolution of 1688, when Parliament gained supremacy over the monarch, the political order has gone through several important periods of transition. Gradually Parliament gained control over the ministers and made their tenure in office dependent upon its will. Subsequently, Parliament itself came to be controlled by the electorate, mainly because of the extension of the suffrage, which had the further result of elevating the House of Commons to its predominant position.

The development of political parties, and of a two-party system, made possible the periodic and orderly transfer of political power from one to another dominant group in the society. This transfer was epitomized in the nineteenth century by the alternation in power of Gladstone and Disraeli, the former a leader of the Liberals and the latter of the Conservatives. The "ins" and the "outs" changed places without serious or damaging shock to the system. At the same time, the system accommodated the gradual demise of the Liberal party and its replacement by the Labour party as one of the two major political groups.

The British system was flexible in another way. The political preferences of the electorate could shift and change in response to economic and social changes. Parties once dedicated to free enterprise could accept social welfare legislation. Governmental intervention in the economy was never rejected out of hand, but considered in the light of national needs. The Conservatives and Liberals, for example, inaugurated some social welfare legislation early in this century. At the end of World War II both major political parties accepted the necessity of an increase in governmental intervention, although Labour was dedicated to a more thorough revamping of the economic system, and it was after the Labour victory in 1945 that certain industries were nationalized and additional social services provided. It is significant, however, that when the Conservatives returned to power, virtually all of the Labour legislation was retained. The Conservatives "denationalized" the steel industry, but this was a piece of Labour legislation that had not yet been implemented.

These profound political and social changes have been wrought in Great Britain without violence. Neither of the two major political parties has threatened to refuse to go along, or to seek to disrupt the system, because it could not have things its own way. Arguments there have been—sometimes sharp ones—but in the end a consensus has been arrived at through discussion, debate, and the ballot box.

The British system has long been of special interest to political scientists for other reasons. Not only was it the first system to develop the forms of political organization that we now call the cabinet type of constitutional government; it has very widely been accepted as the classic model of this type. Many new nations all over the world have attempted to pattern their systems after the British. Understanding it and the respects in which it differs from other major systems is therefore of special importance when we try to compare political institutions and processes in different countries to arrive at a more general understanding of government.

What are the consequences of differences between the cabinet system as exemplified by Great Britain, the presidential system of the United States, the parliamentary system as exemplified by the French Third and Fourth Republics, and the peculiar form of presidential-parliamentary government instituted by the Fifth? How are these consequences related to other differences between some or all of these systems and such regimes as those of Nazi Germany or Soviet Russia? Can non-Western societies in the modern age expect the same results from the adoption of similar political institutions?

Familiarity with the structure and working of the British system is indispensable to the consideration of such questions. But it is only through comparative analysis of many systems that we can begin to answer them. We turn next, therefore, to an examination of the American system, which, though historically an offshoot of the British, has developed distinctive characteristics clearly differentiating it from the British type of constitutional democracy.

SUGGESTIONS FOR ADDITIONAL READING

AMERY, LEOPOLD, *Thoughts on the Constitution* (London: Oxford University Press, 1953).

BAGEHOT, WALTER, *The English Constitution* (London: World Classics Edition, 1928).

BEER, SAMUEL H., *British Politics in the Collectivist Age* (New York: Alfred A. Knopf, 1965).

GUTTSMAN, W. L., *The British Political Elite* (London: Macgibbon & Kee, 1963).

JENNINGS, SIR IVOR, *The British Constitution*, 4th edition (Cambridge, Eng.: Cambridge University Press, 1961).

————, *Cabinet Government*, 3rd edition (Cambridge, Eng.: Cambridge University Press, 1959).

LASKI, HAROLD, *Reflections on the Constitution* (New York: Viking Press, 1951).

MACKINTOSH, JOHN P., *The British Cabinet* (London: Stevens & Sons Ltd., 1962).

MCKENZIE, R. T., *British Political Parties: The Distribution of Power Within the Conservative and Labour Parties*, 2nd edition (New York, London: Frederick A. Praeger, 1964).

MORRISON, HERBERT, *Government and Parliament: A Survey from the Inside*, 3rd edition (London: Oxford University Press, 1964).

Chapter 3

THE GOVERNMENT
OF THE UNITED STATES

It may seem strange that many and perhaps most of the classic descriptions of American government have been written by non-Americans, men like Tocqueville and Bryce. This is more understandable, however, when one considers how difficult it is for the American who stands in the midst of the political trees to discern and describe faithfully the broad sweep and contours of the governmental forest. In many ways our own political world is "too much with us" for us to see ourselves as others see us. This chapter will nevertheless attempt to take a broad view of American government, following the pattern of the previous chapter in seeking to understand American constitutional development, the social forces and political groups at work in the United States, and American governmental institutions in theory and practice.

Constitutional Development

It is easy to forget, in our understandable pre-occupation with the present and the immediate past, that our nation was a part of the British Empire for nearly as long as it has been separated from it. Though the framers of the Constitution were creative and inventive in many respects, they were strongly conditioned by their British heritage and the American colonial experience.

Colonial Beginnings. The early British colonists came to America with new hopes, but they also brought old traditions, the social system of seventeenth-century England, belief in the importance of constitutionalism (as embodied in the Magna Carta), trial by jury and due process of law, British ideas of representation and parliamentary government, and the British common law. The New England colonies were strongly influenced by Puritan ideas of theocratic government, in which power resided in a spiritual aristocracy. Religious requirements for voting and holding public office were established, and Calvinistic standards of morality were enforced upon all citizens; indeed, government in New England became as intolerant, religiously, as the British government and the established Anglican church from which the colonists had fled. Yet the seeds of democracy were also present in New England, in the democratic pattern of congregational church government, with each congregation electing its pastor and church officers; in the direct democracy of the New England town meeting (at least for those who were qualified voters); and in the colonists' leanings toward the social contract theory, as practiced in the Mayflower Compact and espoused by Roger Williams when he established what later became Rhode Island.

The southern colonies were largely spared a religious issue because their settlers were chiefly Anglicans—younger sons of wealthy English families. These young aristocrats succeeded in establishing in the southern colonies something like the English socio-economic pattern: an agricultural economy based on landed estates (plantations), with Negro slaves for manual labor. The middle colonies, like Pennsylvania and Maryland, differed in important respects both from theocratic New England and the aristocratic South. The Quakers who founded Pennsylvania, and the Catholics who founded Maryland, along with the followers of Roger Williams in Rhode Island, pioneered in granting religious freedom. Interestingly enough, Pennsylvania and Rhode Island were also leaders in the development of political democracy.

Revolution and Confederation. Despite the differences among the thirteen colonies, broadly similar lines of development—with respect to political attitudes, experiences, and needs—began to congeal during the eighteenth century. The political ideas we usually associate with the American Revolution and the years immediately following were strongly reinforced by (as well as owed to) political controversies, events, and writings in England and France. The ideas of social compact and popular sovereignty were encouraged by the English Glorious Revolution of 1688 and the writings of John Locke in support of it. The colonists' ideals of civil liberty found support in the English Bill of Rights of 1689, and the concepts of natural law and natural rights had similar support in French philosophical writings. Such ideas as separation of powers, checks and balances, and rotation in office had French and English origins in the writings of Montesquieu and Harrington.

But little real sense of unity developed among the colonists until the years immediately preceding the Revolutionary War, when controversy with the mother country developed and the end of the French presence in Canada removed the most compelling need for British protection. Until now the colonists' loyalty had been to the British Crown and to their own colonies, but not to America. Concerted colonial action had received little encouragement, either from the English government or from local colonial leadership. The early experiment with the New England Confederation (1643–1683) and Benjamin Franklin's Albany Plan (1754) for continental government inspired little lasting support.

But grievances against the British mercantile system's restrictive effect on colonial trade finally came to a head at the conclusion of the Seven Years' War (1763). Although the agricultural South was less aroused over these restrictions than the northern seaboard area, a British "get tough" tax policy and the quartering of British troops at colonial expense united the thirteen colonies in resistance. Early protests were primarily legalistic in nature, involving charges of denial of trial by one's peers and of taxation without representation. When these protests failed, leadership began to pass into the hands of more radical men, such as Samuel and John Adams, Patrick Henry, Thomas Paine, and Thomas Jefferson. Their arguments were more philosophical and moral than legal, emphasizing the natural rights of man, the social contract theory, popular sovereignty, the "consent of the governed," and, indirectly, the right of revolution.

The Declaration of Independence and the events of the Revolutionary War do not need to be recounted here. We should note, however, that as the fighting began the new "states" replaced their colonial charters with constitutions containing strong statements of popular sovereignty, bills of rights, and severe limitations on the power of government generally. This understandable but extreme reaction to their recent experience with strong government resulted in weak government bordering on anarchy, both within and among the new states. The state governor was a mere figurehead, elected in most states by the legislature for a one-year term and deprived of any veto power or appreciable appointing power—a direct reaction to the recent symbol of external oppression, the colonial governor. By contrast the colonial assemblies, which had been the champions of popular causes, were succeeded by state legislatures authorized to exercise the bulk of state powers. Bicameralism was adopted in eleven of the original thirteen state constitutions, with both branches being popularly elected. Yet despite the strong democratic character of the new state governments, suffrage continued to be limited to property owners. The colonial court system was changed but little.

The national government provided by the Articles of Confederation in 1781 was even weaker than the state governments. Though it rested on a written constitution and managed to preserve at least the idea of unity, it lacked such fundamental powers as the taxing power and the power to regulate interstate and foreign commerce. It could not require the states to honor either their own commitments or those made by

Congress, and—probably basic to all its other weaknesses—it could not pass laws applying directly to the individual citizen. Furthermore, the Articles provided no executive branch or national judiciary; required unanimity among the states for passage of amendments; and gave each state one vote in Congress, with members of Congress being appointed and recalled by their state governments.

Under such a regime economic and political conditions within and between the states grew increasingly chaotic. Each state's currency became so badly depreciated that it was refused by all the other states as well as by foreign merchants. Interstate and foreign trade was paralyzed by separate state tariff walls. The absence of a national judiciary made it impossible to collect interstate debts. Debtor-controlled legislatures began to pass "stay laws" extending the period for the payment of mortgages and inflationary currency measures, though such measures did not prevent violence (Shays' Rebellion) by desperate debtor-farmers seeking to prevent the foreclosure of mortgages on their farms.

Against this background of weak government, domestic difficulties, and foreign threats, the radicals who had been so prominent in the Revolution began to lose power. The conservatives—property owners, creditors, shippers, and "solid citizens" generally—began to talk of ways of strengthening the Union, protecting property rights, and promoting business development. Eventually representatives from five states, meeting in convention at Annapolis in 1786, petitioned Congress to call a convention of delegates from all the states to meet in Philadelphia in May 1787, "for the sole and express purpose of revising the Articles of Confederation."

The Constitutional Convention. Though the convention had been called only to "revise" the Articles, the fifty-five attending delegates (out of seventy-four appointed) soon concluded that a wholly new charter had to be drafted. Average attendance at the sessions was about thirty or thirty-five. The convention was thus a small body, quite distinguished but hardly representative of the country as a whole. The membership consisted of successful merchants, bankers, lawyers, planters, and statesmen, and came primarily from urban rather than rural areas. The majority owned public securities; many were money-lenders, slave-owners, and speculators in land. The more active and influential participants in the convention were Alexander Hamilton of New York; George Washington, James Madison, Edmund Randolph and George Mason of Virginia; Benjamin Franklin and Gouverneur Morris of Pennsylvania; John Dickinson of Delaware; and William Paterson of New Jersey. Many of the delegates were young men—Hamilton was only 30 and Madison was 36. Benjamin Franklin, at 81, was the oldest delegate and, though considered "too democratic" by most of the delegates, served as a stabilizing force during moments of tension and bitterness.

Conspicious by their absence were many of the important figures of the time, particularly such leaders of the Revolution as Thomas Jefferson, Samuel and John Adams, John Jay, Thomas Paine, Patrick Henry, Richard Henry Lee, and John Hancock. Jefferson, Jay, and John Adams were absent on other duties, and Samuel Adams was not appointed a delegate from Massachusetts. Patrick Henry was appointed but refused to serve because he "smelt a rat"—a suspicion shared by the Rhode Island legislature, which refused to send any delegates. The more radical spokesmen for democracy were thus represented only by the aged Franklin, and virtually all of the convention's leaders warned of the dangers and evils of democracy. But despite the delegates' general distrust of direct democracy, they knew that it would be politically impossible to stray very far from the essentially democratic principles expressed in the Declaration of Independence.

It took the delegates only five days to decide that mere amendments to the Articles would be inadequate and that "a national government ought to be established consisting of a supreme legislative, executive, and judiciary." The days which followed were devoted in large measure to compromising the serious differences among the various groups, especially to those resolved in the three famous compromises. The first, the so-called Connecticut or Great Compromise, was a compromise between large and small states over representation in Congress. The Virginia Plan had favored the large states by basing a state's representation on population; the New Jersey Plan would have given each state equal representation. The deadlock was broken with a proposal for a bicameral legislature with a lower house based on population and an upper house in which each state would have an equal vote. The large states considered this to be a serious setback, but finally accepted it as the small states' price for union.

The second or Three-Fifths Compromise ended a dispute between North and South over how to count slaves for purposes of representation in the lower house. To increase their quotas in Congress, the southern states wanted to count slaves, while the northern states, having few slaves, did not. At the same time the question of counting slaves for purposes of apportioning direct taxes was involved, with southern states now opposing their inclusion. The resulting compromise made use of a practical, if less than humane, formula, previously used by Congress in requesting funds from the states: a slave was counted as three-fifths of a free person, for purposes of both representation and taxation.

Southerners feared the possibility that their predominantly agricultural interest might suffer at the hands of a northern majority in the passage of export duties, the negotiation of unfavorable treaties of trade and commerce, and even the abolition of the importation of slaves. The northern states, in turn, were keenly interested in having a government with full power to regulate trade and navigation, levy import and export duties, and ultimately to eliminate the infamous African slave trade. The outcome was a compromise that gave Congress broad powers to regulate interstate and foreign commerce and to levy duties on imports but not exports, and that forbade prohibition of the importation of slaves before 1808. In addition, the southern delegates secured as further protection the requirement of a two-thirds majority of the Senate for consent to the ratification of treaties.

But in understanding the politics of constitution-making it is perhaps more important to examine the areas of *consensus* among the delegates than it is to look at the well-publicized *conflicts* and compromises. The general conservatism of the delegates was reflected in substantial agreement that the right to vote should not be extended to those who did not own property and the establishment of voting requirements should be left to the states. The concepts of a written constitution and of limited government were not subjects for debate, even by those few delegates who favored a monarch. Similarly there was no real conflict on the basic principle of federalism. Finally, the framers were in strong agreement that provision for stability and balance in government was far more important than provision for change. This consensus is reflected in the various checks and balances built into the system to ensure that no single interest would prevail over others. The separation of the executive, legislative, and judicial powers and the provision of a difficult method of amending the Constitution were the products of a conscious effort to promote stability. Few of the delegates would have disagreed with Gouverneur Morris' statement that protection of property was "the principal object of government."

The Struggle over Ratification. Even though the framers of the Constitution departed from the rule of unanimity prescribed by the Articles of Confederation for passage of amendments and called for approval by only nine of the thirteen states, ratification was by no means assured. The outcome in such important states as Virginia and New York was very doubtful, even after nine other states had ratified. A close victory in Massachusetts was won only after the opposition of Samuel Adams and John Hancock had been cleverly appeased and the passage of a series of amendments to protect individual rights (the Bill of Rights) was promised. Virginia's ratification came after a debate between two groups of delegates who were almost as illustrious as those in the Constitutional Convention itself. Patrick Henry, George Mason, James Monroe, and Richard Henry Lee led the opposition, and James Madison, Edmund Randolph, George Washington, and young John Marshall were the principal supporters. New York became the eleventh state to ratify, but its two-vote margin came only after a masterful campaign by Alexander Hamilton, John Jay, and James Madison, who wrote a series of essays which have come to be known as *The Federalist.* The eighty-five essays, published in the leading New York newspapers, have since been hailed by historians as one of the most profound treatises on government ever written. North Carolina ratified in 1789, and Rhode Island made the Union complete in the spring of 1790.

An interesting question, though now a purely academic one, is whether the method of adoption of the Constitution was really "unconstitutional." The delegates were authorized only to revise the Articles, not to write a new constitution; they represented only twelve of the thirteen states; the Articles' requirement of unanimous ratification was not followed, at least initially; and ratification was by special conventions rather than by the state legislatures. Because of these procedural violations, some historians speak of the Constitutional Convention as a *coup d'état* or as a second American revolution, with Federalists winning over anti-Federalists. Others say the people simply decided to "start over again" and were successful. While little is gained by debating such a question, the twentieth-century student of government can profit from an awareness of the Founding Fathers' greater concern with finding practical solutions to real problems than with the procedural legalisms of the Articles of Confederation. The American constitutional literalists of today can find little support for their position in the history of the framing and adoption of the Constitution.

AMERICAN CONSTITUTIONAL PRINCIPLES

The American Constitution is extremely brief, as written constitutions go, and comes closer to the ideal of being concerned only with "fundamentals" than do most modern constitutions, especially American state constitutions with their clutter of details. What are these fundamentals? Most are by no means unique principles of government in the sense that they are to be found only in the United States, but it can be said that the American *combination* of these "basic rules of the game," discussed below, *is* unique and has no counterpart elsewhere in the world.

Popular Sovereignty. "Sovereignty" is a troublesome word for political scientists because of its emphasis on supreme and final *legal* power rather than on actual or practical *political* power. Nevertheless, the presumption of popular sovereignty—supreme power residing in the people—runs throughout the Constitution, and an understanding of it is essential to an understanding of American constitutional development. Tocqueville described the classic idea of American popular sovereignty when he wrote that the qualified voters reign in the American political world "as the Deity does in the Universe."

The principle of popular sovereignty is clear, but it runs into difficulty in practical application. Was sovereignty transferred from the English king and Parliament directly to the American people as a whole or to the people of the thirteen states separately? The familiar controversy between nationalists and states' rights advocates over nullification and secession is related to this question, and the nationalists won only after the bloodshed of the Civil War. Does popular sovereignty support the right of revolution? During the early days of the Republic the right to revolt was strongly defended, but more recently support for it cannot be found, in official pronouncements at least. One of the most recent official concessions to the right of revolution was the Supreme Court's distinction in 1957 in the *Yates* case between theoretical belief and revolutionary action, with punishment limited to the latter.

Representative Government. The Constitution provides for a representative system, rather than pure or direct democracy. Although the initiative, referendum, and recall are used in varying degrees in state and local government and although town meetings continue to be held in parts of New England, the pattern for the nation as a whole is one of government by elected representatives. There is no national initiative or recall, and no national referendum as such, except for the very limited use of the referendum in such cases as a farm vote on crop controls.

Separation of Powers; Checks and Balances. The separation of powers —that is, a division of functions among the executive, legislative, and judicial branches of the national government—is supported by an elaborate system of checks and balances. Thus the legislative body is not the central agency, as it is in those countries having a parliamentary form of government, in which the prime minister and his cabinet serve at the pleasure of the parliament and in which the courts may not invalidate parliamentary action. Although the Constitution does not state specifically that the powers must be separated, this is the practical effect of the language used in creating the three branches in Articles I, II, and III.

The system of checks and balances makes each branch of government responsive to different political groups. Thus Congress is checked by the existence of two houses, by Presidential veto, and by judicial review. The President is checked by the right of Congress to enact appropriations, override a Presidential veto, and impeach the President; by the right of the Senate to approve treaties and certain appointments; and by judicial review. The judicial branch is checked by Presidential appointment of judges and by the congressional power to impeach and to determine the size and appellate jurisdiction of the courts.

A Federal System. The American adoption of a federal, rather than a unitary, form of government was in effect predetermined by the circumstances of 1787. Although federalism was not an American invention, nor unique in any theoretical sense, it had never before been tried in the governing of such a large area. It involved the distribution of powers between the national government, which was given delegated or enumerated powers, and the individual states, which under the Tenth Amendment were guaranteed all reserved or residual powers not specifically given to the national government. The constitutional definition of national powers has been given room for flexibility and growth by the "necessary and proper" clause (Article I, Section 8), which authorizes Congress to make such laws as may be necessary and proper to carry out its expressly delegated powers. Thus the broad range of powers of the national government is based on both expressed and implied powers.

Technically speaking, "federal government" refers to the whole governmental system, including national and state governments, and it is incorrect to use the term "federal" to designate only the national level. In common American usage, however, in such terms as "federal courts," "federal administrators," and "federal Congress," "federal" refers to the central government.[1]

Supremacy of the National Government. With the near anarchy of the Articles of Confederation fresh in their minds, the delegates to the Constitutional Convention placed the authority to settle jurisdictional conflicts between the national and state governments in the hands of the national government, specifying that the Constitution, acts of Congress, and treaties are the "supreme law of the land."

Judicial Review. The right of the courts to declare acts of Congress unconstitutional has been exercised almost since the beginning of America's history as a nation—since 1803, in fact, when in the case of *Marbury* v. *Madison* the Supreme Court first declared that an act of Congress violated the Constitution. The fact that the Constitution does not specifically grant the power of judicial review has made the practice the subject of considerable controversy through the years. Nevertheless, the preponderance of historical research indicates that the framers of the Constitution thought judicial review was clearly implied in the language they used. Acceptance of the principle has made the United States Supreme Court more powerful than any judicial agency in the world and has helped make the doctrine of separation of powers more than mere theory.

Limited Government. The American fundamental law also embodies the idea that there are some things which *no* government, national or state, may do. The principle of limited government, like those of federalism and separation of powers, is not detailed in any one place in the Constitution. But a written constitution is itself a manifestation of the idea of limited government; more particularly so are the Bill of Rights and the Civil War amendments (the Thirteenth, Fourteenth, and Fifteenth), which place certain individual rights "out of bounds" insofar as action

[1] For a fuller discussion of federal government in the United States and elsewhere, see Chapter 8.

by either level of government is concerned. In addition, the limitations on Congress stipulated by the Bill of Rights have been increasingly incorporated by the courts into the Fourteenth Amendment as limitations on the states. Examples of other specific limitations include the prohibition on export duties by the national government, the ban on state laws impairing the obligation of contracts, and the prohibition on both levels of government against the deprivation of life, liberty, or property without due process of law. In these and other limitations the framers of the Constitution were seeking to solve the age-old problem of how to have a government which has the necessary power to coerce its citizens, yet which ensures a maximum degree of personal liberty.

Constitutional Change: Formal and Informal. The Constitution provides two methods of proposing formal amendments and two methods of ratification. Only one method of proposal has ever been successfully used—that of a two-thirds vote of both houses of Congress. Proposal by a convention called by Congress upon petition by legislatures in two-thirds of the states has been tried on numerous occasions unsuccessfully. Amendments may be ratified by legislatures in three-fourths of the states or by conventions in three-fourths of the states; except for the repeal of prohibition, all amendments have been ratified by legislative action.

The first ten amendments, known as the Bill of Rights, were promised to leaders in the reluctant states during the campaign for ratification, with pro-Constitution leaders pledging action by the first Congress (see page 79). The next two amendments settled certain difficulties which arose early in the nation's history, by providing that a state cannot be sued by a citizen of another state, and for separate balloting in the electoral college for President and Vice-President. The Civil War amendments (the Thirteenth, Fourteenth, and Fifteenth) prohibited slavery; defined citizenship and placed restrictions on the states pertaining to interstate citizenship, due process of law, and equal protection of the laws; and prohibited restrictions on voting on account of race, color, or previous condition of servitude.

A forty-year drought in amendments ended in 1913 when a progressive income tax was authorized by the Sixteenth Amendment. In the same year popular election of senators was provided in the Seventeenth Amendment. Shortly after World War I the Eighteenth Amendment authorized the short-lived experiment in prohibition of the liquor traffic and the Nineteenth Amendment provided universal woman suffrage. Two amendments were passed in 1933. The Twentieth moved back the date for inaugurating a new President from March 4 to January 20 and fixed the term of a new Congress to make "lame-duck" sessions virtually impossible. The Twenty-first Amendment repealed prohibition. The Twenty-second Amendment (1951) came as a reaction to the breach in the two-term tradition by the four elections of Franklin D. Roosevelt and limits a President to two elected terms in office. Residents of the District of Columbia were permitted to vote in Presidential elections by the Twenty-third Amendment, ratified in 1961. The Twenty-fourth Amendment, outlawing the poll tax as a requirement for voting, was ratified in 1964. A Twenty-fifth Amendment, prescribing procedure in case of Presidential disability, in 1965 passed the congressional hurdle toward ratification.

It is clear from this brief history of formal amendments that such changes are not easy, and that many amendments have been of relatively minor significance. By far the greatest changes in the American governmental system, particularly the relative increase in the powers of the central government, have come about by methods other than formal constitutional amendment. Judicial and executive interpretation, legislative elaboration, and usage or custom have all played vital roles in making the basic "rules of the game" what they are today.

There is much evidence, for example, to support a contention that judicial interpretation has been far more influential than formal amendments in shaping American institutions. The oft-quoted statement of former Chief Justice Hughes that "we are under the Constitution, but the Constitution is what the judges say it is," may be shocking to some, but it is basically true. It is the judges, for example, who decided that the preamble to the Constitution provides no grants of power, that an income tax is a "direct tax," that Congress can create a national bank, and that acts of Congress may be declared unconstitutional by the courts. Different courts have always given different meanings to the Constitution, but some of the most dramatic reversals of the rule of *stare decisis* have been made by the Supreme Court in recent years. Thus a party primary is now considered an election, whereas once it was not; minimum wage laws for women once violated the due process clause, but now they do not; federal regulation of interstate commerce at one time did not extend to manufacturing, mining, or agricultural production, but now it does; state segregation laws until recently did not violate the Constitution, but now they do; and required prayer and Bible reading in the public schools have only recently been declared unconstitutional.

Congress too shapes the development of the Constitution as it spins a legislative web in and around the general phrases found in the document. Various "holes" in the Constitution, such as Presidential succession if there is no Vice-President, the functions and interrelations of the executive departments, and much of the organization of the federal court system all have been filled by congressional action. Thus the Constitution is also, in some respects, what Congress says it is.

And through the years various Presidents have construed the Constitution in particular ways; often their interpretations have prevailed. The Louisiana Purchase was consummated by Jefferson without prior consent of Congress, even though the Constitution does not expressly enumerate such a Presidential power. The use of federal troops within a state to enforce federal law and protect federal property was asserted as a right by President Cleveland. Congressional restrictions on the removal of executive employees were contested with some success by Andrew Johnson, Woodrow Wilson, and Franklin D. Roosevelt. Although not all executive actions go unchallenged, as is illustrated by Truman's unsuccessful "steel seizure case," many do escape successful challenge, and by virtue of the precedents they set become virtually a permanent extension of the Constitution.

Many other unwritten provisions of the Constitution have come to be accepted simply through habit, custom, and the mere passage of time. Political parties have become an indispensable part of the basic rules of the game, but they are nowhere mentioned in the Constitution. Although the framers of the Constitution considered the electoral college a brilliant invention, it has not functioned as they intended since as early as 1796. Other important institutions which are the product of custom are the President's cabinet, legislative committees, and the tradition that members of the House of Representatives must be residents of the districts from which they are elected.

These formal and informal methods of constitutional change have made possible what is often called "a living Constitution," able thus far to keep pace with radical changes in American social, economic, and political life. Its combination of flexibility with stability has made it a truly remarkable document in world history. We do not really leave this subject as we turn to a consideration of the major social forces which have been instrumental in shaping the American governmental system.

Social Forces

American political behavior and institutions are in large measure a composite of such factors as the hopes, fears, customs, tensions, and drives of the American people. Any discussion of legal doctrines like federalism, separation of powers, and judicial review is hollow indeed without taking into consideration the social context within which they operate. Population characteristics, social stratification, religion, geography, economic forces, and national security tensions all have a close, continuous, and important relationship to American politics.

POPULATION: GROWING, MOVING, CHANGING

Population Growth. From an initial population of 4 million at the time the Constitution was written, the number of Americans has grown, through the effects of immigration and natural increase, to about 195 million in 1965. In 1790 there were 105 members of the United States House of Representatives, each representing about 35,000 people; in

1965, in a House of 435 members, each member represented on an average almost 450,000 people. The rate of increase in the nineteenth century seldom dropped below 25 per cent per decade. It began to slacken in the 1920s with a curtailment of immigration and a decline in the birth rate, reaching an all-time low of 7.2 per cent during the depression decade of the 1930s. With a return to prosperity, a sharp increase in the birth rate has caused demographers to abandon their earlier predictions of a "flattened out" population curve for the United States. The rate of increase in the 1940s was 14.5 per cent, more than double that of the previous decade, and rose even further between 1950 and 1960 to 18.5 per cent. Public schools in particular are feeling the population pressures, and the Bureau of the Census predicts no relief, forecasting a population of 235 million by 1975.

The American population is aging as well as growing, a fact with important implications for politicians and welfare administrators. The median age of Americans was only 16.7 years in 1820, but rose to 22.9 in 1900 and reached a peak of 30.2 in 1950. It dropped slightly to 29.5 in 1960—a reflection of the booming birth rate rather than of any decline in life expectancy. The percentage of population sixty-five years of age and over increased from 6.8 per cent to 9.2 per cent between 1940 and 1960. There is every indication that the proportion of American population in the older age brackets will grow increasingly large in future years.

Immigration and the "Melting Pot." Immigration from other nations has been the very lifeblood of the United States. The movement of 40 million Europeans to this country in a little more than a century is a development unparalleled in world history and has made America a fabled "melting pot." The sources of immigrants during the 1800s were mainly Great Britain, Germany, and Scandinavia, but beginning about 1880 Italy and the Slavic countries of Central and Eastern Europe began to provide the bulk of new arrivals. The early need for labor and the abundance of land supported a national policy of open doors to immigrants, but the disappearance of the land frontier in 1890, coupled with the growing power of organized labor and the recurrence of depressions, contributed to an eventual reversal of this policy.

With the possible exception of the American Indians, the American people today are all descendants of immigrants who brought with them and retained in varying degrees the political, economic, and social traditions of their mother countries. They are a complicated mixture of nationalities, races, and religions, whose outlooks have not all been reduced by the melting pot into one "American mind." Concentrations of peoples sharing the culture of a particular country—Irish, Italian, or Polish settlements, for example—still constitute important political blocs in some parts of the United States.

.   .   .

Race. In 1960, 88.6 per cent of the American population was white. Though the 1960 census reported 524,000 American Indians and 700,000 people of Chinese and Japanese origin, American non-whites today are predominantly Negroes. Assimilation of the Negro into the American polity and society has been a most difficult problem throughout the nation's history, and the race problem today has no small place in both national and international politics. The American Negro's persistent drive from his former role as a servile adjunct to Southern agriculture to a position of full equality, whether in the North or South, continues to be one of the stronger social forces shaping American politics.

Urbanism, Suburbanism, and Metropolitanism. The United States population is not only growing; it is moving around and changing in ways possibly more influential on American politics than mere growth. Among the more important kinds of change are the three "isms" of population movement: urbanism, suburbanism, and metropolitanism. The amazing shift of population from rural to urban areas is seen unmistakably in the following figures from past census reports:

Year	Per Cent Urban	Year	Per Cent Urban
1790	5.1	1880	28.2
1800	6.1	1900	39.7
1820	7.2	1920	51.2
1840	10.8	1940	56.5
1860	19.8	1960	69.9

This change from 95 per cent rural to nearly 70 per cent urban helps explain much about modern American government that is often misunderstood: the expansion of governmental functions, taxes, and expenditures, for example, and the feeling that even local government has lost much of the "personal touch" it had when grandfather was a boy. It is the crowded, dependent, insecure urban wage-earner who invites and even compels an ever-growing number of governmental activities to serve and regulate all phases of his daily life. Until the Supreme Court's landmark case of *Baker* v. *Carr*, the new urban areas were frustrated in their efforts to obtain equitable representation in state legislatures and, to some extent, in Congress.

An added dimension to American urbanism has been the flight to suburbia of more than 50 million people, a flight vastly accelerated in recent years. Thus while centripetal forces have been luring millions from farms to cities, centrifugal forces have been scattering still more millions into sprawling suburbs. Indeed, the suburbs of the great metropolitan areas in the United States are fast overtaking the central cities in population. While the central cities were gaining only 5.6 million (7.1 per cent) between 1950 and 1960, the metropolitan suburbs gained 28 million (almost 50 per cent) during the same decade. Many core cities are already outvoted by their suburbs, and the total population of central cities in 1960 was 58.0 million, compared with the only slightly lower total of 54.9 million for the suburbs. Of the ten largest American cities in 1950, all but one (Los Angeles) were reported in the 1960 census as actually losing population.

The rise of suburbia and the decline and blight of the central city have had an important impact on local government, an impact which has required the coining of such new words as "metropolitanism" and "metropolitics." A metropolitan area usually includes a core city of 50,000 or more, plus areas from the surrounding county (or counties) which are reasonably urbanized and are contiguous and interdependent with the core city. In 1960 the Census Bureau identified 212 "Standard Metropolitan Statistical Areas," a substantial increase over the 168 listed in 1950, and reported that 62.9 per cent of the nation's population resides in these areas. They account for about three-fourths of the nation's economic activity—79 per cent of all bank deposits, 78 per cent of all manufacturing payrolls, and over 70 per cent of all local tax revenue.

Metropolitics is concerned mainly with the struggle to secure area-wide decisions concerning governmental services and regulations in metropolitan areas fragmented into many (often hundreds) of autonomous decision-making governments. The stakes are high, involving such problems as mass transit, tax rates, crime control, local self-government, control of zoning, and metropolitan planning, with the proponents of metropolitan reform warning that the only alternative to more coordination among localities is state and federal intervention.

Even as the "metropolitan area" is just beginning to gain acceptance in laymen's and journalists' language, some sociologists and political scientists have begun to talk about the developing "super-metropolitan area," or "megalopolis," formed when two or more metropolitan areas grow closer together. A 600-mile long "linear city" on the eastern seaboard is the most publicized, stretching from lower New Hampshire through Boston, New York, Philadelphia, Baltimore, Washington, and northern Virginia, reaching into ten states and containing 31.5 million people. A similar linear city is developing on the west coast from Los Angeles to San Diego, and perhaps eventually as far as San Francisco.

Other Population Movements. Other kinds of mass movements of population, past and present, are important factors in any explanation of American politics. Several parts of the nation have been affected by special types of internal population movements having racial, economic, and political overtones. Population mobility has become an important political fact. Florida is becoming a haven for the aged; New York City has received a swelling tide of job-seeking Puerto Ricans; and Miami has been flooded with thousands of Cuban refugees. There has been a massive migration of Negroes from southern farms and towns to cities outside the South, with the total exodus of non-whites reaching an all-time high of 1.5 million between 1950 and 1960. Of this total California received the largest number (345,000), with New York (282,000) and Illinois (189,000) ranking next. In 1960 only about half the United States Negro population still lived in the eleven states of the "old Confederacy." More Negroes—1.4 million—live in the state of New York than in any other state.

CLASS AND CASTE

A classic distinction between American and European society is supposedly the absence in America of a rigid class system. Certainly no class of landed gentry has flourished in the United States since the fall of the southern plantation system, nor can we point to closed aristocracies consisting of public servants, the clergy, or the military. And in further support of those who would deny the existence of any class system is the failure of the Marxist appeal, so warmly received by masses of European wage-earners, to generate any real response from the bulk of Americans.

Nevertheless, in some ways American society *is* stratified, and repeated studies of American communities have revealed a kind of class system based largely on wealth. People with comparable income, occupation, or social position tend to associate with each other and to vote alike. Although more than 80 per cent of American people *consider* themselves members of the "middle class," studies of voting behavior reveal that a large number tend to fall into a "working class" consistently different from the middle and upper classes.

Even more abhorrent to most Americans than the notion of classes in their society is the idea of a caste system—that is, a system of class based on birth and from which there is no escape. Yet the position of certain minority groups—the Negro in particular—has undeniably had many of the characteristics of a caste system.

RELIGION

The religious traditions and affiliations of the American people contribute to the shape and direction of their political system, both in its historical origins and in the current issues of the day. Protestant Christianity is either the professed religious faith or the unprofessed tradition of the great majority of Americans, giving both religion and politics the individualistic and anti-authoritarian spirit of the Reformation. Nearly one out of every four persons are Roman Catholics (based on an estimate of 45 million adherents), and an estimated 5.6 million are Jews. The Catholic minority in the nation is actually a majority in some cities and states, where the pressure for public support for the parochial school system has become strong.

CHANGING ECONOMIC PATTERNS

Political scientists and historians generally point to economic change as the most significant influence on the development of the American political system since the adoption of the Constitution. The growth of the large-scale industrial corporation, the continuing technological revolution, with its accompanying specialization of labor and increased interdependence of men, the divorcement of most of the people from the soil, and the growth of powerful labor unions—all have contributed to a governmental system that Thomas Jefferson would hardly recognize. American democracy has come to require its government to serve as the protector of the rights of weaker parties in economic struggles, particularly if the economically weak may be politically strong. This trend has been reflected in the development of the independent regulatory commissions, the "trust-busting" responsibilities of the Justice Department, the guarantee of collective bargaining rights to organized labor, and, on occasion, in the creation of such public enterprises as the Tennessee Valley Authority.

The American economy is characterized by private enterprise, but it is hardly the pure capitalistic system implied by so many civic club speeches. Any realistic description of the close affinity of politics and economics in the United States must conclude that the system is a mixture of private, public, and hybrid enterprises. Although no "laissez faire" separation of government from the economy has ever really existed in the United States, even in its early years, governmental regulation and intervention have steadily increased throughout the past century, tending to parallel the growth of big business and big labor.

Depression and inflation have come to be the twin devils of American politics. Both conservative and liberal economists now recognize the American government's responsibility to do whatever it can to prevent "boom and bust" cycles in the economy. Governmental provision of "built-in" stabilizing forces is increasingly accepted as a permanent fixture of our political economy. Discussion in recent years has shifted somewhat to questions of economic growth rate and the possibility that the once-burgeoning American economy has reached a plateau of maturity. One economist, John Kenneth Galbraith, suggests that the struggle for private affluence in the United States has been largely won, but that we have a paradox of *public* shortages and *public* poverty. He contrasts private luxuries and public blight as follows:

The family which takes its mauve and cerise, air-conditioned, power-steered, and power-braked automobile out for a tour passes through cities that are badly paved, made hideous by litter, blighted buildings, billboards, and posts for wires that should long since have been put underground. . . . They picnic on exquisitely packaged food from a portable icebox by a polluted stream and go on to spend the night at a park which is a menace to public health and morals. Just before dozing off on an air mattress, beneath a nylon tent, amid the stench of decaying refuse, they may reflect vaguely on the curious unevenness of their blessings.

Is this, indeed, the American genius?[2]

WAR AND THE "GARRISON STATE"

The impact of war—preparation for it, participation in it, and recuperation from it—should be mentioned before concluding this discussion of social forces, even though its manifestations are found in most of the topics already discussed. War contributes to mass population movements, affects the birth rate, increases governmental costs and taxes, stimulates economic inflation, and tends to contract economic and political freedom. The cold war has similar effects, to a lesser degree, perhaps, but for a longer time. Thus, many political observers speak with apprehension of the possible growth of a kind of "garrison state."

Interest Groups and Political Parties

In spite of all the fun poked at the multitude of clubs and organizations formed in the United States for almost every imaginable purpose—from pious moral reform leagues to super-patriotic veterans' organizations— interest groups play an important and even essential role in the political system. They are undoubtedly more important than similar groups in other countries, possibly because Americans are more nearly incurable "joiners" than other peoples, but more likely because such factors as economic specialization, a history of continuing technological revolutions that impinge on special interests, and a legal tradition of respect for the freedom of association, have all contributed to their growth. In many respects the role of interest groups in political decision-making is far more significant than the more publicized role of American political parties.

THE "INTERESTS" OF GROUPS, ORGANIZED AND UNORGANIZED

A distinction should be made between *unorganized* groupings of people with nevertheless discernible common "interests" and the *organized* in-

[2] John Kenneth Galbraith, *The Affluent Society* (Boston: Houghton Mifflin, 1958), p. 253.

terest groups. We will therefore look first at the major discernible communities of interests, or interest groupings, in American political history.

Within the broad category of "economic interests" it is customary to speak of "the business interest," "the labor interest," and the "agricultural interest"; but these communities of interest are much less homogeneous than is commonly believed. There was no single "farm interest" in the long struggle to repeal a federal tax on colored oleomargarine, for the dairy farmers opposed any measure to help the sale of a "cheap imitation of butter," while the cotton farmers favored eliminating this "artificial restriction on the use of a cotton seed product." The clash of interests between different groups of farmers—wealthy ranchers and small renters, corporation farmers and single-family farmers, cotton farmers and hog farmers—makes it hazardous to speak with any certainty about the "agricultural interest." Yet, on the other hand, any congressman who seeks to promote the "consumer interest" by introducing a bill setting maximum prices for all agricultural products would doubtless find the diversified farm groups suddenly united in defense of the "agricultural interest."

Labor and business interests must be considered with similar caution. True, the common appeal of higher wages and a shorter work week has traditionally united most industrial wage earners; but seeds of rivalry are found in the diverse interests of specialized labor groups—artisans and craftsmen versus large-scale industrial workers, New Englanders versus Southerners, coal miners in favor of the St. Lawrence Seaway versus longshoremen opposed to it, and on occasion, white laborers versus Negro laborers. Similarly, businessmen generally unite in the interests of lower taxes, curbs on "labor excesses," less government regulation, and less governmental centralization. But the "business interest," too, must be subdivided into such particular interests as those of union and non-union companies, of importers and exporters, of big business and small business, and of groups of businesses competing with other groups in the same field of service or sales.

Just as one can oversimplify the special interests of agriculture, labor, and business, it is a common error to assume that all interests are economic. But national origin, for example, has always played a prominent role in American politics and, emotional or perhaps irrational though it may be, it is a kind of interest which does not quickly die. The first Henry Cabot Lodge secured support for the defeat of the League of Nations by appealing to the Italian-Americans' interest in an Adriatic port for Italy, and to the Irish-Americans' interest in a united and free Ireland. A mayoral candidate in some cities may help his chances by supporting freedom for Poland, and in other cities Finnegan will beat Jones every time.

Religious interests have an impact separate and apart from national interests, though the two obviously overlap. Religious interests are no less real simply because some of them are seldom if ever challenged, which is usually the case in American politics. The two constitutional doctrines of separation of church and state and freedom of religious faith and practice have tended to keep the bulk of religious interests away from the floodlight of political struggles. From time to time newspapers will report a case of Jehovah's Witnesses, or members of some other religious sects, claiming freedom from certain laws of the community. Less frequently, but with more massive impact, the "Protestant interest" or "Catholic interest" will rise above the surface in a political campaign—as in 1928 and 1960, when Catholic Presidential candidates, Alfred E. Smith and John F. Kennedy, respectively, encountered powerful religious opposition in strongly Protestant areas. It is particularly in state and local governments, however, that clergymen and lay denominational leaders frequently speak out for religious interests in legislative and administrative matters.

Many other interests of particular groupings of people in the United States could be mentioned: racial and ethnic interests, geographic and sectional interests, and community or neighborhood interests. Some of these are seldom organized on any permanent basis; but all it takes is a commercial "spot-zoning" proposal in an all-residential neighborhood to discover that a community interest is there.

ORGANIZED INTEREST GROUPS IN THE UNITED STATES

Labor Groups. Although not all labor unions are combined in a single political interest group, the 1955 merger of the American Federation of Labor and the Congress of Industrial Organizations resulted in an organization of some 15 million members, overshadowing all others in the world of labor. The miners, teamsters, and railroad brotherhoods are the major independent unions outside the combined AFL-CIO, and are powerful in their own right.

The American Federation of Labor was organized in 1886 by skilled workers and craftsmen. During the next half-century it stressed the economic weapon of the strike more than political action and worked as a genuine confederation, with the individual craft unions (carpenters, machinists, and so on) giving up only limited power to the parent body. Samuel Gompers, founder of the AFL, supported lobbying activities and political action when necessary to oppose hostile governmental action, but preferred to avoid any kind of alignment with a particular party.

The CIO was organized in the 1930s as an outgrowth of a conflict within the AFL over the industrial versus the craft basis of organizing unions. The industrial unions, led by John L. Lewis of the mine workers, withdrew from the AFL and began vigorous unionization campaigns in such mass-production industries as steel, automobiles, rubber, and textiles. For twenty years the rival organizations competed for members, with no great difference in their membership totals, but with the CIO entering more aggressively into the political arena in support of a broad range of New Deal and Fair Deal programs. The objectives of both organizations both before and after their 1955 merger have been much the same—the improvement of wages and working conditions, the extension of social security programs, and the protection of unions from hostile governmental regulations. Whether American labor will follow the pattern of labor movements in other countries and form a separate political party probably depends upon how well they feel these objectives are being met by working through such organizations as the Committee on Political Education (COPE). Pressure for a labor party has been comparatively weak thus far within the American labor movement.

Farm Groups. Farmers too have organized into several groups for the purpose of promoting their common interests. The most powerful of these is the American Farm Bureau Federation. The Farm Bureau, a federation of county farm bureaus actively promoted and virtually organized by the county agents in many states, has had a remarkable growth since its beginnings in 1920. Much of that growth is due to the agricultural extension program of the U. S. Department of Agriculture and the land grant colleges and universities. The organization is particularly strong in the Midwest and South, tends to represent the relatively prosperous farmers, and speaks with a vigorous and demanding voice in the halls of Congress on such subjects as price supports, research, production controls, and trade regulation.

The National Farmers Union is a smaller organization, founded in 1902 and influential in the Missouri River Valley. It claims to speak for the smaller farmers. It has had a close association with cooperatives of various types, and has a reputation for taking a more liberal position than the Farm Bureau. The National Grange dates back to 1867, but has lost much of its earlier strength and aggressiveness. Many other organizations are active in the promotion of agriculture in specific commodity fields—for example, the American Soybean Association, the National Wool Growers Association, and the National Beet Growers Association.

Business Groups. The "Big Two" of the organized spokesmen for business interests in politics are the Chamber of Commerce of the United States and the National Association of Manufacturers. The Chamber, organized in 1912, is a federation of between 3,000 and 4,000 local chambers of commerce and trade associations of merchants, financial and service institutions, and manufacturing establishments. Although its membership is sharply divided on many issues, the Chamber crusades vigorously on such common interests as lower taxes, rigid economy in government, aids to business, curbs on labor, less governmental centralization, and in general "less government in business and more business in government."

The National Association of Manufacturers (NAM) is even more aggressively anti-labor and opposed to social legislation than the Chamber of Commerce; it carries on extensive public education programs through the mass communication media. The NAM was organized in the 1890s; although composed of all types of manufacturing firms— more than 20,000 in number—it has come to be more or less dominated by the larger manufacturers.

Like the farmers, manufacturers and other business groups have organized themselves into hundreds of trade associations to promote the interests of particular types of manufacturing or other business enterprises, from tombstone-cutting to automobile-manufacturing. Although some of their activities have the practical effect of price fixing and other practices of doubtful legality, their lobbying function is quite legitimate.

Professional Groups. Professions such as medicine, law, and architecture cannot claim the mass membership of the giant farm, labor, and business organizations, but they are important because of their prestige and their ability to focus their undivided attention on a single issue. Many professional organizations can become powerful pressure groups when they see a need to do so, as the American Medical Association did in the 1940s, when it organized to oppose national health insurance (successfully), and in the 1960s, when it opposed Medicare (unsuccessfully). The National Education Association actively lobbies for more financial support for education and for legislation raising educational standards. The American Bar Association speaks out on a variety of matters of interest to lawyers, such as court organization and procedure, administrative regulatory procedures, and standards for licensing lawyers.

Other Groups. Many strong interest groups are based on non-occupational interests: veterans organizations, patriotic societies, moral reform groups, ethnic groups, religious groups. It can readily be seen that such groups often have memberships that overlap with each other and with the occupational groups discussed above; thus a person may be a union member, an active Catholic, a member of the VFW, and a member of the Cherry Heights Community Improvement Association. Also, separate groups with varying emphases and approaches are found within the same field of interest.

One other category of groups which deserves mention in any discussion of pressure group activity is the bureaucracy itself, frequently found represented before legislative committees and in various kinds of inner circles for purposes of planning, pushing, and compromising legislation in its fields of special competence or interest. This role of special pleading by governmental officials for particular causes is bitterly resented by many Americans, but others defend it as providing the most dependable voice for the general or national interest on a public question, in contrast to the propaganda of special or fractional interests.

AMERICAN PRESSURE GROUPS: METHODS AND SOURCES OF STRENGTH

The methods of political interest groups in the United States are probably better known to the student of government than are the factors determining a given group's strength or weakness. The lobby that seeks to influence legislators and administrators directly is well known, but increasingly the most effective lobbying begins by seeking to influence the public at large through mass-media educational campaigns, with a resulting indirect pressure on legislative and administrative bodies. Intermediate techniques between these two are campaign assistance to friendly candidates for public office or opposition to unfriendly candidates, and efforts to influence political party platforms and the selection of party candidates. Techniques alone are not enough, however, and are less important ultimately than several other critical factors, in determining the pressure group's strength: its size, cohesion, geographic distribution, status, organization, leadership, program, and political environment. The most obvious source of strength is size, but size alone is not a guarantee of strength if certain other factors, particularly unity and cohesion, are lacking. Labor unions, for example, seldom exhibit the same cohesion in politics that they do in collective bargaining. The effects of geographic distribution of membership cannot always be predicted, because concentration within one city may result in great influence at the local level but pull no weight in a state legislature or Congress. Conversely, a well-distributed national or statewide organization might be hard put to influence a particular city council or mayor.

A less tangible but perhaps even more important factor is the prestige or status of the group in society. Doctors, bankers, and lawyers, and particularly the leaders of their professional associations, will usually enjoy easier access to the decision-making circles of government than the representatives of lower-status groups. Finally, the ideological content of the interest group's program has an important effect on its power position, with certain programs doomed to hard sledding no matter how much professional public relations assistance is employed. A clear-cut goal of "fair play," "correcting a wrong," or "supporting the weak but worthy," will give a group a decided edge over the group whose program has earned the brand of "obvious special privilege."

One other factor should be mentioned in explaining the strength of pressure groups in the United States in contrast to the power of such groups in other countries. The American political environment, the context in which interest groups operate, is responsible for much of the strength of pressure groups and of the system itself. Such American phenomena as the separation of powers, the federal system, less disciplined political parties, and the multiplicity of independent agencies and popularly elected officials (at the state and local levels) have provided an abundance of access points for interest groups, and thus encourage organized efforts to be heard.

AMERICAN POLITICAL PARTIES

In recent years the growth of very large pressure groups in the United States, particularly organized labor, has made it appear that the distinction between political parties and pressure groups is either thin or non-existent. Yet a basic distinction does remain: the political party seeks control of government by electing its candidates to office, whereas the pressure group seeks control only of certain governmental policies and does not nominate and place on the ballot candidates for office. A pressure group may seek support from all parties, and may provide campaign support for specific candidates from different parties who are "right" in their attitude toward the group's goals. Particular pressure groups in particular election campaigns may behave almost like political parties, recruiting, nominating, and supporting candidates for office, but in the total picture there continues to be a meaningful distinction between these two kinds of political groups.

Few political institutions have been so criticized and yet have shown such persistence as the American party system. To speak of party *membership* is almost meaningless, because the two major American parties have no formal enrollment (except in several states where declaration of one's party is required in registering for primary voting), no dues, no rules of behavior, and no prescribed sanctions for improper conduct. Party "identification" is probably a more meaningful term than membership, in that it expresses the voter's leanings and his tendency to support one of the parties regularly with his vote.

Furthermore, American political parties have assumed great importance in spite of the fact that the Constitution is entirely silent about them. In the early days of the Republic, George Washington and others warned against the "baneful effects of the spirit of parties." In some respects the popular American image of political parties through the years has been no more favorable than that held by the Founding Fathers. This "traditional image" of American party politics has consisted of four major elements: a belief that there are no real differences in program between the two major parties, resulting in only a "tweedle-dee-tweedledum" choice between them; the party organization's obsession with patronage and spoils; party irresponsibility, as characterized by "invisible government" and behind-the-scenes bosses; and a reputation for corruption as a major means for getting and retaining power. Many would contend, however, that this characterization of American party politics is unduly harsh and does not accurately reflect the political realities of the 1960s, when, according to one point of view, a "new type of party politics" emphasizing program or policy rather than patronage or spoils is developing in the United States.

It is still too early to know whether a totally new species of party politics is replacing the traditional system. Probably the most accurate picture is a mixture of the old and the new. Certainly old-time bossism and patronage are not what they used to be, but irresponsibility, corruption, and lack of genuine commitment to policy have a persistent quality which must be recognized.

The Development of the American Party System. From the beginning of American history the electorate has tended to divide into two groups over political issues. Our English forebears had resolved most of their political issues into Tory versus Whig alignments, and the early alignments in the colonial struggle for independence were between the Loyalists and the revolutionaries. The fight for a strong constitution to replace the Articles of Confederation was accompanied by cleavage between the Federalists and the Antifederalists. The first real party lines began to develop toward the end of Washington's Presidency. Hamilton and Adams retained the Federalist label for a new grouping of business, industrial, and financial interests in New England and the Middle Atlantic States; Jefferson and Madison organized the planters, small farmers, and artisans into a party which by 1816 had eliminated the Federalists. Known successively as Antifederalists, Jeffersonian Republicans, Democratic Republicans, and Democrats, this party is today one of the world's oldest.

After the demise of the Federalists, the major conflicts were intraparty rather than interparty until early in the Jacksonian era, when the Whig party was organized and took up the fight from about 1832 to 1856. The slavery conflict split the northern and southern wings of both the Democratic and Whig parties, the Whigs ultimately disintegrating under the blow. The southern Whigs joined the slave-holding Democrats and the northern Whigs joined the new Republican party, which first captured the Presidency in 1860.

Today's Republican party is the natural successor of two earlier parties—the Federalists of Hamilton and Adams and the anti-Jacksonian Whigs. The party of Lincoln succeeded in bringing together a coalition of northern industrial and financial groups and midwestern farmers and almost completely dominated national politics for the next half-century, as the Democratic party found it difficult to throw off the image of rebellion. It was the economic distress of farmers and laborers in the 1920s and 1930s which led more of these groups into the Democratic fold and provided the basis for the modern Democratic party. Each party has held the Presidency approximately 50 per cent of the time during the past half-century.

This amazing persistence of two major political parties, rather than the rise of a multiplicity of parties that might seem logical in a country of such great size and sectional, religious, and economic diversity, has inspired a variety of explanations. The English heritage, a natural inclination to compromise, greater religious homogeneity, and the nature of the American electoral system are among the more common. The last must be accorded an important place, if not the most important place, in any explanation of the American two-party system. The single-member district plan for electing legislators tends to encourage coalitions of diverse groups within each district, as well as to overrepresent the majority and make it hard for a third party ever to gain a foothold. Similarly, the all-or-nothing basis of casting a states' electoral votes for the Presidency makes it easier for the two major parties to convince the voters that supporting a third party is "throwing your vote away." In addition, there is simply the force of momentum which favors the retention of the two-party system in much the same way that family tradition continues church and club affiliations, vocation, and sectional attachment.

What, then, has been the fate and impact of third parties in American history? Although the Republican party is the only one to rise from third-party status to be one of the two major parties, it would be wrong to conclude that third parties are unimportant. Through the years they have played an important role as innovators of policy, with the major established parties taking over vote-getting planks of third-party platforms (such as those of the Populists, Greenbackers, Socialists, and Progressives) when it became apparent that the smaller parties were making serious inroads into major party strength.

Both of the major parties today stand close to the middle of the road ideologically. The demarcation line between the Republican and Democratic parties is badly blurred, and each party is divided into various wings, such as left and right, or northern and southern, with more unity often found *across* party lines in Congress than within each party. Party discipline in Congress is invariably strong in matters of personnel and organization but often weak in matters of substantive policy. Furthermore, even though the major parties have clearly differed on particular issues at particular periods in history, these differences have changed through the years and complete reversals have taken place, such as the Republican and Democratic "swap out" in the field of states' rights and national power.

Some differences, however, do exist in the policy position of the Democratic and Republican parties today, even if only in the location of each party's "center of gravity." The modern Democratic party is in large measure a coalition of the industrial workers and minority groups of the metropolitan areas, particularly in the North and the Midwest, along with the predominantly conservative southern leaders. Additional elements in this strange coalition are many farmers, ranchers, and miners of areas farther west. The modern Republican party has combined its traditional upper-income support from manufacturing and financial interests with strong sectional support from New England, the northern Great Plains, and the rural and small-town areas of the Midwest and Middle Atlantic regions. In spite of policy diversities within each party, however, it is usually safe to predict that in Congress a greater percentage of Republicans than Democrats will be found voting against proposals for government regulation of business, social legislation, and expenditures for international assistance.

It is not easy to explain to foreign observers a party system in which southern Democrats may join with the Republicans in defeating legislation proposed by a Democratic President and promised in a Democratic platform. Some explain it in terms of a two-party system in Presidential elections and a multi-party system in the workings of Congress. Others have argued that the American party system is basically a four-party system consisting of Congressional Republicans, Presidential Republicans, Congressional Democrats, and Presidential Democrats, each having its own institutional characteristics, policy positions, and voter constituencies. Under this interpretation the national decision-making processes, such as choosing a President or enacting a law, are the occasions for ever-changing coalitions among the four "parties."

Party Organization and Nominating Procedure. The "paper organization" of both parties gives them every appearance of being broad-based pyramids, with disciplined chains of command from the national committee at the top, through state, county, city, and ward committees, down to the lowly precinct captain. But such a picture is highly inaccurate, and in many respects the actual power relationships involve a reverse flow of influence, or at least veto power. Perhaps the most important factor in the organization of American political parties is the principle of federalism, whereby only a limited amount of national machinery holds together a loose association of state and local organizations. The precinct captain may be at the bottom of the pyramid, but in the large urban areas he is a highly important figure in the party's efforts to develop a core of loyal voters. His job is to dispense favors and win friendships in a way that will "carry his box" on election day. The work of precinct leaders is commonly coordinated by a ward committee, which in turn is coordinated by a committee for the entire city. In rural areas, and occasionally in urban areas, the county committee is the principal local party organization.

State and national committees of the party are seldom powerful in themselves: the real direction comes from an individual party leader. At the state level this leader may be the governor, a United States senator or, occasionally, an actual party boss. Any notion of a hierarchical chain of command is least applicable when applied to the party national committee, for a gulf frequently exists between the national party headquarters and state and local party organizations. The relationship must be cooperative rather than authoritative, with cooperation commonly at its highest level during Presidential campaigns and considerably lower at other times. The mere fact of fifty separate sets of state regulations for party machinery and elections places strong inhibitions on centralized party operations.

Many other factors make for great diversity of party organization and procedure from state to state and city to city. Some states or sections of states have a long tradition of one-party politics, which becomes virtually no-party politics insofar as meaningful organization is concerned. The elaborate party organizations of Chicago, New York, or Philadelphia would hardly be understood by party leaders in many southern cities, even less so in rural areas, North or South.

In carrying out their principal function of selecting candidates they will try to elect to office, American parties have used several different devices through the years. The first was nomination by a caucus of party leaders gathered informally in a home or more formally as the members of one party in the legislature. After "King Caucus" fell into disrepute as not sufficiently representative of the party membership, the delegate convention was tried as a more representative system of deciding on nominations. Criticism of the convention as subject to machine manipulation resulted in a movement for the direct primary, and the great majority of states have now abandoned the party convention. But both parties retain the national convention for nominating the Presidential candidate, and it remains to be seen whether the floodlight of television on this circus-like spectacle will result in altering or even abandoning it. Although the direct primary at the state and local levels was hailed by many as a cure for party corruption, it has more recently come in for criticism as an obstacle to the development of more disciplined and responsible parties.

Many of the criticisms of American political parties mentioned in the preceding pages (bossism, corruption, irresponsibility, preoccupation with spoils, and the absence of significant policy differences) are closely related to the degree of interparty competition at the state and local levels. Recent studies indicate a significant trend toward real two-party competition in states once considered "safe" one-party states. Such factors as the nationalization of political campaigning, greater mobility of the American voter from one section of the country to another, the growing industrialization of previously agricultural and rural states, and a general decline in sectionalism all seem to be contributing to a decline in one-party politics. Whether this will contribute to the development of the "more *responsible* two-party system" called for by a committee of the American Political Science Association remains to be seen.

Governmental Institutions

THE PRESIDENCY

Two opposing but seemingly equally plausible interpretations of Presidential power emerge from contemporary literature on the American Presidency. One is that the American President is the most powerful single official in the world, with broader personal discretion to make decisions in vital matters than the chief executive of any other nation. The other is that the Presidency is becoming so "institutionalized" with surrounding staffs and more or less permanent agencies that advise on highly technical and complex matters, and subject to so many virtually uncontrollable pressures, that in reality the President has far less discretion or freedom of choice within the American political system than is commonly imagined. In understanding the Presidency it is important to look at each of these paradoxical elements.

Presidential Powers. The constitutional grant of powers to the President is made in general language without great detail. The "executive power" is vested in him; he has power to appoint officials, subject to the advice and consent of the Senate (except where Congress waives the confirmation requirement); he is authorized to require opinions of such officials. He is charged with seeing that the laws are faithfully executed and with keeping Congress informed of the state of the Union. He can veto legislation, call Congress into special session, and make treaties with the advice and consent of two-thirds of the Senate. He is commander-in-chief of the armed services, and has the power of pardon in all federal cases except impeachment.

But the realities of Presidential power are better seen in the history of what Presidents have actually done with these constitutional grants. George Washington established early precedents when he asserted Presidential control of the cabinet, responsibility for suppressing domestic disorder (in the Whiskey Rebellion), and a Presidential monopoly on communications with foreign governments. Jefferson's initiative in the Louisiana Purchase without advance consent of Congress was mentioned earlier. Jackson made his mark as a vigorous law-enforcer, a vetoer of legislation on policy grounds (not merely on questions of constitutionality), and a strong leader of his party.

President Lincoln combined the roles of law-enforcer and commander-in-chief in ways that greatly expanded Presidential power. He blockaded ports, summoned state militias, and freed the slaves, all without congressional action. Presidents Theodore Roosevelt, Woodrow Wilson, and Franklin Roosevelt were influential in the growth of "administrative legislation" (rule-making by administrators of federal agencies, having the force and effect of law) and "administrative adjudication" (dispute settling by federal administrators, resembling judicial procedure). Much of it is performed by semi-independent agencies, such as tariff rate-making or unfair trade practice determination, but subject to varying degrees of Presidential influence. The depression of the 1930s, followed by World War II and the cold war, provided further impetus to the expansion of Presidential power and a doctrine of "crisis leadership." President Truman, in recalling General MacArthur, dramatically reasserted Presidential and civilian control of the military, but he exceeded the judicial limits of constitutionality when he seized the steel mills without congressional authorization.

Eisenhower's use of troops to enforce school integration in Little Rock left little doubt about the extent of Presidential power in civil rights disturbances. Kennedy's dramatic roll-back of Big Steel's price increases in 1962, and Johnson's less dramatic but equally decisive encounter with the aluminum and copper industries in 1965, demonstrate the withering impact of the formal and informal Presidential power that can be mobilized in a contest with a segment of American industry.

Clearly, these examples of the assertion and expansion of Presidential power are thoroughly bipartisan in character. The powers of the Presidency have increased in response to such factors as war, depression, the failure of Congress to act in time of crisis, and popular demand for leadership, without regard to the party of the White House incumbent.

The Growing Institutionalization of the Presidency. Though Presidential power is obviously vast, recent studies of Presidential decision-making have described a growing tendency toward institutionalization of the Presidency, and some even suggest that the bulk of Presidential decisions are actually made by the variety of staffs surrounding the President and even controlling him. He is surrounded not only by his immediate staff, or White House secretariat, but also by a complex of agencies whose heads report directly to him and which are grouped together in what is called the Executive Office of the President. These agencies include, among others, the White House Office, the Bureau of the Budget, the Council of Economic Advisers, the National Security Council, the National Aeronautics and Space Council, the Office of Emergency Planning, and the Office of Science and Technology. Not all of these executive agencies and assistants surrounding the President are of equal importance or influence. The Bureau of the Budget ranks near the top in importance. It is not only the central control agency determining the financial needs of all government agencies but the President's policy clearinghouse for all proposals to Congress from the various administrative agencies. In addition, it is the President's arm for making "O and M" (organization and methods) studies aimed at achieving administrative efficiency. The Council of Economic Advisers is potentially as important as the Bureau of the Budget because of its responsibility for advising the President on measures necessary to keep the nation's economy sound and growing, but its role in practice cannot compare with that of the Bureau of the Budget.

The National Security Council was created in 1947 to help the President coordinate military and diplomatic policy with domestic resource mobilization capabilities and policies, and was given responsibility for direction of the Central Intelligence Agency. President Eisenhower made much use of the National Security Council, but its utility as a coordinating mechanism has been subjected to a considerable amount of criticism, and President Kennedy relied on it much less than his predecessor. President Johnson has not restored it to its earlier prominence. Other agencies having close relationships with the President in his role as chief administrator are the Civil Service Commission and the General Services Administration (GSA), which is concerned with purchasing, construction, and other housekeeping activities in the government establishment.

Although members of the President's cabinet are obviously important officials, the cabinet in the collective sense has been vastly overrated as a political institution for advice, coordination, and decision-making. Most studies conclude that cabinet members operate independently of any significant procedural or policy guidelines laid down by the cabinet as a whole and that their relations are more directly with the President. Thus the collective judgments required by the President have come to be institutionalized in the staff relationships referred to above.

Are we to conclude that the American President has become a highly individualistic and powerful ruler—or is he rather so surrounded by specialized staff experts and institutionalized "pre-decision" centers that he is really their prisoner, an expendable "organization man" whose death or political replacement would not significantly change the course of governmental policies and administration? As the reader has doubtless concluded, the true picture lies somewhere between these extremes. It is conceivable that a particular President might rely so heavily on the surrounding institutional forces that he would come to have virtually no mind of his own. It is less likely that any American President could or would make highly individual decisions that would not be modified by these institutional forces. The particular pattern of decision-making carved out by any given President will depend in large measure on his own ability, personality, and flair for politics and administration.

CONGRESS

Although the paramount function of Congress is legislative, it has constituent powers relating to the proposal of constitutional amendments, electoral powers in certain Presidential elections, impeachment powers, investigatory powers, the power to admit new states to the Union, and, in the case of the Senate, certain administrative powers, such as the confirmation of executive appointments and the giving of advice on and consent to treaties. The powers of Congress through the years have increased in some respects, particularly as state powers have been eclipsed; but in other respects it has also lost out to the President, whose legislative leadership and quasi-legislative powers have taken away much of its policy-making initiative.

Bicameralism is an important factor in any comparison of Congress with legislative bodies in other countries. Congress shows no signs, for example, of following the British parliamentary pattern of steadily reducing the power and influence of one of the two houses. The 100-member Senate and 435-member House of Representatives remain virtually equal in legislative powers; such differences as exist between them stem more from their respective sizes and methods of electing members than from formal powers.

The role of House and Senate committees as "little legislatures" is also important to understand—especially for the tourist who expects to find an impassioned forensic battle going on when he arrives in the House or Senate gallery. He will be less disappointed at what he sees and hears if he knows that the main work of legislative decision-making is done in committees. Congressional committees generally have the power of life or death over bills. The House of Representatives is especially dependent on its standing committees, twenty in all, with an average membership of about thirty; the Senate has sixteen standing committees, varying in size from seven to twenty-six members. Some committees are so large that they are divided into specialized subcommittees, some of which have come to have considerable power in themselves.

One of the "sacred cows" of Congress in both House and Senate is the seniority rule governing the selection of committee chairmen. Thus the men who fill these important positions are in effect locally chosen and locally responsible, because seniority depends upon the decision of voters within individual districts to send their legislators back to Congress time after time. The result has been a preponderance of southern chairmen when the Democrats are in the majority, and a preponderance of rural midwestern chairmen when the Republicans are in control. This helps to explain the four-party theory mentioned earlier in this chapter. The party leaders in each house are not chosen on the basis of seniority, however; the Speaker of the House, for example, is elected every two years by a majority vote of the members of the majority party.

A "sacred cow" peculiar to the Senate is the strong tradition of virtually unlimited debate, with a resulting right of "filibuster" for minority groups determined to block a given piece of legislation. The larger size of the House has necessitated stricter rules limiting debate, but in the Senate cloture, or a vote to end debate so that the legislation before the Senate can be voted on, is a very rare event. As a result, either filibuster or the threat of filibuster by an organized Senate minority is sufficient to block the chances of certain kinds of legislation—particularly, until very recently, civil rights legislation. It should not be concluded, however, that only conservative Southerners use the filibuster, for in recent years small groups of liberal senators have availed themselves of unlimited debating privileges. For example, Senator Morse of Oregon and nine other liberal senators filibustered in 1962 in an effort to block the communications satellite bill.

Though he is the head of the executive branch, the President normally plays an important role in the work of Congress, both by virtue of constitutional provisions and by his traditional extra-constitutional powers. The constitutional powers include the sending of messages to Congress, the proposing of legislation, the veto power, and the power to call special sessions. Extra-constitutional devices for influencing legislation include the threat of veto, discriminating use of the patronage power, personal persuasion through individual contacts with key congressmen, the use of the lobbying capabilities of administrative agencies, and direct appeals to the public through televised speeches, press conferences, and the like. While there are obvious limits to what a President can obtain from the Congress, skillful use of these legislative powers can make him the chief legislator in actuality.

Throughout American history, Congress as an institution has been criticized more seriously than the Presidency, and for a greater variety of offenses. Overrepresentation of certain areas, groups, and interests, particularly rural areas and the party in power, has been a major offense. The device often used by state legislatures to accomplish this purpose is gerrymandering—the practice of drawing congressional district boundaries so as to augment the strength of one group at the expense of another. Even when compelled by the Supreme Court to apply the one-man–one-vote principle in determining the size of congressional districts, state legislatures may create a small number of congressional districts with an urban-rural population ratio of 10 to 1, for example, and a larger number of districts with a rural-urban ratio of 3 to 2. But on the whole, because the number of congressmen allowed each state has been revised equitably by Congress after each decennial census, rural overrepresentation has been less of a problem in Congress than in the state legislatures.

The requirement of the consent of a two-thirds majority of the Senate for the ratification of treaties has received sharp criticism, particularly when a minority of the Senate was able to keep the United States out of the League of Nations. In more recent years many important policies have been put into effect by executive agreements which do not require Senate consent, and by joint (simple majority) action by both houses. The European Recovery Program and the Point Four

Program, for example, were both authorized by legislation rather than by formal treaty.

Congressional investigations, particularly during the McCarthy era of loyalty investigations, have occasioned some of the severest criticisms that Congress has received. Few would deny that the investigatory function of Congress is an important and even indispensable corollary to law-making; many congressional investigations have brought to light important misconduct in and out of government. But in recent years several factors, not the least of which is television, have led to the use of investigations for the personal aggrandizement of certain committee members, or for campaign ammunition, or partisan malice. One committee in particular—the House Un-American Activities Committee— has been the subject of bitter controversy, both for its indiscriminate attacks on groups holding unpopular political and economic beliefs, and for its questionable methods of conducting hearings. The Supreme Court has indicated that there are limits to the investigatory power and that it will not compel testimony if these bounds are overstepped.

One other frequent criticism of Congress is that too much of a congressman's time is required to run errands for constituents. Congressmen have consistently refused to relieve themselves of this chore, for the fairly obvious reason that doing countless individual favors for constituents is one of the best ways to secure re-election. Even though being an errand boy makes it difficult for a legislator to perform his major task, law-making, there are some rather sophisticated arguments in support of congressional errand running. As big government gets bigger and seems more cold and impersonal to the citizen, the congressman can and does assume an invaluable humanizing role as mediator between the bureaucracy and the citizen.

THE JUDICIARY

Foreign students of the American governmental system never cease to marvel at the power and prestige of the American judiciary. There is probably no single reason for the great influence of American judges, though an important one is their possession of the power of judicial review. Judges have many more functions than reviewing the constitutionality of legislation, however, and probably spend only a very small part of their time in cases involving judicial review. Most of their activities center around the ordinary function of settling disputes on the basis of law and fact.

The Founding Fathers provided specifically for only one federal court, the Supreme Court, but authorized Congress to establish inferior federal courts and to determine their size, as well as the size of the Supreme Court. Congress ultimately set up a hierarchy of district courts, courts of appeal, and the Supreme Court. In spite of the principle of national supremacy as a general feature of American government, the relation of the federal court system to the fifty state court systems is not entirely a superior-subordinate relationship. Only state courts have jurisdiction over some kinds of cases; only federal courts have jurisdiction over certain others; and both court systems have jurisdiction over other kinds.

The Supreme Court was initially made a six-member body by Congress, but the number of justices has gradually been increased to the present total of nine, with one member serving as Chief Justice. All federal judges are appointed by the President with the advice and consent of the Senate for an indefinite term of "good behavior." Appointments have been made largely on political considerations from the very beginning; even John Marshall's main qualifications consisted of his loyal and able service as a Federalist politician. Roger B. Taney had a more distinguished legal background than the inexperienced Marshall, but he too was appointed Chief Justice (by Jackson) because of his political services in the cabinet. President Grant made sure his prospective appointees were prepared to reverse a previous court decision declaring the Legal Tender Acts unconstitutional. Presidents in all periods of our history have paid attention not only to the party affiliation of prospective appointees, but also to their political, social, and economic views.

We cannot escape the conclusion that judges are, in the true sense of the term, politicians. Their appointment with partisan and policy considerations in mind, their inescapable attachment to particular economic, social, political, and religious values, and their full knowledge of the important political implications of judicial decisions clearly makes them actors in the American political process. Judicial eyebrows are still raised by such a statement, but it has become increasingly common to recognize that judges do often *make* the law, rather than simply *discovering* it. There is a danger, to be sure, of overstating the case and concluding that judges are no different from other participants in the contest for the stakes of politics. Important differences do exist, for judges are considerably less accountable to elected legislatures and to executives than other political actors; and the avenues of access to, and bargaining with, judges by various political groups are restricted by formal judicial procedures, the strong weight given to legal precedent, and the ethical norms of the profession. But on the whole it is more likely that the student of politics will fail to recognize judges as participants in the broad contest for the rewards of politics than that he will fail to recognize certain differences between judges and the various other participants in American politics.

THE BUREAUCRACY

It is a common mistake to think of the mass of federal employees as part and parcel of the executive branch of government and directly subordinate to the President in a hierarchical structure. Actually, because of the complex combination of the principle of separation of powers with the principle of checks and balances, the bureaucracy has an identity of its own and is characterized by dual and even triple responsibility—to the President and Congress as well as to the judiciary—under the law. This mixed pattern of bureaucratic responsibility is further complicated by such factors as responsibility to profession, pressure groups, political parties, and public opinion.

It is also common to think of those 2.5 million bureaucrats "in Washington," but the fact is that the great majority of them are *not* in Washington; they are scattered throughout regional, field, and local offices in every state. More than half of them—all civilians—work for the Army, Navy, Air Force, or other defense agencies, and only about 10 per cent work for so-called welfare agencies; the welfare state is still relatively "small potatoes" in terms of the proportion of employees involved. An even smaller number work in agencies responsible for economic regulation.

The organization of the bureaucracy is rather heterogeneous, encompassing the eleven "cabinet departments," more than a score of government corporations, such as the Tennessee Valley Authority and the Federal Deposit Insurance Corporation, a group of independent regulatory commissions such as the Interstate Commerce Commission and the Federal Trade Commission, and close to forty other agencies of varying degrees of independence. The independent regulatory commissions are set apart primarily to keep them relatively free from Presidential influence in their exercise of quasi-legislative and quasi-judicial powers.

AMERICAN FEDERALISM IN PRACTICE

The formal constitutional picture of national-state relations in the United States often leads the unsuspecting student of American government to adopt a rather rigid, "layer-cake" analogy of a careful parceling out of functions either to the states or to the national government, with the states in turn parceling out some of their functions to local government. Professor Morton Grodzins contended that a "rainbow" or "marble cake" analogy gives a far more accurate image of the federal system in practice, since it symbolizes better an inseparable mingling of functions at all levels, vertically, diagonally, and in whirls. Whether the layer-cake analogy was at one time true or not (Grodzins thought it never was), few would deny that federal-state-local relationships today are characterized far more by cooperation, coordination, and the sharing of power than by separation and competition. Issues of "states' rights" are seldom a concern when national, state, and local governments get together in joint action on a highway project, in fighting an epidemic, or in running down a "public enemy number one." The occasional controversy between a state and the national government over the administration of a "federal aid" program is an occurrence sufficiently rare to evoke newspaper coverage.

The inevitable question in any discussion of this "new federalism," or "cooperative federalism," is whether or not constitutional federalism in the United States as it once was known is now dead, or at least on its deathbed. It should be quite clear that in the *formal constitutional* sense federalism has lost much of its vitality, not only because of the impact of grants-in-aid and other recent changes, but because of issues settled as early as the days of Jefferson and Lincoln. Nevertheless, in the *political* sense the states still play a prominent part in shaping the character of national party nominating conventions, determining the makeup of Congress, and influencing the selection of judges. Thus the political facts of American life are frequently "state" rather than "national" facts such as one might expect to find in England, France, and other nations not having a federal form of government. Although formal constitutional federalism seems to be withering considerably in the United States, political federalism remains vital principally because of the political vitality of the fifty states *as states*.

SUGGESTIONS FOR ADDITIONAL READING

AMERICAN ASSEMBLY, Wallace Sayre (ed.), *The Federal Government Service: Its Character, Prestige, and Problems* (New York: Graduate School of Business, Columbia University, 1954).

BAILEY, STEPHEN K., *Congress Makes a Law* (New York: Columbia University Press, 1950).

CAMPBELL, ANGUS, PHILIP CONVERSE, WARREN E. MILLER, and DONALD E. STOKES, *The American Voter* (New York: John Wiley & Sons, 1960).

CORWIN, EDWARD S., *The Constitution and What It Means Today*, 12th edition (Princeton, N.J.: Princeton University Press, 1958).

DAHL, ROBERT A., *A Preface to Democratic Theory* (Chicago: The University of Chicago Press, 1956).

HEARD, ALEXANDER, *The Costs of Democracy* (Chapel Hill, N.C.: University of North Carolina Press, 1960).

KEY, V. O., JR., *Politics, Parties, and Pressure Groups*, 5th edition (New York: Thomas Y. Crowell, 1964).

MACMAHON, ARTHUR W. (ed.), *Federalism: Mature and Emergent* (New York: Doubleday & Company, Inc., 1955).

MURPHY, WALTER F., and C. HERMAN PRITCHETT, *Courts, Judges, and Politics* (New York: Random House, 1961).

NEUSTADT, RICHARD E., *Presidential Power: The Politics of Leadership* (New York: John Wiley & Sons, 1960).

TOCQUEVILLE, ALEXIS DE, *Democracy in America*, Phillips Bradley (ed.), 2 vols. (New York: Alfred A. Knopf, 1944).

Chapter 4

THE GOVERNMENT
OF FRANCE

Constitutional Development

The most striking feature of French constitutional development has been the inability of the major social groups in the nation to agree on their fundamental values and institutions. In all political systems a clash of interests takes place through channels provided by a constitution; France is one of those nations where the constitutional arrangements themselves are in dispute.

Events since 1958 have highlighted the continuing disagreements among the French on their political institutions. In that year General Charles de Gaulle stipulated as a condition of his return to power that he be given a mandate to draft a new constitution, to be approved by the people in a referendum. The new Constitution introduced a number of structural changes in the republican regime, but its adoption did not still public debate; if anything, controversy over the Constitution increased in intensity. Opponents of the Gaullist regime criticized its hybrid nature, and proposed either a return to the parliamentary government the new regime had replaced, or an experiment with a presidential system. Former prime minister Pierre Mendès-France, in a widely read book, advocated a parliamentary system based on the Scandinavian and Dutch experience. Even supporters of the Gaullist regime suggested constitutional reforms, mainly to strengthen the presidential character of the Fifth Republic. Only four years after the adoption of the Constitution, General de Gaulle himself proposed an amendment providing for popular election of the president. Although the amendment was approved by a majority of the people in a referendum, the campaign revealed that the major political parties were opposed to popular election of the president—and that no regime in fact would have the approval of all major political forces. In the 1965 presidential campaign all the candidates took different positions on the regime, in addition to the usual stands on policy. Whether France will evolve toward presidential government after General de Gaulle's tenure as president, or will return to a parliamentary form, is an open question. All that is certain is the lack of consensus on the basic institutions themselves.

This lack of consensus is reflected in the tumultuous history of the French during the past two centuries. Since the Revolution of 1789, France has had nineteen constitutions (the exact number being a matter of dispute, since several of these documents never came into force). In succession the nation went through the following stages: limited monarchy (1789), assembly government (1792), a directorate (1796), consulate and empire under Napoleon (1801), restoration of monarchy (1814), return to limited monarchy (1830), the Second Republic (1848), the Second Empire (1852), the Third Republic (1875), an authoritarian regime (1940), the Fourth Republic (1946), and the Fifth Republic (1958).

In spite of this apparently ceaseless experimentation, certain broad trends of development can be discerned. A long period of constitutional stability (over a thousand years) under the old regime was followed, from 1789 to 1875, by a series of regimes none of which was able to win lasting support from all the social forces within the nation. The partisans of monarchy, drawn mainly from the landed aristocracy, were pitted against the advocates of parliamentary republicanism, representing the commercial and industrial middle classes and later the workers. As some French observers have pointed out, the seesaw contest produced two similar cycles (1789 to 1814 and 1814 to 1870) in which limited monarchy led to a republic, which in turn degenerated into dictatorship.

In 1875, with the creation of the Third Republic, the French achieved a compromise which slowly won the adherence of the people. After stabilizing itself in the latter part of the nineteenth century, however, the Republic was increasingly subject to criticism. The Vichy government of 1940 had the support of certain groups alienated from the Republic, though its establishment was due to foreign conquest. One of the most important movements for reform after World War II finally culminated in the Gaullist constitution of 1958.

The perennial constitutional debate in France reflects an inability on the part of the principal social classes to "agree to disagree" within the framework of a common set of institutions. In other terms, the French state since the overthrow of Louis XVI in 1789 has lacked "legitimacy," that is, universal acceptance. The original conflict between the advocates of monarchy and a republic was resolved with the establishment of the Third Republic in 1875, but the issues shifted and a lasting national consensus never materialized. The regime created by General de Gaulle in 1958 is but the last in a long line of efforts to forge institutions that might receive the allegiance of all the people.

Constitutional instability in France historically has reflected the cleavages between "the Right" and "the Left"—terms whose exact meanings are not clear, but which are useful in denoting the existence of polar extremes. In the eighteenth and early half of the nineteenth centuries the Right contended that the unity and interests of the French people were incarnated in the person of their king. The legitimate ruler, educated expressly for his supreme post, above the everyday passions and selfish interests of his subjects, alone was capable of perceiving the ultimate good of the nation (as distinguished from the temporary advantages which might accrue to politicians). The Left, however, argued that legitimacy derived from no source other than the people, who were the only reliable judges of their own interests. A regime can thus be justified only to the extent that those who hold power are representative of, and responsible to, the people. For the Right, legitimacy derived from the reality of the French nation and its history; for the Left, recognition could be accorded only to those governments emanating from the popular will as expressed by universal suffrage through representative assemblies. Advocates of monarchy won out on several occasions (notably 1814, 1830, and 1851) but eventually lost their mass following, largely because of internal divisions.

One of the permanent historical achievements of the nineteenth century was national acceptance of the principle of universal manhood suffrage. First vindicated in 1789, the participation of the people in political affairs through elections was thereafter admitted (even though frequently under severe limitations) by all regimes. Since 1875 the opponents of this principle have been an insignificant, minuscule group. A second historical achievement of the nineteenth century, one which has greatly complicated French politics, was the creation by Napoleon Bonaparte of a far-flung, highly efficient, and rational administrative system. The advantages of the administrative system are so great that all political groups accept its existence as essential to the governance of the nation. But the conflict between the Left and the Right continues in terms of the relative importance ascribed to a parliament representative of the people and an executive that administers according to a rational definition of the public good—a definition not necessarily accepted by the people at a given time. In Rousseauean terms, it is the difference between the "will of all" and the "general will." The Right has long since ceased to oppose the Republic; instead it seeks to strengthen the position of the administration and the executive by affording them independence of action. The Left does not question the potential utility of expert administration, on condition that the political head of the executive is directly responsible to, and readily removable by, parliament.

CLASSIC PARLIAMENTARISM IN FRANCE

In recent years the classic parliamentary system, which came into being in 1875 with the Third Republic and continued in 1946 under the Fourth Republic, has been subject to a steady barrage of criticism. Even the self-proclaimed defenders of "republican legality" during the days of crisis in May, 1958, went out of their way to denounce certain of the distinctive features of the Third and Fourth Republics, particularly cabinet instability, the multi-party system, weakness of the executive, and the lack of popular identification with the state. Yet the kind of parliamentary system which came into existence in France after 1875 represented a workable compromise among major political and social forces, and also conformed to profound historical traditions.

The National Assembly elected in 1871 for the purpose of negotiating a settlement with Germany had a monarchist majority. But this majority was split between the partisans of the Count of Chambord and the Count of Paris. When agreement was finally reached in favor of the former, a new difficulty arose: the Count of Chambord refused to accept the tricolor flag. As a temporary expedient, executive power was vested in a president, on the assumption that he would willingly yield his position as soon as the king made his appearance. This hope was not unrealistic, since the "Chief of the Executive Power" was Marshal MacMahon, a convinced monarchist. But inability to reach an agreement with the pretender to the throne at length (after four years) induced the Assembly to create a republic—by one vote! The institutions of the Republic were then established by three fragmentary "organic laws." Thus in a prosaic, halting fashion the parliamentary system was launched by monarchists, and during the last part of the nineteenth century taken over by the republicans. After the Liberation of France in 1944, the French people in a referendum voted overwhelmingly against a simple return to the Third Republic. A Constituent Assembly considered proposals to establish either a strong executive or an omnipotent assembly (proposals identified with the Gaullists and Communists, respectively), but neither alternative could muster the required majority in both the Assembly and the nation. A draft constitution providing for a strong assembly and a weak executive was rejected decisively by referendum. And so, in much the same spirit that characterized its predecessor in 1875, the Assembly of 1946 arrived at a compromise—the classic parliamentary system providing a balance between executive and legislature. The modifications introduced under the Fourth Republic were relatively minor.

The basic structure of the French Republic, from 1875 until 1958, resembled that of a constitutional monarchy—with a president of the Republic in the role of the constitutional monarch. Executive power was shared by the president and a Council of Ministers (or cabinet); and legislative power was divided between lower and upper houses

(Chamber of Deputies and Senate under the Third Republic, National Assembly and Council of the Republic under the Fourth Republic). The upper chamber was elected indirectly, and its power was reduced in 1946, though in the last years of the Fourth Republic it regained some of its former importance. The lower chamber was elected by universal suffrage, and was considered to be the expression of popular sovereignty. The President of the Republic was elected at a joint session of parliament (not by the people). He in turn designated a prime minister, who formed a cabinet, subject to the approval of parliament. Of crucial importance were the relations between executive and parliament, for here was the distinctive character of the French republican system.

It was originally the hope of the monarchist majority in 1875 that the president of the Republic would become the dominant force within the system, thus facilitating the transition to a monarchy. The president, for example, was given the power to dissolve the Chamber of Deputies (with the consent of the Senate). These hopes were not realized, however. President MacMahon used the power of dissolution on May 16, 1877 (the celebrated *seize mai*), but in the election which followed, the republicans scored a decisive victory and virtually compelled Mac-Mahon to resign. Since that time it has been an article of republican faith to select a "weak" president, that is, one who confines his activities strictly to the performance of ceremonies, and who does not attempt to wield political power. The requirement that acts of the president be countersigned by a minister made it possible to enforce the custom.

Executive power then devolved upon the prime minister and his cabinet. In order to prevent the utilization of the highly centralized administrative services for political purposes, parliament enforced continuing responsibility upon the political heads of the executive. A rough balance came into being between the executive (cabinet and bureaucracy) on the one side, and the national sovereignty (expressed through universal suffrage and parliament) on the other. Whenever there seemed to be danger of an abuse of power, parliament could overthrow the cabinet with relative ease. Whenever a majority in the Assembly came together on a particular problem or issue, the cabinet had sufficient power to accomplish whatever was required to achieve a specific objective. Majorities shifted, however, according to issues; hence the cabinet crisis became a technique of adjustment enabling the legislature to deal with a series of different problems.

The French parliamentary system worked remarkably well until the end of World War I. Under its auspices a succession of strong personalities was able to establish the Republic on firm foundations (against the attacks of monarchists and assorted Rightists), reconstruct the shattered economy, pay off the reparations imposed by the Germans, establish a far-flung system of secular schools, build up the armed forces, create a diplomatic coalition that eventually brought about the isolation of Germany, and consolidate an empire in Africa and Asia. These achievements, crowned by victory over Germany in 1918, all redounded to the glory of the Republic.

After having surmounted brilliantly the opposition of the Right in the nineteenth century, the Republic succumbed to the lesser challenges of the interwar period. The delicate balance between executive and parliament was upset. On one hand parliament, in the eyes of the public, became increasingly capricious in enforcing the responsibility of the cabinet. Confidence was withheld on the basis of partisan considerations which appeared unrelated to the serious task of constructing majorities. The specialized standing committees of the legislature encroached on the policy-making power of the cabinet. On the other hand, pressing needs of the economy and society necessitated reinforcement of the executive. The practice developed of vesting the government with the power to legislate by decree. After the pro-fascist riots in 1934, the decree power was invoked regularly, even though it obviously violated the spirit if not the letter of the Constitution. There was no real alternative, since the legislature was unable to muster a durable majority.

What caused the failure of the Republic after the victory of 1918, in such sharp contrast to the success achieved after the defeat of 1871? It is doubtful that the explanation can be found in the structure of the regime. The French have demonstrated on numerous occasions their ability to combine universal suffrage, parliamentary control, and bureaucratic centralization in an effective manner. Institutions began to function badly because the major social and political groups were unable to maintain sufficient unity to sustain effective government, and were incapable of providing dynamic political leadership. Growing ineffectiveness of government and the rapid military collapse of 1940 were both reflections of a deep crisis within the French nation.

The Fourth Republic, in the course of its brief twelve-year history, seemed to go through the same cycle as did its longer-lived predecessor. It was launched without any noticeable popular enthusiasm; it gradually met a number of serious threats from both the Left and the Right, consolidated popular support, and scored some respectable achievements; but in the end it lost contact with the masses and disappeared almost entirely unlamented.

The most serious threat confronting the Fourth Republic in its early years came from the combined strength of its opponents. Communist votes accounted for over 25 per cent of the electorate, and in the municipal elections of 1947 the Rally of the French People (which, under the leadership of General de Gaulle, rejected the Constitution) swept almost 40 per cent of the vote. But politicians of the democratic Center managed, with considerable skill, to isolate both Communists and Gaullists and reduce the combined opposition vote in the election of 1951 to such an extent that republican government could continue. The mere existence of the Fourth Republic after 1947 was no mean achievement in itself!

On the more positive side, the Fourth Republic presided over an impressive expansion of the French economy, on the basis of moderate economic planning. Immediately after the war a *Commissariat-général du plan,* with Jean Monnet as chairman, drew up a master plan for rapid modernization and development of the economy. By 1952 national production amounted to 45 per cent over that of 1938, and by 1957 the increase amounted to 104 per cent.

However, the Fourth Republic failed in one crucial respect: it was unable to enforce an equitable social division of the benefits deriving from this increased productivity. Wage levels remained below prewar levels until about 1951, and even with expanded social security benefits, continued to lag behind the general rate of economic expansion after that date. Programs of social reform would have brought down delicately balanced cabinets and perhaps, in requiring new elections under adverse conditions, might have precipitated a crisis of the regime. In the field of colonial policy a major reversal of French attitudes led to a partition of Vietnam and, in North Africa, to the grant of autonomy to Tunisia and Morocco by the Mendès-France government. In 1956 a "framework-law" for Africa at long last granted a large measure of home rule to French colonies and pointed the way to independence.

In spite of hesitations and equivocation, the Fourth Republic introduced basic reforms that modified French economic, social, and colonial structures. The regime functioned relatively well until it came up against the grave problem of Algeria. Inability of a series of governments either to suppress the rebellion or negotiate a peace with the rebels guaranteeing French rights led to an explosion of nationalist sentiment and the overthrow of the Republic.

On May 13, 1958, a demonstration took place in the city of Algiers protesting the investiture of Pierre Pflimlin (who, it was widely believed, advocated negotiations with the rebels) as prime minister. Activist groups composed of French settlers in Algeria managed to break through police lines and seize public buildings. The police and armed forces fraternized with and then joined the insurrection. Together with a group of Gaullists (who had long been planning for just such a development), the army and activists formed a Committee of Public Safety, and demanded the return of General de Gaulle to power. In order to implement that demand, the French army in Africa prepared to invade Metropolitan France. General de Gaulle himself stated that he was ready to assume the powers of the Republic, but only if the people desired it and if it could be accomplished legally. After ascertaining that it was impossible to avoid civil war, the leaders of the government finally decided to negotiate with De Gaulle and bring him back to power. The forms of republican legality were respected, though in reality the pressure exerted by the army proved crucial. On June 1, for the first time in almost thirteen years, General de Gaulle entered the National Assembly. He read a statement requesting investiture as prime minister and full powers to govern the nation and revise the constitution. Confidence was accorded by a vote of 329 for, 224 against.

The institutions of a new, Fifth Republic were established in short order. Within three months a new constitutional text was drawn up by General de Gaulle's cabinet, and on September 28, 1958, it was approved by the people in a referendum (79 per cent for, 21 per cent against). On November 23 and 30 elections took place for a new National Assembly; on December 21 General de Gaulle was elected President of the Republic; and on January 15, 1959, a cabinet with Michel Debré as prime minister was formally invested by the National Assembly. The new Republic differed greatly from its predecessors. In establishing a powerful presidency, it represents a significant departure from the classic French tradition of parliamentary government.

Social Forces

A major reason for French constitutional instability following the Revolution was the failure of the dominant social groups to devise political forms capable of gaining the support of their opponents. The landed aristocracy remained devoted to the principle of hereditary monarchy, while the new middle class and the workers tended to be republican. As we have seen, the Third Republic represented a compromise between monarchists and republicans, which gradually stabilized itself and won widespread acceptance. Yet the old social and ideological divisions continued to bring into question the forms of the state. The social groups which previously had supported the monarchy or Bonapartism—notably the aristocracy, clergy, army officers, elements of the peasantry, and part of the middle class—clamored for a stronger executive. On the other hand, the workers and the more recently prosperous elements of the middle class tended to identify the Republic with the dominance of universal suffrage, as expressed through parliament. The rough balance in the classic French parliamentary system between parliament and the executive (including the civil service) reflected an underlying equilibrium between opposing social forces. The "immobility" of French cabinets has been but one of many manifestations of a deeper social immobility.

The social structure of France has changed less than that of any other major Western nation in the past two centuries. Since 1789 the population of the United States has increased fifty times, from 4 million to 195 million and that of Great Britain has tripled; but France's has grown only about 50 per cent. Furthermore, the industrial revolution has had less of an impact in France than elsewhere in northern Europe. Thus the agricultural sector is far more important in France than it is in Britain or Germany, and the industrial sector is proportionally less important. In political terms this means that the new social forces generated by advanced industrialization (a managerial class, skilled workers, technicians, engineers, and the like) play a relatively limited role in France, while the traditional social formations (the peasants, small shopkeepers, landed aristocracy, family business groups, and unskilled workers) retain much of their old political power. It also means

Table 4.1

Relative Size of French Population Sectors, 1906, 1936, 1954

Population Sector	1906	1936	1954
Total population*	39	42	44
Active population*			
Agriculture and forestry	8.8	7.2	6.4
Manufacturing	6.0	5.8	6.8
Commerce and services†	5.3	6.3	6.7

* In millions.
† Includes commerce, transport, and public as well as private services.
SOURCE: From *Tableaux de l'économie française* (Paris: Institut National de la Statistique et des Études Économiques, 1960), p. 83.

that classic ideological controversies (involving, for example, the form and activities of the state and the position of the church) have had a longer life in France than in other advanced nations.

The figures in Table 4.1 are instructive. They show, for one thing, that the number of people engaged in agriculture has declined in the past fifty years by about 25 per cent, but nonetheless represents one-third of the working population. The increase in the number of people engaged in manufacturing and services corresponds with the trend in other advanced nations, but has not been as marked. Also, the family shop or enterprise remains a prevalent form of economic organization. Again, the political implications are obvious: in France the working class and managerial groups are less important, and the peasantry more important, as voting blocs and political forces than in most other Western democracies.

Stability of the social structure is also reflected by figures on the distribution of the population between rural and urban areas. According to the census of 1962, only 25.6 per cent of the population live in cities with more than 50,000 inhabitants, while 32.7 per cent live in communes with less than 2,000 inhabitants (of which 11.8 per cent live in communes with fewer than 500). Paris is the only city with a popula-

tion of over 1 million and, with 3 million people within the city limits
and 5 million in its metropolitan area, is only one-third to one-half the
size of either London or New York. Rural areas in France are more
populous, and hence more powerful politically, than in the other advanced democracies.

THE POLITICAL ORIENTATION OF SOCIAL FORCES

Governments and even constitutions come and go in France, but the
principal social groups remain in place and manifest their political
views with remarkable fidelity, if not monotony. Under the Fifth Republic, as under the Fourth and the Third and indeed in every election
held since the Revolution of 1789, certain communes and even *départements* (basic administrative units roughly comparable in size to large
American counties) have voted to the Left, others to the Right. For
example, the peasants of the east (along the German border) and the
northwest (Normandy and Brittany) tend to be conservative if not
reactionary, while the peasants of the south and the center tend to be
radical. In many areas of central and southern France, the peasantry has
always voted for the party on the extreme Left—Radical Socialist in
the late nineteenth century, Socialist until 1939, and Communist thereafter.

The working class, like almost every large professional, social, or
economic group in France, is split along ideological or party lines. A
majority of the industrial workers have been voting Communist since
World War II, though there is significant working class support for the
Socialist party and the Christian Democrats. It is impossible to identify
the other social groups with any one party or political orientation. In a
country with so many parties and ideological divisions, there are partisan and ideological organizations among all classes and groups. Thus
there are Socialist teachers, shopkeepers, workers, civil servants, and
veterans at the same time that there are Communist, Christian Democratic, and other organizations among the same groups. Nonetheless
certain social groups *tend* to vote or support certain parties more than
others. Teachers and civil servants tend to be on the Left, although the
higher civil service is generally on the Right. Workers are on the Left,
but they frequently respond to nationalistic appeals, as is evidenced by
General de Gaulle's success among them. The peasants are on the Left
or the Right according to region and income; the landed aristocracy and
capitalists on the Right; businessmen sometimes in the Center but more
often on the Right. The clergy and the religious faithful were historically
on the Right, but since World War II a segment of the Catholic community has supported the Christian Democratic party. Veterans are
organized into literally dozens of groups, but the dominant note among
them recently has been extreme nationalism or Gaullism.

Despite this long history of stability in social structure and political alignments, however, sweeping changes have been taking place in the French economy and society in the past fifteen years. It is likely that the historic orientations of both geographic regions and social groups will be utterly transformed as a result. Since 1949 France has been experiencing a remarkable economic expansion. Table 4.2 indicates the general out-

Table 4.2

French Economic Growth, 1938–1959

Year	National Revenue	Industrial Production	Retail Prices	Average Salary, Steel-workers, Paris	Value of Imports	Foreign Trade Exports
1938*	100	100	100	100	100	100
1945	58	50	401	277	34	10
1948	100	113	1449	798	98	81
1952	132	145	2347	1524	116	161
1957	168	204	2511	2165	175	223
1959	173	220	3067	2512	170	280

* 1938 is the base year. Other figures are percentages based on 1938.
SOURCE: From *Tableaux de l'économie française* (Paris: Institut National de la Statistique et des Études Économiques, 1960), p. 95.

lines of this impressive economic growth, showing, for example, that industrial production about doubled in the period 1948–1959. In certain key sectors of the economy—railroads, aviation, electricity, chemicals, and automobiles—technological progress has approximated or surpassed that of Western Germany and the United States. Between 1949 and 1959 production of electric energy doubled; production of aluminum tripled; production of steel went from 9.1 million to 15.2 million tons; production of agricultural tractors from 17,000 to 78,000; production of automobiles from 286,000 to 1,283,000; and the number of new housing units from 51,000 to 320,000. In the first five years of the Fifth Republic (1959–1964), national production increased by an additional 29 per cent. Table 4.2 also shows, however, that the wages of industrial workers have not kept pace with either prices or production.

The widespread use of modern household devices and ownership of private automobiles are changing shopping and living habits. Many uneconomic family enterprises are disappearing. The rapidity with which the "Quick Lunch" and "Self-service" have caught on in France attests to a major revolution. The tempo of life is shifting from a traditional to a modern pace. Work incentives and leisure time aspirations are increasingly similar to those of the more advanced industrial states. France as a result is losing some of her "old world charm"—which is regretted by the foreign tourists, but not by the French. Despite losses during World War II and in both the Indochina and Algerian wars, France's population is growing rapidly and undergoing a structural change as well; by 1970 France will have the youngest population of any country in Western Europe. "Dynamic France" is winning out over "static France."

Many observers of the French political scene—Gaullists in particular—have hailed these social and economic developments as presaging an inevitable transformation of French political life as well. They reason that the newly created or expanded social categories—technicians, managers, economists, scientists, engineers, rural elites using modern techniques, white collar workers—are no longer interested in the old, sterile ideological quarrels. The hope has been expressed that the political parties will respond by becoming more pragmatic, that is, by proposing practical solutions to pressing problems without regard to old ideological issues.

Paradoxically, however, the center of political gravity in the Fifth Republic (which is above all an attempt to create dynamic government) originally was to be found among the inhabitants of the small communes of France. The Constitution provided for election of the president and the Senate by electoral colleges consisting largely of mayors and municipal councilors. In 1958 communes with less than 1,500 inhabitants, representing one-third of the French population, elected 51 per cent of the presidential electors in Metropolitan France and 53 per cent of the senatorial electors. These people continue to be preoccupied with agriculture and wine-cultivation; their major concern is still the protection of the small artisan and the family farm or business; their political experience has been gained mainly by extracting favors or concessions from the state while taking care to shift the tax burden onto others. These are the social elements least affected by the industrial revolution —the most likely indeed, to resort to violent protest against programs of modernization. However, with the adoption of the constitutional reform in 1962 providing for popular election of the president, it is possible that the center of political gravity will shift away from these groups in the future.

In the long run, modernization of the French economy is bound to bring with it changes in political parties and opinions. But so far there have been few signs of such change. Public opinion in the latter part of 1959 was once again raised to fever pitch over the hoary issue of state aid to religious schools. Indeed, the most ideologically oriented party in France—the Communist—recovered a good part of its electoral support in the legislative elections of 1962 and the municipal elections of 1965. In other words, the traditional political parties have not freed themselves of concern with doctrinal and ideological disputes, nor have they been successful in recruiting the elite of the new social groups. On the contrary it appears that President de Gaulle's total domination of policy-making since 1958 has undercut or partially paralyzed the parties. Perhaps only after the parliamentary institutions of the nation have been revivified will the process of modernization include the parties and public opinion as well as the economy and the social structure.

Political Parties and Interest Groups

The French party system often appears to the Anglo-American observer more complicated than in fact it is. Part of the difficulty is that the term "party" does not refer to quite the same phenomenon in France as in Britain or the United States. Major parties in a two-party system like the British or American invariably consist of coalitions of groups, interests, and forces—each of which is more akin to a French party than is the whole British or American "party." On the other hand, the French parties collaborate—frequently in election campaigns and always in cabinet coalitions—and this collaboration corresponds to the process of compromise which takes place *within* the major parties of the English-speaking countries.

French parties traditionally enter into alliances with each other for electoral purposes, much as the various factions making up an American party will unite temporarily every four years in order to nominate a candidate for the Presidency. Under the Third Republic candidates for the lower chamber were elected only if they received an absolute majority of the votes cast on the first ballot. In the event no candidate received this majority (which was usually the case), a run-off election (or *ballottage*) was held two weeks later; on the second ballot only a plurality was required for election. This practice permitted the parties of the Left, Center, and Right to regroup, generally in support of the candidates of each trend who won the largest number of votes on the first ballot.

After the Liberation a system of proportional representation,[1] based on multi-member *départements* rather than single-member districts, eliminated the possibility of electoral collaboration. When General de Gaulle founded a political party in 1947, however, the Center politicians calculated that under a system of straight proportional representation the Gaullists and Communists together would have a majority of both popular votes *and* parliamentary seats. To prevent this, they modified the electoral law to permit parties to form alliances (*apparentements*) in

---

[1] Under proportional representation seats in a legislative body are divided among political parties according to the percentage of votes they have received. In contrast, the single-member district system usually awards legislative positions to the candidate winning a mere plurality; thus the composition of the legislative body may not reflect the percentage of votes cast for the parties.

each *département*. If any party, or coalition of parties, received a majority of the votes in that department, it would win *all* of the seats. Coalitions were formed throughout the nation, mainly by the Radical Socialists, Popular Republicans, and Socialists. In the election of 1951, majorities were achieved in almost one-third of the *départements*, and the Center parties were thereby enabled to maintain their control of parliament. A smaller number of alliances were registered in the elections of 1956, mainly because the break-up of the Gaullist party had reduced the danger to the Center parties.

One of the key decisions of General de Gaulle's cabinet preparatory to the first elections under the Fifth Republic was to revert to the traditional single-member district with *ballottage*. On the second ballot in 1958 there were over 50 straight fights between two candidates, and an average of three or four candidates in all districts. In 1962 there were only 889 candidates for 369 seats on the second ballot—with straight fights in 227 districts. Thus under the Fifth Republic, French voters generally have been presented on the second or run-off ballot with a choice almost as limited as that in two-party systems.

Collaboration by the parties is continued in cabinet coalitions, though not always on the same basis as the electoral alliances. After 1947, when the Communists were compelled to resign from the cabinet, a Center coalition retained power until the overthrow of the Fourth Republic. Ministerial crises involved relatively minor shifts of emphasis within the coalition, rarely any brusque reversal of course. Thus, despite the apparent complexity of the French party system, the choice presented to the voter is frequently narrowed on the second ballot; and the participation of the parties in cabinet coalitions also serves to channel the conflict between major political forces.

LEFT AND RIGHT

In the competition for mutually profitable electoral alliances, in negotiations preceding the formation of a cabinet, and in general political discourse, the classic distinction between the French Left and Right remains of overriding importance. The issues between these two political families and the social groups composing them have changed significantly in the course of the past century. Nonetheless, public opinion remains divided along Left-Right lines, and party coalitions necessarily reflect these divisions.

As we have seen, the original issue between Left and Right involved a choice between hereditary monarchy and the Republic. Throughout the nineteenth century legitimists (partisans of the former monarchy) and Bonapartists strove to re-establish a monarchy. Although they were profoundly divided over the nature of the monarchist regime and the choice of a king, they almost succeeded in gaining their objective on several occasions under the Third Republic. The success of the Republic in consolidating popular support eventually led to the elimination of the monarchist threat, but the social groups making up the classic Right remained opposed to the parliamentary system. In the twentieth century the principal constitutional issue between Left and Right has been the relative power to be accorded to parliament and to the executive.

A second major issue dividing Left from Right relates to the status of the Catholic Church and of religious schools. The clergy and the practicing Catholics tended to be monarchist throughout the nineteenth century, though in 1891, Pope Leo XIII advised them to "rally" to the Republic; Catholics who eventually accepted the Republic generally supported the moderate Right. In order to win over the youth, the Third Republic established a universal system of free, secular (and, in practice, frequently anti-clerical) education, which further antagonized the Catholic faithful. A new development, however, was the creation during and after the Liberation of a pro-republican, socially progressive party of Catholic inspiration—the Popular Republican Movement (MRP). In matters of social and economic policy, the MRP has been close to the Socialists—that is, Leftist. But the issue of state aid to the religious schools during and after the election of 1951 revived all the old doctrinal quarrels of Left and Right over the relationship between church and state, and provoked a realignment of political forces reminiscent of the classic Left-Right dichotomy.

A third Left-Right split has resulted from the social turmoil of industrialization. French business interests have traditionally sought to block state interference in the economy (except, of course, when interference has taken the form of special subsidies or protection for industry), while the French working class has historically demanded state regulation or ownership of industry and also measures guaranteeing an equitable division of the national income. Broadly speaking, the Right favored laissez faire, while the Left urged either socialism or far-reaching regulation and reform of the economy. Similarly, on issues of colonial policy, the Left, at least in recent decades, had tended to favor "decolonization" while the Right has been generally nationalistic, resisting the grant of autonomy or independence to French possessions.

One of the striking features of the Left-Right clash in France is that the lines of demarcation shift with the issues. "Left" and "Right" are not solid and permanent blocs, opposing each other on any and all issues; rather, groups which stand shoulder-to-shoulder as "Leftists" on one major issue may well find themselves bitterly opposing each other as "Left" versus "Right" on another. Thus middle-class Radicals are on the Left as far as the republican regime and the status of church schools are concerned, but on the Right with respect to social and economic policy. The MRP is Left on the regime and economic policy, Right on church schools. To complicate matters further, moreover, Left-Right splits have been taking place *within* most parties, particularly under the Fifth Republic; thus Algerian policy, the events of May, 1958, leading to General de Gaulle's return to power, reform of the Constitution, and state policy in stimulating economic expansion have caused controversies within almost all the traditional political groupings.

MAJOR POLITICAL CURRENTS AND PARTY GROUPS

The broad divisions of organized opinion among the French electorate have remained remarkably constant since the Liberation, though successive changes in the electoral system have produced sharp variations in each party's allotment of parliamentary seats. It is possible to discern three fairly stable currents of party opinion since World War II: the Communists and Socialists on the Left; the Radical Socialists and the MRP in the Center (that is, Left on some issues, Right on others); and the Independents, Gaullists, and assorted smaller groups on the Right. Each of these parties has been able to count on a solid nucleus of supporters, with about two million voters shifting about between the parties or into abstention.

Parties of the Left. The French Communist Party (PCF) was founded in 1920 when the Socialist party split over the question of adhering to Lenin's Third International. By and large, the militant revolutionary section of the Socialist party of that time went over to the Communists. An organization was created resembling that of the Soviet Communist Party, with the members compartmentalized in "cells" linked to the leadership (but not to each other) by a series of intermediary bodies. Hence the Party is organized admirably for carrying out the orders of the leadership by mass action without too much risk of dissension. The Communists greatly increased their electoral support during the Popular Front period (1934–1936) and after the Liberation, when they emerged as the largest party in France. Under the Fourth Republic the PCF consistently received about 25 per cent of the vote.

The PCF espouses the classic Left position on the nature of the regime, the status of the church, and the role of the state in regulating the economy. The other parties of the Left fear, however, that the Communists are interested basically in coming to power (preferably unaided, but otherwise through the agency of the Soviet Union) and then legislating into existence one-party control—which is hardly compatible with the democratic ideals of the Left as a whole. A chasm has therefore opened up between the Communists and the other groups on the Left and Center.

The Communists made an effort to break out of political quarantine after Stalin's death by offering cooperation to other parties of the Left. The gap between the PCF and the others was too great to be bridged, however, until 1962. Then, in order to prevent a landslide Gaullist victory in the elections of that year, the Socialists and Radicals negotiated limited agreements with the Communists on the second ballot (see p. 133). One of the consequences of the deep division within the parties of the Left has been, quite naturally, to drive the balance in parliament to the Right.

In the elections which took place immediately after General de Gaulle's return to power in 1958, the PCF suffered a significant reverse, its vote going from 25 per cent to 18.9 per cent of the total. Many of the Party's working-class supporters were won over to De Gaulle's emotional brand of nationalism, while they remained completely unaffected by Socialist and Radical programs of reform. But the Party recovered much of its mass support in 1962, winning 21.8 per cent of the vote.

The second major party of the Left, the French Section of the Workers' International (SFIO), or Socialist party, was created in 1905 by a fusion of revolutionary and moderate Socialist factions. It was the first party, historically, to organize a mass of supporters. Its structure represents a balance between the "democratic centralism" of the Communists and the rule by members of parliament and local elites characteristic of the Right. Local sections are grouped into "federations" within the *départements;* the federations elect delegates to a National Congress; and an Executive Committee runs current party affairs.

The SFIO remained in opposition to the "bourgeois" regime for thirty years after its founding (except during World War I, when it participated in a government of national unity); it nonetheless collaborated with other Leftist parties during election campaigns (for example, by agreeing to rally behind common candidates on the second ballot). In 1936 the SFIO, under the leadership of Léon Blum, formed a cabinet based on a Popular Front agreement between the Socialists, Radical Socialists, and Communists. Although the Popular Front was overthrown within two years, the event was significant in that it marked the entry of the Socialists into the political system.

Since the Liberation, the SFIO has participated intermittently in cabinet and electoral coalitions with other parties of the Left and Center —consequently losing considerable support among the workers and Left-oriented intellectuals. After the 1956 elections, the Socialists formed a government under the presidency of Guy Mollet, with the support of the Popular Republicans, Radicals, and a few Gaullists. The party leadership became increasingly nationalistic, favoring the expedition against Egypt and the suppression of the Algerian rebellion, policies which reflected a general drift to the Right. A majority within the party went along with General de Gaulle after his return to power; indeed, Guy Mollet became one of his ministers. But after the formation of the Debré government in January, 1959, the SFIO went into opposition. The leadership of the party at first drew a distinction between President de Gaulle, whom they supported, and Prime Minister Debré, whose government they freely criticized, but their position rapidly shifted to one of hostility to De Gaulle himself. Socialist intellectuals have become increasingly restive over the party's inability to implement its doctrine when in power and its failure to check the Right when in opposition. Many Socialist intellectuals, and several important leaders, have recently seceded from the party and formed the more radical Unified Socialist party (PSU).

Parties of the Center. The Center parties play a crucial role in the French political system. They are the "hinge" parties, ready and eager to collaborate with both Left and Right, depending upon the issues and the chances for success. A center party must have both Left and Right wings, so that it can move in either direction without too much strain on its organization. In France the model hinge party has been the Radical Socialists. One faction of this party is oriented towards the Left, particularly as regards defense of the principles of 1789 and opposition to the church; another, and perhaps dominant faction, combines fervent republicanism with conservatism on social and economic policies. Their inability to evolve a concise doctrine or a disciplined organization actually facilitated the rise of the Radicals, who constituted a buffer between the divided Left and the resurgent Right of the Fourth Republic, and formed an essential element of most coalitions.

In 1954 Pierre Mendès-France attempted to bring about a far-reaching reform of the Radical Socialist party. He wanted to create an ideological movement, committed to state direction of the economy and based on forward-looking elements of the middle class. The clash between Mendès-France and the more traditionally oriented Radical leaders led to the break-up of the party. Some of the conservative elements withdrew and formed a splinter group, and Mendès-France himself resigned his leadership in 1957 and later joined the Unified Socialist party. The present Radical leaders have quietly laid to rest all the ambitious schemes for renovation. Despite the party split, the Radicals continue to retain the support of close to 12 per cent of the electorate, largely as a consequence of the personal following of the party's "notables."

After the Liberation a second Center party was created: the Popular Republican Movement (MRP). Its historic importance was to eliminate the identification of French Catholicism with the political Right. MRP doctrine is republican, and also tends to be critical of capitalism on ethical grounds. In matters of social and economic policy, the MRP advocates a kind of Christian socialism which has the support of a sizable segment of the working class. Ideological tensions are reflected, however, by the social composition of the MRP: Catholic intellectuals and working-class militants infuse the movement with a sense of fervor and social mission, while its traditionally pro-clerical and conservative supporters in the west and northeast are more interested in the status of the church than social reform.

Until 1947 the MRP, in cooperating with the Communists and Socialists, veered to the Left; but like the Socialists, the party was virtually compelled to participate in a Center coalition after 1947. A turning point seemed to be reached in 1951, when parliament debated a law providing subsidies to both public and private (that is, religious) schools; at that time the MRP swung sharply to the Right. On the Algerian question and during the events of May, 1958, however, the MRP took a position at least as far Left as that of the Socialists. The party entered the Debré government in 1959, attempting to form the "left" wing of the cabinet coalition, but broke with De Gaulle in 1962 over his policy on European economic and political integration.

Parties of the Right. Parties of the Right in France traditionally have been more divided and less well organized than those on the Left. Under the Third Republic the chief conservative "parties," the Republican Federation and the Democratic Alliance, were in reality combinations for electoral purposes which broke up into half a dozen groups in Parliament. They had no mass organization and no militants. Under the Fourth Republic they worked mainly within a grouping called the National Center of Independents, which managed to achieve a measure of discipline and organization only in 1954.

The Independents are roughly comparable to the right wing of the American Republican or British Conservative parties. They advocate a laissez faire policy untarnished by Keynesian heresies, reduction of taxes and a balanced budget, an end to nationalization of industry, stimulation of private investment, and in general creation of conditions favorable to capitalist development. They supported General de Gaulle's return to power and made up, with the Gaullists, the principal support of the Debré government. But they became increasingly critical of the government's Algerian policy, and by 1962 they were in the anti-Gaullist camp. They suffered a crushing defeat in the 1962 election.

The Bonapartist or anti-parliamentary trend within French public opinion has expressed itself since World War II largely through the Gaullist parties and smaller activist groups, the latter having been especially important in Algeria. In January, 1946, General de Gaulle unexpectedly resigned as head of the government, and campaigned against adoption of the Constitution of the Fourth Republic. The following year he personally founded the Rally of the French People (RPF), dedicated to the reform of the French political system. The RPF offered a vision of a republic above the parties, with a chief of state embodying the superior interests of the nation. The working class would be reintegrated into the nation by a network of capital-labor associations, thus reducing Communist influence; the state would be rescued from the selfish interests; and France would regain its influence in the councils of the world. At the end of the year (1947), the party scored impressive victories in local elections.

The Center parties were temporarily successful, however, in staving off the double menace of Communism and Gaullism. A "Third Force" coalition managed to stay in power for four years, and in the 1951 elections the RPF returned only 120 deputies, not enough to carry De Gaulle back to power. A number of Gaullist deputies broke away to support a conservative cabinet. In May, 1953, General de Gaulle abandoned leadership of the RPF and withdrew from active political life.

The RPF's place on the Right was then partially taken by the Poujadists, who won a surprising victory (about 10 per cent of the votes) in the election of 1956. Pierre Poujade, a small-town bookseller, began his political career as a champion of the interests of shopkeepers, particularly in their efforts to prevent tax collectors from examining their records. His movement rapidly attracted the support of anti-parliamentary and right-wing groups. Poujadist deputies cut a poor figure in parliamentary debates, however, and the movement lost its momentum. In the 1958 election the party virtually disappeared as a political force. But the Poujadists established links with activist and conspiratorial groups in Algeria, playing a role of some importance in the May, 1958, Algiers uprising which led to the overthrow of the Fourth Republic.

After General de Gaulle's return to power in 1958, his supporters created a new party, the Union for the New Republic (UNR). This time, however, De Gaulle dissociated himself from all partisan activities, whereas he personally had led the old RPF. Leaders of the UNR claim that they are not on the Right but in the Center. "We are neither Gaullists of the Right nor Gaullists of the Left," commented one UNR founder, "but just Gaullists." The party's election program was simply approval of all political positions taken by General de Gaulle in all domains ever since June, 1940. Its supporters include left-wing intellectuals who desire social and economic reforms, activists who participated in the May uprising, traditionally oriented conservatives, and many youthful nationalists. The Leftist Gaullists have founded their own party, the Democratic Union of Labor (UDT).

In the elections of November, 1958, the UNR scored an unexpected victory, receiving 17.6 per cent of the votes on the first ballot and 26.4 per cent on the second ballot. Out of 465 seats in Metropolitan France, the UNR won 189, and the adherence of a few independents finally brought the figure to 206. For the first time in the modern history of republican France a single party approached a majority in parliament. Many of the old RPF voters had gone over to the MRP and Independents; their place was taken by former Socialists and even Communists (perhaps half of the 1.6 million votes lost by the Communists went to the UNR). Compared to the old RPF, the UNR included a greater number of former supporters of the Left and a smaller number of traditional conservatives; it was less a party of the Center than a meeting of extremes. Right-wing activists gradually deserted the UNR after it became clear that De Gaulle was pursuing a policy of Algerian independence.

The UNR and UDT won an astonishing success in the 1962 election, when they polled 31.9 per cent of the votes on the first ballot and 40.5 per cent on the second ballot, gaining 223 seats. Together with 41 deputies from other parties who had received the endorsement of the Gaullists, they constituted a solid majority of 274 in an Assembly of 482 members.

On the extreme Right there is a proliferation of small activist groups, rarely able to do well in elections but with an important following among intellectuals, students, veterans, and army officers. The deterioration of France's position in Algeria led to a revival of extremist sentiment, represented by such organizations as the Young Nation, the Indochina Veterans, and the Secret Army Organization (OAS). Activists belonging to such groups have made a number of attempts to assassinate General de Gaulle.

French Parties since World War II. Viewed broadly, there have been three significant phases in the evolution of the French political situation since the Liberation. (See Table 4.3 for a schematic presentation of election results and coalitions in the period 1946–1962.) From 1944 to 1947 three parties of the Left and Center, together controlling almost three-fourths of the seats in the National Assembly, formed a "tripartite" government. The Communists, the Socialists, and the MRP divided administrative and political tasks among themselves and attempted to bring some economic order out of the chaos inherited from the war. Cooperation with the Communists became increasingly awkward, however, and in May, 1947, a Socialist prime minister, Paul Ramadier, forced his Communist partners out of the cabinet.

A second phase then began which lasted until the fall of the Fourth Republic, with many minor shifts and changes resulting from the constant reshuffling of parties in parliament. Basically, the parties between the extreme Left and the extreme Right pooled their resources in order to maintain and defend the Republic. In 1947 the Socialists, the MRP, and the Radicals together had a bare majority of the seats, but were able to form a stable coalition which remained in power for four years. After the election of 1951 the Center coalition had to be widened to include the Independents. Indeed, moderate conservatives formed cabinets with the support and later the participation of the Gaullist party, the RPF, and were able to do without the Socialists; the balance within the Center coalition then swung to the Right. When Mendès-France came to power in 1954, the balance swung Left again, since the Socialists accorded him their support.

In the election of 1956 the Gaullist RPF virtually disappeared, but the Poujadists won 9 per cent of the seats and the Communists 26 per cent. Thus the parties between these two extremes were again compelled to continue their collaboration, since the defection of any one of the four Center parties (Socialists, MRP, Radicals, Independents), coupled with the permanent opposition of the Communists and Poujadists, would have brought down the government. The Socialists assumed cabinet leadership in 1956 and 1957, but the Independents exercised a virtual veto. The last cabinets of the Fourth Republic were presided over by Radicals and by a member of the MRP. But the pattern remained constant: the Communist Party and the extreme Right were both isolated and power rested with the four major parties named above. Coalition agreements between these four shifted according to the issues involved; for example, the MRP joined the Center-Right in 1951 in order to help secure state subsidies for religious schools, and the Socialists came to the support of Mendès-France in 1954 in order to bring about a cease-fire in Indochina and economic reforms. The margin for maneuver, however, was greatly restricted by the existence of a sizable representation for the Communists and the extreme Right.

A third phase began after General de Gaulle's return to power in June, 1958. It was originally his intention to preside over a government of national unity, and his first cabinet included members of all Center formations—Socialists, Radicals, MRP, Independents, and the former RPF, excluding only Communists and Poujadists. But the election of 1958 gave the UNR 40 per cent of the seats in parliament and the Independents 28 per cent. The cabinet formed by Michel Debré consisted mainly of UNR and Independents, with some participation by the MRP. The parties making up the prewar Popular Front (the Communists, Socialists, and Radicals), who together received an absolute majority of the popular vote in the three elections under the Fourth Republic and about 47 per cent on the first ballot in 1958, were all in the opposition. When the Independents turned against the government over Algerian policy, Prime Minister Debré reshuffled his cabinet without permitting the reshuffling to reach the proportions of a cabinet crisis. But his successor as prime minister, Georges Pompidou, found it increasingly difficult to construct a majority around the UNR, especially after the defection of the MRP over European policy. By October, 1962, there was a "negative majority," and the Pompidou government was defeated on a censure motion. In the elections which followed, however, the Gaullists scored an impressive victory, and Pompidou reconstituted his government with the support of the UNR, UDT, and Republican Independents.

Thus since 1958 there has been no need for a full-fledged cabinet crisis as a means of bringing about a new party alignment. But the significance of this evolution is reduced considerably by the fact that policy-making in the Fifth Republic has remained largely in the hands of General de Gaulle. In a sense, the third phase in the evolution of the party situation might be described as the transfer of power from the parties to the President of the Republic.

Table 4.3

Election Results and Cabinet Coalitions in France, 1946–1962*

Party Groupings	1946		1951		1956		1958		1962	
	VOTES	SEATS	VOTES	SEATS	VOTES	SEATS	VOTES	SEATS	VOTES	SEATS
Left										
PCF	28%	29%	26%	16%	26%	26%	19%	2%	22%	9%
SFIO	18	17	14	17	15	16	15	9	13	14
Center										
Rad. Soc.	11	10	11	15	14	13	13	8	8	9
MRP†	26	26	12	14	10	13	12	12	9‡ +	6‡ +
Right										
Ind.‡	13	12	13	16	14	17	20	28	4‡	4‡
Gaullist**	1	—	22	19	4	3	18	40	32	49
Poujadist	—	—	—	—	11	9	—	—	—	—

* All figures are percentages, and approximate. 1958 and 1962 figures are for the first ballot.

† Includes Christian Democrats in 1958.

‡ The Independents split in 1962; the National Independent Center candidates won 8.9% on the first ballot and the (pro-Gaullist) Republican Independents won 4.4% of the vote.

** RPF in 1951, Social Republicans in 1956, UNR in 1958, UNR and UDT in 1962.

SOURCE: For detailed figures, see R. C. Macridis and B. E. Brown, *The De Gaulle Republic* (Homewood, Ill.: Dorsey Press, 1960), p. 258 and *Supplement to the De Gaulle Republic* (Dorsey, 1963), p. 82.

Note: Table 4.3 presents the results of the four elections since the Liberation. The various coalitions are indicated by brackets—which does not mean that these parties were all members of the same cabinet, but that they were involved in negotiations for cabinets and generally either supported or participated in them.

The disparity between popular votes and parliamentary seats in 1958 and 1962 is accounted for by the electoral system in effect for these elections. In each of the 465 districts into which Metropolitan France was divided, a candidate was elected on the *first* ballot only if he received an absolute majority of the votes cast; otherwise a *second* ballot was held one week later, and the candidate with the greatest number of votes was then declared the winner. Between ballots, many candidates withdrew or desisted in favor of better-placed parties of the same general tendency. Isolation of the Communists worked to their severe disadvantage in the run-off in 1958. For example, in Paris the Communist candidate received almost twice as many votes as her nearest rival. One week later only three candidates were left in the field. The result on the second and decisive ballot: the UNR candidate was elected; runners-up were the Communist (first) and the Socialist (second). In most cases the UNR or the Independent was preferred by the majority of the voters to ensure the Communists' defeat.

But in 1962 the Communists and Socialists (joined by some Radicals) collaborated in a number of *départements* in order to beat the UNR and to survive the tidal wave. To cite a widely publicized example, the Socialist secretary general, Guy Mollet, would surely have been beaten in his district had it not been for Communist support. On the first ballot, the Gaullist candidate received 14,233 votes; Mollet, 12,944; a Communist, 11,362; and an MRP, 5,960. On the second ballot two candidates were left: Mollet, 24,375 and the Gaullist, 21,810. In 1958 the anti-Communist reflex united all the other parties, whereas in 1962 an anti-Gaullist reflex drove the parties of the Left together. The run-off ballot thus forced the electorate to choose between drastically limited, clear-cut alternatives.

INTEREST GROUPS

Social interests put forward their demands through a complex network
of pressure groups as well as through the political parties. Under the
Fourth Republic, pressure groups were very much in evidence. Each
major lobby could count on a core of solid support in the National
Assembly and on established contacts with the appropriate administrative agencies. Some groups (especially labor unions, business interests,
and religious organizations) were loosely affiliated with political parties.
Cabinet instability frequently made it difficult for governments to resist
the demands of interest groups, since the small margin of a government's parliamentary support might be destroyed if even a few of its
supporters deserted it in response to a group's demands. Perhaps the
most notorious example of pressure politics under the Fourth Republic
was the success achieved by the alcohol lobbies, made up of beetgrowers,
wine cultivators, and distillers, in maintaining state purchase of alcohol
at premium prices. It has been estimated that 4 million people in France
derive profit in some way from the manufacture, sale, or transport of
alcohol. Reform of the *Service des Alcools,* which at one time was buying
up twice as much alcohol as the market could absorb, was prevented
by parliamentary pressure; indeed, a cabinet was overthrown in May,
1953, partly because it had requested special powers to cope with the
situation.

The chief organized groups in France include those speaking for
broad socio-economic interests: business interests such as the National
Council of French Business and the Union for the Defense of Artisans
and Shopkeepers; trade unions such as the General Confederation of
Labor (pro-Communist), the Democratic Federation of Labor (pro-
MRP), and the pro-Socialist *Force Ouvrière* (Workers Strength); and
agricultural groups such as the National Federation of Farmers Unions.
Each of these can draw support from a significant portion of the population—6 to 8 million workers, 8 million farmers, and several million
people engaged in commerce and business. In addition, there are a host
of more specialized groups: veterans, religious faithful seeking subsidies
for schools, secular champions of the public schools, students, and so on.

These groups utilize techniques we are familiar with in the United
States: mobilization of public opinion, provision of information to administrators, and especially application of pressure upon parliamentarians and ministers. Recourse to drastic measures (refusal to pay
taxes, blockade of roads by the peasants, strikes, seizure of public
buildings, and sabotage) has not been infrequent since World War II.
The army's intervention in politics as an aftermath of the uprising of
May 13 and the resort to terror by conspiratorial associations in both
Algeria and France since then may be considered spectacular examples
of the recourse to violent methods by pressure groups.

The framers of the Fifth Republic anticipated that the power of lobbies would be reduced under the new constitution, and to a certain extent their claims have been borne out. Since the government rests essentially upon a solid bloc of deputies, it need not court the support of small coteries defending particular interests. But the great interests, and many smaller interests as well, are largely represented *within* the UNR and allied parties. Thus the alcohol-producing groups, the associations in favor of religious schools, the business groups in general, and the peasants have many defenders in the new Assembly and within the cabinet. And if the army is considered a pressure group, its role if anything was more important after 1958 than before. The most important interest groups whose political power has declined under the Fifth Republic are the labor unions, since the parties with which they are affiliated, particularly the Communists and Socialists, have had their parliamentary representation substantially reduced.

Political Institutions

When General de Gaulle returned to power in June, 1958, he immediately requested, and was granted, constituent (that is, constitution-making) powers. He assured parliament that the new constitution would respect the principle of universal suffrage, maintain the responsibility of the government before parliament, and establish effective separation between the legislative and the executive. The elaboration of a text took only three months.

The Constitution of the Fifth Republic was largely inspired by the ideas of two men: General de Gaulle and Michel Debré (who was chairman of the study group which drew up the first draft and who later became the first prime minister of the new regime). De Gaulle had outlined his views on the constitutional question twelve years earlier during the national debate over the Constitution of the Fourth Republic. He argued that in France political parties were too divided to provide effective, dynamic leadership for the nation. Hence it was essential to create a chief of state whose authority came from some source greater than parliament (but not directly from the electorate) and who could function as a "national arbiter." He would embody the superior interests of the nation and dispose of significant independent power, especially in the event of an emergency similar to the war situation of June, 1940. In addition, there would be strict separation of power between the judiciary, the legislature, and a "government that governs."

Debré's main concern was to create governmental stability by means of constitutional provisions reinforcing the position of the cabinet and restricting (or "rationalizing") the role of parliament. These two seminal ideas—an independent executive and a "rationalized" cabinet system—are the source of the originality of the new constitution, which departs from the classic French model and yet differs radically from both the American Presidential and British parliamentary systems.

As an indication of its new emphasis, the Constitution deals first with the president, next with the government, and then with parliament (whereas under the previous constitution the order was parliament, economic council, president, and council of ministers). The basic structure of the institutions is unchanged: executive power continues to be vested in a president and a cabinet, with the latter responsible to the legislature. Legislative power is shared by two chambers, the National Assembly and the Senate. But the powers of each institution, and the relations among them, are significantly different.

The President of the Republic. When he presented the new Constitution to the French people for approval by referendum, General de Gaulle summarized the nature of the presidential office:

> A national arbiter—far removed from political bickering—elected by the citizens who hold a public mandate, charged with the task of ensuring the normal functioning of the institutions, possessing the right to resort to the judgment of the sovereign people, accountable, in the case of extreme danger, for the independence, the honor and integrity of France and for the safety of the Republic.

Unlike the presidents of the Third and Fourth Republics, the president of the Fifth Republic has political powers which he may wield personally, without the need for ministerial countersignature. As "national arbiter" he may, for example, dissolve parliament at any time and for any reason (but not twice within the same year), subject only to "consultation" with the prime minister. Under the Third Republic the president's power of dissolution required ministerial countersignature and the approval of the Senate, while under the Fourth Republic it was in effect transferred to the prime minister. General de Gaulle used the threat of dissolution on several occasions in order to strengthen the position of the Debré government. When the National Assembly censured the Pompidou government in October, 1962, De Gaulle immediately dissolved parliament.

The president can also bring certain issues before the people in referendum. According to the Constitution (Article 11), the president *may* submit to the people any bill dealing with the organization of the public powers or the community (consisting of former French colonies electing to retain a special relationship), on the proposal of the government or on joint resolution of parliament. But he is not compelled to call the referendum; hence this too remains a personal power. General de Gaulle has used the referendum extensively as a means of establishing a direct relationship with the French people, without the intermediary of parliament; he has stated that the referendum is now part of the political *mores* of the people. In the course of the first legislature, referendums were held on three occasions: January 8, 1961, on the text of a government bill to grant some kind of autonomy to Algeria (15.2 million Yes, 5 million No); April 8, 1962, on the Evian accord granting independence to Algeria (17.5 million Yes, 1.8 million No); October 28, 1962, on election of the president by universal suffrage (13.1 million Yes, 8 million No). The referendum of October, 1962, was the occasion of a political crisis; a majority in parliament voted to censure the Pompidou government specifically because De Gaulle submitted a constitutional reform to the people without first allowing parliament to pass on it.

According to Article 5, the president "shall see that the Constitution is respected. He shall ensure, by his arbitration, the regular functioning of the governmental authorities, as well as the continuance of the State. He shall be the guarantor of national independence, of the integrity of the territory, and of respect for Community agreements and treaties." This sweeping grant of power implies a virtual presidential veto over all policy-making. The president may refuse to sign a decree or make a nomination: he may also send parliament personal messages which do not require ministerial approval or countersignature.

In addition the president retains the traditional powers of the office: the right to designate a prime minister; the appointing power, legally defined in a more sweeping fashion than before; and the power to request the parliament to reconsider a law. In a concession made to the classic parliamentary system, the Constitution does *not* give the president power to dismiss a cabinet, which remains solely responsible to parliament. By exercising his power of "mediation," however, the president could probably make it impossible for a cabinet to continue in office. Michel Debré resigned as prime minister in April, 1962, at the simple request of President de Gaulle.

In accordance with General de Gaulle's concern that the chief of state have legal power to act on behalf of the nation in circumstances similar to those of June, 1940, the Constitution gives the president broad emergency powers. He can take "whatever measures are necessitated by the circumstances" in the event that the independence of the nation is threatened or the functioning of its institutions interrupted. He is required only to "consult" the Constitutional Council and inform the nation by message, but he may not dissolve the National Assembly during this period. This power was invoked by General de Gaulle in April, 1961, when four retired generals attempted to seize power in Algeria with the aid of a few military units.

In order to place the president above the welter of political and party interests which in De Gaulle's view sap the nation's unity, provision was originally made for the election of the president by a restricted electoral college consisting of members of parliament, municipal and general councilors, and representatives of member states of the Community. General de Gaulle was chosen in December, 1958, by approximately 81,000 electors, most of them municipal and general councilors in Metropolitan France, who themselves had been elected in 1953. He received 79 per cent of the vote, while the Communist candidate won only 13 per cent, and another candidate of the Left won 8 per cent.

The increased importance of the presidency was further accented by the 1962 constitutional amendment providing for popular election to that office. Electoral procedure embodies the traditional French practice of the run-off (*ballottage*), so that voters are able to express their specific preference among any number of candidates on a first ballot. In the event that no candidate wins an absolute majority, the choice is narrowed down to only two candidates (those polling the highest number of votes, taking into account possible withdrawals) on the second ballot two weeks later. Nominations are made simply by petition of 100 French citizens who are members of parliament, of the Economic and Social Council, of the general councils, or who are mayors.

The problem confronting the opposition parties was to overcome their disunity and translate their popular majority in the country (about 60 per cent of the votes in the 1962 legislative election) into a majority against General de Gaulle. The Socialist mayor of Marseilles, Gaston Defferre, entered the race a full two years before the election, and sought to rally all elements of the Left and Center. His effort failed, however, because of reluctance on the part of the Communists and Christian Democrats to cooperate. After Defferre's withdrawal, the Socialists and Communists threw their support to François Mitterand, a deputy, leader of the UDSR (a small Center party closely linked to the Radical Socialists), and a bitter critic of General de Gaulle. Other candidates included Senator Jean Lecanuet (leader of the MRP), Senator Pierre Marcilhacy (supported by a small liberal faction), J. L. Tixier-Vignancour (a spokesman of the activist Right) and Marcel Barbu (unsupported by any party, whose sole purpose apparently was to dramatize the housing crisis). After some suspense, General de Gaulle announced his own candidacy only one month before the election.

Never before in the history of France had a president of the Republic been elected by direct popular vote. The campaign was unprecedented and, as it turned out, full of surprises. Each candidate was offered two hours of television and two hours of radio time—a large increase over the ten minutes allotted to each major party in legislative elections. General de Gaulle made only one short speech, and remained aloof from the campaign. Both Mitterand and Lecanuet, however, made full and effective use of their broadcasting time. On December 5, General de Gaulle received only 43.7 per cent of the vote, a total below an absolute majority, and was forced into a run-off. Mitterand did far better than generally anticipated, winning 32.2 per cent of the vote, while Lecanuet carried 15.9 per cent. Tixier-Vignancour did less well than predicted, with only 5.3 per cent, and Marcilhacy barely edged out the unknown Barbu with 1.7 per cent.

In the two weeks between ballots, General de Gaulle changed his tactics. He delivered a hard-hitting campaign speech on radio and television, frankly soliciting votes. Tixier-Vignancour urged his supporters to beat De Gaulle by voting for Mitterand (in spite of the latter's Left affiliation). Lecanuet refrained from endorsing Mitterand, but advised his followers not to vote for De Gaulle. A few MRP leaders advocated a blank or invalid ballot. The line between Left and Right was thus blurred on the second ballot; the extreme Right and extreme Left supported Mitterand, while the Center was split. On December 19, General de Gaulle received 54.5 per cent of the vote and Mitterand, 45.5 per cent. In gaining 3 million votes on the second ballot, Mitterand obviously retained most of his original Left votes, and received considerable support from the extreme Right. Most of Lecanuet's voters went over to General de Gaulle and thus provided the margin of victory. The results of the two ballots are shown in the table below.

| | First Ballot | | Second Ballot | |
	NO. VOTERS	%	NO. VOTERS	%
Registered, total	28,233,167		28,233,198	
Abstentions	4,231,206	15.0	4,360,545	15.5
Invalid	244,292	0.9	665,141	2.3
Votes	23,757,669	84.1	23,197,512	82.2
De Gaulle	10,386,734	43.7	12,643,527	54.5
Mitterand	7,658,792	32.2	10,553,985	45.5
Lecanuet	3,767,404	15.9		
Tixier-Vignancour	1,253,958	5.3		
Marcilhacy	413,129	1.7		
Barbu	277,652	1.2		

In spite of General de Gaulle's triumph, the election raised a number of disquieting questions about the Fifth Republic. It was demonstrated that a presidential election is not a referendum and that a majority in favor of a policy is not identical with a political majority in favor of either a candidate or a party. Many of those who voted for De Gaulle as a presidential candidate are likely to vote for opposition parties in the 1967 legislative elections. Yet, the continued tenure of General de Gaulle in office depends upon control of the National Assembly by the UNR and its allies. De Gaulle's election in a paradoxical way underlined the fragility of the political majority upon which his regime rests.

The Cabinet. The Constitution creates a "Government" vested with the power to "determine and conduct the policy of the nation." It further declares that the "Prime Minister directs the action of the Government," is responsible for national defense, assures the execution of the laws and exercises extensive decree powers. The traditional character of the parliamentary system is preserved in that the prime minister submits a declaration on his program to the National Assembly and is invested only after his program is approved. Theoretically the government, and especially the prime minister, dispose of important powers and may rival the president; in practice, however, the government has lost some executive power to the president and gained considerable legislative power at the expense of the parliament. Compared to the Third and Fourth Republics, the cabinet today is weaker in relation to the president, and stronger in relation to the legislature.

The Legislature. The parliament of the Fifth Republic, like those of the Third and Fourth, is bicameral. A National Assembly, consisting of 465 deputies from Metropolitan France and 17 from the overseas departments and territories, is elected by universal suffrage. Legislative power is shared with a Senate, whose members are elected mainly by municipal and departmental councilors and serve for nine years, one-third of the membership being renewed every three years. The Senate is not empowered to introduce a motion of censure. In case of disagreement between the two chambers over the text of a bill, the prime minister may convene a joint conference committee to work out a compromise text. If discord between the chambers continues, the prime minister may ask the National Assembly to rule definitively; thus the government in effect decides whether or not the Senate is able to exercise a veto.

The new Constitution attempts to eliminate some of the abuses of the past, and also strengthens the cabinet's hand in dealing with the National Assembly. The parliament is now limited to two sessions per year—two and a half months beginning in early October, and three months beginning in late April. Thus the parliament can sit for a maximum of five and a half months during the year, whereas under the Fourth Republic it generally sat most of the year. An extraordinary session may be convened at the request of the prime minister or of a majority of the members of the Assembly. But President de Gaulle refused to convoke an extraordinary session of the Assembly in March, 1960, even though requested to do so by the requisite majority.

The law-making power of parliament is now restricted to regulations concerning matters specifically listed in the Constitution. On all other matters the government may legislate by decree. It also draws up the agenda of the National Assembly, thus determining the order of business. In order to prevent encroachment upon the executive power by the Assembly's committees, the Constitution allows for the creation of only six committees. Instead of being *ad hoc*, that is, created for the purpose of considering specific bills, these are standing, specialized bodies, ranging in size from 60 to 120 members. Above all, debate in the Assembly must take place on the government's text of a bill and not, as in the past, on the committee's counter-proposal. The Constitution also provides for an "executive budget." Proposals by members of parliament entailing "diminution of public resources or an increase of public expenditures" are not receivable. Complicated constitutional provisions make it possible for the government to adopt the budget by simple decree if the National Assembly and the Senate have not given their approval within seventy days after its presentation. To prevent members of parliament from profiting by the overthrow of a cabinet, and to create a separation of powers, the Constitution requires a member of parliament to resign his seat if he enters the cabinet.

In spite of these numerous limitations upon the power of parliament, it must be stressed that the cabinet remains responsible before the National Assembly. If it loses the Assembly's confidence, it must, as in the past, resign. After being nominated by the president, the prime minister presents his program to the National Assembly, which must approve the program by a simple majority before the cabinet can be invested. If the government is invested, however, a determined effort has been made to provide for cabinet stability while preserving the principle of cabinet responsibility; a motion of censure must be signed by 10 per cent of the Assembly. The motion carries only if an absolute majority of the members of the Assembly vote for it—that is, abstentions count for the government. If the government makes the text of a bill a matter of confidence, that bill becomes law unless a motion of censure is carried within 24 hours by an absolute majority. Thus a law may be passed with no vote at all, or because the opposition, while it might have a simple majority, is unable to muster an absolute majority. An innovation of the new Constitution which enhances the role of the National Assembly is the setting aside of one session each week for questions by members of the Assembly and answers by cabinet members.

The Judicial System. The distinctive features of French judicial organization remain unchanged under the Fifth Republic. The judiciary is very different from its Anglo-American counterpart, although the differences appear to be lessening as the systems borrow practices from each other. French law is based on the Napoleonic Code, which in turn is influenced by Roman jurisprudence; that is, the principles which govern large areas of human activity are codified and applied in specific cases by trained judges. Juries are used only in criminal trials involving serious offenses.

There are two distinct court systems: a hierarchy of regular courts, culminating in the Court of Cassation, which deals with the usual civil and criminal matters; and a system of administrative courts, headed by the Council of State (*Conseil d'État*), which handles disputes involving the state and also gives the government technical advice on the drafting of bills and decrees. In the event of a question over the nature of a dispute, a Tribunal of Conflicts decides whether it is to be tried in the regular or administrative courts.

Under the French system it is relatively easy for the individual citizen to sue the state in the event of abuse of power by a civil servant. The procedure is inexpensive and effective. Since World War II, however, the Council of State has not been able to clear away a huge backlog of cases, so that redress of administrative wrongs is rather slow at present. The French system of codes, specially trained judges, and administrative law has been widely copied throughout the world.

An innovation of the Fifth Republic is the Constitutional Council, composed of nine members appointed by the President of the Republic and the two presiding officers of parliament, who serve for nine years, renewable by one-third every three years. The Constitutional Council's main function is to decide whether bills are compatible with constitutional provisions relating to the organization of the public powers. Cases may be brought up only upon the request of the president, the prime minister, or the two presiding officers of the parliament. In other words, an individual cannot challenge a law's constitutionality on the grounds that it deprives him of his rights. To cite one example of the Council's procedure: In November, 1962, the President of the Senate, Gaston Monnerville, formally requested the Constitutional Council to declare the referendum on popular election of the president null and void on procedural grounds. The Council, by a vote of 6 to 4, declared that it was not competent to strike down a law voted directly by the sovereign people. Under the Fifth Republic the main role of the Constitutional Council apparently is to enable the government to prevent the legislature from encroaching upon its domain.

Local Government. Though France is probably the most highly centralized democracy in the world, local government is vigorous and important. Elections are held in 90 *départements* and over 38,000 communes for councilors, who compose the council of each *département* and commune. Local elections are hotly contested by all political parties. Each municipal council elects a mayor, who has considerable prestige and power, particularly in the large cities. A host of party leaders and deputies serve as mayors of smaller cities or communes. Some leading politicians on the national scene are mayors of large cities (for example, Gaston Defferre in Marseilles, Pierre Pflimlin in Strasbourg, Jacques Chaban-Delmas in Bordeaux).

The municipal and departmental councils deliberate on a variety of questions, including local public services, the budget, public works, public enterprises, and cultural activities. They are subject, however, to pervasive central control from Paris. The main agency through which

this central control (or "tutelage") is exercised is the departmental prefect, an officer of the Ministry of the Interior. The prefect has the power
to veto any decision of a municipal or departmental council. He is
himself the president of the departmental council, and he may dismiss
or suspend the mayors. The prefect is the chief of all national government employees in the department, and is responsible for coordinating
their work; he also may exercise police power to maintain public order.

The prefect is thus the link between the central government and
the multitude of local units. The French system provides less scope for
local initiative and imagination than do the American or British systems,
but on the other hand it makes possible effective implementation of
national policy throughout the land. The recent tendency to encourage
industrial development outside of the Paris region may eventually lead
to a greater devolution of power upon local units of government. But it
is unlikely that the prefect's "tutelage" power will be reduced in the
near future.

THE LIVING CONSTITUTION

Any critique of the new institutions in France must take into account
a fundamental assumption of the framers: that the kind of party
divisions that existed under the Third and Fourth Republics will probably make impossible the formation of an effective and dynamic majority bloc in parliament. The problem of French government and politics
then is to achieve governmental stability in the absence of a parliamentary majority. Essentially, the Fifth Republic's solution is to buttress
the cabinet's authority with respect to parliament by constitutional
guarantees, and then to create a chief of state vested with sufficient
power and prestige to protect the government in case of difficulties.
The personal powers granted to the president do not concern the daily
business of government, which remains the province of the cabinet;
they rather permit the president to occupy a position above the rancor
of party politics, from which lofty place he may descend from time to
time in order to separate the combatants and remind them of their
duty to the nation.

But political responsibility in a democratic system cannot easily
be evaded. It is conceivable that a monarch, whose legitimacy derives
from the identification of his family with the history of the nation,
might be able to play an active role in politics. But monarchical regimes
in the nineteenth century proved unstable; power either surged to the
politically responsible ministers and parliamentarians, or became increasingly concentrated in the hands of the king or emperor. In a
democracy, where basic political decisions are referred to the people in
elections, it is exceedingly difficult to preserve a sphere of political
irresponsibility. Assume, for example, that the President of the Republic
exercises his power to dissolve the National Assembly or calls for a

referendum to strengthen the government's hand. If the government's policy is approved by election or referendum, then the cabinet's dependence on the president is accentuated—that is, the regime becomes increasingly presidential. This indeed was a noticeable consequence of the three referendums in France in 1961 and 1962 and of the dissolution of October, 1962. In all these instances, General de Gaulle's policies were vindicated by the electorate. But what if the government is repudiated in the future? Then the triumphant opposition may associate the president with the defeated cabinet and compel him either to "give in or get out." Political pressures are therefore likely in the long run to force the regime into one channel or the other—to become either presidential or parliamentary.

In practice, the clear trend ever since De Gaulle's inauguration in January, 1959, has been towards concentration of power in the president's hands. The office of the presidency has become the driving force of the political process. De Gaulle presides over the important meetings of the Council of Ministers. Small inter-ministerial committees then implement decisions arrived at by the president. Major policy directives are announced by General de Gaulle, frequently in press conferences, and obviously have taken his ministers by surprise on several occasions. During the Algerian conflict policy on Algeria was virtually the province of the president alone; in the crises caused by the insurrection in Algiers in January, 1960, and the attempted seizure of power by army elements in April, 1961, the president and not the cabinet made the crucial decisions. The replacement of Michel Debré by Georges Pompidou (a close personal associate of General de Gaulle) has further emphasized the presidential character of the regime. At the same time the government has used the full range of powers made available to it by the Constitution in order to "manage" the National Assembly. Parliament has not been permitted to overstep the narrow limits within which it is required to function by the Constitution. However, the cabinet's success in maintaining legislative leadership has been due only partially to the new procedural rules. The Debré and Pompidou governments were maintained basically because they had the confidence of the President of the Republic, who in turn was supported by a majority in both the country and in parliament (at least until the censure vote of October, 1962). In the first years of the Fifth Republic, real power was vested in General de Gaulle.

But a constitution is not made for one man. What will happen after General de Gaulle departs the political scene? Assuming that the Constitution remains in force, strong pressures will be at work for a return to the parliamentary system. General de Gaulle's legitimacy does not derive only or primarily from the election of December, 1958, but also from his role in the Liberation of France, and the overwhelming acceptance of his policies in the referendum—really a plebiscite—of September, 1958. But a future president will not be invested by "history," but by men. The constitutional reform of 1962, providing for direct election of the president, is a step in the direction of presidential government. Wholly apart from the difficulties which will be encountered in mobilizing a majority behind some one candidate other than De Gaulle, it is doubtful that any future president, even if popularly elected, will be able to wield the power De Gaulle now enjoys. In any event, the legitimization of its institutions remains perhaps the most serious task confronting the Fifth Republic and its creator.

The French Political System in Perspective

The most persistent feature of French political life has been the intensity of political debate, which involves not simply alternative policies but even the nature of institutions. In the century following the Revolution of 1789, rivalry between monarchists, Bonapartists and republicans produced a series of regimes none of which won the support of all major social groups. Towards the latter part of the nineteenth century the republicans seemed to win out, but agreement failed to emerge on the exact balance between executive and legislature. Strong parties have always existed on both the revolutionary Left and the nationalistic Right, repudiating the principles of moderate republicanism.

Yet in spite of the fragility of the consensus on which the political system rested, techniques were developed by the Center parties enabling them to formulate policies and govern the country with reasonable effectiveness. A centralized bureaucracy, the main structure of which goes back to the old regime and Napoleon, furnished an essential element of continuity and expertise. While no one party enjoyed a stable majority in parliament or in the country, coalitions were formed which provided majorities on important issues as they arose. Once a decision was made and a new issue called for attention, the old coalition broke up and was replaced by another. Hence through the institutionalized "cabinet crisis" the party system was able to produce policy even though no one group or party constituted a majority. Above all, the democratic system was preserved and the extremes prevented from coming to power. But the constant shuffling of cabinet posts and of party coalitions frequently left the public bewildered or confused. Some of the real achievements of the Fourth Republic—economic progress, colonial reforms, freedom in which the creative arts were enabled to blossom— were obscured or even negated in the confusion generated by the system.

The Fifth Republic is an attempt to create effective and dynamic government in a country which lacks a stable party majority. Unquestionably, one change has been striking: the Debré cabinet lasted longer than any under the Third and Fourth Republics (three years and three months) and this record was bettered by the Pompidou cabinet. Such stability was perhaps somewhat misleading, since there were numerous "little crises": in just over a year, half of the original members of the Debré cabinet had either resigned or changed posts. But the continued tenure of General de Gaulle as President of the Republic and of Debré and Georges Pompidou in the post of prime minister has given the impression of stable government.

Moreover, a number of reforms, delayed by the negotiations and bickering of the previous regime, were enacted in the first years of the Fifth Republic, especially in the fields of finance, housing, education, organization of the judiciary, and relations between France and her former colonies. Even though most of these reforms were actually continuations of policies formulated and partially implemented under the Fourth Republic, the Fifth Republic can claim a major success in resolving one monumental problem—that of Algeria, which had brought down the Fourth Republic and led to the army's involvement in politics.

On the other hand, the grant of independence to Algeria antagonized the same forces which had opposed official policy in 1958. The Gaullist regime was severely shaken in January, 1960, when barricades were erected in the city of Algiers in protest against the government's policy. An even graver crisis was precipitated in April, 1961, by the open rebellion of part of the army in Algeria. Increasingly, power was assumed by the President of the Republic in order to deal simultaneously with the Muslim rebels, Algerian settlers, extremists in Metropolitan France, and a refractory army. General de Gaulle used this power to make his policy prevail, and to crush the activist opposition to his regime. But even after the ratification of the Algerian peace settlement, the role of parliament remained rigorously circumscribed. General de Gaulle has not seen fit to create a responsible majority party, nor has he offered the opposition an honorable role to play within the Republic. By resorting to the traditional Bonapartist technique of the referendum, De Gaulle has undercut and undermined the nation's representative institutions. The choice presented to the French people in the legislative elections of 1962 and the presidential election of 1965 was between a national hero and the maligned "parties of yesteryear," rather than between government and opposition. In the long run, perhaps the most important challenge facing the Fifth Republic is to provide an institutional alternative to General de Gaulle's personal rule.

SUGGESTIONS FOR ADDITIONAL READING

BROGAN, DENIS, *France under the Republic* (New York: Harper & Row, Publishers, 1940).

DE GAULLE, CHARLES, *War Memoirs,* 3 vols. (New York: Simon and Schuster, Inc., 1958, 1959, 1960).

DUVERGER, MAURICE, *The French Political System* (Chicago: University of Chicago Press, 1958).

EARLE, EDWARD MEADE (ed.), *Modern France: Problems of the Third and Fourth Republics* (Princeton, N.J.: Princeton University Press, 1951).

EHRMANN, HENRY W., *Organized Business in France* (Princeton, N. J.: Princeton University Press, 1958).

HOFFMAN, STANLEY (ed.), *In Search of France* (Cambridge, Mass.: Harvard University Press, 1963).

LORWIN, VAL R., *The French Labor Movement* (Cambridge, Mass.: Harvard University Press, 1954).

MACRIDIS, ROY C., and BERNARD E. BROWN, *The De Gaulle Republic: Quest for Unity* (Homewood, Ill.: The Dorsey Press, 1960); and *Supplement to the De Gaulle Republic* (Homewood, Ill.: The Dorsey Press, 1963).

SHARP, WALTER R., *The Government of the French Republic* (Princeton, N. J.: D. Van Nostrand Company, 1939).

THOMSON, DAVID, *Democracy in France: The Third and Fourth Republics* (New York: Oxford University Press, 1952).

WILLIAMS, PHILIP, *Crisis and Compromise: Politics in the Fourth Republic* (London: Longmans, Green, 1964).

——, and MARTIN HARRISON, *De Gaulle's Republic* (London: Longmans, Green, 1960).

WRIGHT, GORDON, *The Reshaping of French Democracy* (New York: Harcourt, Brace & World, 1948).

Chapter 5

THE GOVERNMENT
OF THE FEDERAL REPUBLIC
OF GERMANY

Germany poses many controversial problems for political scientists. Western democracy has been closely linked with a developing technology and high standards of living and education, but the recent history of Germany demonstrates that these factors alone do not ensure democratic government. For although German achievements in science, technology, industry, education, philosophy, and music have been outstanding, its political achievements have been much less successful. Twice within thirty years the nation's industrial and technological might was used to heap destruction upon its neighbors. Its extermination of millions of Jews and other Europeans during World War II has surpassed anything in the records of modern barbarism.

Both world wars ultimately brought calamity to the Germans, but after each their recovery was remarkable. Today they are enjoying prosperity and what appears to be a stable government. But German political history, the short experience of the Bonn Republic, and Germany's geographic position on the frontier of the conflict between East and West all caution against an easy assertion that stable democratic government has at long last been achieved in the German Federal Republic.

Constitutional Development

THE EMPIRE (1871–1918)

Several unique factors in its constitutional development help explain why Germany has differed significantly from its Western European neighbors. Crucial among them is the relative lateness of its national unification, for modern Germany dates only from the end of the Franco-Prussian War in 1871.

Although the trend toward modern nationalism was intensified throughout Europe by the French Revolution and the Napoleonic Wars, "Germany" was a mere geographic expression for a region of central Europe composed of diverse kingdoms, principalities, duchies, and free cities. The so-called Holy Roman Empire existed formally in this area, but Napoleon merely proclaimed a fact when he declared its termination. The Congress of Vienna, which met in 1815 to make the peace treaties after Napoleon's defeat, reduced the total number of independent states in central Europe to the thirty-nine which joined together in the German Confederation. This feeble organization, which existed from 1815 to 1866, was essentially a congress of ambassadors rather than a government, and as a result of the rivalry between its two strongest members, Prussia and Austria, it was unable to function effectively.

In 1848 a wave of national and liberal revolutions spread through most of Europe and in many countries led to a significant increase in popular participation in government. In the German states middle-class liberals tried to unify the nation and bring about a liberal democratic government. To achieve these ends, a German Constituent National Assembly was held at Frankfurt in 1848, but the liberals' efforts failed when King Frederick William IV of Prussia refused to accept a crown offered to him by this popular assembly rather than by his fellow princes.

The failure of the middle-class liberals to achieve unification from below meant that ultimately it would be imposed from above. This was accomplished by the first minister of the king of Prussia, Otto von Bismarck, who brought about the unification of Germany under Prussian dominance.

Through a complex series of maneuvers, Bismarck succeeded in expelling Austria from Germany and in extending Prussian dominance over the German states. He finally achieved unification by provoking a war with France which brought the South German states into a close cooperation with Prussia and evoked such a surge of national sentiment that the final goal of unification was reached. During the concluding phases of the Franco-Prussian War, on January 18, 1871, King William of Prussia was proclaimed Emperor of Germany at Versailles.

The German Empire Bismarck created in 1871 had a central government of limited powers, with a minimum of concessions required from the princes of the states. The Empire was a federal system composed of twenty-five states: four kingdoms, eighteen principalities and duchies, and three free cities. The central government had jurisdiction principally in foreign affairs and indirect taxation. The states retained control over direct taxation, their own educational systems, and even their postal systems. The Kingdom of Bavaria, the second largest state after Prussia, was allowed to retain additional special rights.

The members of the upper house of the parliament, the Federal Council (Bundesrat), were essentially ambassadors of the ruling families of the various states. The fifty-two seats were apportioned to give Prussia seventeen. Thus, although Prussian dominance was assured through the positions of the emperor and chancellor, it alone could not control the Council. The federal character of the system was further manifested in the practice of having the cabinet institute legislation in the parliament only after prior secret deliberations with the members of the Federal Council.

The constituent states of the Empire remained essentially aristocratic institutions. With relatively few restrictions, the princes were able to appoint their ministers, and the parliaments continued to give greater representation to the upper classes.

Even though the princes retained many of their powers, the emperor and his chancellor were the dominant forces in the German Empire, and their positions assured Prussian dominance. Just as the king of Prussia was the emperor of Germany, so the chancellor was first minister both in the Empire and in Prussia. Chancellor Bismarck ruled with little interference from Emperor William I, who died at the age of 91 in 1888. However, his grandson, William II, dismissed Bismarck in 1890 and assumed a more active role in government.

The emperor had the power to appoint the chancellor and other principal officials. The chancellor, in turn, appointed members of the cabinet, who, like the chancellor, were responsible to the emperor rather than to parliament. Although initiated by the cabinet in consultation with the Federal Council, legislation was of relatively less importance than in other countries of Western Europe, because the emperor had power to issue emergency decrees and in his capacity as commander of the army could even determine whether the country would be at war or at peace.

The Imperial Assembly (Reichstag) was the lower house of parliament. Its 397 members were elected, under a system of universal male suffrage, in single-member districts. The election system (similar to that used in the Third and Fifth French Republics) required a second election if no candidate received a majority in the first election. Although the franchise was more liberally granted in Germany for these Reichstag elections than in most of the rest of the world, the apportionment of seats was based on the census of 1869 and thus increasingly discriminated against the growing urban population.

In practice the relations between the chancellor and the Reichstag were somewhat ambiguous, but on the whole he was not dependent on the confidence of this parliamentary body. Although Bismarck was defeated in the Reichstag in 1878 and in 1887, he dissolved it each time and won the subsequent election. Some years later, a government was able to remain in office despite its lack of a parliamentary majority; this seemed to confirm the fact that the chancellor and his cabinet were responsible only to the emperor. The Reichstag did have power to vote the budget and loans, but this power was restricted by the exclusion of the most important expenditure, the military budget, which grew at a staggering rate up to World War I. Here again Bismarck's precedents did not augur well for parliamentary control of the budget; he had achieved unification by disregarding the Prussian parliament's rejection of his budget, but after he had won a couple of small wars, the parliament approved his violations of the laws retroactively.

Thus there was considerable difference between the formal constitutional system and what Sigmund Neumann called the "unwritten and real constitution" of the Empire. This real constitution he describes as the extra-parliamentary forces which actually exercised power in the system: the landed aristocrats (Junkers), the army, the bureaucracy, and sometimes the industrialists.[1]

Among the political events of the Empire deserving attention in this brief summary was the Kulturkampf of 1871 to 1879. This was the German nationalist struggle against the internationalism of the Roman Catholic Church. Fortified by about a two to one Protestant majority in Germany, Bismarck used this "cultural struggle" campaign against the "un-German activities" of Roman Catholic educational institutions, religious orders, and the clergy. Although some damage was inflicted on the Church and its subsidiary institutions, the campaign was given up, in part because Bismarck needed the support of the Catholic Center party for some of his other programs. In fact, the long-range consequence of the cultural struggle has been a conviction among German Catholics that political activity is necessary to protect themselves in a Protestant nation.

Bismarck also crusaded against socialism. Again he was fighting a form of internationalism (in this case Marxist), but, as a Prussian Junker, he was also fighting against his class enemy. This crusade led to the Anti-Socialist Law, which the Reichstag adopted in 1878 and re-enacted periodically up to 1890. Nonetheless a Marxist Social Democratic party was founded at Goetha in 1875 and continued to grow as Germany became industrialized and developed an increasingly large working class. When finally permitted to participate freely in elections, the Social Democratic party became the largest single German party and ultimately obtained the constant support of approximately one-third of the voters, a percentage which it maintained in the Empire before World War I, in

[1] Sigmund Neumann, "Germany," in Taylor Cole (ed.), *European Political Systems,* 2nd edition (New York: Alfred A. Knopf, 1959), p. 346.

the Weimar Republic, and now in the Bonn Republic. Although Bismarck's crusade against the socialists was a failure and ultimately played a crucial part in providing William II with a pretext for his dismissal, it has had a continuing effect in intensifying class conflict in Germany.

On the other hand, the constructive side of Bismarck's program for defeating the Marxists has had an opposite, but equally lasting, effect. As a master politician he knew that he could not defeat the socialists by repression alone. Therefore he sought to outflank them and obtain support from the working classes by instituting a widespread social welfare system. Thus, the Prussian Junker created the first welfare state, some principles of which still exist in the Bonn Republic.

Ultimately, however, the politics of the German Empire was dominated exclusively by the imperialist rivalry which was to lead to World War I and the collapse of the Empire itself. Under the bellicose leadership of Emperor William II, Germany embarked on an aggressive campaign to build up its military establishment, perfecting and expanding its long-standing system of compulsory military service, constructing a large navy and merchant marine, and acquiring a colonial empire in Africa and the South Pacific. By 1914 this nation-state, which was less than fifty years old, was the strongest on the European continent. Its industrialization had proceeded so swiftly that Germany seriously threatened British naval, commercial, and colonial dominance and was a threat to French influence on the Continent as well. But in the world war touched off in 1914 by the attack on Serbia by Germany's faltering ally, Austria-Hungary, the Empire found itself waging a losing two-front war against the British and French (and later the Americans) on the West and the Russians on the East. After four years of fighting, Austria-Hungary collapsed, Emperor William II then abdicated and fled, and an armistice went into effect on November 11, 1918. The German Empire had come to an end.

In 1919, representatives of the new German Republic were compelled by the victors to sign the Treaty of Versailles, which reduced German territory on the European continent by one-eighth and reduced its population by over 6 million. Its provisions placed 3 million ethnic Germans in Czechoslovakia and 1 million in Poland, and forbade the union of the German-speaking remnant of the Austro-Hungarian Empire with Germany. The Saar region was placed under League of Nations control with a guarantee of special rights there for France and a proviso that its ultimate status would be determined in 1935. The entire German colonial empire was lost. The army was to be reduced to merely 100,000 men and the navy to 15,000, with a further restriction on the number and type of vessels allowed. Perhaps most significant, Article 231 of the treaty obligated Germany to accept responsibility for the losses and damages of the war and to pay reparations to the victors. This war-guilt clause was regarded as the ultimate humiliation of the German people. Thus, the Empire, which had raised the Germans to such heights of accomplishment, brought them ultimately to ruin and humiliation before the other nations of the civilized world.

THE WEIMAR REPUBLIC (1919–1933)

Following the surrender of the nation and the flight of the emperor, a republic was rather hastily proclaimed. The Social Democrats, who had assumed the initiative in founding it, restored order by cooperating to some extent with their traditional rivals, the army. In 1919 a constitution for this first German republic was drafted in the quiet little town of Weimar. This lengthy document (181 articles) was hailed by some as the most democratic constitution in the world.

The government established by the Weimar Constitution preserved some forms of federalism, but essentially it created a highly centralized system. Prussia lost its unique position, although it remained the largest and most populous state.

The Weimar Constitution established a parliamentary system but also delegated significant power to a strong, democratically elected president. Its fundamental organs included a chancellor and a cabinet who were appointed by the president but responsible to the Reichstag, the lower house of parliament. An upper house representing the states was retained, but its status was considerably reduced from that of the imperial Federal Council.

As is also true of the Constitution of the Fifth French Republic, the Weimar Constitution, by providing both for a strong president and for cabinet responsibility to the parliament, was somewhat ambiguous. Three provisions that strengthened the powers of the president were the long term of seven years, direct popular election, and special emergency decree powers.

The Reichstag was elected on a nationwide system of proportional representation[2] for a term of four years. Proportional representation was allegedly one of the most "democratic" features of the constitution; but, in fact, it contributed to an increase in the number of small splinter parties which often made it impossible for the chancellor to obtain a majority. Moreover, no parliament served its full term; because of the instability of the cabinets, the chancellor was frequently forced to dissolve the parliament in the hope that new elections would result in a coalition of parties which could obtain a majority.

The Weimar Constitution also provided for an impartial judiciary and guarantees of individual rights. Here again these provisions were originally hailed as progressive democratic reforms, but the record of actual achievement fell far short of the goals.

2 See note, p. 163.

Some observers have maintained that the Weimar Republic was doomed from the beginning, but others insist that this experiment in democracy might have succeeded. Whatever the case, it is clear that the circumstances that Germany faced at the time, rather than its particular form of government, created insurmountable obstacles to constitutional democracy. Although the war had not been carried to German soil, the country had suffered serious losses of men and was in a state of economic and social upheaval. The loss of European territory and overseas colonies and the decline of its commerce compounded the problems of readjustment. German efforts at making reparations payments were a serious drain, although these payments were far less than what the allies expected and demanded. A ruinous inflation in 1923 led to default on reparations, and France, Belgium, and Italy retaliated by occupying the industrial Ruhr. Inflation also contributed to social instability by wiping out the savings of many members of the middle class and by intensifying German nationalist resentment, upon which radical political elements could play. The depression which swept the world in 1929 had particularly acute effects in Germany and presented the last Weimar chancellors with problems they never succeeded in solving.

These problems, which might well have brought about the collapse of more effective governments, were too much for the first feeble German attempts at democracy. The many minor parties in the parliament made it at first difficult and ultimately impossible for a chancellor to obtain a majority which was committed to preserving the system. In the earlier Weimar period, this instability led merely to many cabinet changes and frequent elections. Later chancellors relied increasingly on the emergency decree power of the aging president, Field Marshal von Hindenburg, whose support of democracy was suspect.

As conditions in Germany became worse, the strength of radical parties increased. Resentful of defeat in war and of the peace terms imposed on them, more Germans began turning to Adolf Hitler and his National Socialist German Workers (Nazi) party. The lower middle class in particular, threatened from above and below, fell prey to Nazi propaganda, while elements of the upper classes encouraged the movement in the hope that they could control it. At the same time, Communist strength was increasing, partly because the Socialists, by their efforts to work with others in making the Weimar Republic succeed, had lost some of the support of the working class. Thus the Nazis and the Communists, who together had almost half the votes in the elections of 1932, could combine in opposing the government, but of course could not collaborate to govern the nation.

Ultimately, on January 30, 1933, President von Hindenburg called Adolf Hitler to serve as chancellor. With Hitler's appointment, the Weimar Republic in effect came to an end, although some of its legal forms were in theory still valid until the complete destruction of the German government in May, 1945.

THE NAZI DICTATORSHIP (1933–1945)

Upon assuming the chancellorship, Adolf Hitler began to establish a one-party Nazi state under his dictatorship. A mysterious fire which destroyed the Reichstag building on February 27, 1933, provided him with a pretext for terminating civil rights; the following day President von Hindenburg was prevailed upon to sign the Decree for Protection of the People and the State, which restricted freedom of assembly, association, speech, and press and authorized searches without warrants and confiscation of and restrictions on property.

The last elections were held on March 5, 1933, under conditions of strong Nazi coercion. Nonetheless, the Nazi party, while it increased its popular support by 5½ million to a total of over 17 million votes, received only 44 per cent of the votes and thus had less than a majority. But with the support of the Nationalists, who had polled over 3 million votes, the Nazis could muster a majority in the Reichstag. However, they still lacked the two-thirds necessary to amend the constitution. In order to achieve this, Hitler had the Communist members of parliament arrested, thereby reducing the total membership. When he put his fundamental constitutional revision to a vote on March 23, only the Socialists summoned the courage to vote against this act, so German democracy was "legally" terminated by a vote of 441 to 84. This enabling act, whose official title was "The Law for Removing the Distress of People and *Reich*," transferred from the parliament to the cabinet the authority to legislate, to determine the budget, and to amend the constitution. It even specifically authorized the chancellor to draft legislation that deviated from the constitution.[3]

In accordance with this delegation of power, Hitler's government decreed on July 14, 1933, that the Nazi party was the only legal party in Germany and that those seeking to maintain or to organize other parties would be imprisoned. Upon the death of President von Hindenburg in the following year, Hitler consolidated his power by combining the office of chancellor with the office of president. Step by step he further consolidated all the important positions of the state. Although it is questionable whether any one person could actually carry out the tasks of all these offices, legally speaking the government of Germany at this period was a one-man dictatorship.

Under Hitler's leadership Germany embarked on major domestic recovery programs and large-scale remilitarization with remarkable success. After violating one provision after another of the World War I peace treaties, he was able in 1938 to annex Austria and the Sudetenland of Czechoslovakia without war. However, when German armies in-

[3] A popular history of this period is William L. Shirer, *The Rise and Fall of the Third Reich* (New York: Simon and Schuster, 1960). Shirer's work is a source of Nazi documents easily accessible to the student. However, his interpretations are subject to various serious criticisms. See Klaus Epstein, "Shirer's History of Nazi Germany," *The Review of Politics*, XXIII (1961), 230–45.

vaded Poland in 1939, Britain and France came to the aid of the Poles, and World War II began.

During the first two years of the war, the German armies spread over most of the European continent. But when Hitler ordered the invasion of the Soviet Union and declared war on the United States in 1941, he overextended himself. Once the Allies were able to muster their resources for war, the preponderance of power was against Germany and its Japanese and Italian allies. Long after defeat was certain, however, Hitler insisted on a suicidal policy of continuing the war, which lasted until the Allied armies overran Germany and completely destroyed its institutions of government.

OCCUPATION AND THE BONN REPUBLIC

Hitler's "Thousand Year Empire" had been crushed after only twelve years, leaving a country almost totally devastated and completely without political institutions. This void was filled at first by the Allied armies of occupation, which assumed the functions of government in their respective zones.

Germany was divided into four zones, each of which was governed by one of the four principal Allies: the Soviet Union, the United States, Britain, and France. Berlin, an enclave within the Soviet Zone in East Germany, was given a special status, under which authority over it was also divided among the four occupying powers. Under the agreements made by them these arrangements were to be temporary and were to last only until a new German government could be organized and a peace treaty negotiated with it. But these temporary arrangements, insofar as they involved the division between the Soviet Zone and the three Western zones, have become a permanent feature of the post-World War II period. The cold war which developed so quickly after the hot one has made it impossible for the Soviet Union and the Western countries to agree on the conditions for a peace treaty with a united Germany. Thus the country has been split, and Berlin, divided between East and West and surrounded by Soviet-dominated East Germany, has been a source of constant conflict.

Immediately after the war, the Soviet Union initiated policies directed toward making Communist satellites of East Germany and the other countries in Eastern Europe. When they began their occupation, the Western powers concentrated on de-Nazifying Germany and dismantling what was left of its industry. However, in response to the Soviet threat, they quickly changed their policy and focused their efforts on helping the West Germans to rebuild their economy and to establish their own institutions. First, over Soviet protests, the Western powers established economic cooperation among their three zones under an arrangement called "Trizonia." Then they set about helping the Germans to establish their own political institutions, first at the local, then at the state, and ultimately at the national level. In 1949 the German Federal Republic was established in what had been the Western zones. (This government was given complete authority over its territory in a series of agreements made with the Western powers in 1955.) In the same year the Soviet Union countered by forming the German Democratic Republic in East Germany. Each of these governments continues to exercise authority in its own territory, and there is still no general peace treaty ending World War II.

The constitution promulgated in West Germany in 1949 was drafted in Bonn, now the temporary capital, by German representatives of the states and was subject to the approval of the occupation authorities. It is called the "Basic Law" rather than the constitution in order to emphasize its temporary nature, for the drafters assumed that a genuine constitution could be drawn up only after Germany was reunited and all Germans were given an opportunity to be consulted on their form of government. This terminological distinction does not, however, conceal the fact that, for all practical purposes, the Bonn Basic Law is the constitution of the German Federal Republic.

Some of the basic characteristics of the Bonn constitution are suggested by the country's name, German Federal Republic. It provides for a republic by establishing a president, elected by a special electoral college, as chief of state, and for a federal government rather than a unitary government by specifically reserving certain powers to the states. One of the conditions specified by the Western powers was that the states must be kept strong. Although the Germans increased some of the powers of the national government after the occupation ended, the essential characteristics of federalism remain. In addition, by guaranteeing an elected parliament to which the chancellor is responsible and by prohibiting anti-democratic political activity, the constitution provides for democratic government. It also contains a bill of rights with such traditional features as a guarantee of freedom of speech, press, and assembly as well as certain novel provisions, such as those guaranteeing economic freedom. Various guarantees of the rule of law are also included, and for the first time in German history, a constitutional court with powers of judicial review is able to guarantee the rule of law against encroachments by the organs of government. Another distinctive feature of this constitution is its authority to transfer functions to international organizations.

Social Forces: Cohesion and Cleavage

GEOGRAPHY AND POPULATION

The German Federal Republic is only 95,000 square miles in area and thus corresponds in size with the American state of Oregon, but its population of 53 million people (not counting West Berlin) is thirty times that of Oregon. The most important reason for this high population density has been the influx of German refugees and others from the East into the Federal Republic; they now constitute approximately one-fourth of the population. Like industrial societies everywhere, the German population is becoming increasingly urban. Geographically the Federal Republic can be divided into three sections: the North German plain along the North Sea, the midland plateaus, and the mountains in the South. These geographical divisions, plus the distinctive characteristics of the industrial concentrations in the Ruhr and the more agricultural lower Rhineland, provide greater variety than the small total area of the country would lead an American to expect. In broadest outline, the Ruhr–North Rhine region is the industrial center of the nation; the North German plains are more agricultural; and South Germany features agriculture and scenery.

West Germany has many natural advantages for industry, which give it a more favorable situation than Britain, France, or Italy, although, aside from coal, it does not have the mineral resources for all its industrial requirements. The agricultural situation is less favorable because the partition of Germany cut off 55 per cent of the arable land. Its agriculture is characterized by small peasant holdings (averaging less than 20 acres) worked only by the peasants and their families. Since it is more difficult to increase production on these small holdings than could be done on the large estates of East Germany, the country must now import approximately 30 per cent of its food.

REGIONAL AND RELIGIOUS DIFFERENCES

Because of the country's geographic diversity, the German people have tended to maintain strong attachments to their native regions. This is one reason for the late unification of the country. The extent of regional identification is perhaps best indicated by the fact that although there is only one written language, known as High German, dialects of this language spoken in one section of the country are not understood by people in another.

Some of the boundaries dividing the ten states were drawn rather arbitrarily at the end of World War II, and thus many of them no longer coincide with the historic regional boundaries. To some extent, this has diminished some aspects of regional identification.

Closely related to regionalism is the more divisive issue of religious differences, an issue which has resulted in many conflicts—from the Thirty Years' War, through Bismarck's Kulturkampf, to current conflicts over religious education. Before partition Germany was two-thirds Protestant and one-third Catholic; but now in West Germany the two groups are almost equal in number.

Religious cleavage has generally re-enforced regional particularism. The formula of the Peace of Augsburg, 1555, which imposed the religion of each German prince on his subjects, provided a geographic basis for religious affiliation which has continued down to the twentieth century. Political parties are thus compelled to use involved systems of ticket-balancing so that both Catholics and Protestants are represented. The critical political conflicts based on religion center around state support of religious education and religious institutions.

PARTITION AND REFUGEES

Potentially more explosive than religion were the problems which derived from partition and the influx of refugees from the East. In 1961 it was estimated that 13 million people, almost 25 per cent of the population of the Federal Republic, were exiles and refugees. For a country which had just been devastated by war, the problems created by millions of people pouring in with only the clothes on their backs would have seemed insoluble. Simply housing these refugees in an area in which 22 per cent of the housing units had been destroyed might have seemed impossible. Moreover, the differences in economic status between those who had been completely dispossessed and those who still had some property could have added to the social tension.

Yet West Germany rose to the challenge and has been largely successful in absorbing these refugees. The most important single step was the Equalization of Burdens Law, which provided that those who still held property in 1948 would be required to pay one-half its value in installments over a twenty-year period in order to compensate for those who had nothing. This equalization fund has been used to provide housing, welfare assistance, and compensation for lost household goods.

"THE ECONOMIC MIRACLE"

Nobody could have predicted the success the Germans have had in rebuilding their economy since World War II. At the end of the war Germany lay prostrate, with its factories and its transportation and communications systems destroyed. Organized social life had come to an end, and the Allies had to provide aid simply to keep the population alive. The first few years after the war were very difficult, but beginning with the currency reform of 1948 rapid progress was made in rebuilding the economy through a combination of government action and free enterprise known as the "social market economy." From 1950 to 1958 the gross national product, the total of all goods and services produced, increased by 110 per cent. The annual rate of growth has exceeded that of any other country in Western Europe, and exceeds that of the United States. From 1949 to 1960, over 6 million new jobs were created; and over 50 per cent of the population is employed, the highest percentage in Europe. Thus West Germany has not only absorbed the refugees, but it has so successfully achieved full employment that it now must use some migrant workers from other countries to complement its own work force.

Some of the specific achievements of the West Germans help to make clearer the extent of the economic miracle. Twenty-two per cent of the 10 million homes in the area of the Federal Republic were destroyed during the war; from 1950 to 1960, 5½ million new housing units were constructed. Over 2 million motor vehicles have been manufactured annually since 1960, and production of passenger vehicles now exceeds that of the United Kingdom. West Germany's share of world trade has risen at such a rapid rate that it is now about three-fourths that of the United Kingdom, and the country is a serious competitor in international markets.

These economic achievements have enabled the Germans to re-establish their extensive social welfare programs, the expenditures for which now amount to 12.5 per cent of the gross national product.

Thus, the most tangible element in German cohesion is the economic miracle which has produced such a high standard of living for everyone that the regional, religious, and other differences have not become explosive. With more new cars, TV sets, and houses, and one of the most comprehensive social insurance systems in the world, the Germans are less inclined to social conflict than they were earlier. The economic miracle is not, however, the sole basis for cohesion in West German society. Less tangible but perhaps equally important factors are a strong national patriotism and the necessity for maintaining a united front in a country on the frontier of the worldwide East-West conflict.

Political Groups

In Germany, as in other democracies, political groups include both interest groups and political parties.

INTEREST GROUPS

Although Germany also has the kind of voluntary associations which characterize American society, (chambers of commerce, farmers' associations), an outstanding feature of its interest groups is that some of them are established by public law and membership in them is obligatory. These are business, farmers', and workers' organizations. For example, a handicraft worker must join a handicraft council, a manufacturing business an industrial council, and in some states all farmers are required to belong to the state agricultural council. These organizations act not only as pressure groups in promoting the interests of their members but also perform such regulatory functions as setting standards, licensing, and educating apprentices. They are organized in a hierarchy on local, state, and national levels. For example, the German Handicraft

Trades Diet has 9,500 local guilds, one branch in each county for each handicraft.

In addition to the public law bodies in which membership is compulsory, there are many other interest groups. Almost every German business concern is associated with one or more business organizations. One national group of business organizations, the Federation of German Employers Associations, has a membership in its local branches that takes in 80 per cent of private enterprise. Another, the Federation of German Industry, represents 90,000 employers. These two organizations in turn support another one, the German Industry Institute, which is the propaganda organization for business interests. Businessmen also support the Civic and Sponsors associations, which are the overtly political agencies of business. Among their political goals, business groups naturally favor lower taxes, but their position on government regulation is ambivalent, in that they seek more restrictions (on competition, imports, new products) favorable to their interests as well as fewer restrictions unfavorable to their interests.

The German Farmers Union favors higher subsidies and high tariffs for agricultural products, and thus has hampered German steps toward a common agriculture policy in the Common Market. Although, unlike the state agricultural groups, membership is not compulsory, almost all farmers belong to it.

There are several labor organizations, but the largest is the German Trade Union Federation with 6 million members in 16 industrial unions. This federation has adopted an official party neutrality, which it finds difficult to maintain at times, however, since most of its active leaders are Social Democrats. In addition to such traditional goals as seeking higher wages and better protection for workers, it has sought to increase the power of organized labor. It has been particularly active in promoting "co-determination," the German term for workers' participation in the management of industry. Under the laws of the Bonn Republic, labor names half the members of the boards of iron, coal, and steel concerns, and one-third of the members of the works councils in private plants outside these basic industries. The unions now seek an extension of this legislation to include union participation at the board level in private industries as well, and into more fields of economic activity.

Because the heritage (or origins) of the German Trade Union Federation has long been associated with Marxism, some Catholics have organized the Christian Trade Union, which now has almost 2 million members. In addition, the Salaried Workers Union and the German Civil Servants Union each have almost a half million members.

More clearly than in America, the German churches and their auxiliary organizations are political interest groups. The intimate relations between the churches and the government require that religious groups concern themselves with politics. For instance, the states collect church dues with regular taxes and provide religious instruction in public schools and state aid for parochial schools.

The Roman Catholic Church, whose membership is 45 per cent of the population, has long been involved in German politics. Bismarck's struggle against it impelled its members to organize a political party for their defense, the Catholic Center party. Thus Catholics have participated in politics as Catholics since the beginning of modern party organization in Germany.

Although bishops and priests have been somewhat restrained in overt support for Catholic candidates in the Bonn Republic, Catholic auxiliary organizations such as the Christian Trade Union movement have been quite active. The Catholic Workers movement and the Köpling Family movement have been particularly active in politics and together have usually elected about fifty members of the Bundestag.

Although 51 per cent of the population is Protestant, German Protestant traditions in politics have been quite different from those of the Catholics, in that Luther's stress on salvation by faith alone has led many of his followers to be less concerned about the social order. However, Hitler's persecution of Protestants and the catastrophe he brought to the country have convinced many of them that their Christian duty does require a greater concern about the social order. Therefore in 1948 they organized the Evangelical Church in Germany. This organization of twenty-seven state churches divided along geographical and denominational lines has no clear-cut political position other than a defense of Christianity and a particularly great concern about reunification, which would bring back their Protestant co-religionists in East Germany. As far as voting habits go, Protestants are distributed among all the German political parties.

Interest groups in Germany do much more than simply trying to persuade members of parliament or executive officials to adopt their policies. At one extreme, they actually regulate certain activities, as is the case with the public law bodies described at the beginning of this section. Sometimes the interest groups are even given an official role in the state government. For example, Bavaria, the only state with a bicameral legislature, has an advisory upper house composed of representatives of organized economic and religious groups, local governments, higher education, and others. Two other states have economic chambers composed of representatives of interest groups; these representatives are empowered to advise the legislature and consult with the cabinet.

In addition to those activities, organized groups have a role in partisan politics—in the selection of candidates and in campaigning. By offering financial support and campaign assistance to the parties at elections, they try to place their own officials in the Bundestag or state legislatures and onto the appropriate committees. Business groups have formed associations to provide contributions to the non-socialist parties. For example, it has been estimated that more than one-half the campaign money for the four non-socialist parties in national elections has come from these associations.[4] Farm groups have been equally active in supporting right-wing parties and in placing their officials in legislative bodies and on the agricultural committees. The Trade Union Federation has been more circumspect in its relations with the Social

Table 5.1

Bundestag Election Results, 1949–1965

			Year		
Party	1949	1953	1957	1961	1965
Christian Democrats (CDU/CSU)	31%*	45%	50%	45%	48%
Social Democrats (SPD)	29	29	32	36	39
Free Democrats (FDP)	12	10	8	13	9
Others	28	16	10	6	4
Total	100	100	100	100	100

* Percentage of valid party list votes received.
SOURCE: *Das Parlament,* Bonn, Vol. 15, No. 38 (Sept. 22, 1965).

Democratic party, but its officials have been elected to offices and its functionaries have "unofficially" campaigned for Socialist candidates at elections.

Besides taking an active interest in parties and elections, the interest groups maintain close relationships with officials in the executive branch of the state and national government. In some cases these relationships are formalized by allowing the organized groups to name members of advisory bodies attached to executive departments. In other cases, the relationships involve informal but regular consultations with the officials. But however it is done, it is customary for executive officials to consult the organizations that might be affected before issuing administrative orders or proposing legislation. Because executive action is so important in Germany, lobbying in executive agencies is more extensive than it is in legislative halls.

POLITICAL PARTIES: THE CHRISTIAN DEMOCRATIC UNION

The Christian Democratic Union (CDU), with its Bavarian wing, the Christian Social Union (CSU), has always been the strongest political

4 U. W. Kitzinger, *German Electoral Politics* (Oxford, Eng.: Oxford University Press, 1960), p. 215. The discussion of parties and interest groups in this chapter relies heavily on Kitzinger's work.

party in the Bonn Republic. It obtained a majority in parliament in 1953, the first time in history that any German party achieved this goal. In 1957, it established another new record by winning a majority of votes in the election and thus increased its majority in parliament. Although the CDU did not win a majority in 1961 and 1965 (see Table 5.1), it remains the strongest party and continues to dominate the national government.

The origins of the CDU extend back to the Catholic Center party established during the Bismarck era. However, Konrad Adenauer succeeded in bridging the religious gulf after World War II by organizing a new party which brought a large number of Protestants into association with the Catholic nucleus of the prewar Catholic Center party. Thus, today it is Christian in a broad rather than in a denominational sense. In addition to bridging the religious differences, the party has had some success in bridging class divisions by enlisting the support of some workers for a party closely associated with business and farm interests. This was a notable gain because in prewar Germany political parties had been based on class interests. Therefore, with support from both religions and from diverse social elements, the CDU has made a genuine attempt to form a majority party.

This diversity, however, is both the party's strength and weakness. Before 1950 it was merely a collection of local notables in each of the states. It was not yet a national party in an organizational sense during the first elections under the Bonn Basic Law in 1949. But in 1950, Adenauer organized a national party which brought together the various state parties except for that of Bavaria, which has retained its own separate but associated organization. Since then the party has become somewhat more centralized, especially because the national party has controlled funds obtained from business associations. Nonetheless, the party is not so centralized as its principal rival, the Social Democratic party. The national party cannot dictate the naming of candidates for office, although state and local organizations, which nominate candidates, may voluntarily cooperate with the national organization. Thus the CDU has remained a cadre party rather than one with a mass membership; the Social Democrats, who command less electoral support, have approximately twice as many members as the CDU, whose membership has varied between 230,000 and 350,000 members.

Geographically, the CDU/CSU has been strongest in Catholic Bavaria and the Saar and weakest in Protestant North Germany. There is a significant correlation between the percentage of Catholics in the population and the percentage of CDU votes in each state. Economically, the CDU has commanded more support from businessmen and from farmers than from workers. It has also drawn more support from women than from men and from older people than from younger ones. Its vote is lower in state and local elections than it is in national elections, when a higher percentage of people vote. This suggests that the party draws considerable support from people who vote only in national elections and are therefore not particularly interested in politics.

As a broad collection of diverse elements, the CDU has tended to stress general principles and promote popular candidates rather than to spell out issues in detail. Its election tactics have been directed to trading on the popularity of Adenauer and Erhard and to pointing with pride to the prosperity associated with Erhard's economic policies. Campaign slogans have included "No experiments" and "You never had it so good." However, in a general sense, one can describe the party's position as pro-Christian, pro-West, and pro-free enterprise.

In spite of its electoral successes, the CDU has been less cohesive than the usual German political party. This is due mainly to the diversity within the party. When it selects candidates, the ticket must usually be balanced so that the various groups are represented—somewhat like the ethnic considerations of American city politics. Religious balance is the chief consideration, but representation of important interest groups is also given attention. However, these candidates are often more loyal to their own groups than to the party. Thus, after they are elected, they often vote along group rather than party lines in legislative roll calls, and this is contrary to the norm in German politics, where party discipline is usually strong. This is particularly true of representatives with working class backgrounds or those who are active in trade union organizations. Thus, Chancellors Adenauer and Erhard have not had a monolithic organization on whose support they could always rely. Erhard has had the additional problem of having his policies as chancellor attacked by his predecessor Adenauer.

POLITICAL PARTIES: THE SOCIAL DEMOCRATIC PARTY

Although the Social Democratic party of Germany (SPD) is its oldest party and the one with the largest membership, 1961 was the first year it polled over one-third (36 per cent) of the votes cast in a national election (see Table 5.1). Although it has increased its percentage of votes in the last four national elections, its electoral strength in the Bonn Republic has always been less than that of the CDU.

It was founded as a Marxist party in 1875. In spite of Bismarck's attempts to outlaw this working class movement, the party could soon depend upon the support of one-third of the voters in election after election. Although it has changed its philosophy over the years, moving from orthodox Marxism through revisionist Marxism to a repudiation of Marx, it can still make some claim to being a continuing organization that has outlived the Empire, the Weimar Republic, and the Nazi dictatorship.

The Social Democratic party has a more centralized organization than the CDU. Its mass membership of over 600,000 is organized into 7,500 local organizations, which have some of the characteristics of social clubs. Its members pay dues monthly, and many participate actively in election campaigns. Thus the financial support and personal activities of its members help the party to compensate for the advantages which the other parties derive from large financial contributions from business organizations. Moreover, it is permanently organized on the national, state, and local levels, having a group of full-time permanent party functionaries.

The core of Social Democratic support is still the working class, although the party has neither succeeded in obtaining the support of all workers nor confined its appeals exclusively to them. The party is strongest in North Germany, and it has often dominated the state governments in Bremen, Hamburg, Hesse, and Lower Saxony. It has more Protestant than Catholic supporters and even more support from among those who are unaffiliated or only nominally affiliated with churches. It is stronger among young people than old and stronger in cities than in rural areas.

In the early postwar period the Social Democratic party called for a fairly large-scale program for nationalizing industries. It also opposed Adenauer's foreign policy, which concentrated on developing closer ties with the West, and urged instead greater efforts toward unification with East Germany. The prosperity brought by the social-market economics of the Christian Democrats, and the intensification of Soviet pressure did much to discredit both the domestic and foreign proposals of the Social Democrats. Therefore they made an all-out conscious effort to readjust their program and to present themselves in a new light in preparation for the 1961 elections.

In November, 1959, the party formally turned from Marxism and adopted a program that endorsed some free enterprise. The slogan eventually used by the party was "As much competition as possible—as much planning as necessary." Instead of nationalizing industries, the party proposed "Peoples Shares," a plan such as that used for Volkswagen ownership, in which preferential prices for lower income groups would make corporate shares available to the masses. In November, 1960, it formally endorsed a pro-Western foreign and defense policy. In 1961, instead of putting forward party chairman Erich Ollenhauer as its proposed candidate for chancellor, the Social Democrats endorsed Willy Brandt, the popular young mayor of West Berlin. This change was calculated to appeal to some middle-class voters who regarded Ollenhauer as a traditional Marxist party functionary and associated him with older discredited Socialist policies. The specific proposals announced by the Social Democrats as their campaign issues in 1961 included improvements in pensions, health insurance, family allowances, and public housing.

Despite its increased share of the vote in the 1961 and 1965 elections, these efforts to appeal to a broader segment of the population have created some dissatisfaction, for the party's program called for less socialism than the majority of party members want.

OTHER POLITICAL PARTIES

The largest of the minor parties in the Bonn Republic is the Free Democratic party (FDP). It is difficult to characterize the FDP. It is compounded of nationalism, nineteenth-century liberalism, sheer opportunism, individualism, and anti-clericalism, with the actual combination of these elements varying from state to state. Its support of big business and lower taxation has meant that its appeal has been greatest among upper income groups. Like the Christian Democratic Union, it is a cadre party. Because it has not been able to hope for a majority, it has directed its efforts to becoming the decisive factor in power struggles between the major parties.

It achieved its objective in 1961 and 1965 by being able to dictate the terms on which it would join the CDU in a coalition. As the only minor party to succeed in electing members to the Bundestag, it achieved this power with less than 10 per cent of the popular votes in 1965. When the Christian Democrats failed to retain their parliamentary majority, the decision of the FDP to join a coalition with them was the crucial factor in allowing them to form another government.

No other minor party elected members of the Bundestag in 1965, although some continue to be represented in state legislatures and local governments. These other minor parties have all become victims of the so-called splinter-party clause in the German election law (see p. 170). The combined voting strength of the minor parties in the national elections of the Bonn Republic was as follows: 1949, 28 per cent; 1953, 16 per cent; 1957, 10 per cent; 1961, 6 per cent; 1965, 3.6 (see Table 5.1). The number of parties represented in the Bundestag also declined from ten (plus independents) in 1949 to three in 1961 and 1965.

Two extremist parties, the neo-Nazi Socialist Reich party and the Communist Party, were outlawed by the Federal Constitutional Court as unconstitutional organizations seeking to overthrow the government. The Communists had polled 6 per cent of the votes and elected fifteen deputies in 1949, but their vote declined to almost 2 per cent in 1953, and they elected no deputies. The court outlawed the Party in 1956.

Two other parties, of some importance earlier since they elected deputies and served in early Adenauer governments, were the German party (DP) and the League of Homeless and Those Deprived of Rights (BHE). Although each of these parties had elected deputies in the past, their combined efforts under the title United German party (GDP) brought them less than 3 per cent of the total national vote in 1961. The German party had its base in the rural areas of Lower Saxony. In general more conservative than the Christian Democrats, it was especially concerned about subsidies for farmers.

More interesting for the significance of its demise was the BHE, the refugee party, primarily composed of refugees from beyond the Oder-Neisse line. In 1953 it achieved more than 5 per cent of the national vote and elected twenty-seven deputies; in 1957 it fell somewhat below 5 per cent and the party lost its parliamentary representation (see p. 170). In part the decline of this group reflects both the successful renewal of German society and the ability of the other German parties to absorb these refugee elements.

Governmental Institutions

The Bonn Republic is a parliamentary government as distinguished from a presidential government. It has a president who is considered chief of state, and his role is mainly a ceremonial one. The chancellor as chief of government is the one who actually heads the government. Thus, the German president has more in common with the British Queen or the presidents of the Third and Fourth French Republics than with the President of the United States or the De Gaulle Republic.

The president is elected by an electoral college composed of the members of the Bundestag (the lower house of the parliament) and an equal number of electors designated by the legislatures of the states. A majority vote is required on the first two ballots, but if no candidate obtains a majority, a plurality (the greatest number of votes even if not a majority) suffices on the third ballot. He is elected to a five-year term and is eligible for re-election to a second term. A third term is not permitted.

The president has few functions aside from the ceremonial ones. His most important official act is selecting a chancellor in the event that no candidate has an obvious majority in the Bundestag. Closely related to this is his power to dissolve the Bundestag if it rejects his nominee for chancellor and fails to elect another candidate by a majority. In that event the president may either accept the candidate who has achieved a plurality on the third ballot or dissolve the Bundestag and thus require new general elections. All his other official acts must be countersigned by a cabinet member.

Although the Bonn Republic is a form of parliamentary government, it is neither a cabinet system like the British model nor a chamber democracy like the model of the Third and Fourth French Republics. It may be designated as a chancellor system. In brief outline, the citizens elect a Bundestag (lower house), which in turn elects a chancellor. He alone is responsible for the government and continues to serve unless the Bundestag elects a successor by majority vote. We shall look first at the Bundestag, since it elects the chancellor, but we must keep in mind that the chancellor and not the Bundestag is the most important political institution.

BUNDESTAG

The two houses of the German parliament do not have equal powers. In fact, authorities differ on whether the German parliament should be called bicameral or unicameral. Most of the powers are held by the popularly elected Bundestag, which has the principal legislative authority and elects the chancellor. Although the Bundesrat (upper house) has some legislative authority, it functions chiefly as an agent of the states. It is therefore more appropriate to discuss it in the subsequent section on federalism.

Members of the Bundestag must be at least twenty-five years old and are elected for four-year terms in democratic elections in which all citizens twenty-one years of age or older may vote. In the Fifth Bundestag (elected in 1965) there are 496 members plus 22 non-voting delegates from West Berlin.

The Bonn Basic Law sets forth requirements for democratic, free, and equal elections, but it does not specify the number of members of the Bundestag or contain the specifics of an electoral law. These provisions are set forth in laws passed by parliament. The electoral system is one of the novel features of German government because it provides for both single-member districts and for proportional representation, with approximately one-half the members being elected under each system. Each voter has two votes: one for a member from his district and one for a party list in his state. There are 248 single-member districts, and voters elect one person from these districts by plurality, just as elections are conducted for the U.S. House of Representatives and the British House of Commons. In addition, each of the ten states is assigned an additional number of Bundestag seats equal to the number of single districts in the state. These additional seats are allocated on the basis of proportional representation, the election system which assigns seats to political parties in proportion to the votes which they have received.

Each state party organization submits a list of proportional representation candidates for its statewide slate and ranks them from first place down for the total number of seats for that state. Position on the lists is of great importance, because those on the bottom of the list are not likely to be elected. The rank on the lists is also important, for if a member dies or resigns during his term, the next person on the list just below the last member elected becomes a member of the Bundestag.

The voter casts one vote for a single representative in his district; he casts a second vote for a party list in his state. The number of seats won by a party in single-member districts is calculated in determining the number of additional seats to which a party is entitled under proportional representation.

To cite a hypothetical example, if there are ten districts in a state, there will be ten additional statewide proportional representation seats.

Let us imagine what happens with the following election results: the CDU wins 6 district seats, the SPD wins 4 district seats, and the FDP none; on the state party lists, the CDU wins 50 per cent, the SPD 40 per cent, and the FDP 10 per cent. Accordingly, the total to which each party is entitled would be CDU, 10 (50 per cent of 20); SPD, 8; and

Table 5.2

Composition of Fifth Bundestag, 1965

| Member | Party | | | |
	CDU/CSU	SPD	FDP	TOTAL
District	153	95	0	248
State P. R.	92	107	49	248
Total	245	202	49	496

SOURCE: *Das Parlament*, Bonn, Vol. 15, No. 38 (Sept. 22, 1965), p. 1.

the FDP, 2. The CDU has already won 6 seats in the districts, so it is entitled to 4 more from its state list. The SPD has won 4 in the districts, so it is entitled to 4 from its state list. The FDP, which has won in no district, receives the two seats to which it is entitled from its state list.

To prevent splinter parties from disrupting the government, the Bonn electoral law relies on a modification of straight proportional representation. In order to qualify for any seats at all, a party must win 5 per cent of the total national vote on the state party lists or win in three single-member districts. The tightening of these provisions, especially the requirement of winning 5 per cent in the entire nation rather than in one state, has been the primary reason why the number of parties represented in the Bundestag was reduced from ten in 1949 to three in 1965 (see Table 5.2).

There are no primary elections. Party organizations in local districts nominate local candidates, and state organizations prepare lists of state candidates and determine the positions of the candidates on the ballot. However, the parties are required to prove that their organizations have used democratic methods in selecting their candidates.

In 1965 the Free Democratic party failed to elect a single member in a district but achieved 49 members through proportional representation. The Christian Democratic Union, the strongest party, won in most of the single districts. These results indicate why the CDU favors a complete single-member district system and why the Free Democrats and other minor parties favor proportional representation.

Businessmen and farmers comprise the largest single occupational groups in the Fifth Bundestag, and civil servants are heavily represented. Lawyers, who are always a majority in an American Congress, have only forty-one members. Businessmen are heavily represented in the CDU and FDP, and laborers predominate in the SPD. There are thirty-eight women in the Fifth Bundestag, and the average age of all members is approximately 50.

The Bundestag has certain powers of election and appointment: it participates in the election of the president; it appoints federal judges; and, as noted earlier, it has the important function of electing a chancellor. Its primary functions, however, are legislative. Most of the bills it considers are introduced by the government and a few are initiated by the Bundesrat, but the Bundestag itself also has authority to introduce bills. In addition, it has the authority to question members of the government and to conduct investigations, but these powers have not been much used.

Government bills are sent first to the Bundesrat and then submitted through the cabinet to the Bundestag. Bundesrat proposals are submitted to the Bundestag through the cabinet. Proposals originating in the Bundestag must be introduced by a *Fraktion,* which, under the rules, is a group of fifteen members. Each of the three parties now represented in the Bundestag constitutes a *Fraktion.* Individual members do not have the right to introduce bills.

Proposals are considered in three stages or readings. First, the basic principles are discussed and a vote is taken simply on these principles. If the proposal overcomes this hurdle, it is sent to a committee, where the specifics are discussed in greater detail. There are thirty-six standing committees with chairmen, members, and alternates assigned in accordance with the proportional strength of the *Fraktionen,* or parties, in the Bundestag. There are no public hearings on bills, but the committees may call expert witnesses, ministers, and civil servants to appear before them. The committees do much to work out compromises among the parties and among the groups affected by the legislation; indeed, the latter are often represented directly on the committees by interest group functionaries who have been elected to the Bundestag. After the committee has worked out the details, the bill is returned to the Bundestag, where the second consideration is rather general. The third and final consideration is the longest and provides an opportunity to vote on each item of the bill as well as on the complete bill. Voting is by show of hands, by standing, or by roll call in which individual votes are recorded. The prevailing norm in German parliamentary practice has been *Fraktionszwang,* the requirement that each member vote in accordance with the party position. However, there has been considerably more deviation in the CDU and FDP in the Bonn period than there was in past German parliamentary history.

Bills passed by the Bundestag are sent to the Bundesrat, whose consent is required if they affect the states. Constitutional amendments require the approval of a two-thirds majority in both the Bundestag and Bundesrat. But simple bills not affecting the states can be passed without Bundesrat consent. A bill rejected by a simple majority in the Bundesrat may become law by a second simple majority vote in the Bundestag, but a bill rejected by a two-thirds majority in the Bundesrat requires a two-thirds majority in the Bundestag to become law. Disagreements between the two bodies are often worked out by a mediation committee, a joint standing committee composed of members of each house. Compromises through the mediation committee are necessary for legislation affecting the states and in the case of ordinary legislation they obviate the necessity of overriding vetoes. The mediation committee has become especially important because the Bundesrat has insisted that proposals affecting the states be interpreted rather broadly. Thus the committee has considered most of the bills in dispute between the two houses and has worked out compromises for almost all of them.

In the main, the German Bundestag is not a strong legislative body. It can be characterized as a decision-legitimitizing institution rather than as a decision-making one. It held only 168 plenary sessions in the four-year period from 1957 to 1961. Of the 424 bills which it passed, 348 were introduced by the cabinet, as compared with only 74 formally introduced in the Bundestag itself (and some of these may have been initiated by the cabinet) and 2 proposals of the Bundesrat. Moreover, in the Third Bundestag, 87 per cent of the cabinet proposals became law as compared to only 36 per cent of its own proposals.

Adenauer's treatment of the Bundestag diminished its prestige. He refused to explain his policies to the body to which he was formally responsible, and he at times ordered ministers to refuse to appear before it or its committees. This policy of the first chancellor is principally responsible for the relative unimportance of parliamentary investigations and questions in Germany as compared with Britain, where these devices provide members of Parliament with important opportunities to influence government policy. Erhard is not so high-handed in dealing with parliament, but Adenauer established precedents which will continue to determine practices in the Bonn Republic.

THE CHANCELLOR AND CABINET

The chancellor is the chief of government in the Bonn Republic and the commanding personality in the entire system. This authority stems both from the constitution and from the personal characteristics of Konrad Adenauer, who held the office for the first fourteen years.

The constitution intentionally established a strong chancellor, partly in reaction against the weak ones who were unable to maintain stability during the Weimar Republic. One means to this end was to weaken the president by providing for his election by an electoral college rather than by popular vote; thus he does not compete with the chancellor for popular support. Similarly the Bonn chancellor was given the emergency-decree power of the Weimar president, but with some careful safeguards.

More important in the long run may be the unique tenure which the Bonn Constitution provides for the chancellor. After the Bundestag has elected him, he can be removed only if that body elects a successor by majority vote. This "constructive vote of non-confidence," as it is called, is intended to prevent a repeat of the Weimar experience in which parties of the extreme left and extreme right joined in overthrowing governments even though they obviously could not agree on establishing a new one.

After a new Bundestag is elected, the president nominates a chancellor. If the nominee obtains a majority in the Bundestag, he assumes office. If he fails to obtain a majority and the Bundestag elects another candidate by a majority, the president must appoint the Bundestag's choice. However, if no candidate has achieved a majority after two weeks, another ballot is conducted. After this ballot, the president can choose either to appoint the candidate receiving a mere plurality or to dissolve the Bundestag and thus require new general elections. These alternate provisions have not yet been used, because both Adenauer and Erhard have been named by the president and elected by the majority in the Bundestag.

The chancellor and the cabinet constitute what is officially designated as the federal government, and its powers are extensive. In addition to executing the laws, the government can also make laws. As we have seen, it initiates most bills passed by the parliament. It determines the budget, which is subject to Bundestag approval. (But the latter body cannot increase expenditures or revenue beyond what is proposed by the government.) The government also makes laws directly by issuing decrees. Furthermore, many laws passed by parliament simply establish general lines of policy; the government implements these policies by filling in the details with decrees, which do not have to be approved by the Bundesrat unless they affect the states.

In an emergency the government could exercise even greater decree-making powers. With the approval of the president and the Bundesrat, it may declare a legislative emergency. Under these circumstances, the Bundestag must approve legislation proposed by the cabinet in four weeks or it becomes law merely upon the declaration of the government and the approval of the upper house. However, a chancellor may exercise these emergency powers for only six months during one term of office. As further safeguard, emergency decrees cannot be used to amend the constitution. Nonetheless, if exercised, these emergency powers would signify the temporary suspension of parliamentary government.

Extensive as these powers are, they are not shared jointly by the chancellor and the cabinet. It is the chancellor who determines the general lines of policy of the federal government, and he alone is responsible to the Bundestag. He nominates and recalls the members of the cabinet, although the president performs these acts formally. Cabinet ministers therefore play a subordinate role. Since the cabinet is not a collegial body with collective responsibility as in Britain, the German chancellor's status far exceeds the position of the British prime minister.

Cabinet ministers are not required to be members of the Bundestag, but most appointments have been made from this body. Although a few ministers without administrative responsibilities have served, most of them have been in charge of an executive department. The cabinet sworn into office in October, 1965, a coalition of the CDU/CSU and the FDP, was made up of 22 ministers, including 18 from the CDU and its Bavarian affiliate, CSU (13 CDU + 5 CSU), and 4 from the FDP.

The Adenauer regime, in particular, showed up the weakness of the cabinet. He did not use the cabinet as a decision-making institution. Officials in the chancellery often appeared to exercise more influence on top policy decisions than the cabinet ministers, who were merely charged with running specific departments. At times, Adenauer publicly criticized his cabinet ministers, and they often had public disagreements among themselves. A further step away from cabinet responsibility resulted from Adenauer's dependence on the Free Democrats to obtain a majority for his election in the Bundestag in 1961. The Free Democrats insisted on a specific coalition contract as a condition for their joining Adenauer's government; this contract involved the formation of a coalition committee which was to make all basic decisions. However, this committee was not drawn from the cabinet as such, and the Free Democratic leader was not even a member of the cabinet. Thus, even when a coalition required some collective responsibility, the cabinet was not selected as the agency for bargaining among the coalition leaders. Ludwig Erhard, who is less dictatorial and more human, has shown a greater willingness to consult others. He succeeded in bringing the leader of the Free Democrats, Erich Mende, into the cabinet, where some interparty negotiations can be conducted.

FEDERALISM: STATES AND BUNDESRAT

The Bonn Republic is a federal system composed of ten states. In addition, West Berlin is associated with the Republic, but national laws are valid there only if approved by the occupying authorities. The states, known as *Länder*, range in size from North Rhine-Westphalia with over 15 million inhabitants to the city-state of Bremen with less than 1 million. Table 5.3 lists the states, their sizes, and their populations.

Table 5.3

The States of the Federal Republic of Germany

State (from north to south)	Capital	Area (sq. mi.)	1958 Population (000)
Schleswig-Holstein	Kiel	6,057	2,275.8
Hamburg		288	1,807.6
Lower Saxony	Hanover	18,290	6,515.6
Bremen		156	677.5
North Rhine–Westphalia	Düsseldorf	13,111	15,458.6
Hesse	Wiesbaden	8,150	4,651.5
Rhineland-Palatinate	Mainz	7,656	3,354.7
Saarland	Saarbrücken	991	1,040.2
Baden-Württemberg	Stuttgart	13,803	7,433.0
Bavaria	Munich	27,239	9,278.0
Total		95,742	52,492.5

SOURCE: Helmut Arntz (ed.), *Facts about Germany* (Bonn: Press and Information Office of the German Federal Government, 1960).

The pattern of German federalism is exceedingly complex and cannot be explained in any one simple formula, such as "delegated powers to the national government and reserved powers to the states." In general, however, German federalism has much in common with what has been called "cooperative federalism" in America. Under this arrangement the national government enacts general legislation, provides funds, and sets standards; the states, on the other hand, enact more specific implementing legislation and administer programs. In the main, Germany exhibits more national legislative authority than the United States, but the states there have more administrative authority.

The Bonn Basic Law spells out the specific areas in which the national government has legislative authority. These areas can be broken down into three general categories: (1) Those in which the national government alone has the power to legislate. In all, the Basic Law lists eleven of these, including foreign affairs, defense, communications, and public transportation. (2) Certain areas in which both the national government and the states can legislate. The most important of these are legal, economic, and fiscal matters. However, the states may exercise legislative authority in these fields only if the national government fails to act. (3) Areas in which the national government can pass skeletal laws establishing general standards; the states are then permitted to pass laws that will carry them out. Examples are the civil service, the press, and motion pictures.

Those legislative powers not granted to the national government are reserved to the states. Included among them are: local government; police protection; cultural affairs; and, most important, education. In these fields the states can legislate and administer their own programs.

In addition, the states can exercise considerable discretion in establishing and regulating local governments. The forms for the intermediate units, roughly corresponding with American counties, have varied widely. On the municipal level, however, the prevailing pattern is an elected council which chooses the mayor and some other local officials.

Although state governments differ somewhat in their forms and in the names of their various institutions, they have many similarities. Except for Bavaria, which has a two-house legislature—members of the upper one appointed by interest groups, churches, local governments, etc.—each state has a democratically elected, unicameral (single-house) legislature. This legislature elects a minister-president, whose functions correspond roughly wtih those of the chancellor at the national level. His state cabinet consists of a group of ministers, each with jurisdiction over one or more departments. The party composition of state governments has included almost all possible combinations. The Social Democrats, who have never been included in the national government, have dominated some state governments and have served in coalitions with their principal opponent, the Christian Democratic Union. The Free Democratic party has participated in coalitions with the CDU and also in coalitions with other parties opposed to the CDU.

A unique feature of German federalism is that the states have a protector in the national government. That is the Bundesrat, the upper house of Parliament, which acts as an agent of the states in defending their interests against the national government. Since it derives its membership from state executives and performs significant non-legislative functions, the Bundesrat is discussed here as an aspect of federalism rather than as a house of parliament.

Its forty-one members (plus the four consultative delegates from West Berlin) are not elected representatives of the voters but, instead, are ambassadors of the ten state governments. The four largest states have five members, the three intermediate-sized states have four, and the three smallest states have three. There are no fixed terms of membership; each state appoints and recalls its members, who are state ministers or their deputies. Voting is by state delegations acting under instructions from their governments rather than on an individual basis.

In its capacity as defender of states' rights, the Bundesrat exercises concurrent legislative authority with the Bundestag over eleven categories of legislation which affect federal interests (see pp. 175–76). Examples would include territorial changes and the establishment of new federal agencies. Such legislation cannot become law without the consent of the Bundesrat, and its broad interpretation of what constitutes legislation affecting the states has made this power important. In other legislative fields, the Bundesrat exercises only a suspensive veto, which can be overridden by the Bundestag by a vote proportional to the vote against the measure in the upper house—for example, if two-thirds of the Bundesrat vetoed the measure, a two-thirds vote would be needed in the Bundestag to override the veto. However, even in ordinary legislation the Bundesrat is given an important advantage because the cabinet must submit its proposals to that body before transmitting them to the Bundestag. This gives the Bundesrat an opportunity to seek modifications favorable to the states. For example, in the Third Bundestag (1957 to 1961) it sent more bills back to the government with suggestions for modifications than it accepted without modifications. The Bundesrat has a further opportunity to seek modifications favorable to the states through the mediation committee.

In addition to its legislative functions, the Bundesrat performs others such as the amendments to the Constitution which require the consent of two-thirds of its membership as well as two-thirds of the Bundestag members. In addition, it has the power to appoint half the members of the Constitutional Court and to approve both ordinary decrees affecting the states and emergency decree powers.

Although observers have agreed that the ministerial specialists and their technical assistants in the Bundesrat have effectively represented the states, the injection of state agents into the national government has nevertheless tended to diminish state autonomy. Because the party composition of state governments determines the party composition of the Bundesrat, national issues become vital questions in state politics. Both in state elections and in the formation of state governments attention is directed toward the effects of state actions on the national government rather than merely on what might be most expedient for the state.

ADMINISTRATION AND JUDICIARY

In contrast to the complexity of legislative functions in Germany, administrative and judicial functions are organized in a clearer basic pattern. At the risk of oversimplifying this pattern, one may describe it as involving a few key national institutions with most of the work carried out at the state level.

Functions such as foreign affairs and defense are administered by the national government alone. In domestic affairs, however, the basic German administrative system is a skeletal national ministry, with the states administering the programs in the field. Thus, German ministries do not traditionally have field offices throughout the country to perform the actual tasks assigned to their jurisdiction. State and local administrators perform these services and deal with the general public. The national ministry is concerned with planning, setting standards, and supervising administration. Its officials promulgate decrees and participate in the legislative process; they may, for example, appear before the Bundestag and its committees. The top officials in the ministerial hierarchy therefore play an important role in making government policy. Yet the minister himself is usually the only political appointee in his department. The other high officials are drawn from the top level of the civil service and are thus not subject to the same democratic controls as an elected or appointed official.

Although government by bureaucratic experts raises serious questions of democratic responsibility, few persons question the competence of the civil service. Germany in the nineteenth century was the first nation to establish a professional bureaucracy, and it early developed a tradition of honesty and efficiency. However, the values which it maximized were antithetical to democracy, and its reputation later suffered from the willingness of many officials to serve the Nazi regime unquestioningly.

The civil service, both at the national and state levels, is regulated by national law. There are four classes, based primarily on level of education, and a person does not move up from one class to another: higher service (university education), elevated service (high school education), middle service (junior high school), and simple service (grade school). In order to obtain tenure in the two top categories, one must pass special examinations after three years of probation. Since legal education is the prevailing preparation for the higher civil service, German bureaucrats generally have an almost exclusively legalistic approach to administrative problems.

Although appointments and promotions are based on qualifications rather than the spoils system, civil servants may participate in politics. If they serve in the Bundestag or in state or local elective offices, they may go on leave and retain their civil service seniority and pension rights. Similarly, a civil servant may preserve his rights while accepting employment from an interest group whose activities he may have been regulating in his capacity as a government official.

The judiciary has much in common with the civil service as a professional career, but aside from the Nazi period, it has preserved a non-political status. Judges are not elected, nor are they drawn from the ranks of experienced lawyers; rather, the judicial service parallels the civil service as a career: law graduates enter the hierarchy at a bottom level and are promoted up through the ranks in accordance with their professional qualifications. The national and state ministries of justice administer the judicial system and determine its personnel policies.

German law is based on legal codes that are enacted by the national government to ensure uniformity throughout the states. However, most of the courts are operated by the states. These state court systems include local courts with a single judge, state courts of both original and appellate jurisdiction with three judges, and state supreme courts of appellate jurisdiction divided into civil and criminal divisions, each of which has three judges. Juries are not used, but lay assessors may sit with the judges and vote with them, and in important cases, more than one judge is used. Thus, even though there is no jury system, litigants are not subject to the whim of one person.

Only a few courts exist at the national level. The Supreme Federal Court has approximately eighty judges, who sit in sections of five judges each. This court is primarily an appellate court which ensures uniformity throughout the nation by reviewing decisions of state courts. One section of the court, however, has original jurisdiction over a few categories of offenses which are national crimes. Judges of this court are appointed by the minister of justice. He is assisted in his selections by a committee representing the Bundestag and the state ministers of justice.

More significant as a new feature of German government is the Federal Constitutional Court, which has been given explicit powers of judicial review—powers that did not exist before the Bonn Republic. Its jurisdiction extends to conflicts between the national government and the states, conflicts between states, interpretations of the respective rights of the national government and the state governments, interpretations of the rights of national government organs (president, cabinet, Bundesrat, Bundestag,) and interpretations of the constitutionality of national and state laws. Some cases may reach the Federal Constitutional Court on request of the lower courts. However, questions can also be brought before the Constitutional Court by request of the national or state governments or by one-third of the members of the Bundestag. Thus, unlike American practice, the Court can render opinions without waiting for litigants in specific law suits to raise constitutional questions.

The Bundestag and the Bundesrat each elect one-half the judges of the Court. Some members must be chosen from among federal judges, and they serve for life, while other members serve for eight years and are eligible for re-election. The judges are divided into two panels, each with ten members. Each panel exercises jurisdiction over specified categories of cases, and the two panels meet only if one wishes to deviate from a previous decision of the other.

This constitutional tribunal has played a significant role in the Bonn Republic. Its jurisdiction clearly authorizes it to decide questions which American courts would avoid as "political" and therefore not subject to judicial determination. Accordingly, the Court has ruled on some of the most controversial political issues, such as the status of civil servants, remilitarization, outlawing extremist parties, and consolidation of the Southwest states.

In addition to the regular courts, there are various special ones. The most important of these are the administrative tribunals, which hear claims based on wrongful state action. Like the regular court system, these lower courts function on the state level, and a federal administrative court is primarily charged with maintaining uniformity throughout the country by hearing appeals. Other special tribunals include labor courts which deal with labor-management conflicts.

The System in Action

The Bonn Republic was dominated throughout its first fourteen years by Konrad Adenauer, who was elected when the government was first established in 1949 and was re-elected in 1953, 1957, and 1961. Some features of the system derive exclusively from this strong-willed and skillful politician, whose precedents are bound to leave a permanent imprint on the system.

Adenauer weakened every other political institution in the Republic by concentrating power in his own hands. His motives had been to overcome the evils of the Nazi heritage and to establish strong ties with the West, but his methods were widely condemned as autocratic.

The prestige of the presidency was well established by President Heuss (1949–1959). In 1959, Adenauer first announced that he would seek the presidency, then suddenly changed his mind and indicated, in effect, that the position was not worth having. As a result, the prestige of the office has declined.

Adenauer treated the parliament and the cabinet in a cavalier manner. He refused to explain some actions to the Bundestag and sometimes ordered ministers to refrain from answering questions. When the Bundestag refused to adopt some of his proposals, he achieved his goals by skillful manipulation and use of alternative methods. He used his cabinet members as mere subordinates and refused to take them into his confidence. Although it was clear that the octogenarian's days were numbered, he tried to prevent the grooming of a successor. He spoke disdainfully of Erhard in public, even when it was clear he was the obvious successor.

In his capacity as chairman of the Christian Democratic Union, Adenauer dominated rather than led the party. In 1961 he imposed a coalition agreement which was clearly opposed by the majority of CDU deputies. His primary motive for conceding much to the Free Democratic party was to obtain its consent to his staying longer in office, for he was convinced that he alone could deal with the crises facing his country. In the same manner, the Chancellor weakened the states by intervening in their politics to ensure state political alignments consistent with his national policies.

Adenauer's methods did little to convince observers that democratic government is assured in Germany. On the other hand, his regime brought prosperity and stability and thus may have contributed to democracy by providing the conditions under which a democratic government could exist.

Ludwig Erhard, who succeeded Adenauer as chancellor in 1963, conducts business in a much different style. Most important, he is willing to consult others before making decisions. But the legal powers of the office are so great and the precedents for the chancellor's authority are so strong that Erhard has imposed his policies in circumstances where it has not been clear whether the majority in the cabinet and in his party agreed with him. One notable development is that Erhard has been able to withstand the attacks which Adenauer continues to direct at his foreign policy. Thus, the difference between the two chancellors appears to be in their style rather than in their actual authority. Erhard, whose method and power are best characterized by his new nickname, "the rubber lion," has succeeded in creating and maintaining a working style of government independent of his predecessor.

Although the orderly transfer of power to a new chancellor has been successful, the question of whether the social basis for democracy now exists in the German system is still open to speculation. Admittedly, extremist parties have had relatively little success in the Bonn Republic, and the Nazis have been discredited by the catastrophe which they brought to the country. However, many former Nazis are active in politics and serve in the government. Other doubts about the future of democracy derive from the inadequate education for citizenship in the German schools. Therefore, although a democratic system of government is functioning, some observers have wondered whether it functions simply because Germans have turned from an obsessive interest in politics to pursuing their private goals.

As important as this question may be, however, the ultimate fate of the German Federal Republic will probably be determined by outside forces. Germany's position on the frontier between West and East in the cold war may mean that the decisions made in Washington and Moscow will be more important than those made in Bonn.

SUGGESTIONS FOR ADDITIONAL READING

DEUTSCH, KARL, and LEWIS EDINGER, *Germany Rejoins the Powers* (Stanford, Calif.: Stanford University Press, 1959).

GOLAY, J. F., *Founding of the Federal Republic of Germany* (Chicago: University of Chicago Press, 1958).

HEIDENHEIMER, ARNOLD J., *Adenauer and the CDU: The Rise of the Leader and the Integration of the Party* (The Hague: Martinus Nijhiff, 1960).

HISCOCKS, RICHARD, *Democracy in Western Germany* (London: Oxford University Press, 1957).

KITZINGER, U. W., *German Electoral Politics* (London: Oxford University Press, 1960).

LITCHFIELD, EDWARD H. (ed.), *Governing Postwar Germany* (Ithaca, N.Y.: Cornell University Press, 1953).

MERKL, PETER H., *The Origin of the West German Republic* (New York: Oxford University Press, 1963).

PLISCHKE, ELMER, *Contemporary Government of Germany* (Boston: Houghton Mifflin Company, 1962).

POLLOCK, JAMES K. (ed.), *German Democracy at Work* (Ann Arbor, Mich.: University of Michigan Press, 1955).

WELLS, ROGER HEWES, *The States in West German Federalism* (New York: Bookman Associates, 1961).

Chapter 6

THE GOVERNMENT
OF THE USSR

Unlike the countries studied in the preceding chapters, Russia (now formally called the Union of Soviet Socialist Republics) is a dictatorship. Dictatorships are nothing new, and there are many of them in the world. The Soviet Union has been selected for consideration primarily because of its importance in the world and its challenge to democracy, and because it represents a type of dictatorial rule that is in some ways an innovation of the twentieth century. This type of authoritarian rule has come to be called totalitarianism or totalitarian dictatorship.

Constitutional Development

Russia has a long history that can be divided into more or less distinct epochs, set off by crises or decisive turning points. But two chief themes persist throughout: the expansion of Russia into a large empire and the retention of autocratic political systems. Not until this century did democratic constitutionalism make a brief and uncertain breakthrough, only to be eclipsed by the Soviet dictatorship in 1917.

THE AUTOCRATIC TRADITION

The history of the Russian state goes back to the period when the chief city of Russia was Kiev, an era that lasted from about the ninth century to 1240. The conquest of Russia in that year by Mongol hordes ushered in a period of Tartar rule which continued for some 250 years. The re-establishment of Russian rule in the sixteenth century under the leadership of the princes of Moscow was accompanied by autocratic rule and internal troubles. Ivan IV (the Terrible or Dreaded), who ruled from 1547 to 1584 and was known for his ruthlessness, was the real unifier of Russia in the post-Mongol period. After his death, the country entered a period of strife—the "Time of Troubles"—when civil war and palace intrigue threatened to undo Ivan's work. But the election of the first Romanov as Tsar in 1613 ended this epoch. The rule of the Romanovs, which came to an end in 1917, saw Russia expand into a great empire and rise to a position of power among the nations.

Most of Russia's achievements in the Romanov period are associated with a few of her great rulers, particularly Peter I (the Great), who ruled between 1682 and 1721 and whose overriding aim was to Europeanize Russia in one lifetime. But these rulers did not tolerate, much less promote, democracy. Some were less ruthless than others, but all ruled by autocratic methods, and even the weaker ones did not readily accept limitations on their power. Even Alexander II, who ruled between 1855 and 1881 and who is known for his liberation of the serfs, would accept no restrictions on his absolute power.

The most vocal defender of tsarist absolutism was the Russian Orthodox Church, whose leaders viewed Western influence as inimical to Russian interests. Nurtured in the Christianity of Byzantium, Russian church leaders saw the West as hostile to "Holy Russia," the true interpreter and defender of Christianity. Thus the church early became an ally of Russian nationalism, although a full-blown Russian version of the divine-right-of-kings theory was not developed until late in the nineteenth century.

Another source of support for tsarist absolutism was the landowning, serf-holding aristocracy. Although it was initially illegal to sell serfs apart from the land, the practice had become so common by 1675 that it received legal sanction. More and more voices came to be raised against serfdom, however, and it became the most persistent issue during the long history of Russian autocracy. The reforms of Alexander II (1861) offered some promise of resolution, but many things were left undone, and no final and acceptable solution to the most acute problem of Russian society was ever found under the tsarist regime.

Protests against serfdom and Russian autocracy took several forms. In the seventeenth and eighteenth centuries they consisted mainly of intermittent and small-scale peasant revolts, although two revolts of major proportions were led by non-peasants (Stenka Razin, 1667–1671; Emilian Pugachev, 1773–1774) and were brutally put down. In the nineteenth century protests were mainly literary and political. The first major political protest, known as the Decembrist Revolt, occurred in December 1825, and was led by non-peasants, chiefly nobles and army officers who had fought against Napoleon. It, too, was quickly and ruthlessly suppressed. The intellectual atmosphere which made the uprising possible, however, also gave rise to a literary protest against the evils of tsarist autocracy. This literary upsurge produced Russia's greatest writers, among them Pushkin, Gogol, Lermontov, Herzen, Chekov, Turgenev, Dostoyevsky, and Tolstoy. The intellectual protest against serfdom and tsarist autocracy was also the forerunner of late nineteenth-century political revolutionary movements, among them the Russian version of Marxism.

STEPS TOWARD REFORM

Although reforms were slow in coming to Russia, those inaugurated by Alexander II gave considerable promise at the time they were promulgated. The emancipation of the serfs in 1861 was hailed as a great act and earned for Alexander the title "Tsar-Liberator." In actuality, however, the serfs were only partially emancipated. The government bought one-half of the land owned by landlords, but the peasants who received this land had to pay for it over a period of forty-nine years, an obligation which was to prove increasingly burdensome. As time went by, moreover, it became evident that more and more land would have to be bought from the landlords if peasant needs were to be satisfied, but this the government failed to do.

Another great reform of Alexander II was his partial democratization of the institution of local government (the *Zemstvo*) in 1864. This reform was in large part the consequence of the emancipation of the serfs, who were no longer content to see the landlords govern the local communities. The reform of the judiciary in the same year fell in somewhat the same category: it was intended to give the free peasants a share in the dispensing of justice. Among other things, juries and *lawyers* were introduced for the first time.

Other notable reforms made the budget public (1862), introduced self-government in the universities (1863), reorganized municipal government (1870), and placed military conscription on a non-class basis (1874). Additional reforms were under consideration when Alexander was assassinated in 1881.

Unfortunately, the assassination of the "Tsar-Liberator" doomed prospects for further reform and ushered in a period of reaction, during which some of the reforms were reversed or made less meaningful. Alexander III and his anti-reform advisers hit hard on all fronts, but especially at education and the press. The political police (*Okhrana*) were given far-reaching authority. And the procurator-general of the Holy Synod of the church developed a Russian version of the doctrine of the divine right of kings.

THE BEGINNINGS OF CONSTITUTIONALISM

Although for the most part it could not be manifested publicly, there was a good deal of political ferment in Russia in the last decades of the nineteenth century. Few political movements could function openly, and those that could were not productive of change. More and more energetic people were therefore driven to work in underground organizations, some dedicated to democracy, and others to direct action and violence. Among the former were the Social Revolutionaries and the Constitutional Democrats. Among the latter were the Russian Marxists, officially called the Russian Social Democratic party, who found new ammunition in the evils resulting from the industrialization that had recently burst upon Russia.

But political ferment in itself would not have produced the Revolution of 1905. This was triggered by the disastrous consequences of the Russo-Japanese War (1904–1905). The revolution was brought about by the *Zemstvos*, the local assemblies whose work had in the past been impeded by the government. The first All-Russian Congress of *Zemstvos* met in the capital in November, 1904. It demanded the creation of a representative assembly with real legislative powers, the elimination of class and racial discrimination, and the protection of civil liberties. As things were going from bad to worse, both at home and on the war front, the Tsar in June, 1905 promised a joint deputation from the *Zemstvos* and municipal councils that he would convoke a national assembly "as soon as possible." But when it was announced in August that the *Duma* (legislature) would have only consultative powers and that it would be chosen on the basis of a narrow franchise, the unrest grew, culminating in a general strike in October.

Although his initial answer to the revolution was the imposition of martial law, the Tsar at the same time proclaimed a moderate constitution. Russia, in theory at least, became a constitutional monarchy. The *Duma* was to have legislative powers and would be elected on the basis of universal manhood suffrage. Moreover, a cabinet of ministers was made responsible to it, and guarantees of free speech, press, assembly, and conscience were promulgated.

Because of these new-found freedoms, the underground political groups came out into the open. All of them promoted active discussion of contemporary political, economic, and social problems. Through meetings, newspapers, and political tracts, they attempted to propagate their views and their programs for reform.

But the promise of this seemingly auspicious beginning for representative government was not to be fulfilled. The Tsar refused to play the role of a constitutional monarch. From the outset he committed unconstitutional acts, among other things dissolving the first *Duma* within three months of its convening, although it had been elected for a term of five years. A second *Duma*, newly elected, was convened in March, 1907, but met a similar fate four months later. The electoral law was then changed, without consulting the *Duma*, to do away with universal manhood suffrage. By thus manipulating the electoral regulations, the government was able to facilitate the election of two conservative *Dumas*, both of which served their full terms. But the *Duma* did not become a true parliamentary body. It never was able to call the ministers to account, nor did it gain control over finance. Moreover, administrative officials continued to ignore it and to make use of emergency powers that were still on the statute books.

THE COLLAPSE OF THE OLD ORDER
AND THE BOLSHEVIK SEIZURE OF POWER

In spite of these halting steps toward a constitutional regime, Russia by 1914 was making progress in the economic, social, and political realms. To be sure, there were some discouraging situations, but on the whole the signs were favorable. Had it not been for World War I, the revolutions of 1917 might never have occurred. But war did come, and with it the whole tsarist structure was swept aside.

Initially, the war against Germany was not unpopular. The spirit of resistance was strong, and in spite of heavy losses the Russian army fought well. As the war progressed, however, and particularly as evidence of general inefficiency on the home front piled up, dissatisfaction spread. As the situation deteriorated at the front and seeming helplessness prevailed at home, leaders of the *Duma* and the *Zemstvos* demanded the appointment of a responsible cabinet, but their call went unheeded.

The beginning of the collapse came with food riots in the capital in March, 1917. When the troops refused to fire on the rioters, tsarist authority was at an end. The *Duma* thereupon asked for and got the Tsar's abdication. Tsarism was therefore overthrown with very little bloodshed. The *Duma* leaders quickly formed the Provisional Government, which was to exercise a tenuous authority until its overthrow by the Bolsheviks in November, 1917.

For the overthrow of tsarism engendered a struggle for power between two competing forces, the Provisional Government and the Soviet (Council) of Workers' and Soldiers' Deputies.[1] The latter organization had come into existence with the collapse of the old order, and from the beginning sought to share in running the country. Its famous Order Number One, for example, asked military units to obey the Provisional Government only to the extent that its orders did not conflict with those of the Soviet. Although the Soviet allegedly sought to help the Provisional Government, the latter found itself increasingly harassed by the former.

In its struggle with the Soviet, the Provisional Government was handicapped by two crucial decisions it had made when it first came to power: to continue the war against Germany and Austria-Hungary, and to postpone domestic reforms until the end of hostilities. With no decisive victories at the front, the Provisional Government was increasingly

---

[1] The first soviets, or councils, grew out of the strikes in the spring and summer of 1905, as bodies to represent the workers in a number of cities throughout Russia. They were not associated with any political party.

challenged by those who wanted to get out of the war and to get on with needed reforms at home. These forces gathered momentum in the newly-formed soviets in various cities throughout Russia, particularly in Moscow and Petrograd.

In the early months of the struggle between the two authorities, the Bolsheviks, the Lenin-led maximalist wing of the Marxian Russian Social Democratic Workers' party, were skeptical about working in the Soviet, which they believed to be too close to the Provisional Government. But as the Soviet began taking an increasingly independent stand, the Bolsheviks started to work among the various local soviets, seeking to take them over; by September, 1917, they had succeeded in gaining majorities in the soviets of Petrograd and Moscow. Thereupon they determined that the soviets should have military revolutionary committees. Although the Bolshevik leaders had serious doubts about their prospects of success if they sought to seize power, one of them, Vladimir Lenin, insisted that they must do so. On the eve of the Second Congress of Soviets in Petrograd, the Bolsheviks struck, seizing the government buildings, the railway station, and the telephone and telegraph networks, and arresting the members of the Provisional Government. The next day (November 8, 1917), they asked the Congress of Soviets to install them as the new government of Russia.

Once in power, the Bolsheviks proceeded to consolidate their gains, a process that required several years. The Provisional Government had promised the election of a Constituent Assembly to determine the future form of government in Russia. The Bolsheviks permitted this election to take place, even allowing the Constituent Assembly to convene in January, 1918. But since they could not control it (they had about 25 per cent of the seats), they disbanded it by force. Moreover, they concluded a separate peace with Germany (the Treaty of Brest-Litovsk), which many Russians regarded as treason to their allies. Many of the military commanders actually sought to rally their forces against the Bolsheviks. The result was several years of civil war, which the Bolsheviks finally won.

The young Bolshevik regime was led by Lenin until his death in 1924. Thereupon a struggle for power ensued among several leading Communists, principally Leon Trotsky and Joseph Stalin. By 1928 Stalin was firmly in the saddle, but several more years elapsed before he liquidated his main enemies (real and imagined) and established a personal dictatorship that lasted until his death in 1953.

SOVIET CONSTITUTIONALISM

Soviet ideas of constitutionalism have been consistently different from those found elsewhere. In the West, for example, constitutions historically have come to be looked upon as instruments by which government is restrained and the rights of citizens are protected. In addition, Western constitutions have provided for procedural safeguards to prevent abuses in the exercise of the powers granted to governments. The Soviet concept of constitutionalism contains none of these ideas. The Soviet Constitution provides neither limitations on the powers of government nor any meaningful procedural safeguards. In the Soviet view, the constitution is an instrument for defining governmental goals and citizen duties, as these are conceived by the leaders of the totalitarian state.

When the Bolsheviks came to power, they did not have a blueprint of the type of government they wanted. Lenin and other Marxists had insisted that it must be a dictatorship of the proletariat, but even this was not precisely defined. According to Marxist theory, the dictatorship of the proletariat was to be temporary—the transition stage between capitalism and communism. Once private property, the basis of all class struggles, was abolished, classes would cease to exist. The state, the instrument of the dominant class in any epoch, would no longer be needed, and would wither away. The dictatorship of the proletariat would thus pave the way for a classless, stateless society, which, according to Marxist doctrine, is the ultimate in social development.

In the early months of their rule, the Bolsheviks operated their "dictatorship of the proletariat" without a constitution. After they disbanded the Constituent Assembly by force in January, 1918, they went about drafting a type of constitution, which came into force in July, 1918.

This first Soviet constitution in effect ratified the evolving governmental structure based on the soviets. It proclaimed the revolutionary nature of the regime, declaring power to rest in a dictatorship of the urban and rural proletariat. Moreover, it announced the inauguration of socialism and the suppression of the bourgeoisie. Political power was to be exercised through a hierarchical organization of executive committees of the soviets, culminating in a Council of Peoples' Commissars at the top.

The first constitution was for Russia proper, or the Russian Soviet Federated Socialist Republic, as it then was officially called. After the end of the civil war, parts of the old Russian empire were forcibly brought back under Russian domination, and a Union of Soviet Socialist Republics was created in 1922. A new constitution, not too different from that of 1918, was ratified by the Congress of Soviets in January, 1924. Although technically a federation, the USSR was a highly centralized state, all powers of significance being vested in one central government.

In 1936, a completely new and much heralded constitution, which still remains in force, was adopted. The building of the new society had presumably proceeded to such a point that a new constitution was needed to reflect the changed state of affairs. A drastic economic and social transformation had in fact taken place. But the drawing up of the new constitution seems actually to have been motivated more by external factors, particularly the rise of Hitler in Germany. To counter the Nazi-Fascist threat, the Soviet Union needed allies in the West. By providing proof of an allegedly evolving democratic system in Russia, the Soviet leaders hoped to convince the Western democracies that they had something in common with the new Soviet regime, and that therefore they should cooperate in meeting the Nazi-Fascist challenge. Moreover, the Soviet leaders hoped to gain a propaganda victory abroad with a constitution that contained declarations of universal suffrage and workers' rights, and provided for secret elections.

Under this constitution the regime remained a dictatorship, but its constitutional forms were altered. All legislative power continues allegedly to reside in the Soviet structure (that is, the series of local, regional, and national assemblies). At the national level is the Supreme Soviet, made up of two houses, the Council of Union and the Council of Nationalities. Both are popularly elected, the former based on population, the latter is designed to represent national units (the republics and other subordinate units). Each of the republics, as well as each local unit of government, city and rural, has a unicameral soviet, also popularly elected.

Executive power is divided. The formal executive functions are vested in a Presidium of 33 members, elected by the Supreme Soviet and exercising the latter's powers when it is not in session. Powers of government are allegedly vested in the Council of Ministers, elected by and responsible to the Supreme Soviet. As we shall see, however, all of these governmental institutions are but instruments of the party dictatorship.

In April, 1962, the Supreme Soviet approved the appointment of a large committee, headed by Nikita Khrushchev, then Chairman of the Council of Ministers, to draft a new constitution for the USSR. Perhaps because of its association with Stalin, many of whose acts and policies had been denounced by Khrushchev, the 1936 Constitution had to go. But Khrushchev's ouster in 1964 leaves the future of this project in doubt. If his successors do promulgate a new constitution, the changes are apt to be more in form than in substance.

Social Forces

The various social forces that normally exist in every society do not have free play in a dictatorship. Some may be repressed and others favored, but a façade of unanimity is usually erected. In a communist dictatorship the aim is allegedly a classless society: hence the elimination of competing social forces. The extent to which this goal is being achieved in the Soviet Union is, however, open to question.

THE CLASSLESS SOCIETY

Marxism teaches that any system of private property divides society into hostile classes, with the capitalist system simplifying the conflict into one of the proletariat versus the bourgeoisie. Once the working class seizes power it will proceed to socialize property and liquidate the bourgeoisie, a move which will lead to a classless society, the best of all possible worlds, where there will be no need for the state, or for compulsion of any kind.

It was to be expected, therefore, that in the initial years of the new regime the Soviet leaders would rant against the surviving capitalists. As a matter of fact, the so-called "remnants of capitalism" became the scapegoats for nearly every failure of the new regime. The alleged discovery of innumerable "wreckers," "spies," "diversionists," and other malefactors produced countless trials, executions, and imprisonments. But although the Soviet regime is in its fifth decade, there is still no sign of the abolition of classes and the consequent withering away of the state. Wide social and economic differences persist in the Soviet Union. There are wide disparities in earning power, perhaps wider than those found in most capitalist states, with consequent disparities in standards of living. The few privileged—members of the Communist Party, the higher bureaucracy, university professors, military officers, top writers and artists, and the technical-administrative intelligentsia—live relatively well. The bulk of the people, however, are on one common level, with a standard of living considerably below that of most (if not all) Western European countries.

Thus while most private property is abolished, privileges continue. This is made possible because the "new class" (the Communist ruling group) can manipulate property even if it does not "own" it. The justification is that this is a temporary situation, and that the leaders need better living conditions if they are to contribute to the maximum of their ability. At some future date, presumably, there will be plenty for all; in the meantime, the top leaders decide who "needs" to share the available privileges with them—that is, who is most needed in the pursuit of the aims of the regime.

In other words, although the actual structure of Russian society may have altered in the years since the Revolution, social classes continue to exist. It is only natural, after all, that those who share the available material privileges should develop a feeling of oneness—a class consciousness—and should be loath to give up their privileges. They know, however, that they owe them to the high Party leaders, and are consequently careful not to offend the Party.

Their less fortunate fellow-citizens constitute groups which in Western democracies would organize for political action to promote their interests. But in the Soviet Union these groups are immobilized. They are given "crumbs," and constantly told that their day will come. But as the day recedes more and more into the future, awareness of class differences becomes stronger, and the regime's promises develop a hollow ring.

CHANGE AND STABILITY

Without admitting it openly, the Soviet leaders have learned that basic social conflicts cannot be assumed away. They therefore seek to keep them in check by a rigid organization of society in which nothing is left to chance. All organizational life is controlled and directed by the Party. There can be no autonomous groups or organizations, only those the Party sanctions. The Party, because it seeks a total transformation of society along definite lines, gives direction to all group activity, and attempts to prevent any it considers inimical to its aims.

The Soviet system, particularly during the rule of Stalin, seemed cast in a totalitarian mold that permitted little change. Not that the new system was not affected by the past; the Russian social inheritance cast a significant shadow over it. The predominance of the Great Russians under tsarism, for example, so much criticized by both Lenin and Stalin, strongly reasserted itself under the latter. Similarly, the Bolshevik leaders were critical of the anti-Semitism of the Empire, yet anti-Semitism was to reappear in various forms under Stalin, and there is some indication that it continues today, although perhaps to a lesser degree. These are but two examples of how past inheritance affects even the most rigid of systems, one that aims at the total transformation of society.

At the same time, the totalitarian pattern is subjected to change by new forces. Industrialization has produced a new class of engineers, technicians, and managers with a stake in the new system. Because they are so necessary to the system, the Party, as we have seen, has accorded them great privileges in the form of higher salaries, better housing, and a host of fringe benefits, advantages it has also accorded to artists, authors, and others it judges to be of great potential usefulness. And there is no telling what further significant changes will be wrought in the system if and when the rank and file citizens are able to enjoy material abundance.

Political Groups

In every society there is competition for the things that society has to offer. In democratic societies people are relatively free to compete individually and in groups, although the government acts as a kind of umpire, enforcing the rules under which competition takes place. (And there is also competition to see who will do the umpiring, as exemplified by the struggle for power among political parties.) But many rules and norms of conduct are not government-imposed or government-enforced. In short, there are a number of forces at work, a situation which has led some to describe modern democracies as "pluralistic societies."

Pluralism also exists in totalitarian dictatorships, but it is of a different order. Although there is still a struggle for goods and services, the limits of this struggle are carefully defined and rigidly controlled. In the Soviet Union the controller is the Communist Party. It is the self-appointed rule-maker and umpire, and no one can challenge its decisions. Consequently, in the Soviet Union what is generally described as politics takes place primarily *within* the Communist Party.

THE BOLSHEVIK CONCEPT OF PARTY

The Russian Communists still adhere to the original Bolshevik concept of what the Party ought to be. First, although it has grown to between 10 and 11 million members, it is considered relatively small in that it includes only about 8 per cent of the adult population. It was Lenin who set the standard when he said that the Party should consist of a small group of dedicated revolutionaries. In his opinion a large party would be unwieldy; numbers, he asserted, were not nearly so important as discipline and dedication.

Second, the Bolshevik concept of party also holds that the Communists alone are all-wise. Therefore, to permit competing parties would be to introduce obstacles to the attainment of desired objectives; consequently, Communists must have a complete monopoly of power. More than that, the Communist Party must speak with one voice; hence no factions within the Party are permitted. Communists often speak of the Party as being monolithic, in other words, it cannot be split into factions. Factions have nevertheless arisen, as we shall see, but they have been ruthlessly suppressed.

Third, the Party is organized on the hierarchical principle. At the base of the Party pyramid are some 300,000 primary organizations (once called cells). Above these are a number of levels of Party organizations, each subordinate to the one above it. This means that there are local, area, and regional organizations, in addition to the Party organizations at the republic and national levels.

AUTHORITY WITHIN THE PARTY

Theoretically, the Party is governed according to the principle of "democratic centralism." Lesser Party units elect members of higher units, which in turn elect others until the topmost level is reached. Hence the notion that all Party bodies and Party officers are democratically elected, and the corollary notion that lesser Party units must obey the instructions of those above them.

In actual practice, however, democratic centralism has never worked this way, except perhaps at the beginning, when there was some semblance of election of persons to party congresses and to the Party's Central Committee. Since that time, however, those at the top have controlled the election of those below. Perhaps the only exceptions are Party secretaries at the local level, who are chosen by secret ballot. But no one is "elected" to the highest governing bodies of the Party except on the recommendation of those bodies themselves.

The supreme authority in the Party is ostensibly the Party Congress, which is supposed to meet every four years. But Soviet leaders have been able to avoid convening the Congress for as long as a dozen years. Moreover, congresses are large and unwieldy affairs. Even when they meet, they are in session only a few days, most of which are consumed by speeches from the Party leaders. There are no debates and no contested resolutions. The delegates are there to hear the leaders and to applaud their statements; the leaders are there to report on their achievements, to urge increased efforts in behalf of new or existing programs, and perhaps to signal new turns in the Party line.

Much more important than the Congress is the Party Central Committee. It consists of approximately 175 members, theoretically elected by the Congress and theoretically in charge of Party affairs between congresses. In the early years of the Soviet regime, the Central Committee met with reasonable frequency, and considerable discussion of Party affairs took place. But because factions began developing, and because these could not be tolerated, meetings became less frequent and began to resemble the Congress in that no dissent occurred. During Stalin's reign, the Central Committee was not even called into session for long periods of time. Since his death, however, it has met with greater regularity, although there is little indication that it cannot be completely controlled by the top leaders.

The most important body in the Party is the Presidium of the Central Committee (formerly called the Politburo or policy bureau). Although its size varies from time to time, it generally consists of about twelve members and five candidates. The Presidium is a self-perpetuating body. Although technically elected by the Central Committee, no one is ever proposed for membership except by the Presidium itself. Its members are the most important Communists in the Soviet Union. From them emanate all important decisions and many lesser ones. As a general rule there is a division of labor within the Presidium, each member being responsible for an important area or field of activity (for example, agriculture, agitation and propaganda, and so on).

The implementation of Presidium decisions is left to the Secretariat, generally headed by from six to ten secretaries, several of them Presidium members. The most important person in the Secretariat, and hence in the Presidium, is the First Secretary, at present Leonid Brezhnev. While Khrushchev was not a one-man dictator in the Stalin pattern, he was generally conceded, in the words of George Orwell, to have been "more equal" than the other members of the Presidium. This is probably true of Brezhnev as well.

Working under the supervision of the Secretariat is the Party bureaucracy, consisting of some 200,000 *apparatchiki,* or full-time paid Party officials. (The figure is based on information supplied by Moscow to foreign Communists, and may be too small; some Soviet defectors insist it should be larger.) This body of Party workers utilizes many part-time Party volunteers, both as sources of information and as a means of conveying the Party message. The bureaucrats' essential task is to see to it that Party orders are transmitted all the way down the line and to report on their observations of how Party and government agents are carrying out their assigned tasks.

RECRUITMENT OF PARTY MEMBERS

Anyone who has reached age 18 may be recruited for Party membership, provided he is recommended by three Party members who have been in good standing for at least three years and who have known the applicant professionally and socially for at least one year. Before full membership is granted, however, the applicant must pass through a one-year proba-tionary period, referred to as "candidacy." The principal recruiting ground for Party membership is the Young Communist League (*Kom-somol*). One becomes a member of the *Komsomol* after progressing through other organizations designed for younger age groups; the most promising youngsters, numbering close to 20 million, end up in the *Komsomol,* and from this elite organization are chosen most of the future members of the Party. As can readily be appreciated, the various youth organizations constitute a long and careful screening process.

STRUGGLES FOR POWER WITHIN THE PARTY

According to Communist theory, the Party is a monolithic organization and is therefore free from factional quarrels. In practice, however, all Communist movements have been beset with such conflicts. Because there are no democratic procedures for resolving them peacefully, they have been, in the main, resolved by force.

In the initial years of the new regime, there were those who believed that intra-party democracy (democratic centralism) could be a workable principle. At first a group calling themselves "Democratic Centralists" attempted to offer opposition to the course being followed by the Leninist Central Committee. Next another group, the "Workers' Opposition," sought to exercise a voice in Party affairs. Both these groups were silenced by Lenin, who had the Party Congress pass resolutions pro-hibiting activities contrary to the Party line—a prohibition extending even to top Party leaders who might have disagreed with Lenin and his close collaborators.

Although Lenin did not actually execute or imprison those colleagues who did disagree with him, he removed them from positions of responsibility and banished them to remote regions of the country. He thus paved the way for the harsher actions of his successor, Stalin, who did not hesitate to imprison and execute even on the merest suspicion. Stalin's purge of the Party reached all ranks. No one was spared. Countless members of the Politburo and the Central Committee were shot, often without any case being proved against them. Thousands of innocent comrades paid the supreme penalty, as no less a figure than Khrushchev has admitted. At one point even Stalin admitted that the purges had gone too far, but he blamed this on anti-Party elements who had allegedly infiltrated the Party.

It was easy for Stalin to order the liquidation of lesser Party figures. For those of higher rank, however, he employed different tactics. At first he aligned himself with one group, which carried the fight against certain deviationists (left and right) from the Party line; with these successfully removed, he aligned himself with another group, which worked against the first. Thereafter, Stalin even adopted as his own the program of the latter group. He was thus able to discredit and remove all of Lenin's one-time colleagues, in the meantime securing the appointment of people loyal only to him. As Secretary General of the Party, he managed to control the election of delegates to Party congresses, choosing candidates who would side with him in intra-Party conflicts. In the end he made himself the unquestioned dictator of the Party and therefore of the government.

The purging process continues, although under Khrushchev it was not the bloody affair it was under Stalin. Since Stalin's death, aside from the Stalinist head of the secret police, Lavrenti Beria, and a number of his alleged associates, no one reportedly has been tried and executed. Many Party leaders have, however, lost their posts or have been demoted; many have been criticized and have resigned. But there have been no reports of mass trials, confessions, and executions of the kind that occurred under Stalin. The purging process evidently has been tamed; Khrushchev's own ouster, for example, seems to have been achieved without bloodshed.

Political Institutions

THE DUALISM OF PARTY AND GOVERNMENT

Since, as we have seen, the Communist Party is the decision-making body in the Soviet Union, the governmental apparatus operates as an adjunct of the Party, carrying out its decisions. The result is a twin hierarchy of Party and government (see Figure 3). At all levels there are Party and government bureaucrats, with the latter consulting Party

Figure 3

Interlocking Pyramids

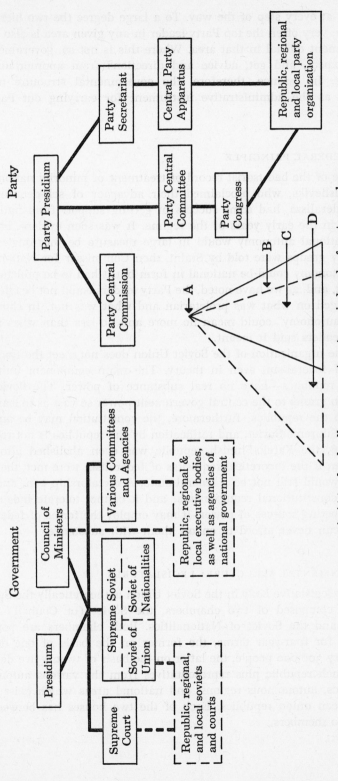

A At top levels all government posts are in hands of party members.
B Some party members do not hold any government posts.
C Most party members hold government posts.
D Many government posts held by nonparty members.

Key: ---- Government pyramid   —— Party pyramid

leaders at every step of the way. To a large degree the two hierarchies overlap; very often the top Party leader in any given area is also the top government official in that area. Where this is not so, government officials expect, and get, advice and directions from appropriate Party officials. In essence, therefore, the governmental structure may be viewed as the administrative instrument for carrying out Party decisions.

THE FEDERAL PRINCIPLE

Because of the bad tsarist record of treatment of minority nationalities, the Bolsheviks, who proclaimed their advocacy of self-determination and federalism, had some success in getting support from nationality groups in the early years of the regime. It was soon evident, however, that national autonomy would in large measure be meaningless. Nationality groups were told by Stalin, then Commissar for Nationalities, that autonomy could be national in form but it had to be proletarian in content, and, as we have noted, the Party leaders could not be effectively challenged on what was proletarian and what was not. In short, "national autonomy" could mean no more and no less than what the top Party leaders said it meant.

The organization of the Soviet Union does not meet the traditional tests of federalism, even in theory. The main component units—the fifteen republics—have no real substance of power. The Soviet constitution grants to the central government power so vast as to leave very little to the republics; furthermore, the constitution may be amended by the Supreme Soviet, and ratification by the republics is not required. In 1956, the Karelo-Finnish republic was even abolished altogether. But even if the theoretical requisites of federalism were met, the Soviet Union would still not be a federal state. A dictatorship can, and does, ignore constitutional requirements; and it cannot tolerate independent or competing sources of power. It may employ the forms of federalism, but it can never afford to endow them with substance.

GOVERNMENTAL STRUCTURE: LEGISLATURES

The top legislative body in the Soviet Union is theoretically the Supreme Soviet, composed of two chambers, the Soviet (or Council) of the Union and the Soviet of Nationalities. Both chambers are popularly elected for four-year terms, the former on the basis of one delegate for every 300,000 people, the latter on the basis of twenty-five delegates from each republic plus representatives from the various autonomous republics, autonomous regions, and national areas which exist within the fifteen union republics. Each of the two houses has between 600 and 700 members.

The Supreme Soviet is supposed to meet twice annually, although it has not always done so. Its sessions are brief, averaging no more than five or six days; many are joint sessions, taken up mostly with speeches from Party leaders, who also present proposals to be voted upon. Voting is perfunctory, and there are no opposing speeches, conflicting amendments, or proposals for new legislation. Under the circumstances, the Supreme Soviet cannot be viewed as a true legislative body; it is rather the epitome of a "rubber-stamp" legislature.

Each of the union republics has a unicameral body called the Soviet, which in theory is the republic's legislature. There are also soviets at the regional and local levels. All are part of the administrative apparatus, charged with carrying out decisions and policies determined at the center.

GOVERNMENTAL STRUCTURE: THE EXECUTIVE

The Supreme Soviet elects a presidium (not to be confused with the Party Presidium) which acts as a formal collegial executive. It is composed of a president, a secretary, fifteen vice-presidents (the presidents of the presidiums of the fifteen republics), and fifteen members. Several top Party leaders are always members. The presidium receives the credentials of diplomatic representatives, confers titles of honor, awards decorations, and performs other functions associated with a chief of state. At the same time, as a permanent nucleus of the Supreme Soviet, it is authorized to perform most of the functions of the parent body when the latter is not in session.

The Supreme Soviet also elects the Council of Ministers, the directing body of the huge bureaucratic machine. The size of this bureaucratic giant can only be appreciated if one bears in mind that in addition to the normal governmental bureaucracy in a large industrialized nation, there are millions of people who operate the vast and far-flung network of government-owned economic enterprises. Following the pattern of development of Soviet governmental forms, which have so often been modified as a result of trial and error, the Council of Ministers, which is comparable to the cabinet in Western governmental systems, has been reorganized many times. It has varied in size from sixty to fifteen members (the latter being its present size). The reduction is somewhat deceptive, however, because many former ministries were replaced with committees and some non-ministers have ministerial rank.

As might be expected, the Council of Ministers seeks to carry out Party decisions. Although technically responsible to the Supreme Soviet, the ministers are in reality responsible to the Party Presidium. No votes of confidence are ever taken in the Supreme Soviet, nor do its members propose motions of censure. Furthermore, several ministers are usually also members of the Party Presidium, and hence are responsible to no one but themselves.

THE JUDICIARY

According to Marxist theory, in any given society the legal system is the instrument of the dominant class. Be that as it may, the Soviet leaders have made it clear that their system of law and their courts are the instruments of the Party dictatorship. Soviet courts and judges are under no illusions on this point. It would be erroneous, therefore, to expect an independent judiciary in the Soviet Union, for the Soviet judiciary, like other governmental institutions, is but an arm of the administrative apparatus that seeks to implement Party decisions. The job of the courts is to preserve the regime and to facilitate the promotion of its programs, and conversely to strike down all those who would stand in the way.

Soviet law is code law, following in the Roman law tradition of the tsarist regime. Much has been added, however, because of the vast complexities of the Soviet system, particularly its rejection of the concept of private economic enterprise and the state's assumption of all responsibilities in the economic sphere; new categories of crimes (for example, "economic" crimes) have been added to the code as a result. But the system operates much more along the lines of a Roman law system than do the American and British systems.

The Soviet court system consists of local, intermediate, and supreme courts in each of the fifteen republics, and a supreme court of the USSR. The lowest or local court, called the people's court, is presided over by a judge and two lay assessors; it has original jurisdiction in less important civil cases and in minor criminal cases. The judge is supposed to have legal training and is popularly elected for a term of three years; the assessors are chosen for two-year terms by convocations of citizens at their place of residence or work (not at a regular ballot-box election). Decision is by majority vote; there are no juries.

The intermediate courts are based on the autonomous regions, areas, territories, and autonomous republics. They are presided over by five judges, elected by the soviets of the respective geographic unit for five-year terms. They also have panels of people's assessors, but these are employed only in cases of original jurisdiction. These courts hear appeals from the local people's courts and exercise original jurisdiction in more important civil and criminal cases.

The supreme court of each union republic has five judges and a panel of people's assessors, all elected by the supreme soviet of the republic for five-year terms. It has appellate jurisdiction, as well as original jurisdiction in civil and criminal cases of major importance; it also supervises the functions of the lower courts.

The Supreme Court of the USSR, elected by the Supreme Soviet for a term of five years, consists of a chairman, two deputy chairmen, and nine members. In addition, it has a panel of twenty assessors. Its functions are said to be purely appellate, although the presence of the assessors would seem to suggest that there may be cases in which the Supreme Court exercises original jurisdiction—perhaps in those cases it may wish to remove from the dockets of the supreme courts of the republics. In addition, the Constitution stipulates that the Supreme Court will supervise "the judicial activities of all judicial organs of the USSR and of the union republics," thus insuring a uniform, centralized and disciplined judiciary.

In addition to the regular courts, there are certain special courts which are not a part of the formal judicial hierarchy. The most widespread of these are the so-called comrades' courts, which are supervised by the local people's courts. They are to be found in such places as factories and apartment houses, and handle minor offenses, such as insults, petty theft, and small damage charges. They have the power to reprimand and to impose small fines. There are also military courts which deal with military offenders and violations of military regulations. Other special courts, now allegedly abolished, included transport and secret police courts.

In the late 1950s and the early 1960s, extra-judicial law enforcement was broadened with the creation of anti-parasite tribunals and a voluntary citizens' militia. The anti-parasite tribunals have the power to exile to the more remote regions of the nation individuals who evade socially useful work or who live on unearned income. These sentences may be for as long as five years of forced labor and possible confiscation of property not acquired by labor. The anti-parasite tribunals are not courts in the normal sense, but mass meetings of local citizens who convict by majority vote of a specified quorum.

The members of the voluntary citizens' militia, sometimes referred to as "public-order squads," are supposed to patrol the streets during the evening hours for the purpose of combatting drunkenness, rowdyism, and similar breaches of the peace. The members of these squads are recruited mainly from the Communist youth organization, and they operate under the guidance of Party organizations and the police.

The prosecutor-general is given "supreme advisory power to ensure the strict observance of the law by all ministries and institutions subordinated to them, as well as by officials and citizens of the USSR generally"—which suggests far broader powers than are usually associated with the office of prosecutor in the Anglo-Saxon world. The prosecutor-general is chosen by the Supreme Soviet for a seven-year term. He in turn appoints the prosecutors-general of the republics, regions, territories, and autonomous republics, who serve for five years. Prosecutors at the area, county, and city level are appointed for a like period by the prosecutors of the republics, subject to approval by the prosecutor-general of the USSR. In the performance of their duties, officials of the prosecutor-general's office are in no way subordinate to local organs of authority. There is some question, however, as to where the prosecutor general's authority may be infringed upon by the secret police.

Judicial Practices. Even Nikita Khrushchev has pointed out that many innocent persons have perished at the hands of Soviet justice. Although Khrushchev also claimed that judicial reforms have put an end to such instances of injustice, the conduct of Soviet legal proceedings embodies practices which to any Western observer must appear incompatible with the impartial administration of justice. First, the Soviets employ the inquisitorial approach, in which the judge proceeds on the presumption that the accused is guilty, so that the latter has little or no opportunity for meaningful defense. Such an approach, which compels the accused to take the witness stand, is not necessarily bad, and it is employed in all countries whose legal systems are derived from Roman law. But without a free press and a free legislature to act as guardians of justice, it may and does become a tool of tyranny. The accused may be browbeaten by the judge, and has no opportunity for effective protest against the judge's actions.

Second, there is no right or privilege of habeas corpus in the Soviet system. This permits long pretrial incarceration, people being held for months, sometimes even years, with no formal charges being brought against them. Closely related to the absence of habeas corpus, and in part made possible by its absence, are forced confessions. During long periods of detainment a prisoner can be put through all sorts of torture to extract a confession, often being led to realize that such treatment will end only if he agrees to confess. Moreover, there is no protection against double jeopardy: a person may be tried any number of times for the same offense. And milder sentences may be appealed in favor of stiffer ones.

Other judicial practices, now allegedly abolished, should also be noted. One involved the sentencing of persons to work camps, for varying periods of time, by administrative authorities (generally the secret police). The usual charge was that they were "socially dangerous," although there was no legal definition of such an offense. As we have seen above, however, the present anti-parasite tribunals exercise much the same type of function. Another practice was that of sentencing persons for acts not legally forbidden but analogous to forbidden acts (crime by analogy). Still another was that of holding members of a family responsible for acts of one of its members; such a charge was applied particularly to the families of soldiers who defected to the West.

In the light of such practices, the Soviet Constitution's guarantee of a public trial and defense counsel constituted a hollow mockery.

For many offenses, it was not necessary for the accused to be present at the trial, nor was it necessary for a defense attorney to represent him. Countless trials were held in secret and unpublicized. Consequently, even theoretical guarantees are something less than meaningful.

CIVIL RIGHTS

The Constitution's bill of rights is one of the principal bases of the Soviets' claim that theirs is a democratic constitution. But even in theory these rights are not guaranteed as they are in democratic countries. The article (125) dealing with these rights begins with the words, "In conformity with the interests of the working people, and in order to strengthen the socialist system . . ." Hence, the citizen is severely limited in advance as to the ends for which he may use the freedoms of speech and press. And the Communist Party is the sole judge of what is in the interests of the working people and what will strengthen the socialist system.

In a similar vein, Article 126 states: "In conformity with the interests of the working people, and in order to develop the organizational initiative and political activity of the masses of the people, citizens of the USSR are guaranteed the right to unite in public organizations. . . ." Among the public organizations mentioned are trade unions, youth associations, and other societies. The only political party mentioned is the Communist Party, which is said to constitute "the vanguard of the working people" and the "leading core of all organizations of the working people, both public and state." It seems evident, therefore, that the only type of organizational life that can exist in the Soviet Union, even in theory, is that which meets with the Party's wishes and desires.

Other provisions of the bill of rights are subject to similar limitations. There is freedom for anti-religious propaganda, but not for pro-religious teachings. There is the right to work, but no right to strike. And there are a number of enumerated duties, such as military service and the duty to abide by the Constitution, to observe the laws, and to maintain labor discipline. In sum, therefore, the Constitution not only specifies the purposes for which "rights" may be employed, but in addition insists that the furtherance of these purposes is among the primary duties of the citizen.

The System in Action

The Soviet system, as a totalitarian dictatorship, is concerned with two broad classes of domestic problems. The first concerns the question of how to harness the people to the dictatorship, that is, how to get them to do the things that the wielders of power desire. The second concerns the organizational setup and management of the far-flung Soviet economic apparatus. While these two problems are intimately related, it is more convenient to treat them separately, beginning with problems of organization and administration.

THE ADMINISTRATIVE STATE

Before the Revolution Lenin believed that administration could be a part-time affair. Anyone who knew the four rules of arithmetic, he said, could qualify as an administrator; and as the new society was built, the state would wither away. But, Soviet reality came to bear little or no resemblance to this blueprint. The bureaucracy, instead of withering away, has grown. It is difficult to estimate its size, for in one way or another nearly everyone works for the government. Of course the very size of the country would require a large bureaucracy under any political system; but how much larger an apparatus is required by a dictatorship that sets out to remake society in its entirety, and that believes that nothing should be permitted to happen by accident and that private enterprise is not to be tolerated. No wonder, therefore, that the Soviet system constitutes an administrative state *par excellence*.

The Soviet administrative apparatus is the instrument of the one-party state, with centralized control and direction. The Communist Party issues a constant stream of directives, often changing with changes in the Party line or simply as experience proves one solution to a political or administrative problem unworkable and dictates that another be tried. These latter directives indicate that the Party is engaged in a constant effort to check on the performance of the bureaucracy.

The bureaucracy is recruited under the Party's watchful eye. There is a civil service commission, but its task is not recruitment; rather it is concerned with classification of personnel and with promoting efficiency and greater effort on the part of employees. Recruitment is more and more carried out on the basis of specifications put forth by individual ministries, which in many instances dictate the curriculum of institutions from which employees are to be recruited. At higher rungs of the administrative ladder, however, the Party takes an increasing interest in the assignment of personnel. No important posts are filled without the knowledge and consent of the Party Secretariat, perhaps including the first secretary himself.

The bureaucracy, as we have seen, works under the direction of the Council of Ministers. In the Council there are two types of ministries, all-union and union-republic. The former are vertically organized and operate through their own employees down to the lowest level; the latter are organized vertically and horizontally, but operate in the main through corresponding ministries in each one of the republics.[2] As has been noted, the number of ministries represented in the Council has varied; today there are about fifteen, although the general areas of a number of former ministries are now under the supervision of committees, with chairmen of ministerial rank. The deputy members of the State Planning Commission now also have ministerial rank.

But the present organization, which in general dates from 1957, does not mean that the administrative apparatus is withering away. The 105 regional economic councils which were then set up to supervise the activities of their respective regions in 1962 were reduced to seventeen. Supervision and direction were still to come from the center, though regional authorities exercised more discretion in the way they implemented Moscow's directives. This resulted in some particularism, with local interests being emphasized at the expense of national; to remedy this situation, penalties were provided to punish regions which failed to deliver needed goods to other regions. By late 1965, Khrushchev's successors had abolished the regional councils. Thus, the trial-and-error principle still operates.

The Soviet economy is operated on the basis of plans. After they seized power in 1917, the Bolsheviks sought to have the government take over the entire economy. The result was chaos, so, in 1921, Lenin launched the "New Economic Policy" (NEP). During the NEP period (1921–1928) many of the capitalist managers were called back, and peasants were allowed to sell their produce at market prices. Economic recovery ensued, but also the emergence of some relatively well-to-do persons; therefore, in order to combat the reappearance of "capitalistic" features in the economy, the regime in 1928 launched a series of Five Year Plans, signifying its intent to establish rigid control in industry and agriculture. The general principle of the Five Year Plan has continued to be used; recently, for example, Khrushchev launched a Seven Year Plan, one aim of which was to catch up to and surpass the United States economically. And his successors seem to be devising new plans, unannounced at this writing.

The basic goals of the plans are determined by the top Party leaders; the means of achieving them are left to the State Planning Commission (*Gosplan*), which supervises a considerable bureaucratic apparatus. Ministers, statisticians, Party secretaries, factory managers, engineers, technicians, and other experts are consulted with a view to producing plans that call for maximum effort all along the line as well as the best possible utilization of resources. Historically, the State Planning Commission had also exercised a great deal of authority in seeing to it that the plans were implemented. In late 1962, however, its functions were confined largely to long-range planning and co-

[2] The term "vertical" is employed here to suggest a single, unified hierarchical organization. The term "horizontal" is employed to indicate two levels of organization, one national and the other republic. The internal organization of the latter, however, is hierarchical.

ordination of annual economic plans. At the same time a new agency, the Council on National Economy, was created and given extensive authority to implement plans and to make prompt decisions on resource reallocation and other problems of day-to-day management.

The management of economic enterprises is characterized by two primary principles: the single-manager concept and capitalist patterns of reward. In the early years of the Soviet regime there was an attempt to run industries through trade-union committees, but it was largely unsuccessful, and by the 1930s, the single-manager idea had won firm acceptance. Just at this point, however, the purges consumed many of the managers and created a fear of assuming managerial responsibility; virtually every decision was referred upward, so that Moscow found itself deciding minute details. In the past decade, however, the freedom to manage has largely been restored, although primary decisions are still taken in Moscow. Managers are now less afraid to use their own discretion and imagination in implementing decisions.

Marx had said in the *Manifesto* that in a Communist society each person would be expected to contribute according to his ability and would in turn be rewarded according to his need. Lenin, in the initial years of the Soviet regime, talked of paying everyone workingmen's wages. Stalin and other Soviet leaders soon learned, however, that the only way to increase production significantly was to introduce capitalist patterns of reward. Piece rates were introduced, with special bonuses to those who exceeded the established norms, and managers were accorded bonuses for over-fulfillment of planned output. Engineering and technical personnel were rewarded at rates considerably above those of the average worker. The general result has been a wide disparity of reward, but there is no evidence of the development of a market economy, although some experimentation with certain market mechanisms (for example, interest) may be indicative of other changes to come.

In Soviet agriculture the dominant theme is collectivism. Although the Bolshevik slogan at the time of the Revolution was "all land to the peasants," they did not intend to foster private ownership of land. Following the NEP period, and in line with the Five Year Plans, the regime inaugurated collective farming. Organizationally, it took two forms: collective farms and state farms. In the latter, the government was the owner and manager; farmers were ordinary wage-earners. In the former, the members of the collective held the land in common, not owning it, but having its use in perpetuity. Management was by a board, theoretically elected by an assembly of all the members of the collective, which had to conform to basic governmental rules concerning the operation of collective farms in general.

Members of collective farms are rewarded according to their work, that is, according to the number of work-days they accumulate in a year. There is a daily norm for various types of work, and the farmer who surpasses the norm accumulates more work-days—the agricultural equivalent of piece rates in industry. In addition, members of collective farms are permitted small garden plots, whose produce is their own, and also, possibly, a cow and a few chickens. Because so many farmers would spend a disproportionate share of their efforts on the private plots, the government has from time to time initiated measures to discourage them, hence progressively diminishing the area of private initiative in agriculture. To ease shortages, however, Khrushchev's successors were forced to make additional concessions to the peasants.

While the bulk of the land is in collective farms, events of the past few years seem to indicate that the regime was favoring state farms. For example, all of the area opened up in the 1950s, the so-called "Virgin Lands," was organized into state farms. But Khrushchev's successors have indicated that the collective farms will be preserved for some time to come.

In summary, then, it can be said that the Soviet administrative machine is large, and growing. The very vastness of this machine, to say nothing of the many different efforts of the Party to check on its performance, has resulted in confusion concerning responsibility. Too many people have their fingers in the administrative pie at too many places, making it difficult for even the Party to assess responsibility. But someone must take the blame when things go wrong; consequently, many administrators have, in self-defense, entered into so-called "protective alliances" to help and protect each other. Evidence of bungling and inefficiency, together with Party meddling, is ample—none of which makes for popular trust in the bureaucracy.

HARNESSING THE MASSES: REPRESSION

It was obvious from the beginnings of the new regime that opposition would not be tolerated. To the Soviet authorities, whoever was not for them was against them, and real and imagined opponents were to feel the brutal repression of a systematic police regime. This repression took three primary forms: liquidation (summary execution), imprisonment, and surveillance by the secret police. All three came under the jurisdiction of the CHEKA, the secret police organization whose formal name was the Extraordinary Commission for Combating Counter-revolution, Espionage, and Dereliction of Duty.

Those considered most dangerous to the Bolsheviks—chiefly former government officials and church and business leaders—were soon liquidated, many without the benefit of even a perfunctory trial. The blood bath was extensive, but no one, not even the Communists, knows how many perished. The Bolsheviks took Lenin at his word that they should not be squeamish about spilling blood. In city after city, persons who had been prominent as judges, teachers, church officials, or administrators felt the terror.

Those who were considered slightly less dangerous, who were suspected of opposition but not marked for immediate liquidation, were thrown into prison. Some were put on trial and others simply sat in jail, uncharged. Some were sent off to labor camps and forgotten; many simply vanished without a trace. Often records were not kept, or were imperfectly kept. Those who were accidentally caught in the web suffered the same fate as those intentionally removed from circulation, for no one in authority really bothered or cared. Some people were fortunate enough to be released after a brief span of time, but this was due more to fortuitous circumstances than to any established judicial procedures.

In a third category were those who were suspect but not considered dangerous enough to warrant either liquidation or imprisonment. Literally millions in this category were subjected to secret police surveillance and the ever-present eye of the informer. Secret police tactics varied. In some cases there were brief periods of incarceration and questioning, accompanied perhaps by police brutality; in others, people were simply asked to report to a secret police office, where they were questioned and released. Often the invitation was repeated, with the victim not knowing when it might mean a more permanent stay.

Secret police surveillance was a deliberate tactic, designed to intimidate all those who might think, however remotely, of working against the regime. The network of police informers, reaching into every office, apartment house, and group gathering, was designed to reach every possible dissident element. No one knew who the informers were, but all knew they existed. Often informer was pitted against informer as a means of cross-checking. Sometimes people were pressed into informing, while at other times they volunteered their services, perhaps in the hope that such voluntary activity might stand them in good stead in less fortunate circumstances.

The secret police and the informers are still very much a part of Soviet society, but they are less openly in evidence than during Stalin's time. More important, the powers of the secret police have been curbed, and they are feared less. The Khrushchev decade (1953–1964) witnessed a declining number of secret police repressions, a change which has led most experts on the Soviet Union to conclude that no present or future Soviet ruler could resort to the type of brutal rule so characteristic of the Stalin period.

HARNESSING THE MASSES: PERSUASION

In their efforts to get the people to do the regime's bidding, Communist leaders have supplemented their techniques of force and fear with a massive attempt at persuasion. This persuasion takes several forms. First, the regime seeks to mobilize public opinion through ownership and control of the public opinion media. The extent of this control cannot be appreciated unless one realizes that in the Soviet Union there are no privately owned newspapers or publishing houses, no privately owned radio or television stations or privately produced programs, no privately owned theaters or privately produced plays, and no privately owned movie houses or privately made motion pictures. In the public opinion media field, the Communists own and control everything.

In order to reach and involve every important segment of society, the Party has created appropriate propaganda instruments, such as the *Literary Gazette*, a newspaper specifically created for writers and artists. A writer therefore cannot plead that he does not want to get into political polemics in the political organs of opinion, for the Party has been particularly solicitous: it has created a special outlet just for him. How could he not show his gratitude by using it to extol the privilege of being a writer in a Communist paradise? Similarly, a university professor cannot refuse to praise the virtues of science in a Communist society, because the Party has created another special newspaper just for him. And if he should be busy, the Party will find someone to write a piece for him.

Everyone who contributes to the propaganda output in the Soviet Union is provided with ample guidance by the agitation and propaganda section (*Agitprop*) of the Party's Central Committee. *Agitprop* furnishes themes which should be stressed, slogans that need to be utilized, problems that need to be emphasized; and in many instances it provides texts of feature pieces or editorials. Those in the radio-television and newspaper fields receive a steady flow of materials to be utilized. Almost nothing is left to chance or to individual choice.

In addition to mobilizing and monopolizing the instruments of pubic opinion, the regime pursues its persuasion campaign through the so-called mass organizations. On a number of occasions these organizations have been described by Soviet leaders as "transmission belts" by means of which the Party machine operates. Here the people are harnessed in a variety of ways to work for the regime's goals and programs. The most widespread of the mass organizations are the soviets. As local administrative bodies the soviets, guided by a core of faithful Communists, mobilize countless non-Communists to help in the pursuit of Communist objectives. Soviet trade unions operate similarly. Rather than performing the tasks usually associated with labor unions, they are more concerned with promoting the regime's economic or other goals; in addition, they administer a large part of the social security program.

Many other organizations serve similar functions. The Writers' Union, for example, is given the task of keeping writers in line. As the Party's outpost among this important group, the Writers' Union sees to it that literary output conforms to what the Party currently wants in literature. The same can be said for the association of artists.

Of special importance are the youth organizations. In some ways the regime's major effort is concentrated on youth, because it realizes that unless youth is won over the outlook for communism will not be bright. Young children are organized into the Octobrists, where their first indoctrination begins. Next, they become Pioneers, and are subjected to more subtle propaganda about Soviet leaders, the Soviet Union, and the outside world. The more promising among the Pioneers are selected for membership in the Young Communist League (*Komsomol*), which then becomes the principal recruiting ground for new Party members. At every step of the way, through special newspapers, lectures, movies, and other means, the Party seeks to inculcate the "right" attitude among the young, to steer them toward the communist way of life.

Third, the regime also pursues its persuasion campaign by regimenting the schools. The Western tradition of free inquiry is totally foreign to the Soviet educational system. Everything must fit into the concepts of the one and only true "science," the science of Marxism-Leninism. Moreover, there is great stress on science and technology, and little opportunity for liberal learning. Everything in education must point to specific goals and achievements, laid down by the Party and supervised and directed by the ministries of education in each of the republics. Teaching materials and the teachers themselves are carefully screened by the ever-watchful Party. All this is understandable, for the Party views the schools as simply another instrument in the ultimate harnessing of the masses to do the regime's bidding.

Finally, the Party seeks to neutralize or destroy all competing influences. The most important of these are religion and the home. In its campaign of repression, the Party destroyed many churches or turned them to other uses, and countless clergymen were liquidated or imprisoned. At the same time, the Party embarked on a systematic campaign, through ridicule, the establishment of "atheistic" museums, and the like, to minimize the effect of religious teachings. Subsequently, while continuing to heap scorn and ridicule on believers, the regime set about guiding and controlling the remaining clergy, in an effort to render them less harmful. And although the regime is in its fifth decade, there has been little letup in its anti-religious campaign.

Similarly, the regime has conducted a systematic campaign to minimize the influence of the home. Initially, it encouraged children to inform on their parents; now it seeks to combat home influence chiefly by taking children out of the home as much as possible and as early as possible. From the outset women were encouraged to work when the government provided places for mothers to leave their young ones during the day. More recently, the regime has inaugurated week-care centers, where children may be left on Monday morning and picked up Friday night or Saturday morning. In this way, the Party can begin to shape the young generation at an early age, and with less competition from the home. All of this is in addition to the children's and youth organizations, to which reference has already been made. In short, the regime overlooks no opportunity in its efforts to produce the "new communist man."

SUGGESTIONS FOR ADDITIONAL READING

ARMSTRONG, JOHN A., *The Politics of Totalitarianism: The Communist Party of the Soviet Union from 1934 to the Present* (New York: Random House, 1961).

BAUER, RAYMOND A., et al., *How the Soviet System Works* (Cambridge: Harvard University Press, 1956).

BRZEZINSKI, ZBIGNIEW K., *Ideology and Power in Soviet Politics* (New York: Frederick A. Praeger, 1962).

DJILAS, MILOVAN, *The New Class: An Analysis of the Communist System* (New York: Frederick A. Praeger, 1957).

FAINSOD, MERLE, *How Russia Is Ruled*, rev. ed. (Cambridge: Harvard University Press, 1963).

HUNT, ROBERT N. CAREW, *The Theory and Practice of Communism* (New York: The Macmillan Co., 1958).

MC CLOSKY, HERBERT, and JOHN E. TURNER, *The Soviet Dictatorship* (New York: McGraw-Hill, Inc., 1960).

MEYER, ALFRED G., *The Soviet Political System: An Interpretation* (New York: Random House, 1965).

MOORE, BARRINGTON, JR., *Soviet Politics: The Dilemma of Power* (Cambridge: Harvard University Press, 1950).

SCHAPIRO, LEONARD, *The Communist Party of the Soviet Union* (New York: Random House, 1960).

ULAM, ADAM B., *The New Face of Soviet Totalitarianism* (Cambridge: Harvard University Press, 1963).

WALSH, WARREN B., *Russia and the Soviet Union, A Modern History* (Ann Arbor: University of Michigan Press, 1958).

WOLFE, BERTRAM D., *Three Who Made a Revolution*, rev. ed. (Boston: Beacon Press, 1955).

Chapter 7

THE POLITICS
OF DEVELOPING NATIONS

Students of comparative government have traditionally concerned themselves with the Western world alone, and above all with such major European nations as those treated in the preceding chapters. One reason for this limited focus is that the study of politics has, in modern times, been a peculiarly Western discipline. The major concepts available for examining political problems have been Western concepts, developed by Western thinkers in the specific context of Western civilization. The seeming irrelevance of these concepts to non-Western areas led many observers to conclude they had little to observe or learn by studying such strange societies.

Another important reason for the bias of students of comparative government can be found in the course of world history. Until the thirteenth century, the "known world," so far as Europeans were concerned, was little more than Europe itself. As this known world began to expand through travel and exploration, especially after the end of the fourteenth century, European politics tended to become world politics. Through their crushing superiority in military technology, based in turn on a more advanced economy, European peoples were able to bring large areas of Asia, Africa, the Middle East, and America under their political control and into *their* international state system. And although many non-European nations did manage to maintain their independence throughout the modern period, even they could not escape the pervasive influence of the dominant Western powers. Thus it was natural for political observers to concentrate on Europe and North America, where the important decisions affecting the fate of the world were made. Nor is it surprising that, until recently, scant attention was paid to other regions except by those interested in colonial administration.

But the international position of Europe began to weaken in the period following World War I. Japan blazed a new path by rapidly assimilating European technology and establishing hegemony over part of Asia. Throughout the areas under the political control or tutelage of European powers, economic and social developments took place which had the long-range effect of undermining the whole colonial structure. By building schools, roads, hospitals and factories in their colonies, Europeans were facilitating the transition to modern economies in these areas and also arousing the political consciousness of the masses.

During World War II colonialism received a staggering blow. Japanese armies defeated the Americans in the Philippines, the British in Malaya and Burma, the Dutch in Indonesia, and, later, the French in Indochina. The myth of Western invincibility was shattered. In order to secure the loyalty of India in the face of Japanese preparations for an invasion, the British promised her independence. And once Indian independence was conceded, the other colonial powers were hard put to withhold similar pledges. After the Axis defeat the chief colonial powers were in any case so exhausted by the war that they were incapable of reimposing their rule in colonies overrun by the Japanese. The native populations of Asia demonstrated an ability and willingness to resort to guerrilla warfare rather than permit their former European rulers to return. Furthermore, the Western European countries were no longer the dominant powers of the world after 1945. Power had shifted to the United States and Soviet Russia, both of which courted the support of former colonial peoples. Thus the European nations were not only physically unable to regain control over other continents, but were also prevented from doing so by the new world powers.

The achievement of independence by peoples who had once been under the domination of European states is one of the most significant historical developments of our time, comparable in importance to the French Revolution, the industrialization of Europe and North America, the extension of European influence in the world, and the Communist seizure of power in Russia. All these events transformed the social, cultural, and political environment, and were reflected in intellectual movements as well. The resurgence of the formerly subjugated peoples of Asia and Africa has likewise created a new dimension in world affairs and calls for a new focus of interest in the study of comparative politics. The extension of inquiry into Asia, Africa, and Latin America has drastically affected the whole field of political science. Traditional questions and problems in comparative politics can now seem irrelevant or trivial. True, a comparison of British and American institutions is of some utility because the two countries have roughly the same kind of culture. But a comparison of institutions in Great Britain and Ghana can be misleading. It is more important to examine such matters as the extent of literacy and urbanization, the level of economic and technological development, educational opportunities, class differences, the state of mass communications, and the degree of national unity. The fact that 75 per cent of the people of Ghana are illiterate and that only 3.5 per cent live in cities with more than 100,000 inhabitants is perhaps more important than the adoption of certain British political practices.

Traditional and Modern Societies

Are there any significant differences between the "Western" and the "non-Western" political processes? As far as institutional arrangements are concerned, it is difficult to identify important differences, for all of the leading Western systems have been imitated by one or another of the new nations. Examples may be found of presidential government, parliamentary government, federalism, multi-party systems, charismatic leadership, code law and common law—and so on endlessly—in Asia, Africa, the Middle East, and Latin America, as well as in Europe and North America.

It is obvious, however, that such states as Ghana, Nigeria, India, Indonesia, and Ecuador—to pick a few at random—share certain common characteristics in contrast to those shared by Great Britain, France, Germany, the Soviet Union, and the United States. In the first group of nations the population is largely illiterate; life expectancy is low; per capita income is abysmally low; the mass of the people lives in villages; religion or magic usually governs daily existence; and the principal occupation is subsistence agriculture. In the second group virtually the entire population is literate; life expectancy is high; per capita income is relatively high; a significant percentage of the population resides in urban centers; and the values of science and technology underpin the industrial sector of the economy. And these general conditions prevail quite apart from the institutional differences that may exist among the nations of the two groups.

For analytic purposes it may be useful to distinguish between two "ideal types" or models of societies: the *traditional* and the *modern*. Ghana, Nigeria, India, Indonesia, and Ecuador, for example, tend to be more traditional in every way (economic, social, cultural) than Britain, France, Germany, the Soviet Union, and the United States. The distinction does not imply any judgment of inferiority or superiority regarding individuals or cultures. A traditional society may include a large number of highly educated individuals whose level of culture and social grace is higher than that of the mass of inhabitants in any modern society. Furthermore, these terms, as we will use them, refer only to abstract "ideal types" and *not* to any actual society. The United States, for example, is a predominantly "modern" society, but there are many "traditionally" oriented groups in its population.

The distinction suggested here is a familiar one in social science literature. Similar definitions have been put forth by such eminent theoreticians as Sir Henry Maine, Ferdinand Tonniës, and especially Max Weber. Essential to all these classifications is a contrast between the simple and the complex, status and contract, immemorial custom and rationality. Thus, Sir Henry Maine compared societies where rights and obligations are defined by the individual's status or membership in a group as opposed to those where individuals voluntarily join large organizations and assume contractual obligations. Along the same lines, Max Weber distinguished three types of claims to legitimacy: *traditional* (belief in the sanctity of traditions and of those exercising authority under them); *charismatic* (devotion to an individual endowed with exceptional personal qualities); and *rational* (belief in legality and obedience to institutions rather than to persons). These are the types of beliefs that are established and cultivated in order to secure acceptance of and obedience to a system of authority. From Weber's scheme may be drawn the implication that the three types correspond to stages of historical development from simple to more complex societies. Usually a people will break out of its traditional or primitive condition under the leadership of a charismatic chief, whose power, as the society becomes more advanced, is devolved upon rational institutions.

THE "IDEAL TYPE" OF TRADITIONAL SOCIETY

In both traditional and modern societies the individual is a member of groups and associations, but there are marked differences in their nature and importance. In a traditional society the economy is agricultural and more or less self-sufficient. Virtually the entire population is engaged in agriculture, hunting, or fishing in order to provide the society's sustenance. There is no knowledge of technology or science, no accumulation of food reserves, little cultural or artistic activity. The dominant social organization is the family and the family type group—*primary* organizations whose members are in a face-to-face relationship. An individual's status in society is determined by his family's status. He is fed, educated, and nurtured by his family, and usually finds his life work within the family.

Family values permeate the whole society, which prizes such qualities as devotion, respect, courage, and reverence. Personal relations are influenced greatly by irrational beliefs in witchcraft, taboos, and the like. Custom regulates the actions of the population in minute detail. Men live close to nature, even as part of nature. They see their lives inextricably bound up with the stars, the seasons, or external events over which they have no control.

Political organizations tend to be an extension of the family. Chiefs, elders, and kings are obeyed in the same way and for the same reasons as fathers; legitimacy of the leaders, like parental authority, derives from a superhuman or divine source and is enshrined in custom and tradition. The governing class in traditional societies is sharply set off from the rest of the population, its position buttressed by myths of divinity and sacredness. "Politics" is the continual rivalry of families and clans for economic and military domination. As the economy develops, the dominant class may intensify its exploitation of the rest of the population; it is characteristic for government in traditional societies to be viewed as a coercive device for the exploitation of the laboring peasantry. (A distinction is frequently drawn in popular literature and ballads between the beloved monarch and the hated tax collectors.) Because it is exceedingly difficult for a traditional society to rule large areas from any one central point, local rule is usually vested by the paramount chief in some loyal supporters or clans. Relationships between regions or areas are therefore often feudal, dependent on the degree of personal devotion inspired by the ruling families. Alternatively, as in traditional China or ancient Egypt, a disciplined bureaucracy and army developed as instruments by which central power was extended.

Examples of societies exhibiting "traditional" characteristics in greater or lesser degree may be found at present throughout Asia, the Middle East, Africa, and Latin America. Even in more economically advanced nations, there are pockets of traditionally oriented people: the American Indians, for example, and the Sicilian peasantry. In Africa anthropologists have distinguished between two main types of traditional social organization, the pastoral and the agricultural. Pastoral societies predominate in eastern, central, and southern Africa; agricultural societies, in west Africa. In pastoral societies status is measured by the number of animals owned. The tribes live entirely off the meat, milk, and labor of their animals and tend to be self-sufficient; hence there is little economic exchange, and there are no large cities. Typical of the pastoral peoples are the Masai, numbering about 200,000, who live on the plains of Kenya. They own over 4 million cows, sheep, and goats.

The agricultural societies of west Africa are characterized by settled populations that produce enough for subsistence, and sometimes a surplus. There is some specialization of labor and exchange of produce. Market places and towns have come into existence. Extensive empires were created in the past, and were maintained for long periods. The Ashanti of Ghana are a typical agricultural people. Their culture is based on the ownership and cultivation of land. Property rights and political rule are determined by a complex system of matrimonial bonds. The chiefs are named by a Queen Mother, although in fact the choice is made beforehand by tribal elders. All chiefs occupy a throne (or stool) in which is said to reside the spirit of the ancestors. Reverence for ancestors is a fundamental myth, serving to buttress the rule of those in authority.

THE "IDEAL TYPE" OF MODERN SOCIETY

The contrast between traditional and modern societies is complete in every respect. In the "model" modern society, the individual gains his livelihood in a factory, office, or enterprise. The family performs only a biological function and tends to take on the character of a specialized association, that is, it is no longer the principal circle within which the individual spends his time. In modern societies there is a proliferation of *secondary organizations*—large, specialized, and impersonal associations like business corporations, labor unions, recreational groups, political parties, churches, and universities. Members of these organizations need not be in a face-to-face relationship, and are rarely in a position to know all their fellow members.

Most of the functions of the traditional family are taken over by the new associations (education by the schools, charity by the state or church, the provision of a livelihood by the business firm, exchange of produce by the banking system, and so on). The state begins to resemble a secondary organization rather than a family. It becomes large, complex, impersonal, and intendedly rational in organization. The civil service recruits able men from all strata of society on the basis of competitive examinations, replacing, with a system of fixed tenure, grade classifications, and specified increments, the former traditional practice of nepotism.

In the realm of values and thought-patterns, the old preoccupation with magic, astrology, and religion yields to science and reason. Religious worship may continue, but it no longer dominates all social activity; men investigate the mysteries of life and the universe, rather than adjust to them. Political legitimacy derives not from divine right but from a more rational concept of popular sovereignty and man-made legality.

POLITICS IN MODERN AND TRADITIONAL SOCIETIES

Let us re-emphasize that the foregoing descriptions are of "ideal types," not of any actual societies. The utility of such concepts is not that they describe accurately any existing society, for they do not, but rather that they suggest relationships betwen economic, social, and political structures which might otherwise escape attention. To return to an example already cited, the newly independent nation of Ghana has a political system modeled after that of Great Britain. But comparison of the relative positions of these two nations on a scale listing present-day societies with the most traditional at one end and the most modern at the other would immediately reveal fundamental differences. The immense majority of the people of Ghana still live in tribal organizations, which are in turn based on mystery and immemorial custom. A small, educated elite is completely set off from these masses and is attempting to lead them out of their traditional way of life. The people of Great Britain, on the other hand, are for the most part literate, rationally or scientifically oriented in many of their activities (although not all), and look upon the government as an agency responsible to them and required to serve their interests. Political parties, bureaucracy, public opinion, and economic activity in Britain tend to reflect a modern, rational outlook, whereas in Ghana they frequently mirror the values of the traditional native culture.

All political systems, whether in traditional or modern societies, perform certain essential functions. Claims are put forward by individuals and groups; in various ways they are channeled through interest organizations or political parties, reconciled within some kind of political structure, and eventually decisions are made. But the nature of the claims, groups, parties, and political structures is quite different in traditional and modern societies. In a modern society, there is a highly developed system of specialized groups, all of which make demands upon the government and compete with each other for political power. In traditional societies, the family is a fairly sufficient economic unit, and politics is mainly the concern of rival clans. Political institutions resemble the social and economic structure in that they are relatively unspecialized and highly personalized.

Perhaps the crucial difference between traditional and modern societies is that all of the latter have developed an *industrial technology*. Rationalization of political authority, development of secondary organizations, and secularization of the culture go hand in hand with industrialization. The major nations of Europe and North America moved into the modern era in the course of the eighteenth and nineteenth centuries as a consequence of the French Revolution and industrialization. Essentially, the rest of the world is now following suit, at a very unequal pace. Most of the nations of the "non-Western" world are no longer "traditional," but they are not yet "modern." They may be considered to be *in transition*. A process of modernization has begun, large cities are springing up, but many elements of the traditional culture persist and give a peculiar flavor to the political process.

Transitional societies are mixed political cultures and systems, containing both modern and traditional characteristics. The extent of intermingling varies enormously from country to country. In some nations the colonial power made a deep impression, leaving behind, after independence, a political structure similar to its own. Sometimes the native elite accepts such institutions and sincerely tries to make them work; more frequently, they are modified significantly in practice; and occasionally, as in Guinea or Indonesia, the entire heritage, except for its technological component, of the colonial power is repudiated. It may also happen that traditional leaders react violently against the whole process of modernization and prevent the society from abandoning its historical or religious myths. There is no steady, ineluctable progression from the old to the new.

The Transitional Process

Within the general category of "traditional" societies there have been an enormous variety of types, ranging from the subsistence agricultural and pastoral societies of Africa to the ancient Egyptian military state, the land empires of Asia Minor and China, the island civilization of the Aegean, ancient Greece and Rome, and the feudal states of Europe. Many of these societies produced remarkably high cultures, including elaborate political structures and efficient administrative systems. Accumulation of surpluses and realization of profits from trade led to the creation of merchant classes, the growth of cities, and the flourishing of the arts. But these societies were not able to sustain regular increases in economic growth through the application of technology. They are thus fundamentally set apart from the societies which came into existence in Europe and North America after the industrial and technological breakthrough of the nineteenth century.

Industrialization in Europe and America was a slow process to which many factors contributed. From the early seventeenth century men were disposed toward the values of thrift and hard work by changes in religious doctrine; a reservoir of manpower was created by the displacement of peasants from the land; a number of brilliant inventors turned their attention to problems of technology; and capital accumulated from commercial ventures was available for investment purposes. Industrialization took place gradually, in response to many pressures.

An immediate consequence of industrialization was to permit or accelerate the extension of European influence over other areas of the world. As has been pointed out, however, one of its long-range effects has been to disrupt the traditional non-Western societies, to arouse the political consciousness of their peoples, and to stimulate a movement toward modernization and independence from European influences. To govern their colonies effectively, the ruling powers created transportation and communication facilities which helped unify the masses. They sponsored education that brought the natives (or at least a native elite) into contact with the modern world. But at the same time a feeling of nationalism was aroused by the mere presence of foreign rulers. Native elites and native masses were united by the desire to end the relationship of inferiority between themselves and the Europeans. The powerful forces thus released pressed against and finally shattered the traditional social structure. The very victory of European arms contributed to the process of undermining established authority, since it demonstrated that the traditional native leaders were unable to maintain the integrity of the nation and its culture.

Even in the absence of a colonial relationship, however, knowledge of the contrast between modern and traditional ways of life has become widespread as a result of travel, education, radio, and motion pictures. Children of middle-class and merchant families have been sent abroad to study. They acquired skills which could not be fully employed in the traditional society of their homelands, and they thus constituted a reservoir of potential revolutionary leaders. Doctrines of egalitarianism also permeated the masses, making them receptive to revolutionary ideas. The convergence of these pressures—the reaction to foreign rule, the example of more advanced nations, the creation of a revolutionary elite, the masses' dissatisfaction—has seriously undermined the social, economic, and political structures of the traditional societies. Throughout the world, these societies have gone through either an evolution or a revolution that has pushed them along the road to modernization—that is, they have entered upon the transitional process.

The political development of all nations has followed this pattern. Britain, France, Germany, Russia, and even the United States were all traditional societies at one time. It must be stressed, however, that the differences among traditional societies may be as important as the fact that they are traditional. America during the colonial period and the tsarist regime in Russia were both "pre-industrial" societies, but they produced altogether different political attitudes. Traditional society everywhere in Europe, including Russia, had disappeared or was breaking up before the twentieth century. But there were important variations in the way in which the new social classes generated by industrialization were integrated into the existing political system. The middle and working classes were more easily absorbed in Britain and the United States than in France, Germany, and Russia. And industrial economies were successfully created under sharply different political regimes—fascism and communism no less than parliamentary democracy are "models" of modernity.

There is thus no clearly marked path of political development for the nations now emerging into the modern world. In many cases the traditional leaders maintain their sovereign control, and reform is introduced piecemeal, if at all; examples are Ethiopia, Jordan, Saudi Arabia, Iran, and Cambodia. In other countries the elite group is committed to the goal of modernization but wishes to preserve the basic values of traditional culture as well. Most of the newly independent nations are in this category, and all are experiencing difficulty in mobilizing mass support and carrying out extensive reforms. The pace of modernization varies greatly from country to country.

In our discussions of Britain, France, Germany, the Soviet Union, and the United States, we gave particular attention to constitutional patterns, political parties, and institutions. It would be less rewarding to place the same kind of emphasis upon constitutions and parties in an analysis of traditional or transitional societies. Indeed, one of the healthy trends in comparative politics resulting from inclusion of the developing nations in the discipline is a renewed emphasis on the interdependence of political, economic, and social factors.

The Politics of a Developing Nation: A Case Study of India

We shall now turn to a case study of India, the most populous and probably the most important of the developing nations in the non-Communist world. In terms of the typological scheme set forth above, we shall consider India as a traditional society (before the arrival of the British), a transitional society (under British rule), and a modernizing society (since independence). All developing nations can be viewed in terms of these analytic categories, and the student is urged to use them in his own analysis of an Asian or African country. It would even be useful to re-examine in this way the historical experience of Western Europe and North America.

TRADITIONAL SOCIETY IN INDIA

When the British first extended their influence and power over India in the seventeenth century, they found a vast, sprawling congeries of peoples whose historical unity went back five millennia. Recent archaeological discoveries indicate that great cities developed in the Indus Valley from 4000 to 2500 B.C., with a level of civilization equal to or exceeding that of Egypt, Mesopotamia, and China during the same era. Some of the elements of Indus culture somehow managed to survive the catastrophe which brought about the destruction of this civilization, and later reappeared in Hinduism. Beginning at about 1500 B.C., the northern and central plains of India were invaded by waves of nomadic Indo-Aryans. The light-skinned Aryans gradually pushed the native Dravidian people, generally dark-skinned, further and further south. A fusion of culture took place, out of which emerged the Hindu way of life. It was during this time that the caste system developed, probably in order to maintain an appropriate distance between Aryan invaders and the native inhabitants. Our knowledge of this period comes largely from the epic literature of the ancient Vedas (religious hymns handed down by word of mouth) and the later Gita (an epic poem glorifying war). The early Hindu society resulting from the Aryan-Dravidian synthesis proved durable and resilient. Successive invaders, including the Greeks under Alexander the Great, were either ignored or absorbed into the national life. A serious challenge was posed, however, by Muslim incursions beginning about 1000 A.D. For seven hundred years the Muslims, with their militant ideology, were a disruptive force. They succeeded in governing most of the country under the Mogul dynasty, founded in

1526 by a Turkish descendant of Genghis Khan. Some of the Mogul emperors, particularly Akbar, were men of considerable skill and talent. But by 1700 A.D., the Mogul empire was in an advanced state of decay. The stage was set for a new period, that of European, or more specifically, British domination.

The economy, social structure, ideology, culture, and politics of India in the seventeenth and eighteenth centuries, at the time of the British invasion and conquest, constituted in every respect a model of the "traditional" type of society. The masses of India lived in some 700,000 villages, each of which was virtually a self-sufficient, self-governing entity, with its own class and caste divisions. A few towns or cities developed as centers of royal authority, trade, or pilgrimage, but the overwhelming majority of the people lived in the villages. Royal authority might be concentrated in the hands of some mighty personage in Delhi or Lahore, but his power was barely felt in the villages, except through the intermediary of the inevitable tax collector. In general a committee of elders, or *Panchayat,* was responsible for order and justice within the village. Minor matters of a personal nature were usually settled by caste councils, while more serious crimes, such as cattle stealing and murder, went before the elders. Invaders, revolutions, monarchs, and empires came and went, but the Hindu village endured because of its self-sufficiency. In the face of a hostile army the villagers would arm and defend themselves; if attacked by superior force they fled, only to return later and take up cultivation again. The astonishing stability of this village system enabled the inhabitants of the Indus Valley to till their land and maintain their culture through 5,000 years of turmoil and troubles.

The dominant activity was agriculture, though some handicraft industries developed, along with manufacture of cloth, under the Moguls. Finished products of cotton and silk and handcrafted silver objects were exported to Europe, and a small merchant class came into being. Yet these activities probably did not involve more than 2 or 3 per cent of the population, nor were the merchant and trader accorded much respect in Indian society, which was led by Brahmans (the priests) and noblemen. Indian farmers produced barely enough for subsistence, husbanding the rain water which fell only during the four months of monsoon. In the event of drought, reduction of fertility, or desolation caused by invaders, famine was practically unavoidable. The lack of a more advanced technology made it impossible to expand the country's resources even to feed a rapidly growing population, let alone improve its lot.

Indian economic and social institutions, like those of all traditional societies, were pervaded by family values. Individuals did not own the land. Rather, the village families enjoyed rights of occupation as a consequence of clearing and cultivating their tracts. In the event that a family died out, all rights concerning their land reverted to the village.

The male played the dominant role, and the household consisted of all his sons, grandsons, and their womenfolk, except insofar as the women married and entered other households or the sons left the village to strike out on their own. The villagers, in a sense, constituted one large or "joint" family, with the committee of elders playing a paternal role.

An element of cardinal importance in traditional Indian society was Hindu ideology, which developed mainly during the period of fusion between Aryan and Dravidian cultures, though some of its elements can be traced as far back as the Indus Valley civilization. Like any "traditional" ideology, it affects and regulates all aspects of human behavior. It is more than a theology; it is a way of life, a code that determines how a man shall live, eat, marry, cultivate his land, share his produce, and raise his children. Much of the morality that informs Hindu ideology may be found in the Vedas and the Gita, and in the religious prose of the Upanishads (the main source of information on the formative period of Hinduism).

The central concept in Hindu ideology has been that of salvation, considered as a release or deliverance of the soul from the endless cycle of birth and death. Life is miserable and evil. Material things are an illusion. The object of religion is to permit the individual to free himself of evil and illusion and to merge with the Absolute, or the World Soul. Until release is obtained, the soul is condemned to wander about the earth incarnated in one body after another—the kind of body depending upon the soul's record in its previous existence. There are almost endless varieties of Hindu beliefs, some stressing the importance of ritual, others emphasizing the gods, such as Brahma, Vishna, and Shiva (representing, respectively, creation, preservation, and destruction). Yet the theme is constant: life is a mystery; nature is to be accepted, not mastered; earthly existence is inherently evil; the true destiny of man is to escape from the melancholy cycle of birth and death through ultimate deliverance. Hinduism provided a scheme of thought which made life a little more tolerable in a society where the average individual could expect to live about twenty years, where famine was regular and catastrophic, and where hunger and unadulterated misery were the everyday lot of the great mass of people. But the striking drawback of Hindu thought, as of most traditional ideology, was that it offered no incentive to improve material conditions, to master and transform nature, to make more bearable the fate of men on earth. Hindu society was able to endure as a consequence of its stability and the widespread acceptance of its values, but it was not able to keep up with the rest of the world in technological development.

A distinctive feature of Hinduism as a way of life is its division of its Indian followers into over 3,000 castes, each with its own rules for eating, marriage, and general behavior. The institution probably derives from the efforts of learned Aryans to preserve their racial purity and culture from contamination by Dravidians. In terms of the theory of birth, rebirth, and incarnation of the soul, caste marks the progression from a lowly to a higher state and, presumably, to liberation from the cycle altogether. There are four main classes or orders in the caste system, each of which contains numerous separate castes. In order of nobility or grace these groups are the Brahmans (the learned or priestly class); Kshatriyas (the warriors and rulers); Vaisyas (the traders and merchants), and Sudras (the serfs). In the past, certain wild tribes and people who performed menial tasks were considered outside this general scheme of things—even below the Sudras—and were called untouchables, or outcastes. There were about 60 million of these unfortunate people in 1950, when untouchability was abolished by the new constitution. But, members of the Scheduled Castes—as they are now officially designated—continue to suffer social discrimination in spite of the special legislation designed to protect them.

The caste system doubtless served a useful social purpose in a land subject to ceaseless invasion. Numerous races, at different levels of development, settled in India. The caste system permitted each group to preserve its identity and yet somehow to coexist wtih the others. Within a caste, no matter how lowly its general status, each member found himself accepted and helped. During periods of foreign occupation there was a natural tendency for the Hindus to defend themselves passively by withdrawing more and more deeply into their separate world of ritual and *dharma* (minute regulations concerning food and relations among the castes). They were thus able to maintain their Hindu way of life against the foreigner. Yet the price paid for survival of the culture was high: Popular energies were devoted to theology and *dharma* rather than to the acquisition of knowledge concerning science and technology and the improvement of economic and social conditions. The caste system also created deep divisions within the society, and greatly reduced the effectiveness of central institutions in achieving national objectives in an increasingly competitive world.

THE IMPACT OF BRITISH RULE

By 1700, the Mogul power in India had virtually disintegrated. No native chiefs or groups at that time were capable of conquering or unifying the nation. The political vacuum was filled at first by European trading companies and then by the European nations themselves. After a period of economic and military rivalry among Britain, Portugal, France, and Holland, the British emerged as the paramount power in India, their dominance registered by Clive's decisive victory over an Indian army at Plassey in 1757. The British steadily extended their power into the interior, defeating one native ruler after another, sometimes permitting an Indian prince to retain his throne, sometimes assuming direct control themselves. The Mahrattas, the Gurkhas, the Sikhs, and the Burmese were all crushed in battle. By 1840 the whole Indian subcontinent was in British hands, with the exception of a few small enclaves retained by France and Portugal.

Thus the inhabitants of a small island off the coast of Europe were able to extend their rule over a vast subcontinent at the other end of the globe, teeming with several hundred million people, and maintain their power there for two centuries. British supremacy was achieved by an amazingly small number of men. During the entire nineteenth century, the British ruled India with about 500 administrators and 65,000 troops. The disparity in numbers—at the most 100,000 Britons ruling 2 or 3 hundred million Indians—reflected the tremendous difference between these nations in military potential and economic power. The British had complete control of the sea, an immense superiority in military equipment and tactics, and above all surplus wealth which could be used to recruit and pay large numbers of Indian troops. They also created a far more efficient administrative system than had existed previously. Divisions between the Muslims and Hindus and among the princely states also enabled the British to play off one region or community against another and to succeed eventually in subduing them all. Their successes were made possible in part by their advanced technology, which produced the necessary wealth, ships, and firearms.

India had managed to absorb all of her previous conquerors, with the single notable exception of the Muslims. But even at the height of Muslim rule the Hindu way of life in the villages was hardly affected by events at the imperial court, except insofar as hostile armies might march through the countryside. British rule, however, profoundly transformed India—economically, socially, and culturally. In the course of the century and a half leading up to independence in 1947, India had changed more than during the preceding five millennia. Large portions of Indian society had been wrenched out of the traditional mold; an irreversible process of modernization had begun.

Some of the earliest British social reforms dealt with the custom of *suttee* (the burning widows on the funeral pyres of their husbands), the institution of *thagi* (organized robbery and murder), and slavery. Gradually a system of English law was established which profoundly affected relations among the castes. But perhaps the most important of the early British measures was the creation of a new educational system and the introduction of English as a kind of national language. There are 15 major languages and more than 500 dialects spoken by the people of India. The Indians were brought into contact with English literature and law and the whole new universe of Western science and technology. In the British scheme as it was conceived originally, the educated Indians were to form a huge intermediary class between the governing elite and the masses and thus to constitute a bulwark of the regime. In fact, this Indian middle class deliberately created by the British eventually led the movement to overthrow British rule. But in any case English education became an abiding source of Western influence in India, upsetting old ideas, introducing modern knowledge, and helping to form a distinct new social class.

British rule also stimulated economic growth. A network of railroads covered the nation by the end of the nineteenth century, and for the first time in 5,000 years the life of the village masses began to stir and change. The railroads opened regions to each other, and India to the world. The mobility of the population was vastly increased; transport of agricultural products made it possible to avert or at least to deal with famine; capital flowed into the country; and a few industries, including coal, iron, jute, and cotton, began to develop. The postal system and the telegraph likewise provided part of the framework for a more modern economy. Population drifted into the urban centers of Calcutta, Bombay, and Delhi. By 1940 there were 58 cities with more than 100,000 inhabitants, and a total urban population of over 16 million. Thus, although India remained overwhelmingly rural, urbanization had become a significant social phenomenon. In terms of foreign commerce, India by 1940 ranked sixth in the world, and had the eighth most important industrial economy, employing over 2 million workers in large-scale industry. However, agriculture was still the direct occupation of over 70 per cent of the population, and 90 per cent of the population continued to live in villages.

These changes—political, administrative, social, and cultural— shook Indian society to its roots. How did the Hindus react to the challenge thrown down by the West? Perhaps the first, instinctive, reaction was to exalt traditional values and seek refuge in a revival of orthodoxy. Some Indians, however, sought to adapt the values of Hindu life to the new conditions. Still others, members of the educated elite, became completely anglicized and lost touch altogether with their ancient traditions. All of these reactions eventually merged into a nationwide drive for independence.

One of the early strongholds of Hindu orthodoxy was, curiously enough, the Indian troops in the pay of the British. These troops were mercenaries and had great pride in their military prowess, but no identification with the British regime as such. Their discipline took the form of a fanatical devotion to religious ritual. When British administrators began to reform Indian society, however, the reliability of the native troops was subjected to great strain. All the irritations and frustrations of the traditional groups burst into the open in the Mutiny of 1857. Its immediate cause was the introduction of the new Enfield rifle, the cartridges of which were smeared with animal fat—said by outraged Hindus and offended Muslims to come from both the cow sacred to the one group and the unclean pig abhorred by the other. Native troops refused to accept the new cartridges, killed their officers, and seized control of large areas of the country. It took a year of bitter fighting to restore order; and the British thereafter were far more cautious in enacting reform measures. Other manifestations of the retreat into orthodoxy were the denunciation of everything European and the glorification of traditional Hindu or Muslim values and society. Among the new middle classes and intellectuals the view became widespread that the West was "materialistic," inhuman, and crass, while the East was spiritual and humane.

But a number of keen Indian observers realized that traditional India could not resist the new invaders, and that the only way to preserve the old values was by reform and purification. Most notable of the early Indian reformers was Ram Mohan Roy, who discerned in the Upanishads a central theme of reason with which practices like suttee, polygamy, and infanticide were declared incompatible. That is, Roy urged social reforms for Hindu, not Western, reasons. The role of the West, he contended, was to supplement, not to supplant, the values of the East. Roy gave Indian intellectuals a new measure of self-respect and pride. Religious and theosophical movements mushroomed, all advocating a return to the essential values of Hinduism or Islam purged of irrational customs.

The various groups within Indian society were initially divided over the questions of Hindu orthodoxy, reform, and the extent of imitation of the West. But they were united in their desire for self-government. At first they demanded only that more Indians be recruited into the Civil Service. The Indian National Congress, founded in 1885 by a retired English civil servant, was essentially a middle-class reformist organization during its early years, and nationalism in India remained largely a middle-class movement until the emergence of Mahatma Gandhi as its undisputed leader around 1920. Gandhi's contribution was to reach out to and arouse the great masses of the people. He understood the Hindu mind, and with a sure instinct, always formulated political demands in a manner the people easily understood. Gandhi built up national pride by exalting native Indian languages and religious values and by defending the spirituality of Indian village life in contrast to the materialism of Western civilization.

The technique Gandhi developed for advancing the cause of independence represented a masterly compromise between the policies of the liberal reformers, who wanted simply to register protests and sign petitions, and those of the extremists, who sought to oust the British by force and violence. Gandhi's supreme achievement was to involve the masses in the struggle against British rule, yet to avoid a direct challenge to British arms, that is, to keep the protest "non-violent." Although his preference for non-violence was couched in religious and ethical terms, it probably did not escape Gandhi's attention that British superiority in military technology made a successful uprising an exceedingly doubtful prospect. His technique of political action was far from passive, however, and indeed "non-violence" is not an accurate translation of *Satyagraha*— a combination of two Sanskrit words meaning "truth-force." Elements of his doctrine were derived from Hindu practices; they also fitted quite nicely, however, the particular needs of the Indian nationalists. The object was to win over the enemy by sympathy, patience, and suffering, by "pitting one's whole soul against the evil-doer." The essence of the technique was *non-cooperation*. Under British rule in this century, 400 million Indians were governed by about 1,000 British civil servants and 50,000 British troops. It would have been utterly impossible for the British to deliver the mail, run the railroads, police the streets, suppress crime, educate the children, or administer the economy without the cooperation of Indian civil servants, troops, teachers, nurses, and so on. Hence in political terms Gandhi's insight was correct: foreign rule could maintain itself against violence, but would founder if the Indian people simply refused to cooperate.

Gandhi's first call for non-violent non-cooperation, immediately after World War I, led to large-scale rioting which was stopped by the mahatma himself. During World War II, circumstances made the British increasingly reliant on Indian cooperation, and thus vulnerable to the threat of non-cooperation. Indian support for the war effort came to depend on a British commitment to independence—which was conveyed as early as 1942 by a special emissary of the British government, Sir Stafford Cripps, though at that time the discord between Muslims and Hindus made it impossible to work out an agreement. Immediately after the war the British Labour government entered into negotiations with Indian national leaders with a view to granting independence. In February, 1947, it was officially announced that Britain would relinquish her sovereignty over India by June, 1948 (and in fact independence came even earlier, in August, 1947). The continuing inability of Muslims and Hindus to agree on common political institutions led to an agreement for partition among all parties concerned and to the creation of the separate states of Pakistan and India.

The independent India which thus came into existence in 1947 was vastly different from the nation first ruled by the British two centuries earlier. In spite of Gandhi's idealization of village life and Hinduism (perhaps necessary for political purposes), the economy and social structure had undergone profound transformations. Industries and cities had sprung up among India's 700,000 villages, and above all a new middle class had come into existence. Independence did not mean restoration of the society which had existed in 1757; it was rather the signal for a new departure.

SINCE INDEPENDENCE: THE DRIVE FOR MODERNIZATION

With independence, political energies in India had to be redirected. Instead of overthrowing authority, the problem was to create it; instead of glorifying the village and denouncing material goods, the goal now was rapid industrialization; instead of opposing power, the need now was to rally popular support behind the government. The new goals were clearly underlined by the Indian government's decision to integrate the 552 princely states, amounting to 40 per cent of the national territory, into the new federation. To gain the support of local elites, the British had entered into agreements whereby the princes' domestic rule was respected, the princes in turn giving up their control over foreign policy and defense. The consequence was an irrational division of the country into areas governed directly by the British and a patchwork pattern of princely states at various levels of cultural and political development. When the Indian Constitution was proclaimed in 1950, this feudal structure was finally eliminated, and all the territories of India were reorganized on a more rational basis. Under the British regime, princely rule was a means of safeguarding local customs and privileges against the foreigners, at least in a few areas; in an independent India the princes were obstructions to national progress.

Political Institutions. The construction of a national authority was undertaken by a Constituent Assembly (chosen indirectly by provincial legislators), which first met in December, 1946. A constitution was promulgated in November, 1949, and took effect formally on January 26, 1950 (the date now celebrated annually as Republic Day). The political institutions outlined by the Constitution are inspired mainly by the British parliamentary system. There is a parliament, consisting of a House of the People and a Council of States, and a president, who is chosen by an electoral college consisting of the parliament and elected members of the state legislative assemblies. According to the Constitution, the president is aided and advised by a Council of Ministers (cabinet), headed by a prime minister.

In practice, the system resembles that of Great Britain: the president is expected to nominate as prime minister the leader of the majority party, who forms a cabinet and seeks the confidence of the House of the People. Members of the cabinet are collectively responsible for all decisions taken by any one of its members. Power is therefore concentrated in the political executive, that is, the cabinet, which is responsible to the parliament, while the president acts as a non-partisan chief of state. The major departure from the British model is the provision for a federal system, dividing powers between the central government and the states. The main powers, however, are held by the center, so that in practice India has many of the characteristics of a unitary system.

Political Forces and Parties. Although Indian institutions resemble those of Great Britain, political life, and especially the party system, is radically different. A large segment of the Indian community, inspired mainly by orthodox Hindu values, repudiates the secular state and views its institutions with contempt. Another element in the community identifies itself with the Communist Party and also rejects these institutions—for other reasons, of course. Thus, the consensus about political institutions and values on which the British system is based simply does not exist in India. Furthermore, the cleavages and contrasts in Indian society are far deeper and more intense than in Britain. A tiny educated elite, Western in education and taste, is set off sharply from a largely illiterate mass attached to a traditional way of life. The gaps tend to be greater all along the line: between the rich and the poor, between urban life and village life, between language groups and religious groups, and so on. There is also a stronger tradition of violence and resort to violence, in spite of Gandhi and perhaps because of the effort required to overthrow the British. Above all, India is still largely a traditional society, only started on its way to modernization, and with all the social, economic, cultural and political characteristics of such a society.

The divisions of Indian society are reflected in the party system. The dominant Western-oriented elite is associated with the Congress party, while the opposition is scattered among a host of smaller groups, including classic liberals, socialists, Communists, and orthodox Hindus. In the first general elections, held in 1952, out of a total of 106 million votes, the Congress party received 47.6 million votes (45 per cent of the total), and won 364 of 439 seats in the House of the People. Despite its complete domination of Parliament, the Congress party is thus *not* a majority in the country as a whole. The three parties which later merged to form a united Socialist party received 17.4 million votes; and the Communists, 5.7 million. In all, twenty-three parties were represented in the House of the People. The pattern remained similar in two subsequent elections (1957 and 1962), with the Socialist share of the vote dropping from 16 per cent to 10 per cent, while the Communists more than doubled their vote and constituted the largest opposition group in the House of the People.

The dominance of a single party, combined with the fragmentation of the opposition parties, the growing strength of communism, the continued importance of orthodox religious movements that reject the secular state, and the frequent recourse to direct action and violence, create a "style" of politics in India quite different from that prevailing in Great Britain. Nonetheless, the holding of three general elections (in 1952, 1957, and 1962) in which several major and numerous minor parties competed is a significant achievement in a nation where so large a proportion of the population is illiterate and uninformed. Pakistan, in contrast, has not had any general legislative election at all since its founding.

Political, Social, and Economic Development. Perhaps the most striking feature of contemporary Indian politics is the commitment of the political leadership to modernization of the nation's economy and rationalization of its social structure. The immediate problems faced after independence and partition were the accommodation of approximately 8 million Hindu refugees from Muslim Pakistan, and then the elimination of the independent power of the princely states. Reorganization of boundaries brought about consolidation of almost 600 territorial units into 27 states. Difficulties were encountered only in two princely states with Hindu populations and Muslim rulers (Junagadh and Hyderabad) and one state with a Muslim population and a Hindu ruler (Kashmir). In all three instances the intervention of Indian troops was necessary in order to bring about unification. Further reorganization of territories took place when the Government of India created 14 states out of the earlier 27, mainly along linguistic lines, with an exception for two important areas, Bombay and the Punjab. There is widespread popular dissatisfaction in both Bombay and the Punjab as a result, punctuated by frequent protest riots.

Remaking the map of India has gone hand in hand with an attempt to reorganize Indian society. The Constitution abolished untouchability and asserted the equality of women. Needless to say, this amounted in practice to a declaration of intent, since the status of the 60 million untouchables, and of the women, cannot be changed overnight. Nonetheless, an act of parliament has unified marriage laws for the entire nation, permitting marriages between members of different castes and providing for divorce. The Untouchability Offences Act of 1955 makes it illegal and punishable to discriminate against members of the untouchable class. Here too, however, the enforceability of a statute is limited. More important are other developments which have the effect of undermining the traditional caste system. The Community Development Program (which now affects almost half the villages in India) is a positive force making for social change. Similarly, the design of new industrial towns does not take caste differences into account. Inevitably, the growing urbanization and industrialization of the nation are creating new patterns of life which weaken the millennia-old social structures.

It is in the economic domain that the heritage from the past has weighed most heavily. Modernization of the social structure is ultimately possible only with a simultaneous modernization of the economy—each process being indispensable to the other. The great leader of the national independence movement, however, was unalterably opposed to industrialization. Gandhi once exclaimed:

> India's salvation consists in unlearning what she has learned during the last fifty years. The railways, telegraphs, hospitals, lawyers, doctors and such-like have all to go; and the so-called upper classes have to learn consciously, religiously, and deliberately the simple peasant life . . . Every time I get into a railway car or use a motor bus I know that I am doing violence to my sense of what is right.[1]

1 Cited in T. Walter Wallbank, *A Short History of India and Pakistan* (New York: Mentor Books, 1958), p. 157.

This attitude may have been sound political tactics during the period when the British rulers, in the eyes of the nationalists, were exploiting the Indian economy. It also represented a concession to Hindu culture—which seeks salvation in liberation from earthly existence, not in improvement thereof. After independence, however, Gandhi's successors had to face the problem of India's mass poverty. Some continued to exalt the virtues of village life and of a poor but spiritual existence. But the leadership of the Congress party, particularly the group around the prime minister, Jawaharlal Nehru, broke completely with the Gandhian tradition. They set about deliberately to create a modern economy through a series of five-year plans. A noted Indian journalist has observed, in this connection: "Posterity will probably rate Gandhi as one of history's magnificent failures."[2] In any case, the drive for industrialization is taking place in a country where poverty is intense and massive, where illiterate, tradition-bound peasants have the vote and therefore can act as a brake on economic development, where the democratic process is novel and fragile, and where religious doctrine discourages improvement of material existence. Herein is the historic importance of Indian politics today.

The term "five-year plan," as it is used in India, covers a multitude of activities, both governmental and private. A Planning Commission in Delhi establishes certain targets and goals, measures progress, and calls attention to shortcomings. By Western standards the amount of money involved is not great—hardly surprising in a nation where the total annual revenue is roughly equivalent to the budget of New York City. But the goal is to launch India into a "take-off" period, so that the economy will gain momentum and expand on all fronts. The First Five Year Plan covered the period 1951 to 1956, the Second Plan carried through 1961, and the Third Plan is now under way.

The emphasis in the First Plan was on expansion of agricultural production; in the Second it was on industrialization. The results so far have been encouraging, more so in industry, however, than in agriculture. In agriculture considerable progress has nevertheless been made in irrigation projects, the reform of land holding, and the construction of fertilizer plants. The Community Development Program and the National Extension Services have introduced cooperative techniques in the villages. But total food production, which increased by about 20 per cent during the First Plan, remains insufficient for a rapidly growing population.

Progress has been more satisfactory in creating the infrastructure of a modern economy—electric energy, locomotive factories, roads, and so on. The advance in industrialization has been remarkable. Three new steel plants are being built by foreign interests (German, Russian, and British). By 1959 industrial production had increased by more than 50 per cent over 1951. Striking growth was achieved by 1959 in iron

[2] Frank Moraes, *India Today* (New York: The Macmillan Company, 1964), p. 89.

and steel (a 63 per cent increase), chemicals (114 per cent), and machinery (324 per cent). India now manufactures automobiles, telephones, locomotives, diesel trucks, and aircraft. The productivity of labor in steel mills and locomotive works approaches European standards. India seems to be repeating the experience of France under the Monnet Plan in that expansion of basic industries has stimulated an impressive growth in the private sector as well. Modern forms of business enterprise are beginning to spread in the private sector, displacing the older artisans and speculator-capitalists.

Although the success scored in the first two Five Year Plans has been impressive, danger signals are flying at many points. Much of the increase in production is consumed merely in keeping pace with the growth of population. Large areas of the nation are stagnating economically, and in these areas the Communists are particularly active and strong. Unemployment is endemic, and the peasantry has barely been touched by the new spirit.

Social diversity, class divisions, and the weight of tradition continue to obstruct the creation of a modern, forward-looking political majority in the nation as a whole. Difficulties in dealing with the problem of surplus cattle illustrate the political potential of orthodox Hindu sentiment. The border disputes with China and Pakistan, resulting in military clashes in 1962 with China and in 1965 with Pakistan, have placed an additional burden on the economy. If India fails to break out of her traditional mold at a time when the Chinese Communists claim to be achieving modernization at a rapid rate, the democratic experiment may fail in all of Asia—and as a consequence, perhaps, in the world.

Democracy and Totalitarianism

Modernization, as has been pointed out, is compatible with either democracy or totalitarianism. Toward which of these models are the transitional societies moving? More important, are social conditions emerging which are conducive to the functioning of parliamentary institutions? There are genuine difficulties in transferring parliamentary institutions from advanced to developing nations. Democracy involves more than the mere existence of a particular political structure. Both the American and British systems of government could easily become dictatorships in the absence of an organized opposition, a free press, deeply rooted traditions of civil liberty, and free elections. Democracy can work only when the values associated with it (particularly those relating to speech and opposition) are fully understood and accepted by all the people. Literacy, education, and enjoyment of wealth must be fairly widespread if the mass of the people are to be in any position to judge and criticize the actions of their governors.

Obviously there must also be a desire on the part of the political leadership of the developing lands to introduce both social reforms and democratic institutions. It is possible to discern at least three different types of leadership, corresponding to political trends, in the developing nations: traditional, liberal, and authoritarian. Traditional leaders in the new countries are sometimes opposed not only to democracy but even to the introduction of modern technology and ideas. Liberal leaders condemn the outmoded practices of the traditional rulers and accept both the goals and the procedures of Western democratic systems. They press for political reforms which will limit the power of hereditary rulers, provide for popular participation in politics, and guarantee basic civil liberties. They are also in favor of industrialization, generally by means of classic techniques of capital investment.

Some authoritarian leaders accept the goals of democracy, but deny that these goals can be achieved in economically underdeveloped nations by adopting the procedures of Western democracies. They distinguish between "formal" or "procedural" democracy (characterized by a two-party or multi-party system, rights for the opposition, and periodic elections) and "genuine" or "substantive" democracy (which supposedly consists of economic development, modernization, equal opportunity for all, moral regeneration, and the like). They deny in particular that an active opposition plays a constructive role. Emphasis is therefore placed on "guided democracy" (in the phrase of President Sukarno of Indonesia) or "personalism" (the doctrine developed by the late Ngo Dinh Diem in Vietnam). Both terms imply the creation of national unity and leadership of the masses by a morally conscious, dedicated elite. Some, but not all, authoritarian leaders hold out the hope that the masses will, at a future stage, be ready for Western-style democracy.

Still other authoritarian leaders are inspired by revolutionary theories and seek to wrench the masses out of their traditional way of life by means of rapid industrialization, sweeping land reform, and stimulation of political consciousness. The people are organized for political purposes through a single political party, which tolerates no rivals. These leaders are more concerned with modernization than protection of individual rights. The new elite tends to be drawn particularly from the ranks of disaffected intellectuals, with some representation of peasants and workers. Its ideology calls for sacrifices and discipline on the part of the people in order to achieve collective goals. Revolutionary elites of this type have come to power, for example, in Cuba, Egypt, Guinea and Ghana.

In the contest for power, the traditional groups seem condemned in the long run to disappear. All of the social and historical trends are against them. Only in such countries as Saudi Arabia, Iran, Ethiopia, and Cambodia are traditional elites still in power. In some situations they may remain in office only by gradually turning political direction over to a more active group. This was the case in Morocco, when Hassan II permitted a limited, and since terminated, experiment with parliamentary democracy. The liberals, too, seem to be at a severe disadvantage. Application of liberal economic doctrine rarely results in rapid industrialization and usually serves only to enrich speculators and merchants. Liberal ideology does not impose the kind of social discipline which makes it possible to direct people, against their immediate will, into productive activities. Liberal elites have had some success in such countries as the Philippines, India, Nigeria, and Lebanon. But in recent years a number of regimes with liberal constitutions and ideologies (including Pakistan, Burma, South Korea, and Turkey) have been overthrown by the intervention of the armed forces, which have vowed to "clean up" politics, eliminate corruption, and launch the nation on the road to modernization. The drift toward authoritarianism highlights the incapacity of traditional and liberal leaders to satisfy popular demands. It also seems to support the view that the social, cultural, and economic conditions for parliamentary democracy do not exist, or do not as yet exist, in many "transitional" societies. The great strength of the authoritarian elites, whether of the left or right, is that they are able to arouse the political consciousness of the masses and then enforce strict social discipline for the purpose of achieving quick modernization. On the other hand, ruthless procedures and irresponsible rule may generate resentment and opposition, which lead occasionally to popular unrest or uprisings.

It would be rash indeed to attempt to predict the future development of the non-Western world. The trend in recent years has been toward authoritarianism of both the conservative and radical variety, but it may not be irreversible. It is barely possible that economic modernization may bring about changes even in totalitarian regimes like that of the Soviet Union, so that eventually they will turn to more liberal practices. Even in those countries where representative institutions are unable to work effectively—because of illiteracy, the fragmentation of parties, the lack of skilled administrators, or the absence of libertarian traditions—the resort to dictatorship may still be avoided. Leaders who tolerate criticism, respect the independence of the judiciary, and refrain from the temptation to regiment the masses can at least keep open the possibility of a future choice in favor of democracy. Turkey, to cite one instance, was guided from theocracy to secularism under an authoritarian leader in a process culminating after World War II in the establishment of a parliamentary regime with a two-party system. Thus under certain conditions authoritarian rule may pave the way for a more democratic form of government. But recent events in Turkey indicate that democratic traditions introduced in an authoritarian manner lack vitality. The firm establishment of democracy is undoubtedly a long-term, gradual development. It would be altogether unrealistic to expect it to happen overnight (or perhaps at all) in nations now breaking out of the traditional mold.

In any case, the societies and economies of the developing nations are so different from those of Europe and North America that some adaptation or transformation of democratic institutions is inevitable. Study of these modifications, and of the interaction between economic, social, and political change in the non-Western countries, is one of the most significant and challenging tasks of contemporary political science.

SUGGESTIONS FOR ADDITIONAL READING

ALMOND, G., and J. S. COLEMAN (eds.), *The Politics of Developing Areas* (Princeton, N.J.: Princeton University Press, 1960).

APTER, D., *Ghana in Transition* (New York: Atheneum, 1963).

ASHFORD, D., *Political Change in Morocco* (Princeton, N.J.: Princeton University Press, 1961).

BRAIBANTI, R., and J. J. SPENGLER (eds.), *Traditions, Values and Socio-Economic Development* (Durham, N.C.: Duke University Press, 1961).

COLEMAN, J. S., *Nigeria: Background to Nationalism* (Berkeley, Calif: University of California Press, 1958).

EMERSON, R., *From Empire to Nation* (Cambridge: Harvard University Press, 1960).

JOHNSON, J. J. (ed.), *The Role of the Military in Underdeveloped Countries* (Princeton, N.J.: Princeton University Press, 1962).

LERNER, D., *The Passing of Traditional Society* (Glencoe, Ill.: Free Press, 1958).

MILLIKAN, M., and D. BLACKMER (eds.), *The Emerging Nations: Their Growth and the U.S. Policy* (Boston: Little, Brown and Company, 1961).

PARK, R. L., and I. TINKER (eds.), *Leadership and Political Institutions in India* (Princeton, N.J.: Princeton University Press, 1959).

PYE, L. W., *Politics, Personality and Nation-Building: Burma's Search for Identity* (New Haven, Conn.: Yale University Press, 1962).

ROSTOW, W. W., *The Stages of Economic Growth* (New York: Cambridge University Press, 1960).

WRIGGINS, W. H., *Ceylon: Dilemmas of a New Nation* (Princeton, N.J.: Princeton University Press, 1960).

Part Two

POLITICAL RELATIONS AMONG GOVERNMENTS

Chapter 8

LEVELS OF GOVERNMENT

Problems of Autonomy, Area, and Service

A system of government can be effective over a substantial area only if it has devised some means to ensure the geographic distribution—or *devolution*—of political power. Even with modern means of communication, one man or a small group of men cannot be everywhere and decide everything. Decisions made centrally must be carried out in many distant localities and adapted to peculiar local circumstances too numerous and varied to be known by a single leader or group of leaders. And in the absence of central decisions—sometimes in the face of them—local and regional leaders and political groups tend to make decisions on local matters for themselves, leaving it to central government to change or overrule them if they wish or can.

The history of governments is replete with examples of ways to combine effective government at local levels with coherence of policy and power over a larger community. The ancient Chinese relied upon a system of tribute levied on surrounding nations to develop and govern their empire; the Mongol tribes sought to rule most of Asia and half of Europe by using couriers who, mounted on swift horses, carried the Khan's orders over roads and highways built expressly for that purpose. While the Greek city-state evolved into a highly effective system of governing small territorially based communities, the Greeks never managed to devise means for making government effective over larger areas. The Romans, on the other hand, were able to build an empire throughout the Mediterranean area and beyond because they discovered, invented, or evolved ways of coordinating political decisions made on an imperial scale with those made at lower levels within the Roman system.

Essentially, then, the problem of levels of government, or of geographical distribution of power, is concerned with unity and diversity. From the viewpoint of the larger political community, the problem is to establish a central government with authority to make decisions on matters common to all the individuals, groups, and communities that make up the larger community. From the standpoint of the towns, districts, regions, states, or other component communities, the problem is to allow decisions to be made on a lower level about those matters on which policy can be adjusted to peculiar local conditions without undoing the unity of the larger community.

All governments, whether totalitarian or democratic, authoritarian or liberal, despotic or constitutional, face this problem. In the Soviet Union, for example, although all decisions of consequence in terms of broad community goals are made at the top level, it has nonetheless been found desirable to provide nominally for a federal form of government in the Constitution, and necessary to have in practice some devolutionary forms of administration. Thus even a system which asserts the desirability of central direction of the entire economy and society has had to experiment with decentralization and adjust to local circumstances while pursuing the goal of efficiency. And it appears that there is in fact no clear-cut, rational solution for making such an adjustment. In 1957, for instance, there was a widespread decentralization of the Soviet economic system in which 100 economic regions were established as the directing units for the economy. In 1962 another reorganization drastically reduced the number of these units. The point here is simply that there is no ideal form for dividing power upon geographic lines, either in general or for any specific country. The constant series of organizations and reorganizations in the Soviet Union indicates that even when no value conflicts can take shape along geographic lines or between levels of government, there are nevertheless constant tensions and problems in adjusting national policy and local circumstances. If this is true in a centralized socialist country with no open political opposition, it is easy to understand how in democratic systems like the United States, where units of government themselves embody certain strongly held values and where democracy makes possible open struggle among people to implement these values by political means, controversies over the sharing of governmental powers become sharper and more serious.

Confederate, Unitary, and Federal Systems

In a situation where a number of governments each has jurisdiction over a very small area and another government has jurisdiction over the entire area which includes all these, an almost infinite variety of relationships among the governments is possible. Lower-level governments may have jurisdiction over some matters, the central government over others; there is no logical or "natural" way to divide up the possible subjects of jurisdiction. Similarly, actions of the lower-level governments may be more or less directly controlled by decisions of the central government, and vice versa. Some spheres of lower-level government may be more or less insulated against influence and control from the center, and the center may be more or less insulated against control and influence from below.

Despite the great variety of possible and actual arrangements, we can nevertheless make rough comparisons among systems with respect to geographic distribution of power. In one the center of gravity of political power may lie closer to the central government, whereas in another it may lie closer to the component governments. Theoretically, we could place all political systems along a continuum according to where this center of gravity lies in each, beginning with the system whose center of gravity lies closest to the central government and ending with the one where it lies closest to the component governments. If we proceed far enough, we come logically to the situation where the center lies so close to the lower units that central government does not really exist. Thus it is the character of the *central* government which above all determines classification and comparison of systems on this point.

Most political systems can be classified, according to the *formal* geographic division of power, into three principal types of arrangement: confederations, federations, and unitary governments. The distinction among them is based upon the formal geographic distribution of jurisdiction and authority and not upon the actual locus of decision-making power, which may correspond more, or less, or not at all to the formal picture.

CONFEDERATE FORMS

In a *confederation*—the weakest form of central government—the central government operates only through the constituent units and has no direct jurisdiction over individuals. On tax matters, for example, a confederate government does not levy taxes directly on individuals but assesses each of its constituent member governments a certain sum of money; the constituent members in turn levy the taxes on their own citizens. Examples of confederate governments include the United States under the Articles of Confederation, the Confederate States of America, and Switzerland in the nineteenth century before it was reorganized as a federal system (even though Switzerland still uses the name "Confederation"). At one time the Commonwealth of Nations could certainly have been classified as a form of confederation. If one regards the United Nations as a government, it too qualifies as a confederate system. (Reflection on these examples will indicate that we are dealing not with objective, clear-cut and absolute "types" of government, but with variations that span a wide range.)

UNITARY FORMS

At the other extreme, a *unitary* form of government exercises all governmental authority directly over its citizens. It may, as a matter of convenience, establish subsidiary units to implement central government functions, but these units are simply creatures of the central government, and such jurisdiction as it chooses to give them it may also take away without their consent.

Unitary government is the most common model found throughout the world. Of the countries described in Part One, Great Britain and France are unitary systems. The subsidiary units within each of these systems exist legally only by the will of the national government; whenever the latter wishes to take over a function exercised by authorities on a lower level, it can legally do so. Thus in Britain there are counties and other local districts, but they exercise only whatever jurisdiction the central government in London has authorized them to exercise. Similarly, in France *départements* and communes are created by the central government and serve simply as part of an administrative apparatus for the central government's convenience.

Within American states, whose governments are themselves unitary, local units such as counties exist on the same basis. A state can abolish counties, consolidate them, or create new ones without regard to the wishes of the citizens of these units—except where the state constitution provides for "home rule" for counties, or cities.

FEDERAL FORMS

A *federal* government involves characteristics of both confederations and unitary governments. Basically, a federal government divides authority between two levels of government, each level deriving its authority from the constitution that establishes the system, and usually with overlapping or concurrent areas of public policy, such as taxation and the police power, shared by each level. A federal government's constituent units, like those in a confederation, have direct relations with the individual citizens in their own jurisdiction; the central government has direct relations with its component constituent units. But in addition, federal governments, like unitary governments, also deal directly with the citizens of the constituent units. Thus a federal government differs from a confederate government by virtue of this direct relationship with individuals; it differs from a unitary government in that its constituent units are not simply creatures of the national government. Federalism, therefore, is the most complex of the three forms of government.

Usually a federal government does not come into being by a simple evolutionary process. Rather it is usually deliberately and, so to speak, "artificially" created; at some point a group of "founding fathers" sits down and determines what the respective jurisdiction and authority of each level of government will be.

Federal governments exist in the United States; in the Soviet Union (where federalism is, however, almost wholly formal); in the German Federal Republic, Austria, and Switzerland; in several countries of the British Commonwealth, such as Australia, Canada, and India; in some of the newly emerging African states; and in some South American countries.

There are several means of defining the federal system constitutionally. In the United States certain powers are *delegated* to the national government, and those powers not delegated to the national government nor denied to the states are *reserved* to the states. The Canadian federal system, in contrast, delegates certain powers to the provinces and reserves certain other powers to the central government. The Canadians established their government in 1867 after the American Civil War. Observing the consequences of the American system, they concluded that they would make a stronger central government by reserving certain powers to it. Subsequent experience in both countries indicates, however, that it is the delegated powers rather than the reserved powers which have tended to expand. In the United States it has been the central government's delegated powers which have increased in scope, while in Canada the expansion of powers delegated to the provinces has become a serious restriction to expanding national authority.

A more complicated federal system, not based on a simple formula of reserved and delegated powers, is found in the German Federal Republic. Here the national government has been delegated exclusive legislative, judicial, and executive authority in some fields; in others both the national government and the states exercise concurrent legislative jurisdiction; in still others certain activities have been delegated exclusively to the states. The most striking feature of West German federalism, however, is that in many fields where the national government exercises *legislative* jurisdiction, the constitution gives the states *administrative* jurisdiction. Thus, in contrast to American federalism, the German national government has responsibility for legislative policy determination, while the German states exercise responsibility for the execution of national policies to a far greater degree than do American states.

Similarly, in the USSR, administrative jurisdiction is probably more important than the legislative jurisdiction exercised by the fifteen constituent republics of the Soviet Union. At the national level there are two kinds of ministries: All-Union ministries and Union Republic ministries. All-Union ministries exercise direct and exclusive administrative jurisdiction over certain fields, such as foreign trade and the railroad system. In the second category, the Union Republic ministries, for each ministry at the national level, such as the Interior Ministry, there is a corresponding ministry on the republic level. Basic policy decisions are made in Moscow, and the administrative implementation of these decisions is carried out at the republic level by the Union Republic ministry there, under the direction of the corresponding national ministry. At the republic level there are other ministries with no national counterparts which exercise a few functions over which the republics have been given greater discretion. Essentially, these functions cover public utilities and other local government services. The republic ministries of communal economy, with authority over water works, sewers, and the like, are examples of this pattern.

A requirement of any enduring federal system is some means to decide disputes over jurisdiction between the central government and a component government or governments. As has been mentioned before, in federal systems the lines of authority are deliberately set down. But it is difficult to fix such lines with finality in a dynamic society, and change requires continual reinterpretations of the respective authority of these units. Most federal systems, therefore, establish courts both to interpret and apply their constitutions to conflicts between levels of government and to enable them to adjust to changing circumstances. The United States, Germany, Australia, and Switzerland all give their supreme courts authority to strike down state-government legislation.

While the right of the court to annul legislation of a national legislature is not a necessary requirement of federalism, it is necessary to have a court which can umpire disputes between the central and component units of a federal system. The fact that these courts operate on the national level, however, raises some question of their impartiality. The trend almost universally seems to be that national courts tend to construe the powers of the national government more broadly and to limit the powers of the constituent units. As one author has expressed it, the umpire is really a member of one of the teams.[1]

Forms of Local Government

Local governments everywhere are legally creatures of the central government and exercise only such authority as it allows them to exercise. In the United States this legal principle is known as "Dillon's rule," after the Iowa judge who first formulated this relationship of states with their subdivisions. Dillon's rule says in effect that in case of any doubt about the respective authority of the state and its subdivisions, the doubt will be resolved in favor of the state. While other countries may not have a

[1] Austin Ranney, *The Governing of Men* (New York: Holt, Rinehart & Winston, 1958), p. 507.

comparable specific rule of this sort, the principle nonetheless is widely accepted that the powers of subdivisions will be narrowly construed.

Forms of local government differ widely. We will confine our discussion, therefore, to a brief look at local government in several of the countries described earlier in this book.

LOCAL GOVERNMENT IN THE UNITED STATES

Almost all the states are subdivided into counties, but the jurisdiction and organization of counties varies widely from state to state. In Louisiana, counties are known as parishes; in Connecticut they have recently been abolished. In Maine, as in other New England states, where the town is the most important unit of rural local government, counties are simply judicial and administrative units. At the other extreme, in the Southern states, counties are the most important units of local government. In the Midwest and the Western states, counties have more power than in New England, but generally less power than in the South. In the main, as we have seen, counties are regarded as administrative units of state government and exercise only such powers as are specifically delegated to them. True, there are a very few states in which so-called county home rule is permitted, but this is a less common pattern than home rule for municipalities.

The forms of county government vary widely throughout the United States, but they usually have a great number of elected officers and provide for little coordination among them. Counties have often been called the least reformed unit of government in America; one writer has characterized them as a "lost world of government."

Below the county level, American states are divided into cities, villages, and towns or townships. Since the majority of American people now live in cities, the city is by far the most important of these units of government. In legal terms there are four types of city government: the weak mayor-council type, the strong mayor-council type, the commission type, and the city manager type. The *weak mayor-council* form prevailed throughout most of America until the end of the nineteenth century. Its essential characteristic was that the mayor did not have exclusive authority over the administration of the municipality but shared authority with a diverse group of boards and commissions which were either directly elected or named by the city council, and which in any event were not directly responsible to the mayor himself. The mayor had no veto power over council acts and ordinances and no control over finance and personnel. Recently many city charters have been changed to increase the mayor's authority in order to centralize administrative responsibility in his office.

The *strong mayor-council* form of government may be conversely defined as one in which the mayor has sufficient authority to be regarded as responsible for the city administration. A strong mayor names his department heads and directs the personnel and finance policies of his administration. As described here, however, both these forms of city government are ideal; probably no system conforms exactly to these models. Systems described in general as strong mayor systems, for example, often possess characteristics usually associated with weak mayor systems.

In the *commission* form of American city government a council is elected whose members collectively serve as the legislative branch of the government while each member is at the same time in exclusive charge of one or more administrative departments. Thus the commissioners combine both legislative and executive functions. Although a number of cities adopted this system after the turn of the century, it is no longer very common in the United States.

The *city manager* form has in recent times become much more popular and has been adopted by many smaller cities. Under this system the people elect a council, which in turn names a city manager who is usually professionally trained for such work. The manager, who holds his office at the pleasure of the city council, has exclusive responsibility for the administration of the city government. While the council exercises legislative authority, the manager commonly provides executive leadership.

Although in this century there has been much discussion in the United States about "home rule" for cities, it is not always clear just what that might mean. Presumably cities authorized to frame and adopt their own charters are by that fact exercising home rule. But the point should again be made that, legally speaking, cities are the creatures of state governments. Thus even where the state constitution or statutes authorize cities to exercise certain general powers, it is always possible for the state to intervene by imposing certain specific regulations. For example, it is common for state laws to grant cities general control over their own police forces, but if the state legislature enacts regulations in this area—let us say, requiring that policemen work only forty hours a week or be provided with certain vacations or certain pension rights—these enactments would take precedence over the general delegation of police authority to city government.

LOCAL GOVERNMENT IN GREAT BRITAIN

Although there is a great variety of units of local government in Britain, the forms of these units are simple and uniform compared to the wide variations found in the United States. In general, within each local government the citizens elect a council, one member being chosen to serve as a presiding officer, with the title of either chairman or mayor depending on the unit. The elected council members may name additional persons to serve with them on the council even though these have not run for office. This process is known as cooptation. Members of the council, elected or coopted, serve without pay. They designate a professional person to hold the office of clerk, a position roughly the equivalent of the American city manager in that the clerk is professionally trained for his office and is not elected.

The United Kingdom is divided into county boroughs and administrative counties. County boroughs exercise both the traditional functions of counties and municipal functions; administrative counties are more like the historic counties, and in fact some of them coincide with the historic counties of Britain. They are in turn divided into urban districts, rural districts, and municipal boroughs (cities). The various county subdivisions each have their own agencies of government. An exception to the general pattern is the London County Council, which performs functions common to the entire Greater London area.

The prevailing characteristic of local government in Britain is close cooperation between the central government in London and the local authority. The national government delegates to local authorities administrative responsibilities for many local functions. Thus local school officials have close relationships with the Ministry of Education, and other local government officials work closely with the Ministries of Housing and Local Planning. In very few cases do the local governments have exclusive jurisdiction over any function; rather they administer national policies locally. But in doing so they work with many central government agencies. There is no single central office or agency in London for supervising or communicating with local governments.

LOCAL GOVERNMENT IN FRANCE

Regional and local government in France is even more centralized than in Britain. France, as we have seen,[2] is divided into approximately ninety *départements*, which are in turn divided into *arrondissements*—administrative, judicial, and electoral districts of relative unimportance. These are further divided into communes, the lowest level of French local government, which vary widely in size of population. As we have also seen, the French *départements* were created by legal fiat and are not necessarily based upon the traditional and historic boundaries of French provinces. Each *département* is headed by a prefect appointed by the Ministry of the Interior. The prefect acts as an agent of the central government in administering national programs at the regional level. There is also an elected departmental council, but its jurisdiction is limited to relatively minor matters; it does not have power to undo the work of the prefect.

Each commune has an elected council and an elected mayor. Although communes may have more autonomy than *départements*, the jurisdiction of commune officials is severely limited; even their budgets can be vetoed by officials of the central government. The mayor is

2 See Chapter 4.

regarded as an official of the central government as well as a locally elected official. He can be removed by the government not only for such an obvious reason as a criminal act but also for poor discretion in administering national programs.

LOCAL GOVERNMENT IN GERMANY

In the main German local government has more in common with French than with American patterns. Since it is a federal system, however, Germany has considerable diversity in its local government patterns, which vary from state to state as well as within the individual states. Germany has as many forms of local government as the United States. A common pattern in South Germany, particularly in the smaller villages, is what is known in America as the weak mayor-council system.[3] In the Rhineland the strong mayor form of government is traditional, but here "strong mayor" means in practice that mayors serve for terms up to twelve years and have considerable responsibility and authority— by American standards almost dictatorial authority—in the conduct of the city government. An arrangement like the commission form of government is used in some states. It provides for both an elected council and a second group usually known as a senate. The senate may act in some ways as a second legislative chamber, but its members individually have authority over departments of the city government. Variations of this pattern exist now in the city-states of Bremen and Hamburg, although since the war the senates no longer exercise legislative authority. A fourth pattern, roughly equivalent to city manager government, was introduced by the British in their zone of occupation after World War II and has been retained particularly in parts of North Rhine-Westphalia. Under this arrangement the elected city council designates a professional administrator to have charge of the routine operations of city government.

Whatever the forms of city government, each unit acts not only on its own in carrying out local programs but also as the agent of the state government. Thus even elected officials, such as mayors, are regarded as agents of the state government in carrying out state-government programs, as well as agents of the local community which elected them.

ADMINISTRATIVE INTERGOVERNMENTAL RELATIONSHIPS

Although the foregoing discussion has been chiefly concerned with the legal relationships established by statutes and judicial decisions, in each of the four countries discussed *administrative* rather than statutory or legal control has become increasingly important in the relations

3 See page 256.

of local governments with central governments. There has been a decided tendency for the national or state government, as the case may be, to set standards and provide for inspection on a continuing, day-to-day basis rather than simply to establish statutory enactments with which local officials are supposed to comply.

A noteworthy development, for example, has been the steadily enlarged financial control exercised in all four countries by national over local governments, often through national *grants-in-aid* to the local units. Grants-in-aid can be *specific*, providing funds to carry out certain programs in accordance with a definite formula—such as specific allotments per child for school-day attendance in the public schools or allotments per mile for roads and streets. They can also take the more general form of *block grants*, sums given to local governments to be spent at their own discretion for their own purposes. Those who are concerned about preserving the autonomy of local units argue for more widespread use of block grants rather than specific grants-in-aid. Another device common in all four countries is the *equalization grant*, by which relatively more funds are provided for those local units with the least resources of their own, so that taxes drawn from more wealthy jurisdictions are used to maintain certain minimum levels of functions in the poorer communities. Naturally, this pattern involves obtaining more tax revenue from urban areas and spending it in rural areas.

Informal Aspects of Geographic Distribution of Powers

Having discussed some of the patterns in the formal, legal relationship between central governments and their subdivisions, we now must look at certain aspects of the actual workings of the political process. As we have continually stressed in this book, institutional forms simply set the boundaries of political behavior. A knowledge of the formal factors is a precondition for intelligent political analysis—but it is only a precondition.

CENTRALIZATION AND DECENTRALIZATION

As important as knowledge of whether a system is formally federal or unitary is knowledge of the extent to which a system is centralized or decentralized in practice. We have seen that the Soviet Union formally regards its system as federal; legally speaking, it even gives its constituent units the right to secede—an attribute of confederation. More important, however, is that not only the formal right of secession but most other rights and powers of the Soviet republics can not really be exercised. The Soviet Union is actually a highly centralized system in which almost all major decisions are made by the Central Committee of the Communist Party or its executive nucleus, the Presidium. While the formal appearance of federalism may make the Soviet regime more palatable to the diverse nationality groups in the USSR, it is only a facade for a highly centralized political and administrative system.

On the other hand, British government, which must be classified formally as unitary, must, when compared with the Soviet system, be categorized as highly decentralized. In Britain the national government not only relies on local authorities to a considerable extent but allows them to exercise broad discretion in administering national programs. Similarly, when we compare Britain and France we are comparing two formally unitary systems. But British local government is much more decentralized in practice than French. The British have a strong tradition of active citizen participation in local units of government, in contrast with the French pattern where centralization not only exists in theory but is embedded in the expectations and political habits of French citizens. Accordingly, if we rank the five countries we have been considering in terms of extent of centralization, the Soviet Union would be the most centralized, followed in order by France, Germany, the United Kingdom, and the United States. Such a ranking is quite different from the formal or legal classification of these same systems.

Among other important non-legal factors is the extent to which institutions other than the government itself may be decentralized. In the United States the fact that American political parties are decentralized to the state level, with the most important power centers often at a level even below the state, makes parties an important instrument for maintaining American federalism. In contrast, the increasing centralization of German political parties is an important contributing factor in the growing centralization of that government, notwithstanding its continuing federal structure. Thus, in order to understand where decisions are made, one must understand the structure of political parties and interest groups and how power is distributed within them.

COOPERATIVE FEDERALISM

Traditionally federalism has been conceived of as a system in which power is divided between two levels of government, each independent and each exercising exclusive jurisdiction over the functions assigned to it. This conception was most clearly expressed in the United States in the doctrine of *dual federalism,* which for a time was even applied by the American Supreme Court. According to this doctrine the reserved powers of the states are a restriction on the delegated powers of the national government.

More recently, however, it has come to be recognized, not only in such countries as Germany and Switzerland where the states administer national government programs, but also in the United States, that neither level of government can in fact be completely independent.[4] In the 1930s Jane Perry Clark described the modern pattern of American federalism as "cooperative federalism,"[5] a felicitous phrase to describe the actual relations between the national government and the states. Another authority, Professor William Anderson, has amplified this concept by stressing that the national government and the states are partners rather than rivals.[6]

Examples of such cooperative relationships are those activities in which the national government provides outright grants-in-aid to the states: the several categories of public assistance, the interstate highway system, and agricultural extension programs (research and education). But even in fields such as education, which are reserved to the states, the national government participates in some basic decisions. At least since 1954, for example, the national government has insisted on applying the constitutional principle requiring equal protection of the laws and thus prohibiting segregation in the public schools. And as far back as 1787, the Northwest Ordinance set aside certain lands to be used for schools. The Morrill Act of 1862 provided for national grants to establish schools for agriculture and mechanical arts. Since 1958 the National Defense Education Acts have provided grants for students as well as grants to schools for teaching certain subjects, and in 1965 Congress approved a broad program of aid for elementary and secondary schools.

Thus the study of federalism in the United States and elsewhere may perhaps be better conceived of as a study of intergovernmental relations rather than of separate units of government. In many matters the relations between national governments and states in federal systems have much in common with the relations between national governments and their subdivisions in unitary systems, or with states and their subdivisions in federal systems.

VERTICAL FUNCTIONAL INTEGRATION

Although conflicts in society may involve governmental units at different levels, such as a conflict between a state government and a municipality, some of the most important policy conflicts do not primarily involve units of government as such. Some, for example, may concern the relative amount of money to be spent for any given function of government. In a sense at least, education, welfare, and highways are competitors for funds. Those who put a particular premium on any one of

[4] M. J. C. Vile, *The Structure of American Federalism* (Oxford: Oxford University Press, 1961).
[5] Jane Perry Clark, *The Rise of a New Federalism* (New York: Columbia University Press, 1937).
[6] William Anderson, *The States and the Nation: Rivals or Partners* (Minneapolis: University of Minnesota Press, 1955); President's Commission on Intergovernmental Relations, *Report* (Washington, D.C.: Government Printing Office, 1955), Vol. I, Part I.

Figure 4

Vertical Functional Integration

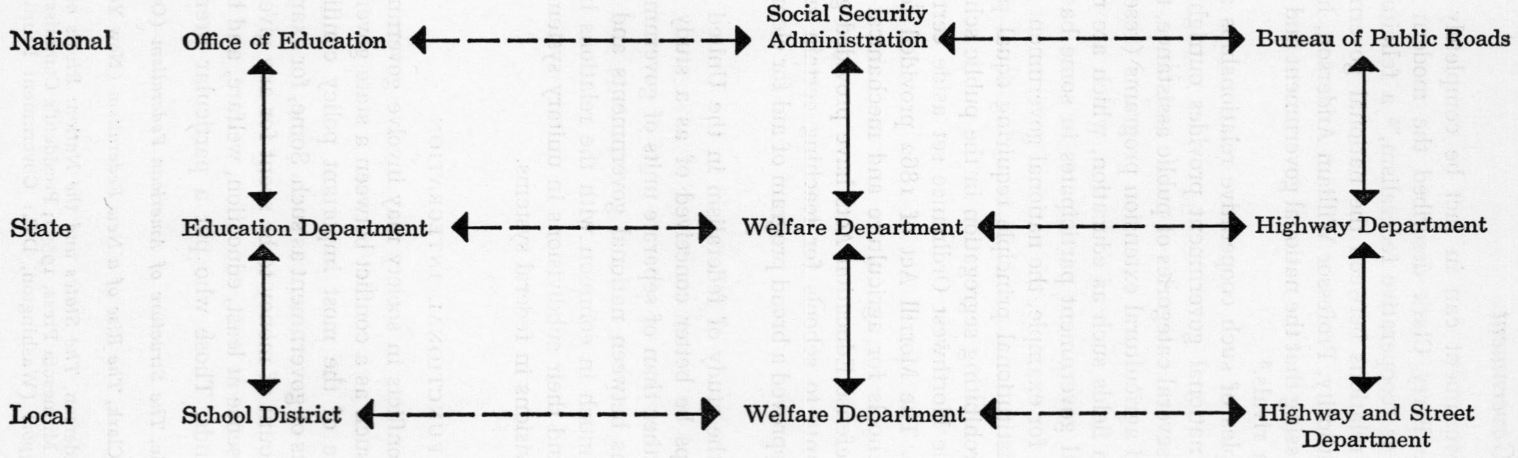

National   Bureau of Public Roads   Social Security Administration   Office of Education

State   Highway Department   Welfare Department   Education Department

Local   Highway and Street Department   Welfare Department   School District these activities will tend to be far more concerned about the size and adequacy of a given program than about the units of government which carry it out. This phenomenon is known as vertical functional integration.[7]

Figure 4 presents a pattern indicating what the relationships in so-called vertical functional integration may be. The diagram shows that at the national level people involved in education are active in the United States Office of Education (in the Department of Health, Education and Welfare), on the state level in the state departments of public instruction, and at the local level with school boards, superintendents and principals. Similarly in the welfare field, people must work at the national level with the federal Social Security Administration and at the lower levels with state and local welfare departments. Again, in the highway field, people are involved at the national level with the Bureau of Public Roads, in the states with state highway commissions and locally with public works departments. What people engaged in any one field of government have in common, because of their involvement with this field, may be more important than what they have in common with other officials at the same level of government in which they may operate. Thus the local school superintendent shares a primary concern about education and possibly even a philosophy of education with state school officials and education officials in Washington. He is far more concerned with his educational colleagues at all levels than with his counterparts in the highway or welfare departments at his own level. Similarly, the highway engineers, who have had the same kind of education and training, meet one another regularly and talk together about their technical and "shop" problems. Understandably the function of government in which they are engaged may be more important to them than the level of government at which they happen to be employed.

In each functional field, then, the value conflicts between on the one hand those who are engaged in it and on the other the groups engaged in attacking, supporting, or seeking to change policies in the field, are probably the most vitally important conflicts for all concerned. Units and levels of government become for them the institutional forms within which these conflicts take place. In politics one notes time after time that when a functional group loses in a conflict at one level of government, it immediately attempts to transfer the decision to another unit of government where it believes the chances of success may be greater. Recent political research in America, Germany, and Britain shows how prevalent such functional conflicts are, regardless of country.

[7] See the penetrating analysis in Edward W. Weidner, "Decision Making in a Federal System," in Arthur W. Macmahon, *Federalism: Mature and Emergent* (New York: Doubleday and Company, 1955), pp. 363–83. Weidner writes: "The disagreements and conflicts that do arise and that may be encouraged by federal structural features are not basically clashes between state and national governments. Instead, they are clearly between much smaller groups of people and the opposing groups are located within a single governmental level as often as not."

Trends in Intergovernmental Relations

CENTRALIZATION

If there is a prevailing trend in intergovernmental relations, it is toward increasing centralization—a consequence of the increasing complexity of industrial society, in which economic systems require greater
centralization. Centralization is made possible by improvements in transportation and communication and intensified, in most countries, by the
great demands of foreign affairs and national defense. The federal governments of the United States, Germany, Switzerland, Australia, and
Canada, among other countries, have all witnessed increasing gravita-
tion of power to the national government.

The trend toward centralization is both a cause and a consequence
of changes in communication. In the eighteenth century Thomas Jefferson could argue that citizens would know most about their local
governments and would be best informed about what their local governments were doing; they would know second best their state governments, and they would know least about their national government
which was so far away. Jefferson argued that every function of government would be best performed at the lowest level of government possible,
closest to the people. In the twentieth century, however, the evidence
increasingly indicates that citizens are best informed about their national governments. People who cannot name their aldermen or their
mayor may be well informed about the President's pets or the latest
activities of Luci Baines. One study of voter understanding of and
interest in government indicates that citizens knew most about and
were most interested in the national government, were second most
knowledgeable and interested in their city government, third in their
state governments and least in their county governments. Further
evidence for this pattern is presented in the voter turnout in various
kinds of elections. In the democracies we are studying, the turnout in
local elections is almost always less than for national elections.

Many observers have lamented this trend toward increased centralization in government and have urged various steps to halt or even to
reverse it. Such efforts have not been successful. In the United States
President Eisenhower in 1953 appointed a Commission on Intergovernmental Relations to determine what functions should be returned to the
state governments. After two years of work the commission concluded
in effect that very few functions then performed by the national government could be returned exclusively to the states. Similarly, in postwar
France and Italy efforts to decentralize parts of the national administrations have so far been abortive. The new West German Republic set
up in 1949, at the insistence of the Allied powers, was more decentralized than the Weimar Republic which preceded it after World War I.

However, as soon as Germany was free to amend its own constitution, many functions originally delegated to the states were reassigned to the national government. Thus even conscious efforts to halt the trend toward centralization have not been successful.

Here again one encounters the question of whether the substantive conflicts in our democratic societies do in fact take shape in terms of units of government. In the United States many of the arguments to transfer certain functions from the national government to the states are in fact arguments against having a given function performed. Thus advocacy of so-called "states' rights" may be a mask for an argument against action rather than a sincere assertion that a given function should be performed by the state government. The course of debate over states' rights well illustrates the tendency for conflicts in society to be moved up and down between levels of government, depending on the respective power of the competing groups at the various levels of government. The fact is that each level of government represents a different constellation of political forces and groups who may lose in conflicts at let us say the national level, but may be strongly enough entrenched to win at another level.

Political parties and interest groups change their positions on the respective claims of various levels of government. In the United States the Democratic party was for years a "states' rights" party. In the past thirty years the Democrats have been the national majority party, and they have talked more of the need for national action while the Republicans have argued more strongly for states' rights. Similarly, in Germany the Christian Democratic Union was in theory committed to federalism and strong powers for the German states. The Socialists, on the other hand, have urged a strong central government. However, since the Christian Democratic Union has become the dominant party in the national government, the Socialists have taken refuge in some defense of the rights of the states, largely because the Socialists have been in opposition at the national level while still able to control several of the state governments. Thus substantive conflicts of interest and power between the parties appear to be more important than their principles concerning the distribution of power between levels and units of government.

CONSOLIDATION OF GOVERNMENT UNITS

Another general trend in intergovernmental relations is a reduction of the number of units of government through consolidation. The need for such consolidation is particularly apparent in metropolitan areas. As cities and industrial societies grow to staggering proportions, what is economically one metropolitan area may be subdivided into a hodge-podge of political jurisdictions. Means of dealing with the resulting problems include annexation of surrounding areas by the city, consolidation of governments, or the establishment of another level of government to bring about some coordination among the jurisdictions within the metropolitan area. The adoption of any one of these proposals has relative advantages and disadvantages for all groups involved. Proposals for reform or maintenance of the status quo give rise to lively controversies. A common pattern in America is that of a core city, left with lower socio-economic groups, attempting desperately to annex wealthier adjacent suburbs. This pattern is certainly not the only one in America, but it is probably the image most widely held in city-suburban relationships. In Europe, on the other hand, because of differing patterns of city and suburban relationships, controversies on these issues more frequently take the form of adjacent, urban fringe areas seeking unsuccessfully to be incorporated into the core city. In Europe it is more often the adjacent urban fringe that is a financial liability.

A solution to some of these problems is the creation of a metropolitan government, which performs some functions common to the entire metropolitan area but which allows constituent units within the metropolitan area to continue to exercise other functions of government at a neighborhood level. In Berlin, for instance, there is a government for Greater Berlin, but in addition there are units of government within what is essentially one city, and these units of government perform some municipal functions. Each is headed by an elected council and a mayor having some autonomy in making limited decisions and some authority to direct his own administration. A comparable pattern is that of the London County Council, already mentioned. The London pattern served as a model for Toronto, Canada, which established a metropolitan government for the entire Toronto area but allowed some of the previous constituent units within the metropolis to continue to perform certain functions. The Toronto plan has served as a model for some American cities, most notably Dade County, Florida (the Miami area); and it is now being proposed for many other American cities. A more radical consolidation, which in effect not only merges several municipal governments but combines them with the county government, has recently been effected in Tennessee, where the governments of Nashville and Davidson County were consolidated.

Another example of the reduction in governmental units is the consolidation of special districts, notably school districts. This trend has been most pronounced in the United States, although there are comparable examples in the other democracies. In the nineteenth century, when an elementary education was adequate, it was possible to provide this education on a neighborhood level in a rural school district. Now, however, modern societies require much more extensive educational systems, and such small districts are unable to perform these modern educational functions. There has been a sharp decrease, especially in the United States, of the number of rural school districts in order to provide consolidated school districts capable of offering more extensive and diversified educational programs.

On matters such as the consolidation of metropolitan governments or school districts, it is possible for planners to sit down and devise rational solutions; but the mere fact of their rationality does not ensure their acceptance. In dealing with matters of this kind, one is dealing with deeply held value preferences as well as economic and other advantages of the affected groups. These controversies and the compromises which they may require can result in solutions which no objective observer could regard as rational.

FEDERALISM IN EMERGING NATIONS

Just as federalism was the means for achieving both unity and diversity in building such governments as those of the United States, Switzerland, Canada, or Germany, so today federalism appeals to many of the emerging nations as a possible solution of their problems. In many of the new nations these problems are compounded by the fact that there is geographic contiguity but little cultural unity. India, for example, has adopted a federal system as a means of reconciling the disparate racial, linguistic, and cultural groups of which it is composed. But even in its first ten years there have been serious examples of the difficulties faced by such efforts, and once, when the national government attempted to change some state borderlines, violence broke out between the groups involved. In the new African nations there are even more serious problems of racial and tribal political conflict. Many of the so-called countries of Africa are simply geographic expressions rather than cultural and economic units. Nigeria, for example, is clearly composed of three separate and distinct countries. Drastic problems of this nature were brought to the attention of the world in the former Belgian Congo. Here efforts to establish an independent government in the province of Katanga led to forceful United Nations intervention to compel the province's participation in the Republic of the Congo left by the Belgians. Difficulties in formulating a constitution for Kenya reflected comparable problems in attempting to define the relationships among the tribal kingdoms which make it up.

To make matters worse, many of those very African nations having difficulty in establishing governments within their present borders appear to be too small to be economically viable when confined within those borders. Perhaps, in the long run, further federal combinations could be a means for establishing viable units. But the efforts which have been made toward establishing a broader federation in West Africa have so far come to naught. More hopeful are the prospects for a federation in East Africa, where Tanganyika, Uganda, Kenya, and Zanzibar have indicated some desire to work toward the establishment of such a federation. The wish, of course, is not necessarily father to the act. In the West Indies, for example, when Great Britain agreed to the independence of its colonial possessions there, the formation of a West Indies Federation was contemplated. Formal steps were actually taken to set it up, but by 1962 it had become clear that such a federation was not possible because two vital components, Jamaica and Trinidad, insisted on their independence. Federation is certainly not an automatic, ideal, or certain solution to the problems of the emerging nations.

FEDERALISM IN EUROPE

More promising developments toward the establishment of federalism in larger areas can now be observed in Europe. Since World War II, cooperation among the European countries has progressed to an extent which prior to the war almost no one would have believed possible. So far most of this cooperation has taken the form of *functional integration* for specific functions. Thus perhaps the most effective supranational institution is the European Coal and Steel Community. The community arose out of an agreement among the Benelux countries (Belgium, the Netherlands, and Luxembourg) and Germany, France, and Italy to set up a supranational authority to regulate and manage these basic industries. A similar authority, Euratom, has been set up for the development of atomic energy. More important in the long run may be the success of the European Common Market. Begun with the same six countries that compose the Coal and Steel Community, the Common Market is now prepared to discuss admission of other countries. The Common Market looks forward, by a series of stages over a period of ten years, to virtually complete abolition of tariffs and trade restrictions among its members, and thus to the establishment, in economic terms, of a United States of Europe. In 1962 the rules for the direction of the Common Market were changed to provide that a majority decision would be binding on all members, thus discarding the traditional arrangement by which unanimity was required and each sovereign country in effect had a veto.

Post-World War II functional integration has been so successful in Europe that now many Europeans are looking forward to political unification by means of a genuine European government. Until now the Council of Europe, the political equivalent of the functional body, has been purely consultative, but some European leaders look forward to the establishment of a political federation of Europe. German leaders have been sympathetic to this proposal, but President de Gaulle of France, unlike most of his predecessors in the Fourth French Republic, has opposed it. Moreover, if Great Britain were to join the Common Market and then later were to join a European political organization, such an organization would probably have to be weaker than the ideal which European federalists have been urging. In any event, in spite of De Gaulle many observers believe that there will be increasing political consolidation in Europe in the future. Depending upon how such consolidation is brought about, it might be a step toward what has long been an ideal of mankind, namely, world federation.

SUGGESTIONS FOR ADDITIONAL READING

BOWIE, ROBERT R., and CARL J. FRIEDRICH (eds.), *Studies in Federalism* (Boston: Little, Brown and Company, 1954).

COMMISSION ON INTERGOVERNMENTAL RELATIONS, *A Report to the President for Transmittal to Congress* (Washington, D.C.: U.S. Government Printing Office, 1955).

CLARK, JANE PERRY, *The Rise of a New Federalism* (New York: Columbia University Press, 1938).

FESLER, JAMES W., *Area and Administration* (University, Ala.: University of Alabama Press, 1949).

HICKS, W. K., et al., *Federalism and Economic Growth in Underdeveloped Countries* (Fair Lawn, N.J.: Oxford University Press, 1961).

LIVINGSTON, WILLIAM, *Federalism and Constitutional Change* (Fair Lawn, N.J.: Oxford University Press, 1956).

MACMAHON, A. W. (ed.), *Federalism: Mature and Emergent* (New York: Columbia University Press, 1955).

MCWHINNEY, EDWARD, *Comparative Federalism* (Toronto: University of Toronto Press, 1962).

RIKER, WILLIAM H., *Federalism* (Boston: Little, Brown and Company, 1964).

ROBSON, WILLIAM A., *Great Cities of the World* (New York: The Macmillan Company, 1955).

WHEARE, K. C., *Federal Government,* 3rd edition (Fair Lawn, N.J.: Oxford University Press, 1953).

Chapter 9

WORLD POLITICS

World politics has two fundamental and striking characteristics which set it apart from the politics between communities at the levels discussed in earlier chapters. The first difference—although it is not an absolute one—is the frequency with which there is resort to armed violence in order to resolve conflict. The institution of war is crucial to the practice of international politics.

The second is an absolute difference. Unlike domestic politics, world politics lacks the framework of a recognized higher authority, whose rules are generally obeyed. Structurally, the striking aspect of world politics is its decentralization. For we must recognize that the independent state is "the most important actor in the international system,"[1] and that the patterns of relationships between states are best explained in terms of relative power.

Those two concepts—of state and of power—are most usefully analyzed within the framework of political science. It is increasingly clear, for example, that the kinds of foreign policies a nation pursues are deeply affected by the nature of its political system, and that the effort to understand political systems is much of what political science is about. Thus one of the best roads to an understanding of politics among nations is to analyze and compare the processes of determining foreign policy within major nations. International politics in the Pacific area before World War II, for example, could not be understood very well without a prior analysis of the internal foreign policy machinery of both Japan

[1] Morton A. Kaplan and Nicholas de B. Katzenbach, *The Political Foundations of International Law* (New York: John Wiley & Sons, 1961), p. 88.

and the United States. In the case of Japan, it would be crucial to grasp the particular significance of the military in determining Japanese foreign policies. In the case of the United States, it would be necessary to understand the distinctions in popular attitudes toward Europe and Asia generally, particular American interests in China, and finally, the historic attitudes of the U.S. Navy toward this country's Pacific role. The ensuing clash of these two nations fundamentally altered global politics from that time down to the present.

It is at least clear, therefore, that relations among states can best be studied as one field of political science. But we want also to stress the fact that international politics is analytically different from politics at other levels. In this chapter we hope to make those differences clear. We shall do that by discussing four subjects: first, the nature of the "international world"; second, the institution of conflict among nations; third, the phenomenon of the nation and "nationalism"; finally, some of the methods by which conflict among nations is limited and channeled.

The International System

It is very basic to ask, "What is the nature of the international world?" Even the use of the terms "international relations" or "world politics" implies that we have some picture in our minds of patterns or regularities. The words "world politics" presumably evoke an image of interaction that is different from other forms of interaction—or else they would have no meaning at all. There *are*, of course, some regularities in the concept of the "international world"; we pointed to a basic one when we suggested that the nation-state is the prime focus of attention in the study of world politics. While there are arguments to be made for focusing on other levels of human organization as well, the nation is still the central concept in world politics.[2]

THE "TRADITIONAL CONCEPT"

Let us be clear, however, that the traditional conception of world politics —a political globe of independent but interacting nations—is only a few centuries old. We may take it for granted today that "nation-states" have an inherent right to independent existence, and even beyond that, a right to popular self-government, but we should recognize that the acceptance of this doctrine dates only from 1648, when the Treaties of Westphalia

2 All students of world politics must struggle with this question. In one of the most interesting and sophisticated efforts to bring together the newest thinking on the problem, J. David Singer has also had to deal with the "level-of-analysis" problem. He concludes, in the introduction to his study, "I still consider the nation the most important and most useful choice, and will use that level of social organization as my actor in this book." J. David Singer (ed.), *Human Behavior and International Politics* (Chicago: Rand McNally & Company, 1965), pp. 35-36.

were signed. It was from those peace treaties, which terminated a particularly barbaric series of wars, that there flowed general European acceptance of this important principle: that states have a right to continued independent existence.

It is also from about 1648 that we can date in Western thinking the notion of a society of states. After Westphalia, the ideal of a single hegemony over Europe, whether of a secular or an ecclesiastical nature, was no longer acceptable. Instead, states were believed to have the right to determine their own internal affairs, and it was assumed that, after any conflict, the defeated states—whatever they had to pay in territory and in treasure—would continue to exist.

That assumption points up an important difference between then and now in both the concept and the practice of international politics. After World War II, for example, both Germany and Japan temporarily ceased to exist as independent political systems. The present governments in Tokyo, as well as in Bonn and Berlin, are the direct outgrowth of patterns and procedures established by the victorious occupying powers. The decisions that determined the choice of German and Japanese leaders, made major transformations in their economic structure, and set limits on German and Japanese rights to self-defense were products of administrations established by the conquerors. No such interventions in the affairs of even defeated governments would have taken place before this century.

The assumption of a "society of nations" did, however, make considerable sense during the seventeenth, eighteenth, and nineteenth centuries. Its ideals, moreover, continue to influence present-day practices and thought in international politics. For that reason, some of these "traditional" concepts need to be understood today.

Characteristics of the Ancien Régime. One striking difference between that time and the present is that, during earlier centuries, and even among very different countries, there was a pervasive similarity of political outlook on the part of diplomats and rulers. The sources of political authority, for example, were not very different in Russia, France, Prussia, Austria, and England, in that all were ruled by king or emperor. There was a common diplomatic language (French); there were important ties of religion; and there was considerable intermarriage among elite groups. Most important, there seems to have been a self-conscious recognition that the states of Europe did in fact comprise a family of nations.[3]

Some of the best-known doctrines of international law emanate from that period and that set of attitudes. Thus the doctrine of "international comity"—by which is meant the non-formal rules that nations follow in their dealings with one another, and which are based upon

3 Kaplan and Katzenbach, *op. cit.*, pp. 30–41.

courtesy and convenience—implies the existence of an underlying bond among nations. More importantly, the rules of war, and especially those codes and practices that have helped limit war, stem directly from the period 1648–1914.

War, Rules, and Law. With the important exceptions of the American Civil War and certain Napoleonic practices, warfare in the Western world followed patterns during that period which today seem very strange. In the first place, comparatively few people were involved in most of the frequent European conflicts of the period. Except for the *levée en masse*, a form of conscription that was instituted by Napoleon at the start of the nineteenth century, armies in the seventeenth and eighteenth centuries were generally made up of mercenaries. Since these armies were expensive, they were small. Civilians were altogether out of the picture. Moreover, the weapons employed were neither efficient nor effective, so that casualties were not excessive. As a further factor, not only was the fighting season short (there were neither winter campaigns nor night battles), but generals, in maneuvering for decisive strategic positions, often put a premium on *avoiding* actual hostilities. Finally, up to the time of Napoleon, most wars lacked the passions and hatreds that are characteristic of war today. In a word, these wars were limited: in their scope, objectives, cost, commitment, and consequences.

At non-violent levels too, the international political world was characterized by a formalism, an apparent civility, and a general non-involvement on the part of plain people—all of which are strange to contemporary thinking. In the eighteenth century, for example, it was not unusual for nationals of country X to live in country Y during a time when X and Y were at war with each other. Today, by contrast, it is hardly likely that, during the course of a war between the United States and the Soviet Union, Americans would continue to reside in Moscow or Russians in New York. Indeed, in the United States during the First World War, Americans of German descent (not only German aliens) were sometimes unwelcome in their own communities. More strikingly, American citizens of Japanese descent who were living in California in 1942 found themselves forcibly transported to detention camps in other states. This contrast is striking, in that the earlier practice indicates a lack of individual involvement, or concern for the war's outcome, that certainly does not fit the contemporary world. It illustrates as well the fact that, historically, wars were primarily the concern of ruling groups —not of national populations.[4]

Those ruling groups conducted their affairs with one another

4 Thomas Jefferson wrote in 1809 that "these (scientific) societies are always at peace, however their nations may be at war. Like the republic of letters, they form a great fraternity spreading over the whole earth, and their correspondence is never interrupted by any civilized nation." Quoted in Hans J. Morgenthau, *Politics Among Nations*, third edition (New York: Alfred A. Knopf, 1960), p. 104.

through highly regularized channels; in the absence of mass literacy and mass communication, the only significant contact between nations was brought about by virtue of infrequent travelers and diplomatic correspondence. The conduct of diplomacy itself, in contrast to present-day thinking on the subject, was regarded as distinctly within the province of professional diplomats, rather than heads of state or even their ministers. That may have been more justified than it would be now, for by contrast with the situation in today's world, the subjects with which diplomats dealt in earlier times were seldom intimately connected with the actual survival of the nations involved.

CHANGES IN THE SYSTEM

It is perhaps that factor—the issue of national survival itself—that most clearly separates contemporary international politics from that of earlier periods. Force, or the threat of force, has of course always been at the heart of politics among nations, just as the possibility of ultimate resort to legitimized force underlies any domestic political system. But in terms of modern history, only in the twentieth century have both leaders and observers realized that the consequences of political action can be such as to negate the political systems that make up the international world.

Interdependence. This fact—that war today can destroy much of civilization—impresses on contemporary world politics a tighter or more systematic context than it functioned within during the past. Especially in the affairs of the two great powers, it is clear that the actions of one almost inevitably and immediately lead to identifiable reactions on the part of the other. Consider, for example, the impact of the first Russian sputnik on American educational, space, and missile efforts. School programs at state and local levels were boosted, there were intensive hearings in Congress, and American spending for its space programs for the first time took on a systematic, planned, and permanent character. This simply emphasizes the fact that, in the making of American foreign and domestic policy, the thinking of Soviet Party Chairman Brezhnev is at least as much an input as is the thinking of Foreign Relations Committee Chairman Fulbright in the United States Senate.

Put another way, what this means is that modern world politics is characterized by great interdependence among the nations—and this interdependence extends far beyond the superpowers alone. Thus a Canadian decision to sell trucks to China has caused irritation in Washington, and Moscow has been disturbed by a Malayan decision to work more closely with Thailand and the Philippines. Partly, of course, this reflects the fact that the great powers construe their vital interests today to include far more of the globe than before. By contrast with earlier periods in history, the leading states are much less able today to divert their conflicts to areas far removed from their home territories. That was still the pattern, however, when the control of Canada and India changed hands after Franco-British conflicts in the eighteenth century. And Imperial Germany, anxious to assert herself on the world scene in the nineteenth century, but equally anxious not to provoke directly the other major powers in Europe, expanded her interests in Africa and the Pacific in a great wave of fairly short-lived colonialism.

Today there are no uncontested areas remaining on the globe. Since World War II, and until very recently, world politics has been dominated by Russia and America—a condition that has come to be known as *bipolarity*. In a bipolar world, the states not tied closely to either of the two poles (they are part of what is sometimes called the "third world," or the "grey" areas) have become the source and focus of basic conflicts between the two major powers. The overriding reason for this, of course, is that both the United States and the Soviet Union see themselves as engaged in a contest of ideologies and conceive of their interests in global terms. That belief—that what is good for the nation is also good for the world—is sometimes referred to as "nationalistic universalism"; it has tended once again to transform international relations.

One result of nationalistic universalism is that contemporary world politics, like European politics before 1648, is once again dominated by ideological struggle. Ideological conflict, in turn, has changed the meaning of many of the traditional concepts of international politics, forcing us thereby to rethink our approaches. Consider, for example, the hallowed doctrine of traditional international politics long known as "neutrality," and along with it the "rights of the neutral nation."

Neutrality. Neutrality has generally been regarded as applicable only during war. It meant, for example, that a nation that declared its neutrality while a war raged could continue to trade with all countries— under specified conditions, even with the parties engaged in the war. Underlying this approach to neutrality were two convictions: first, that wars were an inevitable, even if distasteful, consequence of international relations; second, that these wars were primarily the concern of those nations that were actually doing the fighting. Thus any non-belligerents, if they so decided, could "respectfully abstain." Out of this set of assumptions about international politics grew highly formalized and detailed codes, basic to the study of international law, which attempted to define the rights and obligations of neutrality. For example, if England and France were at war, this question might arise: Could a French ship in need of repair call at an American port to be outfitted and rehabilitated? And could American shipowners and merchants sell any goods to France without England protesting?

In order to answer such questions, the doctrine of "contraband" was developed so that, insofar as that was possible, normal commerce might continue even during war. As the term was defined in the famous Jay Treaty of 1794, Britain and the United States agreed that contraband included:

> All arms and implements serving for the purposes of war, by land or sea, such as cannon, muskets, mortars . . . and generally all other implements of war, as also timber for ship-building, tar or rozin . . . and generally whatever may serve directly to the equipment of vessels, unwrought iron and fir planks only excepted . . .[5]

Modern technology, of course, would require a far different list of materials to be designated as "implements of war," if indeed there are any materials at all today that are not related to war.

Nevertheless, during the seventeenth, eighteenth, and nineteenth centuries, the technology of military and national power was seen in a much narrower light than it is now. By and large it was thought that only materials directly related to the battlefield should be regarded as military commodities. Add to this the conviction that neutrality is a feasible and respectable national policy, and it becomes clear that defining contraband posed pressing practical problems. Uncounted diplomats, jurists, lawyers, and professors worked to resolve these questions, and out of their labors (embodied in the treaties, decisions, commentaries, and customs that they wrote and adopted) grew the body of generally accepted international law.

The doctrine of contraband is, of course, only one of the features of traditional neutrality, and it is now quite clear that that concept has been rendered obsolete. Do we see as clearly what this century's experience has done to our conceptions of both war and neutrality?

Neutrality was based on the assumption that war is the constant byproduct of a traditional, multi-centered international "society," and on the further assumption that any nation has the right to stay out of a war if it so chooses. Statesmen also took for granted, as we have noted, the right to existence of the other members of the "society." They attempted, therefore, to channel even their violent contacts with one another through somewhat civil forms. The Hague Conventions of 1899 and 1907, which attempted to soften the horrors of war, serve as examples of these efforts. They were the final steps in a process that was by that time at least a century old.[6]

Today this concept of a society of nations, so well embodied in the Hague Conventions and in other similar attempts at international legislation, seems no longer applicable. The interrelationships of states today are so much tighter than in the past, and the resulting interdependence is so crucially related to the continued existence both of individual states

---

5 Article XVIII of the Jay Treaty, reprinted in Dorothy Burne Goebel (ed.), *American Foreign Policy* (New York: Holt, Rinehart & Winston, 1961), p. 32.
6 J. L. Brierly, *The Law of Nations*, fifth edition (Fair Lawn, N.J., and Oxford, Eng.: Oxford University Press, 1960), p. 93.

and of modern human organization, that we would be better advised to view the framework of contemporary international politics not as a "society" but rather as tending toward a political system.

Conflict in World Politics

From what point in time can the demise of international society, with its concern for rights and its limits on violence, be dated? At first glance it might seem that the new stage in world politics began in 1933, when Hitler came to power, for it was under his tutelage that Germany's international behavior became an utter denial of the Western tradition. Yet the basis for the new era had been laid earlier—at least around World War I.

The words of Woodrow Wilson, in his request for a congressional declaration of war in 1917, illustrate perfectly my contention that perspectives on both war and neutrality were changing drastically. In Wilson's view, the war could no longer be regarded simply as an affair between several of the great European powers: "The present German submarine warfare against commerce is warfare against mankind. It is a war against all nations."

In a "warfare against mankind," there is little room left for neutrality, and later in his speech Wilson anticipated what would become the modern view of it:

> Neutrality is no longer feasible or desirable where the peace of the world is involved and the freedom of its peoples, and the menace to that peace and freedom lies in the existence of autocratic governments backed by organized force . . . we have seen the last of neutrality in such circumstances.[7]

In this view, the very existence of non-democratic regimes becomes a threat to world peace. In the face of that threat, those who love peace must adopt goals far different from the traditionally limited ones of changing boundaries, striving for certain resources and rights, or otherwise seeking to "adjust differences among nations." Instead, it becomes necessary to change the shape of world politics by establishing only such governments as will—if they are responsive to their peoples—renounce force. In Wilson's words, "a steadfast concert for peace can never be maintained except by a partnership of democratic nations."

The orthodox Marxist view is not altogether different, except insofar as it maintains that lasting peace cannot be looked for until socialism is universally established.[8] Both views, of course, see the contemporary

---

[7] Message of President Wilson to Congress asking for a Declaration of War, reprinted in Goebel, *op. cit.*, pp. 221–22.
[8] According to *Pravda*, August, 1957, former Soviet leader Khrushchev said: "In the contemporary world there is a fierce struggle going on between two ideologies, the socialistic and the bourgeois, and in that struggle there can be no neutrals."

conflict as one between good and evil. From either perspective, the ethical justification and practical chances for maintaining a neutral position become very difficult to maintain. Consider, for example, the "uncommitted" nation that has the temerity to believe that a war growing out of today's ideological conflict is not a holy one, and decides, therefore, to declare itself neutral. Is it likely that the belligerents—each of whom feels its cause is sacred—will respect the neutrality of the uncommitted?

Thus the prospects for neutrality do not seem bright, although, as Eagleton has written, "the neutral was always at a disadvantage."[9] Nevertheless, in an age of ideological conflict and technological revolution, these disadvantages have rendered it exceedingly difficult for any significant nation successfully to practice neutrality, and the very concept itself has become suspect.

We should be clear, of course, that the term "neutral" applies today not only to a condition of actual hostilities (the traditional view), but also to the "cold war." That war, as we have said, has been characterized by a loose bipolarity, in which the two polar powers have striven constantly to win the commitment or allegiance of the smaller, and often uncommitted, nations. Thus India, Indonesia, Ghana, Cambodia, Egypt, and many others have been wooed—with economic aid, offers of alliance, state visits, and many other means—by Russia and America, and more recently by China.

To the extent that the uncommitted or "neutral" nations are in fact affected by the favors offered to them by either of the two poles, and weaken in their non-alignment, the condition of loose bipolarity tends constantly in the direction of a tight bipolar structure for world politics.[10] In 1964–1965, for example, a conflict between Indonesia and Malaysia illustrated this tendency. Malaysia, a member of the British Commonwealth, was engaged, with the aid of troops from Australia and Britain, in defending herself from terrorist attacks that were being supported by Indonesia. Indonesia had been equipped militarily by the Soviet Union, and had adopted policies that placed her in an increasingly close relationship with Communist China. A localized hostility between Indonesia and Malaysia might, therefore, have "escalated" into a conflict between the great powers. Even the United States could have been implicated, through its relationship in the SEATO military alliance with Australia and Britain, while Russia—if Indonesia suffered military setbacks— might have felt called upon to support its associate.

This tendency toward tight bipolarity means that not only such small far-off conflicts, but also indirect confrontations between the great powers—as in Vietnam—pose the threat of global conflagrations. In the face of this possibility, our traditional assumptions about war itself require a new look.

9 Clyde Eagleton, *Analysis of the Problem of War* (New York: The Ronald Press Company, 1937), pp. 89–90.
10 Morton A. Kaplan, *System and Process in International Politics* (New York: John Wiley & Sons, 1957), p. 36.

WAR TODAY

Do we accept today the traditionally accepted proposition that war must be regarded as an expected byproduct of international politics? Traditional diplomacy and international law were based on the inevitability of war, and therefore devoted merely to limiting war's excesses and consequences. Traditional thinking seldom dared to suggest that war itself might disappear. Thus the pattern of thought that has come down to us is that, in the final analysis, nations may decide to resort to armed violence. Today, however, war is less widely regarded as a necessary method or an inevitable product of international politics. This is a new element; it helps clarify, for example, the observation that, if the U.S. Strategic Air Command is ever required to launch its nuclear-armed missiles and aircraft, it will have failed its primary purpose.

It has often been said in the past, of course, that new weapons have made war too awful to contemplate: some such conclusion followed the adoption of the machine gun, the tank, and the heavy bomber. Nevertheless, only in the twentieth century has warfare come to be regarded as criminal; only in this century have statesmen increasingly concluded that war does not serve national purposes.

The most famous early statement of this position is in the Kellogg-Briand Pact of 1928, which was negotiated originally between France and the United States and eventually ratified by sixty-four nations. In that remarkable document, the signers declared that they "condemn recourse to war . . . and renounce it as an instrument of national policy in their relations with one another."[11] This act of renunciation did not deter these same nations from engaging in major war just over ten years later; yet the pact cannot be too quickly dismissed. The Kellogg-Briand Pact upset traditional thinking about war. Whereas war had been regarded, as Eagleton says, "as a providential visitation to be compared with plague or flood or fire,"[12] Kellogg-Briand established a precedent from which it later became possible to view war *as a criminal act*.

This precedent was cited at the end of World War II, when the Allies convened the series of war trials known formally as the International Military Tribunals of Nuremberg and Yokohama. The Nuremberg trials, which were designed to assess responsibility among Germans for specific acts of war guilt, referred repeatedly to the no-war pledges that had been incorporated in the Kellogg-Briand Pact. Partly as a result of those war trials, it is now widely held that "aggressive war" is a crime.

The Nuremberg doctrine raises some rather difficult questions for the student of politics. It was not Hitler's Germany and Imperial Japan, as states, that were charged in the trials; it was the German and Japanese political leaders, and their military officers, who were indicted. Yet

11 From Article I of the Kellogg Pact, in Goebel, *op. cit.*, p. 257.
12 Clyde Eagleton, *International Government*, third edition (New York: The Ronald Press Company, 1957), p. 455.

international practice had never before recognized individual men as subjects or actors in world politics; only nations, or states, had been traditionally included. Does the doctrine of Nuremberg, which led to the execution and imprisonment of scores of Nazi leaders and German soldiers, mean that today individuals *are* to be regarded as parties in world politics? If so, what is the effect on our traditional conception of military obedience to superior orders? Do orders from a superior officer afford immunity?[13] And, even assuming that we know what "aggressive" war is, we must ask: In what ways, if at all, is future international behavior likely to be affected as a result of the Nuremberg precedent that aggressive war is criminal?

The establishment of this precedent assumes, of course, that some significant portion of people, and the leaders of some nations, give credence to the doctrine. The Kellogg-Briand Pact, which purported to "outlaw war," dates only from 1928, but even in its own time the pact was not really taken seriously. A leading American professor of international law wrote about it, less than a decade after it was signed, that "it has become an object of ridicule."[14]

But whether the Kellogg-Briand Pact itself deserved to be ridiculed is of far less importance than the doctrine it embodied, for that same doctrine is being expressed once again today: that somehow resort to war among states must stop. Especially since 1945, and the advent of nuclear weapons, it is not uncommon to hear the remark that today war is really unthinkable. A variant thesis is the judgment that nations simply do not benefit from wars.

Both of these premises seem to have had great influence on the policies of Russia and America. Both countries, of course, stand ready for the prosecution of war and possess enormous strategic forces equipped with thermonuclear weapons, yet both sides have demonstrated an exceedingly great measure of restraint. Never was this better demonstrated than when the Soviet Union removed its missiles from Cuba. And neither side seems willing to act as if it thought general thermonuclear war were really a viable goal of policy. It was not until 1958, for example, that the Soviet government told its people any important facts about nuclear war and the consequences of nuclear bombing. Similarly, the American people still remain extremely reluctant to think in terms of defending themselves during such a war, and civilian defense recommendations have nowhere been taken seriously.[15]

[13] At his trial in 1961 Adolf Eichmann said: "I was in the iron grip of my oath to continue my assignment. . . . I regarded myself not guilty because I was under orders. . . ."

[14] Eagleton, *Analysis of the Problem of War*, p. 85.

[15] Herman Kahn, a high-level consultant to the Pentagon, has commented precisely on this point: ". . . the planners seem to care less about what happens after the buttons are pressed than they do about looking 'presentable' before the event. They show slight interest in maintaining an appreciable operational capability on the second day of the war . . ." Herman Kahn, *On Thermonuclear War* (Princeton, N.J.: Princeton University Press, 1960), p. 18.

THE BENEFITS OF WAR

It may, of course, be true that no nation today can benefit from war, but since that conclusion has been reached before this, and nations have gone to war anyway, the judgment itself must be examined.

During the First World War, for example, and later as a direct result of that war, both Japan and the United States benefited greatly. The war induced a spurt in the industrial development of Japan and the United States that was of great significance for their economies during the 1920s. Moreover, World War I changed world financial, political, and market patterns in such a way as to inject both countries into the small circle of great powers. Indeed, the later clash between Japan and the United States in World War II is a direct consequence of the position each had achieved as a result of World War I.

Consider the more recent case of Russian development. If ever there was a phoenix that arose from the ashes, this was one: it is clear that the Soviet Union's present state of power, and its leadership of world communism, is directly traceable to the consequences of World War II. Aside from the fact that its occupation forces literally stripped defeated territories of any remaining industrial plant, the total defeat and demoralization of Germany meant that only the Soviet Union could hope to establish hegemony over much of Europe. Furthermore, the destruction and the dislocations that afflicted much of the rest of the globe in the wake of World War II vastly enlarged the audience for the appeals of communism and widened the scope for its expansion. Thus, despite the enormous cost in men and wealth, it might be said that, in a sense, the Second World War has been the biggest single boon so far to Soviet goals. Such a conclusion forces us, therefore, to question the usual contention that "nobody benefits from a war."

In the 1960s, however, no major power (save perhaps one) seems willing to conclude that on balance a war is likely to further national goals. Only China, Mao Tse-tung is reported to have said, can face the cost of 200 million dead and perhaps still conclude that the price is not exorbitant. For the rest, and especially for the United States and the USSR, the ideals of the Kellogg Pact—however unreal they may have been in 1928—seem for the first time to have a practical immediacy. It is not too much to say that, because of the advent of thermonuclear weapons and missile delivery systems, general unrestricted war among the great powers has become the most unlikely of possibilities.

This becomes credible when we recognize that for almost two decades the policy of the Western bloc of nations has been designed, not for any eventual military "defeat" of the Soviets, but for "deterrence"— which, in the words of one of its leading interpreters, is the notion that "no nation whose decision makers are sane would attack another nation which was armed with a sufficiently large number of thermonuclear bombs."[16]

DETERRENCE

This is indeed a new factor in international politics. The concept of deterrence suggests, of course, that states can be dissuaded from taking certain kinds of action; but it is not that that is new. What is new is that deterrence is based not primarily on the likelihood of the *use* of violence, but instead on the threat—that is, simply the possession—of enormous force.

Deterrence, let it be said at once, is a crude concept, and inevitably raises a wide range of crucial and difficult questions. Is it reasonable to expect, for example, that the possession by one nation of enormous force will deter *all* provocative actions by any other nation—even smallish ones? Furthermore, how large is a "sufficiently large number of thermonuclear bombs"? The answer might well depend upon who was doing the estimating of the numbers, and that in turn on their view of reality. Thus we might ask, what constitutes "sanity" among leaders whose nations are threatened, and under what conditions may they be regarded as not sane? Finally, what become the consequences for international politics if the deterrent fails to deter? These are only a few of the relevant problems, but it should be clear even from this that deterrence has heavy overtones of the bargaining process, and as such is a peculiarly political phenomenon. What sets it apart in the context of traditional international politics is that, as Schelling has explained, "a theory of deterrence would be a theory of the skillful *non-use* of military force."[17] Once again, President Kennedy's behavior in the Cuban missile crisis provides an object lesson.

This factor lends a quality of unreality to the use of major force today, for the "skillful non-use of force" presses the actual resort to violence into the background. And with violence thrust into the background, some of the classical assumptions and practices of international politics are challenged. For, as we suggested earlier, deterrence forces the great powers into tighter, more *systematic* patterns of interaction than ever before. To an unprecedented degree, their actions, and their responses to each other's behavior, must be more carefully calculated than ever before.

One aspect of this interdependence is that nations that can exercise deterrence, those that possess thermonuclear weapons and a convincing means for delivering them, seem on the face of the matter to share a certain mutuality of interests. For example, since accidental war in the thermonuclear age is a particularly horrendous thought, there are objective reasons for supposing that both the Soviet Union and the United

[16] Kahn, *op. cit.*, p. 8.
[17] Thomas C. Schelling, "Toward A Theory of Strategy for International Conflict," (RAND Corporation P-1648, 1959), pp. 8–9.

States would prefer that the "nuclear club" not include too many nations. And indeed, both Moscow and Washington have acted on that basis. They have already signed a treaty prohibiting the atmospheric testing of nuclear devices, and both support in principle the concept of a non-proliferation treaty.

By the same token, both the United States and the Soviet Union share an interest in ensuring that each side has as accurate and foolproof a system of detection and communications as possible. Americans would not want Russians to misconstrue a series of peaceful space shots any more than Russians would want American officials to mistake for bombers, as they once did, the radar "blips" caused by flying geese. Thus, unlikely as this may seem at first glance, the technological conditions of modern conflict seem to force belligerents closer together, rather than to drive them farther apart. One striking illustration of this, of course, is the "hot line" telephone, which connects the American President directly with his Soviet counterpart. This notion of mutuality is central, moreover, to arms control hopes, which rest "on the recognition that our military relation with potential enemies is not one of pure conflict and opposition, but involves strong elements of mutual interests . . ."[18]

The Nation, the State, and Sovereignty

Implicit in the doctrine of deterrence is the conviction that neither side can really defend itself in thermonuclear war. This disbelief in the feasibility of "national defense" immediately calls into question a concept that is traditionally thought to be at the heart of international politics: the principle of national sovereignty.

SOVEREIGNTY

The meaning of sovereignty, and the question of its utility as a concept, are problems that have plagued students of politics for centuries. But the notion is not reserved for the classroom; it also enters into everyday popular argument.

In the United States, for example, groups like the John Birch Society regularly invoke American "sovereignty" against what they believe are encroachments on American freedoms by the United Nations or some of its agencies. Often such complaints focus on the International Court of Justice, for some people fear that American interests may some day be sacrificed by that "world court" on which non-American judges also sit. Americans who share this fear demand that the United States not allow itself to be dominated by the court in any dispute with another state. They insist that, by invoking the "Connally Amendment," the United

18 Thomas C. Schelling and Morton H. Halperin, *Strategy and Arms Control* (New York: Twentieth Century Fund, 1961), p. 1.

States can in fact exempt itself from the court's jurisdiction. For the Connally Amendment provides that, whenever the United States feels that a particular international controversy is a "domestic" American problem, it may ignore the jurisdiction of the world court. Acceptance of the compulsory jurisdiction of the court, which is what many other nations have done, is regarded by these groups as an infringement upon American "sovereignty." Similarly, those who have continued to oppose American signing of the United Nations Declaration on Human Rights base much of their position on what they regard as a threat to American sovereignty.

These attitudes imply a definition of sovereignty that was probably never really accurate in the past but—more importantly for our purposes —has almost no relevance for the present: that "sovereignty" means independence, or the capability for independent action. As we pointed out at the beginning of this chapter, it is a fact that Brezhnev or Kosygin in many ways have more to say about the foreign (and the related aspects of domestic) policy of the United States than do most American officials. As the Vietnamese war escalates, or the Kremlin threatens a crisis, American defense spending is likely to increase, taxes can be expected to rise, and some domestic American programs, such as aid to education, are almost certain to be threatened with curtailment.[19]

It should be clear, moreover, if the United States cannot really be regarded as fully in control of its own actions, how much more this dependence on others must be characteristic of smaller and weaker nations. Without outside military aid, many states have been unable to defend themselves from potential and actual aggression; this was true in the case of Iran, Laos, and Israel. Others, like Thailand, are forced to desist from aggression or aggrandizement. Thailand covets Cambodian territory, yet it does not act for fear of generating American displeasure. Some, like India, could not feed their own populations without massive gifts of food from abroad.

Thus in actuality no nation is independent: the ties and dependencies that result from the patterns of military and political power, of economics and finance, and even of sentiment (to name only a few) require us to recognize that it is interdependence, rather than independence, that characterizes politics among nations.

Sovereignty, therefore, if by that term one implies total control over one's destiny, may be altogether dismissed from today's vocabulary as a useful concept. It could also be maintained that the notion was obsolete almost from the time when it was introduced by Jean Bodin, whose *De Republica* appeared in 1576. The concept of sovereignty that Bodin formulated was a product of his time, designed for the major political

[19] Even the space programs, among the most glamorous, are affected. It was reported, for example, that NASA "can only look to its most spectacular achievements to ward off further cuts in its budget as the Administration and Congress look for ways to reduce the civilian budget *so as to finance the Vietnamese war*." *The New York Times*, December 16, 1965 (italics added).

development of his time: the rise of the territorial state. Thus Bodin stressed the state as superior, not only to the universal claims of emperor and pope, but to the divisive pretensions of the feudal lords as well. The essence of Bodin's "sovereignty" is the idea of a unified government, embodied in an absolute monarch (or "sovereign") whose authority to make and enforce the laws in a given territory is unchallengeable.

Three Changes. This elevation of the monarch was the first of three major transformations that have affected the concept of sovereignty. The ascendancy of the king raised a central problem of international law, and sometimes of diplomacy as well, which arose in this way: If the sovereign, the embodiment of the state, is the supreme law-giver and law-enforcer in the state, can there be any laws or rules to which the state itself is subservient?

In Bodin's own time this apparent conflict was not too difficult to resolve, since it was generally conceded that the absolute internal power of the monarch was legitimized by divine right and natural law. Thus the power of the king was understood to be subordinate to elementary principles of justice and "right" behavior, embodied in what was known as "natural law." The two most famous classical authorities on international law, Hugo Grotius in the seventeenth century, and Emeric Vattel in the eighteenth, also took this position: that international law is reconciled with sovereignty through the principles of natural law. This meant that, when the doctrine of sovereignty was introduced, there was also a framework, or a system of constraint, by which the authority of the state was limited. Bodin himself, though he stressed the authority of the sovereign, specifically included among the laws that bind the sovereign "the law that is common to all nations."

Popular Sovereignty. The acceptance of natural law among the leaders of nations established, we must repeat, a common framework for international politics. It tended to provide a set of limits on the behavior of nations. Soon, however, in the wake of republicanism, monarchs ceased to be regarded as the holders of absolute power in their realms. Yet men were unwilling to give up the idea of sovereignty—which meant that the doctrine of sovereignty was to undergo its second transformation.

This was an attempt to graft onto the "state" itself those sovereign qualities that originally had been the attributes of a personal ruler. It raised the problem that was to bother students of politics for generations —namely, to find the sovereign power in those states in which there was no longer a monarchy, or where the monarch had become largely symbolic. As Brierly was to conclude, "That is a hopeless quest"; yet some scholars have continued to hunt for the location of sovereignty

> . . . as if sovereignty, instead of being a reflection in theory of the political facts of a particular age, were a substance which must

surely be found somewhere in every state if only one looked for it carefully enough.[20]

The problem, of course, was that as kings were displaced, the people themselves came to be regarded as the source of authority in each political system. In brief, after the French Revolution the doctrine of popular sovereignty was accepted. This was an enormously important doctrine, both as a revolutionary slogan and as an expression of the demand that government should serve the people. Analytically, however, and especially in the study of international politics, the doctrine of popular sovereignty has been a source of confusion. For one thing, an uncritical acceptance of the implications of "rule by the people" has given rise to an exaggerated nationalism. When we add to this the traditional belief that sovereignty means absolute power, the result is a conception of the state that does not fit reality.

The Walls Come Down. Yet in its first two transformations the idea of "sovereignty" was a useful practical tool. In its first phase, "the doctrine was of great stabilizing value in the contest between kings and feudal lords";[21] in its second phase, "the conception of popular sovereignty . . . provided the national democratic state with a potent political weapon."[22]

We now seem to be passing through the third phase, and in this era the usual notions about sovereignty seem particularly open to question. For it has been traditionally felt that one essential aspect of sovereignty is that *within* the borders of a state the "sovereign" power is supreme. This supremacy rested on the understanding that the sovereign power had the power to preserve the territorial integrity of the state. In fact, it is this aspect—sometimes called the "impenetrability" of the state—that is often regarded as the distinguishing feature of politics among nations.

One scholar, for example, asks rhetorically, what it is that ultimately sets one state off from another, "permitting us to characterize it as 'independent,' 'sovereign,' a 'power'?" His answer is that the idea of "state" has meaning for us in its "physical, corporeal capacity: as an expanse of territory, encircled for its identification and defense by tangible, military expressions of statehood, like fortifications and fortresses."[23] There is, of course, a certain element of crudeness in that analytical scheme. Nevertheless, it is clear that, in a world in which for several centuries there has been no authority above nations, the state has in fact performed the vital function of physical protection.

It is as a result of this power to protect its population from interference by other governments that the state claims and maintains its

20 J. L. Brierly, *op. cit.,* pp. 13–14.
21 Eagleton, *International Government,* p. 22.
22 Morgenthau, *op. cit.,* p. 313.
23 John H. Herz, *International Politics in the Atomic Age* (New York: Columbia University Press, 1959), p. 40.

authority as supreme law-giver within its territory—its "sovereignty." What, however, is the effect on sovereignty if an overriding "framework" —which at the time of Bodin was derived from natural and divine law— is restored after long absence to the structure of politics among nations?

This is precisely the question raised by the dire predictions about thermonuclear war. According to the nuclear physicist J. Robert Oppenheimer, an accurate simile for thermonuclear war between the two great powers is that of "two scorpions in one bottle."

This phrase, and many others like it, have one fundamental point to stress. They all suggest that, for the first time in centuries, a transcendent, authoritative element has been introduced into politics among nations—namely, that the fear of mutual destruction can serve as a constraint within whose limits international politics must now be viewed. This mutual fear, which Sir Winston Churchill early termed a "balance of terror," is based, of course, on the assumption that states cannot effectively defend themselves in thermonuclear war. If this is so, then that ultimate function that the doctrine of sovereignty helped to reflect—the intent and the capability of the state to erect a "hard shell" around itself—no longer has meaning.

Very briefly, however, we must add here that not all are agreed that effective defense is today impossible. As we pointed out earlier, there has been in the past recent past an analytical tendency to anticipate the products of military technology. For example, the notion of "two scorpions in a bottle" was raised at the very beginning of the nuclear age, when even the United States possessed a very limited capacity to wage nuclear war. Certainly the fear of *mutual* suicide was altogether unreal up to the time when the Soviet Union possessed a thermonuclear arsenal and delivery system sufficient to "destroy" the United States. Yet the notion of a "balance of terror" had wide currency years before such a Soviet capability existed, if indeed it does now exist.

Similarly, it is a fact that until quite recently, both Russian and American strategic power have been dependent primarily on manned aircraft; yet for years discussion has proceeded as if both were in fact capable of push-button missile destruction. Indeed, the idea of the "unthinkable" war is now so widely accepted, that evidence on the other side—that national political survival *is* possible—seldom receives attention. Such evidence has begun to appear,[24] and the student of international politics, faced with claims that world politics today is fundamentally "new" and different from the past, must weigh this evidence. The doctrines both of internal and external sovereignty, and many other notions about world politics, bear re-examination in a world where the destruction threatened by war today does in fact call into question national political survival.

For example, while sovereignty never did mean complete independence, it is nevertheless a profound irony that the great powers are

[24] Kahn, *op. cit.*

perhaps less free in their actions today than at any previous time in modern history. The Soviet Union, which regards a minuscule West Berlin located 100 miles *within* Soviet-controlled territory as an intolerable thorn in its side, still does not feel free to remove the sore. The United States, which regards as a threatening affront a tiny Communist-associated Cuba situated only 90 miles from American shores, is also paralyzed:

> And paradoxically, the most powerful powers . . . are exactly the ones which, as the most dangerous opponents of their opponents, become the natural targets for destruction on their part. Thus utmost strength now coincides in the same unit with utmost vulnerability.[25]

This suggests that there are important limits on the actions of any state, even and especially the most powerful among them. It suggests, too, that sovereignty, as of the time of Bodin, Grotius, and Vattel, can again be understood as existing within certain overriding restraints on national action. Earlier, the conception of natural law and divine legitimacy helped provide the framework within which states acted. Today, in the thermonuclear era, the limiting framework may derive from a mutual interest in avoiding all-out conflict. This does not mean the end of sovereignty, nor does it mean that the doctrine no longer has any utility, since sovereignty is not necessarily inconsistent with certain forms of consensus among states. Instead, let us recognize that the concept of sovereignty has had several different meanings at several different points in time, and that the doctrine is indeed useful only to the degree that it reflects existing political facts.

This means that we must recognize the relative inability of even strong and powerful nations to deal effectively with affronts to their sovereignty, in spite of the fact that they possess the physical and military capacity to take action. The failure of France and Britain to oust the Nasser regime at the time of the Suez invasion of 1956 is one illustration; the continuing thorn that West Berlin represents to the Soviet Union is another; so, of course, is the grudging and tacit recognition that Washington affords the Castro regime in Cuba. Most striking, no doubt, has been the continued existence of the Communist regime in North Vietnam. For that government, which could be destroyed by the United States in a matter of hours with relative impunity, has sponsored actions that have brought great harm to American interests and citizens. This is one more instance of a great power tolerating problems that are clearly within its military and material power to lessen or remove.

The relative inability to act highlights a major restraint on sovereign independence—the problem that is posed today by demands for revolutionary political change. Sometimes the major instruments pressing for such change are actors in world politics that are not sovereign states.

25 Herz, *op. cit.,* p. 41.

This is the problem represented in the war in Vietnam, and by the Viet Cong. It was represented most prominently prior to that in the rebellion in Algeria, and in the "insurgency" in Malaya.

The period since World War II has been plagued by this development, which has been illustrated also in Greece, the Philippines, Laos, Yemen, Nagaland, Cuba, and at least a score of other places. Common to almost all of these is the fact that non-sovereign entities, usually espousing national independence and "self-determination," have resorted to violence in ways that have deeply marked not only international but national politics, too. For years, as the chapter on France has pointed out, the acts leading to the establishment of the Fifth Republic were intimately connected with the existence of the non-sovereign F.L.N. movement in Algeria. That movement had a major impact on international relations as well, for the bulk of French ground forces were in Algeria for several years—which in turn affected the foreign policies of many nations and the military policies of the NATO nations in particular.

Often these struggles have been pictured as the consequences of a particular "nationalism" rebelling against one form or another of "imperialism." Thus the war in Vietnam has been pictured by the Communist nations as a nationalist struggle against American "imperialism," just as the earlier Viet Minh struggle was (more accurately) portrayed as a war against French opposition to full Vietnamese independence. Those two terms—"nationalism" and "imperialism"—are so freely used, and have been subjected to so many meanings, that the student of politics must treat them with care.

NATIONALISM

Marxism maintains that imperialism is the inevitable consequence of capitalism, and that, in turn, it inevitably results in war. But just what is imperialism; is it exclusively the product of economic forces? What, on the other hand, is the contemporary role of nationalism? Both the Marxian and Western world are avowedly "internationalist," but does that fact imply that they are both somehow "against" nationalism? What is nationalism, after all; is it necessarily found in conjunction with imperialism?

To the student of nineteenth-century history especially, the idea of nationalism represents essentially an integrating force—the bringing together of like peoples into some form of political unity. Similarly, international politics is quite cognizant of this integrative aspect of nationalism.

While in general it is correct to view the "nation" as an ethnic and cultural entity, tied together by such forces as common language, history, and outlook, we must also recognize that often the nation is not coterminous with the state. There can be and there have been several "nations" within a single state, as in Malaysia, Canada, and Cyprus. The discrepancy among the ethnic groups within those states has frequently been a major source of tension, and often of bloodshed. The student of international politics, who needs to understand the components of national power, must deal with those divisions. For national "identity," or unity, is one of the elements of the power and capability of nations; it must be weighed alongside such factors as industrial status, population size, territorial configuration, and other elements.

Generally, however, and especially during the nineteenth century, nationalism was an internally important cohesive force. In recent generations, and particularly as the concept has been applied to the formerly colonial areas of Africa and Asia, the term has become evocative of disintegrative and tension-producing forces. Frequently, for example, we hear references to the role in international politics of Asian and African "nationalism." The role of nationalism, moreover, is often stressed as an ingredient in the foreign policies of Russia and China— two states that can hardly be regarded any longer as newly emergent nations. Nevertheless, it is often questioned whether the policies adopted by the Soviet Union and China are the result of Communist ideology or are merely traditional Russian and Chinese policies, newly wrapped in Marxist clothing.[26]

The point is that "nationalism" need not necessarily evoke an image of a recently colonial people, or of a nation that is still struggling to become independent of foreign political control. We would not be doing justice to the major role of the concept if we limited it in that manner, since some of the major states have adopted policies from time to time in which nationalism has seemed to be a crucial element. Germany under Hitler, of course, is a prime example; German nationalism has contemporary relevance because of the tension that has resulted from a divided Germany, a situation that most Germans are presumed to abhor. French nationalism, heavily endowed with an element of prestige, certainly helps to account for the lack of grace with which France has reluctantly dissolved her empire. Finally, Americans tend to overlook an important instance of nationalism close to home. Many of Canada's recent foreign and domestic policies are understandable only in the light of the determination to assert Canadian nationalism against the informal dominance of the United States.

The New Nationalism and World Politics. The nationalism that makes today's headlines, on the other hand, often seems only slightly related to the traditional use of the term. Traditionally, nationalism looked back fondly to a people's historical past, and the relics and attributes of that past. The emphasis of traditional nationalism was on the common

26 One of the most prominent authorities on nationalism has recently commented: "And we should not overlook the fact that nationalism, as well as communism, is a mark of contemporary Russia and China." Carlton J. H. Hayes, *Nationalism: A Religion* (New York: The Macmillan Company, 1960), p. 2.

historical and cultural characteristics, even common myths, that served to differentiate one nation from another. Those common characteristics, refashioned in each case as nationalistic symbols, have been used as the ingredients for welding together the peoples we now know as single nations.[27]

Today, however, we must recognize that, in the "new nations," there is often no common heritage—as, for example, in parts of Southeast Asia and Africa. What we know as the "new nations" today were, in many instances, formed into nations only because the colonial powers (for their own purposes) so structured them. Indonesia is one of the clearest illustrations—it exists as a "nation" today only because of decisions made by the Dutch and the Japanese.[28] More interesting, even where a great and common heritage does exist, some of its aspects may be regarded as obstacles to modernization, as seems to be the case in the United Arab Republic.[29]

There is of course a common experience shared by the new nations: they have all been ruled in the past by alien colonial powers. The Bandung Conference of twenty-nine nations, which met in 1955, is evidence of such shared attitudes. That conference symbolized the effort to construct an Afro-Asian "bloc" in world politics—unified, presumably, by their common colonial experience, their suspicion of the West, and their desire to remain uncommitted and non-aligned in the bipolar conflict. With these as central elements in the attitudes of the new nations, along with the fact that their accession to independence has added enormously to the number of states now active in world politics, it is clear that the student of politics must learn to assess the impact of non-aligned nations on world politics.[30]

The United Nations, for example, which seemed in its early years to be a useful instrument of Western diplomacy, has been transformed by the recent additions (especially since 1955) of several dozen new nations; the greatest impact has been on the General Assembly. The "Afro-Asian" bloc has been the particular focus of attention, and the idea has often been put forward that the West, being roundly disliked in its former colonial areas, could no longer expect to be successful in UN voting, if these new nations took to voting as a solid bloc.[31] Political analysis is eminently suited to determine whether such a bloc could in fact be established and maintained, for this is essentially a question of the conditions that lead to a political coalition. Indeed, recent studies have attempted to determine to what degree, and on what sorts of issues

27 An excellent brief introduction to the subject is Hayes's *Nationalism: A Religion.*
28 See Bernard K. Gordon, *The Dimensions of Conflict in Southeast Asia* (Englewood Cliffs, N.J.: Prentice-Hall, Inc., 1966), pp. 84–86.
29 P. J. Vatikiotis, "Dilemmas of Political Leadership in the Arab Middle East," *American Political Science Review* (March, 1961), esp. pp. 103–07.
30 A good beginning is in Carlos P. Romulo, *The Meaning of Bandung* (Chapel Hill, N.C.: University of North Carolina Press, 1956). For a more recent examination see "Nonalignment in Foreign Affairs," *The Annals of the American Academy of Political and Social Science* (November 1965).
31 Hans J. Morgenthau, *op. cit.,* pp. 488–92.

these nations have in fact been voting as a unit. One analysis concludes that "in spite of the formidable reputation of the fabulous 'Afro-Asian bloc,' there are no groups of states that vote less like a bloc than those from Africa and Asia."[32] Thomas Hovet, on the other hand, asserts that, while the bloc presents "a far from united voting record . . . , it has been fairly effective in 'going with the Assembly majority'."[33] Most important, however, is the point that "the Afro-Asian bloc has but rarely voted as a unit; its vote has typically been split, with some members voting with the American, others with the Soviet bloc, and a very considerable number abstaining."[34]

National Interest. One major reason for the apparent fact that there is no bloc of non-aligned nations is that, despite their common colonial experience, and their similar desire for rapid economic advancement, these nations often have interests that conflict with one another. They are agreed in their determination to preserve their nationalism, but in little else. The most striking illustration of this inability to agree on significant problems was the failure of the non-aligned nations to convene a highly touted conference in Algeria in 1965. Designed to serve as the second instalment in the neutralists' movement established at Bandung in 1955, the conference foundered on the shoals of conflicting national interest. Indonesia was annoyed with India, and Ghana was upset by the Congo's policies; the "spirit of Bandung" was barely remembered only a decade after its establishment.

"Nationalism" must therefore be approached with care: it certainly is no longer the liberal, humanitarian force that it was in the nineteenth century, when it became so readily associated with the desire to rid one's people of the domination of an alien aristocrat. While nationalism among the newly independent states does serve as something of an anti-colonial bond, the sentiment itself has not been capable of transcending the particular "nationalisms" of the several nations that share that sentiment. Some obvious illustrations of this separatist function appear, for example, in the Arab world. Despite the common bonds of language, the oneness of their faith in Islam, their hatred for Israel, and their anti-Western feeling, some of the sharpest exchanges in the Middle East have been between the leaders of Jordan, the United Arab Republic, and Saudi Arabia.

If we consider Southeast Asian "nationalism," it quickly becomes clear that, whatever common experiences do bind those states together, and even despite their many ethnic and religious ties, the region of Southeast Asia is torn by national rivalries. Burma, India, and Cambodia maintain that their preferred method for preserving their national

32 Roderick C. Ogley, "Voting and Politics in the General Assembly," *International Relations* (April 1961), p. 158.
33 Thomas Hovet, Jr., *Bloc Politics in the United Nations* (Cambridge, Mass.: Harvard University Press, 1960), p. 87.
34 Morgenthau, *op. cit.*, p. 491.

independence is to emphasize their non-alignment and neutralism, while Thailand, Pakistan, the Philippines, and Malaysia have joined in military alliances with Western nations. Afghanistan and Indonesia, on the other hand, have important ties with the Soviet Union. These cold-war differences, however, are merely a thin veneer, barely able to hide even more basic tensions among these states—tensions that would exist even if there were no bipolar struggle.[35] Thus Indonesia and Malaysia are engaged in open conflict; the Philippines and Thailand have broken diplomatic relations; and, of course, India and Pakistan have been engaged in a conflict over Kashmir ever since both of them gained their independence.

Moreover, some of the new nations, even aside from the policies they adopt toward Russia, China, and America, have made arrangements with other smaller nations that tend to destroy the myth of "Afro-Asian solidarity." Thus Burma and Ghana, whose spokesmen were in the forefront at Bandung, have very strong economic ties with Israel, whose very existence is anathema to the Arab nations. Similarly, Indian spokesmen defended Malaysia's right to exist while Indonesia was landing troops there—thereby angering President Sukarno. In response to this Indian rebuff, Indonesian leaders then supported China's position when New Delhi and Peking were at odds. Yet India and Indonesia had always been regarded as leaders of the "neutral" nations, and have generally adopted similar foreign policies. Their agreement came to an end, however, when they conceived their nation's interests differently. Their estrangement illustrates once again the fact that the concept of "national interest" seems to override whatever bonds of anti-colonial "nationalism" may exist.

From the standpoint of history we may maintain that, in the contemporary world, this continued emphasis on national interest and nationalism is at best foolhardy, uneconomic, and obsolete, and at worst, downright dangerous; from its standpoint, the Soviet Union also holds that nationalism must give way to the internationalism of the world's working peoples. Yet this advice may sound like an inverted form of "sour grapes" to the new nations—until they too have had their opportunity to taste the fruits of nationalism.

These fruits need not necessarily be armed conflict, since nationalism by itself does not cause conflict, any more than does sovereignty by itself. Yet the twentieth-century form of nationalism, typified best by Hitler and to lesser degrees by Italy and Japan before World War II— the form that we call "integral nationalism"—has often been associated with war. Charles Maurras, writing at the height of the Dreyfus Affair in France, is responsible for the term: an "integral nationalist," he wrote, "places his country above everything; he therefore conceives, treats, and resolves all questions in their relation to the national in-

[35] See Bernard K. Gordon, "Problems of Regional Cooperation in Southeast Asia," *World Politics*, XVI (January 1964) pp. 222–53.

terest."[36] Not surprisingly, "this integral nationalism of Maurras bred hatreds."

Nationalism, therefore, has come full circle. It began as a force for freedom, and has served particularly to liberate minorities from oppression. Yet now nationalism seems to be incomplete until it has singled out a minority that can then be utilized as a target for oppression.[37] It is this extreme form of nationalism, and the "excesses" that it perpetrates, on which so much blame has been laid. Observers have so often noted that the rise of nationalism was accompanied later by the outbreak of violence that some have even concluded that nationalism *causes* war. "Nationalism, whatever its form, makes peace forever insecure,"[38] is one example of this belief; the statement that nationalism is "like war, to which it leads,"[39] is another. These simple propositions are single-factor explanations; they do not take into account, for example, the historic fact that armed violence already existed in the pre-nation and pre-state world.

IMPERIALISM

A similar attempt at single-factor analysis has been made with regard to imperialism, and with equal futility. A major difference, however, is that, while the term nationalism even now evokes favorable connotations, because of its association with nineteenth-century liberalism and twentieth-century anti-colonialism, the label of imperialism is tantamount to slander. The term has become one of opprobrium, as it is used by almost all statesmen; today it has little analytic utility. Russian leaders complain of the plots of the "capitalistic imperialists," at the very same time that the West warns against the dangers of "Communist imperialism." The government of North Vietnam, celebrating the Fifth Anniversary of the Viet Cong movement in 1965, charged that "In replacing French imperialism U.S. imperialism has re-engaged on its own account the same flunkeys, *comprador* bourgeois, reactionary landlords, adventurists . . . and henchmen who successively served the French colonialists."[40] Thus, as one astute observer has said, "Everybody is an imperialist to someone who happens to take exception to his foreign policies."[41] The same writer defines imperialism "as a policy devised to overthrow the status quo."[42]

One prime difficulty surrounding the term is that sometimes imperialism is regarded simply as the opposite, or "enemy" of nationalism —which is too crude a distinction. Another, more important, problem

[36] Quoted in C. J. Hayes, *op. cit.*, p. 137.
[37] Louis Wirth, "Types of Nationalism," *The American Journal of Sociology* (May 1936), pp. 732–37.
[38] Norman D. Palmer and Howard C. Perkins, *International Relations: The World Community in Transition* (Boston: Houghton Mifflin, 1953), p. 56.
[39] Eagleton, *International Government*, p. 26.
[40] *Vietnam Courier*, Hanoi, December 7, 1965.
[41] Morgenthau, *op. cit.*, p. 45.
[42] *Ibid.*, p. 53.

is that too often we accept the Marxist assumption that imperialism is solely the product of economic forces. While there are, to be sure, illustrations to support the Marxist thesis, there are also many illustrations of "imperialism" that cannot be explained in Marxist terms.

There is no difficulty, for example, in finding instances of political change and conflict in which economic motives have been irrelevant. Some of the most prominent motives, historically, have been dynastic ambition, ideology and religion, revenge, and personal glory. All these and more have accounted for organized violence in man's history. And even in the age when imperialism was in its classic form, as some studies have shown, it was the political leaders who egged on the bankers, rather than the other way round.[43] Finally, it should be clear that, with regard to today's central conflict, the Marxist explanation of imperialism seems altogether irrelevant: of all the factors that divide Russia and America, "competition for markets and scarce raw materials" must rank among the least important. Thus, just as "imperialism" does not as a single cause explain world conflict, economic motivation does not by itself explain imperialism.

Moreover, if we accept the definition that imperialism implies fundamental political changes—"the overthrow of the status quo . . . the reversal of the power relations between two or more nations"— then it is also clear that not every shift in world politics can be called "imperialism."[44] There has been a reversal, for example, in the power relationship between Britain and America, but the word "imperialism" hardly seems applicable as a description of the process. Similarly, small nations in South America, Central America, Southeast Asia and Africa, are now contemplating entering into regular forms of regional economic and political cooperation. If those efforts should develop, assuredly the status quo in each of those regions will have been markedly altered, if not entirely overthrown. Yet, once again, the term "imperialism" would hardly seem to fit such changes.

Thus the student of politics will recognize that every viable political system must provide for stability and change; from this recognition our attention is again drawn to the means by which national power is channeled, limited, and controlled.

One way to stifle or channel conflict is, of course, through a Pax Romana, or world empire. Conflicts among the small states of Southeast Asia would no doubt be quelled if they were all incorporated into the Chinese Communist realm. That, in a sense, is "the peace of the grave." But the contemporary rebirth of nationalism suggests that accommodation of conflict at lower levels is called for. The same lesson flows from man's experience with such imperialisms as those typified by Hitler and Napoleon, with their visions of world conquest. And certainly, the

[43] Eugene Staley, *War and the Private Investor* (New York: Doubleday, Doran, 1935); Raymond Aron, "The Leninist Myth of Imperialism," *Partisan Review* (November–December 1951), pp. 464–72.
[44] Morgenthau, *op. cit.*, p. 45.

present ideological conflict makes it plain that means must be found for the control of conflict.

But how is this to be accomplished? One possibility has always been suggested, and that is the extension to the international sphere of an overriding law or rule-making authority, with adequate powers of enforcement. It has failed to take place up to now, however, and despite the growing recognition of interdependence among nations, no institutional framework—or world government—seems likely to emerge in the foreseeable future.

The Control of Conflict

A fundamental task for political science, therefore, is to discern the major political forces at work in the world community, and on that basis to determine at what levels the present and future accommodation of conflicts can be achieved.

BALANCE OF POWER

In recent centuries, for example, both the number and the relative equality of European states, as well as their policy flexibility, permitted the concept of a "balance of power" to have real meaning. There were few ideological attachments to bind one nation to another; unhampered by any need to build, maintain, or alter consensus among mass populations, statesmen in the eighteenth and nineteenth centuries could shift, or threaten to shift, their allegiances in any way believed to be necessary in order to maintain the balance of power among European nations.

There were problems in a balance-of-power system, and some observers now deny that it ever did work in the ways we generally assume. Nevertheless, the fact remains that statesmen at the time believed in its existence and often operated accordingly.[45] It helped sometimes to prevent the outbreak of war, and it certainly helped to prevent the establishment of the hegemony of any one country over the rest of Europe. For our purposes the important point is that the idea of a balance of power was quite well suited to a political world in which there were a limited number of states and a certain consensus on the "rules of the game." Its essential weapon for limiting and channeling national power was simply the element of counterpower. For the balance of power meant that a potential "troublemaker" had to expect to reckon with the threat or the actual use of force by a combination of states opposed to his goals.

[45] For an unsympathetic treatment see: A. F. K. Organski, World Politics (New York: Alfred A. Knopf, 1957). The most modern and sophisticated discussion, and a sympathetic one, on the other hand, is in Kaplan and Katzenbach, op. cit., pp. 30–44.

In the contemporary and near-foreseeable world, however, the classic balance of power has fallen out of context, and the concept itself is often attacked. Admittedly, there were important problems involved in the concept, such as imprecision in measuring the power and the intentions of various elements within a particular system of "balance." These and other difficulties even led many observers to the conclusion that the balance of power was itself among the *causes* of war. Thus Cordell Hull, after helping to lay the groundwork for the United Nations, happily concluded that "there will no longer be need for spheres of influence, for balance of power."[46] A generation earlier, Woodrow Wilson had been even more emphatic in denying that peace could be achieved through setting power against power.[47]

COLLECTIVE SECURITY

The primary result of this disenchantment with counterpower was the development of a widespread conviction that international organization, and its corollary, collective security, could better serve to limit and channel world conflict. But that notion seems to suggest an abdication from reality—a denial that there are fundamental and irreconcilable conflicts of interest among political actors. This thought is not too different from a pattern of thinking that is found at other levels of politics, too, which we would call "non-political." It has attracted many men to the notions of a "leader above the parties" in national politics, and of a "city manager" in urban politics. Similarly, in world politics, conceptions of international organization and collective security—to the extent that they seek to remove the "politics" from international relations—are seeking to deny or to push aside conflicts of interest rather than to deal with them.

In its original sense, collective security was meant to be as nearly universal as possible; it was an essential underlying principle of the League of Nations—the first "universal international organization." The concept of collective security is based on the logically correct premise that a state that is intending aggression probably will not act if *all* the other states of the world are ranged against the act, and the equally correct premise that, if aggression *is* committed, the combined force of the other nations will be sufficient to defeat the aggressor. A classic failure of attempts to invoke collective security—in a sense, a failure of international organization itself—is to be seen in the League's inability to act against Italy in the case of her aggression in 1935 against Ethiopia.

This failure underlined the fact that not all (or even most of) the

46 Alfred Vagts, "The Balance of Power: Growth of an Idea," *World Politics* (October 1948), p. 82.
47 Robert E. Osgood, "Woodrow Wilson, Collective Security, and the Lessons of History," in Earl Latham (ed.), *The Philosophy and Policies of Woodrow Wilson* (Chicago: The University of Chicago Press, 1958), pp. 187–98.

nations have an equal interest in preventing every aggression. It also indicated that not all states are equally willing to impair their relationships with any nation that is likely to commit aggression. Indeed, some bystander nations stand to gain from the aggression of others. As two perceptive critics point out, "The genius of collective security . . . lay in its ability to fragment opposition to an expanding nation . . . it placed an emphasis on collective action . . . when it was to the advantage of some not to act at all. . . ."[48]

Yet these failings in the concept are implicit in the assumptions of its parent, the idea of international organization itself. "International organization," as one of our foremost scholars has stressed, "tends to assume the equality of states"[49]—an assumption that is patently false.

Nations are, instead, vastly unequal—in almost every conceivable respect. They are as unequally endowed in their geography, for instance, as the United States and Poland; as rich and as poor in valuable natural resources as the Soviet Union and Nicaragua; as different in the ideals and ideologies that guide their policies as Australia and Communist China; and they are led by men as different as Neville Chamberlain and Adolf Hitler. It is precisely these inequalities that give rise to international conflict, for some nations have always as a consequence sought to alter and improve their situations. Thus any framework that seeks to control conflict and prevent wars, but lacks an effective instrument with which to bring about relative equality among the contestants (be that instrument force, moral suasion, divine right, or some other "equalizer") will not be heeded by those who expect instead to gain from conflict.

International organization, whether in the form of the League of Nations or the United Nations, has not possessed such an equalizer; it has, moreover, been based on a false assumption of equality. Its failure as a method for resolving or accommodating fundamental conflict can ultimately be traced to that false assumption. Any other analytical concept, or prescription for peace, which similarly fails to take into account the major political forces in the world community will be similarly ineffective. Thus new analytical concepts, if they hope to lead to more success than earlier efforts, must be prepared to break out of the restraints of traditional thought patterns and prior attempts.

The goal, however, is not new: it is to develop or to find the conditions that will encourage the development of a world political system in which there is a tendency toward the reduction of the use of armed violence as a way to settle conflicts.[50] Once we have stated that goal, the parameters of the analysis become clearer. The first step is to discern the major political forces in the world system; the second, to determine

---

[48] Kaplan and Katzenbach, op. cit., p. 43.
[49] Quincy Wright, The Study of International Relations (New York: Appleton-Century-Crofts, 1955), p. 203.
[50] Gabriel A. Almond and James S. Coleman (eds.), The Politics of the Developing Areas (Princeton, N.J.: Princeton University Press, 1960), p. 64.

to what degree the several analytical schemes for understanding and dealing with conflict are consistent with those forces, and at the same time with our preference for a less violent world.

CONFLICT CONTROL TODAY

It seems clear that three major forces threaten the peace today. First of these is the "revolution of rising expectations" or the "new nationalism." Most of the world's people are poor and illiterate, and their leaders are bent upon achieving a rapid improvement of their condition. This means that a revolution is going on all around us and, in any revolutionary environment, violence may be close at hand.

The second force is the still enormous ideological rift between the Soviet bloc and the nations of Western heritage. In recent years that rift has to some extent widened, as Communist China has increased in power and influence, and as the rising expectations of the world's poor nations have clearly remained unsatisfied. Indeed, as is so often pointed out, the gap between the rich nations and the poor nations, rather than growing smaller, has been growing wider. China in particular seeks to capitalize on the resulting frustration; it seeks also to utilize it in its effort to displace the Soviet Union as the leader of world communism. Thus China advocates revolution and violence now, and brands Russian efforts at the achievement of "peaceful coexistence" as a denial of Marx and a conspiracy with the West. The third force, consistently overshadowing the first two, is the awesome destructive capacity of thermonuclear weapons.

When we turn to the analytic concepts that man has previously developed to deal with national conflict, it is clear that the most famous one, the "balance of power," is no longer useful. Both as an analytic tool and as a prescription for peace, the balance of power is not in harmony with the three forces just referred to. It is especially inconsistent with ideologically based conflicts of interest, because ideological conviction and flexibility do not mix well. Moreover, the expectations that flow from balance-of-power analysis have not been borne out by the political realities of this generation.

In the early postwar years, for example, most observers would have expected the tendencies implicit in a balance-of-power framework to lead in the direction of "tight bipolarity," that is, with more and more nations becoming tied closely to either the Soviet Union or the United States. That would have meant a direct and continuing confrontation between the two nuclear giants. Frightening as this prospect is, it might at least have held out an appearance of stability, and stability in the overall system is one of the attractions of the balance-of-power idea. Presumably, that is, Russians and Americans might have agreed tacitly to share and divide global authority among themselves, and not to disturb each other's vital interests. But while Moscow and Washington have sought to avoid unnecessary provocations, it is not a tight bipolar world that has in fact come about. Instead, there has been a tendency, starting from the early bipolarity between Russia and America, to move toward a multi-centered world, as states like China, France, and India have gained in international stature. This tendency has been intensified by the increasingly widespread possession of nuclear weapons.

These are tendencies that Kaplan has described as "loose bipolarity," and the system of the "unit veto." By "loose bipolarity," he means a relatively multi-centered world political structure, and by "unit veto," a world wherein each and every significant state has a decisive nuclear capacity.[51] Both those structures seem to promise less global stability than a tight bipolar world dominated by Moscow and Washington, if for no other reason than the greater difficulty of controlling state be- havior when the number of significant state-actors increases.

The concept of international organization, as we have noted, is another important framework for analyzing world politics. But its assumptions are unreal, and as a prescription for peace the concept of the universal international organization seems very inconsistent both with the "revolution of rising expectations" and with the contemporary ideological split. The Soviet Union, for example, at one time attempted to change the original conception of the United Nations by substituting a proposed three-man or "troika" leadership for the secretary-general. This was done partly because Russia felt discriminated against by Western-supported secretaries-general, and also because it is plain old-fashioned Marxism-Leninism to destroy any parliamentary body that cannot be controlled. Starting from different premises, the United States has also at times been increasingly disenchanted with the United Nations —particularly the ever more important General Assembly, where the principle of "one nation-one vote" has, since 1955, worked against American national purposes in the international sphere.

The view of the new nations regarding the United Nations is also significant. For the first time able to exercise power independently, they are likely to be satisfied with the United Nations only to the extent that it is useful in permitting smaller states to take their independent stand between Russia and America. They seem not to desire the development of the United Nations into a "world government," in which the new nations must be least interested and for which they are in fact least prepared. Thus the new nations, along with Russia and Communist China, also complain that the present structure of the United Nations is inconsistent with today's reality. This is symbolized for them, of course, by the continued exclusion of Communist China from the United Nations, a development for which the United States is chiefly responsible. But it is also clear that the small new nations would rather not have a United Nations dominated by the giants. The developing nations recognize that, if the Soviets and Americans should ever reconcile their

51 Kaplan, *op. cit.*, p. 51.

differences, the United Nations, as an instrument for controlling and channeling conflict, could be dominated by those two states, even if they acted almost alone.

REGIONALISM AND ARMS CONTROL

Our thoughts must then turn to the means by which a "viable international order" (not inconsistent with the three major forces we have suggested) may in fact be achieved. Such an international order would have to be solidly based on a mutuality of interest of these three major forces. It would also have to allow and provide for accommodation of conflict.

Two approaches often suggested in order to meet these requirements are arms control and regional cooperation. The first has particular reference to great power relationships, while the second is seen as particularly applicable to the problems of the developing nations.

Arms-control measures raise immense problems, yet among specialists they are regarded as among the most promising developments in the changing patterns of international politics.[52] A former senior policy-maker in the United States has said that arms control provides "one area where joint action with the Communists may be feasible on the basis of mutual interests even while the underlying hostility persists."[53] The new nations, moreover, also have a great stake in successful methods for achieving arms control. To say the least, the continued progress of their "revolution of rising expectations" is basically dependent on the survival of the two blocs, and upon the ability of the wealthy and powerful nations to continue economic assistance to the new nations. Traditionally, these states have backed attempts to achieve military reductions, and especially to bring nuclear weapons under some forms of control.

And political relations between the United States and the Soviet Union, as we pointed out at the beginning of this chapter, are *not* typified merely by pure conflict and opposition. Their interest in arms control—symbolized, for example, by their agreement on the treaty prohibiting atmospheric nuclear testing—suggests that Moscow and Washington share a strong mutual interest in certain fields. This includes, obviously, a mutual desire to avoid a major war.

This common concern may now serve a function not too different from that which was provided by natural law in an earlier period and by the common consensus on limited means and objectives adopted by states in the balance-of-power era. It is the function of an overriding common interest in survival. Thus a suitable analytical framework for contemporary great power politics may lie in a context of arms reduction

[52] Schelling and Halperin, *op. cit.*
[53] Robert R. Bowie, "Arms Control and United States Foreign Policy," in Louis Henkin (ed.), *Arms Control* (Englewood Cliffs, N.J.: Prentice-Hall, Inc., 1961), p. 74.

and control, which also recognizes the persistence of polar conflict. In such a conceptual framework, hostility is conceded, but the institutions and measures necessary to bring about arms reductions, as others have said, can "lay a foundation for more extensive cooperation if and when that hostility should moderate."[54]

That hope is built upon a familiar hypothesis, which is that, as nations collaborate on narrow, functional issues, their experiences will lead to more broadly based political cooperation. As applied to the concept of arms control, it has been expressed in this way:

> In addition, the operation of agencies for international cooperation, if successful, might in the long run contribute to altering the political climate. This would not require the ending of conflicts of interest or disputes. It would mean rather that all states were prepared to accept the general structure of world order and to settle disputes and conflicts within that framework.[55]

This thesis also underlies much of the present interest, expressed by both statesmen *and* scholars, in the concept of regional cooperation. No doubt much of this interest has been rekindled by the experiences of the European states in the European Economic Community. Efforts toward economic integration there, among nations that have for generations been so much at odds with one another, have in fact assisted in developing striking levels of political consultation and multi-national cooperation. Moreover, these efforts at "community building" have attracted the attention of students of international politics, who see in the European prototype a direction that other nations may follow. Ernst Haas, for example, has said that the study of regionalism challenges the theorist because of its "potentialities . . . for insights into the process of community formation at the international level."[56]

When applied to the problems of the developing areas, the concept of regionalism has special attractions. Not only are these regions of great political instability—which makes them especially susceptible to involvement in the bipolar struggle—but their developmental problems are often greater than any one of them, acting alone, can reasonably handle. Thus regional cooperation, to the extent that it may reduce levels of tension among the new nations and simultaneously assist them in the resolution of their internal problems of economic development, deserves special attention today. This thought has not been lost upon the leaders of the new nations themselves, for among the most interesting of recent political patterns are the groping steps toward multi-national economic cooperation in Latin America, in Africa, and in Southeast Asia. Admittedly, the obstacles in the way of achieving such

---

54 *Ibid.*, p. 75.
55 *Ibid.*
56 Ernst B. Haas, "The Challenge of Regionalism," in Stanley Hoffman (ed.), *Contemporary Theory in International Relations* (Englewood Cliffs, N.J: Prentice-Hall, Inc., 1961), p. 223.

goals are high. In their own way, they are no less difficult to overcome than the problems faced by Russia and America in building arms-control agreements as an instrument for reducing great power tensions.

The student of international politics would be well advised to recognize the renewed interest in regionalism as one of the significant new patterns in international politics. For regionalism as understood today is not a "blue-sky" approach. It does not seek, as earlier dreams of international organization sometimes did, to ignore the differences among nations. Instead, it seeks to build upon the goals and interests of the nations that make up the international system and to find ways of harmonizing those interests. Its emphasis, for example, has been on means by which industrially poor nations can pool their resources in order to attract investment capital and build plants of efficient size. Steps of this kind are readily understood by leaders whose consuming interest is the rapid development of their own nations' economies.

In that sense, contemporary regionalism is an exquisitely *political* phenomenon. It builds upon one of the critical insights of political science: that coalitions or communities are derived from the accommodation of conflicting interests in ways that create new and *common* interests. The process of community-building among nations, however, must reckon with the powerful forces of culture, national traditions, and historically different patterns of behavior. Experiences in building the European Economic Community, for example, have shown that its members were encouraged to participate to the extent that national, or internal, procedures were respected and utilized. "Internal procedures," as Harold Guetzkow has pointed out in precisely this context, are "familiar procedures."[57]

Initial experiences in the Latin American and Southeast Asian efforts at regional cooperation tend to support that conclusion[58]—which makes this one of the most heartening developments in contemporary international relations. For it means that the central problem of world politics—that of alleviating the tensions that lead to armed conflict—may be in process of solution. At lower levels of political organization conflict has been lessened, and communities built, by generating shared goals. If the concept of regionalism, based initially on narrow and functional goals such as economic cooperation, leads to similar processes of community-formation at the international level, a major step will have been taken toward global political stability.

[57] Harold Guetzkow, "Isolation and Collaboration: a Partial Theory in Inter-nation Collaboration," in James N. Rosenau (ed.), *International Politics and Foreign Policy* (New York: The Free Press of Glencoe, 1962), p. 156.
[58] See Gordon, *The Dimensions of Conflict in Southeast Asia,* chap. VI.

SUGGESTIONS FOR ADDITIONAL READING

DEUTSCH, KARL W., *Nationalism and Social Communication* (Cambridge, Mass.: M.I.T. Press, 1953).

GORDON, BERNARD K., *The Dimensions of Conflict in Southeast Asia* (Englewood Cliffs, N.J.: Prentice-Hall, Inc. 1966).

HOFFMANN, STANLEY, *The State of War: Essays in the Theory and Practice of International Politics* (New York: Frederick A. Praeger, 1965).

KERR, MALCOLM, *The Arab Cold War 1958–1964* (Fair Lawn, N.J.: Oxford University Press, 1965).

MORGENTHAU, HANS J., *In Defense of the National Interest: A Critical Examination of American Foreign Policy* (New York: Alfred A. Knopf, 1951).

NYE, JOSEPH S., JR., *Pan-Africanism and East African Integration* (Cambridge, Mass.: Harvard University Press, 1965).

ROCK, VINCENT P., *A Strategy of Interdependence: A Program for the Control of Conflict Between the United States and the Soviet Union* (New York: Charles Scribner's Sons, 1964).

SCHELLING, THOMAS C., *The Strategy of Conflict* (Fair Lawn, N.J.: Oxford University Press, 1963).

THORNTON, A. P., *Doctrines of Imperialism* (New York: John Wiley & Sons, 1966).

WOHLSTETTER, ALBERT, "The Delicate Balance of Terror," *Foreign Affairs*, XXXVII (January 1959), 211–34.

Chapter 10

THE FOREIGN POLICIES
OF STATES

The preceding chapter examined politics among nations from a broad perspective, that of the international system itself. In this chapter we approach the subject with a narrower view, focusing our attention on the states as they act within the system. Everyday experience, of course, indicates that there are great differences among the nations from the point of view of their actions in foreign policy. They differ in the kinds of policies they try to follow as well as in the methods they use to shape and implement them. Do these differences affect the world political system in which they interact; if so, how? The reverse question should also be asked: In what ways does the nature of world politics affect the methods and content of any given state's foreign policy?

To illustrate the complex interrelationship between the system of world politics and the foreign policies of individual states, let us consider certain events associated with the 1961 meeting, sponsored by Ghana, Egypt, and Yugoslavia, of the leaders of neutralist nations at Belgrade. (We must remember that neutralism, as we have seen in the preceding chapter, does not mean neutrality in the traditional sense, but non-alignment with either the Communist or the Western powers in today's cold war.)

It was while the Belgrade meeting was in progress that the Soviet Union resumed atmospheric testing of nuclear devices, thereby breaking a two-year informal moratorium with Britain and the United States against such testing. The Soviet action flew in the face of well-known neutralist sentiment; leaders of most of the neutral nations had repeatedly expressed their opposition to atmospheric tests. The timing of the Russian decision seemed especially odd to some observers at the time. Why should the Russians have chosen to take a clearly unpopular step at precisely the moment when it would seem most likely to alienate neutral opinion? To the surprise, however, of many Western officials who waited for days for the chance to capitalize on this seeming Soviet propaganda error, and of the hundreds of journalists assembled in Belgrade, who prodded the neutralist leaders there for statements denouncing the Russian tests, no vehement protest was forthcoming. The meeting of neutralists instead came to an end after expressing officially only some very tentative criticism of nuclear testing in general, and with almost none of the neutralist premiers and presidents assembled in Belgrade (President Nasser of Egypt was a notable exception) publicly singling out the USSR for beginning the latest round of poisoning the atmosphere. A strong resentment of the neutrals then developed among many Westerners, who felt that if the United States and not the Soviet Union had been the first to break the moratorium, a storm of harsh criticism would have fallen on Washington. Yet the Russians seemed to suffer for their actions little loss of esteem in the eyes of neutrals.

The point of this episode is not that the neutralist leaders are necessarily favorable to the Soviet Union. Rather it illustrates the fact that most statesmen, neutralists included, expected the Soviet Union to disregard widespread sentiment against nuclear testing, to take such actions unannounced, and to act afterwards as if nothing untoward had happened. This sort of behavior would not, on the other hand, be expected from the United States. Part of the reason for these expectations plainly lies in the very different kinds of political system that exist in the two states. The incident illustrates two general propositions: first, that the foreign policy behavior of any given nation is in fact significantly linked with the kind of political system it has; second, that statesmen everywhere, recognizing this relationship, shape their expectations of any country's foreign policy partly in terms of their conception of that country's political system.

These propositions can be further illustrated by several events that occurred in 1956. When Britain and France invaded Egypt during the Suez Canal crisis, the international reaction was generally one of anger and bitterness. The United States found itself side by side with the Soviets in demanding withdrawal of the Anglo-French forces from Egypt, and even members of the British Commonwealth similarly expressed their great displeasure at London's actions. In Britain itself, members of the opposition Labour party (and some Conservatives) opposed the invasion, and a direct consequence of the thwarted landings was Anthony Eden's retirement as Britain's Prime Minister.

Yet at almost the same time, in Budapest, Russian tanks were bloodily suppressing the efforts of lightly-armed street fighters in the Hungarian rebellion. This instance of Russian armed aggression, however, distasteful though it was, apparently was regarded generally as a considerably less serious international crisis than the Anglo-French-Israeli use of force in Egypt. The principal reactions in the case of Hungary were some complaints from the Western world and the abortive appointment of a United Nations investigatory commission, which was subsequently refused permission to enter Hungary. Thus the Russians were able to complete their intervention successfully, with no effective international interference.

A major explanation for this difference between the consequential reaction to British-French intervention on the one hand and the inconsequential reaction to Russian intervention on the other is that statesmen, like average citizens, have come to expect the employment of extreme tactics in the arena of world politics from a dictatorship of the Russian pattern. A Western parliamentary democracy, however, whose policies and personnel are dominated by free political competition, operates in such a way as to lead us to expect not only milder foreign policy methods, but different long-term international goals as well.

Sometimes this general pattern of expectations is upset; in such cases the results prove interesting, as the case of the Berlin Wall illustrates. For the direct Soviet-American confrontation in Berlin has sometimes suggested that a nuclear war might well result from a spark in that city. Yet when the Russians erected their wall in 1961, and thus divided with finality the city of Berlin, the initial Western reaction was at most tentative. When American officials were criticized for their inability to deal effectively with this seemingly permanent division of Berlin, their replies indicated that they had been taken almost completely off guard. NATO planners had long been prepared for any number of the most extreme kinds of Soviet provocations in Berlin, including massive troop movements and the imposition of another blockade. But so outwardly mild an action as the erection of a brick and barbed-wire wall seems to have been overlooked by high-level planners, and no steps had been contemplated to deal with it.

The Role of "Objective Conditions" in National Foreign Policies

One should not conclude from the foregoing discussion that each nation's foreign policy is determined solely by its form of government. Nor should one infer that "democratic" states necessarily have responsible and "moral" foreign policies, while dictatorships inevitably have aggressive and irresponsible foreign policy goals and methods.

It is also clear, however, that there are certain immensely significant objective characteristics which differentiate nations from one another. Among those that obviously affect a nation's foreign policy goals and potentialities are its geography, including its location, terrain, and natural resources; its wealth and economic development; its over-all military capacity, and the history of its foreign relations with neighbors and other nations. We should be wary of trying to explain the foreign policy behavior of states by any one or more of such material factors alone, however, as some writers have attempted to do in the past.

GEOGRAPHY AND RESOURCES

British foreign policy has traditionally been explained in the light of Britain's geography and her historical desire to protect her independence against attempts at European domination by continental powers. Much emphasis used to be placed on Britain's geographic position as an insular state dependent on overseas territories both for supplies of food and raw materials and for markets for her manufactures. It has often been said, for example, that Britain was impelled to maintain a position of naval supremacy in order to keep vital sea lanes open—that is, to maintain the ability to exert her influence at distant points considered crucial to her role as an insular trading nation. The development of the British Empire was thus explained in essentially geographic terms. Indeed, one of the founders of "geopolitics," the conceptual school that seeks to explain political forces largely in terms of geographic determinism, was a Briton, Sir Halford Mackinder. His works, particularly his 1904 essay on "The Geographical Pivot of History," have had considerable influence on scholars and policy-makers alike. When men speak today of the "Eurasian Heartland," or of the advantages of land powers over sea powers, they pay an unknowing debt to Mackinder's influence.

Geographical explanations have also been given for the foreign policies of other nations. The geography of Russia, for example, is said to impose certain permanent demands on her foreign policy; implying that any Russian statesman must follow policies predetermined by his country's location and terrain. Two commonly mentioned factors are Russia's need for a warm-water port and its desire for "buffer" territories between its own borders and the nations of Western Europe. The concern with "buffer states" grows ostensibly from the absence of any natural barriers, such as major rivers or mountain ranges, which might separate European Russia and such major continental countries as Germany.

Germany has been regarded, both by the Germans themselves and by others, as a country whose size and location were inadequate to the dynamism of its society. This notion was most common after World War I, when many felt that the terms of the Versailles Treaty concerning Germany had been too harsh and restrictive. There was sympathy in England and elsewhere for a German foreign policy that aimed at "rationalizing" Germany's borders and restoring the former German economic and political dominance in Central Europe. Hitler, of course, used the slogan of *Lebensraum* ("living space") in support of his demands for more territory. It is interesting, however, that even though the

Germany of today is smaller in size than at any time in a century, and can hardly be said to dominate Europe politically, its people are nevertheless more prosperous and its government more stable than at any time in this same century. It would seem, therefore, that *Lebensraum* as such has little to do with the actual well-being of German society.

Much the same sort of paradox is to be seen in the case of Japan, a nation which by the 1930s had come to regard itself as forced by geography (and destiny) to establish a huge overseas empire. According first to extreme Japanese nationalists, and finally to the leaders of the government, it was geography that demanded that Japan have political control over the iron and coal of Manchuria and the rubber, oil, and food supplies of Southeast Asia; thus Japan was driven to embark on World War II. Yet the result of that war is that Japan does not now have political control over any of those coveted territories, and indeed has even lost territory that it possessed before Pearl Harbor. And still, in the face of "setbacks," Japan today is more prosperous than it ever has been, and its potential for even greater economic growth and wealth has reached new heights.

It should be clear from these illustrations that a nation's role in the international system is not determined, as some historians once thought, solely by its geography or by other "objective" conditions. Rather, conditions such as geographic location help define and shape the limits within which each nation frames its world role. Australia provides an excellent example of this admixture of influences. Geographically, Australia is located on the fringes of Southeast Asia, one of the world's most unstable, densely populated, and poorest regions. Its geographic position therefore impels Australia to seek some kind of coexistence with the dynamic neighboring world of Southeast Asia. At the same time Australia is an all-white country with an enormously high standard (and cost) of living. It benefits greatly from high agricultural production and a very small population and is economically drawn to the markets of Britain, Europe, and Japan, where its agricultural products can be sold at satisfactory prices. Thus Australian foreign policy tends to be ambivalent, and it is clear that geography is only one among the factors that help determine that policy.

TECHNOLOGY

The case of Australia illustrates a further point: objective conditions, such as geography and natural resources, gain or lose importance in accord with the technology of the time. Thus as Southeast Asian nations advance technologically and become more industrialized and wealthy (and perhaps more stable politically), they may become less worrisome to Australia and even provide a market for her expensive agricultural products. In that event, the traditional historical significance of Australia's geographical location will have been greatly altered. As a general proposition, we can say that the level of technology significantly affects the meaning and the utility of such objective conditions as geographic location or natural resources.

The Political System and Foreign Policy

Most important of all in determining how the various factors will blend in shaping foreign policy is the political system of a state. This is the crucial factor that finally sets the shape of a nation's foreign policies, although other objective conditions may have helped frame the outlines of those policies.

POPULAR GOVERNMENT

A cardinal feature of the political system in this respect is the role assigned to the people of the country, its body of citizens at large. This question has become especially important since World War I, when for the first time statesmen had to face the fact that their own countries' foreign policies, and those of other states as well, were no longer the private affair of small elite groups clustering around royal courts, diplomatic circles, and the great international banking and trading firms. The changing character of world politics is well described in one of the novels of C. P. Snow. In *The Conscience of the Rich,* Snow mentions the withdrawal of the March banking family from an active foreign policy role, and describes the family's system of having private business correspondents stationed in the various European capitals: "In 1880, the Marches were still better informed, over a whole area of facts where politics and economics fused, than any newspaper." By 1896, however, their long-standing role in world politics was coming to an end; by that time, "their loans of a million pounds or so to the Argentine or Brazil no longer went very far; they were coming near to a world of preposterous size—a world dangerous, mad, exciting beyond measure."

That is today's world, and in such an environment, foreign policy problems loom larger than ever before in human affairs: the stakes and risks are more formidable, and the number of players is greater, than at any time in history. Whereas traditionally world politics directly affected only limited numbers of people, and the overt effects of wars in particular were restricted, today whole populations are involved. This has come about not only because of the totally destructive capacity of modern weapons, but also because of the almost universal acceptance of popular sovereignty as the basis of modern governments. Whether a particular version of the doctrine of popular sovereignty is oriented toward groups and parties competing freely for power, as in the Western world, or toward a Soviet-type single party that purports to represent and speak for the entire population, this doctrine raises special foreign policy problems.

One of the most difficult of these problems has to do with the gap between, on the one hand, the peoples' will and understanding, and on the other, the views about the necessities of national interest and security that are held by officials directly charged with those responsibilities. This difficulty is most obvious in Western democracies with openly competing party systems, but it is also found in party-dictatorship regimes, where the leaders must assume that they know best what the people want and need, or what they *would* want if they had all the relevant information. For example, during the early years of the Soviet state there was a serious dispute between advocates of the doctrine of continuing world revolution, represented by Trotsky, and those represented by Stalin, who advocated a policy of securing Russia as the "home base" of world communism. In foreign policy terms this meant choosing between Soviet policies designed to help bring about many other revolutions around the world—which would have required the diversion of scarce Russian resources and capital—and a policy of turning inward. Stalin chose the latter, and in his efforts to build and preserve Russia, he found it necessary to establish, even by using the most extreme methods, a new consensus both within the Soviet Communist Party and more widely among the populace generally. The consequence was the establishment of a new orthodoxy and a new "party line."

The gap between popular preferences and the requirements of the national interest, as these were seen by responsible government leaders, was also faced in the United States during the early years of both world wars, at times when the United States was still abstaining from participation in armed conflict. Both the Wilson and Roosevelt administrations came increasingly to feel that American security would be endangered by a German victory, while in each instance it was clear that there was heavy mass sentiment against American involvement in war. The second of these breaks in synchronization, in 1940–1941, is so important a problem that its history and interpretation fill a shelf of books. Most spectacularly typified in the works of Professors William Tansill, Charles A. Beard, and Harry Elmer Barnes is the famous thesis that President Roosevelt deliberately provoked the Japanese into their Pearl Harbor attack. Roosevelt's purpose, according to this interpretation, was to galvanize the American people into fighting a war which the President believed necessary, and in the people's best interests, but which the people did not want.

One reason for the bitterness of partisan debate in such instances is the enormity of the consequences that can flow from foreign decisions. In other areas of governmental activity—say agricultural or tax policy—often the worst that can happen is that the people's resources are unwisely or foolishly expended. Such wrongs can frequently be set right later. But the results of an unwise or inept foreign policy may not always permit a second chance; literally, these can be matters of life and death. The Japanese decision to attack Pearl Harbor, for example, had irrevocable consequences affecting millions of lives; the American decision four years later to drop atomic bombs on Hiroshima and Nagasaki had equally enormous effects.

Thus, as we proceed to examine the methods employed by nations as foreign policy actors in the modern world, it is essential that we bear in mind first, that the audience watching, involved in, and affected by these decisions is much larger than ever before in history; and second, that the stakes involved in the decision-making are huge beyond precedent. With this in mind, we can then ask: How does the structure of government affect the formulation and execution of foreign policy?

GOVERNMENTAL STRUCTURE:
EXECUTIVE AND LEGISLATIVE ROLES

In the United States, many of the problems involved in planning and carrying out an effective foreign policy can be traced to familiar institutional difficulties, and especially to the division of responsibility for foreign affairs between President and Congress. While this responsibility was traditionally thought to be shared primarily by the President and the Senate, since the beginning of the postwar era there has been a considerable change. Today the House of Representatives is in many ways as potent a force in shaping foreign policy as the Senate, in spite of the arguments of Alexander Hamilton and others that the House was too large an assembly to meet the special requirements of foreign policy-making and in spite of the intentions of the Constitution's framers.

This development is largely a reflection of the crucial role played by finances in contemporary world politics. For it is the House, of course, that is initially responsible for revenue and appropriations measures, and representatives are notoriously jealous of their fiscal role. This means that the House today has enormous power in determining the size and shape of the various American foreign aid programs. It further enters the foreign policy field through its similar role in the determination of military appropriations and armed forces policy, key elements in the foreign policy of all modern nations. It is said that former Representative Carl Vinson, for years Chairman of the House Armed Services Committee, was once asked why he had never thought seriously about becoming Secretary of Defense, and he is said to have replied, "Why should I bother trying to run the military from over there [the Pentagon], when I can do it just as well from over here?" Whether it is apocryphal or not, this story illustrates the point that, in certain major areas of United States foreign policy today, the attitudes of some leading representatives are as significant as the views of the most prominent senators.

This is not to deny the continuing importance of the Senate's role in foreign policy. The Constitution does, after all, require that the President seek its "advice and consent" in the negotiating of treaties as well as in the appointment of such major officials as ambassadors, the Secretary of State, and his major assistants. The Senate has rarely, however, objected seriously to such Presidential nominations, although on occasion obvious senatorial coolness to a nominee has had its effect.

The Senate's role in the treaty-making process has been historically more important. The most famous, or perhaps infamous, of Senate actions in this connection was the struggle successfully led by several leading senators to prevent America from entering the League of Nations. But two developments, one of them curtailing the Senate's influence, the other tending to extend it, have altered the Senate's foreign policy role in important respects.

First, the President has increasingly made end-runs around the Senate in his negotiations with other countries, particularly since about 1920. Nowadays, the overwhelming majority of American agreements with foreign states are not embodied in treaties but instead take the form of "executive agreements." It is clear that the treaty, the classical instrument of international commitment, has been significantly downgraded in American practice. The question may be raised, "But what is the difference between a treaty and an executive agreement, and does that difference matter?" No easy answer is forthcoming, for there seems to be no clear dividing line which separates those subjects that must be ratified as treaties from those that can be processed as executive agreements. One thing is clear: that the executive agreement does not require Senate consent. It is strictly the President's affair and is thus more quickly and easily processed. On the other hand, the instrumentality of the treaty is still preferred in American practice when the President wishes to convey to the world, to the American people, and to the particular countries concerned the most solemn commitments of the United States, a preference that probably reflects the time-honored prestige of the treaty.

The Senate's traditional role in the foreign policy process is paralleled by the great prestige that has generally been accorded the Senate Foreign Relations Committee. This committee, studies show, has been regarded by most senators themselves as the most attractive committee assignment, and until recently senators vied for appointments on Foreign Relations. In part this prestige is a reflection of the six-year tenure characteristic of the Senate generally, for longevity of service has meant that committee members built up considerable expertise on foreign policy matters. That in turn is significant when we recall that most executive officials concerned with foreign policy problems—for example, assistant secretaries of state and directors of foreign aid programs— spend notoriously short terms in office. Thus the senators who deal with them are sometimes as knowledgeable as the officials. A more specific reason for the committee's great importance is a conviction, shared by most senators, that they *ought* to exercise a certain prerogative in foreign affairs. As a result committee members conduct frequent and intensive hearings involving the Secretary of State and his assistants; they finance studies of foreign policy problems by universities and other agencies; on occasion some have even attempted to involve themselves directly in the policy-making process. They are thus a group that every President tends to respect.

Nevertheless, the President and his assistants responsible for foreign affairs probably wish at times that there were no Senate at all, and no Committee on Foreign Relations in particular. Early in 1962, for example, a Foreign Relations subcommittee returning from a study trip to Africa issued a report which must have disturbed considerably both the African specialists in the State Department and some American ambassadors in the field. The report frowned on American aid to countries that were unfriendly to Washington's foreign policy and that did not, in their internal policies, respect "basic rights and freedoms." "American aid," the committee concluded, should not "be used to assist governments engaged in the systematic suppression of free expression."[1] The same committee made headlines several years later, when its chairman, Senator Fulbright, was openly critical of President Johnson's intervention in the Dominican Republic in 1965. Another committee member, Senator Morse, declined to participate in the Administration's delegation to an Inter-American conference held soon afterwards because, in the light of his disagreement with the President on this subject, he felt it would be improper to be regarded as part of the President's "team."

Such pronouncements inevitably make life difficult for executive officials charged with implementing American foreign policy. And foreign governments and observers find such criticism especially hard to understand when it comes from avowed supporters of the President and members of his own party. In this respect the American system is unique, since in no other major government are legislative committees so prominent, nor is there such a high degree of public and "official" criticism of the government's foreign policies.

In Britain, for example, committees of the House of Commons are neither specialized nor crucial to begin with, and because of their changing membership, have little opportunity to build up expertise in any one field. Before World War I there were suggestions from time to time that the Commons establish a permanent committee on foreign affairs, but the proposal seldom found wide support. For one thing there was a reluctance to put classified information into the hands of a legislative body; more particularly, there was some question about what the Opposition's role would be if it was able to come into possession of secret data. Probably more important in avoiding any change, however, was the traditional concern in England with maintaining central control of foreign policy—keeping it within the province of the foreign secretary in par-

1 *The New York Times*, January 14, 1962.

ticular and the cabinet generally. Thus no formal structural change has been made in British practice so far.

A number of informal techniques have developed, however, which tend to satisfy some of the pressures for a parliamentary committee on foreign affairs. In the British Labour party, for example, front-bench members meet weekly during parliamentary sessions; at these meetings an "external affairs group" leads a discussion on current foreign policy problems. A roughly similar body operates for the Conservative party; indeed, it seems to have been responsible for one of Britain's major policy changes of the 1930s. The occasion was the Hoare-Laval Agreement of 1936, which would have given London's "approval" to some of Mussolini's early conquests. Members of the Conservative party's Foreign Affairs Committee, however, expressed strong opposition. Amid similar pressures from other quarters, the policy was hurriedly dropped and there was some cabinet reshuffling as well. Such informal party measures, together with the general British determination to keep control of today's complex foreign relations in ministerial hands, have somewhat diluted the earlier pressure for an American-style foreign relations committee.

In France, on the other hand, such a committee does exist. Under the Fourth Republic, and during the final years of the Third, the Committee on Foreign Affairs may have been the most important among the standing committees of the French lower house. While its role should not be exaggerated, the Foreign Affairs Committee of the National Assembly became a repository of considerable knowledge of world politics. During the interwar period, for example, several of the committee's presidents later served as foreign ministers, so that the chairmanship sometimes came to be regarded as a stepping stone to the Foreign Ministry. Under DeGaulle the committee's importance—not great in the Third or Fourth Republics—has declined considerably. It continues to hear the foreign minister and questions both him and the Premier on issues of French foreign policy; but like parliament generally in the Fifth Republic, the committee has seen its role greatly diminished, and its conduct of business has become rather perfunctory.

What can be learned from this glimpse of parliaments in regard to foreign policy matters? Can we say that they have become an anachronism in a thermonuclear era, an obsolete reminder of an age when foreign affairs could be understood and dealt with by the elected representatives of the plain people? While the American Congress, the Senate especially, is the most active among the three legislatures we have considered, even its role seems narrow. The fundamental question is, after all: What kinds of authority can a legislative body exercise in this field? Essentially, the answer has seemed to be: policy initiation, policy reversal (veto), and policy amendment or modification. Today it is only the last that seems to be generally in use.

Case studies show that, in some instances, Congress has initiated aspects of American foreign policy, but in no case have these constituted significant policy changes. Part of the reason, of course, lies in the sheer lack of time that most congressmen suffer from. Simply to understand and keep up with the complexities of world politics requires far more time for the reading of available data than a congressman's other duties allow him. If congressmen want to go further, and attempt rationally to *reverse* some aspects of the President's policies, they face the same problem: by comparison with foreign policy officials in the executive branch, they lack the expertise and the needed information to challenge basic proposals. In 1948, for example, the Senate Republican Policy Committee estimated that it would take each interested senator four or five months to read the assembled material on the proposed Marshall Plan alone— and this material did not yet include the appropriation committee reports! When one considers such intricate foreign policy problems as countering guerilla warfare in Southeast Asia, it is a wonder that Congress manages to keep its head above water. In seeking advice, Congress may be able to muster perhaps a dozen of its own expert assistants on such a matter, while the President and secretary of state can call on the information-gathering and analytical talents of hundreds of trained people serving the executive branch.

The role of the American Congress in foreign policy-making, therefore, is primarily one of amendment and modification, particularly where money is involved. Here Congress has established a pattern of intensive review of executive budget requests for such items as defense costs and foreign aid. The common pattern has been for Congress simply to trim these executive requests, except that on foreign aid items the meat-cleaver has sometimes been used rather than the scalpel. Occasionally, and usually in military programs, Congress has actually appropriated more than the President requested, but in such cases the executive has successfully refused to spend the unwanted funds. The general conclusion remains, therefore, that Congress is insufficiently staffed and informed to compete effectively with the President regarding the many details, seemingly unrelated, that add up ultimately to the substance of both military and foreign policy. Along with other major parliaments, this legislature too has suffered a decline in its powers in this field.

THE "FOREIGN POLICY MACHINE"

This decline means that ultimately the broadest responsibility for formulating and carrying out American foreign policy rests with the President and the executive agencies headed by his principal assistants. Of these, the Department of State is the most important; indeed, until recently, it was correct to say that the State Department was the only executive agency of any consequence in foreign affairs. Once again, however, the changed shape of world politics, plus certain American beliefs about world affairs, have helped change the status of official institutions. No longer do the department and the secretary of state have sole and exclusive control over the shaping and practice of American foreign policy.

The most important of the other institutions involved are the Agency for International Development (AID), which is responsible for foreign aid programs; the U.S. Information Agency (USIA), which is responsible for America's "image" overseas;[2] the Department of Defense, which has become increasingly responsible for American policy in an era of cold-war conflicts; the Central Intelligence Agency (CIA); and the National Security Council, which helps the President to coordinate them all. These groups and several others as well exercise authority today in fields that impinge upon the traditional territory of the secretary of state. As a result, a major problem in the past decade has been to make certain that the activities of other executive departments and agencies, in particular the military, are "coordinated" with the policies and actions of the Department of State.

The need for coordination is by no means new, though perhaps some Americans were shocked to learn that it was the Central Intelligence Agency (CIA), and not the State Department, that had the largest measure of responsibility for the abortive Bay of Pigs invasion of 1961. That affair was only the most recent illustration that the Department of State often does not make or even direct the implementation of American foreign policy. The problem of coordination and of the State Department's role in foreign policy has been a critical one since at least World War II, when it became clear that American overseas activities were often uncoordinated. In particular, the military departments were increasingly entrusted with decisions that vitally affected the shape of postwar world politics. Among the most extreme illustrations of their impact was the set of decisions (or non-decisions) that helped mark off the furthest lines of advance for the American and Russian forces converging into the center of Germany in 1945—and one must include here General Eisenhower's decision not to advance into Berlin. Although these decisions were to have portentous consequences, not always unforeseen, for the postwar political control of Europe, the Department of State seems to have played a relatively minor role in their formulation.

The National Security Council is a direct and unmistakable product of those times. Throughout the war years American officials were impressed with the comparatively smoother working of Britain's politico-military machinery. Most of them concluded that the credit for this contrast was due to Britain's Committee on Imperial Defense, a small subcommittee of the cabinet. Consequently, the United States National Security Act of 1947, in addition to establishing the Department of

2 Both AID and USIA are not "independent," but are loosely responsible to the secretary of state; overseas, AID and USIA personnel, and all other American officials, are ultimately responsible to the ambassador.

Defense and a separate Air Force, also created the National Security Council.

Modeled on the British pattern, NSC represented a striking innovation in American foreign policy-making, for it is by law interdepartmental. Its membership—always including the secretaries of state and defense in a committee chaired by the President—symbolizes again Clausewitz' teaching that military policy and foreign policy are merely different perspectives on the same problem. Yet the actual composition of NSC, its utilization by successive Presidents, and hence its true significance, have been uneven. NSC reached its highest point of importance, when it was termed the "top of policy hill," under President Eisenhower. He personally attended most of the several hundred NSC meetings convened during his administration—meetings characterized by the regular attendance also of the director of the CIA, the secretary of the treasury, the chairman of the joint chiefs of staff, and by law, the Vice-President and the director of the Office of Defense Mobilization. Under Presidents Kennedy and Johnson, however, NSC has been called into session far less often and has, as an institution, become less significant. But its purpose, to integrate the policy views and recommendations of the departments and agencies involved in security problems, while at the same time attempting to ensure the primacy of the State Department, remains a cardinal requirement and a difficult problem.

The problem is aggravated by the American propensity (in other fields of American public administration as well) to establish specialized agencies outside of the regular departmental structure—to create *ad hoc* bodies for specific jobs. The problem of insurgency and war in Vietnam, for example, led to the establishment of the "Vietnam task force"—a group combining military officials, foreign service officers, and officials in the fields of development assistance, intelligence, and information programs, among others. The effect was to remove much of the authority that ordinarily resides in the State Department bureau responsible for individual country affairs. Significantly, this "task force" was initially located in the Pentagon. Only later was it moved to the State Department building and ostensibly put more directly under the control of the secretary of state. Yet even without such innovations, American policy is influenced by a conglomeration of agencies, and the United States is represented abroad by many more bodies than just its local embassy. At one capital there were, several years ago, fewer than 120 State Department and Foreign Service employees but more than 800 Americans connected with other departments and agencies. Thus the task of coordinating the "foreign policy activities" of other agencies with the policies of the Department of State continues to be enormously difficult.

A prime cause of the problem lies in the nature of the office of the secretary of state, whose responsibilities are both ambiguous and complex and involve him in at least three distinct roles. First, he is expected to be the President's principal *adviser* on foreign policy. Second, he is the nation's *chief diplomat and negotiator*. This role has considerably expanded in recent years. First, the era of the "summit conference" has required the frequent face-to-face confrontation of foreign ministers (and sometimes even of heads of state). Second, the entry of the United States and other powers into many institutionalized alliances (SEATO, CENTO, ANZUS, NATO) has meant that if the secretary of state attends any one of their annual conferences personally, he may feel obliged to attend other regional alliance meetings as well. And finally, the advent of jet flight has made it physically possible for the secretary of state actually to conduct diplomacy on three continents in two weeks.

The last of the secretary's "official hats," that of *administrator of the Department of State*, is the one most easily overlooked, and some secretaries have apparently found it the least appealing and most burdensome aspect of their position. Yet the caliber of State Department professionals and the quality of their work is necessarily dependent in some degree upon how effectively the department is run. In particular, if a secretary of state believes that he can carry the department around in his own homburg, performing as chief negotiator, chief planner, and chief adviser all at once, the willingness of excellent people to serve under him tends to decline and general departmental morale tends to suffer. At the same time it must be conceded that the administrative "housekeeping" duties of the secretary can be an enormous chore. Some recent studies have suggested that the secretary of state be relieved of these duties almost entirely. Such proposals are not likely to be seriously considered, however.

But all these tactical considerations should not make us forget that the greatest difficulty faced by any secretary of state and most foreign ministers today is the enormously more complex nature of contemporary world politics. Not only are there twice as many nations to deal with, not only is the prospect of war more horrendous than ever before, but the nature of certain foreign policy questions is itself unprecedented. In negotiations dealing with arms control, to consider just one example, the secretary must understand the problem of detecting underground nuclear explosions, an exceedingly technical subject, and one on which the seismologists themselves disagree. Yet governments must take positions on such matters, and since in the American system the secretary of state is himself the President's chief foreign affairs adviser, there is nowhere above himself that he can look for guidance.

In this respect (and others) the American secretary's job is very different from that of the Soviet foreign minister, for example, who has generally been a career diplomat and nothing more. The same is true now in DeGaulle's France, where there is no question that the President himself makes foreign policy. When we consider such disparities among "comparable" positions in several governments, it becomes clear that foreign ministers' meetings can be very unequal contests. For the American secretary of state (so long as he retains the President's confidence) is enabled to speak for his government almost without reservation, while his counterparts have considerably less latitude. Under President Eisenhower, for example, Secretary Dulles almost single-handedly made much of American foreign policy. Generally, the other foreign ministers are more literally the mere agents of their governments, assigned to carry out detailed instructions. Indeed, Premier Khrushchev once boasted at a meeting in Vienna that he could instruct his foreign minister (Andrei Gromyko) to pull down his pants and sit on a cake of ice—and Gromyko, Khrushchev said, would do precisely that.

Diplomacy Today

In a sense, Khrushchev's expression of complete control over Gromyko, foreign minister and professional diplomat, was only an extreme caricature of the general plight into which diplomats everywhere have fallen. Diplomats still exist, to be sure, but the services they perform and the position they occupy within the broader framework of world politics have changed greatly in the twentieth century. Diplomacy remains, in the words of Harold Nicolson, "the management of the relations between independent States by processes of negotiation," but its methods are different. In particular, the traditional Western attitude that diplomacy is essentially a process of peaceful methods, directed toward the achievement of peaceful goals, has undergone revision.

A famous definition of war, that of General Karl von Clausewitz, will be instructive on this point. Clausewitz regarded war as "nothing else than the continuation of state policy by different means." Unfortunately, the interpretation long put on this statement was that a strict separation exists between those international relations using outright violence (war) and all other international relations (diplomacy). Yet Clausewitz himself did not intend so sharp a dichotomy. Instead, his statement indicates a *continuum* of diplomacy along which states conduct their relations with one another. This diplomatic continuum ranges gradually from friendly, peaceful contact at one end to the threat and use of force at the other end of the scale. The important point here is that violence is but one method of diplomacy, subservient to the broadest requirements of state interest.

Recently, under the impact of the cold war, and especially because of greater Western experience with Russian and Chinese diplomacy, sophisticated observers have come to appreciate this politico-military concept, and as a result, our understanding of both war and diplomacy has been enhanced. Today we find it most useful to regard diplomacy as encompassing the widest range of state actions that affect other nations. Thus the decision, for example, to raise or lower American economic aid to a new nation's development program is obviously a diplomatic step. So is the decision to undertake a new series of nuclear tests, or to build an effective anti-missile system, or a large scale network of civilian defense shelters. For, as we pointed out in the preceding chapter, the major nations today are more closely linked in the international system than ever before. The impact of the actions of any one of them is almost immediately visible in the reactions of another, and the scope of their confrontation is almost total. The conflict today involves their ideologies, their economies, their "image" in the eyes of non-aligned nations, and of course their physical security and integrity.

We can therefore say that diplomacy, which used to be symbolized by a small group of professionals negotiating around the green baize table, is of a different character today. Important changes have occurred with respect to the problem of intelligence and security in foreign policy matters, the functions and tasks of the diplomats themselves, and the character of the whole diplomatic process.

INFORMATION, INTELLIGENCE AND SECURITY

The problem of diplomatic intelligence and foreign policy-making has long confronted democratic governments with an apparent paradox: the nature of politics among nations appears to be such as to exempt many foreign policy matters from the usual democratic assumptions about popular sovereignty. Recognizing this seeming contradiction, Alexander Hamilton urged that in this one field of the new American government's powers the democratically based House of Representatives should play almost no role:

> Accurate and comprehensive knowledge of foreign politics; a steady and systematic adherence to the same views; a nice and uniform sensibility to national character; decision, SECRECY, and despatch, are incompatible with the genius of a body so variable and so numerous.[3]

Hamilton thus emphasized two factors especially important in modern foreign policy: the role played by a good system of intelligence, and the need for quick and effective implementation of policy. Clearly, Hamilton was recognizing and taking for granted the typically unordered and competitive quality of international politics; hence his stress on "secrecy" and "despatch." Both of these are of the essence when the national existence may be at stake.

No government would find it easy to meet these needs, but a democratic government in particular runs into problems. Intelligence, for example, involves both collecting and evaluating as much foreign information as possible and safeguarding one's own sensitive data. If we look for a moment at only the first of these—the gathering of intelligence—it is clear that the moral codes of Western societies can pose some serious questions for policy-makers. American *mores* in particular

3 *The Federalist*, No. 75.

have raised problems for the forerunners of today's CIA. In President Hoover's cabinet, for example, Secretary of War Stimson once indignantly put his foot down against American interception and decoding of foreign diplomatic communications. "Gentlemen," Stimson is reported to have said, "do not read other people's mail." And President Truman, who came to the Presidency suddenly on Franklin Roosevelt's death, was disturbed and apprehensive when he learned for the first time of the scope of America's wartime and early postwar intelligence activities. The new President, unsure whether United States intelligence agencies were engaged in domestic as well as foreign surveillance, asked for assurances that no American "Gestapo" was being built up.

The other side of the intelligence-collection process, protecting one's own information, raises even greater problems. Inevitably the need to suppress and restrict access to government information must conflict with the traditional democratic emphasis on freedom of information. The publication by the *Chicago Tribune* of United States war plans for the Pacific on the eve of Pearl Harbor is a case in point. More recently, it has been charged that detailed American newspaper treatment of Cuban revolutionary training grounds in Florida and Guatemala did not help the ill-fated American-sponsored invasion attempt of 1961. Many newspapermen felt that the Kennedy Administration came to adopt a "restrictive" attitude on the release of news because of the late President's disturbance over the press coverage of that incident. One can also assume that the Johnson Administration was not pleased with the publication of an article in late 1965 by correspondent Eric Severeid. Severeid disclosed that North Vietnam had proposed to meet with the United States in Rangoon, under the auspices of United Nations Secretary-General U Thant, and cited Adlai Stevenson as his source. That disclosure forced the Department of State to concede that, despite numerous earlier denials, North Vietnam had made overtures to discuss the Vietnam conflict—however unacceptable the overtures were.

The desire to protect information has been the occasion for frequent complaints against governments and government officials by journalists and publishers. Thus at the 1962 joint meeting in Paris of the International Press Institute and the International Federation of Newspaper Publishers, newsmen from Western countries commiserated with one another on their common problems with government news policies. The editor of the Chicago *Sun-Times* was of the opinion that Secretary of Defense McNamara distrusted both the press and the intelligence of the American people, while the French Premier, Georges Pompidou, defended his government's practice of seizing newspaper editions that touched on sensitive foreign problems and offered journalists the hope that such seizures might end with the cessation of violence in Algeria. American newspapers are not seized by the government, but American newsmen reacted indignantly to a suggestion by President Kennedy that the press voluntarily censor itself for security purposes.

One American congressman, Representative Moss, Democrat of California, has built a wide reputation on his campaign to relax official secrecy measures.

Dissemination of intelligence within the government is another aspect of the intelligence function that poses serious difficulties for all forms of government. The best intelligence is useless if it does not reach policy-makers quickly and in forms they can readily use. Totalitarian regimes are apparently subject to special difficulties in this respect, for there is danger that the reporting diplomat or intelligence agent may relate to his home offices not what he has actually seen and learned but what he thinks his superiors will want to hear. The reports of the German ambassador to the United States during the Nazi era, Dr. Herbert von Dirksen, well illustrate this point. According to von Dirksen's information, the United States in 1940–1941 was thoroughly saturated with Americans favorable to the Nazi cause, and even numerous high-ranking American officials could be expected to favor Nazi (as against British or French) policies. Such misinformation helped mislead Hitler about American intentions. One can speculate about the similar problem faced by Communist-bloc diplomats stationed in the countries of Western Europe, North America, and the British Commonwealth. Each of these states has major domestic policies that have been designed to solve the unprecedented problems of a complex, modern, urban society—for example, in the fields of education, welfare, and employment. How, then, does the well-grounded Marxist "square" what he sees with what he has been trained to believe? If he reports home in the diplomatic pouch that Walter Reuther's automobile workers are so frustrated with their exploited life that industrial revolt is on the horizon, he will be badly misinforming his government. If he reports the truth, on the other hand, he will daily be forced to make major adjustments in his personal system of beliefs, as well as to contradict official concepts and doctrines.

The problem is not peculiar, of course, to totalitarian regimes; if anything, it is more *objectively* apparent in such a political system as the United States. One of the consequences it was feared might result from the so-called "McCarthy era" in the United States was its effect on the quality of American diplomacy. State Department morale, for example, suffered considerably as a result of the harassment of Foreign Service officers, especially those who had been stationed in China during and immediately after World War II. But more important, it was thought that the objectivity of *future* American diplomatic reporting might be affected adversely. Professional diplomatic practice clearly required that Foreign Service officers analyze and report on the Communist movement in China as well as on the Chiang Kai-shek Nationalist government, and such reporting inevitably at times involved comparisons unfavorable to the Nationalists in certain respects. For example, diplomatic despatches sometimes reported not only that certain Nationalist officials were engaged in corrupt practices, but also that the Chinese Communists appeared to be making a favorable impression on the population of some areas they controlled. And often the Americans, too, were impressed with the vigor with which the Chinese Communists fought the Japanese. Years later, after the Chinese Communist victory in 1949, some of the diplomats who had attempted to report honestly and objectively on these events were subjected to intensive congressional criticism and attack, to the extent that some of them who had reported favorably on aspects of the Chinese Communist movement were branded as naïve, "pro-Communist," or even as traitors. American diplomats today, concerned never to be so branded again, and perhaps with the precedent both of China and Cuba in their minds, may have overreacted since. Thus, in the case of the Dominican Republic in 1965, most diplomatic reporting to Washington strongly emphasized the extent of Communist involvement in Dominican politics, and the potential for a Communist takeover in the wake of a domestic coup there. Newspapers such as *The New York Times* and the *Washington Post* discounted much of this, however, and were later supported by Senator Fulbright, Chairman of the Foreign Relations Committee. Nevertheless, the American ambassador so stressed the imminent danger that events in the Dominican Republic might bring about "another Cuba" that President Johnson, barely consulting the State Department, dispatched troops to Santo Domingo—with consequent damage to America's reputation in Latin America. With such incidents of the recent past in the background, it is not surprising that observers sometimes doubt whether American diplomats are as free to report objectively as they formerly were.

It seems clear, therefore, that totalitarian and democratic regimes share certain difficulties in shaping an effective foreign policy. In the former, the source of the problem may be the existence of an orthodox party line to which officials must conform, as in the Soviet Union. Or the conformity may be to the private preferences of a single individual, and his certainty that he best understands history, as in Hitler's Germany. In democratic states, by contrast, the difficulty may arise from the power of an ill-informed public, whose attitudes are often reflected and heightened by a similar lack of information on the part of their legislative representatives. Either way, it is evident that diplomacy and foreign policy-making are not in the hands of the "experts" alone. The experts must share their power with various amateurs to whom they are responsible.

In the short run these difficulties are greater for Western parliamentary regimes than for dictatorships, of whatever variety. But even among Western governments there are important variations. Thus the British cabinet system meets Hamilton's requirements of consistency, secrecy, and speed in foreign policy more readily than does the looser American form of government. In fact, if we regard such Western democratic essentials as free speech, open debate, and competing parties as capable of becoming obstacles in the way of an effective foreign policy, then the American hurdles seem to be actually the highest of all.

THE DIPLOMAT'S JOB

Of the three major functions of the diplomat—reporting, representation, and negotiation—the principal one has always been the first. When communication was slow, when there were few if any newspapers and no radio, governments learned much of what they knew about other nations through their diplomats abroad. In addition, in the era before popular governments, good diplomatic reporting meant for the most part news of the latest court factions and intrigues. In the modern world, however, even this one task of accurate reporting has become vastly more complex.

First, it became clear early in the modern era that accurate knowledge about foreign governments, and especially their "national power," required detailed information about much more than their politics at the capital. There was now need for data on a nation's agriculture, its natural resources and industrial development, its transportation network, its trade relationships, and so on. The classically trained diplomat was not equipped to gather and evaluate data in these new categories of information. One immediate consequence, therefore, was the addition to embassy staffs of specialists in various functional fields: commercial, agricultural, and military attachés. The British government in particular developed to a high point the science and art of amassing encyclopedic studies on foreign economic data.

A second major problem of modern diplomatic reporting has to do with the diplomat's contact with opposition groups and parties, and the nonofficial elements or strata of foreign society generally. This question plagues diplomats today especially in the new nations, in which "one-party democracy" is frequently encountered. It has always been regarded as rather bad diplomatic practice for an ambassador, say, to be seen too often in the company of persons who are antagonistic to the government to which he is accredited. But it is clear that the diplomat, if he is to report home accurately, objectively, and fully, must keep his government informed on the status and prospects of political opposition movements as well as on the affairs of the incumbent regime.

In many situations, of course, the problem did not arise because diplomats were often not inclined personally to mix with the "out" groups at their foreign post. Thus British diplomats in Europe before 1939 have often been criticized for unintentionally keeping their governments in the dark on this score:

> They reported honestly enough what they knew, but knew pathetically little of what was really going on . . . because they

could not bring themselves to mix with any but the right people. It has been truly said that we were far better informed about social and political conditions on the Continent during the German occupation than we ever were before it because we had no Ambassador to mislead us.[4]

Recently, however, the problem of diplomats' restricting their contacts to the "right people" has taken a new form and become more difficult than before. Especially in the new Afro-Asian nations, governmental leaders tend to identify support of their own regime with patriotism, and any kind of opposition to it as approaching treason. This tendency obviously intensifies the diplomat's dilemma, for regardless of the local sensitivities to foreign diplomats' dealings with opposition groups, it is important that such contacts be made. In the American case it is sometimes charged that the CIA agents in a given country act as a second U.S. embassy, while the official embassy itself maintains a "hands off" attitude. There is little published evidence to support the charge, but if it is true, then at least the American ambassador in each such capital can claim in relative honesty that he knows nothing of any rumored American dealings with dissident or opposition groups. An unfortunate by-product of this practice is that inevitably, American students and scholars who study politics—particularly in the newly-independent nations—are regarded at least initially as undercover intelligence agents.

In still other respects restrictions on diplomatic reporting are much more severe than in the past. There was a time, for example, before the impact of technology on politics was so great or so well recognized, when foreign military attachés were invited to demonstrations of new weapons. Before World War I, Captain Alfred Thayer Mahan, the American exponent of sea power, inspected the German navy's new dreadnought-class capital ships as the Kaiser's guest. Today, by contrast, weapons secrecy is so great that published American estimates of Russian bomber strength have disagreed with one another by two hundred or more.

Totalitarian states have, of course, become expert in making life difficult for the diplomats stationed on their soil. For one thing, such states frequently place very curious travel restrictions on their diplomatic communities. In Soviet-American relations, the Russian tendency to do this has led to great-power behavior that at times has seemed more like the antics of small boys. For years the Russians prevented American diplomats from visiting most parts of the Soviet Union, and for a long time the United States did little more than complain. Eventually, however, the United States retaliated, perhaps in accord with Harold Nicolson's urgings that in dealing with the Russians, one bad turn deserves another. Nicolson argues that Russian diplomacy is most

4 Quoted in Donald G. Bishop, *The Administration of British Foreign Relations* (Syracuse, N.Y.: Syracuse University Press, 1961), p. 287.

akin to Byzantine practices, where retaliation was effective. Thus for several years Russian diplomats stationed at UN headquarters in New York had unlimited access to Manhattan but were not permitted to take the subway to Brooklyn!

Another Byzantine practice adopted by both Hitler and the Russians was the custom of impressing the diplomatic corps with a false array of military might. In the original practice, many thousands of troops were paraded through a public square flying the colors of known regiments. Then, once out of sight of the visitors, these same troops changed their uniforms and flags only to reappear in the parade as new formations—and so the endless circle continued. In modern times the closest parallel was Khrushchev's famous remark that the Soviets had begun the mass production of intercontinental missiles, which led some Western observers promptly to accept Soviet expressions of their *capabilities* for missile production as an index of what they actually would produce. The result was an alleged "missile gap," which apparently did not materialize, but which nevertheless influenced some Western observers to conclude that Khrushchev's "hard line" in the Congo, in Berlin, and in Laos was backed up by a strategic superiority.

If the diplomat's job of reporting and analysis has become terribly difficult, changing circumstances have so changed his second major role, that of negotiator, that we may well wonder about the meaning of diplomacy itself. Traditionally, at a time when it took months for an ambassador's report to reach his home government, diplomats were often pretty much on their own in negotiations. The diplomat's "instructions"—that is, the overall approach that his government wanted him to follow in dealing with another state—might be either broad or else very detailed. But in the application of these instructions, he was necessarily often entrusted with considerable latitude. And most important, as we have emphasized before, the diplomat himself was usually the only channel of contact between governments. All things considered, therefore, the professional diplomat was at the center of traditional negotiations among states.

These negotiations were very different from today's normal pattern in several respects. They were almost always conducted by more or less "professional" diplomats accredited to the particular nations concerned, rather than by political heads of governments; they were private, even secret; they were usually conducted bilaterally (among only two powers) or on some other fairly narrow base; and they were generally concerned with fairly narrow goals. In contrast, negotiations among the powers today are conducted semipublicly, with newsmen attending frequent public meetings of negotiators, vying for information about the less public sessions, and publicizing widely the course of negotiations. Increasingly, negotiations involve not just two or a few interested parties but also their allies and supporters, regional groups, or general meetings of states. The arena of negotiation is frequently a permanent international or regional organization or the headquarters of an alliance of states. The agents in the negotiations, more often than not, are not ambassadors, ministers, or other foreign office personnel, but the personal deputies of foreign ministers or heads of state, the foreign ministers themselves, or even the heads of state. "Summit diplomacy," moreover, means not only that the agents who negotiate are high-level officials, but also that the topics of negotiation are broad and general. Negotiations tend to focus not on narrow and specific issues but on complex sets of issues and on the whole character of the relationship between the parties.

These changes in the mode and methods of negotiation have resulted from a number of more or less recent developments. The advent of popular government, along with the appearance of mass attitudes toward international politics, has made private, secret diplomacy unpopular and encouraged the trend toward publicity and public involvement. The fact that today the stakes of the bargaining are enormously larger than ever before has prompted governments to consider all policy problems at the top level, and promoted the practice of "summit diplomacy." The addition to the world political community of many new nations has made it necessary to consider the interests of more and more countries, and thus broadened the base of any negotiation. The creation of permanent international organizations, alliances, and blocs has, for obvious reasons, heightened the trend toward multi-lateral diplomacy, or "diplomacy by conference." These changes have significantly altered the role and functions of the diplomat in international negotiations. But even more important, they have altered the character of world politics. We must therefore consider several of these developments more closely.

THE DIPLOMATIC PROCESS:
DIPLOMACY AND GOVERNMENT BY THE PEOPLE

The first major indication that popular government would alter the methods of diplomacy came during World War I. It was American insistence that sought to recast the traditional, secret methods of diplomacy into a new mold: "open covenants openly arrived at," in President Wilson's phrase. There was an understandable revulsion at that time against the secret treaties and complex national commitments that seemed to be in part responsible for the outbreak in 1914 of a war that nobody wanted. But despite the failings of "secret clauses" and undisclosed alliances, it is still the opinion of most diplomats and observers of the diplomatic process that hardly anything could be worse than treaties "openly arrived at."

For one thing, any negotiation necessarily assumes some willingness to compromise, and it is difficult to compromise under the glare of publicity from both one's own national press and the world press. In addition, the multitude of newsmen who attend and publicize international negotiations are often so starved for "inside dope" that they sometimes create news, forcing diplomats to deny any intention of taking steps they may actually have been contemplating, and thus restricting their scope to maneuver. Just as troublesome is the diplomats' own temptation to make propagandistic use of the assembled press. It is not altogether unknown for Western diplomats to use this technique, but the Soviets have been especially given to framing their policy statements in a way calculated to appeal to "the people." Faced with this tactic, diplomats often feel that the bargainers across the table are not really there to bargain at all, but instead to "play to the galleries."

The press is of course not the sole villain of the piece. Its presence at international meetings merely symbolizes the interest of mass audiences in the substance of the day's negotiations, and the attitude of mass audiences toward the processes of negotiation is itself a factor that causes consternation among the diplomats. Americans in particular are accused of finding it difficult, for example, to accept the notion of compromise when they are dealing with foreign powers. It is often said in this regard that the World War II policy of "unconditional surrender" may have been very bad wartime strategy but was excellent from the point of view of domestic politics for President Franklin Roosevelt. Both the German and Japanese leaders, some people have argued, might have been willing to surrender earlier in the war, at considerable savings in lives and property, if they had thought that there was some chance of a decent negotiated settlement with the Americans. But Nazi propagandists were able to use the American demand for "unconditional surrender" to convince both German officials and the German public that they had no alternative to complete German victory.

More recently, it seems clear that some of President Truman's problems in the Korean conflict resulted from the inability of many Americans to accept the peculiar requirements of a "limited war." For example, the famous episode of General MacArthur's dismissal by President Truman in 1951 is directly related to this difficulty. The General had actively lent his support to both journalists and public figures who were arguing in favor of a war to "defeat China." The President, on the other hand, felt strongly that the war in Korea was only one among many foreign policy problems and was therefore not to be viewed out of context with the Russian threat in Berlin and other places. He of course wanted the American people to support his Korean policy—but not in the form of "all-out" support for some "all-out" policy. In any case, the attitudes of the mass audience were a critical element in the diplomacy and policy-making involved in this event.

An interesting paradox appears in this connection. In the West, where the *domestic* political culture generally accepts and even glorifies the necessity of compromise, the diplomats' problem appears to stem from the tendency of mass popular attitudes to favor "total victory" and a policy of no negotiation. The Soviet-bloc diplomats, on the other hand, have a corresponding problem which arises not from mass popular attitudes but rather from the ideological imperatives of Communist doctrine. For in Marxist dogma, the "total victory" of socialism is regarded as necessary and inevitable. Thus, speaking about Russian diplomats with whom he had negotiated, a former British Ambassador in Moscow writes,

> It never seems to occur to them that the proper object of a negotiation is not to defeat your opposite number but to arrive at an agreement with him which will be mutually beneficial.[5]

If we put this Soviet goal of total victory in another context, it becomes clear that the Soviet attitude is inimical not only to successful negotiation generally, but also to any kind of permanent international organization designed to serve as a vehicle for the peaceful settlement of disputes. And it should be stressed that international organizations can best be understood as one of the formats within which diplomacy operates. The United Nations, that is, is but the most recent illustration of a pattern of international politics dating from at least 1815, when the Congress of Vienna instituted the concept of "diplomacy by conference."

INTERNATIONAL ORGANIZATIONS
AND DIPLOMACY BY CONFERENCE

It should be stated at the outset that the mere existence of the United Nations, and the League of Nations before it, represents a significant success for important principles of Western thought and political culture. For these international organizations reflect the belief that even national conflicts, with all their attendant potential of patriotism and glory, can be alleviated and perhaps solved by reasoned argument and peaceful persuasion. This is far from saying, of course, that either the League or the UN were founded on a simple principle of majority rule; on the contrary, different forms of requiring unanimity were built into both organizations. In the League Covenant, the need for unanimous consent was absolute: Any negative vote by any state on any substantive issue was sufficient to defeat a proposal. The League had two major "organs," and the principle of unanimity applied to both—to the executive-type Council of the League, which by 1939 had fifteen member states, and to the parliamentary-type Assembly, which at its peak included fifty-eight countries.

In the United Nations, on the other hand, the rule of unanimity is qualified. In the UN Security Council, its "executive-action" body, unanimity applies only to the permanent members, that is, to the United States, the Soviet Union, China, France, and Great Britain. This fact in itself represents an advance over the structure of the League, for

[5] Sir William Hayter, *The Diplomacy of the Great Powers* (New York: The Macmillan Company, 1961, p. 28.

one of the major faults of that organization was the increasing dominance over its business by the smaller states. When the Charter of the UN was drafted in San Francisco in 1945, it was clear that its authors had benefited from the League's history; by restricting unanimity to the five permanent members of the Security Council, the major role of the great powers in the United Nations is frankly acknowledged. Of the three major organs of the UN (the General Assembly, the Security Council, and the Economic and Social Council [ECOSOC]), the Charter gives prime responsibility for settling disputes to the Security Council. It was to be expected that this body would be dominated by the five permanent members, in contrast to the six seats allocated on a two-year rotating basis to all "lesser" states.

The UN Security Council. As an agency for effective political action, the Security Council was admirably constituted. The permanent members, so far as anyone could foresee, were those which would continue to possess the overwhelming portion of the world's industrial and armed might. It was clear that any serious international tension or conflict which threatened world peace would necessarily involve one or more of these great nations. Thus it was hoped that on the basis of their wartime cooperation as the allied powers, these five states would continue to cooperate among themselves in the postwar world. And just as important, it was recognized that no other state would be in a position to threaten world peace if it were faced with the combined opposition and power of the great nations. The basic concept of the Security Council is therefore almost identical with the principles of collective security discussed in the previous chapter. There is the assumption that each of the nations has a mutual interest in keeping the peace and the belief that the specter of enormous military power will deter aggression.

Building on these principles, the Charter gave to the Security Council considerable formal latitude to act as an executive body. For example, it is incumbent on the Security Council to determine whether some international incident constitutes a threat to peace, an actual breach of the peace, or ultimately, an outright act of aggression. Having made the appropriate determination, the Council then has the responsibility to recommend and decide on the measures to be taken. These were not shallow grants of authority. Under Articles 41 and 42 of the UN Charter, the Security Council is granted the right to require members to take the kind of political, economic, and military measures necessary to restore peace. It was expected that UN members would agree to make certain military forces available to the Security Council for this purpose, and thus Article 43 continues to stand as the formal authority to build an international police force, if one should actually be established. Finally, the Council was granted a Military Staff Committee. Ostensibly, this committee is composed of the chiefs of staff (or their representatives) of the five major powers.

The UN General Assembly. The influence of the Council has not grown as the planners thought, however, and when one thinks of the United Nations today, it is not the Security Council but the General Assembly which comes first to mind. The General Assembly was established as the "legislative" organ of the United Nations. It was to be primarily a deliberative and advisory body, and in this sense it comes closest to the concept of diplomacy by conference. Yet it must be emphasized that the functions and reputation of the General Assembly have so broadened since 1945 that by now it has eclipsed all other organs of the United Nations in importance.

A number of negative and positive forces account for this greater role and enhanced prestige. Among the negative forces, the most important is the decline of the Security Council itself. If we glance briefly at the UN's history in the early postwar period (up to about 1948), this trend will become clear. For the one fundamental assumption underlying the Security Council's creation—the expected agreement of the big five—did not materialize. The Soviet Union was during this initial period generally in a tiny minority when General Assembly votes were cast. Thus the Russians were forced to express their opposition to UN proposals by their negative votes (vetoes) in the Security Council. It was from this time that the Russians began building their notorious veto record—which through 1965 had totaled 103 of the 111 vetoes in the whole history of the Council.

In the interest of objectivity, however, we should point out that the Western nations "manufactured" almost half these vetoes simply by proposing new members for UN membership in cases where Soviet opposition was obvious and expected. Nevertheless, it soon became apparent that Russian obstructionism would prevent the Security Council from operating as the Charter seemed to intend—as the peace-enforcing organ. As a result, the Western powers under American leadership turned increasingly to the General Assembly. In that body, because of the large number of Latin-American votes and the British Commonwealth members, pro-American majorities were generally guaranteed.

This turning to the General Assembly met with the full accord of most of the middle-sized and smaller members of the United Nations. From the beginning this group had been jealous of the special privileges accorded the "Big Five" in the Security Council. Indeed, when the Charter was signed in 1945, New Zealand and Australia, by attempting to prevent the veto and "great power domination," had established early reputations as spokesmen for the smaller powers.

As fewer and fewer issues of importance were placed on the Security Council agenda, and as the frequency of its meetings declined, the smaller nations applauded the trend; for along with this decline of the Council, the number of important issues referred to the General Assembly increased, and its meetings were followed with increasing attention. All the while, we should note, the Soviet Union was documenting its position that this trend in favor of the General Assembly was illegal and contrary to the principles of the UN Charter. At face value, these Russian arguments carry considerable weight.

The United States, for its part, was instrumental in the rise of the Assembly. Beginning in 1947, when it asked the General Assembly to consider Soviet intransigence in Greece and Korea and suggested that the Assembly have an Interim Committee to handle between-session business, the United States prepared the General Assembly for its contemporary role. Thus the first development basic to the rise of the General Assembly was a widespread (and especially American) disappointment with the impotence of the Security Council. The United States was even more deeply implicated in the second development. Involved here is the very important "uniting for peace" resolution of November 3, 1950.

The background of this resolution was the odd circumstance that permitted the Korean conflict to be fought under United Nations, and particularly Security Council, jurisdiction. On the day the Council voted to meet Communist aggression in South Korea, the Soviet delegate to the Council was not present (he was boycotting). But later in 1950 it became clear that the return of the Russian representative would make it impossible for the Council to continue to run the Korean conflict under a United Nations umbrella. Thus the United States proposed that the *General Assembly:*

> . . . explicitly assume the responsibility for dealing with threats to the peace, breaches of the peace, and acts of aggression in case the Council was prevented by the use of the veto from acting.[6]

With minor modifications, this resolution was approved, and the General Assembly now regards itself as involved in any threat or breach of the peace. As a direct product of this major transformation in the structure of the United Nations, the General Assembly has "dealt with" the Chinese intervention in Korea, the Suez affair in 1956, the Soviet intervention in Hungary during the same year, the tension in Lebanon in 1958, and the Congo crisis which began in 1960. Indeed, the Assembly has become so active that today we assume it as routine that political crises will find their way onto its agenda. Yet according to the Charter, our thoughts should turn first to the Security Council.

The third development which helps explain the enhanced role of the Assembly is the vastly increased size of the UN membership. This growth began with a major "package" entry of new members in 1956. Since then many other new states, especially in Africa, have continued to expand the size of the organization, so that in 1965, twenty years after it was established, the United Nations had 117 member states.

6 Leland M. Goodrich, *The United Nations* (New York: Thomas Y. Crowell Co., 1959), p. 122.

This was much more than double the original Charter membership. From the viewpoint of American diplomats, however, this greatly expanded membership, along with the much wider province within which the Assembly now feels justified in acting, must sometimes seem to be a kind of Frankenstein monster of American design. For the General Assembly of today, in which so many new states share the common experience of recent Western colonial dominance, has a very different character from the original Assembly. The United States can no longer count on a certain majority, and the Soviet Union, for its part, has probably been the major beneficiary of this change: the constant Russian cries of "Western imperialism" have generally struck a responsive note among the many Afro-Asian states. Thus the General Assembly of today often seems to act as an anti-colonial sounding board. A striking illustration in 1962 was the case of Goa, in which India used troops to evict the Portuguese from their historic enclave on India's west coast. India's clear aggression evoked a far milder General Assembly response than earlier instances of less flagrant Western-connected military actions.

This was of course a frustrating experience for the West, somewhat akin to Western disappointment after the Belgrade conference discussed earlier. In that instance, the new nations seemed to berate Soviet nuclear testing less loudly than American experiments; in the second incident, the UN representatives of these newer nations seemed to turn the other way when one of their own, India, used force in Goa. But we are not primarily concerned here with the policies of the new nations as such; our interest centers instead upon their impact in the United Nations, and beyond that, upon the UN as an institution of diplomacy. In that context we must ask whether events might have been altered had the UN been more energetic regarding Goa. Did it make any difference that the United Nations did not "slap India's wrists"?

The United Nations has, of course, gone on record in such serious matters as the Israeli-Anglo-French Suez invasion, Russia's brutal suppression of the Hungarian rebellion, India's dispute with Pakistan over Kashmir, Egypt's interference with freedom of navigation in the Suez Canal, and so on. In no recent case, however, is there convincing evidence that a UN resolution had any particular effect on the outcome of events. There is, of course, an air of importance that attaches to any United Nations matter, and especially to any subject debated in the General Assembly. But the fact that a critical situation is placed on the UN agenda and argued there is not what gives that situation its importance. Instead it appears that the UN is rather the beneficiary of the currency—world conflict—in which it deals. In other words, one might ask after observing UN proceedings, "This is all very interesting but what does it have to do with diplomacy and foreign policy?" While the answer is far from certain, there seem to be at least three important constructive by-products of UN activity in terms of policy-making.

First, the very existence of the UN, and its apparent permanence as an institution, makes available a place in which states can meet. This is not an insignificant factor, especially for the smaller, new, and generally poorer nations. Americans or Britons may find it difficult to envisage not being represented in every capital in the world, but for many other countries, foreign representation is not only exceptionally expensive, but more important, demands a supply of talented persons that the developing nations do not have in sufficient quantity to fill even their domestic positions. Thus whatever good diplomatic talent a small nation has it can concentrate in New York and in a few other posts.

Second, and especially as the membership of the UN now includes almost all of the political globe, the notion of "world public opinion" has gained acceptance: at least votes can be tallied up and publicized after a General Assembly session! From the standpoint of traditional diplomacy, of course, this is a distinctly negative by-product of the UN's existence, since diplomats tend to avoid the public arena. And in the case of this particular public arena, there is an even further obstacle to sound bargaining: the disproportionate weight given the views of the small nations. For to pass a resolution in the General Assembly, it must often be so framed as to gain their support.

Finally, it can be maintained that a United Nations orientation as such has assumed a more prominent role in the policy priorities of some nations than might be objectively justified. The Republic of China, for example, recognizes that she must cultivate her relationships in UN circles more than most powers. Whether Communist China gets a UN seat and Nationalist China loses her place on the Security Council could be decided by a special majority of the Assembly. British policy in granting independence to some of her former colonies, especially in Africa, seems also to have been greatly influenced by United Nations considerations. And in the case of the United States, it is certainly significant that the American ambassador to the UN has recently attained some of the prestige and status of a formal member of the President's policy-making group. It was perhaps with this enhanced role in mind that Senator Henry Jackson complained in 1962 that the "UN approach" was given too high a place in the formulation and implementation of American foreign policy!

Yet it is part of the Western, and especially the Anglo-American, political culture to place great faith in the parliamentary method. The United States in particular has tended to believe that the major principles of parliamentarianism can be applied to international disputes, and recent American secretaries of state have expressed their attachment to this faith in both their private and public utterances. It was on the basis of these principles that in 1945, when the Charter was being drafted, the American representatives sought to convince their Soviet counterparts that the General Assembly deserved the fairly prominent position it was even then given. As we have seen, however, that attitude has changed as some Americans have become rather disenchanted with the "new" General Assembly.

Soviet attitudes, on the other hand, have remained fairly constant. And when we inquire into the contemporary role of the UN in world politics and in diplomacy, we must recognize that the answer will be determined to a great extent by the position of Communist states generally, and the Soviet Union particularly. In essence, the problem Russia poses for the United Nations is identical with the problem she poses in the context of traditional diplomacy. It may help to recall Harold Nicolson's definition: "The function of diplomacy is the management of the relations between independent States by processes of negotiation." Soviet ideology seems most inconsistent with that statement, since diplomacy so interpreted presupposes a willingness not only to play by the rules of the game, but to play the game of "independent states" itself.

Diplomacy in a Changing, Divided World

The task of Western diplomacy today is doubly burdened. Not only must it seek to accommodate the "normal" differences among states, but it must also search for a viable relationship with a bloc of powers operating from a very different set of premises. Whether the United Nations, as a method of diplomacy, can be helpful in this effort can perhaps be gauged by understanding the Soviet view of the United Nations:

> [It] has followed with iron logic from the world view of the Communist leadership, which refuses to see in the United Nations . . . the budding parliament of man or the instrument of human brotherhood, but instead sees it as essentially another arena for the struggle between the two dialectic opposites of our age.[7]

But it is not only the ideological dogmatism of the Soviet Union that has prevented the United Nations from achieving the high ideals for which it was established. Few nations, and certainly none of the major states, regard the United Nations today as an instrument of government, nor have their leaders actively sought to make it one.

The United States, in its long-standing opposition to Chinese Communist participation, has in effect declined to accept the principle of "universality" for United Nations membership. Communist China itself

7 Alexander Dallin, "The Soviet View of the United Nations" (Cambridge, Mass.: Center for International Studies, M.I.T., 1959), p. 88 (mimeographed), quoted in Lincoln P. Bloomfield, *The United Nations and U.S. Foreign Policy* (Boston: Little, Brown and Company, 1960), p. 111.

has repeatedly disclaimed any pressing interest in membership, taking the position that the structure of the organization no longer reflects the realities of world politics. And even the small powers, which because of their relative weakness have perhaps the most to gain from a world body dedicated to peaceful settlement of conflict, have not always given the United Nations their full support. They have not, for example, pressed for enforcement of the UN rules that require a nation to pay its assessed dues, although major powers such as the Soviet Union and France have declined to pay. And Indonesia, one of the most prominent of the newer nations, resigned altogether from the United Nations when a government not to its liking—Malaysia—was accorded temporary membership on the Security Council.

The thoughtful student will not confuse the immediate problem posed by ideological conflict with more fundamental questions about the nation-state system and the processes of diplomacy. For even in the absence of an ideological schism, would any international organization constitute an effective format for dealing effectively with conflicts of national interest? Would structural changes in the United Nations (for example, elimination of the veto) make it more or less effective? Can we expect that the new nations, which have just begun to taste the fruits of national independence, will readily accept the advice of the nations President Sukarno of Indonesia has called the "old established forces." Those "old established forces" may well say that nationalism, and sovereignty, provide too few benefits to compensate for all the sacrifices they require. But will the new nations listen?

Available evidence so far indicates that they will not, and one can therefore hardly be sanguine about the prospects for peaceful resolution of all conflicts. Thus the student of politics must inquire into the conditions which have in fact led to wars, and into those conditions which have helped avoid armed struggle among states. He would do well to begin by understanding how war has been avoided between Russia and America, and he may find that between these two powers, the "delicate balance of terror" is the explanation. But among most of the other nations of the world, the element of mass terror does not exist; for them, if conflict generally is to be avoided, the prospects for cooperation will perhaps have to overcome the anticipated benefits of violence. One new element in the international environment does give rise to cautious optimism: most nations today are actively dedicated to the improvement of their national economic welfare. To achieve that welfare, a grasp of the most modern technologies, whether in transportation, industrialization, or agriculture, is essential. Yet to the developing nations in particular the newest technologies are so costly, both in skills and resources, that their development may *require* nations to collaborate more fully than ever before. Technology, which has in the past so often had its largest impact on world politics in war, could for the first time become a major contributor to peace.

SUGGESTIONS FOR ADDITIONAL READING

ALKER, HAYWARD R., JR., and BRUCE M. RUSSETT, *World Politics in the General Assembly* (New Haven, Conn.: Yale University Press, 1965).

ALMOND, GABRIEL A., *The American People and Foreign Policy* (New York: Frederick A. Praeger, Inc., 1960).

BOYD, R. G., *Communist China's Foreign Policy* (New York: Frederick A. Praeger, Inc., 1962).

DALLIN, ALEXANDER, *The Soviet Union at the United Nations: An Inquiry into Soviet Motives and Objectives* (New York: Frederick A. Praeger, Inc., 1962).

HOVET, THOMAS, *Bloc Politics in the United Nations* (Cambridge, Mass.: Harvard University Press, 1960).

JACKSON, SENATOR HENRY M. (ed.), *Jackson Subcommittee Papers on Policy-Making at the Presidential Level* (New York: Frederick A. Praeger, Inc., 1965).

KENNAN, GEORGE F., *Realities of American Foreign Policy* (Princeton, N.J.: Princeton University Press, 1954).

————, *Soviet Foreign Policy under Lenin and Stalin* (Boston: Little, Brown and Company, 1961).

MARSHALL, C. B., *The Limits of Foreign Policy* (New York: Holt, Rinehart & Winston, Inc., 1955).

NICOLSON, HAROLD H., *The Evolution of Diplomatic Methods* (New York: The Macmillan Company, 1955).

Part Three

POLITICAL BEHAVIOR
AND
POLITICAL FUNCTIONS

Chapter 11

ADMINISTRATORS:

Bureaucrats and Policy-Makers

In this section of the book we turn to the processes and structures of government. An appropriate place to start is with administration—the process through which public policies become most apparent to citizens. The end results of political policies are made evident by the acts of postmen, policemen, tax collectors, forest rangers, FBI agents, public health physicians, agricultural agents, astronauts, and all the others who carry out the myriad tasks of government. Until it is administered, a policy is little more than words, words whose intent and meaning may or may not be clear. A policy may have unpredictable effects or no effects at all; the way it is administered is crucial in determining the substance and consequences of a policy for those who made it and for those affected by it.

Since administrative processes are integral to every political system, ordinary citizens in every nation encounter some sort of administrative structure. Administrative organizations may take many forms, differing in size, complexity of relationships, uses of authority, and kinds of people employed and the ways in which their talents are used. Usually these organizations reflect not only the particular purposes for which they have been established, but also the cultural, economic, social, and political patterns of their societies. More will be said shortly about these structures, but the important points to underscore here are that administrative organizations are found wherever there is government and that they are usually important points of contact between people and government.

Administrative structures, moreover, are more prominent in political systems today than ever before, even in parts of the world formerly dominated by the great bureaucratic empires. The causes of administrative growth are to be found in the major problems confronting the contemporary world. Nations are struggling as never before to maintain their autonomy and security and to develop themselves economically, scientifically, and technologically. Many factors encourage administrative growth: rising nationalism, increasing international tensions, the industrial and scientific revolutions, the requirements of military policy, international diplomacy, and scientific and economic development. In the prescientific, pre-industrial world of less devastating wars and simpler military technology, of slower communications and lower standards of living, administration was much less complex and less prominent. In a very real sense administrative sophistication is a prerequisite to the political and economic development of a twentieth-century nation as much as it is a result of such development. The ability to construct complex administrative organs enables people to coordinate their energies, skills, and knowledge for greater and more complex accomplishments. The growth of administration, then, is not just a consequence of national development; it is also a catalyst for it.

The Meaning of "Bureaucracy"

Administrative structures are often called "bureaucracies," and their members, "bureaucrats." What are the characteristics of bureaucracy in a general, formal sense? To some critics, the word "bureaucracy" has an essentially negative, distasteful connotation: It represents groups of timid employees mainly concerned with holding onto their desks (*bureau* is the French word for "desk" as well as for the room or office in which it is located) and afraid to "stick their necks out." Bureaucracy in this sense is cautious, bound by precedent and "red tape," and frustrating to the efforts of enterprising people. Other critics berate bureaucracy because they believe that it leads to an irresponsible, even arrogant, use of power by officials. In general, bureaucrats are specialists, chosen for their talents; and their decisions are often impenetrable to laymen, whether representative officials or simply members of the general public. Under the impersonal and often anonymous cloak of bureaucracy, human ambitions for power and status can be advanced by those skilled in the strategies and tactics of the organizational game.

Some critics of bureaucracy attribute such negative aspects to *public* administrative organization but consider private organization free of them. Arguments of this sort are often convenient for those who have an interest in preventing the substitution of public control for private business management. But the truth of the matter is that caution, red tape, ambition for power and status, make-work expansionism, and other pathologies of organizational behavior can and do manifest themselves in both private and public bureaucracies. The essential difference between the two lies in the "markets" within which each must perform. Public bureaucracy operates primarily in a political market where prices, profits, and losses are calculated in terms of the diverse and complex values of power, policy, and program priority; whereas private bureaucracy operates in a market where prices, profits, and losses are calculated in terms of money and the more limited and concrete values which motivate businessmen in the economic system.

True, finance is a part of the public bureaucratic system, and public administrative actions can be represented in financial terms, but public administration is not primarily an economic operation. Simple profit and loss is not the single, or even the most appropriate, standard by which to measure its performance. Furthermore, the ways in which supply and demand are determined in public administration usually modify the buyer-seller relationship extensively, substituting for supply and demand decisions made by and with public authority. For the most part, taxes are collected for general governmental purposes, or for a rather wide range of "public" goals. Then these funds are spent in accordance with decisions made by people who have power to make political rather than "business" choices. For example, many of the functions which the government has to support cannot or will not be supported in a conventional profit-making system of administration, or are considered to be so closely involved with the public interest that they cannot be entrusted to private control. Governments pursue not profits, but public interests variously defined.

Conceptions of bureaucracy that view even the mere existence of administrative structure as necessarily evil—particularly those conceptions which equate "bureaucracy" only with public administration—are not very helpful, then, for describing and analyzing the subject. A more useful and more analytical view is the one put forward by Max Weber and developed by other eminent social scientists. Weber's definition emphasizes, in a way intended to be free of either favorable or unfavorable connotations, the hierarchical nature of bureaucracy, its specialization of functions, and the arrangement of official positions in a purportedly rational manner to perform necessary tasks. By this definition a bureaucracy is a system which has set rules of management and regularized ways of recruiting and appointing people who have the necessary expertise for their tasks. Bureaucrats are people who undertake their assignments as vocations, look at their jobs as careers, and are accorded status and salary. They maintain records, coordinate their operations, and plan and evaluate the effectiveness of their work. In Weber's view, the bureaucratic type of organization advances because it is technically superior to any other form of organization, just as a machine is superior to nonmechanical modes of production.

Most bureaucracies fall short of the "ideal type" depicted by Weber, but the elements he identifies are present to some degree in all of them. Bureaucracies are complex organizations having patterns of authority which establish superior-subordinate relationships, even though their hierarchies may be very irregular and imperfect. They divide the work to be performed and establish hierarchical positions accordingly, although frequently there is duplication, overlapping, and lack of clarity in defining tasks. In general, they recruit and assign people to jobs on the basis of abilities, skills, and interests, although "square pegs" are sometimes put in "round holes." They receive and allocate resources which enable them to accomplish certain tasks, but they do not necessarily do so in the most economical or efficient way. They participate in planning and executing policy to some degree. In doing all of these things, bureaucracies become systems of power, true extensions of the political system.

Early Bureaucracies

Although administration is more prominent in present-day political systems, man's experience in organizing and managing large-scale bureaucracies extends back over several millennia. Archaeological evidence reveals extensive and elaborate administrative systems in ancient civilizations such as Egypt. Almost 5,000 years ago, the Pharaohs required large numbers of well-trained officials to maintain their control over the Nile Valley. The collection of taxes, the forecasting of the annual flood cycle, the re-surveying of land after the waters receded, the massive conscription and coordination of labor for the building of colossal pyramids and splendid palaces—all required unprecedented administrative sophistication. Other civilizations in the ancient Middle East—in Mesopotamia, Syria, and Persia—maintained and, in fact, could not have developed without skilled and organized officials. More than 3,000 years ago a highly developed civilization, already old, existed in north-central China. Of its administrative structure we know little, but surviving artifacts reflect a culture which would have been inconceivable without a fairly well-developed governmental system. About 1100 B.C., a neighboring people gained control and established the Chou Dynasty. During this dynasty such thinkers as Confucius and Mencius appeared; their reflections upon Chou government and administration served as precepts to the officials of later dynasties, when the Chinese imperial bureaucracy reached still greater heights of achievement and refinement. These achievements included competitive examinations as a means of selecting officials, the construction and operation of vast public works, and state regulation and control of the economy.

In pre-Columbian America, the Maya, the Incas, and the Aztecs had centuries of experience in administering city-states and empires—

in the case of the Incas, without the benefit of a system of writing. Closer to us in culture if not in time, the administration of the Roman Empire depended upon a far-flung bureaucracy of skilled officials. The body of law evolved by the Romans for guidance and application by their bureaucracy had a profound impact upon the legal and administrative systems of the nations of Western Europe. Roman administrative knowledge and skills, adapted for different purposes by the Roman Catholic Church, facilitated the survival of the Church after the decline and fall of the Empire in the West. In the East, Roman administration laid the foundations upon which the Byzantine Empire endured until the fifteenth century.

Many other examples could be given from all parts of the world, but those mentioned suggest that public administrative organization is as old as civilization itself. Indeed, it is no exaggeration to say that civilization is impossible without administration. Civilization cannot come into existence without cities, and cities cannot exist without governors, judges, tax-collectors, policemen, watchmen, record-keepers, public-works planners and managers, and so on. When the administration fails or disintegrates, civilization declines—and may disappear.

The last statement may seem too sweeping a conclusion, particularly to those who view "civilization" as the achievement of a high level of artistic creativity and the liberation of the minds and talents of men. But there are two elementary truths which are often overlooked by those who consider public bureaucracies uncivilized, if not unnecessary. One is that civilization, which is indeed manifested in the ways just mentioned, does not develop or endure in chaos and disorder. Man's imposition of various kinds of order on his disordered physical and social environment is an equally important aspect of civilization. It is true that certain kinds of order in too great amounts are hostile to some important elements of civilization. Here the problem is to find a balance. For example, Western civilization has considered its greatest political achievement to be the creation in some societies—and in some of them only precariously or impermanently—of a relatively high degree of political freedom. But this achievement has been possible only in a context of law and order, by sacrifice of some freedoms (for example, the freedom to attain one's individual goals through physical violence against others) so that others may be enjoyed. Thus in a politically free "civilized" society, there is a constant and inevitable tension between the forces of "freedom" and those of "order," just as there is tension between the forces of stability and those of change.

The second point to keep in mind in this context is that the unfavorable connotations of bureaucracy are not so much characteristics of bureaucracy as such as they are pathologies to which some bureaucracies are more prey than others. We seldom find a bureaucracy that is completely free of them; but some historical examples of bureaucracy have been notably freer of such pathologies than have others. Nevertheless, it should occasion no astonishment that the negative features associated with bureaucracy tend to predominate in popular conceptions, for most of man's long experience with governmental administration has been with bureaucracies in which such features were all too obvious.

Over the centuries, bureaucratic control over political and economic life was often pervasive and subject to few restrictions. Bureaucrats— after monarchs and their courts—constituted the ruling class, the political elite. Officials acted for and in the name of the monarch, whose authority was divinely sanctioned; the authority of officialdom therefore partook of divinity, and to question or challenge it was to raise questions of sacrilege. In addition, the bureaucracies of these times often held a virtual monopoly on knowledge, not only of such abstruse matters as law, mathematics, and astronomy, but also of such elemental practical skills as reading and writing. Only those who were somehow able to secure training for entry into the bureaucracy could acquire such knowledge and skills. Moreover, as an essential means of maintaining control and of carrying out their responsibilities, officials monopolized the construction, operation, and use of networks of communication, such as roads and relay systems. Assistance to official couriers was mandatory; interference with them was one of the gravest of crimes. Seldom elsewhere has it been more true that knowledge was power— or conversely that power (and access to or control over communication) was a prerequisite to knowledge.

Given these conditions, is it surprising that officials would attach great value to their posts, that they would go to great lengths to avoid displeasing their superiors, that they would feel themselves innately superior to the unlettered, ignorant masses? If we were such officials, would we not feel strong tendencies to avoid risks, to stick to the letter of instructions, to report favorable news with pride and play down or conceal bad news, to become impatient with "backward" peasants who refuse to recognize the importance of the interests of the monarch? Or, if our compensation were miserably inadequate for the kind of life to which our status entitled us, would we invariably refuse the gifts proffered by well-meaning members of our communities, not grossly to buy our favor but largely to show understanding and respect for our exalted status and heavy burdens as agents of a sacredly inspired ruler?

Attitudes such as these, in the absence of countervailing values and effective institutional restraints, contributed powerfully to the pathologies to which we have referred. To varying extents such attitudes, or others quite similar to them, are present in all bureaucracies, including those of our own period. But in all periods, and again to varying extents, they have been tempered or overlaid by other motivating factors. These include devotion to leaders who embody or articulate broader goals for a group, class, or nation; commitment to ideologies defending a way of life or prescribing a better way; psychological identification with the goals of one's administrative agency or internalization of professional standards of performance. They may also include fear of embarrassment or of punishment for violation of certain norms, a fear whose importance varies with the effectiveness of legal, institutional, or political sanctions operating to punish such transgressions. Thus it has been possible for some bureaucracies to overcome many of their negative aspects, or at least to limit them significantly. Some political systems have been able to develop what Fritz Morstein Marx has called "merit" bureaucracies, as distinguished from "guardian," "caste," or "patronage" bureaucracies.[1]

Among the actual bureaucracies of human history, however, it is the rare one in which the characteristics of "merit," that is, of efficiency and responsible public service, have been predominant. It is appropriate to wonder why this is so, and to raise the question of what factors determine particular patterns of administrative behavior. Unfortunately, not enough comparative research and analysis has yet been done, either on the bureaucracies of earlier times or on those of our own period, to permit conclusive answers to these questions. But contemporary research and theorizing have begun to shed some light on certain aspects of the problem. In the remainder of this chapter we shall attempt to summarize some of the principal points in current thinking about public bureaucracies, beginning with a consideration of the effects of current and past environmental relationships.

Bureaucracy and Environment

Although we have attempted some generalizations applicable to public bureaucracies both in the past and the present, such attempts are, at best, dangerous. As a safeguard, therefore, it is important to see how some environmental conditions affect bureaucratic structures and functions. Administrative systems do not exist in a vacuum. They operate in settings of social and cultural norms, of economic production and exchange, and of political systems, all of which shape the bureaucracy and are shaped by it. In the effort to classify and to explain public administration on some comparative basis, some scholars have particularly noted the importance of a country's position as a society on a scale between "traditional" and "modern," as these are depicted in Chapter 7.[2]

[1] Fritz Morstein Marx, *The Administrative State* (Chicago: University of Chicago Press, 1957), chap. 4.
[2] The reader should be cautioned again about the shortcomings of this terminology. It is particularly necessary to avoid equating "traditional" with "backward" or "undesirable" and "modern" with "higher" or "better." Nor should one infer that important elements of one are not, in actual examples, present in the other. In the absence of better terms, however, these have gained some currency as a means of distinguishing between societies that have not experienced the complex impact of scientific technology, industrialism, urbanism, political pluralism, and all that is implied by these developments, and those societies that have been significantly transformed by them. The reader should also keep in mind that the necessity for generalization and brevity precludes attention to the variations that are found in the "traditional" as well as in the "modern" categories.

Another relevant factor for comparison is the economic system and its stage and rate of growth. Among the relevant political conditions are the country's intensity and style of nationalism, as well as the character of its political power structure and its heritage of governmental institutions. Many of these complex environmental factors—but not all—are brought into play in administration through the values, skills, attitudes, and knowledge of the personnel selected to man the official posts. Thus we can learn something of how these factors work by examining civil service systems, particularly to discover who is recruited and how. All of these will be discussed in the following sections.

DEGREE OF MODERNIZATION

In pre-industrial traditional societies such as T'ang Dynasty China or medieval England, values were relatively stable; primary (face-to-face) relationships were more important than secondary, impersonal ones; status tended to be inherited and mobility restricted; illiteracy was high; and communication was largely by word of mouth. Public administration in such societies reflected these conditions. For one thing, it tended to serve the elite who had wealth and power. For another, appointment and advancement often depended upon family or other personal relationships.

As traditional society moved toward a more modern stage, one of its crucial struggles was for control over the bureaucracy; for those who would overthrow the old elite had to detach the bureaucracy from the traditional rulers, control and re-orient it toward more modern objectives. This same transition has occurred in Turkey and Egypt in this century. If the bureaucracy were limited, those committed to change developed it to accomplish the tasks of modernization, as did the Hohenzollern rulers of Prussia. Also, in traditional societies members of the bureaucracy often enjoyed more favorable rank and privileges than did most of the other classes of society, and government positions were strongly desired as avenues of mobility. When this "transitional" background is found in conjunction with a short supply of educated and skilled persons and primary-group loyalties prevail, the bureaucracy that develops is likely to have the following characteristics: (*a*) a disproportionate share of the trained people in the society, yet an inadequate number of trained bureaucrats; (*b*) a reliance upon nepotism and personal favoritism in recruiting and appointing people to the bureaucracy; and (*c*) more concern with status and position than with broader policies and programs.

The organization and techniques of operation of traditional bureaucracies reflected personal and particularistic influences. Task-oriented, impersonal, and rational organizations were exceptional. Rather, there were intricate networks of friends, relatives, fellow villagers, and the like, many of whom might have done little in their official positions. Such a group's systems of keeping records, communication, and coordinating tasks were primitive by modern standards.

When such a society seeks to transform itself through economic, social, and political development, the bureaucracy is called upon to aid the spread of education and training to large segments of the society. It is expected to plan and implement programs of economic and social change. It must adopt more universal standards of operation and personnel selection, more complex techniques of administrative management and organizational procedure. These changes entail more than mere methods and procedures. Values of great importance to the bureaucrats concerned may be threatened.

It is no wonder that, in predominantly traditional societies attempting to make a rapid transition to a modern state, the bureaucracy is expected to be a major catalytic agent. Yet limitations such as the few mentioned above retard and complicate this catalytic function. Resistance to change and the patterns that change takes are both intimately related to social structure, values, and political power. As a consequence, the crisis of public administration is nowhere more evident than in the transitional nations and in the more traditional parts of modern countries.

All nations are, in the broad sense, somewhere in transition between traditional and modern stages. Rates of change differ, however, and not all move in the same direction. Some may even be moving away from rather than toward "modernity." Well over half are nearer the traditional than the modern end of the scale. Almost half are "new" nations. Among the more modern, older nations the bureaucracies are characterized by greater impersonality and rationality, have a greater supply of administrative talent, and a more marked tendency to handle complicated tasks in ways reflecting longer periods of industrialization and independent involvement in world affairs.

LEVEL OF ECONOMIC DEVELOPMENT

Related to the matter of modernization is the question of the economic systems and the level of economic growth and development of a country. In general to modernize is to alter production methods and thereby to increase the industrial capacity of a nation. Those nations which developed large industrial capacities early and "grew up" with the industrial revolution were also the first to develop modern bureaucracies, both public and private. In fact, the development of administrative skills went hand in glove with industrialization. The first nations to industrialize were those of Western Europe and North America, which operated mainly under some variation of the system of private capital development. As the large industrial bureaucracies of the capitalist systems developed, the governments of these nations eventually developed public bureaucracies to cope with the increasingly complex problems of urban, industrial society, to regulate the industrial combines, and in some instances to operate them when private capitalism was modified by some degree of socialism.

Although such industrial nations as England, France, Holland, and Belgium dominated great land areas as colonial powers, they did not appreciably build up the industrial capacities and capital structures of these areas. They preferred to maintain the colonies of Asia and Africa as sources of trade and raw materials, that is, as predominantly agricultural and extractive economies complementing industrial development in the "home" countries. Concomitantly, the bureaucracies of the colonies were kept in a rudimentary state. In most instances the important positions were staffed by members of the colonial administrations from the "home" countries. In nations which were not colonies but were nevertheless pre-industrial in their economic structures, feudal agrarianism and oligarchical mercantilism were predominant, and the bureaucracies of such countries tended to follow the typical traditional patterns.

At present, in these former colonies and in the predominantly agrarian societies of the Middle East, Asia, Africa, and Latin America, bureaucracy has a special role. As these nations attempt to develop their economies, they find that their problems are more acute than were those of the older industrialized nations. Moreover, they feel the need to build their productive capacity and to industrialize at a more rapid rate in order to catch up. And since they are often dubious that private capital can or will do the job (for they associate it with long centuries of underdevelopment and exploitation), they look to the state as the central organ of economic development. This attitude necessarily means a tremendous growth of the public bureaucracy. Thus in these developing countries, the scope of public administrative activity is generally broader than that in the older industrial nations. Also characteristic of some such countries is a mixture of foreign and indigenous bureaucrats—a mixture that will be characteristic until the quality and quantity of trained nationals is deemed more adequate to the demands being placed upon them.

NATIONALISM

A political factor closely related to the level of economic development is nationalism. The newer nations, recently freed from colonialism, find it essential to develop organizations for the maintenance of foreign relations and for defense. This necessity in itself creates the problem of developing bureaucratic skills formerly supplied by colonial officials. In addition, the surge of nationalistic spirit which usually accompanies a country's independence generates pressure to eliminate the vestiges of foreign control, especially in the bureaucracy. In some instances the search for national identity and dignity may be a stronger motivation for rapid administrative development than the desire to modernize economically.

Nationalism thus can run counter to the tendency noted above to mingle foreign with national talent during the earlier stages of economic development. Indeed, extreme feelings of nationalism may work so that aid in administration proffered by those associated with the old colonialism is accepted grudgingly, if at all, and is poorly used. Actually, a sort of administrative ambivalence can result in which the political ties with the old colonial power are scornfully disowned while the cultural and technical imprint lingers on in many of the forms and methods of running the government. For example, lawyers and judges in many former French colonies continue to follow the modes of procedure and much of the substance of the French civil and criminal codes, while common law institutions and practices remain, at least formally, in nations which were British colonies.

POLITICAL POWER STRUCTURE AND POLITICAL INSTITUTIONS

A country's system of public administration is intimately affected by its political power structure and political institutions. The wish of some that "administration be separated from politics" is at most a kind of political slogan or ideal. Where political power is dispersed, the effect upon the bureaucracy is to disperse and to fragment its authority. Dispersion of power also has the effect of opening up positions in the administration to a larger portion of the members of the society. Where political power is concentrated, the effect is to concentrate bureaucratic authority and to channelize access to positions. A political structure which emphasizes control at the expense of disagreement, or authority at the expense of freedom, and gives to one man or to a small group the power to pursue their own notions is likely to produce a bureaucracy in its own image.

In one-party states, for example, the bureaucracy tends to serve the party, and the key decision-makers will be strongly loyal to the party. In two-party and multi-party states, the bureaucracy tends to belong wholly to no party, at least not permanently. In the early stages of nations with more than one party such as the United States in much of the nineteenth century, the bureaucracy may experience considerable rotation of personnel as parties gain or lose power. Over the long run, however, the necessity of continuity and expertise in bureaucratic performance leads to the establishment of a *modus vivendi* between the bureaucracy and the party in power. The governmental system strikes some sort of balance between party changes in policy direction and bureaucratic stability and routine. In such situations, the bureaucrats may have considerable voice in policy matters, for they stay while party officials come and go. This situation was particularly characteristic of France during the Third and Fourth Republics. Yet under these conditions a single-minded bureaucracy dominating the state is not the inevitable or even the most likely consequence, for the policy battles tend to shift to groups within the bureaucracy itself.

The institutional structure of the governmental system which has been handed down over the years in a nation also affects the administrative system. Illustrations of the importance of this are particularly dramatic when nations without extended experience with the practices and attitudes of democratic politics seek to adopt democratic forms of government—as did Germany after the First World War. The old imperial bureaucracy continued without basic changes, and its entrenched structure and behavior contributed to the failure of this effort to implant constitutional democracy in Germany.

Governmental bureaucracies are not as easily remodeled as are chief executive and legislative institutions. While relatively rapid transformations of the structure of the latter two types of institutions are not infrequent in some parts of the world, in administrative values and behavior the heritage of structure and tradition tend to persist more strongly. In recent years this has been a problem of considerable significance in many of the "new" nations—those emerging to independence from former colonial status. In these nations, even if the former imperial power had provided training and experience for indigenous administrators—as in India—the problems and demands of independent nationhood have inevitably turned out to be different from those of colonial administration. Yet the ingrained patterns of organization and procedure, of values and behavior, tend to linger on.

RECRUITMENT PATTERNS

As already suggested, one of the important means by which environmental factors are brought to bear on public administration is through the people who make up administrative organizations.[3] Although such organizations—and officialdom as a whole—generate norms, traditions, and characteristic practices of their own, the personnel recruited and admitted into the ranks of administration just as obviously bring with them the values, prejudices, skills, and limitations of their upbringing and experience. Thus if we observe that a government's bureaucracy tends to select its recruits and replacements from certain social classes or occupational groups rather than from others, or if various kinds of educational backgrounds are required of entrants, we have significant clues to some of its functioning and behavior. Let us therefore survey briefly some of the principal variants in civil service systems, with particular attention to methods of personnel selection, to ways of organiz-

---

3 Other important means include the demands and information transmitted to officials by extra-bureaucratic individuals, groups, and institutions; other information gathered by administrative agencies; policy directives from other organs of government; and financial and technological resources provided to and/or extended by the bureaucracy.

ing and ranking officials, and to ways in which these matters are related to the social, economic, and political environment.

Administrative recruitment methods are of less importance for political systems in pre-industrial societies, and even in societies in the early stages of industrialization, than they are when commerce, industry, and urbanization have worked their transformation. The range and complexity of administrative tasks is much more limited in pre-industrial societies, the skills and abilities much less specialized, and the tasks much less demanding. Thus recruitment by patronage, purchase, or inheritance, any of which may be desirable for political or financial reasons but which are not designed to result in competent and skilled administration, have been successfully employed singly or in combination by European, Asian, and American political systems at various times. For example, the British employed patronage widely until the latter half of the nineteenth century, when they gradually instituted a system of recruitment by competitive examinations. Up until then appointments based on nomination by politically important sponsors were for life and in many instances provided convenient employment for sons of aristocrats who could not make a go of it in other pursuits.

The American variety of patronage (the "spoils" system) did not produce permanent appointments but rather subjected officeholders to the risk of displacement when the Presidency changed hands. However, the availability of offices as rewards for such political services as mobilizing votes was an important factor in the growth and vigor of the two major political parties and, to a limited extent, remains important. In France before the Revolution, the sale of offices was an expedient by which the monarch sought to stave off financial crisis; and the practice was also resorted to at various times in pre-twentieth-century China. Somewhat akin to this is the ancient practice of granting certain profitable functions (for example, tax-collecting) to the private individuals or firms who offer the highest bids for them. The collectors contract to deliver a certain revenue to the rulers; they keep any surplus above the agreed figure. The practice was common in the early Roman Empire and has appeared in limited form in some economically underdeveloped countries in recent times, such as Vietnam.

The system of inherited office, though it has ancient roots, is a practice clearly inimical to centralized control. Officeholders so little indebted to the central ruler for their positions are less likely to feel obliged to accept his directives. Thus princes and monarchs seeking to tighten their control have usually opposed this means of selection for office where it has appeared. But in some instances where it has not been formally institutionalized, heredity has nevertheless become the decisive criterion—for example, when only the offspring of a narrow officeholding elite are able to acquire the schooling, motivation, or sponsorship which qualify them for office. This situation was common in various periods under European monarchies as well as in some of the ancient empires.

When rulers, for whatever reason, desire technically competent and effective administrative structures, however, more appropriate methods of recruitment must be utilized. Historically, the temple schools of the earliest Middle Eastern kingdoms and empires provided a supply of literate scribes and account-keepers. The Chinese developed the most renowned early system of recruitment, one of competitive examinations to select the most capable men from the tiny literate minority. European rulers of the Middle Ages drew upon the clergy for their indispensable recordkeepers, financial aides, and corresponding secretaries.

To manage the affairs of government under conditions of industrialization and large-scale urbanization, however, requires more than simple literacy and political loyalty, as Andrew Jackson—and, curiously enough, such a different-minded younger contemporary of Jackson's as Karl Marx—seemed to think. Moreover, the inefficiency, favoritism, and corruption that accompanied recruitment by patronage (purchase and inheritance of office had become rare in most Western countries by the mid-nineteenth century) worked to the disadvantage of the rapidly expanding business classes, whose tax burdens were growing. Extension of suffrage and the growth of public education in some countries, notably Britain and the United States, added to the pressures for reformed methods of recruitment. (In Prussia the autocratic Hohenzollern kings had long since recognized the value of trained and competent officials for centralized control of an expanding empire, and Napoleon had laid down the principle of the "career open to talent" for the French.) Thus in more recent decades governments around the world have turned toward the idea, if not always the practice, of "universalistic" recruitment based on merit. The methods by which bureaucracies attempt to ascertain which among the potential recruits possess the requisite merit are several, but two are common: examinations and educational diplomas. Sometimes one or the other is used, and sometimes both are used together.

Examinations vary widely, both in objective and in form. The predominant objective in the United States is often to discover whether candidates have the knowledge and skills required to perform a particular, narrowly defined, type of work. In other countries, such as Great Britain, more emphasis is placed upon identifying persons who have the capacity to advance through a lifetime career to the highest ranks of the broad civil service "class" into which they are recruited. In form, examinations may be oral or written, "multiple choice" or essay, demonstration or performance (for example, typing), competitive or noncompetitive, or any combination of these. The educational diplomas or degrees that are required of entrants normally correspond to the "level" of responsibility and expertise at which they will be expected to perform, if appointed.

In Western Europe it is common to find the whole of the civil service divided into four general personnel classes. The classes are designed so that entry normally occurs at the point at which the student has left school. Thus the highest class (the "Administrative Class" in Great Britain, "Category A" in France, and the "Higher Service" in Germany) is normally open only to university graduates. These men prepare plans and policies and advise ministers. The second category is for those with a secondary education; they manage and supervise the administrative programs that translate policy into action. The third is for those who have left school following the first major secondary school examinations, and constitutes the bulk of governmental employees— clerks, inspectors, typists, and so on. The fourth is for those who have no more than a primary education, whose work is largely unskilled— porters, watchmen, messengers. Particularly for the highest class, but progressively less for the other three because of the younger ages at which they leave school, it is expected that entrants will join the service shortly after they graduate. Thus—and again especially for those in the highest class—admission at more advanced ages is rare, except for the fourth class; and it is assumed that entrants will make government service their lifetime career. As a consequence, the regular civil service in countries with such a system tends to become somewhat distinct and closed off from the rest of society—it has a tendency to develop caste-like qualities. Because of Western Europe's influence on governmental patterns around the world through the colonial system, similar principles in the organization of civil services are now found in many other areas.

In the United States somewhat different patterns have evolved. The systematic division of all personnel into a small number of broad "classes" has been resisted—although the extent of one's education obviously sets rough "floors" for the level at which one enters and "ceilings" for the heights to which one can aspire. The possibility of entering the service at more advanced ages and of substituting certain kinds and periods of "experience" for formal educational requirements has been greater. Another important difference is that people are employed to fill specific "positions," and the status, pay, and other perquisites accorded them depend upon the positions they occupy. Positions rather than personnel are classified—first according to the type of work performed, then according to the level of responsibility and difficulty (for example, Teletypist GS-4 and 5, Supervisory Teletypist GS-5, 6, and 7, Parasitologist GS-7). These classes, which are much more numerous and narrowly defined than the broad categories called "classes" in Europe, are then related to a complex pay plan. By grouping comparably valued classes into "grades," an effort is made to provide "equal pay for equal work." Thus a civil servant's salary depends upon the position he occupies; if he is moved from one position to another, his pay may change. This contrasts with the European practice (and with the United States military practice) of giving ranks with specified compensation and perquisites to individual officials—ranks which they retain while in the service regardless of the organization or work assignment to which they may be attached at a given time.

These procedures of recruitment and classification help to account for some significant differences between public administration in the United States and in some other countries, such as those of Western Europe. For one thing, public employment in the United States is less of a distinctive, separate, and career-oriented kind of work than it is in England or France. There is more interchange of personnel between governmental and nongovernmental sectors. Many government employees do not look upon their jobs as lifetime careers, but expect to move on to nongovernmental employment later. Indeed, the practice of recruiting for specific positions and without consideration of a person's potential for future development tends to hinder the development of career lines. The classification system works similarly, since it is often difficult to arrange positions into "career ladders" which persons can climb through promotion to successively higher levels of responsibility and authority. This situation can cause problems for those civil servants in the United States who *would* like to make a career of government work.

Another implication for bureaucratic recruitment is that in Europe, as well as in most of Asia, Africa, and Latin America, the educational systems are more closely tied to more stratified socio-economic class structures than in the United States. Since a person's chances of getting a university education depend largely upon his family's socio-economic standing and since recruitment is based largely upon the level at which he leaves school, members of the higher civil service are almost exclusively of upper- or upper-middle-class backgrounds. Although civil service systems in such societies often make provision for advancement by examination from a lower class to a higher one, few people are able to make it by this route. Thus the over-all structures of their civil services tend to parallel their characteristically less open and more sharply differentiated class systems. The civil service system of the United States, as well as its educational system, similarly reflects the more open and less restrictive class system of this country.

Such relationships are all the more important in the economically underdeveloped areas of the world, where the level of education tends to correspond with the degree of a person's "Westernization." As a result, bureaucratic officialdom differs more and more from the bulk of the people in education and values as hierarchical rank increases. Also, since business, industrial, and professional career patterns are more limited, the governmental bureaucracy often offers the most obvious pathway to status, wealth, and power. Consequently—and this poses one of the most painful dilemmas for many of the developing countries—recruitment into the most prestigious employment, that of the government, requires an education that produces alienation from the culture of most of one's own compatriots. No matter how good the intentions of the city-bred and educated *criollo* or *mestizo* official of certain Latin American countries, he will find a serious cultural—and hence communication—gap between himself and the Indian villagers in his jurisdiction. The same can be said of most countries of Africa and Asia. Recruitment patterns, which must necessarily favor those with some version of a Western education, tend to result in bureaucracies staffed by personnel whose interests and values are to some extent out of touch with those of the bulk of the population.

Administrative Structure

The problem of organizing public administration is an old one; it has been attacked in different ways by the Egyptians, the Greeks, the Chinese, the Romans, the Catholic Church, and the military (especially Napoleon), and again by modern scholars and practitioners of the art. Historically and theoretically, the problems of organization center on dividing the work and distributing and relating skills, authority, responsibility, and status in such a way that coordinated work can be done within a framework of purposes and values, not all of which may be explicit.

Division of work means specialization on the part of individuals and organizational units, and the administrative structure is the pattern of relationships among the various specialized elements, linking them into a whole. There are many different ways of dividing and coordinating work to accomplish a given objective, and often one way is not demonstrably better than another because the consequences of one or the other may be multiple, mixed, and complex. Nevertheless, a brief survey of some of the more frequently encountered ideas, practices, and structural patterns can provide some insight into how many contemporary administrators deal with problems of structure.

DIVISION OF LABOR

One long-standing practice in dividing up administrative work is to use *geographic areas* as basic units. Virtually every administrative system utilizes this idea to some degree, carving the country into provinces, regions, counties, districts, *départements*, and so on, in which similar administrative functions are carried out in accordance with the general scheme set up by a central office. A second method of dividing the work is according to the *clientele* or "customers" of the organization. Organizations may be set up to serve or regulate farmers, businessmen, veterans, or some other special segment of the population. A third way of dividing work is according to the special *processes, skills,* or *technical procedures* used to accomplish it. This method is often employed in connection with the organization of staff and auxiliary units within larger agencies and departments, such as accounting offices, typing pools, engineering drafting units, and the like. A final way of work division is according to *objective* or purpose. Examples of this would be one organization for all law enforcement units, for all tax collection units, or for all personnel concerned with public health.

A basic problem in these methods of work division, however, is that the four concepts involve ambiguities.[4] For example, depending on one's point of view, a single public high school can be called a geographically based agency (it serves a defined area); a clientele-oriented agency (it serves youngsters within a limited age bracket), an agency organized according to a process it performs or technical skill it employs (most of its employees are persons using the professional skills of teaching), or an agency specialized according to its purpose (education). Moreover, even when there is agreement upon consistent and applicable ways of using these designations, we find that in actual practice most organizations combine these bases of specialization. Ministries or departments in national bureaucracies very commonly reflect purpose or function as the most general criterion of organization, but they sometimes combine this with clientele orientation. An example is the U.S. Department of Commerce, whose primary basis of organization is purpose—to aid and regulate business activity of virtually all types. Its other basis of organization is clientele—it deals with businessmen and business groups. A clearer example of an agency with clientele as its fundamental basis of organization is the U.S. Veterans Administration. Secondarily, however, it is divided into units based on both purpose and process—units that take care of veterans' insurance, medical care, education, and other matters. Within the structures of ministries, departments, or agencies one often finds central headquarters at the capital and regional or district headquarters throughout the country, each performing some or all of the functions of the agency but each operating only within its geographic area. In the U.S. Department of Agriculture, for example, the Washington headquarters is divided into different services according to purpose, and most of these services in turn have field units in each state. Thus we have an agency using a geographical division of purpose-organized units which are parts of a clientele-oriented agency. Again, in most agencies there are special staffs of people in both central and field offices who are united primarily on the basis of the profession or technology they employ, a good example being the personnel offices or divisions found in most departments.

HIERARCHY: CHAIN OF COMMAND AND SPAN OF CONTROL

Whatever the ideas or practices guiding the division of labor, the administrative structure also provides for the more difficult task of co-

---

[4] Herbert A. Simon, *Administrative Behavior* (New York: The Macmillan Company, 1947), pp. 28–35.

ordinating the various specialized activities so that the work of the organization as a whole can be done.

A fundamentally important and universal means of providing this essential coordination—supervision—results in one of the most prominent characteristics of administrative organization—hierarchy. One person can supervise and interrelate the activities of only a limited number of other people. Thus if a hundred men are divided into ten groups, each group performing an assigned portion of the divided work, each has a supervisor to coordinate its efforts. But these first-line supervisors must also carry on their work in coordination with each other, and thus a higher-level supervisor of the first-line supervisors is necessary. Possibly one person can fill this position; if not, two or more are given the job, and a still higher-level supervisor must be provided to coordinate *their* activities. The result is the more or less pyramidal form of administrative structure, in which authority, responsibility, and status increase at successively higher "levels" of supervision. The more nearly the hierarchy is integrated—that is, molded into one over-all unit headed by a chief executive—the more nearly it approximates a neat pyramid with unified direction and rational assignment of duties. In actual practice, however, most administrative complexes, especially civilian public bureaucracies, lack this neatness. The traditions and training of the military, which follow the Napoleonic concepts among others, are more likely to produce a closer approximation of integrated hierarchies. Still, even the military has within its hierarchy, in the United States and in most other major countries, an army, a navy, and an air force hierarchy. The result is a considerable degree of pluralism and competition within the military, making it difficult for one single military authority to command the whole.

Typically, national civilian public administration contains numerous pyramids composed of ministries, agencies, departments, commissions, public corporations, and so on, all coordinated to some degree by a chief executive. The size, structural pattern, and degree of integration of these units vary widely, giving the over-all edifice a rambling and disjointed character. The chief executive may be a strong dictator, a prime minister and his cabinet, a president, or perhaps in some rare instances a plural commission or council. But even in countries such as the Soviet Union, where Stalin and Khrushchev have exercised such extensive executive powers, the structure of the vast bureaucracy lacks the neatness of an integrated army. There are duplications of function and double chains of authority, one through the administration and the other through the Communist Party. In certain geographic and functional areas, the hierarchical authority of the Soviet leadership is less rational and direct than in others. So it is fair to state that national bureaucracies are imperfectly coordinated and pluralistic structures which only roughly approach pyramidal patterns and that in many countries substantial segments of the administration have sizable degrees of autonomy in their relation to the chief executive. The latter situation is particularly true where semi-independent commissions and corporations have been created to regulate or run specific segments of the business community; for example, the American Securities and Exchange Commission.

The process of creating level upon level of administrative units in order to arrange a "chain of command" from the chief executive downward creates problems of control simply because of the difficulty of penetrating ever-multiplying layers of authority. At every level in the hierarchy, one finds the problem of how many different kinds of subordinate a superior can effectively supervise, how many persons, agencies, and activities can be effectively placed within his "span of control." The establishment of this structure requires organizational decisions balancing the need for close direction by the superior with his capacity to exercise such direction at points where problems and choices first appear. If critical activities are buried too far down in the structure, the executive may be frustrated by intermediate levels in his efforts to control them. Yet if he tries to control all activities directly, he will be swamped, and executive direction will be completely lost. So administrative organizers define the scope of official control at each level and indicate which activities are more important by placing them nearer the top of the hierarchy.

COORDINATION: STAFF, LINE, AND AUXILIARY FUNCTIONS

The executives, managers, and supervisors to whom we have been referring have the job of getting their subordinates to work together, to understand how their efforts fit into the general objectives of the organization, and to keep within the defined bounds of their responsibilities. People who perform these roles are often referred to (particularly in the United States) as *line* administrators, for the authority they exercise is considered to be primarily in the direct "line of command" from the head to the lowest level of operation. But in large organizations, line administrators alone cannot perform the herculean tasks of coordination and control. In addition to them, and more numerous at the highest levels of the hierarchy, there are several "overhead units," usually called *staff* units and *auxiliary* units. Staff and auxiliary units are not thought of as being in the direct line of command. Their functions are to investigate, examine, advise, control, and serve line operations. They include such units as those called "planning," "personnel," "budgeting," "accounting," and "purchasing." Although they may have great influence upon line performance, they are without formal command authority. In practice, it is often difficult to tell who is "line" and who is "staff" on the basis of influence exercised; however, it is necessary to know that administrators make this distinction and that it affects their conception of organization and, consequently, the way they behave.

CONCENTRATION AND DISPERSAL OF AUTHORITY

Another aspect of administrative organization concerns the concentration or dispersal of authority to make decisions. This can be thought of in both a geographic and a hierarchical sense. Some authorities prefer to call the geographic concentration of decision-making *centralization,* and apply "concentration" only to the hierarchical aspect. But the terms are relatively unimportant so long as one recognizes that organizations may vary in distribution of authority and that the variations bring significant consequences. In general, a centralized agency reserves most of the important authority to the people in the main headquarters, so that the performers down the line and out in the field have very little freedom of action.

The public administration of the United States is much more decentralized than are most other nations' bureaucracies. The reasons for this are several: First, there is the federal system and the long tradition of state and local responsibility for many matters. The continent was settled and developed by people who were in many instances fleeing from centralized and overbearing governmental rule and who had a built-in reluctance to have anything determined too far from home. Again, the Anglo-American pattern of law was not very conducive to logical planning and systematic organization. Bureaucracy tended rather to grow pragmatically, responding to local political pressures in a pluralistic fashion. Consequently, the system contains a great deal of duplication and follows patterns of consultation and checking with those who are going to be affected. Furthermore, because of the many deliberative bodies and pressure groups that exist in American society, administration in effect takes place in a goldfish bowl. Consequently, few decisions can be made without participation by many people. Such a system can give administrators a great deal of sensitivity to "grassroots" and pressure group opinion. When there is no extensive disharmony between the field administrators and their clientele, the administration process can proceed without delays; but where the clientele is not happy with the organization's actions, decisions can be challenged at many points, and many delays and inconsistencies can follow.

In the French pattern of centralized administration, on the other hand, the kind of decision-making which results is characterized by somewhat more rigorous adherence to instructions and procedures developed at central headquarters and by review and clearance by numerous levels of the hierarchy. Routine decisions can be handled rather quickly under this system, although the requirement that they be reviewed at several levels may bring delays. Unusual questions, however, if they involve on-the-spot exercise of discretion, are more difficult to handle quickly. In many parts of the world, the French pattern is more closely approximated by national bureaucracies than is the decentralized form.

Administrative Behavior

The discussion of administrative structure in the preceding section focused mainly on formal structure, on the different kinds of organizational units and the relations among them that are prescribed by those who plan, establish, or direct the organizations. As we have seen time and again, however, a person seeking to understand any aspect of government—and that includes administration—has to look beyond the organization charts and the formally prescribed structures, rules, and procedures. These provide only limited insights into what goes on in the administrative process. Actual behavior in organizations, although it may be influenced in important ways by the formal establishment, deviates from it in varying degrees.

One way of studying administrative organizations is to view them as patterns of action, or behavior. We may perhaps be used to thinking of organizations in terms of people, because their members are possibly their most tangible distinguishing aspect. But people are much more than just members of the organizations to which they belong. Even during working hours, much of what is done by members of organizations is not related to the organization or to their jobs.

But if we think of organizations not as people or collections of members but rather as embodiments of what they do, of their behavior, then we are in a better position to get at the observable, empirical stuff of administration. Then we can visualize structure not as a set of boxes linked by lines on an organization chart but as characteristic patterns of relationships among interacting individuals and between dynamic groups. When we draw a map of such relationships, we get a much more realistic picture of an organization's structure than is afforded by its formal chart. Such a map would necessarily be less precise and orderly than the formal chart, and it would evolve more imperceptibly over time, but it would indicate that organizations display these same general characteristics. We shall examine some of these common characteristics in the following sections.

OFFICE AND "ROLE"

Moreover, when we raise questions of administrative behavior, matters considerably more complex than formal structure and procedure have to be faced. We need concepts to describe, relate, and analyze these complexities. One concept that has proved to be of considerable utility is that of "role." A person's behavior in any social system is largely patterned or structured by the role he performs. For example, a role is defined for the father in the family, and his behavior will be strongly influenced thereby in many different kinds of family situations. Of course the role is not precisely the same for any two families, nor does it prescribe *all* of a father's behavior as a father. But for families in the same or similar parts of a given society, there is enough similarity in the role definitions of "father" to warrant generalizing about them.

In administrative organizations the concept of role is particularly useful because of the necessity for a fairly high degree of structured, predictable behavior. For a person to coordinate his work activities with the activities of others, he has to know what the others will be doing, and when. He also has to know what the others expect of him in various phases of the work and in a wide range of situations. When he learns what he is expected to do, he will have learned his role. In other words, each role carries with it a set of expectations. Living up to those expectations in the daily interactions between organization members constitutes role behavior.

An important part of administrative role expectations is spelled out in the formal organization chart, the job description, the rules, and the standard procedures. But the extent to which these factors shape behavior in a given organization is an empirical question that can only be answered by systematic observation. Other factors are also important in defining roles, such as unwritten, customary practices and informal relationships between members. Personality is also an important variable; roles may affect personalities by accustoming people to interact in situations for which they previously had little or no experience. Thus role behavior may bring out aspects of personality that had not been obvious before. In the other direction, by his performance over a period of time, a person may subtly redefine his role to fit his personality more congenially. Thus administrative roles, while they tend to maintain stability, are also constantly evolving.

RATIONALITY IN DECISION-MAKING

A basic part of behavior in administrative roles is the making of decisions. All members of administrative organizations are constantly choosing one course of action over other possible ones, responding in one way rather than another to each situation with which they are faced. Of course these decisions range from the many routine, quasi-automatic alternatives that require little or no conscious deliberation to the broader innovating and problem-solving choices that require the contributions—through research, analysis, proposals, and discussion—of many people throughout the organization. Organizational roles tend to be defined and related to one another so that these broader and more important decisions are made by those in the roles of greatest authority and leadership—although empirical observation of particular organizations may reveal significant departures from this pattern. Decision-making is therefore such a crucial aspect of administrative behavior that special attention must be given to it.

An important reason for the significance of decision-making is the attempt of administration to be *rational*. Administrative structures come into being and are operated to achieve specific purposes; to the extent that the purposes, or ends, are actually achieved, that administration is rational. What then are the conditions of rational decision-making? First, the decision-maker must know all the possible choices in a situation. Second, he must be able to foresee at least the probable consequences of each course. Third, he must have a scale of values or desired outcomes that permits him to rank all the sets of consequences, so that he can know which is preferred. Given these three conditions, the decision-maker can then choose the course that will produce the preferred consequences —that will most nearly achieve the ends he seeks with the smallest number of other undesirable consequences.[5]

Little reflection is required to see that seldom, if ever, are human beings in a position to make a completely rational decision. We seldom know, or have time to find out, *all* the possible courses of action we might choose among. And not being gifted with prescience, we cannot predict with great accuracy what consequences will flow from a given choice. Even if we could, our scales of values are seldom defined and ordered precisely enough to indicate a clear choice between alternative sets of consequences when each includes some desirable and some undesirable elements. The outlook for achieving complete rationality in our choices is indeed discouraging.

However, just as administrative organizations come into being to achieve goals through coordinated, collective activity that single persons cannot achieve alone, so do they provide means for increasing the degree of rationality of decisions made through administrative processes. Information on the organization's environmental situation and on the alternative possibilities of action can be funneled in to decision-making centers from a number of subunits in the organization. Similarly, information concerning the probable consequences of many choices can be provided from several sources: files, the specialized training and experience of the members of the organization, and the research and analysis members may conduct in preparing plans and recommendations. Finally, at least some of the organization's more important goals, or sets of preferred consequences, will probably be known to some of the decision-makers, and may have been subjected to enough thought and analysis to afford an understanding of priorities. Thus cooperative effort to produce organizational decisions may extend the range of rational action beyond what would be possible for an isolated individual.

At the same time, and paradoxically, administrative processes impose their own peculiar limitations upon rationality. Specialization, a necessary concomitant of organizational division of work, tends to

---

[5] For more complete discussion of rationality, see Herbert A. Simon, *op. cit.*, and James G. March and Herbert A. Simon, *Organizations* (New York: John Wiley and Sons, 1958), upon which the present discussion is based.

produce identification with specialized techniques and specialized aspects of the overall goals so that many organization members lose sight of the overall goals. Similarly, long-term preoccupation with routine procedures and rules of operation may cause these matters to become as important to some members of the organization as the goals they were designed to achieve; the result is rigidities in behavior that prevent or hamper organizational change and adaptation to new and different situations. Differences in status, necessitated by organizational hierarchy, create problems in communication between superiors and subordinates, just as barriers to effective communication develop between different kinds of specialists and separate subunits. Hence it becomes difficult to ensure that adequate information about alternatives, probable consequences, and preferred outcomes is made available to the right people at the right time. Personal ambitions, insecurities, affections, and hostilities also come into the picture. Not only the organization's goals and values, but also those of individuals and groups, are fed (sometimes deliberately but often unconsciously) into the decision-making process. It cannot be assumed that all members of the organization will at all times exert all their energies and skills in the interest of organizational goal-attainment—nor even that they all have the necessary energy and skill.

If we consider all these factors—and there are still others—we can perhaps begin to comprehend some of the characteristics of administrative behavior—particularly its tendencies toward rationality as well as its shortcomings in realizing that rationality. Even so, our understanding and therefore our ability to explain this behavior must, for the time being, remain limited. Research focusing on administrative behavior is a relatively recent development, and a great deal remains to be done.

Two Fundamental Criteria for Bureaucracy

RESPONSIBILITY

The ways in which we judge the execution of governmental functions are composites of personal prejudice, custom, moral standards, and varied notions about what "ought" to be done, only parts of which can be spelled out in any rational and objective fashion. Yet we do not hesitate to label public actions "responsible" or "irresponsible." The concept of responsibility is very important in public administration, for it has to do with the values the bureaucracy serves. In essence, responsible action is that which proceeds in accordance with legitimate expectations, which seeks to produce legitimate consequences. In this sense one can differentiate between "mistakes" and lack of responsibility. A mistake is an error in calculation of fitting the means to the end, whereas irresponsibility is refusal to be guided by legitimate expectations or failure to consider how an action will affect these expectations, both in itself and in its consequences. Mistakes do lie in the realm of efficiency; an efficient administration will have a low percentage of mistakes.

What are the main sources of legitimate expectations that set the patterns of responsibility for public administrators? Obviously, one is the laws that create agencies, define their legitimate purposes and methods, and confer specific authority on officials. But legal norms are not the only ones which have legitimate claims upon bureaucrats' performances. It is in the nature of administrative decision-making that many choices are left undefined in the laws, so that bureaucrats must "use their discretion" and look elsewhere for standards to guide them. They must look to the norms of the society, to the norms expressed through the political system, and to the norms which they have personally adopted, especially those professional and technical standards inculcated by years of specialization and education. All of these may have some part in setting the pattern of responsibility—and they may conflict.

Administrative Law. We have already mentioned briefly the relationship of different systems of law to bureaucracy. Here we can consider in more detail how they affect a bureaucracy's responsibility. There are two main traditions of the "rule of law" in the Western world and in those nations which have come under its influence—common law in the Anglo-Saxon tradition and civil or code law in the Roman-Napoleonic tradition. Nations in the former tradition have been slow to develop extensive bodies of administrative law and administrative courts that are separate and distinct from the main body of law and the regular courts. The actions of their administrators have been strongly circumscribed by the principles of individual rights and judicial appeal embedded in the common law tradition. In interpreting the statutes which they must enforce, the bureaucrats of nations such as the United States must often go into the courts as parties to litigation to get interpretations by judges on the intent of the law and the rights, duties, and powers involved. It is irresponsible administration to disregard these judicial decisions or any related decisions made in the past. In the Roman-Napoleonic legal tradition, especially as exemplified by France, elaborate and rational bodies of administrative law have been spelled out and codified, and special administrative courts have evolved to see that the bureaucracy carries out its legal functions. It is irresponsible administration for French bureaucrats to disregard the codes and the rulings of the administrative courts.

Both legal systems have produced a high degree of legal responsibility in public administration. The French system has a greater degree of uniformity, consistency, and logic, but to an Englishman or an American it seems unnecessarily rigid and detailed and also a bit inclined to the advantage of the bureaucrat. The British and American systems have greater flexibility and permissiveness in providing ways for a citizen to challenge the legality of bureaucratic action, but to a Frenchman they seem to lack consistency, logic, force. Yet in each the law serves both to direct the bureaucrats and to protect the rights of the citizen.

The definition of responsibility for Western administration tends to place the law ahead of intervention by political groups. In the Soviet system of law, however, the law is in the service of the "interests of the proletariat," and these interests are expressed primarily through the leaders of the Communist Party. The result is that the law is neither a clear and firm guide for the bureaucrat nor a strong protection for the citizen. The Soviet system leaves the patterns of responsibility unclear and encourages various kinds of political intervention. Different levels of political groups can legitimately assert their claims upon the bureaucrats, and consequently, the final and most important source of direction is the Party leadership. And since responsibility is to a great degree extra-legal, clever and indispensable bureaucrats can exercise some independence of thought and action from those who are officially their superiors.

A realistic look at all political systems, however, quickly leads one to see that, in the last analysis, the law is an expression of the norms of the political system. This is true of both Western and Soviet types of law. The reason there is more of a "rule of law" in the former is that the political values and traditions support it. So, in the broader sense, legal responsibility is always dependent upon a political consensus. Furthermore, since laws are always made by men and enforced by men, elements other than the law are inevitably involved in the legal processes. To go one step further, it is also obvious that every administrative system must have some room for political forces to make themselves felt, and it is inaccurate to assert that there is an absolute dichotomy between those nations that have the "rule of law" as the foundation of their administrative responsibility and those that do not.

Political Responsibility. Political expectations of different kinds—party, group, executive, and legislative—play legitimate parts in determining the nature of all public bureaucratic responsibility. The most obvious examples of partisan responsibility are to be found in one-party totalitarian nations, where it is part of the accepted and legitimate pattern for the administration to serve the interests and objectives of the chief political organization of the state. Under this system all other group interests are subordinate to the party interest, and a bureaucrat who deviates from party directives is guilty of the highest form of irresponsible action. The party will have representatives in the bureaucracy to ensure that its wishes are followed.

In nations with more than one party, partisan responsibility is usually less clearly dominant, for it must compete wth other interests. Any party in power tends to be forced to respect the other parties because of the possibility that it may itself be out of power after the next election. Still, multi-party states have various ways of providing for some degree

of party responsibility. The most obvious and extreme system is historically associated in the United States with Andrew Jackson—the
"spoils system," in which the party attitude toward the bureaucracy is
"winner take all." Under this system, the first criterion applied in the appointment of a bureaucrat is party loyalty, and most of the bureaucratic
positions are political appointments. The spoils system has a dual purpose: to promote party responsibility and to provide a means of supporting the party organization. In actual practice, the latter objective
has probably been uppermost. As the bureaucracy grows, however, and
becomes more specialized and sophisticated in its tasks, the spoils system
is harder to maintain. Parties become torn between conflicting interests.
On one hand, they need many bureaucratic positions to hand out as
patronage so as to keep the party materially alive. Yet, they cannot
afford to run a careless and inferior administration because this will
lose them votes.

With the spoils pattern on the decline in modern multi-party states,
party responsibility has had to come to terms with other interests, especially those of particular economic groups and of professional and technical people. The result has been a reduction in the proportion of positions in the bureaucracies for which party responsibility is the major
concern, and an increase in positions in which responsibility to interest
groups and professional groups is very important. Party responsibility is
maintained by a smaller coterie of high-level ministers at the top of the
bureaucratic pyramid. But they too must share administration with
the professional, career bureaucrats who work with them at levels near
the top of the hierarchy. Furthermore, various clienteles and others directly concerned with the special areas of policy handled by an agency
or ministry are usually acknowledged to have legitimate voices to be
heeded in the execution of policies. In some instances their role has been
formally recognized by the creation of advisory committees to counsel
the bureaucrats.

The executive and legislative bodies of government have, of course,
many formal, legal means of maintaining the bureaucracy's responsibility
to them. But they also usually have, as attributes of their status, informal
powers which are recognized as legitimate by the bureaucracy and
which stimulate administrative responsibility. Both the executive and
the legislature can inquire into the actions of the bureaucracy, can
conduct investigations and ask about expenditures and personnel, can
always pass retributive legislation or reduce budgetary items or eliminate
the positions of certain employees. In modern governments, the executive
is especially charged with seeing that the bureaucracy stays on the
proper path, and even more, that it develops and anticipates new paths
which will lead toward the fulfillment of the "public interest." This
leadership, discussed more fully in Chapter 16, is largely extra-legal,
whether in a Western type of constitutional government or in the Soviet

system or in some other form of government. In most governments it is through the executive, also, that party leadership makes itself most strongly felt in the administration.

Ethical Standards. Although bureaucrats are largely held responsible by legal and political norms, they are not robots. They have personal sets of norms, both conscious and unconscious, derived from the culture in which they have been raised and educated, and these basic values are not set aside when they report to work each morning. Consider, for example, the bureaucracies in two different societies: one a puritanical place with strong standards against the sin of bribery; the other a place where many people see officials not as public *servants*, but as august— and feared—representatives of a distant but divinely sanctioned monarch, to whom gifts or offerings are due as a sign of respect or propitiation. In the first society, bureaucrats are expected to do their duty without receiving gratuities. If one accepts a mink coat, freezer, or free plane ride, he may cause a national uproar. In the other society, on the contrary, patrons expect to hand out gratuities and bureaucrats expect to receive them, all without fanfare.

The cultural standards associated with the people recruited to the bureaucracy thus become translated into standards of responsibility in the administration through the constant exercise of personal judgment by the bureaucrats. Bureaucrats make these value judgments on the basis of things learned outside the administration. Among the most important categories of such personal standards today is professional knowledge. Government engineers tend to feel a strong sense of responsibility to the standards of professional engineers. The same thing applies to accountants, lawyers, educators, electricians, and mechanics. They are apt to resist as irresponsible and invalid demands from law or from politicians to do their jobs in ways that violate their professional standards.

From the foregoing discussion it is obvious that a definition of responsibility in public administration is a complicated matter for any government. It is also obvious that the legitimate expectations directed at a bureaucrat may be in serious conflict with each other. One may ask for an easy answer to the question of how these conflicts should be resolved, but none will be offered here. One statement is, however, appropriate: Each society has different balances and combinations of the ingredients mentioned above in its formula of bureaucratic responsibility And to assess the responsibility of its bureaucrats, that formula must be ascertained. Russian administration, for example, cannot properly be called irresponsible simply because it violates American principles of law, or because Americans object to Communist Party rule. The two countries simply have fundamental quarrels with each other over the values which public administration should serve.

EFFICIENCY

We have differentiated between responsibility and efficiency by noting that mistakes or errors in calculation were not irresponsible but rather inefficient administrative action. Efficiency, like responsibility, is a major concern of administration. But efficiency is not the determinant of the values to which administration will respond or of the ends to be served. Its essence, just as in the problem of rationality, is the choice of means to fit ends that are desired or already given. For choices to be made with any approximation of efficiency, rational judgments must be made about the appropriateness of the administrative means to the achievement of the objective.

In the broadest sense, efficiency is synonymous with rationality. However, when *all* the consequences (or costs and benefits) cannot be foreseen, and when the decision-makers are "neutral" to some of the potential consequences, efficiency represents the difference between those (valued) costs and benefits which can be foreseen.[6]

Administrative means generally have two important common characteristics. First, there are usually several seemingly rational alternative ways of reaching the same objective. Second, some of the essential means are always limited or scarce, so that each alternative always has a price tag attached to it. If one way is chosen, it cannot be used in another situation. It might be rational to use any one of the available means, but it is more efficient to use the one that produces the desired results with the least cost. Or, if all alternatives have the same price tag, then it is more efficient to use the one which would maximize the results. Mistakes in these calculations often lead to inefficiency.

The question of efficiency is not often as simple as it might seem at first glance. For one thing, price tag here refers to values, and as we need not emphasize further, values differ—particularly between cultures. Thus to many if not most Westerners, the phenomenal industrialization of the Soviet Union within one generation was a grossly inefficient operation. The costs in freedom and human lives were immeasurably excessive. But to the Soviet leadership—and those Russians who did not have to bear the heaviest burden of the costs, freedom and human lives were secondary values; from their perspective, the operation was much more efficient. And even in those instances in which most costs can be calculated in monetary terms, it is not merely a question of doing things the cheapest way—for example, getting the most work out of the bureaucrats for the least money. The complexity of political ends complicates the question of efficiency as equally as the difficulty of calculating all the costs does. In hiring stenographers and typists for a typical

6 Herbert A. Simon, Donald W. Smithburg, and Victor A. Thompson, *Public Administration* (New York: Alfred A. Knopf, 1950), pp. 490–98. Cf. Robert A. Dahl and Charles E. Lindblom, *Politics, Economics, and Welfare* (New York: Harper & Row, Publishers, 1953), pp. 38–40.

government typing pool in the United States, it may be fairly easy to construct criteria of efficiency. Here the speed and accuracy of their work may be determined, and those with a maximum of both may be chosen. This is an efficient way to set up a typing pool, just as it would be inefficient to hire the less competent typists, at least at the same salaries, or to hire more typists than are needed. But if this is not a typical stenographic pool as one thinks of it in the United States, if there are other legitimate purposes, such as increasing the supply of trained stenographers, developing secretarial skills, and providing employment opportunities in an underdeveloped economy, in addition to turning out the typing needed in the agency, the problems of how to organize it efficiently, and which applicants to hire and at what wages become much more complex.

Or consider the example of road construction in an economically underdeveloped, predominantly agricultural country with dense population. In judging the administration of such a project, a Westerner may be inclined to apply his own criteria of efficiency and to criticize the public works administrators concerned for permitting the project to be undermechanized and for employing far too many workers. The truth of the matter is that in such economies the ratio of manpower to mechanical power is such that manpower costs much less than mechanical power. In addition, the road project may be directed much more toward the coordinate purposes of relieving unemployment and stimulating purchasing power than is usual in similar projects in Western countries (except, of course, during such periods of economic maladjustment as the 1930s in the United States). Efficiency, in other words, is not a fixed, mechanical formula or criterion; it is relative to time and place.

Also a complicated matter is the relationship between responsibility and efficiency, and much documentation and analysis of the situation in different countries remains to be done by students of administration. In modern administration, for example, certain kinds of efficiency are themselves made dominant values, so that to be inefficient is to be irresponsible. This is particularly evident in certain offices and positions in government agencies which have the *responsibility* of ferreting out inefficiencies in organization and methods. The "O and M" (organization and methods) people become the custodians of efficiency in the bureaucracy. But the fact remains that many things that look inefficient superficially actually reflect conflicts in responsibility or, in some instances, sheer irresponsibility. These are problems of policy, of value choices, of conflicting standards. To remedy them, one may have to get political clarification, or even wait for certain basic cultural changes to take place over a long period of time.

SUGGESTIONS FOR ADDITIONAL READING

APPLEBY, PAUL, *Policy and Administration* (University, Ala.: University of Alabama Press, 1949).

CHAPMAN, BRIAN, *The Profession of Government* (London: Allen and Unwin, 1959).

LAPALOMBARA, JOSEPH (ed.), *Bureaucracy and Political Development* (Princeton, N.J.: Princeton University Press, 1963).

LEPAWSKY, ALBERT, *Administration: The Art and Science of Organization and Management* (New York: Alfred A. Knopf, 1949).

MARCH, JAMES G., and HERBERT A. SIMON, *Organizations* (New York: John Wiley and Sons, 1958).

MERTON, R. K. et al. (eds.), *Reader in Bureaucracy* (New York: The Free Press of Glencoe, 1952).

MORSTEIN MARX, F., *The Administrative State* (Chicago: University of Chicago Press, 1957).

RIGGS, FRED W., *Administration in Developing Countries* (Boston: Houghton Mifflin, 1964).

SIFFIN, WILLIAM F. (ed.), *Toward the Comparative Study of Public Administration* (Bloomington, Ind.: Indiana University Department of Government, 1957).

SIMON, HERBERT, A., D. W. SMITHBURG, and V. A. THOMPSON, *Public Administration* (New York: Alfred A. Knopf, 1950).

WALDO, DWIGHT, *The Administrative State: A Study of the Political Theory of American Public Administration* (New York: The Ronald Press, 1948).

Chapter 12

THE JUDICIAL PROCESS

Judicial Systems

The administration of justice was at one time a private affair. The state as such had no machinery for this purpose, instead disputes were resolved by compromise, or by individual or family retaliation. As a result blood feuds developed, the milder ones being settled with money, while the more serious ones often resulted in one of the antagonists' being driven from the community. At one time church officials and feudal lords administered justice in their respective areas and according to their respective precepts. Later the state became the arbiter of custom, and subsequently law-maker and law-adjudicator, and prosecutor and punisher of offenders.

The Beginnings of Judicial Institutions. Although it is possible to trace back to the earliest civilizations the existence of the office of judge— one who was empowered to resolve disputes by applying the "law" in the name of the ruler—it remained for the Greeks to make the distinction between the responsibilities of judicial and other governmental institutions. The Romans went a step beyond that when they elaborated a judicial system, along with a body of professional jurists. Under the Roman Republic, judicial power was first held by the consuls; later, judicial administration came into the hands of an elected magistrate, the *praetor*. Finally, it was the emperor that appointed these magistrates who, however, were required to be learned in the law.

With the development of ecclesiastical tribunals and feudal courts, the administration of justice became more complex; it was complicated further by the decline of the feudal order and the emergence of increasingly powerful monarchs, whose royal courts led to further competition and controversy. Gradually, royal judicial authority was able to supplement, for the most part, other forms of judicial administration. As affairs of state grew in scope and as the administration of property and other personal rights became more complicated, certain officials, expert in legal matters, tended to be set apart from other parts of administration, ultimately forming a separate branch, which we now refer to as "the judiciary."

These judicial officials, especially those in England, gradually gained independence from the monarch. On the continent, courts continued until relatively recently to serve as auxiliaries of the executive branch of government; administratively, they still remain branches of the ministries of justice. Actually, however, we are justified in thinking of judicial officials in all democratic countries as being truly independent.

STATUTE LAW, COMMON LAW, AND EQUITY

Statute or Code Law. Statute law, more frequently referred to as code law or Roman law, is written law. The attempt is made to foresee all possible eventualities, which are then provided for in an authoritative code of general rules. This arrangement is neat and not cumbersome. Presumably there is no question as to what the law is: the judge simply turns to the appropriate place in the code books and reads it there; there is no need to look at past cases to see how they were decided. When a new problem arises that calls for legal regulation, groups of distinguished jurists (usually law professors and officials of the ministry of justice in the country concerned) are assembled to draw up specific provisions to deal with that problem. These new codes then become valid upon enactment by the legislature. Thus in countries that have a code law system the development of the law is in the final analysis left to the legislature.

Code law is associated with Rome and particularly with the *corpus juris civilis,* sometimes referred to as the Justinian Code because it was the Emperor Justinian who ordered the codification in 528 A.D. Its best-known adaptation in Western Europe is the Napoleonic Code of France, although continental Europe in general came under the sway of code law. Imperial Russia also adopted code law, and although the Soviet regime has made significant modifications in its content, it has retained the code law system in all its important aspects.

Common Law. Common law, on the other hand, is unwritten in the sense that it provides no neat code to turn to. From its origin in England, it has been extended to all English-speaking countries. English judges, by applying local custom, evolved a system of law based on individual cases which is sometimes referred to as "case law," because the rules and principles developed in past and present cases are supposed to determine future decisions. Thus precedent is the hallmark of common law, and courts and judges continue to play an important role in its development.

Common law has also been modified by statute, however, and can be so modified at any time in the future. Statutes may be employed to correct or supplement it, thus providing greater flexibility in the legal system. Where such statutes are in conflict with common law rules, the courts have ruled that legislation takes precedence, thereby forestalling serious difficulties.

At the national level, American law is exclusively statute law. But United States courts, when called upon to deal with cases in common law, must apply the common law of the state in which the case arose, although most state common law provisions on criminal cases have been superseded by statutes.

One important advantage of common law is that it enables courts to decide cases on matters on which the legislature has not yet enacted statutes. Thus when new inventions such as television and jet planes have created new legal problems, courts on the European continent could not make decisions on cases arising from them until their legislature had enacted new provisions in the codes. Common law courts, on the other hand, were able to reason from analogy on the basis of precedents and to decide cases even though there was still no relevant legislation.

Equity Law. At an earlier period common law had been modified by equity law, which grew out of appeals to the "King's Conscience" from claimants who believed that decisions under common law rules would result in manifest injustice. In the process of deciding what was "equitable" and providing relief, the key role was played by the king's chancellor; equity consequently is sometimes called chancery law or simply chancery. Because of the growing number of cases involved, a Court of Chancery was established to administer equity, by applying its own body of precedents. Later, however, the court system was reformed, so that today the ordinary courts apply equity as well as other forms of law.

Typical matters of equity include bankruptcy and injunctions, injunctive remedies being perhaps the best examples of the current concept of equity. Under common law a person must prove that he has suffered damages if he wishes to obtain a remedy in court. Under equity, a person who can foresee that an action of another will damage him need not wait until the wrong has been committed; rather he can go to court and obtain an injunction restraining the other person, first temporarily and, after a successful hearing, permanently.

The differences between the common law and code law systems should not be overstressed. Each springs from the needs of a specific society and from the genius of a particular people in meeting those needs. The rules enunciated in the Roman law codes, for example, can be traced back to tribal customs and to the need for adjudicating conflicts—a background not altogether different from that in which common law rules took shape. Moreover, court decisions under the Roman law system have in recent decades made use of precedent, although without referring to it as such. And neither system is unchangeable: both provide for orderly evolution and development. In Roman law countries it is the legislature that is the primary instrument of change; in common law countries this role is shared by the legislature and the courts.

ORGANIZATION OF THE JUDICIAL SYSTEM: JUDICIAL HIERARCHIES

If justice is to be readily available to citizens, courts should exist in every locality. At the same time, in order for justice to be meaningful, it must be universal: there cannot be a different set of legal rules for every locality. Most modern states meet these requirements by having judicial hierarchies. At the base are widely distributed local courts; at the top one supreme court ensures unity and centralization. Between the base and the top of the judicial hierarchy are a number of intermediate courts, some having original jurisdiction in major offenses, while others are concerned with appeals. Of course, not all court systems are so tidily arranged; in the court systems of the American states, especially, there are jurisdictional problems.

There are important differences in the general pattern from nation to nation. In Great Britain, for example, there are two hierarchies of courts, one dealing with civil cases, the other with criminal cases. Above the level of the courts of appeal, however, Great Britain has one single supreme court, the House of Lords, for both civil and criminal cases. In France and Germany there are also two hierarchies, but in those countries one hierarchy is concerned with cases arising under ordinary laws, civil and criminal, while the other—the administrative courts— takes care of cases that arise from challenges to the administrative authority of the state or its agents.

In the United States and most other countries organized on the federal principle, there are also two court hierarchies, but here it is more appropriate to speak of two *systems* of courts: national and state or provincial. The national and state systems are separate, one being concerned with national laws and the national constitution and the other with state laws and the particular state constitution. With fifty state court hierarchies in the United States one can expect differences from state to state, but there is a common denominator—the common law—except in Louisiana, where the French tradition of code law is important. In cases of conflict between state and national courts, the supreme court of the nation is the final arbiter. Among federally organized states, Germany is a notable exception, in that it has one integrated court system. The Soviet Union, a federation in theory only, also does not have two systems of courts: the nationally supervised courts in the republics handle most matters, while the one actual national court, the Supreme Court of the USSR, hears mostly cases on appeal.

Local courts are usually of two types. Those dealing with petty offenses are presided over by justices of the peace or their equivalent (most traffic courts and the "comradely courts" of the USSR would fall in this category). In the second group, sometimes referred to as trial courts, are the state superior courts in the United States, county courts and quarter sessions in Great Britain, the people's courts in the Soviet Union, the court of major instance (*tribunal de grande instance*) in France, and the district courts (*ländgerichte*) in Germany.

Most cases of major importance—which includes homicide in the United States and the Soviet Union—begin in the trial courts. In Britain and France the more serious criminal cases, such as homicide, are tried in what are called assize courts, which rank below the appeals courts and yet are a step above the ordinary courts. In Germany such crimes are also tried in an assize court, which is, however, merely a separate chamber of the local or district court.

Courts of appeal are usually collegial—that is, they have more than one judge—and reach their verdicts by majority vote. They review the law and the procedure in the lower court, but they do not collect additional evidence. They may reverse or affirm the lower court's judgment, or else they may return the case for a new trial.

Above the courts of appeal stand the supreme courts, the highest courts of appeal, for the most part solely occupied with appeals work. The United States Supreme Court has limited original jurisdiction, chiefly in cases involving conflicts between states or between a state and the national government. In the Soviet Union the Supreme Court, in addition to its appellate work, is charged "with the supervision of the judicial activities of all the judicial organs of the USSR and of the Union Republics."

In all countries there are also some courts that function outside the usual judicial hierarchies. The administrative courts in France and Germany have already been mentioned. The constitutional courts of these two countries are also outside of the hierarchy. The Court of Claims in the United States and the special German courts which deal with labor relations, tax disputes, and social security cases are other examples. Mention should also be made of military courts, which have special jurisdiction over military personnel.

Non-judicial Participants in the Judicial Process. Numerous persons other than judges perform functions necessary to the judicial process. Among them are the members of the legal profession, without whom modern judicial systems could not operate. Their work is not arranged the same way in each country. In Britain, for example, lawyers are divided into solicitors and barristers; the former prepare cases and work directly with clients, while the latter present and argue cases in court. A similar division of labor exists in France, but not in the United States. Those who prosecute in the name of the state are paid officials of the government and therefore have a special responsibility to the courts, but defense attorneys are also obliged to accept judicial verdicts in good faith and not to obstruct justice.

Other non-judicial officials of the courts include those persons in ministries of justice in Roman law countries who are involved in the training of justices and in the supervision of the court systems. In the Soviet Union this category would also include the procurator-general who, among other things, may recommend to the Supreme Court of the USSR that it overrule verdicts of lower courts. In a sense he is the supreme overlord of the whole Soviet judicial structure, watching over the interpretation and application of law (especially criminal, but also civil) at all levels. He works through procurators at all levels of the Soviet judicial hierarchy; they are primarily his appointees and are not responsible to local organs of government. The procurator-general is a trusted, high-ranking member of the Communist Party. One occupant of this office once described the procurator as the "watchman of socialist legality, the leader of the policy of the Communist Party and of Soviet authority, the champion of socialism."

Those who carry out the decisions of the courts may be regarded as non-judicial court officials. This category includes such law enforcement officers as marshals and sheriffs, as well as all those persons in positions of executive authority who during the course of their normal duties carry out court rulings. State governors in the United States, for example, are court officers in the sense that they are the highest law enforcement officials in their respective states. The President of the United States, as the highest law enforcement official in the nation, is similarly an officer of the court. Receivers in bankruptcy cases are court officials insofar as they have been appointed and carry out their special tasks under court supervision.

Non-judicial Functions of Judges. Judges in the Anglo-American countries have inherited a number of non-judicial tasks from the administrative functions of the British justices of the peace, and still perform these today. This is particularly true in a number of American states, especially in rural areas and in the South, where the county judges administer poor relief, mental institutions, and children's homes. At the national level American judges may find themselves in effect running railroads that have gone into bankruptcy. In Great Britain, by contrast, most of these functions have now been brought into a form of civil service.

It should be mentioned also that, in the United States particularly, the courts may be a source of political patronage. The right of judges to appoint bailiffs, registers in probate, clerks, and so on may be quite important in determining the personnel of our state judicial systems. At the national level, too, there are patronage implications in the appointments of judges. More important, with a change in the national administration, changes take place in the United States attorneys and United States marshals assigned to federal district courts.

Types of Law

Within the legal orders of modern states, law is classified as public or private. *Public* law is subdivided into *constitutional* law and *administrative* law; *private* law includes *criminal* and *civil* law. Law that applies within a nation is known as *municipal* law, while that which cuts across national lines is known as *international* law. International law is also divided into public and private law.

PUBLIC LAW

Public law is that part of the law that deals with political conditions— that is, with the powers and duties of the state and its agents and with the relationship of these powers and duties to the citizens. Public law is therefore concerned with relations between branches and officials of government as well as with relations between individuals and the state.

Constitutional law. Constitutional law is the body of law that has been built up around the living constitution. It defines and delineates constitutional practices, whether these stem from the original document (the constitution) or from subsequent political usage. It is concerned with such complex questions as the distribution of governmental powers, both functional (legislative, executive, and judicial) and territorial (national and state), the nature of official duties and responsibilities entailed in the exercise of these powers, and the problem of defining and safeguarding the rights of citizens. Because a constitution often deals in generalities, it needs to be interpreted. The resulting interpretations, in the aggregate, are known as constitutional law.

But a constitution is never "finally" interpreted. While it is generally recognized that continuity is necessary, change is equally necessary, if the constitution is to remain a living document. In the words of one Justice of the United States Supreme Court, the Constitution "must be construed in the light of the present." Constitutional law is, therefore, not a constant, not something that can be determined once and for all and then passed on from generation to generation. It is rather something that continually seeks to reconcile the immediate concerns of popular will (the legislature) with the long-run concerns of a fundamental compact (the constitution) that embodies certain basic principles.

These remarks about constitutional law apply particularly to the United States, and in large measure to France and Germany as well. They also apply to Great Britain, but since Parliament can readily revise the British Constitution, judicial interpretation is less important in that country. In the Soviet Union, on the other hand, constitutional law is what the Communist Party decides it should be: since the Soviet judiciary is, like other Soviet governmental bodies, essentially an instrument of the Party, it has evolved a body of Soviet constitutional law that is to some degree consistent with Party objectives.

Administrative Law. Administrative law is the body of law built up around administrative actions and decisions. Since statutes are often written in general terms, executives in administrative agencies find it necessary, and are permitted, to engage in considerable rule-making that has the effect of law. This "administrative law-making" is especially important in regulatory agencies, which in recent years, because of the vast increase in social legislation, have been authorized to apply not-too-precise legislative standards in wider and wider areas.

For a long time Great Britain, and to some extent the United States, refused to recognize administrative law on the ground that it was only the legislature that had authority to make law. But administrative law having now received explicit recognition, it is the problem of appeals from administrative rule-making that has begun to demand increasing attention. This has been especially true in Great Britain, where some acts of Parliament have had the effect of making administrative adjudication final—which has seemed to suggest to some British citizens that a Briton is no longer necessarily entitled to his day in court. In the United States, mainly because of the separation of powers, administrative adjudication cannot be so easily protected from scrutiny by the judiciary. But even in the United States, administrative agencies make countless decisions (in cases of social security claims, for example) that are not subject to appeal in the courts.

By contrast with the British and American reluctance to recognize administrative law, the French have not only accorded it a distinct place, but in addition have set up a whole system of administrative courts, in which any and all administrative actions and decisions may be challenged. The only basis for challenge that is permitted, however, is the allegation that a decision or act is contrary to the law; the law itself cannot be challenged in the administrative courts. A similar system is to be found in Germany and other continental countries. The Soviet Union, however, does not have a separate administrative court system, nor can there be an effective challenge to administrative decisions unless these go contrary to established Communist Party policies (which is unlikely) or unless the Party itself chooses to make changes in its approach to the handling of certain problems.

PRIVATE LAW: CIVIL AND CRIMINAL

Private law concerns itself with relations among individuals as private persons. *Civil* law governs those actions that involve the rights of individuals, in instances where redress for personal wrong is sought by one party from another. The usual areas are property rights, contracts, inheritances, and marriage and divorce. More often than not, it is not the fact of guilt or innocence that is at issue so much as the degree or extent of personal liability for a certain act. It is in the handling of these cases in civil law that Soviet courts come closest to resembling courts in the West.

Criminal law governs actions involving the rights of persons that are considered to be threats not only to them but to the public order and welfare; it is for this reason that redress, or at least assistance, is provided to the victims by the state—which then goes on to exact its own penalties. The usual crimes are murder, rape, arson, and perjury, among others. In national states that have federal forms of government, such as the United States, there are both state and national criminal laws, which often provide parallel legal prohibitions against the commission of the same acts.

INTERNATIONAL LAW: PUBLIC AND PRIVATE

Public international law is concerned with the conduct of independent nations toward one another. It is the body of rules that these nations consider themselves bound to observe. The sources and sanctions of international law are different from those that characterize municipal law. The principal sources are agreements (treaties, international conventions) and custom (for instance, immunity from prosecution for diplomatic representatives). Where agreements or custom do not seem to cover an issue, resort is had to less important sources, such as general principles recognized by civilized nations, judicial decisions, and the writings of established authorities. Sometimes nations seek to change the rules, either in concert with others or unilaterally; for example, a number of nations (including the Soviet Union) are seeking to extend their sovereignty over coastal waters beyond the customary three miles from shore.

The sanctions of international law, even in the most favorable circumstances, are not so reliable as those at the disposal of governments within national states. For the most part, these sanctions boil down ultimately to good faith and national self-interest. In addition, a nation must consider the probability of retaliatory action if it fails to live up to its obligations. And in more recent years, the activity of international agencies has also come to serve as a sanction. It should be noted that a large part of international law is enforced before national courts. France and Germany provide in their constitutions that international law is part of the law of the land.

Because existing international law is, for the most part, the result of voluntary acceptance by nation-states, and so presumably in (or not against) their interests, it is reasonable to assume that they will abide by it. But a nation's concept of its own self-interest may change from time to time. Some nations take their international obligations so seriously that they are willing, in the name of them, to accept momentary inconvenience and temporary costs to themselves. Others may be inclined rather to ask: Do we have more to lose or more to gain by living up to this obligation?

Private international law (sometimes referred to as the "law of conflict of laws") is concerned with what law should be applied in dealings between citizens of countries that have different legal systems. Typical questions include the validity in one country of marriages or divorces contracted in another, the transfer of property, the validity of wills made in another country, and the enforcement of judgments in foreign courts. For the most part, each state determines what it will or will not permit on its territory and in its courts, but reciprocity is often the governing consideration. In some instances there are treaties or other agreements that seek to specify how a conflict-of-laws case is to be handled. In recent years, for example, the stationing of United States troops in Great Britain, France, and other allied countries has led to the conclusion of "status of forces" agreements which specify that United States citizens may be tried for certain offenses and under certain circumstances in the courts and under the laws of another nation.

The Political Functions of the Legal System

We are so used to thinking of the judicial system in narrowly legalistic terms that we tend to neglect its essentially political functions. For example, when the legal system of a democratically governed nation adjudicates in a manner satisfactory to the bulk of the nation's citizens, it performs the vital political function of guaranteeing the stability and continuity of the political order. A similar function is performed by courts in dictatorships, but since they are not independent, their authority is no greater than the power of the dictatorship itself to compel obedience. The legal system also performs an essentially political function when the courts engage in constitutional umpiring, especially in a federal system, with or without a separation of powers scheme. Many judicial decisions have the effect of law-making—again an essentially political function.

CONSTITUTIONAL UMPIRING:
THE PROBLEM OF JUDICIAL REVIEW

Written constitutions that seek in some specific way to distribute powers geographically (federalism), to allocate powers functionally (separation of powers), to impose limitations on the exercise of governmental powers, or to guarantee individual rights, inevitably induce controversy and conflict, the resolution of which is necessary if the system is to endure. The best example of this type of constitution is that of the United States. It is in the United States that we find the earliest development of the power of judicial review, that is, of the authority of the courts to resolve controversies arising from constitutional arrangements. While any United States court may assume this function, the ultimate arbiter is the United States Supreme Court. American state courts also exercise judicial review: The supreme court of each state is the final arbiter in controversies arising from that state's constitution, provided that a given case does not call into question a provision of the national constitution.

In the United States the most important form of judicial review consists in the courts' declaring an act of a legislature null and void because it contravenes some provision of the state or national constitution. But courts do not seek to pass on the constitutionality of legislation on their own initiative or at the request of some official (even the President) or agency of government. An actual case in which the issue of constitutionality has been raised must be brought to the courts in the regular judicial manner.

In Great Britain, where there are no formal limits on the powers of Parliament, there is no judicial review. Laws may be interpreted but they may not be declared null and void. And if a judicial interpretation is not to Parliament's liking, then it can remedy the situation at any time by passing a new law.

France, too, for most of its history, adhered to the concept of parliamentary supremacy. The Constitution of the Fifth Republic, however, has introduced judicial review in a limited sense. The Constitutional Council, which is outside the judicial branch, may pass on the validity of organic laws and on the standing orders of the two houses of the legislature, which are obliged to submit these to the council; it may also strike down any ordinary law referred to it by the president, the prime minister, and the presiding officers of the two houses of parliament. But private persons cannot challenge the constitutionality of laws as they can in the United States. Actually, there is general agreement that the Constitutional Council was created mainly to protect the executive from the legislature, whose powers in the present regime are considerably curtailed by comparison with what they were under the Third or the Fourth Republic.

Germany, too, has established a special court, the Federal Constitutional Court, which is given explicit powers of judicial review. But, unlike the French Constitutional Council, the German court is not limited either in its jurisdiction or in its competence to hear cases that ordinary citizens bring before it. It does have the power to pass on the constitutionality of any national or state statute; it is authorized, moreover, to pass on disputes between national and state governments, as well as on conflicts between organs of government at the national level. And, of course, it has the power to decide cases that allege an infringement of personal rights guaranteed by the constitution. This new institution has worked so well that individual German states have set up their own constitutional courts to pass on state matters.

In contrast with practice in the United States, however, questions may reach Germany's Constitutional Court by request of the national or state governments or of one-third of the members of the Bundestag; the Court can therefore render opinions without waiting for litigants in specific law suits to raise constitutional questions. Moreover, the Court assumes more initiative in determining facts on its own, and rules on many matters that United States courts would avoid as "political" questions.

In the Soviet Union the Presidium of the Supreme Soviet is in theory charged with the "interpretation of the laws." But the fact that there is no judicial review in practice in the Soviet Union should surprise no one. Since the Soviet Constitution, unlike those of the West, is not conceived of as an instrument for limiting or restraining political power, there is no place in the judicial structure for any institution performing that function. Generally speaking, a dictatorship is not a likely place in which to find judicial review in the sense that that term is commonly understood.

JUDICIAL LAW-MAKING AND POLICY-MAKING

In exercising discretionary powers to determine the precise meaning of the law, judges become in effect creators of law through the precedents they establish. This is true above all in the common law countries, where so much law is based on previous decisions, and is particularly relevant in the United States, where national and state courts seek to define the meaning of clauses in the national and state constitutions (for example, "due process of law") that have not received final definition, and to resolve questions that involve conflicting interpretations of these constitutions.

A series of decisions made in the United States during the past few years may serve as illustrations of judicial law-making and policy-making in two broad areas. One has to do with racial segregation, the other with legislative reapportionment. In the former the courts, by taking what they considered to be a realistic view of the "equal protection of the laws" provision in the United States Constitution, have ruled that laws providing for segregation and other forms of discrimination based on race are unconstitutional and cannot be enforced. The most notable decisions in this respect have been in the field of education, but subsequent decisions have extended the principle to other publicly financed or publicly supported facilities. Recent indications point toward the extension of this principle to private facilities operating under public license.

Judicial decisions of equal importance were made in the reapportionment cases. For many years, the United States courts had not considered it within their competence to decide cases involving state constitutional requirements for periodic reapportionment of state legislatures, and had refused to accept suits brought by aggrieved parties. In a 1962 decision (*Baker* v. *Carr*), however, the Supreme Court decided otherwise, ruling that the courts did have jurisdiction, which the Court itself proceeded to exercise in a number of landmark cases. This change of attitude on the part of the Supreme Court constitutes political policy-making of considerable magnitude.

A similar instance of judicial policy-making occurred in 1961 in Germany, where the Federal Constitutional Court declared unconstitutional Chancellor Adenauer's action in setting up a second television network which was to be nationally controlled but financed largely by commercial advertising. The same court was also engaged in policy-making when it outlawed the Communist Party and a neo-Nazi political party.

Some people regard such actions of the judiciary as a usurpation of legislative functions by the courts. But how does one get around the argument that the *interpretation* of constitutional provisions must be performed by someone? Neither constitutions nor laws can be designed so as to envision all possible eventualities; they must of necessity be written in general terms. True, citizens can always change judicial interpretations by amending the constitution or sometimes by legislation alone. But as a practical matter, because constitutions are often difficult to amend, judicial interpretations usually remain the final word on what the law is on the subject at issue.

COURTS AND LAW
IN CONSTITUTIONAL AND DICTATORIAL SYSTEMS

In democratic countries the judicial system is closely identified with the rule of law and the preservation of individual freedom. The purpose of law is to achieve the rendering of justice. Individual rights are protected under the law, to which all are subject, and no one is punished except for violating the law. Moreover, there is a basic belief that the maintenance of individual freedom is worth the hazard of providing punishment or compensation *after* an abuse has been committed; hence, preventive action is held to a minimum.

If individual rights are to be protected and government restrained from infringing upon them, an independent judiciary is indispensable. It is to the credit of democracy that judges in democratic states have been able, with rare exceptions, to maintain the integrity of a system of justice. One overriding reason is that a judge in a democratic country would lose the esteem of his professional brethren if he abandoned his impartiality. Of equal importance, perhaps, is the fact that political leaders who tolerate opposition also respect the independence of the judiciary.

Dictatorial regimes, however, must be able to control the courts just as they control the legislature. The primary function of the judiciary, therefore, is not to preserve freedom under law; it is rather to secure the interests of society as these are conceived by the regime. Instead of being concerned with protecting the rights of individuals, the courts act as instruments for promoting what is, politically and ideologically, the basic philosophy of the rulers. To this end, there is considerable concern by the courts with the motives and general attitudes of citizens.

Since the primary emphasis is on the rights of the state, it is not surprising that, in regard to individuals, dictatorships place considerable emphasis on *duties*. A Soviet law passed in 1938, for example, states that the general purpose of Soviet courts is "to educate the citizens of the USSR in a spirit of devotion to the fatherland and to the cause of Socialism, in the spirit of an exact and unfaltering performance of Soviet laws, careful attitude towards Socialist property, labor discipline, honest fulfillment of state and public duties, respect towards the rules of the Socialist Commonwealth." Those who ignore or work against these duties are considered to be enemies of the state, and if their transgressions are serious enough to be labeled "political offenses," trial before special courts awaits them.

As an arm of the administrative apparatus, the judicial system in a dictatorship seeks to preserve the regime and to facilitate the implementation of its programs; conversely it seeks to strike down all those who might stand in the way. To this end, the political party, particularly in a Communist system, coordinates closely the actions of the courts. The legal profession, too, ceases to be an independently organized group and comes under government control. Special care is exercised in the selection of judges, to say nothing of the fact that their decisions and other actions are closely watched—all of which is in conformity with the Communist philosophy that law as a whole is an instrument of the dominant class.

In a dictatorship as in a democratic system, however, disputes between individuals must be settled, and the laws that pertain to these disputes must be interpreted and applied. In this respect every dictatorship provides its own system of order among private claimants, performing functions essentially similar to those exercised by the courts in democratic countries when they adjudicate private controversies.

COURTS, LAW, AND POLITICAL AND SOCIAL CHANGE

In the political process it is impossible to separate various branches or activities of government from one another and to place them in watertight compartments; they are all related as part of the general political pattern. The law and the courts play a significant political role, for example, by providing continuity and stability and thereby making it possible for political and social change to proceed in a peaceful and orderly manner. To the extent that law and the courts facilitate the resolution of conflicts between groups or sovereignties (for example, national and state), political processes are able to operate without violent eruptions or revolutions.

The courts (and the law) may, however, hasten or delay social change. Because courts tend to be conservative—that is, to preserve the order of things as they are—they often delay change or at least slow it down; a good example was the long reluctance of United States courts to permit the Congress to legislate in social and economic fields. On the other hand, the courts may sometimes trigger social change, as the Supreme Court did in 1954 when it ruled against racial segregation in the public schools.

Sometimes jurists have been the expounders of political doctrines or ideas that have had a great impact on political developments generally. In raising the question of what standard should be used to judge the validity of human laws, jurists were raising an essentially political question. In the Middle Ages they answered their own question by saying that the yardstick was natural law, which at that time they identified with divine will. Subsequently jurists expounded a secular theory of natural law, arguing that man was capable of arriving at the body of natural laws by the use of his reason. Out of this grew the doctrine of natural rights, on which many of our present-day concepts of political rights and duties are based. Thus jurists propounded an idea that first gained political acceptance and was subsequently given legal form and substance.

In the developing nations, political and social changes have been influenced and shaped by the legal systems which these nations inherited. In India, for example, young intellectuals got their ideas of freedom and independence from their study of British law and judicial practice. The Indian civil service, whose crucial role in India's political development cannot be denied, has been manned by people who were first trained in British law and British administrative and judicial procedures. Similarly, the destinies of the developing nations in what was once French Africa have been shaped by men who studied the rights of man and of the citizen under French law, and who learned the elements of French political and administrative organization.

Changes in legal systems are usually related to the overall pattern of political development, and the law and the courts must be seen in this perspective if their role and position are to be properly appreciated and understood. The political process is a process of interaction. When, for example, the early tribal chief settled disputes, he both changed and made laws at the same time. Similarly, when great lawgivers, such as Hammurabi and Moses, proclaimed codes that endured, political systems developed within the confines of these legal boundaries. This is not to suggest that there is a primacy of either the political or the judicial, but merely to show that they are interdependent.

Judicial Procedures and Practices

THE FORMULATION AND PRESENTATION OF CASES

Judicial action is a process of decision-making in specific cases. Such decision-making takes place only when an individual comes into conflict with society by violating its norms or when individuals come into conflict with one another. These conflicts, moreover, must be genuine: courts have refused to hear cases in which there was collusion among the parties to allege that they were in conflict when in fact they were not.

Premises and Bases of Judicial Action. Judicial action, it should be stressed, deals only with specific cases. Although their decisions may affect "others similarly situated," judges rule only on the conflicts between the parties immediately before them in court. Unlike executives and legislators, who legitimately concern themselves with the broadest general principles, judges are expected to decide cases on the narrowest possible grounds.

　　Judicial action is passive rather than active: judges can act only on cases that have been brought before them on the initiative of others. Those who believe that the function of judges is to look out upon the world in order to see where justice needs to be done—that they take the initiative in redressing wrongs—are suffering from a misconception of the judge's role.

　　Where judicial review does exist, as in the United States and in the German Federal Republic, the courts do not examine each legislative act as it emerges from the legislature in order to determine its constitutionality. Questions about the constitutionality of a legislative act can be raised only on the initiative of parties other than the judges. In the United States, such questions can be raised only by litigants in specific cases—a rule which, when coupled with the requirement that the litigant's interest in the matter must be direct and substantial, makes it practically impossible for there ever to be a court decision on some questions.

Moreover, neither the British courts nor the American national courts issue advisory opinions, although the supreme courts of several American states are obliged to give advisory opinions when requested to do so by the governor or the legislature. And since the passage of the Federal Declaratory Judgment Act of 1934, United States courts may issue legal rulings in cases of actual controversy without the parties involved having to go to court to take action on their differing legal interpretations; but once the law has been declared in the matter, it is assumed that these parties will abide by it.

Other important conditions of judicial action have to do with the distinction between criminal and civil cases. Criminal cases, since they are conceived of as a conflict between society and an individual, are initiated by the state. The accusation is made by an official of the state in the name of the people or, in the United Kingdom, in the name of the monarch. In both England and America, grand juries used to be used in most criminal cases in order to determine whether there was sufficient evidence against a person to bring him to trial. If the grand jury brought in a "true bill," the accused was said to be "indicted" and thus brought to trial. Today the grand jury is less often employed in England and the American states, but continues to be used extensively in the federal courts in the United States. The common substitute for the grand jury today is a "presentment" by a prosecutor, whereupon a judge may determine at a preliminary hearing whether the accused should be "bound over for" (required to stand) trial. In any event, whether or not there is a grand jury, the accused in the Anglo-American countries always enjoys the right of habeas corpus, which guarantees that a person accused of committing a criminal act has a right to be brought before a judge to determine whether he is being lawfully detained in jail.

Roman law countries deal somewhat differently with criminal cases, although they start from the same basic principle that the action against the accused is brought by the state. If there is any difference, it is that in Roman law countries, the state is an even more active party in the prosecution of accused persons. Typical of the continent is the procedure used in France by the *juge d'instruction*, who conducts an investigation into all the facts about the crime and the accused before committing the latter to trial. This official plays a very active role in a prosecution, going into much greater detail than an Anglo-American magistrate conducting a preliminary hearing. The objection generally raised against this system is that Roman law countries do not provide for a writ of habeas corpus, so that persons accused of a crime may be held for a long time while pretrial investigations are being carried on. It is not true, as is sometimes alleged, that the Roman law system is based on the principle that a person is guilty unless proved innocent. But the investigation by an official like the *juge d'instruction* is so thorough that there tends to be a presumption of guilt in any case that this official decides should go to trial.

There are no differences in principle between the Anglo-American and Roman law countries with regard to civil procedure. A private person, called a plaintiff, brings an action against another person, called a defendant, for an alleged wrong. Since the state is not regarded as a party in a conflict involving private persons, its role is limited to adjudicating the disputes through its courts.

The democracies generally make a clear distinction between civil and criminal proceedings. The separation is most clear-cut in England, where there are two separate court systems. While the United States, France, and Germany distinguish clearly between civil and criminal proceedings, they do not make clear separations between the judicial organs that hear each type of case.

In the Soviet Union, distinctions between civil and criminal proceedings are often blurred. Although as we have seen there are some cases in which Soviet courts deal with purely private conflicts between individuals, state interests are seldom separated altogether from private interests. Thus in such civil matters as paternity or probate cases, the courts may assert that a state interest has priority over the interests of the private litigants. Similarly, if both a civil and a criminal case arise out of one set of facts, the courts adjudicate all aspects of the matter at one trial. A typical case of this nature would be that of a drunken driver who has injured another person in an accident. In most countries, probably, this set of facts would result in a criminal trial to prosecute the driver for violation of the law and a separate civil trial brought against him for recovery of compensation for private injuries. The Soviet Union, however, does not recognize a realm of "private rights" even in such an apolitical situation as this.

COURTROOM PRACTICES

The purpose of courts everywhere is to adjudicate conflicts by determining the facts and applying the relevant laws. Such an activity can be conducted only under rules that ensure equal rights to all persons to be heard, to present evidence, to subpoena witnesses, and to have legal counsel. These requirements, plus the necessity of protecting the dignity of the court, make a courtroom the scene of rather formal procedures. Some observers object to the complexities that are the result of this formality, but experience of the contrasting informality of certain American and British justices of the peace or of the comradely courts in the Soviet Union would probably convince them that formality does serve the purpose of ensuring an impartial hearing.

Inquisitorial and Adversary Methods. The inquisitorial system is used in courts in the Soviet Union, Germany, and France, where a judicial proceeding is a formal effort by the judges to determine the facts. The judges play an active role in questioning litigants and witnesses, and assume the initiative in bringing into the evidence matters not presented by the parties in the action. They actively direct the proceedings.

In the adversary method used in the Anglo-American countries, the judges have a more passive role—that of serving as impartial umpires of the proceedings. It is the attorneys for the litigants who assume the initiative in questioning witnesses and presenting evidence. The court considers only the evidence placed before it by the private parties. Only when the judge suspects perjury or some action that threatens the dignity of the court does he move on his own.

The Roles of Judges and Lawyers. The activity of judges and attorneys in the countries we are studying can be placed on a continuum. The least active judges are those in the United States. British judges assume a somewhat more active role in judicial proceedings; they sometimes go as far as to make running commentaries on evidence, a practice that would not be permitted in American courtrooms. Judges in the Roman law countries on the Continent are considerably more active than their British counterparts, and the most active judges of all are those in the Soviet Union.

The activity of attorneys lies along a precisely opposite continuum. The attorneys who play the most active role in courtroom procedures are those in the United States. British attorneys are somewhat less important. Attorneys in Roman law countries on the Continent play an even less significant role in trials; they merely sit with their clients to provide legal advice. The attorneys least active in courtroom procedures are those in the Soviet Union. While attorneys do function there, they are under many restrictions and can easily be disbarred for taking any action contrary to what is regarded as the best interest of the state.

Except for special cases such as those involving children and sometimes matters of state security, courts are open to the public nearly everywhere in the world. In all the countries we are studying, witnesses are heard in courtrooms and are required to give some form of affirmation that their testimony will be the truth. In the United States and Britain witnesses can usually listen to what other persons say, and some stress is placed on the right of the accused to hear what the witnesses say. On the Continent, however, witnesses are usually prohibited from hearing other witnesses; they are kept in special rooms and each is admitted to the courtroom only when he is to give testimony.

There are very important differences in the rules of evidence in the different judicial systems, Anglo-American practice having the strictest rules of evidence. Roman law countries, by contrast, allow wide latitude in the admission of testimony, some of which would scarcely be regarded as evidence in the Anglo-American systems. Roman law countries allow witnesses to present as evidence matters of mere hearsay—even neighborhood gossip may be admitted in testimony. Presumably the judges will give such testimony the credence it deserves.

European judges frequently treat litigants and witnesses, particularly those from the lower classes, in a manner that would surprise Britons and Americans. In their efforts to elicit the truth, they may browbeat such witnesses, accuse them of lying, and in many cases actually frighten them. While such practices may shock some Americans, those who have observed the treatment municipal judges in American courts deal out to habitual criminals or drunkards realize that American judges may also sometimes fail to maintain the decorum usually expected of a courtroom.

Another important distinction between Anglo-American and continental courtroom procedures is the number of judges presiding. In the main, in Anglo-American countries only one judge presides at a trial, though in some British courts bodies of justices of the peace hear certain minor criminal cases. On the Continent most trials are conducted by at least three judges, who in some cases may be joined by other officials, called lay assessors.

In all judicial systems a clear distinction is made between trials and appeals. It is only at the trial itself that the parties to the case appear and witnesses are heard; it is the trial that provides the basis for good movie drama. Appeals, on the other hand, are generally dull, formal hearings at which the judges consider only briefs submitted by the attorneys and read the evidence provided in the trial record. In general, appeals do not involve hearing the case *de novo* (from the beginning), although some European countries do allow for this procedure at times. In Britain and America, however, the rule is fairly firm that an appeals court will consider only the evidence and arguments brought out at the trial itself; there is thus only one trial. On the Continent, where appeals courts may consider evidence not presented at the original trial, experts may be called upon to testify. The ultimate in this practice is a procedure of the German Constitutional Court which allows for calling expert witnesses to give testimony involving the constitutionality of laws.

Juries. By juries we mean here trial juries, or petit juries, as distinguished from the grand juries discussed previously. Everywhere in the world today, the use of such juries is declining. They are most extensively employed in the United States, where they are still widely used in both federal and state courts and in both civil and criminal proceedings. Parties to a case may by agreement waive a jury, but in both civil and criminal cases the parties have a right to a jury trial. In Britain the use of juries has declined even more, so that today juries are not used at all in civil cases, but only in major criminal cases tried in the assize courts.

France formerly used juries extensively, but judicial reforms in

1932 and 1941 began combining the decision-making functions of the jurors with that of the judges. In 1959, trial courts, known as assize courts in criminal cases, provided for nine jurors and three judges, a total of twelve. Since a verdict of guilty requires eight votes, at least five jurors must concur with three judges to obtain a guilty verdict. (By contrast with Anglo-American practice, a unanimous decision of the jurors is not necessary.)

The Soviet Union makes extensive use of "lay assessors," who are in some ways similar to jurors but perform a somewhat different role. Lay assessors sit with the judges in the hearing of evidence and then meet with them in making decisions. There is much evidence that it is the judges who determine the decisions, since untrained laymen are unlikely to persist in their opinions as against trained jurists. Germany also uses lay assessors in important criminal trials.

Judicial Decisions and Opinions. In all countries the decisions of the regular courts are matters of public record. A written statement is filed, even if it is no more than "judgment affirmed" or "petition denied." Often, however, longer and more detailed explanations of their decisions are written by the judges and filed with court officials.

There are important differences with regard to the issuing of decisions between the Anglo-American and continental European countries. In Anglo-American courts with more than one judge, each judge may sign his own individual opinion, writing either a concurring opinion if he agrees with the majority of the court or a dissenting opinion if he does not. In the continental European countries, by contrast, there is no formal recognition of the fact that there may have been differences in the judges' opinions, for such recognition would be contrary to the doctrine that the decision in every case is correct and objective. Thus, although we can be sure that judges in plural bodies do not always agree, their differences are not made public; only one opinion is issued by the court, and dissenting judges are not permitted to indicate their disagreement. In the last few years, American political scientists have been doing a number of behavioral studies on the opinions of individual justices; unfortunately, the Roman law system does not permit European political scientists to conduct comparable studies. As a result, we know less about the actual judicial behavior of Roman law judges than we are coming to know about American judges.

Finality of Decisions. There is an important difference between the ways in which lawyers and political scientists view judicial decisions. Lawyers tend to regard them as final, in that they are controlling with regard to the specific situations with which lawyers are concerned. Political scientists, however, look upon judicial decisions as part of the decision-making process; one political scientist has even referred to them as "merely incidents in the production of statutes."[1] What he meant was that an unpopular judicial decision does no more than provide the impetus for a legislative body to change the law; thus each time the United States Supreme Court issues an unpopular opinion, there is a rush in Congress to introduce bills that would nullify it. This occurred recently after the decision of the Supreme Court to prohibit prayers in the public schools, and also after its decision to prohibit states from exercising jurisdiction over Communist groups. Sometimes Congress actually changes the existing law in order to effect a change in a Supreme Court decision; legislation concerning offshore oil is one example of such congressional action.

Another question about the finality of judicial decisions has to do with their effectiveness. For example, even though the Supreme Court decided in 1954 that segregation in the public schools was a denial of equal protection of the laws, as late as 1963 the Governors of Mississippi and Alabama were both able to affirm publicly their opposition to this decision and their intention of blocking its implementation in their states. More than a decade since the Supreme Court's ruling, it is still clear that this decision has yet to be fully implemented. Similarly, the present status of a decision made at the end of World War II about compulsory flag salutes in the schools indicates that the mere fact that a court has issued an opinion does not of itself guarantee that the bodies responsible for its implementation will comply with it.

It is a long way, both geographically and legally, from the marble chamber of the Supreme Court in Washington to rural America, and much can happen in the transmission of legal decisions from one to the other. Although it is difficult to find such flagrant examples of non-implementation in other countries, it is clear everywhere that judicial decisions, especially those that are unpopular, may not be conclusive in social affairs.

JUDICIAL PERSONNEL

Career Lines and Selection. Except for the justices of the peace still used widely in England and in some places in America, judges are trained lawyers. Knowledge of their career lines thus requires some knowledge of what goes into the training of lawyers.

In the United States, prospective lawyers generally attend law school upon the completion of their undergraduate studies. But law school training is not a specialized advanced academic education; it is technical training for the specific occupation of lawyer and enables the person who has completed the course to be admitted to the practice of law, with or without examination, depending upon the state. Judges

---

[1] Bertram M. Gross, *The Legislative Struggle* (New York: McGraw-Hill, Inc., 1953), p. 105.

are in turn selected from among those who are attorneys-at-law.

In the United Kingdom there are, as we have seen, two types of attorneys. Solicitors are general practitioners or "office lawyers," while barristers practice before the courts; the relationship between the two is somewhat comparable to that between medical general practitioners and such specialists as surgeons. After the completion of their regular academic education, barristers obtain their legal training from one of four "Inns of Court," which provide legal education and also continue to exercise jurisdiction over their members throughout their professional careers; there are thus, in effect, four law-training institutions and four corresponding bar associations. English judges are chosen from the most successful among this elite group of British attorneys.

On the Continent legal education is an academic discipline of the universities. After completing preparatory school, students begin in the law faculty of a university and usually achieve a Doctor of Jurisprudence degree. Preparation for this degree does not, however, include adequate training in the actual practice of law; to become a practicing lawyer one must therefore serve an apprenticeship in the courts and a further apprenticeship in a law office. More important, graduates of law faculties at universities are expected to choose between the private practice of law and service in the courts. Those who wish to be judges do not first practice law and only later become judges, as their counterparts do in the United States and England; rather, upon the completion of their legal education, they enter service under the jurisdiction of the ministry of justice and begin an apprenticeship in the courts which eventually leads to their obtaining a position of tenure as a member of their country's judicial service.

By Anglo-American standards it may seem incongruous to send out a recent graduate of the university as a judge to hear cases when he would not even qualify to serve as an attorney. It should be remembered, however, that the system of code law arms the young judge with a set of books that presumably provides for all contingencies. Further, the cases that a young judge would hear alone would be minor civil cases; if he took part in a more important case, he would serve on a panel of at least three judges, one of whom would be a senior presiding judge. In the main, the case law system used in the Anglo-American countries gives the judge far greater discretion than the Roman law system, and requires a more mature judge with much more experience.

Throughout most of the world judges are appointed to their positions and enjoy tenure. Although it is frequently alleged that the election of judges is one significant aspect of democracy, the only democracies that actually do elect judges are Switzerland and most American states. The Soviet Union, to be sure, also has elected judges; Soviet elections being what they are, however, we would hesitate to describe these as comparable to democratic elections.

Judges in U.S. district courts, appeals courts, the Supreme Court, and special courts are appointed for life by the President, subject to approval by the Senate. In the United Kingdom, judges are appointed in the name of the monarch upon the recommendation of the Lord Chancellor, the highest British judicial and legal officer. Judges on the Continent are under the jurisdiction of their respective ministries of justice, and are assigned to positions and promoted according to merit.

Among the countries we are studying, arguments over the relative merits of elected or appointed judges are important only in America. As we have seen, American federal judges are appointed for life, while forty-one of the states have elected judges. Nine American states have modified the purely elective judiciary. The most common modified system is the so-called Missouri Plan, under which judges are originally appointed, and then, after they have served for a period, voters are asked only "Shall Judge X be retained?" If the vote is affirmative, the judge remains; if it is not, the judge is then removed and another appointment made. It is asserted that the Missouri Plan combines the advantages of both election and appointment; its relative popularity is indicated by the fact that a variation of the plan was recently adopted in the new constitution of Alaska.

What little evidence we have indicates that judges who are appointed or who serve for long terms show greater independence and a more non-partisan attitude than those who are elected for short terms. But a more thorough analysis of the career patterns of elected American judges has led some observers to assert that the differences between elected and appointed judges are not so marked. It is common practice for judges to be continually re-elected; it is highly unusual, in fact, for an incumbent judge to be defeated. Moreover, it has become increasingly common for elected judges to retire at a stipulated age, thereby creating a vacancy that can be filled by appointment; for example, in Wisconsin, where judges are elected, 62 per cent of the justices of the supreme court and 40 per cent of the circuit judges were originally appointed by the governor. Some observers therefore argue that the issue in American states is not really that of election versus appointment but that of who is to do the appointing.

There are, however, some important questions about whether judicial elections in fact represent democratic practice. In a recent survey made in New York City it was found that 80 per cent of a group of respondents had voted for a judge in an election, but only 25 per cent of the group had paid any attention to who the opposing candidates were, and following the election, only 4 per cent could remember who it was they had voted for. This may be one reason why incumbent judges are almost always elected. Similarly, only 25 per cent of the electorate even bothered to vote in a 1963 judicial election in Milwaukee. Thus it appears that the electorate itself is not particularly concerned about its right to vote for judges.

POLITICAL NEUTRALITY

Except in the Soviet Union, where judges are clearly recognized as servants of the goals of the proletarian state, judges are presumably politically neutral. The judges in continental Europe are strongest in their pretensions to complete objectivity and in their efforts to avoid what they call "subjective opinions." Even in private conversations, Roman law judges worry about how they can dissociate themselves from their own subjective views in order to assume the objective position of an impartial arbitrator.

Although this conscious effort to be impartial may result in better decision-making than might otherwise be the case, it is not without its own problems. For example, some observers believe that the reason some judges in Nazi Germany were willing to hand down rulings of doubtful validity was that they had dissociated themselves so successfully from their own views of right and wrong that they could simply apply the law as dictated by Hitler and the Nazi party. This extreme of legal positivism, coupled with the judges' view that they were there only to serve the interests of the state, led to consequences far more reprehensible than their stated ideals of "objectivity" might suggest. Many American observers would doubt that these judges can in fact be as impartial as they claim to be. Most obvious are the problems derived from the European class system: since judges are chosen from the very highest groups in a class society, they cannot help reflecting the opinions of their class, whether or not they recognize them as such.

In the United Kingdom and the United States there is now a fairly explicit recognition of the subjective elements in judicial behavior. Nevertheless, in both countries the goal remains judicial independence and impartiality, and to the extent that human beings are able to strive for such impartiality, British and American judges attempt to do so.

There is now, however, considerable evidence that judges are not simply mechanisms for registering what the law is and that the experiences and ideas of persons holding judicial office will be reflected in their opinions. We now have evidence, for instance, that there are differences in the decisions reached by Republican and Democratic judges. Democratic judges are more likely to hand down decisions in favor of employees and against employers, in favor of the government and against business, and in favor of defendants and against prosecutors.[2]

The most dramatic example in American experience of the significance of the nature of court personnel was President Franklin Roosevelt's difficulties with the Supreme Court, which finally resulted in

[2] Stuart Nagel, "Political Party Affiliation and Judges' Decisions," *American Political Science Review*, LV (1961), 843–50.

his ill-fated proposal to enlarge the Court. Until 1937, the Court had been voting in case after case against legislation proposed by Roosevelt and enacted by the New Deal Congress. After two judges had changed their positions and a majority was achieved on behalf of New Deal legislation, the conservative judges began to resign; Roosevelt was thereafter able to appoint judges more favorable toward his program.

One cannot, however, always predict how judges will vote on particular cases, and some judges have actually surprised the Presidents who appointed them. Thus Justice Holmes seems to have surprised President Theodore Roosevelt, who appointed him, in his first decisions on anti-trust matters. Justice Frankfurter, originally appointed by President Franklin Roosevelt as a liberal, ended his term on the Court as a conservative. And President Kennedy's appointment of Justice White was followed by surprises in two of the first decisions in which the new Justice participated. Thus, although politics influences judges' opinions, they do make an effort to be more neutral politically than the other participants in the political process.

SOCIO-ECONOMIC CHARACTERISTICS OF JUDGES

Throughout the world, judges have a high socio-economic status; the mere holding of judicial office puts one almost everywhere in the top socio-economic ranks of society. A possible exception is France, where there are proportionately more judges than elsewhere, and where judges have been less well paid than they are in other countries. Also, judges in France may have a somewhat lower status than their counterparts elsewhere because they do not always serve as judges but may be transferred through the various offices of the magistrature; thus a person may serve at one time as a judge, later as a prosecutor, then in the justice ministry, and then once again as a judge. Under the Fifth Republic, however, efforts have been made to increase the pay and raise the status of French judges. In America judges are relatively well paid. Some of the most successful trial attorneys may make more money than judges, but everywhere an effort is made to pay judges enough to ensure their ability to resist pressures or enticements to leave the bench.

Perhaps more significant than the occupational status of the judgeship are the social origins of judges. Here again a generalization holds true for all the countries we are studying. Judges usually come from high socio-economic origins; analysis of the occupations of fathers of judges—the clearest test of social origins—have everywhere revealed that judges are in no way typical of their societies. In Europe, with its comparatively rigid class system, the distinction is probably more significant than it is in America. In Britain, for example, where the percentage of young people who go on to higher education is lower than the percentage of Negroes who go on to college in America, the very possession of formal education itself indicates that one has one's origin in a select social group. And when one recalls that barristers are the elite among attorneys and that those selected as judges are chosen from among the most successful barristers, one realizes that one is speaking of a group that constitutes less than 1 per cent of the population.

On the Continent, similarly, the mere possession of a judicial education is already indicative of a high social status. The small group, possibly 10 per cent, who go to a university preparatory school are an elite to begin with; those who go on to the university, obtain their law degrees, and are selected for the judiciary are an even more select elite, for such training is possible only for those from families which can afford to allow their children to study instead of going to work. While tuition is low, only a comparatively small percentage of persons on the European continent are able to avail themselves of the educational opportunities offered by the university. Thus judges enjoy a very high social status in the class systems of Europe.

It is no less true that American judges come from groups of high social status. In a study of the ninety Justices of the United States Supreme Court from 1789 to 1957, John R. Schmidhauser reported that the typical judge was white, Protestant, of high social status, and generally from stock originating in the British Isles,[3] and other studies have given a similar picture of state supreme court justices. Thus even in a country with a less rigid class system, judges are likely to come from the highest socio-economic status group.

Judicial Behavior

LEGAL DOCTRINE AND THE JUDICIAL ROLE

At one time—in fact, less than a generation ago—no less an authority than a United States Supreme Court Justice was still able to express the view that, in deciding a case at law, a judge performs the essentially mechanical function of "finding" the law,[4] that is, of determining the legal precept pertinent to the facts of the case and interpreting and applying the precept to the case at hand.[5] This is still a widely held view. We have observed that many legal systems are actually based upon *codes*, simplified digests or compilations of general legal rules supposedly applicable, with a minimum of judicial discretion, to every particular dispute that might be brought to litigation. Indeed, the

---

3 John R. Schmidhauser, "The Justices of the Supreme Court: A Collective Portrait," *Mid-West Journal of Political Science*, III (1959), 1–57.
4 Mr. Justice Roberts, in *U.S. v. Butler*, 297 U.S. 1 (1936).
5 Roscoe Pound, *An Introduction to the Philosophy of Law* (New Haven, Conn.: Yale University Press, 1922), chaps. 2–3. (Paperback edition, 1959.)

very concept of law itself began as the idea that there are fixed and immutable principles, either deriving from divine command or implicit in nature and reason. Such a conception of judicial functions, however, appears too simple and mechanical today, when we see courts producing decisions by bare majorities, along with several dissenting opinions; overruling precedents of many years' standing; passing upon questions they formerly refused to consider because of their "political" character; and implicitly assuming a position of leadership by adapting formal statements of legal principle to changed ideals and circumstances (while the legislature delays or is blocked from doing so). But equally oversimplified would be the other extreme —the idea that the law is nothing but the reflection of judges' personalities, the product of their psycho-physical condition, their life experiences, their economic philosophies, political preferences and obligations, or their personal views about the prevailing canons of justice and morality.

Speculative theories concerning the nature, ends, and functions of law undoubtedly have a powerful effect on the behavior of judges, but they are not very reliable guides to how judges do in fact reach decisions, nor do they provide precise criteria according to which judges ought to make up their minds. And as Jeremy Bentham and other legal thinkers long ago pointed out, in actual life such theories somehow turn into fictions and rationalizations which, even though they may often be both beneficial and useful to society, are nonetheless quite imperfect explanations of the actual behavior and functions of the society's judges.

But if legal doctrines are unsatisfactory explanations of the process of judicial decision, what is to take their place? Modern political and juristic theory suggests that the first step must be a readjustment of perspective. Instead of looking into the nature and function of law in order to see how judges decide, we should inquire into the nature of the judicial function and role. When we analyze what courts and judges actually do, we find that in all legal systems judges "make" law as well as interpret and enforce it; that "the law" must and does change with changes in society, technology, and economic institutions, and that judicial decisions, whether or not they change legal rules, nevertheless create political controversies that have to be faced by the other specifically political branches of government. Finally, the courts, in attempting to give effect to legal principles, rarely try to implement universal and absolute moral ends; more often, they seek ends relative to the time and the place—to be sure, not those of the "fleeting moment," but those of the era, the epoch, or the civilization.

In this perspective, the legal system becomes a distinctive institution. Its special role is to bring about the conscious, deliberate extension and adaptation of the traditional element in the law in order to permit the greatest possible accommodation of the expressed wants and needs of men and groups with the least sacrifice of the conflicting wants of others. On the basis of the facts in specific cases and controversies, courts and judges determine and balance competing interests and claims, and weigh the relevant social values and goods at stake. There are no precise formulas into which the judge, as if he were operating a computer, can insert the appropriate values and come out with the right answer. Judges are subject to human desires and pressures, just as are legislative and administrative policy-makers, even though they work under different procedural standards and sometimes under different conditions of political accountability. While a legal system is a basic attribute of viable political association, it is at the same time an ongoing process of socio-political investigation, an instrument by which "the value of past experience is rendered available to the community for present scrutiny of new perplexities."[6] In short, the judicial role is not fulfilled by an institution that is responsible solely for one particular value, such as certainty or stability; it is rather one of the natural processes of self-government through which human beings seek authoritative statements about the rights and duties binding upon particular individuals in particular cases of controversy.

We must remember that the standpoint from which we are interested in the activities of courts and judges is that of the political analyst, not the professional lawyer. We are concerned with the analysis of political functions and relationships, not with the mastery of legal norms and rules or the technical problems involved in representing clients in legal proceedings. Our attention is focused on how policy issues are brought into the judicial arena; on the personal background, attitudes, and interpersonal relations that influence judges when they have to make their legal decisions; and on the significance and consequences for public policy that follow from judicial decisions. In other words, instead of concentrating upon the substantive meaning and procedural requirements of the law, political and social scientists seek generalized statements about how the judicial process operates, how it functions as part of the political system.[7]

LEGAL REASONING, PERSONAL CHOICE,
AND POLITICAL INFLUENCE

When professional attention was fixed primarily on private law and not on the judicial process as part of the whole political process, it used

---

[6] The phrase is John Dewey's. A compendium of recent jurisprudential writings may be found in Julius Stone, *The Province and Function of Law* (Cambridge, Mass.: Harvard University Press, 1950). A more summary, analytical treatment is W. Friedmann, *Legal Theory* (London: Stevens and Sons Ltd., 1949).

[7] On these points, see J. W. Peltason, *Federal Courts in the Political Process* (New York: Random House, 1955); G. A. Schubert, *Constitutional Politics* (New York: Holt, Rinehart & Winston, 1960); W. F. Murphy and C. H. Pritchett, *Courts, Judges and Politics* (New York: Random House, 1961).

to be said that "most" cases were open and shut as far as questions of law were concerned; that few real issues of policy were decided by judges; that, regardless of the field of action (breach of contract, personal injury, commercial instruments, and so on), the judge in any given case rarely had very much freedom in selecting and applying the relevant legal rule; and that the functions of judges were, therefore, largely "non-political." Even a seemingly "automatic" application of an unambiguous legal rule by the judge, however, serves the political function of satisfying the conflicting claims or interests represented in the lawsuit itself, if not of fixing more generally the boundaries of wider claims represented by the parties to the suit.[8] From the political standpoint, the courts are arenas in which persons and groups make claims upon each other, press their demands upon the government, and seek in some way to make their own desires and wishes into effective public policy.

Courts thus do more than simply referee disputes between private parties. In adjudicating disputes, they contribute to shaping and changing the law itself. History is replete with examples of groups that press in the courts the same causes they press before legislatures and in executive agencies, or that utilize the courts to bring about changes in the law—utilize them, that is, as vehicles for declaring or changing public policy and not merely as "neutral" vehicles for attempting to enforce unassailable decisions made earlier in the admittedly political branches of government. We are all familiar, for example, with the recent and current activities of the National Consumer's League, the National Association for the Advancement of Colored People, Jehovah's Witnesses, and the American Bar Association in initiating court cases or bringing pressure to bear upon the courts to change established doctrines or particular decisions.

The opportunity, indeed the necessity, for the exercise of judicial discretion is present at every step in the judicial process, in all courts and in all legal systems—not only in the United States Supreme Court and in those cases specifically concerned with judicial review of statutes. The necessity for judicial choice, as well as its political or policy implications, are clear when a judge is called upon to decide whether or not a specific government agency has jurisdiction to satisfy a group or class claim arising in a lawsuit or when his decision directly grants or withholds what is being claimed by one of the parties to a case. Evidence of judicial discretion is equally clear at other points. Local police and municipal judges, state and federal district or trial courts, with or without juries, exhibit wide variations in their sentencing of criminals—variations with obvious policy implications for the character and level of law enforcement against crime. As far as civil

---

[8] E. H. Levi, *An Introduction to Legal Reasoning* (Chicago: University of Chicago Press, 1949), pp. 1–7; C. K. Allen, *Law in the Making* (New York: Oxford University Press, 1956); Murphy and Pritchett, *op. cit.*, chaps. 7–9; Jerome Frank, *Courts on Trial* (Princeton, N.J.: Princeton University Press, 1949).

proceedings are concerned, it is necessary only to list the types of disputes that find their way into the courts to show the opportunity that trial judges have to influence the course of industrial, social, and political development in the community: zoning ordinances, eminent-domain actions, taxpayer suits, public utility rate cases, civil liberties and civil rights cases, and cases involving injunctions in labor-management disputes. And of course the judiciary in many communities provides one of the major sources of influence for local political party organizations: jobs, lucrative receiverships, estate appraisals, and minor patronage appointments.[9]

We may safely conclude, then, that the way cases get into courts and the way judges decide whether or not they have jurisdiction are not wholly dependent upon the "private" motives and interests of individual parties to the lawsuit. They are also strongly influenced by the way the judicial system (local, state, or national) fits into and enforces the political power structure; by the degree to which potential litigants perceive the courts (as against the legislature or administrative agencies) as accessible vehicles for contesting public policy issues;[10] and by whatever it is beyond the "automatic" application of legal principles that guides judges in their discretionary judicial activities.

It thus becomes imperative for the political analyst to search out the relationships that may exist between judges' decision-making behavior and such supposedly extraneous factors as their social background, psycho-physical makeup, professional training and career experience; the process by which cases are presented, argued, and decided—including the role of the attorneys, assistants, and associations the judge is in communication with while cases are under consideration; and personal and ideological groupings among the judges themselves.[11] We must emphasize, however, that the discovery of such uniformities by social science research does not prove that any one general tendency is necessarily the major explanatory factor in any particular case.

With this *caveat* in mind, it is possible to say that significant correlations, both positive and negative, do exist between the voting behavior of judges and specified social-background attributes (demographic origin, ethnic and religious affiliation, occupational experience prior to appointment, method of access to office, and political party affiliation). Moreover, enduring solidarity among judges in certain types of decisions they make can be identified according to their attitudes toward the judicial protection of civil liberties and judicial self-restraint

[9] Wallace Sayre and Herbert Kaufman, *Governing New York City* (New York: Russell Sage Foundation, 1960), pp. 522–54.
[10] Herbert Jacob and Kenneth Vines, "The Judiciary in American State Politics," in Glendon Schubert (ed.), *Judicial Decision-Making* (New York: The Macmillan Company, 1963), pp. 245–55.
[11] Glendon Schubert, "Behavioral Research in Public Law," *American Political Science Review*, LVII (1963), 433–45; "Symposium on 'Jurimetrics'," Law and Contemporary Problems, XXVIII (Winter 1963).

with regard to governmental regulation of private enterprise.[12] While these research findings do not exhaust the variables that influence ju dicial decision-making, they nonetheless demonstrate the unquestionable influence of "non-legal" variables on judicial behavior.

In summary, before we turn to a special aspect of the problem of political influence on judges, let us note that to recognize the existence of such factors is not equivalent to asserting that judges are completely free to decide cases any way they like, nor that they are helpless pawns manipulated by mysterious, hidden or evil forces in society. The student and the citizen must recognize it as normal that judges are exposed to and respond to "political" influences; instead of denying the facts of political life, therefore, or shutting one's eyes to them, one should understand the sublety and complexity of these forces. Nevertheless, it is true that their own conceptions of judicial office and judicial roles are among the most powerful influences shaping the behavior of nearly all judges. In other words, we must remember that it is men who think of themselves as *judges* who respond to the kinds of "political" influences we have briefly surveyed above; it is their conceptions of their judicial roles which are most immediately affected by those influences.

THE COURTS AND PUBLIC OPINION

To what extent are the courts guided in their decisions by public opinion—that is to say, by their perceptions of great currents of popular feeling or of established traditions and customs, even to the extent of "following the election returns"? This question is usually discussed in terms of such things as the desirability of judicial review, and the compatibility of such review with the principles of democracy; or the validity of judicial authority when judges who have been appointed for life or good behavior, and are subject only to the check of impeachment and removal by an extraordinary legislative majority, make decisions that are in conflict with the "people's will," or with the interpretation of the Constitution made by the political branches of government. Many thoughtful men, both within and outside the legal profession, have considered judicial review an anomaly in a democratic political system, and have sought to eliminate it or hedge it around with procedural or substantive restrictions, including legislative regulation of the courts' appellate jurisdiction.

[12] C. H. Pritchett, *The Roosevelt Court* (New York: The Macmillan Company, 1948); *Civil Liberties and the Vinson Court* (Chicago: University of Chicago Press, 1954); S. S. Ulmer, "An Empirical Analysis of Selected Aspects of Lawmaking of the United States Supreme Court," *Journal of Politics*, VIII (1959), 414–36: "Behavior Patterns in the U.S. Supreme Court," *Journal of Politics*, XXII (1960), 629–53; "Judicial Review as Political Behavior," *Administrative Science Quarterly*, IV (1960), 426–45; Joseph Tanenhaus, "Supreme Court Attitudes Toward Federal Administrative Agencies," *Vanderbilt Law Review*, XIV (1961), 473–502; H. J. Spaeth, "Judicial Power as a Variable Motivating Supreme Court Behavior," *Midwest Journal of Political Science*, VI (1961), 54–82.

There is very little evidence to show directly whether or not courts do consciously attempt to reflect the contemporary state of public opinion in deciding doubtful questions of law. The overwhelming assumption, of course, is that that is not their business; most judges and lawyers would presumably say that the judicial function consists of interpreting and applying established rules or law, and *not* contemporary opinion, to the resolution of new issues and situations. Indeed, a fairly interesting argument could be made that the periods of the United States Supreme Court's highest prestige have been those in which its decisions have run counter to policies advocated by elected Chief Executives. In the absence of direct evidence on the extent to which judges actually try to grasp the direction of public attitudes and to incorporate them into their decisions, the relation of the courts to public opinion has to be analyzed in other ways.[13]

Our first working hypothesis is that the people of a democratic political system do not aspire to unlimited popular sovereignty. If such a situation did exist, it would be just as much a form of tyranny—albeit a popular tyranny—as exists in undemocratic and totalitarian governments. When the people initiate or ratify a written constitution, they indicate their desire to establish a government of *limited powers* under that constitution. The latter, therefore, has to be interpreted and applied by each of the branches or departments of government in its own way and within the limits of its own designated authority, procedures, and responsibilities. Second, in the same act by which the people exercise their sovereignty by adopting the constitution, they also limit their sovereignty to the instrumentalities established therein and to the procedures prescribed therein for amendment and revision.

That is, the people desire *both* a limited form of constitutional government *and* a democratic form of government accountable to themselves *under the law* they have created in the constitution. In politics there is nothing strange about the fact that the people desire or approve two ends that seem at first to be logically inconsistent; the important question, speaking empirically, is whether they do in fact wish to have both a constitutional, limited government and, within such a framework, democratic modes of procedure and decision.

If it is accepted, or can be demonstrated empirically, that the people desire democratic government under the law of a constitution, then one finds little difficulty in following Hamilton's argument in No. 78 of the *Federalist* that interpretation of the Constitution by the courts does not make the judicial power superior to the legislative power:

> . . . It only supposes that the power of the people is superior to both; and that where the will of the legislature, declared in its statutes, stands in opposition to that of the people, declared in the Constitution, the judges ought to be governed by the latter rather than the former.

13 The following analysis is deeply indebted to E. V. Rostow, *The Sovereign Prerogative* (New Haven, Conn.: Yale University Press, 1962), chaps. 4–6.

It is, of course, quite conceivable in a given case that the people themselves might prefer the legislative interpretation of the Constitution to the judicial one. Nevertheless, the people cannot have the best of both bargains, unless they wish to give up constitutional government altogether for a model based upon the town meeting, in which matters are decided by a single majority vote at any time a quorum can be obtained, or unless they accept the premise that the only true form of democracy is one in which all decisions have to be made or confirmed by popular elections and referendums. Actually, of course, no democracy makes either a referendum or a legislative body completely sovereign, that is, capable of determining anything it desires. As Dean Rostow has pointed out, even the classic Vermont town meeting knows limits on its jurisdiction: "It cannot (legally) deny a resident citizen his right to vote, nor confiscate the land of a Democrat, nor impose a sentence of exile, nor try a lawsuit over the boundaries and habits of cattle."

The nub of the problem is that democratic constitutions by their very nature divide responsibilities and powers among two or more branches and levels of government. This inevitably produces conflict and the necessity for accommodation with regard to the boundaries of each level's jurisdiction. The courts must exercise the power implicit in the judicial function to declare and enforce those boundaries if the words of the Constitution are not to become, in the crucible of political controversy, little more than good advice. When the Constitution has deliberately set up a division of governmental powers, and created thereby a built-in source of possible friction between the several branches over the question of what is the proper interpretation of the Constitution, then it is legitimate to assume that this was done not in order to establish some single, authoritative voice with the power to enunciate once and for all the imagined will of the people. Instead the aim was clearly to protect the people from autocracy by creating a situation in which the designated branches would have to work out a mutually acceptable recognition of the area of responsibility of each with respect to every controversial question of public policy. Such a sharing and mutual accommodation of overlapping powers is possible because each branch acts through a different process and at a different time, and must therefore tolerate the legitimate jurisdiction of the other before it has arrived at its own interpretation, without being able to insist that its interpretation be immediately and completely accepted as controlling by the other two. If anything other than this were the operative principle, a government of separated but mixed powers would indeed be either impossible or intolerable. Thus the people in a democratic political system can not only accept a power of judicial review on the part of the courts, but can also accept the implied limitations on the freedom of action of their elected representatives —provided that both the courts and the elective branches of government recognize the limited character of their own authority and undertake to work out an acceptable accommodation. This is the meaning of "concurrent majority" in a government of separated powers.

Third, it is a legitimate although not a necessary hypothesis that the people may wish to place certain limitations and requirements in the constitution beyond the power of either the courts or the political branches to alter, except by formal amendment of the constitution itself. For example, do the people accept Mr. Justice Jackson's dictum that "one's right to life, liberty and property, to free speech, a free press, freedom of worship and assembly and other fundamental rights may not be submitted to vote; they depend upon the outcome of no elections"? If they do, they recognize that there are some things that a popular majority cannot abridge, repeal, or destroy, unless authorized to do so by constitutional amendment. But if the step of amending the constitution is not politically possible or available, how then are these rights to be protected from abridgment or violation by legislature, executive, or court (there are examples of such abridgment and violations in every country's history), short of revolution—save by the action of one or both of the other governmental branches? Along with citizens under governments everywhere, the people of the United States are faced with the ambiguous character of democratic government: we want both freedom and law— and if freedom is to be defined as the availability of alternative choices under law, we may as well recognize that there is more freedom under a system that permits political agitation, opposition, and discussion of possible changes in authorized interpretations of the constitution than there is under a system that gives the citizen no alternative except to go to jail, into exile, or toward conspiratorial subversion and military revolution.

The constant tension and potential conflict between the elementary concepts of democracy (government by public opinion) and law (constitutional interpretation by an independent judiciary) has finally brought us to a recognition of the fact that the concept of democracy is more complex than the simple idea of absolute popular sovereignty or of taking all public decision by direct majority vote of the people. Law and public opinion are reconciled in democratic political systems by recognizing that the meaning of constitutional statements may change wth the passage of time, but that such changes are better accomplished by duly designated procedures under the constitution than by violations or reversals sanctioned by majorities whenever one can be mustered; that the task of constitutional interpretation is a multiple one, legitimately if differently carried on by each branch of the government, under the shared assumption of the supremacy of the constitution and their own ultimate responsibility to the members of the political community who adopt, amend, and obey it; and that the authorized legal activities and functions of both the judicial and the elected branches of government should be carried on in a vigorous, open, free, and informed climate of group agitation and active public discussion, to the end that the responsible legal actors may have the benefit of as much knowledge and advice as possible on the actual state and trend of public opinion while they are making their decisions.

SUGGESTIONS FOR ADDITIONAL READING

ABRAHAM, HENRY J., *The Judicial Process* (Fair Lawn, N.J.: Oxford University Press, 1962).

BERMAN, HAROLD J., *Justice in the U.S.S.R.: An Interpretation of Soviet Law* (New York: Vintage Books, 1963).

COHEN, FELIX S., *Ethical Systems and Legal Ideals: An Essay on the Foundations of Legal Criticism* (Ithaca, N.Y.: Cornell University Press, 1933).

FRANK, JEROME, *Courts on Trial* (Princeton, N.J.: Princeton University Press, 1949).

FREIDMANN, WOLFGANG, *Legal Theory* (London: Stevens and Sons Ltd., 1949).

MURPHY, W. F., and C. H. PRITCHETT, *Courts, Judges and Politics* (New York: Random House, 1961).

PELTASON, J. W., *Federal Courts in the Political Process* (New York: Random House, 1955).

ROSTOW, E. V., *The Sovereign Prerogative* (New Haven, Conn.: Yale University Press, 1962).

SCHMIDHAUSER, J. R., *The Supreme Court: Politics, Personalities and Procedures* (New York: Holt, Rinehart & Winston, 1960).

SCHUBERT, GLENDON, *Judicial Decision-Making* (New York: The Free Press of Glencoe, 1963).

STONE, JULIUS, *The Province and Function of Law* (Cambridge, Mass.: Harvard University Press, 1950).

Chapter 13

CITIZENS AND THE GENERATION OF PUBLIC OPINION

Although in modern societies the roles of administrators and judges in government are structurally separated, they still share certain common attributes. Both judge and administrator are representatives of the political community in the sense that each performs duties imposed or required by it. The positions of both are established by law; their authority and duties are legally defined and limited. Both are recruited, appointed, compensated, and promoted primarily upon the basis of technical qualifications (special training, competence, experience) rather than political orientation (group memberships, party service, political beliefs). Both judge and administrator hold a *public office*, a position of trust and accountability to the whole community, the occupant of which is expected to do his job in accordance with standards of equity and fairness and to stay within the limits and requirements of his legal authority. The standards and requirements for both judge and administrator are partly professional and technical and partly conventional norms of conduct, but not commands for specific actions in particular situations.

Communications Roles and Skills in Democratic Government

It is not difficult to understand why the political community needs technical, managerial, and legal experts, of the sort we discussed in the previous two chapters, to provide efficient public services and orderly processes of judicial settlement. It is not always recognized, however, that it also needs experts of another kind, persons skilled in the difficult and important arts of public communication. These are the people who possess the skills needed to identify and elaborate genuine problems, needs, and desires among members of the community; to arouse and focus public attention on significant issues; to present relevant information and ideas; to analyze and discuss controversial proposals and their probable effects upon individual and group interests and values; and to formulate policy criteria in order to control the acts of government officials and guide the thinking and behavior of citizens on specific problems.

Democratic governmental processes, in which public policy decisions are arrived at and carried out in accordance with *public opinion*,[1] presuppose that the members of the community and their leaders either possess these skills or have the interest and capacity to acquire them. How many actually do is a debatable question, but practically all democratic philosophers in one way or another predicate their faith upon the capacity of citizens to acquire and use the skills of communication, as well as upon the exercise of intelligent judgment on the part of the "ordinary" citizen, man or woman.

The relationship of the communicative skills to the political process may be visualized in terms of three types of roles played in the formation of public opinion: those of Citizen, Opinion-maker, and Representative. The *Citizen* is a member of the political community not merely in the legal sense, but in the moral and social sense as well; he feels the obligation to inform himself, to frame his own responsible views, and to discuss them with his fellow citizens. A person who performs the role of Citizen passively, ignorantly, or ineffectively belongs to the *mass*, whereas a person who enters into political affairs competently and effectively may become a leader of opinion in his personal and group associations, or may be a member of an attentive public to whom policy-makers in their turn pay attention. An *Opinion-maker* is a person politically influential beyond the limits of the group of his face-to-face friends and coworkers, either by reason of his name, status, and reputation, or because of his frequent and ready access to the mass media of communication. A *Representative* is a person who by virtue of his official position in some private group or governmental organization can express its views authentically and authoritatively. Of course these roles are not mutually exclusive, though it may be difficult to play more than one at the same time. But each role is important in the living, functioning

1 The reader may wish to keep in mind at least three different ways in which the term *public opinion* may legitimately be used in political discussion: (1) The statistical distribution of individual attitudes on an issue within the political community; (2) a presumed agreement on basic fundamental beliefs that constitutes the unifying bond or consensus between the members of the body politic; (3) a "majority will" of 51% or more of the members of a political community about either the legitimate frame of government or the desirable direction of binding public policy.

democratic community, and all thrive on the legal and political conditions of free elections, free speech, a free press, and free association, including the right of political opposition.

Some voices count for more than others in the opinion-forming and policy-making processes, particularly in a highly specialized, bureaucratically organized society. Therefore, without any implication that their opinions are necessarily "better," it is sometimes convenient to refer to *opinion elites*—those categories of Opinion-makers and Representatives whose occupations, status, or public prominence endow their views with unusual political importance.

The connection between the opinion-forming process in the community and the official decision-making processes of government is established when Opinion-makers and Representatives are consulted or share in some other way in the official policy decisions of legislators, administrators, and judges. The vitality of the democratic process is directly related to the climate and level of discussion among individual citizens, informal group and association leaders, the press, and other media of mass communication, for it is in the context of this discussion that responsible public officials reach their own policy decisions.

In this chapter we shall analyze some of the problems associated with government by public opinion. A traditional approach to the question has been to analyze certain basic concepts such as "the public," "public opinion," "representation," and "responsibility," and to deduce from them a set of criteria for judging how people and their leaders *ought* to form their opinions and political actions. Our approach begins in this way but will develop differently, not because criteria of judgment are unimportant, but because analysis should be based upon what we know about the ways people do in fact form, articulate, and transmit their political opinions, and upon what we know of the extent to which policy-makers' decisions do in fact conform to popular views and the technical requirements of any given situation. Therefore, before judging the performance of citizens or officials, of processes or systems, the competent political analyst must answer such questions as the following: How do political and legal institutions affect the ways in which political communication takes place between citizens, opinion-makers, representatives and policy-determining officials? How are people supposed to form political opinions and reach decisions in a given system, and how do they behave in fact? How do the channels of mass communication affect the way leaders and representatives perceive public opinion, and what they try to do about it? How does public opinion affect the making of governmental decisions? That is, do "the people" make policy determinations which are binding upon public officials, or do their sentiments and views constitute but one among many considerations upon which officials make up their minds?

To attempt to answer these questions we shall first analyze the views of theorists about the nature of the opinion process in the political community. Then we shall examine some of the communications link-ages between citizens, opinion-makers, and non-governmental and offi-cial representatives in the policy-making and decision-making processes of government.

Government by Public Opinion: Three Conceptions

The general conception of the role and function of public opinion in a given political system depends on the prevailing attitudes held by people within that system about how public opinion is to be formed and author-itative decisions of public policy are to be made. In Chapter 1 we noted that political systems tend to group themselves around two polar types, the democratic-constitutional and the oligarchic-authoritarian. Oversim-plifying, we can say that democratic-constitutional systems assume, first, that political authority consists of a set of representative institu-tions based upon majority rule, the consent of the governed, and the right of political opposition. The political order permits the voluntary association of individuals into any kind of organization consistent with the public purposes and procedures of the commonwealth, for the col-lective achievement of goals that individuals cannot realize by them-selves. Further, the political system requires the government to enforce and respect certain basic rights and duties of citizenship—all of which presumes that the individual is not only capable of self-government but actively participates in the processes of policy formation by which he is governed.

The parallel assumptions of the oligarchic-authoritarian political system are, first, that political authority emanates from some source above the people—a supernatural being, an idealized conception of a desirable social order, a hereditary ruling class. No opinion-forming organization or policy-making activity is permitted except by sufferance and under the direct control of the legitimate ruler or ruling group. Finally, the individual members of the political community are essen-tially subjects; their role is to perform the duties assigned them by the government or the ruling class, which presumably knows best how to rule for their benefit. Political theorists differ in their conceptions in the same way. With respect to their views about the role and com-petence of public opinion, they seem to fall into not just two but three groups, which may be labeled idealist, skeptic (or elitist), and realist.

IDEALIST CONCEPTIONS OF PUBLIC OPINION

Idealists believe in democracy and fortify their faith with rational definitions and assumptions about the conditions which must prevail if "the people" are to govern themselves. Idealist theories of public opinion may conceive of "the people" as an organic entity with one opinion or voice; as unrelated individual persons; or as persons organized politically, for the purpose of governing themselves, into electorates, parties, and opinion groups.

Idealists have suggested that for the proper functioning of democracy individual citizens should be interested, informed, and active in the affairs of the political community. Considered collectively as a *public*, citizens should possess a common body of determinate moral principles, to which issues involving conflicts of personal and group interest, opinion and power, can be referred for decision. They are capable of perceiving political realities, particularly as this enables them to choose the best-qualified candidates as their representatives and leaders. They engage in public discussion and evaluation of issues in order to arrive at rational decisions. They can recognize the common good and the public interest, and act upon this basis. Finally, they accept the majority principle as the basis for binding action when the constitutionally-agreed-upon conditions for determining the majority have been satisfied, and provided that conditions are maintained whereby the minority may transform itself lawfully into a majority.

Any thoughtful reader can undoubtedly formulate other conditions he would like to add to the foregoing list (or see some he might subtract from it). One outstanding omission is the eighteenth-century conception of the sovereign general will, or natural order, of society, which it was the duty of representatives and legislators to ascertain and execute. It is omitted because the experience of the nineteenth and twentieth centuries has demonstrated how difficult it is to achieve popular, representative government, let alone to ascertain the general will. Modern faith in democracy still finds support in empirical evidence for individuals' capacities for citizenship and the workability of institutions of popular rule, but Rousseau's mystical sovereign has virtually disappeared from the lexicon of twentieth-century social science.

The appeal of the idealists lies in their articulation of the hopes and aspirations of mankind and in their belief that man's highest goals are attainable, exciting, worthy of effort and sacrifice. Their weakness lies in the gap between ideal and fact; individually and collectively, people often do not behave as idealist theories of public opinion say they ought to. Realization of this gap produces such familiar human reactions as self-deception, disillusionment, or cynicism, which in turn find expression in literary phrases like the compulsively sincere "true believer," the righteously indignant "witch-hunter," and the morally corrupt "unbeliever," or nihilist.

SKEPTIC OR ELITIST CONCEPTIONS OF PUBLIC OPINION

Skeptics about democracy start at the gap between the ideals and facts of human political behavior and further assume that democratic self-government is factually impossible, morally undesirable, or both. The skeptics thus include those who prefer a closed system of customary or hereditary rule in a fixed class society, in which participation in government is determined by birth or restricted to a privileged social status, to a society of citizens regarded as morally, legally, and politically equal and who acquire ruling status by ability, effort, and achievement. Another group of skeptics see democracy as mob or mass rule, capable only of mediocrity, catering to the lowest human common denominator, the enemy of knowledge, culture, and individuality. Perhaps most numerous of the skeptics are those who see democracy as a façade, a secular religion that conceals *de facto* rule by demagogues, power-mad adventurers, or a military or economic elite. In a highly differentiated, organizational society, these perceptions of politics may be particularly appealing to frightened, frustrated, confused personalities who seek the kind of simplified solutions offered by a charismatic authority figure, by prophetic threats of divine retributions, by dreams of return to a historical golden age, or by romantic utopias of a completely new social order.

Perhaps the most descriptive name for the skeptics is *elitists*. The category includes the radicals of both right and left who believe in rule by a good, specially gifted, trained, appropriately indoctrinated minority, unhampered by institutions making them accountable to the public. But although elitists may sneer at or deny the existence of public opinion, they unwittingly pay homage to it. They generally advocate and attempt to gain control over the institutions of education, mass communication, art, and entertainment, even while they attack the institutions of popular rule (suffrage, free elections, representative legislatures) as mere ritualistic procedures and devices hopelessly incapable of achieving effective political choice by the whole body of citizens.

REALIST CONCEPTIONS OF PUBLIC OPINION

Realists do not necessarily reject the principle of rule by public opinion, but they recognize obstacles and difficulties in the way of bringing it about. If they are democrats, they tend to concentrate their efforts on discovering or promoting the conditions under which it may be realized. They postulate neither a "majority will" nor an "average" opinion of the man in the street as the standard for judging governmental acts. Instead, they look for actual expressions of opinion by persons and groups in particular, concrete situations. They also seek to understand the social and psychological processes of individual thought and attitude formation.

Like many others, realists believe rule by public opinion is possible only in an institutional context of free elections, in which the public can periodically choose or change its rulers. In such a context, the rulers, once chosen, may be judged by the public according to their acceptance of the responsibilities of governing and their efforts to make decisions in accordance with the distribution of opinion among their fellow citizens. A frequently overlooked but important aspect of the realist view is that democratic rulers must take into account the presumed or known interests and values of minorities and non-participants, both inside and outside the political community, and not just of majority opinion or the opinions of vocal and active elements in the public.

But realists lay equal stress on the attitudes and behavior of citizens. Thus they emphasize that both public policy and the opinions of individuals, groups, and public must be the product of free consultation, public discussion, and mutual persuasion among individuals and group leaders. Similarly, they insist that rule by public opinion requires acceptance by active individuals and groups of the obligation to seek agreement and, in the event of failure to agree, recognition of the legitimacy of compromises made by their political representatives to adjust their conflicting claims. In short, realists see the individual's opinion and political attitude as a complex bundle of perceptions, beliefs, and values concerning the established structure and processes of political authority, not merely as a series of discrete and simple preferences on particular issues of public policy. Public opinion therefore appears to realists as a complex set of diversely shared modes of perceiving reality, as well as attitudes and preferences for ways of reaching agreement on controversial problems, formulated and expressed in diverse and complex ways.

We might summarize these three differing theoretical viewpoints by saying that, viewed by the skeptic, the public appears as an inert mass which can occasionally be mobilized by leaders, elections, or revolutions into "pros" and "cons" but which at other times oscillates between the role of a mere spectator and that of a supporter of "rules of the game."[2] To the idealist, the public appears to be a corporate body possessing a moral authority which it can and will exercise purposefully when it is "sufficiently dissatisfied with the specialist in charge of a particular function."[3] To the realist, the public is a more or less pluralistic network of diverse individuals and groups linked with a particular set of social and political institutions and particular modes of opinion-formation and communication. To the realist, the public is in no sense a corporate entity.[4]

[2] Walter Lippmann, *The Phantom Public* (New York: The Macmillan Company, 1925); *The Public Philosophy* (Boston: Little, Brown and Company, 1954).
[3] C. H. Cooley, *Social Organization* (New York: Charles Scribner's Sons, 1909). An excellent restatement of the idealist position is J. Tussman, *Obligation and the Body Politic* (Fair Lawn, N.J.: Oxford University Press, 1960).
[4] Succinct statements of the realist faith are Pendleton Herring, *The Politics of Democracy* (New York: Harcourt, Brace & World, 1940), pp. 305–35; Rockefeller Brothers Panel Report No. VI, *The Power of the Democratic Idea* (Garden City, N.Y.: Doubleday & Company, Inc., 1960).

What Governments Do About Public Opinion

From a consideration of different theoretical assumptions about the interrelations of the opinion and governing processes of society, we turn now to consider some of the symbolic and institutional mechanisms whereby these processes are linked. One provocative thinker, Harold Lasswell, has suggested that the communications or opinion-forming process in society may be visualized as performing three functions vital to the survival of both the political and the individual human organism: surveillance of the environment, providing continuous information about it; coordination of the parts of the organism involved in responding to the environment; and transmission of the social heritage—the information, values, and skills required for survival—from one generation to the next.[5] In complex societies, these functions are performed by more than one group or organization. Thus in modern societies the surveillance or intelligence function is performed by diplomats, newspaper correspondents, those who conduct opinion polls, social scientists, writers, and artists (and on another level by military spies and secret service agents). The development of interested and informed public opinion and relevant public policies is a function of journalists, news commentators, and leaders of non-governmental groups, as well as of elected representatives and of civil servants. The educational function is carried on by public and private school systems; by public and private research organizations, libraries, and philanthropic foundations and institutes; by private and governmental channels of information and entertainment; and through motion pictures, telecommunications systems, and national and international networks of postal and wire services.

GOVERNMENT AND MASS COMMUNICATIONS

The more differentiated, urbanized, and industrialized a society, the more there tends to develop within it an autonomous, self-initiating structure of non-governmental groups that acquire their own habitual ways of articulating and transmitting their special interests and policies—that is, their opinions. The mass communications media themselves—the newspaper industry, the radio, television, and motion picture industries, the book and magazine publishing industries—may be considered interest groups in their own right, as well as vehicles of information and discussion. We must further distinguish the process of individual opinion formation, which finds expression both through primary-group channels and in such collective forms as mass, crowd,

5 Harold D. Lasswell, "The Structure and Function of Communications in Society," in Wilbur W. Schramm (ed.), *Mass Communications* (Urbana, Ill.: University of Illinois Press, 1960), pp. 117–30.

Figure 5

The Opinion-Forming and the Public Policy-Making Processes

A SCHEMATIC VIEW

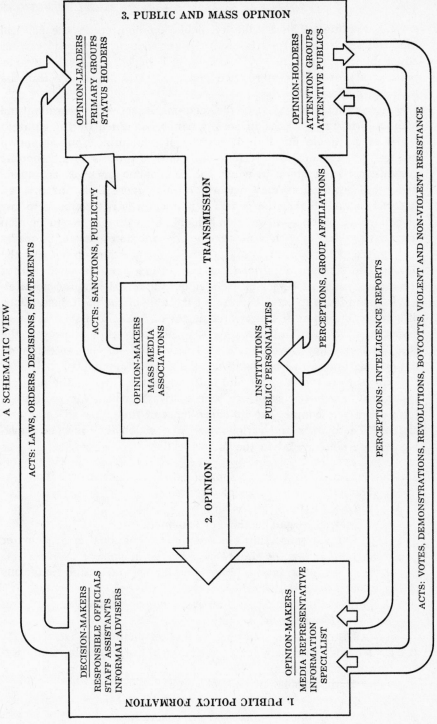

3. PUBLIC AND MASS OPINION

OPINION-LEADERS
PRIMARY GROUPS
STATUS HOLDERS

OPINION-HOLDERS
ATTENTION GROUPS
ATTENTIVE PUBLICS

ACTS: LAWS, ORDERS, DECISIONS, STATEMENTS

ACTS: SANCTIONS, PUBLICITY

TRANSMISSION

OPINION-MAKERS
MASS MEDIA
ASSOCIATIONS

INSTITUTIONS
PUBLIC PERSONALITIES

PERCEPTIONS, GROUP AFFILIATIONS

2. OPINION

PERCEPTIONS: INTELLIGENCE REPORTS

DECISION-MAKERS
RESPONSIBLE OFFICIALS
STAFF ASSISTANTS
INFORMAL ADVISERS

OPINION-MAKERS
MEDIA REPRESENTATIVE
INFORMATION
SPECIALIST

1. PUBLIC POLICY FORMATION

ACTS: VOTES, DEMONSTRATIONS, REVOLUTIONS, BOYCOTTS, VIOLENT AND NON-VIOLENT RESISTANCE

SOURCE: Adapted from J. N. Rosenau, *Public Opinion and Foreign Policy* (New York: Random House, 1961), p. 22.

or public opinion. This last entity, public opinion, enters the political process in institutionalized fashion only occasionally, through elections and plebiscites; but in its symbolic and psychological dimensions it functions as a brooding omnipresence that constantly affects the thinking of policy-makers.

A more adequate view of the relationship between governing and opinion-forming processes in society can be obtained by imagining a series of separable but linked patterns of communication, as shown in Figure 5. The diagram presents the political process as a composite communications system, in which the component processes are linked and some participants may perform roles in more than one process. It should be noted that the generating function is not confined to any one place or process—to opinion-holders, for example, or to opinion leaders (1)—but may start among the transmission agencies or media (3) or the policy-formulators (2), and among either or both of the others. The diagram does not show how diverse and complex each of these component processes is. Neither does it reveal how the political-legal system helps to establish and set the tone of the basic institutions of opinion formation in society (the degree of freedom of speech, press, association, religion, information). At the same time, however, the chart indicates how government itself acts as one of the most influential opinion-forming processes, if not the most influential.

In its capacity as setter and enforcer of the rules of the political system, government acts in three principal ways (which vary, of course, from country to country) to influence mass or interpersonal communications.[6] These ways and various means by which they may be implemented are enumerated in the following list.

I. Government may limit or suppress discussion or information
   A. Through various forms of censorship
      1. Obscene publications
      2. Subversive publications or statements
      3. General censorship (in time of war, national emergency, or martial law, or simply as a matter of policy)
   B. Through libel laws (protection against false and malicious speech or publications)
   C. Through licensing (prior or post-facto restraints)
      1. Radio or television stations
      2. Distribution or showing of motion pictures
   D. Through monopoly (or degrees thereof) of ownership and operation of facilities
      1. Mails, telephone, and telegraph
      2. Air waves (including outer space)
      3. Telecommunications systems generally

[6] Zechariah Chafee, *Government and Mass Communications,* 2 vols. (Chicago: The University of Chicago Press, 1947), pp. *xv*–29.

II. Government may facilitate and improve the flow of information
    A. By requiring equal access to nongovernmental media of communications
    B. By providing equal or non-discriminatory access to governmental facilities
    C. By the protection of authors' rights (copyright regulations)
    D. By compulsory disclosure policies ("corrupt practice" laws, lobbyist registration and reporting)
    E. By the provision of subsidies for research, innovation, and development
III. Government may provide information or facilities directly
    A. Through I (D) above
    B. Through government-conducted research
    C. Through government newspapers, radio and television stations, and movies
    D. Through the information services of government agencies
    E. Through government intelligence services
    F. Through a centralized department or agency of information and propaganda

This catalog of policies and techniques shows how universal are government's responsibilities for regulating and supervising the flow of information and ideas in any society. Where *techniques* are concerned, it is evident that all governments engage in one way or another in each of the major practices we have listed. But in the matter of *policies* on censorship, information flow, and the use of facilities, there is a vast and obvious difference between constitutional and autocratic political systems. Constitutional systems rely upon and encourage as many alternative and competing channels of non-governmental communication as possible, and they deliberately encourage voluntary participation and the honest expression of social interests in the public-opinion and policy-making processes. In countries where such conditions are understood and valued, and the sources and sponsors of communications are clearly labeled and recognized for what they are, the policy of establishing a government-operated medium (for example, the British Broadcasting Corporation) as a yardstick to which the performance of competing media can be compared is not necessarily detrimental to the opinion process—provided that the established medium is not given unlimited monopoly privileges and is constantly exposed to public scrutiny and criticism on such matters as efficiency, partisan group and political influence, or even just dullness. Under such conditions, the standard for judging the political communications system is the extent to which several public and private media, separately and together, strive to give their fellow citizens and their rulers the most accurate and meaningful account possible of newsworthy events and of the world, and the extent to which the responsible owners and managers of the media are trusted to decide what is "newsworthy" without the permission or sanction of a governmental (or any other) censor.

GOVERNMENT AND CIVIC EDUCATION

The political education of their citizens is one of the primary responsibilities of all governments; yet because governments' actions and people's perceptions of them are so often associated with force and propaganda, no function of government is more dissembled and misunderstood. To understand the civic education of citizens in a fundamental sense, we must examine first the relationship between authority and opinion, and second the relationship between educational indoctrination (the transmission of *accepted* skills and attitudes) and propaganda (the manipulation of collective attitudes on controversial, emotion-producing issues). Some inquiring mind will no doubt ask if civic education does not also involve the relation between reason and opinion. The answer is certainly yes, but this question will be dealt with more systematically in Chapters 18 and 19. We are concerned here primarily with the non-rational factors in political opinion.

Force, Consent, and Opinion. Government is so often defined in terms of its monopoly of legitimate violence that some people come to think of it only as an agent of force. Yet if this were true, government would consist entirely of military personnel and policemen. Government does rest upon control of violence, but it would be impotent indeed if it relied solely on physical force. For it symbolizes and embodies emotional force and moral coercion as well as physical restraints.

Government, like any system of organized force, seeks to transform itself from the embodiment of naked power to a symbol of legitimate authority based on consent. Yet if consent is defined as rational, voluntary agreement, few governments historically have relied for their beginnings or survival upon consent alone. They appeal also to the irrational, to deeply felt beliefs in a way of life, to such sentiments as love of country, pride in a common heritage, or fear of a common enemy. Thus they generate the complex attitudes of loyalty, self-sacrifice, and cooperation which, along with the avoidance of physical sanctions, underlie political consent and obedience. Transposed into habit and custom, these attitudes are the foundation for the basic duties of civic obligation: obedience to the procedures of law, payment of taxes, military service. Since their survival depends upon such attitudes, all governments are concerned with them, although central governments frequently leave much of the indoctrination in these duties to local government, the schools and churches, the family, and such unofficial agencies as political parties. And here, where a distinction can be made between the political system itself and the government or party in power, we meet again a basic difference between constitutional and autocratic political systems. The question is, how exclusive, how monopolistic, how absolute, is the governing party's claim to the political loyalty of the individual citizen?

Restating this problem in slightly different terms may help to clarify its implications. Indoctrination of citizens in the basic belief system or ideology is permitted to all political regimes. The tragic conflicts of politics arise when the morally sanctioned demands of the political association—whether we call it the "state," "nation," "country" or "party" —are interpreted to deny or overrule the claims of other cherished associations—family, religion, race, friendships, economic interest, or intellectual conviction. What happens to the political community when two or more political parties, radically different in viewpoint, each sincerely convinced that only it can be trusted with responsibility for the welfare of the commonwealth, assert that recognition of or cooperation with any other party, principle, or candidate is political disloyalty and treason to the system as a whole? If such convictions are carried far enough and deep enough, it is not hard to understand such common observations as: "Political stability does not permit freedom of press and association," or "This country is not ready for self-government." And it is but a short step from such attitudes to a belief in the necessity of rule by a single group, to absolute government control of the machinery of justice and the channels of mass communication, and finally to systematic, strategic use of terror as a physical and psychological weapon.

Moral coercion is of course no natural monopoly of governments. The pages of history are full of examples of non-governmental groups which have fused patriotism, religious absolutism, racial supremacy, and other sentiments to justify exploitation, persecution, expatriation, and even genocide, in the name of the political community. But the question, then, is how many groups are permitted to enjoy full political participation, to share in the process of civic education, to identify their beliefs, practices, and access to political influence with loyalty to the political system as a whole? How many groups thus privileged have enough self-respect and confidence to permit the same freedom to others? Consideration of the relationships between force, loyalty, and group identification enables us to see how fortunate are those political systems in which enough basic consensus exists among the various groups in the population to allow conflicts of power, interest, and opinion to be settled by resort to factual inquiry, free and open debate, and decision reached through public discussion and acceptable compromise rather than through the processes of secrecy and fiat that mark the existence of political-military monopoly.

Civic Education and Propaganda. Probably every reader has noticed on more than one occasion that what is labeled education by one person is called propaganda by another. This semantic difficulty arises because we naturally use the term "propaganda" to refer to the dissemination of someone else's preferred beliefs, never our own. But the confusion may be avoided if we think of "civic education" as the *transmission of attitudes and skills that are accepted in any given society as necessary or desirable,* and reserve the term "propaganda" to refer to *the manipulation of collective attitudes on controversial issues by the use of emotion-producing symbols (words and word-substitutes).* This distinction enables the critical observer to perceive whether it is propaganda or education that is being dispensed in a given situation; it does *not,* however, provide a satisfactory criterion for what government should and should not properly do.

Government, no less than business enterprise, must engage in skillful persuasion; democratic government must also train its citizens in the detection and use of propaganda (including its own) to make them better prepared to analyze and formulate their own values, interests, and preferences and better equipped to engage in political discussion in a relevant and effective manner. The objective of democratic civic education is to enable the individual citizen to think for himself, communicate his thought, analyze issues, and make choices among relevant values. It is with this objective in mind that we apply the negative appellation "propaganda" to governmental or non-governmental communications that aim at persuasion through deception, concealment, and deliberate misrepresentation and that fan the flames of intergroup and interpersonal hatred, blame, fear, and distrust. It is fruitless, however, to expect to destroy propaganda completely or to keep it neatly separated from education and information; the best we can do is to label it, become skilled in its detection, and strive to confine its use to productive and creative ends.

To sum up, then, the functions of civic and political education in democratic societies—whether or not they are divided between government and other groups and institutions—are to enable every citizen to understand his rights, obligations, and values with respect to the system of government under which he lives; to impart the feeling of genuine belonging to, identification with, and prideful participation in a political association without which effective citizenship is lacking; to provide the standards, inculcate the attitudes, and generate the incentives of service and contribution to the public life; and to give every individual the basic information, skills and motivation to think out for himself, and to communicate with his fellow citizens, his ideas on the basic problems of politics. The second and third of these educational functions (and even the first in a limited sense) are found in all governments, democratic or not. But the last of them—the facilitation of individual opinion formation—is not generic to the process of government; rather, it is entailed only by the logic of democracy.

Patterns of Public Opinion and Activity

We now turn to some of the typical patterns that individuals' opinions on public policy may take and to the ways in which these patterns affect the decisions of political leaders and government officials.

By "pattern of opinion" we mean simply what statisticians call a *frequency distribution of opinions* held by people on a particular public issue or question. It is a quantitative description or estimate of the number of persons holding different attitudes toward some more or less controversial group, issue, norm, institution, or the like. The only reliable method of making such a description is a public opinion sample survey. The significance of any opinion pattern we discover by such a survey depends partly upon whether the people consulted constitute a *representative* sample of the relevant population so that the chances of our descriptions being wrong (the "probable error") can be statistically calculated. The significance of the pattern also depends upon the way in which the question was asked, since the meaning of the response depends in large part upon the way the respondents understood the question. The relevant population (or universe) being sampled and analyzed is also very important in determining the significance of an opinion distribution, as well as in making its meaning more precise. These are all technical problems about which much has been learned in the last thirty years, so that the sample survey or opinion poll, when competently conducted, is one of the most valuable systematic devices available for gathering intelligence about popular feelings, desires, values, or information. Polls are used not only for scientific research, but also for estimating the size of consumer demand for a given product or service, determining the extent of advertising and mass media circulation, and ascertaining the concern and direction of opinion on issues of public policy.

INFORMATION AND INVOLVEMENT

The patterns of opinion that officials and opinion-makers must deal with take many forms.[7] Perhaps the most important involves how much people *know* about political questions and how much political matters *concern* them. In the United States, at least, survey after survey has demonstrated the existence of a large stratum of the population, ranging from 15 to 30 per cent, which is neither interested in nor informed on any given question. Another group that may range from 40 to 60 per cent is interested but not informed except in the most general way; and a third group of 10 to 25 per cent is both interested and informed.

[7] The following paragraphs are largely based upon V. O. Key, Jr., *Public Opinion and American Democracy* (New York: Alfred A. Knopf, 1961), particularly chaps. 2–4.

This evidence supports the familiar distinction between the *mass* and the *attentive public*. The mass is composed of both the lethargic apathetic, ignorant sectors of the population and of the so-called attention groups (usually racial or ethnic) who, though not necessarily well-informed, are extremely sensitive to words and symbols with which they have been indoctrinated and who respond quickly and unthinkingly to them. The attentive public is composed of people who are interested in politics and who have well-thought-out views based upon considerable factual information.

The size of these groups varies with the nature of the issue. The American Institute of Public Opinion reported in the fall of 1953 that 60 per cent of its sample had not "followed" and 80 per cent had not "heard or read about" the then controversial amendments to the Taft-Hartley labor law or Senator Bricker's constitutional amendment limiting the powers of the President over foreign relations. And of those who had heard or read about the issues, some had "no opinions." These percentages refer to the total adult population, so that the attentive publics in these instances may have numbered as many as 30 or 15 million people in either case. One may interpret these as either large or small participant publics, but the significance of the figures is heightened by the contrast they present with the idealized picture of a completely interested and informed public. A somewhat similar division of the population seems to exist with respect to participation in American Presidential elections, where less than 30 per cent both vote and engage in other kinds of campaign activity, another 30 to 40 per cent vote but do nothing else, and up to 25 per cent neither vote nor engage in any other kind of political activity.[8] It is a fairly safe presumption that most legislative, executive, and judicial decisions occur in a context of even lower public awareness and information.

PATTERNS OF OPINION PREFERENCE

The direction of opinion for or against a given policy proposal or statement of position may fall into one of several types of opinion patterns, depending on the issue in question. When most people in an opinion survey group themselves closely together on an attitude scale, while a small number scatter widely, the resulting distribution will look on a chart like a "*J* curve" or "double *J* curve,"[9] which seems to describe distributions of opinion where a high degree of consensus on the issue appears to exist. The meaning of such issue consensus is ambiguous,

[8] Angus Campbell et al., *The American Voter* (New York: John Wiley and Sons, 1960), p. 91.
[9] This and the following references to other types of "curves" are introduced to show that it is possible to think more precisely about political concepts by using quantitative "handles," which may also facilitate memory, and to indicate how the results of opinion polls and attitude surveys can be analyzed and expressed more revealingly than by simple percentages, as in Dr. Gallup's syndicated columns.

however. In one case it may indicate that public opinion is negative or *restrictive* on the policy-maker; in another, it may be *supportive* of a given policy, such as social security, and may therefore warn the policy-maker not to oppose it directly or to advocate its repeal. Issue consensus may also be *permissive,* giving the policy-maker considerable discretion with respect to such policies as aid to education, public health, or highways. It may be *directive* or *decisive* at a given juncture of events, as when economic depression requires public expenditures for relief and to create employment, or when military attack sparks an over-whelming demand for reprisal and war. Some analysts, however, feel that "issue consensus" is not consensus at all but a product of public discussion like the Quaker sense of the meeting, and is therefore not to be confused with consensus in the sense of basic political cohesion, agreement on fundamentals, or acceptance of the system. Some have further argued that consensus in the sense of "agreement on a deter-minate set of substantive concepts" does not have to exist for a political system to survive.[10]

In conflict situations, opinion patterns may be sharply divided, taking the form of a U-shaped curve on an attitude scale, which indi-cates that most people hold one or the other of two opposing views and the rest are scattered thinly across the scale in between. Another con-flict pattern is reflected in a W-shaped curve; in this case opinions are grouped around three or more views, each constituting a fairly clear minority position. As in the case of consensus, the implications of these opinion patterns for the policy-maker are ambiguous. A U-shaped (also called a bi-modal) opinion distribution may indicate a highly explosive crisis situation, as in a labor-management dispute or a civil war; or it may describe a two-party presidential election. A W-shaped (multi-modal) opinion distribution may reflect a potentially revolutionary situ-ation, as in the 1860 American Presidential elections or the French elections of 1958; it may also indicate a highly unsettled state of opinion lacking any clearly indicated trend or direction. Some theorists have suggested that the resolution of a public policy conflict depends upon the existence of a multi-modal distribution, so that the central or mod-erate groupings may strategically affect the course of events by altering their ideological positions in the direction of one or the other more extreme position. Alternatively, the middle grouping may draw the less deeply attached supporters of the extreme positions toward the center into the broad consensus reflected in the familiar, bell-shaped, "normal" distribution of the "double *J* curve."

It must be emphasized that these J-, W- and U-shaped opinion dis-tributions are only analytical classifications expressed in quantitative terms. They are not photographic pictures of opinion; they are tools for

10 See Carl J. Friedrich, *The New Image of the Common Man* (Boston: Beacon Press, 1950); Louis Wirth, "Consensus and Mass Communication," *American Sociological Review,* XIII (1948), 1.

understanding how people, classified into different groups, are reacting or might react to significant events, issues, and symbols. Their meaning must be interpreted and articulated by opinion leaders and official representatives in some way that seems relevant and helpful in the particular political situation. Nor do patterns of public opinion *determine* the course of events in and of themselves. However much public officials might wish to be guided by public wishes and desires, events have a certain logic of their own, and responsible leaders must act to meet the requirements of the situation as well as the "dictates" of public opinion. In a democratic society both the people (individuals and groups) and their leaders must recognize the force in decision-making of such factors that have nothing to do with opinion.

The politician's problem, then, is to devise a program of action that is more or less in conformity with public opinion and at the same time furthers the survival and prosperity of the body politic as he sees it. This is a difficult task for even the most consummate politician. Realization of the discrepancy between *public* opinion—the distribution of individual opinions in the population on a defined issue in a given situation—and *political* opinion—the configuration of effective influences actively communicated to politicians and officials (and to which *they respond*)—is a crucial step toward understanding politics for the student, and a probable condition of survival for the practitioner of politics. We shall return to this question in the next section of this chapter.

REFERENCE GROUPS

The policy-maker's problem is further complicated by the fact that opinion patterns do not reflect purely individual reactions to issues, but strongly felt attachments to preferred *group positions*. There is a good deal of evidence that individuals at all levels of age, sex, income, and education look to some group to find their cues about public policy questions, rather than first independently determining their position and then looking for the group or leader that most closely expresses their preferences. This phenomenon leads to a search for the most influential "reference group." Some hold that it is the individual's primary, face-to-face group contacts; others that it is his nationality, racial origin, religion, social status, or income class; still others that it is his experiences and affiliations with an economic (industrial, occupational), professional, social, or esthetic improvement group.

The significance of these reference groups is that the leaders of opinion in each group must be taken into account in analyzing or appraising the state of public opinion at any given moment. In the total process linking opinion to policy formation, the interactions between the significant leadership elements of these groups probably plays a larger part than massive movements of sentiment and belief among the politically responsive population at large.[11]

The initiative in taking steps to provoke changes in either policy or opinion may come from citizen groups, influentials along the channels of mass attention (such as newspaper columnists or television commentators), or political or administrative officials in the government hierarchy. The course of events which shapes the ultimate distribution of public opinion does not occur according to a fixed pattern, and the effective determination of policy may occur at earlier rather than later stages of opinion crystallization. Policy decisions may not wait until some ideal fixed public opinion distribution is determined; the really significant discussions may occur during as well as after the flow of information from government and mass media to the public, and with the continuous feedback of reactions from public to policy-makers.

Exact congruence, therefore, between decisions or public policy and the distribution of public opinion is not to be expected as a normal occurrence but as something that is constantly being more or less approximated. The main factors affecting the extent of this congruence between policy and opinion can be summarized as follows:

1. *The extent of participation* by the public at large in the opinion-policy process. This can be measured by the public's attentiveness (awareness of the issue); its concern (intensity of interest); its possession of considered attitudes based on information; and its transmission of its attitudes (feedback) to policy-makers.

2. *The shape of the distribution of public opinions.* This can be affected by the situation in which a given issue is created or raised; the particular attention groups affected by the issue; the extent to which the members of such groups are cross-pressured by conflicting group affiliations, loyalties, or perspectives; and time—that is, the rapidity of the mass response—and the course of events.

3. *The behavior of opinion leaders and opinion-makers* in taking account of the anticipated reactions of their particular publics and of the general public; in communicating with their own groups and leaders of other groups; in formulating policies and taking the trouble to conceptualize them in ways that will find public understanding and acceptance (a famous example: FDR's "garden hose" analogy to explain Lend-Lease to the British in 1941).

4. *The manner in which information, views, and acts are presented* to the mass public audience by opinion-makers and opinion leaders. This may include such factors as distortions, misrepresentations and mis-

[11] The general, common interest in this view becomes that of a "potential public," constructed out of the configuration of relevant reference groups on each salient issue. Cf. D. B. Truman, *The Governmental Process* (New York: Alfred A. Knopf, 1951). Also H. Ziegler, *Interest Groups in American Society* (Englewood Cliffs, N.J.: Prentice-Hall, Inc., 1964); H. W. Ehrmann (ed.), *Interest Groups on Four Continents* (Pittsburgh: University of Pittsburgh Press, 1958).

understandings, as well as positive, constructive programs for informing and persuading mass audiences by opinion leaders and controllers of communications channels.

The first two of the above factors were emphasized in this section; we turn now to the last two.

Opinion-makers and the Formation of Opinion

Three broad categories of persons influential in initiating and guiding the formation of individual and mass opinions come immediately to mind. These categories, and some (though by no means all) of their possible subdivisions, are enumerated in the following list.

I. Leaders of non-governmental groups
   A. Leaders of associations
      1. Economic interest groups (AFL-CIO, American Petroleum Institute)
      2. Professional associations (American Medical Association)
      3. Societies for moral improvement and civic reform (WCTU, SPCA)
      4. Mass movements (Communist Party, Ku Klux Klan, Congress of Racial Equality)
      5. Political parties (Democratic, Republican, Socialist-Labor, Conservative)
   B. Institutions
      1. Corporation, trade union, and foundation executives
      2. College presidents and educators
      3. Prominent clergymen
      4. Other status leaders
II. Communications specialists (public and private)
   A. Newspaper, magazine, and radio and television executives
   B. Reporters, columnists, commentators
   C. Public relations counselors and executives of advertising agencies
   D. Public information and public relations officers
   E. Certain artists, motion picture personalities and the like
III. Public officials
   A. Elected political representatives
      1. Executives (mayors, governors, Presidents and their advisers and assistants)
      2. Legislators
   B. Appointed officials
      1. Heads of civilian departments and agencies (and their policy advisers and assistants)
      2. The heads of the military establishment
   C. Judges (appointed or elected)

An important category of opinion-maker not included in the above classification is the opinion leader in face-to-face groups, such as the family, church, place of work, neighborhood, or social gathering. Such persons play a very important role, particularly in local communities, in the basic opinion-forming processes of society for persons who constantly look to others for guidance in social attitudes and manners. In the wider political culture, however, when differences in public opinion turn not upon matters of moral consensus, style, or fashion but upon controversial, debatable issues of public policy, issues and attitudes are shaped to a greater degree by leaders of the more remote, secondary attention groups such as those listed above.

Opinion-makers, then, are those people who by virtue of their representative position, their strategic location in the communications process, or simply the sheer frequency of their exposure to mass attention, acquire influence over the formation and expression of significant group perceptions and attitudes. How they develop their views and opinions, and the reasons underlying the typical or unexpected judgments they express, are crucially important for democratic politics. In the next chapter we shall discuss organized group expression, interest groups, political parties and mass movements. For present purposes we are primarily interested in how opinion-makers take public attitudes into account in formulating strategy, long-range programs, and specific policy decisions, and in how they deliberately seek to shape, mold, or prepare public attitudes in a manner conducive to their objectives.

THE INTELLIGENCE PROCESS

That all governments ultimately rest upon opinion is an ancient idea in politics. Insofar as it implies the notion of "consent" it is ambiguous. But it has another meaning; namely, that in every political system there are political intelligence operations whereby rulers and policy-makers discover the range and distribution of public sentiment, estimate its intensity and urgency, and anticipate probable public reactions. "Political intelligence" in this sense refers to the systematic gathering, presentation, and analysis of data and to the interpretation of the significance of these data on public expectations, demands, and morale.[12]

Not all opinion-making is based upon intelligence, and certainly not all opinions find adequate and accurate reflection in policy-making councils, either governmental or non-governmental. This imperfect correlation between information about popular feelings and wants and policy-making or decision-making authority might be asserted as a law

---

[12] This definition follows that of Harold D. Lasswell, developed in several articles written in 1941 and 1942 and reprinted in *The Analysis of Political Behavior* (London: Kegan Paul, 1947), pp. 1–12, 120–33, 296–303, rather than the conception of military and strategic intelligence focusing upon national security outlined by Pettee, Kent, and Hilsman and set forth in Harry Howe Ransom, *Central Intelligence and National Security* (Cambridge, Mass.: Harvard University Press, 1958).

or postulate of politics. The reasons may be technical (for example, the crudity of intelligence-gathering instruments); they may be constitutional or legal (for example, the provisions or customs prescribing the selection and composition of policy-making bodies); or they may be moral and political (for example, societal norms and expectations about how many individuals or groups should participate in the policy-making process). The essential point, analytically speaking, is not whether opinion-makers and policy-makers are inevitably few compared to the whole number of citizens, and therefore oligarchical, but in what ways and to what extent policies are conditioned and shaped by the attitudes and views of the governed, the members of the political society.

Some examples may be instructive. Consider the problem President Franklin D. Roosevelt faced in deciding how the United States, short of war, could render effective assistance to Great Britain after the fall of Norway, Denmark, France, and the Low Countries in the spring of 1940, when the American people were so deeply divided between intervention and non-involvement in European quarrels. Reflect upon the problem of an editor (say of *The New York Times*) deeply convinced that Western Europe in 1947 and 1948 was about to succumb to the forces of internal and international communism unless American economic assistance was somehow brought into the precarious balance of political forces in these countries. Or again, how did the business and civic leaders of Pittsburgh visualize the problem of energizing a whole metropolitan area to attack slum blight at the heart of the central city by deliberate planning and urban redevelopment? In none of the suggested cases was the intelligence process a simple matter of taking an opinion poll and following the course the poll indicated. In the 1941 situation, where that was actually done,[13] the evidence indicated that attitudes were deeply divided; if public opinion had literally been in control in that instance, no course of action would have been clearly indicated, and *inaction* could logically have been inferred. Of course some people and some groups wanted action, others did not, and still others knew or cared little or nothing either way. The problem was whether the inactive and opposition groups could be weakened or placed on the defensive and a feeling of enthusiastic support or passive acceptance generated by the groups organized behind the action program. Intelligence, in short, does not always result in action—it may inhibit it —but it does help to outline the dimensions of a problem more clearly

13 The attitudinal evidence in the case of Roosevelt's foreign policy was reported by Hadley Cantril, "Public Opinions in Flux," *Annals of the American Academy of Political and Social Science*, Vol. 220 (March 1942), 136–52. The policy-making story is told by Henry L. Stimson and McGeorge Bundy, *On Active Service in Peace and War* (New York: Harper & Row, Publishers, 1947), chaps. 14–15. Concerning *The New York Times* illustration, see Lester H. Markel, *Public Opinion and Foreign Policy* (New York: Harper & Row, Publishers, 1949). For the Pittsburgh case, see H. Cohen, "Essentials for Success in City Planning," *The American City*, LXIII (November 1948). For other examples, see Edward L. Bernays, *Public Relations* (Norman, Okla.: University of Oklahoma Press, 1952), part II, pp. 156ff.

and precisely; and it suggests what steps need to be taken if a given policy is to be more nearly acceptable and therefore feasible.

On the basis of political intelligence, then, opinion-makers may visualize several different types of opinion situation, each of which may affect differently the way public attitudes condition policy alternatives. One situation is that of passive, negative obstruction, the result of sheer ignorance, apathy, or irritation. Here the opinion-maker's problem may be to arouse mass awareness or to sharpen attention; it may also be to estimate the possibility (and risk) of enacting legislation or issuing administrative orders without much public reaction of any sort. In another kind of situation the public is divided into two or more sensitive attention groups (the W-shaped or U-shaped distributions described earlier), corresponding to rather sharply opposed views whose latent explosive power can be set off by the use of stereotyped symbols, images, or word pictures. A third situation might be described as that of a predominant predisposition, sometimes hatred, which creates an atmosphere of expectancy or demand that can be whipped up by opinion-makers in such a way as to force policy decisions that responsible officials would prefer not to make. The influence of the "yellow press" in forcing the United States into war with Spain in 1898 against President McKinley's judgment is often referred to as an example of public opinion being "ahead" of its leaders. In its extreme forms—mass hysteria and mob rule—this type of opinion situation inhibits any kind of deliberate, rational adjustment of policy to the requirements of the public interest.

Although the point cannot be proved, it seems possible that in fairly stable political systems combining popular participation with constitutional procedures of representation and deliberation the most satisfactory relationship between public attitudes and official policy-making occurs when the public is in a *state of readiness* to hear debate on specific measures proposed by the government. This readiness is usually achieved through abstract phrases about general aims, the slogans leading the public to accept, if not to embrace, the government's aims. The slogans are constantly repeated in election speeches, party platforms, educational or advertising campaigns, or dramatically staged press and television interviews.[14] All this by no means implies that controversy is eliminated, but when the public has been so educated or prepared to accept debate and discussion of specific measures, controversy is confined to the *methods* of achieving the broad goals formulated by the opinion-makers. Many who admire the British system of cabinet government are impressed above all by the way British electoral politics approximates this type of relationship between public attitudes, electoral propaganda, and official action.

[14] Walter Lippmann, *Public Opinion* (New York: The Macmillan Company, 1922), chaps. 13–15. For a case study illustrating the proposition in the text, see E. E. Witte, *The Development of the Social Security Act* (Madison, Wis.: University of Wisconsin Press, 1962).

PROPAGANDA, PERSUASION, AND OPINION-SHAPING

Opinion-makers may, and often do, seek to influence or change opinions by education, that is, by applying to political persuasion logical and scientific methods of factual observation and reasoning which enable their audiences to determine for themselves the validity of the opinion or policy being advocated. Unfortunately, however, in much discussion of public affairs the conditions of educational communication are utterly lacking. The aim is not to discover the truth but to win an argument; to appeal to emotion, interest, or the desire for power; to convince by crude or subtle means that this or that person or view is "good" or "bad" rather than accurate, competent, or qualified. Broadly speaking, any effort to manipulate, shape, or influence mass opinion by the use of significant symbols is *propaganda*. But some forms of propaganda may be called "black," because they are deliberately based upon deception, falsity of content, and concealment of source and purpose; whereas others may be called "white," because they openly admit their purpose and source and disclose the special interest or group on whose behalf the effort to influence opinion is being made. Under such definitions, most public relations and advertising campaigns may properly be labeled "white propaganda," as can most election campaign publicity, governmental information programs, and corporation and interest group advertising.

In very broad terms, opinions may be changed either by changing an individual's underlying attitudes and perceptions and the terms in which they were learned, or by altering the conditions under which the individual formed or learned them. Propaganda usually resorts to the former procedure. It has an infinite number of tricks and gadgets, but the essence of the procedure of disseminating beliefs or instilling and modifying attitudes consists in certain basic psycho-physical processes:

1. The arousal of attention by inducing a state of anxiety through repeated exposure of the audience to a stimulus-symbol.

2. When a neuro-physiological need or demand for relief of stress and anxiety has been induced, an outlet or focus for this emotional tension in the form of an object of hate, fear, anger, affection, prestige, strength, or awe is provided.

3. The association of this object of emotional attachment or repulsion with a simple, easily grasped and expressed formula of belief, loyalty-ritual, and program.

4. The communication of the symbols of belief, loyalty, demand, and aspiration under conditions that minimize or inhibit rational thought and maximize the suggestibility of the audience, and so far as possible produce sensations of physical gratification, emotional relief, and personal reward of well-being.

The similarity of these propositions to the theory behind Pavlov's well-known experiments on animals requires no elaboration, and explicit application of these techniques to "brain-washing" in politics, medical treatment of battle psychoses, and treatment of prisoners have been dramatically illustrated in such situations as the German concentration camps, the Russian "confession trials," and the experiences of many World War II and Korean prisoners. What requires explanation, however, is not so much the presence of such evils in a world where men can look with equanimity upon the distortion, destruction, and deliberate mutilation of human personality; inhumanity to man is not new in history. Rather, what requires explanation is the everyday presence in modern society of such phenomena as widespread personal alienation and the disintegration of social structure that is reflected in lack of personal and interpersonal standards of respect and obligation; in group hostilities; and in the loss of political identification, the comfort and pride of belonging. It is all very well to assert that men are not mere animals, that the meaning of being human is the capacity of man to symbolize, to think, and to choose the higher over the baser, lower values. And it is all very well to say that man cannot be manipulated according to the simple, conditioned-reflex, stimulus-response model of animal psychology. But society, and particularly the social scientist, must face the fact that the deterioration of social structure, the complexity of economic organization, the inadequacy of education among large segments of the population, and the technological potential in modern mass communications are conditions which make it all too possible that human beings may sink to the level of crowd or herd behavior simply by virtue of their ignorance, apathy, feelings of impotence or incompetence, or lack of training and channels for effectively expressing their wills and choices.

Of course all opinion-makers do not operate upon the assumptions of the fascist, totalitarian conception of power, or seek to dominate and manipulate human beings as if they were so many sheep. Opinion formation proceeds in many other ways and under many other conditions. But political communication—the transmission of personal views and opinions upon issues and objects of public concern—proceeds often enough in the language of propaganda, advertising, and public relations to preclude our assuming that scientific, logical thought and rational discussion is the normal mode of opinion-making in politics. The mode in any system may be more or less rational or more or less propagandistic; and a major problem for those who believe the rational mode to be preferable is to discover and investigate the conditions which promote and inhibit it. But no student of politics can understand the role of opinion in any system without paying attention to the basic theory, technique and conditions of persuasion in its several forms.

The Opinion Process and the Governing Process

In this chapter we have surveyed the institutional conditions, the personal roles of leadership and skill, and the dynamic patterns of behavior which affect the generation and shaping of public demands for political goods and services and the communication of these demands to official makers of public policy. We have rejected the eighteenth- and nineteenth-century theoretical conception of public opinion as a personified general will, the purpose of which should be ascertained and then carried out. At the same time, our analysis has been explicitly related at each step to the theory of democracy.

We have also insisted upon the importance of differentiating the opinion process from the governing process, as well as of constantly visualizing how they are related. In summing up, we can now see that the several different forms or patterns which the opinion process may take bear certain remarkable resemblances to three different models of democracy.

MAJORITARIAN OR MASS DEMOCRACY

The type of opinion situation that exists when official policy-makers are faced with overwhelming demands, obstinate, passive obstruction, or the screaming, hysterical, identification of a mob with the public personalities, propaganda, and agitational slogans of its leaders does not present a pretty picture. We do not project it here as the typical pattern of democratic opinion and policy formation. Yet, viewing the problems of mobilizing a majority opinion in a democratic society of perhaps millions of citizens, it is hard to see how one can avoid using emotional, irrational appeals that inhibit or eliminate those objective considerations that ordinarily divide men into a number of conflicting groups and views. This is not to reject the idealist thesis that a majority opinion or consensus may indeed exist in the political community, or that it really can be produced by rational methods of education and persuasion. Nor is it to reject the principle of majority rule as a practical and expedient basis for reaching decisions when each individual is assumed to count equally as one. We are simply focusing attention upon the difficulties of majoritarian democracy considered as an objective problem in opinion formation under contemporary conditions of mass political organization. We also suggest that the absolute majoritarian position, which views the opinion or policy supported by a presumed majority as right regardless of the methods by which it is produced, is extraordinarily difficult to distinguish from the viewpoint of totalitarian regimes. Such regimes easily produce formal evidence of majority support, although they provide no institutionalized restraints upon opinion-makers, nor any guarantees of individual and minority rights.

ELITIST OR GROUP DEMOCRACY

In a much more frequent type of opinion situation, perhaps as much as two-thirds or three-fourths of the citizenry appears uninterested, uninformed, or unconcerned about an issue that stirs the remainder, the attentive citizens and active policy participants. Under these conditions, the formulation of public policy appears to be a genuine process of adjusting, negotiating, and compromising the interests and policy positions of the well-informed and closely affected individuals and groups. If this conception is considered to be the typical model of how public opinion and policy are formed, however, we are faced with the problem of reconciling our democratic values with what is really minority rule, or oligarchical democracy. For under the conditions we have just described, the forms of democracy are manipulated by the leaders of the most active, influential, and powerful groups, because both long-range political stability and short-range policy decisions depend upon agreement or consensus among these powerful minorities. The realization of how much public opinion and policy-making actually approximates this pattern leads both cynical and realistic observers to say: "All government tends to be of the many by the few, that is, by minorities or oligarchies." Acceptance of this view as either inevitable or right leads to the conclusion that democracy is impossible or undesirable.

CONSTITUTIONAL, PLURALIST DEMOCRACY

If the analysis in the present chapter is correct, however, men and societies do have a choice between domination by minorities and genuine participation by the governed in the formation of opinion and control of policy-makers. The necessary conditions for effective participation by citizens, for effective democratic linkage between the opinion process and the governing process, would appear to be, first, explicit recognition of the need for and the costs of political leadership and participation through organization; second, comprehension of and skill in the techniques of political communication on the part of opinion-makers and leaders of group and official opinion; and finally, popular respect for and maintenance of institutionalized standards and restraints upon opinion-makers and policy-makers.

These standards and restraints, in the last analysis, rest upon deep and abiding belief, shared by both leaders and followers, in the democratic values: in the worth of every individual personality, and in the necessity for certain basic guarantees of fairness and justice in treating individuals' physical, material, moral, and spiritual interests. The viability of democratic processes, then, depends upon the development of official and group leaders who believe in the supremacy of public values over personal and private interests and in the development of citizens who possess both competence for political participation and moral commitment to democratic incentives and institutional restraints.

SUGGESTIONS FOR ADDITIONAL READING

ALMOND, G. A., *The American People and Foreign Policy* (New York: Harcourt, Brace & World, 1950).

——, and S. VERBA, *The Civic Culture* (Princeton, N.J.: Princeton University Press, 1963).

CATER, D., *The Fourth Branch of Government* (Boston: Houghton Mifflin Company, 1959).

INKELES, A., *Public Opinion in Soviet Russia* (Cambridge, Mass.: Harvard University Press, 1950).

KORNHAUSER, W., *The Politics of Mass Society* (New York: The Free Press of Glencoe, 1960).

LANE, R. E., and D. D. SEARS, *Public Opinion* (Englewood Cliffs, N.J.: Prentice-Hall, Inc., 1964).

LOWELL, A. L., *Public Opinion and Popular Government* (New York: The Macmillan Company, 1915).

LINDZEY, G. (ed.), *Handbook of Social Psychology* (Cambridge, Mass.: Addison-Wesley Publishing Company, 1954).

MEAD, G. H., *Mind, Self and Society* (Chicago: The University of Chicago Press, 1934).

MERRIAM, C. E., *The Making of Citizens*, and other volumes of the Civic Training Series (Chicago: The University of Chicago Press, 1931).

SMITH, B. M. et al., *Opinions and Personality* (New York: John Wiley and Sons, 1956).

Chapter 14

ELECTIONS, GROUPS, AND PARTIES:

The Representation of Political Interests

In the preceding chapter the relation between citizens and the official makers of public policy was viewed, primarily from the standpoint of the citizen, as a process of communication. But important as it is to understand the process of *articulating* social and political interests and to realize the consequences of differing conceptions of how public opinion is or should be formed, it is also necessary to recognize another aspect of the political process. This is the historical fact that at any given time a political society or system possesses a set of formal rules and informal habits for selecting its rulers and arranging for their orderly displacement and succession. A considerable portion of the constitutional history of Western democracies in the nineteenth and twentieth centuries was concerned with struggles over the electoral arrangements whereby previously hereditary, customary, or elective rulers were subjected to more democratic choice by popular election—a fact which helps to explain why the formal electoral system is a central feature of most governments calling themselves democratic. But elections are not automatic, self-executing, mechanical devices; they have to be managed, set up, and put into operation, and they must be meshed with the non-electoral parts of the governmental system. As a rule, governments do not explicitly differentiate these processes of *leadership selection* and *system management* from the expression of interests and formulation of public policy. This chapter attempts to show how the electoral and party systems (or *subsystems*, from the standpoint of the political system as a whole) affect in advance the citizen-government relationship.

The Electoral System

The Electoral Function. After his study of how political opinion is formed, transmitted, and translated into governing decisions, the reader is not likely to be satisfied with a simple definition of democracy as "rule by the people." To supply some rational basis for democracy, he needs answers to a new set of questions. For instance, how many and what type of governmental decisions should be made by the electorate? Are the meaning and interpretation of the constitution determined by formal decision of the voters? Political systems around the world exhibit countless varieties of detailed arrangements that might provide answers to such questions, yet we find uniformities in the operation of systems that appear to be ideologically quite different, if not opposed.

Generally speaking, governments that derive their claim to legitimacy from the people as the source of ultimate authority reserve to the electorate certain authorizing functions: the adoption and amendment of the constitution or organic laws establishing the basic features of the political system and the selection of the personnel who compose the highest law-making and executive bodies. The election of high political officials is considered a legitimizing process. While elections need not be held at fixed intervals, some relatively frequent renewal of the popular mandate is thought necessary in a democratic system. The interval for consulting the electorate on constitutional change is somewhat longer. In the United States, only New York and Michigan follow Jefferson's advice that there ought to be a constitutional revolution, in the form of a convention, every generation (their constitutions require a convention every 20 years); and there has been no comprehensive national constitutional revision since 1789. Except for parliamentary systems, in which the amending process is virtually identical with the legislative process, constitutional amendments are almost everywhere submitted either to specially chosen conventions or to the electorate for approval.

Evidently, few political systems follow in practice the dictum that the people *en masse* should make most of the governing decisions; on the contrary, most systems minimize the number of decisions made directly by the voters, preferring to expand the scope of legislative and administrative decision-making. Practical reasons are generally cited for adopting this course. A few political jurisdictions, however—Switzerland and California, for example—do just the opposite and seriously attempt to let the electorate decide as many legislative questions as possible. To this end they make use of the *initiative,* a formal petition, signed by a required number of voters, to enact or amend statutory law; this is followed at the next general or special election by a *referendum,* a yes-or-no vote on the question contained in the initiative petition.

When fundamental policy questions are submitted to the electorate the term *plebiscite* is sometimes used.

Critics of the initiative, the referendum, and other institutions of "direct democracy" often point to the simple, yes-or-no, either-or character of the choice presented to the voters; to the lack of face-to-face discussion of often very complex questions; to the fact that the voter has little information about the issue and little inclination to analyze it; to the usually low level of voter participation; and, above all, to the difficulty of presenting an adequate formulation of the issue when most political decisions of the sort submitted to referendum involve extremely technical, many-faceted considerations. And indeed, as we have seen, the principle of "rule by consent of the governed" generally means that the people through the ballot shall elect their rulers and approve the basic frame of government. To support this principle, an electoral system must fulfill certain basic requirements. It must first produce a government—a set of responsible political leaders capable of acting in concert and of agreeing upon policies with a substantial degree of direction and stability. The purposes and policies of elected governments must find substantial support from a majority of the electorate. The main segments of opinion in the electorate must feel that their views are effectively reflected in those participating in the decision-making process.

Yet these requirements raise a host of difficult problems. Are they mutually incompatible? If, for example, preference is given to the criterion of strong and effective government, will the objective of adequate reflection of the shades of electoral opinion be sacrificed? Can the requirements be satisfied simultaneously? If not, which have priority over the others? We shall not suggest that there is an easy and ready answer for the student, let alone for the practicing politician; but if political institutions are to be shaped by man it seems clear that he must keep these criteria in mind and decide upon the effects he wishes his institutional arrangements to produce.

Suffrage and Political Participation. The right to vote has always been defined by law, statutory or customary. Extension or restriction of the suffrage has been the subject of political and constitutional controversy at least since the period of the Greek and Roman city-states. Regulation of the suffrage has been a means for establishing a preferred role in political affairs for some categories of citizens as against others, presumably with a view to achieving some kind of balance or ranking among groups and classes in the political society. Over the long run, the world has witnessed steady movement toward the criterion of equal adult suffrage, not only in Europe and the Americas but in the developing countries of Asia and Africa.

The advent of democracy in large-scale governments at the end of the eighteenth century foreshadowed universal suffrage but did not

immediately produce it. True, the principle of political equality acknowledged by these governments did alter the older class-based forms of
political discrimination, such as the restriction of the suffrage to certain types of property owners or to adherents of certain religions; at the
same time, however, it introduced new forms. A minimum age limit for
voting was usually adopted, and frequently a higher one was required for
office-holding. Women were not permitted to vote for many years—in
some "modern" countries like France, not until the middle of the twentieth century (1944). At present citizenship and some arbitrary length
of residence within the political jurisdiction is an almost universal requirement. Many political jurisdictions disqualify voters for "mental
incapacity" and for conviction of a felony. From 1918 to 1936 the USSR
excluded from political participation members of the Tsarist dynasty and
ruling class, persons employing hired labor for profit, persons living
on unearned income, private businessmen, monks, clergymen, and
agents of the Tsarist police.

In addition, election laws sometimes set up special qualifications
that may have a disqualifying or a "weighting" effect. These may be
based upon education, in which case they are usually called literacy
tests (although the simple principle of literacy may have far wider
implications); upon income, property ownership, or taxpaying differen-
tials; or upon status, defined by the holding of certain public offices,
occupations, or titles. Similarly, the wealthy or specially favored groups
may be given extra votes. In elections for the Reichstag under the Second
German Empire (1871–1918), for example, voters were grouped into
three categories based upon tax payments, with one-third of the votes
allotted to the minority paying the first third of tax receipts, and so on.
Other examples are the British practice of allotting Parliamentary seats
to Oxford and Cambridge Universities before 1948, and the plural vote,
such as the short-lived "Coutts franchise" in Kenya, which gave men
from one to three votes depending upon their ability to qualify under one
or more of seven special categories.

One final point deserves particular emphasis: the administration
of the suffrage has a tremendous effect upon voters' attitudes. Regardless of the letter of the suffrage laws, their application necessarily affords
an opportunity for manipulation by election officials. How the suffrage
is administered, as much as who formally has the right to vote, determines the quality of expectation, competence, and meaning that the
individual citizen brings to the act of voting. This is why, also, "free"
elections are never supposed to be administered by the military.

Apportionment and Majority Rule. How shall the members of the electorate be classified for purposes of choosing their representatives and
rulers? This depends a great deal upon the conception of society prevailing in a given political system at the time its electoral system is
established, as well as upon the conception of the purposes of elections

entertained by the politically influential groups that participate in making the constitution.

In medieval societies, representatives were generally considered to be corporate representatives of "society." That is, the several politically important "estates" or "corporations" of the realm, such as the nobles clergy, and "commons" (which last term might mean non-noble landowners or merchants or guildsmen, but never "common people"), were the proper units of representation. Modern variations of the medieval idea are the guild-socialist conception of functional group representation —the election of representatives by all those working in a given occupation or industry, by professional associations, or by specially-defined entities like the Italian Fascist "corporations" (1922–1944) and the German Nazi "service frames" (1934–1945).

In the nineteenth century, utilitarian-democratic theory produced the conception of individual or numerical representation. Individuals, grouped into legal entities like counties, boroughs, or districts roughly equal in population were considered to constitute the appropriate electoral unit. Whereas this idea of numerical representation assumed fixed, geographic constituencies, more recent refinements have centered around a notion of mathematically determined, voluntary, mobile constituencies. In principle, under this system, generally called proportional representation or "P.R.," any group of citizens who feel a strong enough common interest are entitled to have their representative or representatives in the government. This can be accomplished by ensuring that any number of people who can mobilize a "quota" (a number of votes roughly equal to the total electorate divided by the number of representatives to be elected) can elect a representative. To this end, multi-member constituencies must be utilized. Then if, say, 100,000 people are to elect 10 representatives, 10,001 Baptists who agree on one representative could elect him; so could 10,001 machinists, 10,001 farmers, 10,001 Democrats, 10,001 Irish nationalists, or any other 10,001 people who could agree to vote for a common candidate. And each representative so elected would represent a constituency formed voluntarily and not tied to any specific geographic area or established functional group. Thus the constituencies represented would not necessarily be the same from one election to the next, but would change (or be "mobile") as people's conceptions of the interests they want represented change.

From these examples it will be seen that the choice of the unit of representation conditions the electoral system, partly to protect the interests of established groups within the system and partly to ensure whatever balance in the formal governing or legislative structure is deemed desirable by the political influentials who designed the system. In democratic, national states some combination of the territorial and population units of representation is almost universally conceded to be the proper embodiment of the principles of individual participation and general consent of the governed. In predemocratic societies, on the other hand, individual voters have frequently been classified on some "communal" basis, so that they vote separately by tribe, for example, or religion, caste, or racial community. Unless the sentiment of national loyalty transcends these communal bodies, electoral organization based upon them is likely to deepen and re-enforce the older, more narrowly-based loyalties, with deeply divisive effects upon the unity and cohesion of the larger political entity. The same comment applies to the use of functional group representation in more advanced countries.

Another form of electoral organization is the device of *indirect* election, that is, the election of officials not directly by the voters but by electoral colleges composed of other public officials or of some similar relatively small group of persons who have themselves been chosen by the voters. Before the widespread acceptance of the democratic ideology, indirect elections were frankly justified as a means of securing the "better judgment" of a small body of citizens more qualified than the "mass" of ordinary citizens; in *The Federalist,* No. 68, Alexander Hamilton offered just such an explanation of the American electoral college. Today, indirect elections are rarely the principal means of electoral participation, but they are by no means uncommon as supplementary devices. In some systems they are used to provide a means of securing control of higher political bodies by some non-electoral political group, as the Communist Party controls the Soviets in the USSR. In others, such as the French Fifth Republic, Holland, and Sweden, they provide a different base of representation for choosing second chambers of the national legislatures. In some of the newer African states, where there is no sense of national political identity, indirect elections restrict local electorates (such as village meetings) to choosing representatives to a higher, territorially more inclusive body (district or regional). This higher body in turn elects representatives to the state or province level, and that still higher body, to the national body. Russian Soviets are constituted on such a four-step basis, which facilitates infiltration of these bodies by Party nominees.

Another important characteristic of an electoral system is the number of representatives chosen from the constituency. Advocates of a single-member (as opposed to a multi-member) district system argue that it is more important to provide a legislative majority, which the single-member system presumably ensures, than to secure fair and accurate representation of minorities, the presumed effect of multi-member districts. (Note that the issue does not arise in the case of electing a single executive or judicial officer.) But the question of which is preferable is complicated by how many or how few effective party organizations there are, by the presence or absence in the country of habits and attitudes permitting party government, and by the fact that a single-member system does not necessarily follow from a two-party system, nor a multi-member system from a multi-party system. The multi-member district system, also called the general-ticket system, could conceivably utilize the entire country as one electoral district, with the whole national electorate considered the unit of representation; for practical reasons, however, a country under this system is usually divided into an arbitrary number of territorial units.

Two final characteristics of an electoral system are the type of ballot it employs and its method of calculating who wins. Again, the usual basis for evaluation is the preference for majority government *versus* fair and adequate representation of minorities. Broadly speaking, there are three balloting methods—majority, preferential, and proportional—with almost limitless possibilities for variation and combination. These are presented in Table 14.1, with a brief indication of their major purposes and effects.

There is a great deal of historical and statistical evidence to indicate that the single-member district, coupled with the plurality winner principle, tends to favor the election of a legislature composed of a majority and one minority party. In contrast, proportional representation systems encourage the formation and continuation of a number of minority parties of varying sizes, none of them likely to obtain a working legislative majority. Research has been unable to prove, however, whether the electoral system is the cause or the result of a particular kind of political system. It would indeed be more plausible to argue that the managers of a political system tend to adopt the kind of electoral devices that will promote the survival of the representative system they know or prefer. Thus the need to recognize several political subcultures —monarchist, clericalist, liberal, and socialist—probably made some form of proportional representation essential in most continental European countries. The English-speaking countries, by contrast, preferred the single-member plurality system, because in addition to providing local, sectional, and group representation, it also furnished an effective counterweight to the executive power. The issue, then, is not simply whether a legislative majority is preferable to a coalition of legislative minorities, although it has classically been debated in such abstract, formal terms.[1] The English-American preference for majority-minority representation arose from the need to make an historically achieved separation of legislative and executive powers effective as well as representative; the continental European preference for P.R. was a response to the problem of legitimizing and protecting minority political opposition and counterbalancing the tradition of an absolute executive supported by a highly centralized bureaucracy.

Criteria for Judging Electoral Systems. Some further questions may be asked about electoral institutions and expectations. What kind of representatives do they produce? What attitudes do they generate on

---

[1] The classic statement of this controversy can be found in John Stuart Mill, *Representative Government* (London: J. M. Dent & Sons, Everyman's Library edition, 1910), chap. 7 (first published 1861); and Walter Bagehot, *The English Constitution* (London: Oxford University Press, 1928), chap. 5 (first published 1867).

the part of the elected representatives toward the dual problems of representing and of governing? What effects do they have in educating and training voters to their responsibilities as citizens?

The concept of representation is basic in any theory of democratic government that is applied to a larger domain than the town meeting or small group, yet it is as ambiguous as almost any notion in political science. What is being represented? The term *constituency* usually refers to those for whom the representative acts or speaks in his district, but this may mean his close friends and supporters, or more broadly the voters who nominated and elected him, or in ideal terms, it may include the entire population of his district. But other factors are involved in the representative relationship.[2] One is how the representative in practice goes about ascertaining the will of his amorphous principal and thereupon arrives at his decisions. Another is how he views his function in the legislative structure or system—that is, how he answers the question: "What am I personally here to do?" Fourth, what attitude does he have toward the powerful group influences, external or internal to the legislative system, that influence his thinking and voting on policy issues? Fifth, certain functions are performed by legislators and legislative bodies that do not involve "representation" in the sense of articulat-

Table 14.1

Electoral Units and Type of Ballot, Related to Objective of Electoral System

Electoral Unit	Type of Ballot, Method of Count	Objectives or Effects
Single-member district Multi-member district may be used with each voter having as many votes as seats to be chosen.	*Single vote* 1. Relative majority or plurality winner ("first past the post") 2. Absolute majority (50.1% or more) a. Repeated ballots b. Second ballot or "runoff" (several variations) among leaders on first ballot. c. Alternative ballot.	*To produce majority winner* 1. Tends to narrow voter's choice to available or probable winner. 2. Favors best-organized electoral minorities. 3. Majority of popular vote tends to be over-reflected and minority under-reflected in number of seats won. 4. Gerrymandering and population shifts produce inequities in value of vote between districts.

[2] Elaboration of the multiple aspects of the "representational role" is a distinct contribution of Heinz Eulau, in John C. Wahlke et al., *The Legislative System: Explorations in Legislative Behavior* (New York: John Wiley and Sons, 1962), chaps. 11–13.

Table 14.1 (Continued)

Electoral Unit	Type of Ballot, Method of Count	Objectives or Effects
Multi-member district	*Preferential ballot* (Plurality Winner) 1. Single, non-transferable vote 2. Limited vote Voter has fewer votes than seats to be chosen. 3. Cumulative vote Voter has as many votes as seats, but may cast them at will for one candidate or divided among several. 4. Preferential vote Voter numbers candidates by order of preference, and candidates are awarded votes weighted accordingly.	*To permit representation of minority candidates* 1. May result in either majority or minority representation, with tendency toward latter. 2. Minority political groups may manipulate the system so as to distort and frustrate individual voter's choice.
Multi-member district Electoral quotient required to elect (total vote divided by number of seats to be chosen.)	*Proportional representation* (I) 1. List system Voter casts one ballot for entire party list. Parties nominate as many candidates as there are seats, and seats are awarded to parties a. As many times as party vote contains quotient, and then in accordance with largest remainders. b. By highest average vote per seat after each seat is allocated one by one.	*To secure representation of political groups in proportion to ratio of total vote* 1. Minority groups secure representation in rough proportion to share of total vote. 2. Method of allocating remainders has discriminatory effects on large and small parties. 3. Value of vote varies between parties.
Multi-member district Quota necessary to elect determined by dividing total vote by number of seats plus 1 and adding 1.	*Proportional representation* (II) 1. Single, transferable vote Voter ranks candidates in order of preference on ballot; seats allocated by successive choices; lowest ranking candidates are successively eliminated and votes redistributed according to alternative choices until quota has been obtained by number of candidates equal to number of seats.	*To reflect most accurately gradations of individual voter's preferences* 1. Reflects most accurately of all systems individual voter's intention. 2. De-emphasizes parties and emphasizes individual candidates. 3. Produces mobile constituencies based on small party group or class lines rather than fixed, territorial boundaries.

Note: For elaboration of electoral mechanics and effects, see E. Lakeman and J. D. Lambert, *Voting in Democracies* (1955); and W. J. M. Mackenzie, *Free Elections* (1958).

ing the opinions of constituents on general laws or public policies at all, but have to do with such mandatory duties as helping constituents, participating in legislative management, investigating executive agencies, and informing and educating constituents. These problems are considered further in the next chapter; for the present, these five dimensions or aspects of representation can be taken as criteria for judging representatives' behavior.

Surprising as it may seem, there is almost no systematic empirical research into the social and personal qualities of legislators prior to the present century. An early example of such research is a comparative study of the English cabinets of 1801 and 1924 by Harold J. Laski.[3] The study sought to assess the representativeness of these ruling groups in terms of their members' social origins, education, and career lines. Laski's finding that the personnel of democratically elected legislative bodies are not typical of the populations they represent has been confirmed by almost all subsequent research.[4] Legislators elected under the single-member district plurality system are generally older, better-educated, less representative of women, wage earners, ethnic and minority groups, and more representative of professional (largely legal) occupations, business, farm proprietors, and managers, than of the general population. And at least one study has suggested that legislators are "better adjusted," at least in the sense that they have a greater capacity for "assessing reality," than the voters who elected them.[5] These findings might be interpreted as testimonial to the capacity of voters to select representatives as good as or better than they are themselves; but they also support the proposition that legislators are less representative of the dominant minority groups in society under democratic institutions than were representatives in the days of class rule and restricted electoral participation. Empirical research thus reopens an old question: Should representatives reflect accurately the kind of people who compose their electorates? Should they represent a dominant stratum of the population or society? Or should they reflect a norm or ideal which the electorate desires or ought to desire? We shall return to such questions in the next chapter.

Empirical evidence has thus far reinforced the general proposition that the effect of the single-member district plurality electoral system upon the quality of legislative representatives depends upon the party-competitive situation, the demographic composition of the district, and the political-cultural environment reflected in the legislator's personal background. In the United States, for example, the electoral system

[3] Harold J. Laski, "The Personnel of the English Cabinet: 1801–1924," *Studies in Law and Jurisprudence* (New York: 1932).
[4] Charles S. Hyneman, "Who Makes Our Laws?" *Political Science Quarterly*, LV (1940), 556 ff.; Donald R. Matthews, *The Social Background of Political Decision-Makers* (New York: Doubleday & Company, 1954); Norman Meller, "Legislative Behavior Research," *Western Political Quarterly*, XIII (1960), 131 ff.
[5] John B. McConaughy, "Certain Personality Factors of State Legislators in South Carolina," *American Political Science Review*, XLIV (1950), 897 ff.

seems to produce a relativistic, realistic, moderate, "mediator" type of representative rather than the moralistic, idealistic, logically extremist, "ideological-advocate" type. Critics of proportional representation have argued, but scarcely proved, that P.R. systems reverse this tendency.

Finally, what are the effects of an electoral system in terms of the political education of citizens, of encouraging them to participate responsibly in elections? Again, answers based on speculative fancy outnumber those based on tested knowledge. But it seems that single-member district plurality systems, insofar as they do produce legislative party majorities, have the salutary effect of making voters feel some direct responsibility for the kind of government they get. On the other hand, the P.R. systems which produce legislative minority-party fractions require coalition governments formed through negotiations among party leaders, and these produce governments constituted on grounds quite different from those which were the issues the voters faced during the election campaign. The single-member district plurality system seems to be associated with a greater degree of voter apathy and lack of information and concern than the P.R. systems. But the formal electoral system may not be the critical factor here. Many others are involved, such as the number of parties and the degree of party competition, the influence of crisis situations, and political and cultural differences extending all the way from such minor factors as attitudes toward Sunday voting to deep-seated social cleavages, differences in economic and educational levels, and differences in exposure to mass communications media.

"Free" Elections: Some Unsettled Questions. We have seen that even democratic governments make voting contingent upon certain requirements and qualifications. Yet how much and what kinds of restriction on the suffrage are compatible with democracy? How many decisions can be removed from electoral action by vesting decision-making authority in executive, legislative, judicial, and administrative officials? Must democratic elections be associated with fixed terms of office and with governmental regulation and conduct of nominating procedures? Can a democratic regime exclude anti-democratic, extremist groups from the ballot—or from any form of political participation—and remain democratic? Is political stability preferable to a system of elections that produces weak governmental regimes that are continually breaking down and contributing to domestic strife and international tensions? Is democracy possible when elections are conducted under military auspices or under the imminent threat of being nullified by military forces led by uniformed officers or civilian politicians?

That such questions are still worth asking does not mean that democracy or the various forms of authoritarian ideology have found no answers to them, nor that political science is ignorant of what kinds of institutional arrangements are associated with what patterns of order and behavior. Such questions are, rather, perennially pertinent to the problems facing both the individual. citizen and the political leader—of whatever ideological preference and conviction—in the twentieth century. Today's citizens need not only awareness, but competence and comprehension if they are to achieve free and representative self-government.

Social Structure and Political Groupings

Constitution-makers in the eighteenth and nineteenth centuries tended to assume that there was a direct, almost mechanical relationship between formal governmental structure, the electoral system, and the informal structure of society and the economy. Although political history and political theory in the nineteenth and twentieth centuries have brought greater sophistication and awareness of the complexities of governing, it is still difficult to specify exactly what we mean when we refer to the *political* functions involved in governing or managing people organized into political societies or communities. Political processes tend to be covert and hidden rather than open and manifest; political techniques are thought to be matters of practical experience and judgment rather than theoretically explicit. And rightly or wrongly, as much in professional literature as in everyday discussion, political management is often associated with authority and force, personal ambition, and compromise and corruption of principle. It is so commonly thought to be somehow incompatible with personal integrity and technical proficiency that many persons readily take for truth the quip that the only good politician is a dead statesman. But notwithstanding such obstacles to objective identification and analysis of the governing function, it is essential for the student of politics to come to grips with the nature of political management. A tentative list of activities and skills that compose the political role is suggested in Table 14.2.
The Political Class. It is probably a mistake to assume that a single group, let alone a single person, monopolizes or controls all these functions, even in the most centralized of political societies; and it is no less erroneous to assume that they are performed in a single, linear process of decision. Some may be fixed by custom and tradition, others by formal constitutional provision, executive acts, judicial decisions, or statutes. Even the most static societies have to be regulated, and the people who participate in performing the political functions constitute the "elite,"[6] or *political class*, of that society. The political class may be coextensive with a particular economic or social grouping; in a complex, industrial, organizational society, however, politicians more

[6] Note that the term "elite," as used by political scientists, does not mean "the best people." It is a neutral term which usually refers to those relatively few people in any system who perform most of the system's political activity.

probably come from many socio-economic and professional groupings. The membership and the boundaries of the political class are fluid, dynamic, and changing; the principal criterion of membership is participation in the making of important decisions that affect the distribution of influence and power in one or more of the functional categories listed in Table 14.2.

Table 14.2

Checklist of Political (Governing) Functions

General Function	*Specific Activities*
1. Political education	1. Socialization; inculcation of loyalties; ideological indoctrination
2. Leadership recruitment and training	2. Control of nominations to public office
3. Regulating the succession to top policy-making offices	3. Timing and contesting of appointments and elections
4. Directing and coordinating the official structure of legitimate authority	4. Control of: (a) Military and police (b) Organs of civilian decision-making (c) Machinery of administration
5. Raising money to finance political activity	5. Financing of election campaigns
6. Formulating or establishing the understandings between political groups which determine the stability of the regime	6. Participation in basic political decisions: (a) Constitutional "conventions" (b) Political negotiations (c) Formulating the "program" of the government, party, or administration

The political class need not be ideologically or demographically unified and homogeneous. Conflicts of interest and power among its members do, in fact, grow out of their ideological, demographic, and other differences. Such differences help to explain the autonomy of legal and administrative structures within a political system and the access to influence of all kinds of political groups whose interests are specialized, narrow, and spasmodic, rather than generalized or aiming at continuous political control. There is a continuing "great debate" between those political and social theorists who see political structure as a unified hierarchy dominated by a small group of decision-makers at its apex and those who see it as a large, somewhat amorphous group of men, drawn from the top strata of a number of representative groups, who reach decisions by a process composed partly of rational calculation, partly of bargaining based on economic sanctions, partly through skills of communication (public relations) and negotiation, and partly upon management skills derived from control of large-scale organizations resting on both professional authority and legitimate violence.

Political Groups. In the United States the term "ruling class," or even "rulers," is somehow felt to be abhorrent, inconsistent with the beliefs and values both of individualism and democracy. Policy-makers, public and private, are therefore careful to avoid the language of class separation and domination. On the other hand, "groups" and "interests," while also suspect terms, are admitted to have a necessary role in politics, so long as they are not monopolistic and their activities are open to public scrutiny. Such notions are commonly attributed to America's historic lack of hereditary land ownership, titles of nobility, and relatively fixed social classes, all of which are associated with feudal Europe. Yet these attitudes are often held concurrently with recognition of the fact that wide differences of status and influence do in fact exist and with acceptance of what is coming to be called "the organizational society." Groups and organizations—the spontaneous, informal, *ad hoc* variety as well as highly legalized, complex, institutional structures—are an outstanding feature of American society and politics, as Tocqueville noticed as early as a century and a quarter ago.

The generic role of interest groups in political communication and in the formation and transmission of opinion was portrayed in Chapter 13. Here we are concerned with the role of political and social structure in the recruitment of political leaders and the exercise of governing authority. If we think of the term "political groups" as including all those formal and informal associations in society which seek to nominate or influence the selection of governing officials, to influence the formulation of public policy, or to do both, the classifications in Table 14.3 may be useful.

Of course in practice few groups restrict themselves to any one primary interest or function. Their activities overlap, and the lines of classification are not mutually exclusive. Interest groups, for example, concern themselves with the nomination and election of candidates; political parties engage in political education and indoctrination; mass movements develop organizational units concerned both with violence and conventional election practices; and modern totalitarian ideologies explicitly assert the desirability of compulsory political unification and monopolization of political techniques through a single political group or class. Interaction between political groups is an important political function, as we saw in Table 14.2 (No. 6). Nevertheless, the classification can help direct attention to important problems for analysis, so

Table 14.3

Types of Political Groups and Their Major Interests

Group	*Primary Interest, Objective, or Functional Activity*
Interest group	Protection or promotion of particular objectives of members by influencing the content of public policies
Political (electoral) party	a. Nomination of candidates to public office b. Conduction of election campaigns c. Assumption of responsibility for conduct of government
Mass movement a. Race or national groups b. Comprehensive world views (ideologies)	a. Political education and indoctrination b. Cultural (ethical, religious, social) transformation or protection
Militarist or conspiratorial organizations	a. Overt or symbolic violence b. Monopoly of effective political power

long as one does not close his eyes to the possible variations and combinations of political functions. Finally, it is important to remember that at least three other kinds of organizations—the military and civil bureaucracy, the mass communications media, and the judicial hierarchy—although they may be professedly and institutionally "nonpolitical," have important political effects and interests in the making of public policy, and that some political cultures sanction the participation of these organizations in the contest over the personnel and conduct of government.

Societal Pluralism and Political Unity: The Emergence of Political Parties. To put the problem of political representation in greatly oversimplified terms, we may start from these three "conceptual facts": the *society*, characterized by a variety of cultural and economic groups and classes; the *formal governmental structure* in the society, which claims effective control over the instruments of legitimate coercion and is expected to establish as much moral and intellectual integration as is necessary for the political community (the society and government taken together) to cohere; and *political groupings* developed by the various social groups or classes and by occupants of positions in the official governing system as well, to act for them and to enter into alliances with other groups for the purpose of choosing political leaders and influencing public policy. The membership boundaries of these political groupings may or may not be identical with those of other social groups or classes; that is, there may be overlapping membership among many groups and types of groups, a phenomenon that constitutes one of the basic problems of political leadership and representation. No less fundamental, however, is the problem of maintaining the viability and stability of the integrating and unifying governmental regime in the midst of the struggle for control of its formal structure among the cultural, economic, and social groups seeking to protect or extend their interests and power.

The four types of political groups distinguished in Table 14.3 suggest some of the forms and methods that political activity may take. In modern times, constitutional democracies have tended to assume that the "normal" method of group representation is a competitive political party system, supplemented by the publicity and lobbying activities of pressure groups which articulate more precisely the aims of functional, status, or other types of social groups. Before the nineteenth century, however, rule by political parties was rare; and in the twentieth we have observed the rise of demands for the elimination or at least the reduction of "party politics," for direct representation of groups in administration, and for the compulsory unification of all groups in a single "party," which then becomes not a party but a bureaucratic apparatus controlling both government and society in the name of an ideology attributed to "the People," "the *Volk*," or "the Masses."

It may be helpful at this point to outline some of the ideas about representation that have accompanied the historical development of political institutions. In simpler, relatively static societies with practically no mobility from class to class, the unity of the commonwealth was usually represented by a monarch (or oligarchical council), to whom was attributed "virtual representation," that is, the right to speak for citizens or groups of citizens by virtue of his office as head of the body politic. Many political functions and practices were regulated by custom, but devices were found to represent the class groupings or "estates" (nobles, gentry, burghers, patricians, plebeians, equestrians, knights) of the realm, sometimes in an advisory capacity, sometimes in a legislative one (through such institutions as the Roman Senate or the British *Curia Regis*), and sometimes in judicial and administrative roles (such as the Roman censors, praetors, tribunes, quaestors, and aediles). The formal governmental structure of political authority was considered virtually identical with the structure of society, the dominant social class or classes naturally assuming governmental office to exercise their powers.

With the rise of absolute kings and emperors, who were elevated above all social classes and whose power rested upon control of military organization and the money-raising and judicial bureaucracy, a separation of governmental and social structure developed, although the imperial monarch sought to ally the upper classes with him through his capacity to reward with honors, titles, and privileges. Under these conditions, social position and political interests were indeed secured through military and administrative services to the king; but they were also secured through factional intrigue ("court politics"), in which groups sought access to or control of the royal presence and favor, and through diplomacy. The king's difficulties with the great landed nobles often drove him into alliances with the mercantile, financial, and industrial interests of the towns; thus the requirements of a successful "absolute" ruler came to include the ability to counterbalance opposing groups within the system of status, wealth, and power that prevailed in his realm. The separation of governmental and social structure not only resulted from the rise of absolute political regimes, but seemed in some cases to contribute to it. In France, the monarchy absorbed all authority, all honors, all power; the king became both State and Society. In contrast, in Great Britain the Tudor and Stuart theories of absolute monarchy were rejected. Further, in the seventeenth and eighteenth centuries, within the upper, influential classes there arose a historic conflict between the Tory and Whig theories of representation, the former upholding the sovereignty of the king, the latter that of Parliament, through which the landed, industrial, financial, and municipal interests might exert their influence more effectively and reduce the king's status to that of a symbolic, constitutional monarch. The results of the British "compromise" between these Whig and Tory views in the eighteenth and nineteenth centuries produced a model of parliamentary-cabinet government that has strongly influenced many political systems all over the world.

Before these developments reached fruition, however, there arose two other theories of representation which were associated with the rise of democracy and which strongly modified the formal governmental institutions of monarchical and legislative representation. One theory reflected the rediscovery of the importance of the individual, the other, the importance of society; both challenged the representativeness of the formal governmental apparatus of the time. The *liberal democratic* theory argued that executive and legislative representation should be based not upon hereditary or traditional forms of authority or upon election by groups or classes, but upon election by numerical majorities of voters, organized as nearly as possible into electoral units containing equal numbers of voters, so that each voter's vote would count equally. Later in the nineteenth century the *radical democratic* theory held that representative democracy consisted not so much in the formal relationship between voters and representative, but in the relationships between the voters as members of political parties and their party leaders, who were in a better position to translate majority opinion into legislative content than were individual legislative representatives. The liberal democratic idea of representation had retained the conception of the representative as a trustee for those who elected him; the radical democratic notion saw the party organization and leadership *outside the government* as an intermediary which should formulate and interpret the voters' views to the elected officials, whose views and judgment should be subordinated to the people's will. From the radical conception of democracy, based upon the masses of voters but asserting the need for leadership by individuals or party organizations, it was but a simple step, logically speaking, to transfer discretionary authority from the people to an authoritative ideology. The ideology might be justified as "the people's will," but in practice it could be reliably expressed only through some political party's program and policy, which had to be made controlling upon the action of formally elected legislators and executives. Professor Samuel Beer calls this the *collectivist* theory of representation.[7] The term seems applicable to Communist, fascist, racist, or any absolutist ideology which places higher value on the dictates of some received doctrine than on decisions reached through the democratic process of continuous opinion-formation and interaction between the people and representative group and official leaders.

We may now realize how crucial the problem of representation becomes when social and governmental structure become differentiated, and why the nineteenth-century experience with democracy in Western Europe and America established such a central role for the political party. Before the American and French Revolutions, what were called parties were really court factions or legislative interest groups. But the extension of the suffrage resulted in the formation of large-scale organizations of voters for the purpose of creating legislative majorities, presumably emanating from and responsible to the people.

As long as it is assumed that basic political decisions should be made peaceably by methods of discussion and persuasion and in accordance with electoral opinion ("ballots instead of bullets"), it is difficult to see how political parties can be dispensed with. But if it is assumed that not the whole people, but a minority group propagating a racial or religious doctrine or a secular ideology, or a mass movement espousing an ethical ideal, is preferable to the people as the legitimate source and agent of political authority, then the problem of representing society and government is solved by assumption, and electoral devices lose all significance as instruments of representation. From the assumed identity of society and government, it follows that competitive party government may be replaced by a "one-party state," by some form of authoritarian or corporate society, or by a military-industrial-political bureaucracy (oligarchy)—in each of which it is assumed that conflicts within the social and governmental structure should be resolved by the binding decision of a ruling group in the name of an ideology, myth, or formula.

[7] Samuel H. Beer, "Representation of Interests in British Government," *American Political Science Review*, LI (1957), 613 ff.

If it is impossible to return to the old "virtual representation" theories of monarchical or legislative representation, and if we reject the sovereignty of such contemporary absolutist conceptions as society, race, nationality, proletariat, or party as either impossibly partial or as idealized myths that necessarily produce dictatorship in practice, we are forced to resort to some system of institutionalized competition between political parties in order to perform the fundamental tasks of governing and of representing or articulating the conflicts between legitimate social interests. The late Professor Sigmund Neumann, an astute political analyst, suggested that the older conception of parties as factional groups for purposes of "individual representation," coupled with a divided, balanced governmental structure (the political theory of the American Federalists), is being replaced by parties of "social integration," coupled with a much more streamlined, unified governmental structure.[8] The meaning of this statement will become clearer when we study party organization. At this point, we conclude the discussion of political representation by re-emphasizing the importance of the values and forms whereby the official wielders of "the power to govern" are associated with the centers and groups of autonomous power in society, while both are subjected to the broad directives and limits of popular expectations and consent.

Political Parties: Electoral and Governmental

Edmund Burke's famous definition of a political party as "a body of men united for promoting by their joint endeavors the national interests upon some particular principle on which they are all agreed" is the classic conception of the political party stated in terms of ostensible purpose or program.[9] Today we would say that the definition more accurately describes an interest or pressure group, and the language is sufficiently elastic to include mass social movements as well as militarist or conspiratorial organizations. Burke also seems to have thought of the party as an "opinion group," but nowadays this function is perhaps more adequately performed by other political groups. The central, vital functions of the modern political party are electoral: to nominate candidates for the principal elective and appointive offices; to conduct election campaigns (and sometimes to run the election machinery as well); to educate the voters through comparison of the alternative candidates offered by the parties (personality evaluation) and through analysis of the issues insofar as this is possible from the candidates' statements of what their election will mean for the conduct of government.

Burke's definition virtually ignores the vital role of the party

8 Sigmund Neumann, *Modern Political Parties* (Chicago: The University of Chicago Press, 1956), pp. 404–05.
9 Edmund Burke, *Reflections on the Revolution in France* (New York: Dolphin Books, 1961). First published 1890.

organization, with its clear differentiation between, on the one hand, the officers and the professional workers and activists, and on the other, those who passively support the party—the general run of voters who identify with the party's program and goals. A satisfactory conception of a political party must recognize that it performs not only electoral functions, but non-electoral functions as well: it recruits leaders from all social groups and geographical sections for governmental offices; it provides welfare services to citizens and voters; and it transmits opinions about government policies between voters and public officials. Some authorities insist upon still another function: the actual formulation and coordination of governmental policy. We should note that the political party plays this role in a very different manner when the legislature acts autonomously in law-making and when it is wholly subservient to a single party or to the executive. Moreover, when the party is only partially, but not exclusively, responsible for governmental policy formation, the relations between the electoral branch of the party (which deals with the voters) and the intra-governmental or parliamentary branch pose critical organizational problems.

The Electoral Party: Membership and Ideology. In most countries membership in political parties is neither defined nor regulated by law (except for certain outlawed parties whose members may be subject to penalties). Parties are considered to be voluntary associations, and their membership, structure, and control are considered their own internal affairs. The American states are an outstanding exception, having adopted extensive, detailed laws on ballots and primary elections to regulate the procedures whereby candidates are nominated to appear on the general election ballot under the party label.

At the same time, however, the legal meaning of "party membership" in the United States is very loose. A voter may simply declare his intention to vote in a given party's primary election, or may enroll on the party's official membership list. The social-psychological meaning of "party membership" in the United States is correspondingly vague and broad. Current voting behavior research uses the term "party identification" to signify the degree to which the voter feels at home in a party, has positive emotional associations with its symbols and leaders, and would normally support its candidates or issues even if he knew nothing about them. In the United States, nothing prevents someone belonging to or identified with one party from voting for another party's candidate if he so desires; and in about one-fourth of the states, so-called open-primary laws actually permit voters to vote in the primary elections of any party they choose. In contrast, party membership in most Western European countries remains quite unregulated but involves a strong degree of emotional commitment, solemn oaths or written pledges of obligation and consent to discipline, the periodic payment of dues and the carrying of up-to-date membership cards, and joining and working with all kinds of auxiliary party organizations and functions.

Contemporary research in political behavior supports the view that most people tend to identify with a party first, accepting its principles and candidates on emotional (not necessarily irrational) grounds, rather than look around for a party which most closely approximates their reasoned, independently formulated principles and preferences. The motivations for a voter's choice of party are manifold, and may include the influences of family, geographical section, residence, status group aspirations, and income level, as well as the psychic rewards that people get from political participation. For whatever reasons, it appears that the intellectualized, rational grounds for party preference perform a supportive, reinforcing function for the individual, whose beliefs and views are initially shaped by his life experiences and situation.

In a strict sense, the policies and programs advocated in the platforms and campaign speeches of electoral parties are not ideologies in the sense that they are not general advance commitments to certain actions regardless of time and place. Such commitments somehow seem irresponsible and irrelevant to the duties of governing representatives who are supposed to be responsive and accountable to their constituents, to their offices, and to the requirements of particular situations. The campaign pledges of electoral parties are, therefore, tentative statements of attitude and preference, rather than of quasi-religious belief and absolute obligation. But this is a difficult line to draw, and the student may observe examples of parties and candidates who consider their beliefs and pledges to be absolute and binding to the point of eliminating all personal discretion and of yielding everything to the claims of the party doctrine and leadership.

Such behavior is appropriate to what may be called *doctrinal*, rather than electoral, parties. Doctrinal parties may be of several kinds. One example is the single-interest party, such as an independence movement, a racial or religious party, or a nationality group dedicated to achieving political separation and autonomy for itself. Mass movements are particularly susceptible to the doctrinal label, partly because they so often come into being as agencies for bringing about a new social order or disseminating a particular ethical view of the world, but partly also because they place the aims of the movement above other loyalties and try to make politics a subservient tool of some supreme moral imperative. Their demand for absolute loyalty and discipline from their members further distinguishes totalitarian mass political organizations from democratic electoral parties. The ideology of the democratic political party recognizes the pluralistic quality of democratic loyalty, which requires support for a political system that tolerates dissent and guarantees equality of individual rights, imposing standards of respect for other groups upon each group that claims such rights for itself.

Interest group or *factional* parties may exhibit all the absolute, fanatic qualities of doctrinal political parties—one reason why the founders of constitutional political systems, including the American, distrusted and suspected them. But most leaders of interest groups such as workers or farmers, employers or doctors, in order to preserve the "purity" of their doctrinal positions as well as the material benefits of their offices and organizations, work through and upon regular political parties when such exist, using publicity, financial, and pressure tactics upon party and public officials. As unabashed advocates of an "interest," they can avoid the multiple, ambiguous responsibilities of party politicians and public officials.

Consideration of problems of ideology and group membership explain why the electoral party is the normal type of political party under constitutional, democratic political systems. The electoral party recognizes the need for differentiating, morally and structurally, governmental offices and their personnel from the personnel and organizations of the competitive interest groups and party organizations in the electorate, the full-time functions of which should be the mobilization of loyalties, the education of voters, and the election of political leaders. We do not mean to say that government leaders cannot be recruited by institutional devices other than the competitive struggle for votes between electoral parties. But where democratic government is based upon popular elections, no better means than political parties has yet been discovered which combines in satisfactory proportions the requisites of stability, progress, and responsiveness to public opinion.

The Electoral Party: Structure and Control. Electoral party organization probably originates from the desire of an individual, faction, or group to predetermine as far as possible who will be elected to a given office or offices in a given electoral unit or district. Legally, most political jurisdictions require potential candidates to meet certain statutory requirements of age, sex, citizenship, and residence. And to become candidates officially, aspirants must usually file petitions, signed by a given number or percentage of voters in the district concerned, with the appropriate election board or office; they must also pay a filing fee fixed partly to eliminate non-serious candidates and partly to help defray the costs of the elections. The practical problem immediately suggests itself: What significant choice exists in a contest for a single office when 9 candidates have filed the required petitions in proper form, or for 9 legislative seats to be filled at large in a district where 56 candidates have qualified? The answer that immediately suggests itself is *organization.*

In electoral politics, organization begins with *caucusing*—meeting, planning, negotiation, and agreement on a plan of action before the formal vote by a number of politically active persons in a position to influence a significant number of votes. Such organization is almost sure to win when there is no opposing organization or caucus among the remainder of the voters. If an opposing organization forms, it expands the effective range of choice from one to two "organization" candidates or slates. If three or more organizations are actively in the race, rules become necessary to determine whether a relative majority (plurality), an absolute majority, or some kind of minority quota will determine the winner. Paradoxically, then, party organization arises to fill a need to limit the voter's theoretical freedom to vote for any candidate to freedom to vote for a candidate who can poll an absolute majority, a plurality, or an arbitrarily-fixed quota.

Historically, electoral parties have organized primarily, though not exclusively, around legislative electoral units, such as the British parliamentary constituency, the French *département*, the Swiss canton, or the American state assembly or senatorial district. The lowest unit of electoral, and hence party, organization is the precinct, or primary voting area, consisting of several hundred voters in a neighborhood. This is where basic party organization starts, in the person of a precinct committeeman or captain thoroughly familiar with voter predispositions at the "grass roots." Control of the party hierarchy, however, as distinct from control of votes, usually begins at the next higher level. In urban areas this may be the ward or *arrondissement*, or a state legislative or parliamentary district. In larger geographical areas or rural districts, however, the country canton, or *département* is likely to be the basic unit of party organization above the precinct. Above this may be one or more regional levels of party organization, for purposes of communication and coordination (in federal systems these would be the state, province, or constituent union republic organizations); these in turn will report to a national level or organization. Control in party organization usually means the power to appoint or remove authorized party workers or agents at the next lower level of organization, or to select from a lower level of organization the delegates to the party convention or congress at the next higher level.

At the lowest level of party structure, three formal elements of organization appear. One is the meeting of party members (the caucus or convention). Second, there is usually an executive committee, formally responsible to the membership of the convention but in practice a managing or directing body appointed by and responsible to a party leader at the same or a higher level (or even to influential people, such as financial contributors, outside the formal organization). Finally, there is a party secretary—or chairman of the executive committee or leader—who directs the work of the full-time party officials. Formally, this individual acts on behalf of the executive committee; in practice, he may vary from a figurehead to an all-powerful executive who completely dominates the committee and is responsible only to higher levels or to outside influence.

The actual location and exercise of power among party agencies at the same level is problematic, but experience indicates certain trends. The party meeting or convention, being large and unwieldy, tends to take place infrequently (annually, biennially, even quadrennially), so that its functions are usually formal, ceremonial, and ratificatory. The strength and influence of the executive committee turn upon the degree of *de facto* decentralization in the organization, upon the vigor of the representative-delegates, and upon the methods of appointments, rewards, and promotion in the party hierarchy. Since executive committee members are usually party executives in their own right, with their own affairs to tend to, they meet only periodically, in the intervals turning over the direction and conduct of party affairs to a full-time secretary, leader, or chairman. The natural tendency in party organization among agencies on the same level, therefore, is to delegate responsibility to a single secretary, leader, or "boss." The degree to which reality conforms to this model, or "ideal type," however, varies widely from one electoral unit to another, from one level to another, and from system to system.

Above the precinct level, conventions of all party members are scarcely feasible, so representative conventions usually constitute the formal link between lower and higher echelons. Delegates may be elected by party members, nominated and elected by delegates, nominated by executive committees or leaders ratified by the convention, or appointed from above. In most countries these arrangements are regulated by party rules; in the United States, however, state laws frequently govern the selection not only of state party officers, but of delegates to the national convention as well. Of course, there are informal, customary meetings and communications among party officials at different levels, and these may effectively supplant the formal procedures required by law. The methods of coordinating and integrating party activities at different levels are informal, complex, and vary widely from one type of party to another.

Generally speaking, party conventions and committees at each level seek to control nominations for public office at their own level. In different party systems, however, there are great differences in the control that higher levels can exercise over delegate and candidate nominations at lower levels. For example, in Great Britain the national party executive is very influential in the process whereby the local parliamentary district association names the party candidate for Parliament. In the United States, on the other hand, neither the national nor the state party committee interferes in a congressional district's nomination of a party candidate for Congress.

How much interlevel control is practiced in making delegate and candidate nominations is a principal criterion for determining how centralized a party organization is. Other factors are governmental structure (federal or unitary), sources and methods of money raising, and ideology. Ideology is especially important, and interesting, here. The ideologically more revolutionary, conspiratorial, or militaristic parties tend to be the most centralized, operating by appointment and vertical command from the top down. Next come the doctrinal parties, which assume the purity and primacy of the central dogma but permit local and regional autonomy in the election of delegates and in the expression of variations in opinion and of problems emanating from the mass membership. Greater decentralization is characteristic of the more pragmatic parties, whose major interests are winning elections and controlling offices, regardless of the level of government or of regional variations in doctrine or program. Paradoxically, the least centralized party organizations are also extremist in doctrine, including parties of an anarchist, nihilist, or highly individualist persuasion; local concentrations of opinion and voting strength at the expense of national membership; and parties of geographic and economic sectionalism.

Party Organization Within the Government. We have referred several times to the functional separation of the electoral organization of a political party and its intra-governmental organization. This separation would not occur if the electoral party organization could simply nominate and appoint from its own membership legislators who would accept the directions of party leaders, or conversely, if the elected representatives had complete control over the electoral party. But when citizen-voters not only directly elect their legislators but look with pride and emotional attachment upon the official bodies and offices of government (cabinet, prime minister, president, parliament, or congress), considering them as *their* representatives, the occupants of these positions may properly claim a direct line of responsibility to the people. And they may confine their responsibility to their electoral party organizations to being discretionary agents, for whom the electoral party is merely one (albeit an important one) of the sources of opinion that influence their official judgment. The subsystem of party organization within each legislative chamber, as well as the partisan devices of executive-legislative coordination, therefore constitute autonomous units of governmental party organization which present the electoral party organization with distinct problems of coordination and control.

There is usually a governmental party organization in each chamber of the legislature, consisting of the leader of the party in the chamber, his two or three deputies or assistant party leaders, the "whips" responsible for ascertaining legislators' opinions and transmitting the "line" determined by the leaders, and the rank and file of party members. The presiding officer of the chamber may be nonpartisan, merely applying the chamber's rules (as in the British and French parliaments), or he may be a party leader, like the Speaker of the American House of Representatives. In parliamentary governments, the prime minister and members of the cabinet are heads of the major government departments at the same time that they act as members of the executive committee of the parliamentary party, so *de facto* political coordination of the executive and legislative branches of government is secured through cabinet meetings and decisions. In presidential governments, the chief executive is outside the legislature and coordinate with it, or even above it. Consequently, a variety of formal and informal arrangements are necessary to bring the action of the party organization in each legislative chamber into line with the policy of the head of the executive branch. The most common forms of coordination are informal meetings with the legislative party leaders, but the president, not being a member of the legislature, is limited to the use of his personal prestige and persuasive powers, in addition to his position as party leader and his powers of appointment and administrative supervision, in winning the support of the legislative party and its leaders. The degree of party discipline in each legislative body—that is, the obligation each representative feels to vote according to his party leaders' decisions instead of according to constituency or interest group demands or his own independent preferences —has important effects on the ability of governmental party leaders to act in a concerted, responsible manner consistent with their public statements of party policy.

In political systems where the direct identification of people with governmental structure is strong and where there is a strong constitutional and parliamentary tradition, the status of electoral party organizations may be reduced to that of subservient appendages of the governmental organization. Perhaps the best example of this type of relationship is the British system, where the majority party organization in Parliament, whether Conservative or Labour, asserts substantial autonomy in deciding upon the content of the legislative program in any given session. The national conventions of each party and their executive committees and chairmen are practically reduced to the status of ratifying bodies and campaign sounding-boards for the reports and recommendations of the parliamentary leaders. Not that in actual practice the process is in any way dictatorial; there is much opportunity for intraparty factional and policy groups to influence internal party communications. The delegate machinery and research organizations of the electoral party contribute much in the way of ideas for policy, particularly when the party is in opposition. In general, however, the pattern in both British parties is one of a centralized electoral party, headed by a national executive committee and its chairman, who report to a national party conference and who at the same time act as the electoral agents of the party leader and the parliamentary party organization. In Britain the parliamentary rather than the electoral party asserts the ultimate responsibility for formulating the legislative program and anticipating the verdict of the voters.

The United States provides a sharp contrast with Britain's formal-informal mechanisms for integrating the electoral and the governmental party organizations. Even when one party controls the Presidency and both houses of Congress, the President as *de facto* party leader may experience the greatest difficulty in mobilizing united party action in support of his program. The chairman of the national committee serves at the President's pleasure and usually supports him, but the national chairman has very little influence, by virtue of his office, upon how in either the House or the Senate the members of his party vote on issues. A major reason is that both the party and electoral systems support the responsibility of the congressman or senator, rather than of the national party leadership, to ascertain voter sentiment and to decide how to cast his vote. The national chairman's influence on a member of Congress is restricted to such sanctions as he may have through information he can bring to bear, his advice to the President on matters of patronage, his ability to influence placement of government contracts in the congressman's district, his political connections in the district, and perhaps a legislator's own political ambition (which the President may be in a position to satisfy or deny). The leaders of the President's party in the House and Senate pay relatively little attention to the national chairman unless he is on especially good personal terms with them.

The rules, traditions and practices of each house of Congress establish the patterns of party behavior within that house, and such cohesion and discipline as do result come about only to the extent that the individual congressman or senator feels obliged to place loyalty to a party leadership above personal convictions or the interests of his state or district. The rules of each body provide for party caucuses, but these rarely meet oftener than once a session to elect the leaders; the rules also expressly provide that members are free to vote in accordance with the interests of their states or districts as well as with the decisions of their legislative leaders. The autonomy of the great standing committees in each house gives their chairmen a strong bargaining position with respect to the party leaders. The Rules Committee of the House, the steering committee for formal legislative debate in that body, is appointed by the Speaker but can be influenced only informally by him because he cannot remove its members. The majority leader of the Senate is chairman of the steering committee of his party and can usually control it, but the rule and practice of floor debate limit him to negotiation and persuasion, through his lieutenants and whips, in getting party measures out of the autonomous standing committees and in mobilizing votes from senators of his party. Under these conditions it is amazing that voting along party lines occurs even to the extent that it does in the American Congress. And it is not surprising that on all major measures involving any degree of public attention and controversy, there are always substantial blocs of party members who "cross over" to vote with the majority of the other party. Perhaps if national party conventions met oftener than every four years, as some Americans urge,[10] intra-party discussion and debate would result in resolutions or expressions of party policy that would have greater influence on members of the House and Senate. But it seems more likely that the same influences now operating on Congress would be felt in the annual or biennial party conventions, and might even have the reverse effect of revealing intra-party disunity to a degree that would undermine such cohesive influences as the President and congressional leaders are now able to bring to bear.

In multi-party systems like the French and the German, a different type of relationship exists, contrasting sharply with both the British example of close cooperation between the electoral and governmental party organizations and the American example of extreme disunity. In these systems the relationship between electoral and governmental party organizations may be called rivalry. The party congresses in these systems meet annually or oftener, and their executive committees feel little hesitation about passing resolutions which are in effect directives to their parliamentary representatives on how to vote on critical measures. Thus decisions of party central committees can effectively make or break party coalitions in the national legislature because the party's members in the legislature feel keenly the pressure of centralized party organization. Experience in France and Germany since World War II indicates that strengthening the position of the president and premier can reduce the degree of cabinet instability, and thereby the secessionist influence of party central committees, but apparently at the price of heightening the influence of government officials, centralizing their control over the parties, and lowering the vitality of democracy within the parties. Before generalizing too much from the French and German multi-party systems, however, we should note the so-called stable multi-party systems—those, for example, in Belgium, Holland, Switzerland, and the Scandinavian countries—where four or more parties over the years have established relatively enduring blocs within the national legislature, and both the composition of the cabinet-executive and controversial public policies are worked out primarily through negotiation among party leaders. Thus in democratic, constitutional political systems the trend seems to be in the direction of enhancing the power of the governmental party officials and lessening that of the national electoral party organization. The form and method of their interaction continues to be vitally important to the survival of democracy.

In totalitarian political systems, as we have seen, the theory of party leadership and responsibility outside the government reduces the relative position of governmental officials to a ministerial role of executing party directives. Thus in the Soviet Union the Central Committee of the Communist Party (or more precisely, its executive committee or Presidium, or even simply the Party chairman) appoints the major

[10] American Political Science Association, Committee on Political Parties, *Toward a More Responsible Party System* (New York: William Sloane Associates, 1950).

governmental officials, and in consultation with the reliable members of the party apparatus in each governmental agency, establishes policies for the government. Full Central Committee meetings are resorted to only in crisis situations, and then only to register prearranged decisions; full party conventions or congresses meet only to listen to and ratify changes of doctrine and program (the "party line") by the leadership. Nevertheless, over the years, as the regime has become established (so far as limited access to documentary sources and published facts permit us to tell), there appears to be a tendency for party leaders to assume official positions within the government (notably the Council of Ministers and the planning and coordinating agencies) and to arrive at party decisions directly through the official machinery of government. If this tendency were to continue, however, it would indicate not only a totalitarian integration of the machinery of party, government and economy, but a symbolic elevation in prestige of the governmental structure, and hence further diminution of the prospects for "withering away of the state."

Democracy and Competitive Political Recruitment

In this chapter we have tried to show how the electoral machinery established by the constitution and statutes of a political system affects patterns of voting behavior and methods of selecting political leaders and representatives. We have considered how the separation of the legal, official structure of government from the structure of economic and social influence makes necessary a political group to manage and coordinate the processes of selecting representatives and formulating public policy. We have seen how the operation of a system of legitimized force resting upon free elections results in, or seems to require, a partly legal, partly extra-legal subsystem of competitive political groups claiming to represent the interests of influential and important segments in society. We have noted that what we call the party system refers to a more or less differentiated set of groups specializing in electoral politics, whereas economic and reform interests take the form of bargaining, pressure, and mass educational movements; hence the responsibility for intergroup coordination in public-policy formation rests upon the electoral parties that control the nomination and election of political representatives. Finally, we have seen how the degree of centralization within the electoral parties and the relations between these parties and those of their leaders who occupy official government positions, largely determine the operative type of political system.

Not all political systems are democratic; a difficult and important problem, however, is to determine why certain systems may not be democratic. The ostensible reason is that they are based on force, but this is only a superficial explanation; all governments, including the democratic varieties, are based partly on force. Culture, the most comprehensive concept for explaining differences between societies, comes from anthropology, and political scientists sometimes use the term "political culture" to refer inclusively to popular attitudes toward the legal authority system, group loyalties and expectations, the norms and practices of leadership recruitment, and representative decisions on behalf of the political community as a whole. Until progress in the discipline of comparative politics provides us with much sharper meaning for the term "political culture" as an analytical concept, however, we are forced to rely upon more conventional criteria in attempting to classify political systems. Such classification must take into account at least three crucial factors: the relation between governmental and socio-economic structure reflected in the electoral system, the operative relationships between constitutional form and actual practice in leadership recruitment, and the number, composition, and interactions between public (politicians and administrators) and private (economic, professional, and opinion group) leaders in legislative and administrative policy-making. The complexity of these processes warns against the attractively simple notion that all governments tend toward either more or less competitive oligarchy or mass democracy requiring more or less one-party dictatorship.

Without attempting to present a final classification of political systems, we can suggest that it is helpful to analyze them in terms of *the competitiveness of their party systems.* For developed political systems, such analysis can begin simply by identifying the number of political parties (one, two, or many). But this is not very satisfactory as a theoretical conception, because in many systems the significant political groups participating in leadership recruitment and policy-making are not electoral parties but military organizations, non-elective bureaucracies, and irresponsible leaders of mass movements; the concept also leaves out of account the subtle workings of the legal-constitutional-administrative order. Nevertheless, if the student probes the historical factors and the societal, organizational, and governmental arrangements underlying the contrasts between two-party and multi-party systems, or between one-party and competitive party systems, he will gain a fundamental insight into the problems of unity through diversity in the first instance, and democracy versus dictatorship in the second. The different kinds of one-party systems, moreover, are especially helpful in highlighting the conditions for establishing and maintaining democracy, and suggestive of the range of alternative possibilities through violent or evolutionary transition from one system to another.

Fundamental, continued cleavages of ideology and outlook, based upon historic conflicts of nationality, religion, region, or class, provide a natural setting for a multiplicity of parties. Irredentist movements and revolutionary international conspiracies contribute another set of potential party subdivisions. A series of political revolutions effectively coinciding with great transformations in social structure is likely to have lasting effects upon political organization. When political ruling groups over scores of years are able to maintain an official system of representation that secures valued rights and privileges to the major social groups, the effect is that of a "divide-and-rule" policy; in the political warfare of group against group a stabilizing force to maintain "normal" conditions of order is needed lest the political contest break down into open violence and military suppression.

But many of these conditions also characterize two-party systems, so we must look for some historical explanation of why social groupings come to accept the confused and inaccurate expression of their interests implicit in a two-party system. One such condition is thought to be a socially homogeneous ruling class that divides politically into two factions, each of which succeeds in mobilizing a substantial proportion of all the remaining groups in the population. Another possible condition is open recruitment and vertical mobility into the two ruling groups. A third is political continuity, that is, a long tradition of negotiated settlements between leaders of the two political groups at strategic moments, before the basic consensus on which the regime rests is destroyed. A fourth factor is the overriding importance of contests for a single office, such as that of prime minister in Britain or the American Presidency, over which the grand stakes of political power are wagered. But whatever the historical reasons for the development of a two-party system, the conditions of its survival seem to be the congruence of societal authority with governing authority patterns, as well as a competitive system of leadership recruitment which reconciles the complementary needs of political integration and freedom for the expression and realization of individual and group demands.

The central feature of a one-party system is an imposed, compulsory unification of the system of political recruitment and responsibility, pending the establishment or re-establishment of a cultural cohesion and economic organization which will permit maintenance of the political regime and opening of the arena of political conflict to free, intergroup competition. If the one-party system is so conceived, it is easy to understand why many such systems arise in pre-industrial, developing countries. The most extreme modern form of the one-party system is the Communist and Fascist totalitarian control of all political, economic, and social activity, centralized in the top stratum of the single, ruling party. Another type is the highly stratified, paternalistic society, like those of Iran, Pakistan or Thailand, in which the top stratum seeks to maintain its authority by a monopolistic combination of military, religious, and educational organization. Between these extremes, Turkey (since 1923 under Ataturk) and Mexico (since 1934 under Cardenas and his successors) symbolize the industrializing society seeking to transform itself culturally and economically through a federal-ized, one-party political structure. For almost a hundred years following the Civil War, the eleven states of the American "Old South" presented a special case of a one-party system exhibiting the most extreme political factionalism on all issues except the dogma of racial supremacy upon which the system rested.

There are other varieties and conditions of one-partyism, but all have in common an emphasis upon the values of security and order; and the threat of force is assumed to be a necessary condition of political stability. Interestingly enough, the democratic, competitive party systems assume that freedom of political entry and participation is a condition of *their* political stability.

Is there an inevitable tendency for any of the different types of party systems to evolve into another type? Does the one-party system, for example, tend to decentralize and develop federalistic, autonomous, competitive political groupings of a two-party or multi-party character? Or does the multi-party system contain within itself certain inherent tendencies toward one-party unification? Does the two-party political system move toward multi-partyism or one-partyism? And is there any cyclical movement through history connecting the three forms? From the data and evidence in this chapter, our answers would be highly speculative. Scientific, educational, technological, and organizational trends in society and government would have to be taken into account, as well as trends in international organization and foreign policy. If one political scientist is correct in his characterization of "the world revolution in our time," the state of political knowledge justifies the prediction that political systems will change far more than is now imagined in any particular formulation about the shape of political institutions in the making.

SUGGESTIONS FOR ADDITIONAL READING

DE GRAZIA, A., *Public and Republic* (New York: Alfred A. Knopf, 1951).

DUVERGER, M., *Political Parties* (New York: John Wiley and Sons, 1954).

ELDERSVELD, S. J., *Political Parties* (Chicago: Rand McNally & Company, 1964).

HERRING, P., *The Politics of Democracy* (New York: W. W. Norton & Company, 1940).

KEY, V. O., JR., *Politics, Parties and Pressure Groups* (New York: Thomas Y. Crowell Company, 1958).

LEISERSON, A., *Parties and Politics* (New York: Alfred A. Knopf, 1958).

LIPSET, S. M., "Party Systems and the Representation of Social Groups," *European Journal of Sociology*, I (1960), 50–85.

MC KENZIE, R. T., *British Political Parties* (New York: St. Martin's Press, 1955).

NEUMANN, S. (ed.), *Modern Political Parties* (Chicago: The University of Chicago Press, 1956).

NEUSTADT, R., *Presidential Power* (New York: John Wiley and Sons, 1960).

SCHAPIRO, L., *The Communist Party of the Soviet Union* (New York: Random House, 1959).

SCHATTSCHNEIDER, E. E., *Party Government* (New York: Holt, Rinehart and Winston, 1941).

WILLIAMS, P. W., *Politics in Postwar France* (London: Longmans, Green & Co., 1954).

Chapter 15

LEGISLATORS
AND THE FORMULATION
OF PUBLIC PURPOSE

The legislature is the principal institutional device for realizing government by consent in modern democracies. It is in the legislative forum that the political interests (the articulation of which by parties and groups was described in the preceding chapter) confront one another most visibly and most dramatically. And it is there that the formulas expressing the agreements of these different interests on public purpose are constructed.

Although representative bodies existed in ancient Greece and Rome, the legislature as a separate institution is a modern development, intimately related to the development of democratic government itself. Indeed, two of the most important concepts for understanding democratic government are legislation and representation. It is therefore appropriate to begin our study of the modern legislature and its functions by surveying its history.

Legislative Bodies: History and Trends

EARLY DEVELOPMENT

The popular assemblies of Greece and Rome were forerunners of modern legislatures in that they embodied, to some extent at least, the idea that the people had a voice in the business of government. The concept of *representative* government can also be traced back to Greece and Rome: the juries and councils of Athens and the Roman Senate were composed of a relatively small number of citizens who acted on behalf of all the citizenry. However, these institutions performed such diverse functions that it would be misleading to classify them as legislatures in the modern sense.

The Greeks and Romans never succeeded in developing clear-cut theories of representation. Thus they could not devise means for institutionalizing the consent of the governed once expansion beyond a city-state made popular assemblies impossible. Nor did the Greeks develop concepts of legislation, that is, of *making* law—having a definite organ of government determine authoritative rules. The Romans, however, did. First popular assemblies, then the senate, and later the emperor were considered by the Romans to perform a legislative, or law-making function.

But, this notion of making laws, as distinguished from finding or *enunciating* rules that transcended human decision about them, was lost sight of during the Middle Ages. Then man tried to determine what the law was by seeking indications of God's will and by interpreting customs derived from the status relationships of feudalism. Law was thus conceived of as "given" rather than "made." The medieval period, therefore, represented a setback from incipient Roman notions of law-making. During this same period, however, the Church did make some contributions to institutionalizing representation, a concept about which the Romans were never clear. The Church held synods in provinces early in its history and later held councils throughout its domain. These councils, which have been called "religious parliaments,"[1] reached a high point in the fifteenth century, when proposals that the Church should be governed by these assemblies were actively promoted by many churchmen.

Originating within the Church, medieval representative bodies were extended to include other "estates." Rulers called assemblies at which the Church, the nobility, and territorial units were represented. The higher clergy and higher nobility participated directly in these assemblies, whereas frequently the lower nobility and territorial units were represented by a few persons chosen from these estates. This participation by persons regarded as spokesmen for others in their estates was a forerunner of modern notions of representation. These spokesmen, however, were regarded as representing estates rather than individuals.

Although none of these medieval bodies could be regarded as a lawmaking body in the modern sense, some of them did achieve a high level of development as agencies of representation. The *Cortes* in some Spanish-speaking countries, for instance, provided notable examples of institutionalized popular consent and of the representative's role as agent of his constituency. But continental European representative institutions

[1] Robert Luce, *Legislative Principles: The History and Theory of Lawmaking by Representative Government* (Boston: Houghton Mifflin Company, 1930), p. 55.

declined after the fifteenth century. By the age of absolutism in the eighteenth century, they had disappeared almost entirely.

Developments in England, however, were far different from those on the Continent. And to find the most direct and immediate historical origins of the modern legislature, we must look to the evolution of the English Parliament. This institution was originally a court, that is, an adjudicating body and had counterparts on the Continent. But while in France the *parlement* remained only a court, the English Parliament evolved into a legislative body which was ultimately to provide a model for the world.

The transition of Parliament from court to legislature stemmed from the kings' practice of hearing petitions for redress of wrongs in councils where they were joined by leading nobles and clerics. Originally these assemblages conceived of their task in the familiar medieval fashion, as one of merely finding and interpreting law. But the councils also gave the nobles an opportunity to insist on their feudal rights and oppose the unlimited authority of the king. In 1215 King John was forced by the barons to concede in the Magna Carta that no taxes beyond the traditional feudal aids could be imposed without the consent of an assembly of nobles and clerics. The enunciation of this principle in written form, reflecting a clear imposition of the wills of representatives of one class of society on the king, already foreshadows the deliberate policy-making and law-making that the modern term "legislation" implies. In 1295 the membership of the English assembly was expanded so that it became more nearly a representative body. In addition to summoning the nobility and clergy, King Edward I directed every sheriff to send two representatives from each shire, city, and borough. This expanded assembly very shortly began to sit as two separate groups, with the nobles and clerics eventually becoming the House of Lords, and representatives of the territorial divisions ultimately forming the House of Commons. The right to approve taxation, together with the ancient right of petitioning the king for redress of grievances, gave Parliament the means for acquiring more rights and more influence in the governing process. In more and more of the meetings convoked by the king to obtain revenue, Parliament presented him with petitions and lists of grievances and insisted on obtaining concessions from him as a condition of approving his tax proposals. In time, Parliament began to draft the orders and regulations it wished the king to issue. Such drafts are the direct antecedents of modern legislative bills.

The notion of law-making was still slow to develop, however. As late as the seventeenth century Sir Edward Coke, one of England's most eminent jurists, argued that the common law, based on customs, was a higher law than parliamentary statutes. But Coke was the last to express this doctrine. From his time on there was a more or less clear understanding that statutes were new formulations rather than simple declarations of customs and traditional rights and that statutes took precedence over customs and common law. Here then, in the seventeenth century, we can finally recognize the modern doctrine that legislative bodies make laws.

Equally significant, by the end of that century the supremacy of the English Parliament had been established. The medieval ambiguities on the respective rights of the king and parliament were resolved in 1688–1689, after almost a century of conflict. The Glorious Revolution and Parliament's calling William and Mary to assume the throne demonstrated that in the event of differences with the king, Parliament was superior.

Thus in the eighteenth century, as the monarchies of the countries on the European continent became more absolute, England was developing a constitutional system of balanced powers. The king had some prerogatives, but his authority was limited by the Lords Spiritual and Temporal and the Commons in Parliament. Further, the Act of Settlement of 1701 provided for an independent judiciary by granting life tenure to judges. When the French observer Montesquieu analyzed the English government in the middle of the eighteenth century, he explained that its success in preserving liberty and maintaining stability was based on its separation of powers. John Locke had already described English government as one of separated legislative, executive, and "federative" powers; but Montesquieu changed these categories to the now familiar trilogy of legislative, executive, and judicial powers. Although Montesquieu inaccurately interpreted the English system of the eighteenth century, he did provide the basis for the modern analytical concept of the legislative function. As he conceived it, the legislature is an institution separate from the executive and judicial institutions; it alone has the function of making laws, and it is restricted to this function.

The Amercan government established at the end of the eighteenth century institutionalized this concept of a separation of powers with a clear delegation of legislative powers to Congress. Some of the former American colonies had gone even further by establishing legislative supremacy, but eventually they adjusted to the separation of powers for which the national government was a model.

On the Continent the French Revolution of 1789 and its aftermath shook the old institutional forms and eventually led to the universal establishment of legislatures. In France, where *parlements* had remained courts and where the Estates-General had practically disappeared before 1789, the English Parliament was used as a model for the development of new institutional forms. Some of the English forms were adopted in France and later in other countries, but transplanting institutions that had evolved in another culture frequently produced something far different from the model. The British pattern has been most effectively transplanted to the former British colonies, such as Canada, Australia, and New Zealand, but there are important variations even among these countries.

In any event, legislatures were established in all the democracies by the nineteenth century. In fact, an established legislature became the criterion of democratic government.

THE NINETEENTH CENTURY:
THE HIGH POINT OF LEGISLATURES

Legislative supremacy was the prevailing tendency in Western Europe and America during the nineteenth century. After representative institutions had been established, the conflicts within democratic societies were over issues which could be resolved by relatively simple statutory enactments. It was even possible for the legislative bodies to cope with the details of budget-making, because the sums devoted to governmental expenditures were small. Economically, the nineteenth century was characterized by policies of laissez faire, which reduced the state's functions to minimal ones of policing a market that operated itself.

In America these nineteenth-century developments made credible the fear of the Founding Fathers that Congress would become the predominant governmental body and draw "all power into its impetuous vortex."[2] In 1885, Woodrow Wilson wrote that, although American government was formally based on the separation of powers, it was in reality a "Congressional Government."[3] Congress not only legislated, but, through its committees, dominated the President and cabinet and controlled the details of administration. Wilson argued that American practices compared unfavorably with contemporary English practices as described by Walter Bagehot, an English writer whose interpretation of English government was then in vogue. The superiority of the English system was that both in theory and fact it was based on legislative supremacy.

Bagehot regarded the English cabinet as a mere committee of the Parliament and explained that Parliament controlled the cabinet, made the laws, and prepared the budget.[4] But his interpretations of nineteenth-century English government were doubtful even in his time. The mere fact that they were accepted, however, suggests the broad extent of Parliament's authority.

In France, after many constitutional experiments, the nineteenth century ended with the establishment of assembly government (see page 114). In the Third Republic the cabinet was clearly subordinate to parliament, which changed cabinets frequently and assumed considerable initiative in legislation and finance.

Even at the high point of legislative supremacy, however, some astute observers noted the inability of representative bodies to perform the functions they attempted. Writing as early as 1861, John Stuart Mill ex-

---

2 *The Federalist* No. 48 (New York: Modern Library, 1937), p. 322.
3 Woodrow Wilson, *Congressional Government* (New York: Meridian Books, 1956). First published in 1885.
4 Walter Bagehot, *The English Constitution* (London: Oxford University Press, 1928). First published in 1867.

plained that a legislature was not capable of general administrative functions, and then went on to argue that "a numerous assembly is as little fitted for the direct business of legislation as for that of administration." Instead Mill argued that the "proper" function of a representative assembly "is to watch and control the government."[5]

THE TWENTIETH CENTURY:
THE DECLINE OF LEGISLATURES

Developments of the twentieth century have to some extent justified Mill's analysis. The changed status of the legislature at this time was symbolized in the change in Woodrow Wilson's perception of American government. Writing in 1908, Wilson no longer regarded Congress as supreme. He stressed instead the potential power of the American Presidency.[6]

There are several reasons for the decline of the legislature and the growth of the executive in twentieth-century democratic government. Basically they derive from the technological advances of expanding industrial societies, which have created demands for more and broader government activities. This increased scope of government authority has required more regulation and more complex types of regulation than representative bodies can provide by simply passing laws. This growth has also led to a great expansion of the bureaucracy. Technical decisions, which have now been delegated to bureaucratic experts, may often be more important than the general principles determined by the legislators.

On the other hand, technological advances have also made mass education and mass communication possible. These developments have in turn led to more popular participation in government, which also tends to reduce the status of legislators. If a political party appeals to the electorate by its commitments to specific policies, legislators elected by the party are generally expected simply to register approval of these policies. Although this concept of responsible political parties achieves a democratic goal of popular participation in a decision-making process, it does reduce the importance of legislators.

Thus, where democracy has been successful, legislative bodies have declined in status. And in those countries where representative institutions have been unable to cope with the challenges of the twentieth century, parliaments have been so altered that they can no longer be called "legislative bodies" in any meaningful sense. Thus Fascist Italy and Nazi Germany reduced their legislative institutions to insignificance, and only the forms of these institutions remain in Soviet-dominated Eastern Europe. In 1958 the French acknowledged the failure of assembly government and established a strong president who is authorized to exercise

[5] John Stuart Mill, "Representative Government," in *Utilitarianism, Liberty and Representative Government* (New York: E. P. Dutton and Company, 1944), pp. 235, 239. First published in 1861.
[6] Woodrow Wilson, *Constitutional Government in the United States* (New York: Columbia University Press, 1908).

many powers previously exercised by parliament. The nation with the most clear-cut system of parliamentary supremacy has thus moved further toward executive domination than most democratic countries.

In those countries where legislatures have survived "intact" in the twentieth century, their primary function is probably that which Mill advocated: to watch and control the executive. When they can perform this task, they ensure the democratic goal of government by consent.

Legislative Functions

LEGISLATING AND NON-LEGISLATING LEGISLATURES

The student of comparative political institutions, we have often said, must be particularly careful to distinguish between formal prescription and actual political processes. Formally, the Supreme Soviet of the USSR and the Congress of the United States are comparable institutions. Chapter 6 of this text makes clear, however, that the Supreme Soviet does not perform the functions the American Congress performs. One must distinguish, therefore, between legislating and non-legislating legislatures.

But after determining that representative bodies in the Communist countries or in some of the emerging African states do not legislate, one has not exhausted the points of comparison between these institutions and legislating ones. Their very existence indicates that they perform some functions. It is the task of the political scientist to determine what these functions are.

Let us take the Supreme Soviet as an example. Elections to this body provide opportunities for propaganda and for mobilizing popular support for the regime, activities that are consistent with the Soviet policy of engineering consent. The Soviet of Nationalities, the upper house, contributes to the achievement of these goals by serving as a symbol of the government's concern about minority nationality groups. The brief sessions of the Supreme Soviet provide an impressive stage for major policy announcements by the rulers—speeches made at these occasions attract considerably more attention than would mere press releases. However, the role of the members is not merely a passive one. The Supreme Soviet is a forum for the limited kind of criticism and self-criticism which Soviet rulers have found to be functional. Such criticism keeps officials alert and active and thus helps prevent the bureaucracy from becoming stagnant.

Other non-legislating representative bodies have performed comparable functions. Hitler and Mussolini used them as impressive backdrops for speeches and as symbols of national unity. The charismatic rulers of the newly emerging African nations find parliaments useful for these same purposes. But these new nations would probably have parliaments even if they did not serve this purpose, for they have become one of the accoutrements of government, along with flags, embassies, and other symbols of civilization. Although legislatures have declined in status during the twentieth century, they appear to be more widespread than ever.

LEGISLATING BY OTHER INSTITUTIONS

Subsequent parts of this chapter concern legislatures which do in fact legislate. But in no country is the body formally designated as the legislature the exclusive source of legally enforceable regulations. The classic doctrine that legislators make law, executives enforce law, and judges interpret law has never been a valid description of governmental processes in any country; but the notion that legislators alone make law is the most doubtful part of all in this formula.

Executives everywhere perform important functions in law-making. To begin with, they are important sources of legislative initiative. In cabinet governments, executive initiative in legislative proposals is direct; the cabinet is expected to have comprehensive legislative programs, and most of the proposals considered by the legislators emanate from this source. Furthermore, most cabinets can ensure priority for their own proposals through their control of the parliament's time. In presidential governments, executives may not be able to introduce proposals directly in legislatures, but this fact is a technicality which scarcely cloaks the importance of executive intitiation of legislative proposals. American Presidents and governors, for instance, are now expected to have legislative programs; and these executives are frequently judged more on the basis of their legislative successes and failures than on their administrative ability. Even career civil servants may be sources of legislative proposals; in their experience in administering laws, they see where new statutes are needed and find the means of having legislators introduce their proposals.

Moreover, as legislators deliberate on proposals, executives seek to influence their decisions. In the cabinet system the influence is direct, because cabinet members participate directly in the parliamentary debates and may specify that the parliament's confidence in the government hangs in the balance. In the presidential system, executive influence may be indirect, but it is no less important. For instance, the American President has a staff agency (the Bureau of the Budget) analyze bills being considered by Congress to determine whether they are consistent with his program. The President uses persuasion, patronage, and appeals to the public to induce reluctant congressmen to vote in accordance with his policies.

After a legislative body has enacted a statute, the administration of its provisions involves a subsidiary form of law-making in the application of general principles to particular cases. Even if the legislature has attempted to spell out details in the statute, the administration of these details is a form of policy-making. Frequently, however, legislators make the compromises necessary to secure passage of a bill by using vague formulas which provide broad discretion for administrators. Increasingly in the twentieth century, legislatures specifically delegate subsidiary law-making functions to executives. Examples in the United States include executive orders of the President and cabinet members and rules promulgated by the independent regulatory commissions. In Britain, a standard device is the statutory instrument promulgated by a ministry to implement parliamentary enactments. On the European continent, parliaments have granted increasing decree-making powers to cabinets. Decrees are usually made pursuant to statutes and must cite the statutory authorization for their promulgation, but provisions for emergency decrees, such as those in France or Germany, actually delegate full legislative authority to the executive for stipulated periods of time.

Courts also make laws. The broadest judicial authority in the world is probably that exercised by the German Constitutional Court, which has ruled on most of the important controversial issues in the politics of the Bonn Republic. The United States Supreme Court, with its powers of judicial review and of umpire of the federal system, also exercises broad law-making authority. Even if courts do not exercise such broad discretion, their interpretation of laws inevitably involves law-making. The common law in English-speaking countries was entirely judge-made law. The interpretation of statutes, especially if the legislative intent is not clear, is also a form of law-making. In Britain, where courts do not have powers of judicial review, judges may so narrowly construe the intent of Parliament that they nullify Parliament's legislation.

In addition to executives, administrators, and judges, there are others who may share law-making authority with legislators. Citizens may participate in direct legislation through the initiative and referendum. Some American states and Switzerland authorize such direct legislation, but in the main, few observers regard these devices as having been particularly important. More important has been the delegation of some law-making functions to organized groups. The most far-reaching powers of this nature are exercised by the "economic chambers" in Austria. All those engaged in certain occupations there are required by law to belong to their respective occupational chambers. These chambers, in addition to advising parliament on proposals affecting them, actually promulgate rules which have the force of law. The German organized groups described in Chapter 5 exercise comparable but not so extensive powers of law-making. In the United States, the Supreme Court set limits on this method of delegating legislative powers to private agencies by its decisions which found the N.R.A. codes unconstitutional. However, within the American states the practice of establishing boards which license and police certain occupations often leads to the exercise of authority by private groups, because these boards are frequently appointed by such groups and their decisions are legally enforceable. Examples include state medical associations and state bar associations.

But even in those cases where we find non-legislative agencies—executive or administrative agencies, courts, private organizations—actually doing some or even most law-making, the legislative body may yet play an essential part in the process. The express or tacit *ratification* of such decisions by the legislative body may be a necessary ingredient in the decision's legitimacy, whether the ratification be in the form of specific advance delegation of authority, of ex post facto approval of rulings which have the force of law, or of mere refraining from making decisions to upset rules made by non-legislative agencies. Some constitutional democracies have very precise rules about the process of legislative ratification of this kind, such as the rules in Great Britain concerning statutory instruments. Even where such rules do not exist formally, or apply only to particular topics (for example, the requirement for legislative ratification of certain administrative reorganization orders in the United States), constitutional democracies usually assume that what we might call "constructive ratification" takes place through the day-to-day legislative scrutiny of the administration. On the other hand, a convenient index to the actual status and power of the legislature in any system is the extent to which legislative ratification is dispensed with. Thus despite the formal requirements of the Soviet Union's 1936 Constitution, not only have general decrees of the Presidium of the Supreme Soviet become law without even the pretense of ratification by the Supreme Soviet (whether by ex post facto approval or tacit acceptance), but so have constitutional amendments and various decrees and orders of the Presidium of the Communist Party. Indeed, many Soviet "laws" are made without the supposed legislative body even being aware of them.

NON-LEGISLATIVE FUNCTIONS OF LEGISLATURES

The law-making authority which the twentieth-century legislature has lost may be compensated for by the increase in its non-legislative functions.

Executive Functions. Legislative control of the executive is clearest in parliamentary systems in which the cabinet must have the confidence of parliament to remain in office. But in presidential systems, legislatures also have means of controlling the executive. In the United States, for example, the requirement that Congress must approve the annual budget is an effective means of legislative control. Legislatures may also influence executives in both systems by the opportunities they have to question, to criticize, and to attract publicity. By these means they can influence government policy and exercise some influence on administration.

As the modern state has exercised increasing authority over activities affecting the daily lives of most citizens, legislators have become increasingly involved in the details of administration in specific cases. Citizens seeking benefits from the government turn to their elected representatives for assistance. American congressmen and French deputies have long devoted considerable time to running errands for their constituents. Austrian legislators, whose law-making functions are minimal, devote the greater part of their time to intervening in the administrative processes. Although these practices have been severely criticized, they do increase the authority of legislators by reminding administrators that their actions may come under the scrutiny of the people's elected representatives at any time.

Electoral Functions. Most legislative bodies perform some electoral functions. In most parliamentary republics, legislators participate in the election of presidents. Many legislatures also participate in the elections of other executive officials and of judges.

Constituent Functions. Most legislative bodies perform important functions affecting the constitution. Many can amend it by means of extraordinary majorities, and most can initiate amendments. All legislatures perform constituent functions by enacting statutes which fill in the gaps of the document or documents regarded as the written constitution.

Judicial Functions. Most legislative bodies perform some judicial functions. It is common to authorize legislatures to serve as courts in the impeachment of chiefs of state or other officials. Legislators are also involved in the judiciary through their functions in naming judges, determining their compensation, establishing courts, and setting the jurisdiction of courts.

Investigatory Functions. Although closely related to the authority of the legislature to control executives, the investigatory function is coming to be a special one in the twentieth century. The legislative investigation, which is provided for in other countries but not used as widely as in America, is a means of attracting widespread attention to problems that might otherwise go unnoticed. Although the American legal doctrine is that there must be a legislative purpose for investigations, the practices of the American Congress have not always respected this limitation. In other countries, this limitation does not exist even formally. Thus, the investigatory powers of legislatures may be regarded as a non-legislative function.

LEGISLATIVE FUNCTIONS OF LEGISLATURES

Although legislators are neither the only law-makers nor are they only law-makers, their primary formal function is enacting statutes, which are, by definition, laws made by legislatures. Statutes rank below the constitution in the hierarchy of laws, but they take precedence over other formulations of law, such as executive decrees, administrative orders, and the common law made by judges.

In the nineteenth century, the primary legislative function was that of enacting general rules for the society. Financial legislation is probably the most important in the twentieth century. Almost all government activity now requires expenditures, and the budget is the blueprint for a government's program. Thus, as Parliament originated in the requirement that the king obtain consent for taxes, so the modern legislature's most important power is the requirement that it approve the budget and the taxes required for these expenditures.

Admittedly, legislatures are no longer capable of dealing with the details of budget-making. And amateurish legislators in many American states are not even capable of considering budgets, although the sums may be insignificant as compared with the national budgets of the United States or of Great Britain. Nonetheless, the requirement in democratic countries that legislatures must consent to finance legislation provides a legal basis for exercising such powers as their competence allows.

In discussing earlier how legislatures often simply consent to the most important legislation they formally enact, or merely ratify important decisions made elsewhere, we pointed to an important analytical distinction which is again relevant here. Legislative functions include both decision-making and decision-legitimizing actions. *Decision-making* is a process in which conflicts in the society are deliberated, classified, and ultimately resolved by agreement on some policy, some imperative to action (or to inaction). In the American Congress and state legislatures, legislators may perform major roles in decision-making on some matters. In European parliaments, opportunities for private members' bills and free votes provide legislators with comparable but less frequent opportunities. In many systems, committee action allows legislators to participate in decision-making. But all these opportunities notwithstanding, decision-making as defined here is frequently performed outside the legislature; the resolution of the conflict is simply brought to the legislature for approval. In these circumstances, the legislature is essentially a decision-legitimizer rather than both a decision-maker and decision-legitimizer.

Although decision-legitimizing is only one of many legislative functions, it is perhaps the most critical factor in maintaining the concept of the consent of the governed and thus in ensuring the full popular acceptance of decisions. In other words, even though a decision may not be "made" by the legislature, it is formal ratification by the legislature which, more than anything else, gives the decision its authoritative character in the eyes of the governed.

Legislative Institutions

Legislative institutions set the boundaries of legislative behavior. The study of these institutions tells us little of what legislators actually do, but it does indicate the terrain on which action takes place and clarify the rules which are accepted to guide and limit that action. Thus a knowledge of legislative institutions is a precondition for an understanding of legislatures, but a student should be warned at the outset that arguments over institutional forms are frequently a cloak for more substantive conflicts in a society.

BICAMERAL AND UNICAMERAL LEGISLATURES

Legislatures may consist of one chamber (unicameral) or two chambers (bicameral). Where two chambers exist, the one with the most democratic elections (and usually shorter term of office) is called the lower house. This name, which in some modern legislatures is now of more historical than practical meaning, was acquired in a day when that house was considered "closer to the people," by virtue of the methods used to choose its members. The other chamber, with a less democratic basis for membership (at present or in the past), is called the "upper house." The bicameral legislature is the almost universal pattern for national legislatures, but unicameral ones are found in such diverse parts of the world as Denmark and New Zealand. Unicameral bodies are found most often at regional and local levels, as with Nebraska (the only unicameral American state legislature); all the West German Länder except Bavaria; the Soviet republics; and the various councils below the national level in the French system.

There are many variations in the respective powers of the two houses in bicameral systems. In the United States and Switzerland, for example, the houses have almost coordinate powers, and in Italy the cabinet is responsible to both houses. But the more common pattern is a lower house with powers far exceeding those of the upper house. In parliamentary systems especially, the prevailing practice is that the cabinet is responsible only to the lower house. Britain, France, and Germany are examples of this pattern.

Arguments over whether legislatures should consist of two houses or one have been endless. The most persuasive argument for having two houses has probably been the desire to provide two different bases for representation. Thus upper houses such as the Italian and Canadian senates and the British House of Lords have been used to obtain members who would not be expected to seek election but who might be expected to make some contribution to parliamentary deliberations. The appointment of such persons lends itself to the argument that these upper houses are undemocratic, and such accusations have contributed to the decline in their status. A more influential reason for the establishment of bicameral legislatures in federal systems has been the desire of constitution-makers to preserve the authority of the constituent territorial units (states) by providing them with representation in their corporate capacity. Other arguments on this question include claims that "two heads are better than one" or assertions that a two-house legislature encourages irresponsible "buck passing." These institutional arguments, however, usually derive from substantive conflicts between those who wish to expedite government action and those who wish to restrict it, or between those whose interests are better represented in a less democratic upper chamber and those whose interests are better represented by a more democratic lower one.

CABINET GOVERNMENT OR PRESIDENTIAL GOVERNMENT

Another important institutional feature of legislatures is their relationship to executive institutions. To analyze the operation and functions of any legislature, we must distinguish between the legislative institution in a cabinet system and that in a presidential system. The world's model for cabinet government has been Great Britain. From there the system has been transplanted to former English colonies throughout the world and has served as a guide for other European countries. The United States has been the model of presidential government for some South American countries and for Liberia and the Philippines. These and other governments do not, however, always adopt every feature of the original model. The Fifth French Republic, for example, combines features of both presidential and cabinet government.

In the traditional model of cabinet government, the executive is derived from the legislature and retains its position only so long as it retains the confidence of the majority in the legislature. If a cabinet loses its majority, it must either resign and allow another group to form a cabinet or dissolve the parliament and appeal to the voters. Thus, cabinet government concentrates responsibility for executive and legislative functions. Presidential government, in contrast, is said to separate responsibility by providing separate executive and legislative institutions. According to the classic theory of separation of powers, the legislature makes the laws and the executive carries them out.

As the reader has already learned, however, the American President, cabinet members, and administrators perform legislative functions. Here one need only add that an American President who has a definite program and who has a majority of his party in Congress also pledged to that program can be certain of its enactment. As an example, President Lyndon Johnson could be almost as certain of support from Congress in 1965 as

the British cabinet could be. Moreover, since World War II even the opposition party in Congress has accepted most of the President's decisions
in foreign affairs, with the result that Presidents facing even a Congress
dominated by the opposition party can be almost as certain of support for
such policies as the British cabinet is.

On the other hand, analysis of the actual operations of the cabinet
system suggests that it also operates differently from the formal institutional theories. Given the present patterns of British politics, it is unthinkable that a majority party would vote down the cabinet. Until it decides
to appeal again to the electorate for a new mandate, the government can
be as certain of its tenure as the American President. Thus, the formal
distinctions between the cabinet system and the presidential system may
not be as important as their operational similarities.[7]

BASES OF REPRESENTATION

Legislative institutions vary widely in their bases of representation. These
institutional variations include representation of territorial units, of
organized groups, and of individuals, according to the various methods
of election described in the preceding chapters, especially Chapter 14.
Another variation involving only a loose concept of representation is the
appointment of persons of special talents, such as the life peers in the
British House of Lords.

The territorial unit as the basis of representation is most commonly
associated with the federal system, in which the constituent units are conceived as having specific interests deserving representation. However,
territorial representation is not limited to federations; it is even urged by
critics of the United States Supreme Court's "one man one vote" decisions
that such artificial constructs as American counties must be represented
in their corporate capacities in state legislatures.

As we have seen, the representation of organized groups has a history that dates back to the medieval representative bodies based on the
estates of the realm. The modern concept of functional representation,
envisaging occupational groups as the units of representation, tended to
be discredited by its supposed use in the corporate states promulgated by
the Italian and Austrian fascists in the 1930s. Nonetheless, an upper
house based on functional representation was established in the German
state of Bavaria after World War II. And the Fourth French Republic, as
well as the Weimar Republic, had advisory economic councils incorporat-
ing the same principle.

Representation of individuals has become the prevailing practice in
modern democracies. Although the theoretical justification for a system
which conceives of society as a collection of atomized individuals is subject to many criticisms, this type of representation has become the pre-

[7] Eric C. Bellquist, "Congressionalism and Parliamentarism," *The NUEA Manual,*
XXVII (1953), 13–29.

vailing democratic norm. However, the bases of representation are the subject of considerable controversy among those committed to the basic concept of representation of individuals. Among all the systems of individual representation discussed earlier (see Table 14.1, pp. 434–35), the most critical differences, as far as their effects on the legislative operation are concerned, appear to be those differentiating preferential P.R., partylist P.R., and single-member-district elections.

There are many variations in the application of these election systems. Countries using proportional representation often require that a party must obtain a minimum percentage of votes to win any seats; such requirements reduce the number of parties and thus are contrary to pure proportional representation. Moreover, special provisions which give advantages to certain parties are a common feature of P.R. election laws; postwar Italy and the Fourth French Republic experienced many electoral law modifications calculated to benefit the parties controlling the parliaments.

It is often said that the single-member district system prevails in the United States. However, the conduct of elections at-large to the U.S. House of Representatives, and the diverse multi-member district systems used in state legislatures and city councils, makes this generalization rather meaningless. The cumulative voting system used for the Illinois House of Representatives, for example, is an adaptation of some features of proportional representation.

Arguments about the desirability and effects of various election systems have been endless. (Some of the purported effects of the different systems are listed in Table 14.1.) There is some evidence for the claim that the single-member district system encourages a two-party system, since plurality elections distort the results in favor of the majority party. Accordingly, the advocates of this system argue that it ensures governmental stability by discouraging the confusion of multi-party parliaments. On the other hand, advocates of P.R. urge that there are more than two sides to the controversial questions of modern society and that other opinions should be represented in the legislature. They also point to the distortions resulting from the plurality system and argue that a more accurate reflection of the opinions in the electorate is more democratic.

No objective observer can hand down a conclusive judgment on these arguments, because they derive from varying concepts of legislative functions and from varying substantive interests. As simple examples, one might mention that major parties tend to favor the plurality system and third parties to favor P.R. Thus, the British Liberal party saw no reason to change from the plurality system when it was in power at the beginning of the century, but it now inveighs against the injustice of a system in which, as a result of its third-party status, it achieved less than 2 per cent of the seats in 1964, although it received more than 11 per cent of the votes.

It is even difficult to determine with certainty the effects of various electoral systems. Although single-member districts are associated with the two-party system, the Third and Fifth French Republics demonstrated that a multi-party system can exist with single-member districts. Similarly, there is evidence that the party-list system of P.R. increases the party responsibility of legislators by making them more dependent on the party for their position on election lists than they are on voters in their districts. Nonetheless, some French parties in the P.R. system used in the Fourth Republic were not cohesive, and one study at least indicates that in the German Bundestag, CDU members elected on P.R. deviated more from party policies than those elected in single-member districts.[8] Thus, although political scientists have used the study of election systems as an opportunity to be "scientific," it is evident that they have not yet succeeded in isolating all the variables and arriving at validated conclusions. Another controversial aspect of representation in legislative institutions is apportionment. Since the controversies leading to the passage of the Reform Act of 1832 in England, the problem of apportioning legislative seats in accordance with the population has plagued democracies. The movement of people from rural to urban areas has long been the prevailing trend in industrial societies. Accordingly, rural areas are overrepresented in many countries. Constitutional factors such as minimum and maximum representation of counties in American state legislatures and the formulas for the participation of French municipal councilors in the election of the Senate increase rural political power. However, such factors alone do not account for the difficulties of achieving the democratic formula of "one man one vote." The responsibility for reapportionment often falls upon the legislators. Yet they have a vested interest in the status quo and are frequently reluctant to displace their own members in favor of others by reapportioning seats in accordance with population changes. Similarly, reapportionment may involve changing the balance of power among the parties in a legislature. These factors may lead to a failure to act or an intentional geographic distortion known as a "gerrymander," an attempt to draw district lines in such a way as to give an unfair advantage to one's own party.

Perhaps the easiest method of achieving apportionment in accordance with population is to increase the membership of a legislature, but that step is sometimes prohibited by constitutions. And even if not prohibited constitutionally, such increases raise questions of how large a body can be and still operate effectively. Some observers claim that the U.S. House of Representatives (435 members), the German Bundestag (496 members), the French National Assembly (552 members), the Italian Chamber of Deputies (596 members), and the British House of Commons (630 members) have already become unwieldy.

Because legislators' own interests are at stake, apportionment in accordance with population is most likely to be achieved if another insti-

[8] George Rueckert and Wilder W. Crane, "C.D.U. Deviancy in the German Bundestag," *Journal of Politics*, XXIV (1962), 477–88.

tution performs this function. The British have used a special commission composed of representatives of both parties. In the United States the distribution of seats among the states in the House of Representatives in accordance with the determinations of the Census Bureau and the reapportionment of state legislatures by officials outside the legislature have been means of more nearly achieving representation according to population than the results of action and inaction by state legislatures. Since the United States Supreme Court ruled in 1962 that state legislative apportionment was justiciable, American federal and state courts have assumed responsibility for compelling reapportionment of state legislatures.

However, reapportionment controversies, like controversies over the number of legislative chambers and types of election systems, reflect more substantive conflicts in the society. The apportionment of a legislature affects the kind of decisions made by the legislators, and calculations of these effects are frequently more important than abstract notions of democratic norms.

LEGISLATIVE ORGANIZATION AND PROCEDURES

Students who visit legislatures are almost invariably disappointed by what they see. In America, they frequently find few members in the chamber; a bored presiding officer looks on while one member speaks and a few others read newspapers or write letters. In European parliaments, the visitor is often confronted with a dull routine in which speakers file to the podium, and read formal speeches that do not seem to relate to the equally dull speeches which precede or follow them; or, when there is excitement, it can descend to name-calling and the hurling of ink wells.

Plenary Sessions and Debate. The student will begin to understand the legislative process as soon as he discards the notion that legislatures are deliberative assemblies to which members come with open minds to hear debates on the basis of which they will make their decisions. With the exception of those minor matters or unanticipated amendments which are often brought up in American state legislatures, the floor activity which the visitor can observe has little to do with the legislators' decision-making processes. Veteran American congressmen have insisted that they know of almost no speeches which changed a vote on a roll call. And if speeches do not determine votes among the relatively independent American legislators, one can hardly expect British M.P.'s with their strong sense of party responsibility or Germans with their *Fraktionszwang* to cast their votes in accordance with speeches.

What, then, is the purpose of debates in legislatures? Among the subsidiary purposes, speeches help to intensify decisions already made; and they provide those already favorably disposed toward the measure being debated with the slogans and explanations necessary to justify their decisions to voters and others. Debates may also be used to delay votes in the hope that further time will be helpful to a given cause.

For the most part, speeches in legislatures are directed to the public outside rather than to the members, for the most important function of legislative debates is to establish a record for the next election. Debates in the British House of Commons reflect this function most clearly, because they are structured so that there is a clear presentation of alternatives. Such a direct confrontation offers considerable drama and can arouse public interest, but the result is never in doubt: the government's majority will prevail. The debate, however, has required the government to justify its proposals and has given the opposition an opportunity to present alternatives. As a result of this debate, the voters will have a clearer basis for deciding between these alternatives at the next election.

The legislative process is accordingly much more complex than it might appear to the visitor attending the formal sessions. It involves a series of procedures that begin long before the formal meetings at which decisions are ratified. Participants in these procedures include party members, interest groups, government executives, and many others besides the legislators. Thus the following description of legislative procedures is primarily an outline of institutional forms, beneath which are so many complex processes that no one observer can follow them.

Legislative organization and procedures are usually determined by the rules and practices of the legislatures themselves. The basis for these institutional *forms* is therefore different from the constitutional basis which determines the institutional *factors* discussed in the preceding sections of this chapter. Like constitutional provisions, however, legislative rules and conventions set limits on the behavior of legislators.

Leadership Structures. Legislative rules determine the formal legislative leadership. The roles of presiding officers differ considerably in different legislative bodies. One model is the Speaker of the British House of Commons; he is an impartial presiding officer who disassociates himself from all party activities. A contrasting model is the Speaker of the U.S. House of Representatives. Although as a presiding officer he is expected to allow some privileges to the minority party, he is the leader of the majority party in his chamber. There are various modifications of these models: the President of the German Bundestag, for instance, is not so impartial as the British Speaker nor is he so active in his party's leadership as the American Speaker.

Parliamentary rules frequently provide for other leaders. Steering committees, councils of elders, or other groups may be given formal leadership status. Legislative rules may also determine patterns of party organization in parliaments. A rule in the German Bundestag, for instance, sets fifteen members as a minimum for establishing a *Fraktion*, and only a *Fraktion* is authorized to introduce bills and to exercise other rights. This rule reduces the individual member to impotence except as a member of a party.

British M.P.'s are also organized into parliamentary party organizations, and these are strong and cohesive. In the United States, legislative caucuses (the organization of all members of one party in a legislature) differ greatly from time to time, from party to party, and from chamber to chamber. It is almost always certain that members of a party will vote together in organizing the legislative body and naming its officers, but from that point on, the influence of party organizations in legislative bodies is uncertain. Nonetheless, party organizations exist in most American legislative bodies.

There may also be other organized groups in legislatures. In the Third French Republic, deputies frequently joined together to promote interests which cut across party lines. Such organizations have now been prohibited, but of course they continue to exist informally. The farm bloc and the silver bloc in the American Congress are comparable examples of bipartisan groups whose informal cooperation has sometimes been more important than formal party organization.

Bill Procedures: Introduction and Assignment. Legislative rules set forth the procedures for considering proposals. The basic steps of formal legislative procedure are introduction, deliberation, and decision.

The initiative for legislative proposals may stem from many outside sources, but the rules set forth requirements for the formal introduction of bills in the legislative body. There are many variations in these rules. In the presidential system, the executive may not be authorized to introduce its proposals directly in the legislature. American executives, for instance, must rely on legislators to submit bills embodying their proposals. In the cabinet system, on the other hand, the cabinet may introduce its bills directly.

Rules on the introduction of proposals affect the balance of power in legislatures. On one hand, the complete freedom given to American congressmen and state legislators to introduce proposals gives them an important forum for their pet projects. On the other hand, the restrictions on individual members in some parliamentary systems reduce their influence. For instance, the British House of Commons has increasingly restricted the scope and time allowed for private members' bills. And as we have already seen, the German Bundestag's requirement that fifteen deputies must join in introducing a bill has important consequences in diminishing the influence of individual deputies.

Once introduced, bills proceed through a series of steps in the process of deliberation. It is customary to refer to these steps as "readings," a term derived from the British Parliament. Before literacy was general, clerks actually read proposals in Parliament three times in order that members would understand their contents. Today, although literacy and modern printing methods make it unnecessary for the bills to be read aloud, this terminology is still widely used throughout the world to indicate the steps in legislative procedure. There are many variations in legislative rules. In America, Germany, and France proposals are sent to committees immediately after they are introduced. In the British House of Commons, however, the most important deliberation on the principles of a bill takes place prior to committee action; it is sent to committee only after its general principles have been approved by the full house.

Committee Action. There are, therefore, many variations in the power of committees in modern legislatures. The strongest committee system is in the United States Congress. Here, after a bill is sent to committee, the decision of the committee, especially its chairman, is the most critical factor in determining whether the full house will ever have an opportunity to consider the proposal. Even when the American congressional committee does release a bill, it frequently rewrites it completely. Since each committee has a subject matter jurisdiction (like foreign affairs, taxation, and so on), its members acquire considerable competence in their subjects as they acquire more seniority. The seniority system itself enhances the power of committee chairmen and often results in having this power wielded by a member whose views are not consistent with the majority in his party. Thus the committees exercise an independent power in determining the fate of proposals.

German committees also have considerable power, since they have jurisdiction over specific subjects and are composed of experts in their respective fields. But, these committee experts confine themselves to working out the specific details of proposals, and thus they do not exercise the authority of American committees.

The change in the rules on French committee authority indicates the importance which was attached to the committee system by those wishing to change the balance of power between the executive and the legislative branches. In the Third and Fourth Republics, French committees had much in common with American ones. They were composed of subject specialists who exercised considerable discretion in initiating proposals and in changing government proposals submitted to them. Among the changes made in the De Gaulle Republic is a requirement that committees must submit the original government proposals to the chamber for consideration before committee amendments are considered.

The British House of Commons has the weakest committee system. The five standing committees are designated simply A, B, C, D, and Scottish Bills. With the exception of the last, these committees have no subject jurisdiction and are frequently composed on an *ad hoc* basis for each bill submitted to them. More important, they receive bills only after the general principles have already been approved on second reading. Thus, the committees may consider only the specific details for implementing proposals already accepted. When a proposal comes back to the House, often little time is spent in deliberating on it, and it is then passed.

Scheduling, Floor Control, and Voting. Other important variations in the deliberation procedures established by formal rules concern the control of time in plenary sessions and the order for considering amendments. The U.S. Senate is unique in allowing almost unlimited freedom of debate. Traditions plus procedural difficulties make cloture (limitation of debate) rare. Other legislative bodies have provisions for cloture which allow the majority to stop a minority from delaying passage of a bill by talking. The absence of an effective cloture rule in the U.S. Senate and the unique absence of a rule requiring that all speeches must be germane allows for the filibuster.

Most legislatures allow the majority to limit debate after a certain period of time. Other institutional arrangements include time limits established by the Rules Committee of the U.S. House of Representatives, the power of the British Speaker to terminate debate on his own initiative, and in many European parliaments formal agreements among party leaders concerning allocation of time. Variations in these rules have important consequences in determining the respective rights of majorities and minorities.

Variations in the rules for the control of time also affect the respective rights of executives and legislators. An American President or governor has no institutional means for ensuring that legislators will give priority to his proposals because those proposals must be introduced by legislators. These bills must then compete on an equal basis with all other bills, and the legislators are under no legal obligation to consider them. But in most parliamentary systems, including France now, priority for cabinet proposals is assured. The cabinets control the allocation of time. Although opposition parties are consulted and time may be allotted to them and to private members' bills, the cabinets make certain that their proposals are considered.

Rules setting forth the order in which the general principles, specific details, and amendments are considered also have important consequences. As noted earlier, there are no provisions in America for considering the general principles of a proposal before proceeding to the details. Thus, when a bill comes up for a final vote, a legislator who favors the general concept of a bill but opposes some of its details has no opportunity to indicate this position. He must vote for or against the proposal as it has been "engrossed;" that is, with all the amendments which have been added. American congressmen and state legislators may therefore be compelled to vote against bills which they have themselves introduced because the amendments have changed important details. In most European parliaments, on the other hand, there are deliberations on the general principles of a proposal before the specific sections and amendments are considered.

Decision follows deliberation in the formal procedures of all legis-latures. This procedure is now assumed everywhere, but the logic for it was apparently not self-evident. Early French assemblies used a system in which each member cast his vote and then gave his explanations. Jeremy Bentham, whose analysis of legislative procedure has great in-fluence beyond his native England, set forth clearly the reasons why de-cision should follow debate. This principle as well as such other prin-ciples as the requirement that only one motion should be before the legislature at any one time have been universally accepted since Bent-ham wrote.[9]

Most legislative bodies use several different methods of voting to express their decisions. When nobody objects to some routine and in-consequential matter, unanimous consent can be used to suspend all the usual formalities to pass a bill. Other matters of minor importance may be decided by voice votes, a show of hands, or by standing. Frequently, the results of these votes are certain and obvious to everyone before they are conducted. On important matters on which the result is in doubt or on which the parties wish to establish a record, a formal roll call is used. Such a roll call can be conducted by calling the names of each member to have him express his vote individually, by walking into division lobbies where names are recorded, by casting written ballots, or by using electric voting machines.

The differences in voting methods may affect the results. Legislators may vote one way if their names are recorded and another way if they are not recorded. Electric voting machines in which all members vote simultaneously create different patterns of adjusting to how others vote than the patterns of an alphabetical voice roll call. Similarly, the French practice which allowed party leaders to cast proxy ballots for absent members produced different results than the more customary require-ment that members must be present in order to vote.

LEGISLATIVE SERVICES AND COMPENSATION

Legislative services and compensation are also institutional factors which vary considerably from country to country, and from state to state in the United States.

American congressmen are provided with the best facilities and services in the world; their large offices and staffs are the envy of legis-lators elsewhere. In sharp contrast, the British M.P. has no office and no staff; he must arrive early at the House of Commons even to find a seat, because the House does not have enough room on the benches for all its members. In addition to his own personal staff, the U.S. congress-

---

9 Jeremy Bentham, "An Essay on Political Tactics, or Inquiries Concerning the Discipline and Mode of Proceeding Proper to be Observed in Political Assemblies," *The Works of Jeremy Bentham* (Edinburgh: William Tait, 1843), Vol. II, pp. 299–373. This citation is to the first English publication, but the essay was first published in France after the 1789 revolution.

man is served by large committee staffs, a bill-drafting service, and the Legislative Reference Service of the Library of Congress. Many American states also provide their legislators with bill-drafting and legislative reference services. In contrast, few other countries provide their legislators with these services. These differences affect the relative status of legislators by making those without their own assistance and services more dependent on the executive or on outside organizations.

There are also great variations in the compensation of legislators. U. S. congressmen, with annual salaries of $30,000 plus liberal expense allowances, are the best-paid legislators in the world. This compensation allows them to devote full time to their legislative tasks, whereas members of many European parliaments and of most American state legislatures must supplement their legislative incomes with other employment.

Until this century, there was a general reluctance in most countries to compensate legislators. The notion that legislative work should be a voluntary public service rather than a salaried career was associated with the idea that government should be conducted by gentlemen. At any rate, inadequate pay or the absence of pay restricts the potential membership of legislative bodies. More recently in Europe interest groups such as trade unions have provided money for legislators who could not otherwise afford to serve, so the social base of parliamentary representation was broadened even before regular salaries were provided. However, the dependence of legislators on interest groups gives these groups special advantages. Thus, inadequate compensation can result in corruption rather than ensuring that only public-spirited gentlemen will serve.

Legislative Behavior

The bases of action taking place within legislative institutions is known as legislative behavior. Our knowledge of these norms and patterns has been scant until very recently, when there has been increasing study of legislative behavior and the development of a body of knowledge about individual legislators as legislators—their roles, their group life, and their patterns of decision-making.[10] Some of what we have learned is presented in the following sections.

SOCIAL AND ECONOMIC BACKGROUNDS

The social backgrounds of legislators throughout the world are not typical of the populations from which they come.[11] Legislators every-

[10] A recent bibliography of this literature is offered in Norman Meller, "Legislative Behavior Research," *Western Political Quarterly*, XIII (1960), 131–53.
[11] Donald R. Matthews, *The Social Background of Political Decision-Makers* (Garden City, N.Y.: Doubleday and Company, 1954).

where have a higher social status than the populations they represent. Moreover, women and minorities are not represented in proportion to their numbers in the population. But not only do the social origins of the legislators set them apart from others in the population; their individual characteristics have the same effect. They have been interested in politics early in life (most frequently as the result of family influences), and, compared to the people they represent, they are more upwardly mobile than the average person.

The occupational status of legislators, while higher than average everywhere, varies considerably in different countries. American state and national legislators are predominantly lawyers; in no other country do lawyers constitute such an overwhelming majority as they do in the American Congress. French parliaments have been characterized by a large percentage of "intellectuals," including many teachers—and lawyers too, but as a percentage of total membership, the lawyers have averaged only around 15 per cent. In Germany the largest single group in both the Weimar and Bonn parliaments has been professional party and interest-group officials. However, civil servants have also played an important role there; they have averaged around 20 per cent of the total membership. The composition of the British House of Commons is considerably more diverse than the American, French, and German legislatures; no one occupational group predominates. Britain, however, does demonstrate vividly the differences that can exist between parties in the predominance of workers in the Labour party and the almost complete absence of them in the Conservative party. Other European parties also reflect this pattern of strong labor representation in the left-wing parties and higher-status occupations among right-wing representatives. In contrast, occupational differences between Republican and Democratic congressmen in America are negligible.

Although there is evidence that the social origins of legislators affect their decisions, this evidence is not clear-cut. Nor is it certain that occupational origins determine quality of representation. American lawyers, for example, are occupationally trained to represent their clients and thus may represent the case for manual workers better than a manual worker could. The crucial factor may be that a representative must have skills in bargaining and negotiating. Professional negotiators like the lawyers and real estate dealers who are often elected to legislative office in America are practiced in these skills. Similarly, the professional party and interest-group officials elected in continental Europe have acquired their negotiating skill through years of political activity prior to serving in the legislatures.

Recruitment and career patterns also differ among democracies. Many American candidates for legislative positions are self-propelled: they decide by themselves that they will run for office. Weak party organizations and the practice of holding primary elections make this course of action relatively easy. On the other hand, in Europe the parties play a much more prominent role in the selection of candidates, and this perhaps provides some explanation for the greater cohesion of European parliamentary parties.

The actual course of a political career can also be affected by patterns of party organization and competition.[12] If the party organization is weak, a person who is just entering politics can run for a fairly high office, whereas a stronger organization is more likely to require a long apprenticeship in a non-elective or lower-status elective position. In the United States, the political apprenticeship needed for legislative office may depend on the degree of competition between parties. Thus in a one-party state, a man without any previous political experience may be elected to Congress. In Europe contrasts between the recruitment patterns of the strong Socialist organizations and the weaker conservative party organizations reflect critical party factors. Socialists require a longer apprenticeship in the party before naming persons as candidates. Differences in the course of careers may provide some explanation for the traditionally greater cohesion of left-wing parties.

ROLES

Most of us expect people in certain offices or positions to behave in certain ways. Social psychologists and sociologists use the concept of "role" to explain this. Thus the kind of behavior expected from a legislator by all the people in any way concerned with his office—his constituents, his fellow legislators, other state officials—all help to determine his role, and, in effect, influence his behavior. Thus legislators—like the rest of us—behave to some extent in the way in which they are expected to behave. But equally significant is the legislator's own concept of what his role is—that is, how he as a legislator should behave.

Different legislators will, of course, entertain different concepts of their roles, depending on their previous experiences, their particular views of the world, and so on. Moreover, a legislator's concept of his role is not static; it varies, depending on the people he is dealing with. For example, with his constituents he may behave in one way, with the governor in another, and his behavior may be altogether different when he is dealing with his fellow legislators.

A recent study by four American political scientists has explored the actions of state legislators in several states in an effort to determine how their behavior affects the functioning of legislative institutions.[13]

[12] Heinz Eulau et al., "Career Perspectives of American State Legislators," in Dwaine Marvick (ed.), *Political Decision-Makers* (New York: The Free Press of Glencoe, 1960), pp. 218–63.
[13] John C. Wahlke, Heinz Eulau, William Buchanan, and LeRoy C. Ferguson, *The Legislative System: Explorations in Legislative Behavior* (New York: John Wiley and Sons, 1962).

The importance of clarifying different types of roles is indicated by the contribution which this analysis has made on a classic issue concerning the role of the representative.[14] Since the eighteenth century, observers have argued over an issue presented by Edmund Burke. As a member of the British House of Commons, Burke had acted against the wishes of his constituents at Bristol and defended his action in a letter which has been widely cited ever after.[15] Burke argued that the representative should represent the entire nation and therefore should not accept instructions from his constituency. Although many subsequent writers have defended Burke's view, others have argued that the democratic goal of rule by the majority is achieved if each elected representative acts in accordance with the wishes of the majority in his district. Burke's conception of the proper role for a legislator has been described as that of a "trustee"; his opponents' conception, that of a "delegate."

Analysis of legislators' role concepts in the study mentioned showed that Burke's formulation of the problem is inadequate, since it confuses two aspects of the legislative role which are analytically distinct: the style of representation—whether a legislator should exercise his own judgment or follow instructions from some person or group—and the focus of representation—whether he should aim at protecting or advancing the interests of the particular district or group which elected him, or should think in terms of the entire community which is collectively represented by the whole legislature. Several of the findings about American state legislators on this point are worth mentioning. As might be expected, with respect to the style of representation, some legislators saw themselves as trustees; others favored the style of delegate. But some attempted to fuse the two or to apply one or the other depending on the situation—a possibility Burke overlooked. Also, as might be expected, it was found that some legislators were district-oriented (felt primary loyalty to their district), others were state-oriented (felt primary loyalty to the state) while still others (again, a possibility not considered by Burke) attempted to combine both orientations. Burke's formulation of the problem of representation is wholly unable to account, however, for some further findings. For example, so-called delegates might respond to instructions not of their constituency, but of some special group in it, or outside it, or of a governor of their own party or some party agency. Even more interesting, so-called trustees might use their own judgment not to promote the interest of the whole community, but to act as trustees for the district. In other words, Burke's "trustees" and Burke's "delegates" are only two of the several possible role types with respect to Burke's

14 *Ibid.*, chaps. 12–13. See also Heinz Eulau et al., "The Role of the Representative: Some Empirical Observations on the Theory of Edmund Burke," *American Political Science Review*, LIII (1959), 742–56.
15 Edmund Burke, "Letter to the Sheriffs of Bristol (1777)," in *Selected Works* (New York: Modern Library, 1960), pp. 177–224.

problem. Thus his formulation has had to be modified to account for the actual behavior of legislators.

Although no similar studies of other legislatures have yet been made, what we know about some of them does suggest certain speculative comparisons here. It would appear, for example, that more American than European legislators are primarily loyal to their districts. However, there are indications that it works the other way around, that more European than American legislators are delegates, for the Europeans usually expect to accept instructions from their parties. There is also some evidence that the legislator's concept of his role is associated with the degree of party competition. For example, legislators from competitive districts are more likely to be responsive to district instructions than those from safe districts.

GROUP LIFE OF LEGISLATORS

The legislator has a special set of role relationships with his colleagues. The legislature is not simply the forum for the confrontation of stimuli from the outside; it is a group in itself. And as a human group, it has a group life of its own; its members have interests of their own as distinguished from the interests of outsiders whom they represent. Accordingly, legislatures have sometimes been called exclusive clubs.

As in all other groups, legislators have their own informal norms of behavior, their unwritten rules. These norms prescribe the patterns of their relationships and regulate behavior. Interviews with national and state legislators in America and in Europe indicate that there is some uniformity in these norms. Everywhere new members are expected to serve an apprenticeship, during which they must be relatively quiet. All members usually understand that they should not talk too much or about subjects on which they have little knowledge; they know that they are expected to compromise to reach agreement with their fellow legislators and that they must maintain respect for the legislative institution.

Other norms may vary somewhat in their relative importance in different legislatures. American legislators, who are relatively free to make many individual decisions, place a high premium on predictability, especially on honoring one's commitments. European legislators may not be so concerned about predictability, since they simply assume conformity to caucus decisions. On the other hand, European legislators place a high premium on norms requiring hard work, especially work on dull and unpublicized committee tasks, for they regard this as a duty to their closely knit parties.

There are always members whose behavior does not conform to these norms. Such deviation is subject to sanctions which vary somewhat among different legislative institutions. American legislators are subject to social ostracism and may find it impossible to secure passage of their bills. European legislators can also be ostracized; but, more important, party organizations may threaten to drop a deviating member as a candidate at the next election.

Another aspect of the group life of legislatures concerns informal leadership patterns. (Formal leadership patterns have already been discussed earlier in this chapter.) However, mere occupancy of a leadership position does not ensure that one is in fact a leader exercising strong influence on the decision-making processes. Although some formal leaders may have great influence, formal and informal leadership patterns do not always coincide. Thus in some legislative bodies, members who do not hold formal leadership positions may exercise more influence than the formal leaders. One of the first tasks of a perceptive new member of a legislative body is to determine what the actual power structure of the institution is.

Group norms and informal leadership patterns are said to be functional when they help the legislature to achieve its purposes. In simplest terms, the legislators are involved in processes of bargaining and negotiating directed toward achieving the broadest possible consensus. Those engaged in these processes recognize that an opponent today may be an ally tomorrow, and thus conflict must be kept within limits to permit subsequent cooperation. Personal relationships must be conducted accordingly and lines of communication maintained. Consequently, American legislators from opposite parties often become close friends. But even European legislators from opposite parties may ultimately address one another in familiar rather than formal fashion after they have served together for a long time on committees. These personal relationships facilitate both understanding and any necessary compromises and thus contribute to the public acceptability of legislative decisions.

ROLL CALLS

The final record of a legislature's activities is the roll call, which is the formal announcement of the individual decisions of legislators. Although a roll call may conceal as many important facts as it reveals, it is measurable data which is easily obtainable and which can be used to determine some patterns of legislative behavior.

As early as 1901, A. Lawrence Lowell, one of the first important American political scientists, conducted a comparative study of roll calls in England and America and presented empirical evidence that party cohesion in the British Parliament was greater than in American legislative bodies.[16] Subsequently, Stuart A. Rice developed more refined techniques for determining the relative cohesion of various groups

---

[16] A. Lawrence Lowell, "The Influence of Party upon Legislation in England and America," *Annual Report of the American Historical Association for 1901*, I (Washington, D.C., 1902), 319–42.

in legislative bodies.[17] Following these pioneering developments of quantitative measures and the subsequent widespread use of computers, there has been a voluminous literature on roll calls of legislative bodies throughout the world.

Roll call studies demonstrate that American parties are less cohesive than most parties in other countries. British parties, on the other extreme, are among the most cohesive; even when free votes are allowed, party cohesion is high. German parties, with their so-called *Fraktionszwang*, were traditionally more cohesive than British parties; and the Social Democratic party of Germany still amost always achieves perfect unanimity on roll calls. However, the Christian Democratic Union and the Free Democratic party have become much less cohesive; many deputies of these parties have often voted against their party's position. French parties also reflect considerable diversity. The traditional French pattern had much in common with the contemporary German one: the left-wing parties were more cohesive than the right-wing. More recently, however, the patterns are increasingly complex, and a right-wing party inappropriately called the Independents has been one of the most cohesive parties. Some issues cut across party lines even in this multi-party system.

Although American parties reflect less cohesion on roll calls than most parties elsewhere, even here party affiliation is the most important single factor in legislative voting. However, research has revealed other factors that determine roll call behavior. Some of them include the following: rural-urban differences, sectional differences, social-economic composition of election districts, degree of party competition in election districts, and the legislator's membership in cliques and factions within the legislature. The relative importance of each of these factors differs with the issues being voted on.

In France and Germany there are also patterns in the deviations of roll calls from party positions. In France, local interests such as wine growing may determine the vote of a legislator. In Germany, the social origins and occupational interests of legislators have been a determinable factor in explaining deviation from party positions on roll calls.

Simple yes or no votes on roll calls do not, of course, indicate the intensity of legislators' support or opposition; nor do they indicate the extent of effort expended by legislators in supporting or opposing a proposal. But the measurable data provided by roll calls probably provide the best basis for beginning studies of legislative behavior.

[17] Stuart A. Rice, *Quantitative Methods in Politics* (New York: Alfred A. Knopf, 1928).

SUGGESTIONS FOR ADDITIONAL READING

CAMPION, LORD, and D. W. S. LIDDERDALE, *European Parliamentary Procedure: A Comparative Handbook* (London: George Allen and Unwin, 1953).

GROSS, BERTRAM M., *The Legislative Struggle: A Study in Social Combat* (New York: McGraw-Hill, Inc., 1953).

JENNINGS, IVOR, *Parliament* (New York: Cambridge University Press, 1957).

JEWELL, MALCOLM E. (ed.), *The Politics of Reapportionment* (New York: Atherton Press, 1962).

KEEFE, WILLIAM J., and MORRIS S. OGUL, *The American Legislative Process: Congress and the States* (Englewood Cliffs, N.J.: Prentice Hall, Inc., 1964).

LIDDERDALE, D. W. S., *The Parliament of France* (London: Hansard, 1951).

SCHUBERT, GLENDON, *Reapportionment* (New York: Charles Scribner's Sons, 1965).

ULLMANN, R. K., and STEPHEN KING-HALL, *German Parliaments: A Study in the Development of Representative Institutions in Germany* (London: Hansard, 1954).

WAHLKE, JOHN C., and HEINZ EULAU (eds.), *Legislative Behavior: A Reader in Theory and Research* (New York: The Free Press of Glencoe, 1959).

—— et al., *The Legislative System: Explorations in Legislative Behavior* (New York: John Wiley and Sons, 1962).

Chapter 16

POLITICAL EXECUTIVES

Leadership and Coordination

In this survey of the principal actors in the political process, we come finally to those most prominently in the public eye, the officials who for most people are the prime symbols and spokesmen, and sometimes even the personification, of their governments. These are the men at the executive pinnacles of government, men who by virtue of their positions are regarded as the foremost political leaders, and who are presumed to command the vast structures of the civil and military power of the state. Indeed, not too long ago the study of political power very often began and ended with the chief executive and the privileged few who advised or otherwise directly influenced him. But the five preceding chapters have shown us in some detail how distorted a view such a procedure would give us of contemporary political systems—and, as a corollary, how much more complex and difficult the task of political analysis has become. Nevertheless the roles of political executives not only remain important, but have become increasingly so in even the most democratic of political systems.

The Executive in Contemporary Political Systems

The turbulent changes of the twentieth century have produced some of history's most extreme examples of concentration of political power in single leaders. While Hitler, Stalin, and Mussolini may now have passed into history, even today the political systems of most Asian, African, Middle Eastern, and Latin American nations tend to be authoritarian or dictatorial, with political executives only slightly or not at all responsible to their peoples. The Communist regimes stretching from Central Europe to the Pacific are, of course, leading examples of concentrated executive power. And in Spain and Portugal, Western Europe has its representatives of systems with little or no popular or constitutional restraints upon their chief executives.

Indeed, even in those countries with the longest and most ingrained traditions of responsible and constitutionally restrained executives, those which continue periodically to hold reasonably free, fair, and competitive elections, the trend toward increased power and prominence of chief executives has been increasingly clear in this century. In England the decline of Parliament's power vis-à-vis the prime minister and his cabinet has been unmistakable. In France the experience with weak executives in the Third and Fourth Republics led to the executive-dominated constitution of 1958. In the United States, the twentieth century has witnessed marked growth in the role and power of the President, reversing the situation of the latter part of the nineteenth century, when Congress tended to dominate the executive. And in West Germany, a more recent recruit to the camp of democratic and representative government (yet the nation with the bitterest experience of a too-powerful executive), the constitution adopted after World War II effectively limited the Bundestag's power to dismiss the chancellor. It also avoided the split of powers between president and chancellor that had weakened the executive under the Weimar Constitution.

The underlying reasons for this worldwide trend are not difficult to discern, and need be outlined only briefly here. For one thing, periods of rapid and far-reaching change and of frequent domestic and international crises require quick and decisive political action: executives can provide it more effectively than legislative assemblies. Technological advances in communication, transportation, and weaponry only underline this requirement. In fact, technological developments across the whole spectrum of man's activity—political and economic as well as the more narrowly scientific—require the use of many kinds of highly specialized knowledge in policy-making; such knowledge is more accessible and more easily fed into the policy-making process in executive bureaucracies than in legislative assemblies. And public policy-making, which in the eighteenth and nineteenth centuries was largely concerned with the organization and distribution of political power (extension of the suffrage, representation, and so on) is now, by virtue of increased governmental responsibility for economic and social welfare, much more concerned with issues of what is to be done through the exercise of governmental power. The attempt to cope with complex economic and social problems depends crucially upon the intelligent use of such technical and specialized knowledge. Finally, conditions of change and crisis, experienced by increasing millions of people in urbanized, industrialized environments, are conducive to anxieties and tensions. Often people so affected seem to find some relief through focusing attention upon leaders whose images and pronouncements can bolster confidence, lessen fear, symbolize unity, and express aspirations—including aggressive aspirations. The development of mass political parties, mobilizing millions of voters, facilitates and reinforces such tendencies.

But whatever the reasons for the trend toward the increased power of political executives—and the reasons given above suggest it is a trend not easily checked or reversed—it poses a rather fundamental question for the relatively few political systems which have achieved and maintained democratic processes. Will they be able to survive as democratic systems, or will the increased power and importance of political executives gradually reshape them in the direction of authoritarianism until the freedoms, rights, and powers of their citizens are smothered? In other words, in the twentieth century is constitutional democracy obsolescent? A more terrifying question applies regardless of the democratic or autocratic character of a regime: will its leaders be able, given the onrushing complexity of political and military developments around the world, to perform their incredibly complex tasks of decision-making and leadership without triggering a hydrogen holocaust? From this perspective, the quality, skills, and organizational effectiveness of Soviet and Chinese political executives are as important to Americans and Europeans as those of their own leaders. A third question has direct implications for the preceding two: will the leaders of the "have not" nations be able to devise the strategies, make the choices, and direct the operations that will lead to the living standards, respect, and security that their peoples are clamorously demanding? The degree of their success or failure will have important consequences in world politics, and thus for the survival of democratic government—and conceivably of mankind itself.

To answer these questions would of course presuppose the gift of prophecy. Lacking that gift, however, we can still hope to gain some insight into the probabilities of different answers by examining the roles and functions of political executives and the dynamics of the political processes that affect them. Let us begin with a clarification of terms.

By political executives, we mean not only chiefs of state and heads of government—presidents, prime ministers, dictators, kings, and others we can call "chief" executives. The category also includes "secondary" executives: the members of cabinets, councils of ministers, supreme revolutionary councils, presidiums, or whatever else may be the institutional title of the inevitable body of men and women who participate in the making of policy and direct and control the bureaucratic agencies charged with its execution.

Even these general criteria unduly narrow the field when we look at some political systems. Where a significant degree of effective decentralization exists or where, as in some federal systems, some autonomy in certain spheres of action is maintained, the category of political executives includes those who hold executive positions in the subordinate but relatively autonomous units. Such, for example, would be the governors and some of the department and agency heads in state governments of the United States, some of the same officials in Brazil, even the mayors of many great cities—as well as the secondary executives who surround these officials. In the most inclusive sense, political executives are distinguishable by three criteria: they exercise significant discretion in the making of public policy decisions, they occupy official positions at the head of governmental bureaucracies or of distinct organizational components of such bureaucracies, and they are not members of career or professional civil services. In this chapter, however, we shall restrict our attention largely to the chief executives of national or independent political systems.

Types of Political Executives: Selection and Roles

The way they come to office and the kind of role they perform are convenient, if not entirely systematic, bases for distinguishing different types of chief executives. Both criteria depend largely upon the "type" of political system in question—and we have no wholly satisfactory typology of political systems. We shall therefore proceed by surveying the conventionally distinguished types of political chief executives, a method that at least has the virtue of revealing both the range of variety among chief executives and some of their important common characteristics.

HISTORICAL CHIEF EXECUTIVES

Selecting chief executives by inheritance is one of the oldest means on record. It most probably developed as political systems evolved from patriarchally or matriarchally ruled clans, tribes, and villages. Since the earliest political rulers also performed religious functions and were often thought to be endowed with divinity, their subjects could easily assume that divine sanction was passed on to a ruler's offspring. Such a means of transferring power would also, presumably, tend to prevent the crisis of succession that would otherwise occur whenever a ruler died or left office. Yet the histories of the world's monarchies and monarchical empires, East and West, are studded with usurpations of power, assassinations, and palace revolutions. And although some dynasties have been able to maintain unbroken lines of succession for as long as several centuries, all have eventually been displaced by other ruling families.

Hereditary recruitment has appeared in several different types of political systems, ranging from ancient despotisms and absolute monarchies (whether enlightened or benighted) through the various feudal systems to the constitutional monarchies maintained in some nations even today. In the constitutional monarchies of modern Europe effective power has passed from the hands of royal families to other political executives; that is, these hereditary monarchs are no longer political executives. It is significant that nowhere has hereditary monarchy survived as an effective means of ruling industrial urban societies without such transference or sharing of power. Societies in which traditional hereditary monarchs are still chief executives, such as Iran, Ethiopia, Saudi Arabia, and Nepal, are still predominantly agricultural or nomadic.

A closely related means of selection, used, for example, by some of the Roman emperors, is cooptation. By this method, the ruler, who may be without an heir, designates his eventual successor and may adopt him as a son, thus strengthening the younger man's claim on the throne. Modern parallels to this practice, although less formal and stopping short of legal adoption, can be seen in the occasional efforts of an elected chief executive to "build up" a protégé in party circles and in public opinion so that the protégé will later have a good chance to win the office for himself. One recent (but unsuccessful) attempt to do this was President Eisenhower's effort before and during the 1960 presidential campaign to pass the mantle of leadership to Vice-President Nixon.

Election of the chief executive is not a recent invention. In ancient Byzantium, Mexico, and China, new rulers were sometimes chosen from the kin of a deceased or deposed ruler through election by a council or other limited elite group. This practice, of course, reflected no democratic tendencies, but was merely an institutionalized means of overcoming the crisis of succession where the principle of inheritance was not operative. The group from which the ruler might be chosen was extremely limited, as was the group which chose him.

All these procedures, however, are more or less formalized and *nonviolent* methods of determining who shall succeed to executive leadership. Historically, the question has very often been determined by military conquest, assassination, *coup d'état,* or more or less extensive revolution. The varieties of violent change of governmental leadership will be examined in the next chapter, in the wider perspective of the manifold processes of political change. Here we need note only that coercive and violent processes have historically been very common means of settling the question of who shall rule. In any system, aspirants for power who are excluded or ineligible under the established procedure for choosing political executives have only two other avenues to power—changing the procedure or resorting to violence; and the former alternative can conceivably entail the latter. As a corollary, it would seem that where eligibility is not too narrowly restricted and effective alternative channels or pathways to legitimate political power have been opened up through such institutions as parties and elections, the resort to violence would become less necessary and frequent. But the key word here is "effective": in many political systems "parties" exist and "elections" are held, but under conditions in which no genuine alternatives are submitted to popular choice, or in which competition for political leadership is so unequal or tightly controlled that formal party processes and elections have little if anything to do with who wins. Thus the ancient patterns and practices of succession through violence live vigorously on into the present.

Given the wide and fascinating variety of personalities, historical situations, and cultures of these predemocratic, preconstitutional, pre-industrial political executives, what general statements can be made about their roles? What common characteristics can we find that would permit us to lump together in one category such historical and culturally different personages as European absolute monarchs, Roman emperors, Egyptian pharoahs, and Chinese emperors? Bearing in mind that our comments apply to *most* and not *all* such executives and that patterns or tendencies manifest themselves in differing combinations and with differing degrees of clarity, we can still discern surprising similarities in the roles of most of the myriad political chiefs of established tribes, principalities, kingdoms, and empires over the course of pre-democratic and pre-industrial history.

For example, one of the most striking elements in the roles of these political chief executives was the religious. Most of them claimed, and were accorded, divine origin, or at least divine approbation and sanction—from the "Heavenly Mandate" of the Chinese emperors to the "divine right" of European monarchs. Most had religious functions to perform (presiding at ceremonies or consecrating holidays and festivals). Consequently, there was a wide and unbridgeable gap between the ruler and the ruled, with the awe of the latter reinforcing the aloofness or arrogance of the former. Such beliefs on both sides fostered the general tendency to ritual and pomp, which were maintained even when more realistic or cynical observation and insight had eroded the validity of the sacred pretensions. In the process of executive decision-making itself, it was not uncommon for augury, revelation, or other religious techniques to have important if not decisive weight.

Under such conditions a ruler's power was limited by only three factors: the technological means at his disposal; the countervailing power of other groups, institutions, or rulers in his political environment, both domestic and foreign; and his own self-restraint. In some political systems these factors combined to produce evolution toward constitutional or limited power of chief executives; in others the trend was toward dictatorial or despotic rule. In any event, the destiny of the people ruled by such regimes was more dependent on the ruler's personality, preferences, and decisions than is the case in contemporary constitutional systems.

Two distinctive patterns of power distribution are to be noted in these earlier political systems. In one the exercise by a limited number of subordinates of independent control over territory, manpower, or both denied the ruler absolute power over these subordinates—in fact permitted them to impose restraints upon the ruler. In these conditions, as during the feudal period in Europe, a system of mutual or reciprocal obligations and loyalties evolved, with the subordinate feudal vassals owing loyalty, tribute, and certain services to the ruler, who in turn was obligated to protect his vassals and to respect their rights to rule and exploit their own territories. Similar arrangements have appeared in many other parts of the world at various times; and even most of the absolute monarchs of Europe were subject to some checks by the landed aristocracy and the church. In the other pattern, central rulers were able to overcome the restraints on their rule imposed by such subordinate landowners and leaders, and thus were able to exercise much less restricted power. Such was the organization of the bureaucratic empires of old, and to a lesser extent, of some of the absolute monarchies.

Rulers of these earlier periods were often called upon to decide not only major questions of policy but also many petty disputes among their subjects. Certain times were often set aside during which the ruler heard the petitions and appeals of the aggrieved. In this way conscientious rulers could maintain a limited amount of contact with the ruled—and from such practices judicial systems grew. Nowadays political chief executives periodically make similar gestures, such as personally answering letters or receiving visits from "ordinary" citizens—children are favorites here—with appropriate attention from press secretaries or propaganda ministries.

Typically, there was little or no distinction between the ruler's personal household affairs and those affairs of the realm which we would today call "public." No clear distinction was drawn between the personal attendants and retainers of the ruler and those subordinates concerned with looking after governmental matters, between "personal employees" or servants and "public employees." In fact, the same people often engaged in both kinds of activity. Similarly, the ruler's personal income was not usually differentiated from what we would now consider public revenues.

Finally, it is worth noting that although intrigue and covert maneuvering for favor or advantage are common around any seat of power, such behavior was probably even more pronounced in the entourages of the class of rulers we are considering here, for several reasons. The courtiers and officials were more frequently and to a higher degree dependent on the favor and patronage of the ruler for their own wealth, position, and future. Furthermore, opportunities for some of them to extend their influence to the point of dominating even the ruler himself were not infrequent: if the accidents of heredity put a weak or malleable person on the throne, a Rasputin in the shadows or a mistress in the royal bedchamber might not find it difficult to plant ideas, suggestions, and requests that could influence or determine the ruler's decisions. Such positions are easier to reach and hold where the political system includes no representative legislature maintaining a critical scrutiny of executive affairs, no independent judiciary reviewing executive actions, and no free press inquiring into such actions and reporting to a literate and politically signficant populace. Indeed, the façade of pomp, ritual, and the court on occasion made it possible for rulers whose interests lay elsewhere to turn over to more willing hands the job of weighing alternatives and making decisions.

MODERN DICTATORIAL CHIEF EXECUTIVES

The selection of chief executives by birth is increasingly rare; the prevalent patterns today are forceful seizure of power and competitive or controlled election. As has already been suggested, however, the mere holding of elections does not necessarily indicate that an electorate is actually expressing a free choice among alternatives. Thus while most contemporary dictatorships were established more or less by violence, many of them have employed elections, referenda, and plebiscites to legitimize their power, increase public acquiescence and support, express national unity, and perpetuate themselves in office. Modern means of organization, of control and manipulation of the important media of communication, and of coercion make it possible for dictatorial regimes to hold elections without risk to themselves.

While the roles of dictatorial chief executives share some important elements and characteristics, it is essential to recognize several distinctions. A basic one is the degree to which the regime of a dictator is "totalitarian." Many dictators, concentrating political power in their own hands, seek to extend their control over their subjects only so far as is necessary to prevent threats to their continued exercise of power, leaving relatively untouched many aspects of life and society—the religious, the cultural, or even the economic, for example. To the extent that political control is extended throughout society, regulating and controlling additional spheres of activity, the system approaches the totalitarian end of the scale, as in Nazi Germany or Soviet Russia. Obviously there are degrees of totalitarianism; compare, for example, Hitler's regime with Mussolini's, or Stalin's with Khrushchev's. But all these totalitarian dictatorships are significantly different from the typical authoritarian dictatorships of, say, Central and South America.

A second important variation among dictatorial chief executives lies in the nature of their ideological orientation and the intensity of their ideological commitment. The more militantly ideological dictators, such as the twentieth-century Communist, Nazi, and Fascist leaders, give prominence in their policy statements and propaganda to doctrines that designate goals for the community, indicate the means for achieving them, and justify the ends and the means. Such ideological systems, not inaccurately described as "political religions," function as sources of inspiration and guidance for political leadership. When they include enough popular symbols and are widely disseminated through the mass media and educational systems, they can serve as means for the integration and mobilization of political communities. In contrast to the democratic ideologies, their exaltation of ends leads them to deny that the means to these ends have moral as well as purely instrumental significance; thus they can establish the ethical and intellectual groundwork for justifying concentration camps and mass terror.

With few exceptions, the most ideologically committed dictators have established the most totalitarian political systems. Although the word "totalitarian" was coined by an Italian Fascist to describe Mussolini's regime, it was Hitler and Stalin who provided the most thoroughgoing examples in practice; under their leadership was achieved the most nearly total penetration and control of all aspects of private life by the state. The unreserved fanaticism and submission of mass-based corps of partisans; the control and manipulation of the armed forces, the police, and the mass media of communication; the infiltration and subjugation of all significant institutions and organizations; and the systematic and uncompromising use of terror distinguish the ideological totalitarians from the less ideologically committed dictators.

In this latter category are such leaders as Franco in Spain, Salazar in Portugal, Vargas in Brazil, Gursel in Turkey, or Sarit in Thailand. Although such men have held political ideologies, their ideologies have not been as explicitly totalitarian and have played a much less prominent part in their regimes.

Falling at various points between these extremes are many of the remaining modern dictators: Korea's Park, Indonesia's Sukarno, Ghana's Nkrumah, Egypt's Nasser. Their ideological orientation may be described as militant nationalism. But while the commitment to nationalism may be strong, leading them in some instances to more stringent domestic policies or more provocative foreign policies than their less ideological counterparts espouse, it does not carry them to the heights of control, repression, and terror reached by the classic models of totalitarianism.

An interesting ideological variant among twentieth-century dictators is manifested by those who found it expedient or necessary to organize parties or movements and to endow them with more or less *ad hoc* ideologies. Ideologies of this type were associated with the regimes of Juan Perón in Argentina and of Ngo Dinh Diem in South Vietnam. But where dictatorial leaders have come to power first and only afterward developed an ideological "doctrine," it appears that it is the power or popular appeal of the leader rather than the ideology which is important.

A third factor important in making distinctions among contemporary dictators is the question of whether a dictator's career background is military or civil. Regimes in which the chief executives are military men have been common throughout history; indeed, many dynasties of earlier epochs were established by military leaders. And in many parts of the world down to the present, the "man on horseback" or the military "junta" have been leading actors in the political drama. Especially in Latin America and the Middle East have military intervention and control been frequent in recent decades. It is interesting, however, that the "militarism" of some military political leaders in such parts of the world tends to be of a different brand from the militarism associated with European traditions. European militarists in the name of "national honor" defended the status quo and/or sought to conquer their neighbors, whereas in the economically less developed areas the most technologically advanced and development-minded elements of the population are sometimes to be found among the armed forces' officer corps. Rather than embarking upon military conquest and expansion after seizing power, such groups often justify their action as having been necessary to speed economic development by removing it from the hands of corrupt or bumbling civilian politicians. While they are by no means "democratic," they promise more decisive, efficient, and honest administration of governmental programs.

But political and military leadership and management differ, even in systems accustomed to autocratic traditions. Chief executives recruited from the professional armed forces frequently find their new roles less simple and congenial than they had anticipated. Used to greater discipline, more automatic obedience to commands, and more concrete problems of strategy and tactics, they are frustrated by unavoidable political requirements of more subtle maneuver, negotiation, and compromise and by the greater intractability and more lackadaisical compliance of civilian bureaucracies. Sometimes they underestimate the importance of imaginative articulation of policies and of the manipulation of symbols to catch the attention and fire the enthusiasm of large segments of the population—skills more commonly possessed by civilian political leaders, even those whose other skills and integrity may be open to question. And often military leaders have little familiarity with the intricacies of economic theory and fiscal policy, on which so much depends in economic development. Thus when military leaders control a government, and even when they are committed to progressive developmental policies, they may find themselves having to resort more frequently to the violence and force which brought them to power in the first place. On the other hand, when a military leader happens to have or can acquire sufficient charisma and can learn to deal with the technical aspects of economic and social problems—as did, for example, Colonel Gamal Abdul Nasser in Egypt—a military regime may be able to overcome such handicaps and institute significant political, economic, and social changes.

The foregoing is not meant to imply that the older-style military dictatorship has passed from the scene. To the contrary, many continue to seek to perpetuate pre-existing social and economic patterns. In the Western Hemisphere, Paraguay provides a leading example of a military regime less interested in development than in maintaining a status quo beneficial to the military élite and its aristocratic allies. Until fairly recent years, in fact, military regimes of this type were much more the norm throughout Latin America.

Dictatorial regimes in which the chief executive and his principal subordinate officials come from non-military backgrounds have also been frequent in the twentieth century. In many ways they resemble the militaristic regimes we have just discussed, but it is worth noting a few important points on which they differ. For one thing, the non-military leaders usually have had greater experience than the military in such political arts as persuasion, public speaking, informal leadership, and party organization, for the chances are that the vehicle that carried them to office was a party or a mass movement. Thus they may be able to communicate with and respond to wider segments of the populace than can most military leaders. This is not always an asset, however; popular demands sometimes exceed the practical capacity of a government to satisfy them, or they may be of such a nature (for example, for consumer goods) that their satisfaction would interfere seriously with more basic programs of economic development.

The civilian dictator also faces a problem in establishing and maintaining control over the armed forces that is obviously different from that faced by the military dictator, who brings his military authority with him to the post of chief executive. The civilian can seek to win over the military commanders by granting special privileges and rewards to the military as a whole or to key officers, by "politicizing" the military by infiltrating it with political spies and secret police and making promotions contingent upon the officers' political reliability, and by playing the separate branches of the armed services off against one another. Obviously, however, key members of the armed services are in strong bargaining positions vis-à-vis a non-military chief executive, all the more so if they maintain a united front. If they have their own political ideas and interests to advance or protect, the outcome may be that the civilian dictator is more or less dominated by military commanders.

The differences we have noted among dictatorial leaders are of great importance. But we must also note certain general characteristics that seem to be exhibited by all or most dictatorial executives. A few generalizations about their recruitment (using that term broadly) and their roles can be offered here, but more systematic comparative research is needed to qualify such generalizations and to establish others.

A large proportion of dictators—certainly all the most spectacular twentieth-century examples—have come from rather humble family backgrounds. And whether they have moved to governmental posts from the leadership of military or civilian groups, almost all have come to power during a period of crisis and instability.[1] A partial exception is Antonio de Oliveira Salazar of Portugal. He was first appointed minister of finance (1928), in which office he became a powerful polit-

1 For some leading examples, see Chapter 17.

ical figure; by 1932, when he was appointed prime minister, he had already all but transformed his constitutional office into one of dictatorial proportions. In Latin America, likewise, elected presidents have sometimes transformed their regimes into dictatorships. But wherever a dictatorial regime is established, its character virtually guarantees that the next change of leadership will come in conditions of crisis or violence or perhaps both. Seldom do dictators, whatever their variety, willingly and peacefully step down.

In some ways the role of the modern dictator is similar to that of the earlier autocratic rulers. Whereas the latter sought legitimacy in religious terms, the twentieth-century dictator's ideological terms of reference are predominantly secular—but, particularly in totalitarian regimes, they may be taken just as seriously as was the doctrine of divine right. Though ceremony, ritual, and pomp may have lost much of their religious or superstitious overtones, they can be used to manifest the symbols of legitimacy and unity; and in focusing deferential attention upon the ruler, one may surmise, they gratify his ego as well as engendering popular acceptance or support.

Like the rulers of earlier times, the contemporary dictator's power is limited only by the technological means available, the power of others, and his own self-restraint. But the relative importance of these three factors has changed dramatically because of technological advances, which have vastly extended government's capacity to manipulate and oppress the governed. High-speed, almost instantaneous communication, fantastically more thorough and elaborate intelligence-gathering and record-keeping, centrally controllable mass media of communication, extremely rapid transportation, much more accurate and powerful weapons, far more sophisticated knowledge of individual psychology and social organization—all of these have made tyranny possible on a scale undreamed of by the despots of old. Indeed, totalitarianism on the scale of Nazi Germany was a technical impossibility as recently as one hundred years ago. In the absence of effectively exercised countervailing power or self-restraint on the part of modern dictators, the logical consequence of the technological revolution and some of the ideologies it has spawned is "1984."

Another important contrast with the autocratic rulers of old is the tendency of present-day dictators to invoke symbols referring to the interests of "the people" in political discourse and to make parallel efforts to establish links with the anonymous masses. Through party organization, elaborate "front" associations, and propaganda in all accessible channels of communication, the symbols of democracy are sedulously disseminated and manipulated, often in careful complement to those slogans and reports calculated to foster a "cult of personality" around the supreme leader. But even when dictators are sincere in the conviction that they govern *for* the people, they do not tolerate government *by* the people.

Regardless of the degree of totalitarianism or the brand and intensity of ideology, and regardless of whether the regime is military or civilian or of the technological resources available, chief executives in dictatorial systems confront problems with their principal subordinates, advisors, and assistants not unlike those of the earlier rulers. The second-echelon political executives depend for their power and position on a combination of the favor of their chief and their control of or support by certain significant elements and organizations in the political system. Sometimes these elements are a church or a party; often they are the police or one or more branches of the military. Thus when factions develop within the leadership group, as they almost inevitably do, the chief executive may have to face the delicate problem of maintaining an equilibrium among several powerful contending forces.

If the chief executive is in firm control of the main instrumentalities of power, he has another problem, the equally difficult task of distinguishing between genuine and sycophantic affirmations of loyalty and support. For political power is always and everywhere an object of competition and rivalry: One who "holds" a large share of it can never lose sight of the desires of others to take it from him. In political systems which lack institutionalized and peaceful processes for transferring power, the stakes are particularly high. To lose one's power or to fall from grace often means to lose one's life or liberty as well—politics is "played for keeps." Thus the central arenas of decision-making are pervaded with much more acute and explosive tensions than those in constitutional political systems.

RESPONSIBLE CHIEF EXECUTIVES

The differences between dictatorial political executives and executives in constitutional, democratic systems can perhaps best be summed up by reference to the concept of responsibility discussed in Chapter 11. In the constitutional democracies, political executives are responsible and accountable—in a relatively effective and not merely formalistic sense—to the citizenry as a whole. That is, periodic opportunities occur for the citizenry, acting in conditions of relative freedom, to remove and replace them in an orderly and peaceful manner. Thus the mode of selection of responsible chief executives is, with few exceptions, elective. Moreover, between elections political executives are subject to institutionalized demands and restraints that reflect the interests of broad segments of society, and how they respond can be the critical factor in whether they keep or lose their offices.

Thus the power of executives in this type of political system is subject to definite limits. The limits may not be precisely understood in all areas and situations, but awareness of their existence conditions political and administrative calculations and actions. Such limits are significantly narrower than in the dictatorial systems; reciprocally, the limits of the citizenry's individual and collective freedom of thought, communication, and action—and thus of its power—are significantly broader. Of great importance are the ideologies and legal systems of such societies, accepted by their political executives themselves, which demand and reinforce such arrangements.

In reality, however, the broad criteria we have noted do not always indicate clearly into which category a given executive falls, for in no political system does the *entire* citizenry participate (for example, through elections) in holding the chief executive accountable. Wide differences in such factors as literacy, wealth, political experience and awareness, and exposure or access to relevant information mean that some electorates are much more effective than others, and that within electorates some individuals and groups are much more influential than others. In some systems differences in the strength of interest groups, opposition parties, or institutional checks on the executive may require greater reliance on executive self-restraint if responsibility is to be maintained. Even in unquestionably democratic systems, chief executives command powerful organizational and technological means with which to influence opinion; their very prominence gives them enormous advantages. Thus competition between candidates when one is an incumbent is sometimes severely unequal. Finally, the legally exercised authority of democratic executives may in some areas or in some times of emergency be so broad as to earn the appellation of "constitutional dictatorship."

In spite of the differences between systems, however, the role of political leadership imposes certain requirements and expectations on dictatorial and responsible executives alike. These will be examined more systematically in the following section; here we need simply note that neither the democratic nor the autocratic executive can escape the demand that he lead. As we shall see, the trappings of formal authority are in the final analysis little more than a weak crutch unless a political executive is also able to carry along with him in his aims and strategies his political and administrative colleagues and subordinates and a significant portion of the politically active population. For in the constant and competitive struggle for influence and power that characterizes the arenas in which executives work, they must assert and maintain the initiative or others will.

As with the dictatorial class of chief executives, certain important (although different) variable conditions affect the roles of responsible executives. Three of the most important are: the character of the constitutional system (parliamentary, presidential, or "mixed"); the character of the party system; and the strength and powers of the representative legislature with which the executive must work.

If the constitutional system is parliamentary, as in England or Germany, the executive branch is headed by a chief of state, a prime minister (or premier or chancellor) and a cabinet or council of ministers. Of these, the prime minister is the effective chief executive; the chief of state is a monarch or president whose powers, other than that of designating the prime minister, are only formal, advisory, and ceremonial. And in designating the prime minister, the chief of state has little or no discretion when one party or bloc controls a majority of seats in the principal legislative body; designation of the leader of the majority is automatic. Otherwise, as in multi-party systems or when a prime minister dies or resigns without having lost the confidence of the legislative majority, the chief of state may be able to exercise a choice among several potential replacements. But in any event the person designated must be acceptable to a legislative majority.

The prime minister, on the other hand, designates the other members of the cabinet, takes the leadership in policy formulation, and is the major strategist and spokesman for the government. He and the other ministers accept responsibility *to* the legislative body (and the electorate) *for* the direction and management of public affairs. Responsibility is maintained by the relationship of confidence: as long as a legislative majority has confidence in the chief executive and his cabinet, they remain in office; when the confidence of the majority is no longer forthcoming, the government resigns, to be replaced by another. Sometimes it may be necessary to hold new elections to the legislature in order to settle the question of the majority there, or it may be possible to form a new majority in the legislature by negotiating new alliances among the parties represented. But even without a formal loss of support by the legislative majority, such systems require new elections to the main legislative body before the lapse of a specified number of years.

Such relationships with the legislative body emphasize the importance of the prime minister's experience and skills in leadership and negotiation. In Great Britain and most other parliamentary systems, he is invariably a man who has risen through years of experience in the legislative assembly to a position of leadership in his party. However, he is elected to his legislative seat not by the country at large but by a single limited constituency.

The presidential chief executive, on the other hand, is elected by a nationwide electorate, and in him are combined the powers and responsibilities that in parliamentary systems are divided between the chief of state and the prime minister: he is both ceremonial chief of state and effective chief executive. He may not have had prior legislative or even governmental experience (although most often he has), and he holds office independently of the legislative assembly or of his ability to command the confidence of a majority of its members. His responsibility is thus directly to the electorate, rather than indirectly via the legislative body. But this circumstance can pit him against the legislative body in a conflict the intensity of which varies in proportion to the effective political strength of the latter. Thus where the legislature is composed of men whose bases of political power are different and to a large extent independent of the president's, as in the United States, the president has as much need of skills in legislative strategy, bargaining, and leadership as does the prime minister in a parliamentary system. But whereas the most important legislative leaders in a parliamentary system are to be found in the cabinet and at the head of the departments and ministries of the executive branch, in the presidential system of the United States, such legislative leaders are excluded from the cabinet (which is accordingly a less significant organ). In such a system presidential influence must be directed toward the cabinet members on the one hand, and toward legislative leaders on the other. For like the prime minister, the presidential chief executive is also chief legislator, and his success depends on being able to induce legislative majorities to accept his proposals.

The Fifth Republic in France can be considered an experimentally "mixed" presidential-parliamentary system. The French president, since a constitutional amendment of 1962 elected directly by a national electorate, exercises important executive powers. He does, however, appoint a prime minister and cabinet to serve as the government, making policy and directing its implementation, and this government must receive and retain the confidence of the legislative assembly in order to remain in office. But in spite of this parliamentary type of responsibility, members of the cabinet cannot at the same time hold legislative seats. Thus the executive powers and personnel are separated from the legislative and are divided between president and prime minister, the latter, with his ministers, being held responsible to the legislative body. As was shown in Chapter 4, however, the personality and leadership of President Charles de Gaulle overshadow the formal constitutional arrangements of the Fifth Republic to such an extent that one of the few safe predictions that can be made in political affairs is that the Fifth Republic, if it is not superseded by a Sixth, will function in a decidedly different manner when its second president takes office.

A second basic condition affecting the roles of responsible chief executives is the character of the party system. A number of variables are important here. The number of parties is one factor: whether there is a single dominant party, as in India or Mexico; two genuinely competitive parties, either of which has a realistic chance of controlling the government, as in Great Britain or the United States; or three or more parties, none of which gains a majority of electoral support or legislative representation, as in Brazil, Italy, and France under the Third and Fourth Republics. Also important is the degree of unity and discipline of the party or parties (for example, relatively high in Britain, fairly low in the United States, and markedly higher in some than in others in France and Italy). A third important consideration is the presence and relative strength of totalitarian parties—and related to this, the degree of ideological conflict or consensus among the most important parties.

These variables combine in different ways in individual political systems, and the consequences are crucial for executive roles. Where the chief executive's party in a parliamentary system controls the legislative assembly, as in Great Britain or India, the government would seem to be in a much more advantageous position to have its major measures voted by the assembly. But if majority-party control is as dominant as it is in India, the prime minister is much more likely to face rival factions within the party, with the result that policy proposals reflect the least common denominator of agreement among the party's factions, raised as high as the prime minister's negotiating and leadership skills allow. The situation of the responsible chief executive in a democratically oriented one-party system is likely to be more similar to that of the same figure in a multi-party system than to that of the chief executive in a relatively disciplined two-party system. Such a chief executive must expend a large portion of his time and energy in negotiating compromises among the various wings of his own party, just as the multi-party executive must do among the various parties in his coalition. Both lack the unifying tonic of a strong and cohesive opposition; cabinet meetings, for example, cannot but be affected when the representatives of several different and competing parties or factions are sitting around the table.

Similarly, if in a two-party system the cohesion and discipline within the parties is low, the chief executive must negotiate and exert pressures to hold his own legislative party together on important votes in the congress or parliament. In the United States, the President is often compelled to go outside his own party and seek support in the opposition party—all the more so if the opposition has a majority in Congress. Indeed, because of the tendency of both Democratic and Republican parties to divide into liberal and conservative wings in Congress, there is some justice in describing the congressional pattern as a four-party system.

The presence in significant strength of totalitarian parties or groups in the party system, as in France and Italy, creates special problems for the democratically responsible chief executive. Because Communist or Fascist parties, under whatever label, are highly disciplined and seek ultimately to destroy the more or less liberal, competitive, and constitutional political systems in which they operate, they constitute "indigestible" forces of opposition. Their presence in legislative bodies reduces the responsible chief executive's field of maneuver, as most of the time they can be counted on to vote against his proposals. Thus he must obtain among the non-totalitarian or "constitutional" parties majorities large enough not only to overcome those in such groups who may oppose him, but also to outweigh the anti-constitutional totalitarians.

The latter also contribute to instability in the system because of their extremist views and their tactics which reflect fundamental contempt for parliamentary "rules of the game." If the combined strength of totalitarian groups in a legislative body approaches 50 per cent of the seats, they can, even though they may be bitterly opposed to each other, very nearly bring about legislative paralysis. The outcome of such a situation may be governmental *immobilisme* in which the only means remaining to deal with the most pressing issues is the executive decree, whether or not authorized by the constitution or the legislature. Obviously, the presence of totalitarian parties implies important ideological cleavages in a society—an absence of consensus on the basic question of the nature of the regime and on the ground rules of political conflict. Whether such lack of consensus stems from contemporary conditions, such as economic dislocations or incapacity of the political system to settle important demand conflicts among powerful groups, or from historical crises whose issues have never been satisfactorily resolved— for example, a revolution or civil war—it increases the problems of political leadership because of both the instability and the obstacles to compromise it engenders.

But even among the "constitutional" parties, and whether totalitarian parties are significant in the system or not, ideological differences may be strong enough to seriously impede the formation of majorities in support of effective leadership. For example, the Revolution of 1789 and the separation of church and state have still not been accepted by all Frenchmen. And the issues of racial prejudice, discrimination, and segregation remain as a disturbing legacy of the Civil War in the United States, a century after the war's end. The party systems of both countries reflect these old divisions. No doubt there will always be ideological differences and conflicts of some sort within any human society (political life would be monotonous, indeed, without them); but when the divisions are as deep as these are, political executives are unavoidably required to face extremely delicate—and potentially highly explosive—problems in formulating policies and resolving contradictory demands.

The party system may contribute to or impede the resolution of such problems. If it is a predominantly two-party system, for example, the competition of each party for a majority of electoral support tends to force both toward moderate positions as each seeks to appeal not only to its own regular supporters, but also to the decisive category of uncommitted or "independent" voters between them. But if each of several major ideological tendencies has evolved its own partisan organization, so that none can reasonably expect to gain support from a majority of the voters, each party organization may become more concerned with ideological purity and the doctrines which distinguish it from the others. In the first instance an important part of the problem of resolving ideological differences may be handled within the parties and thus not rise to the level of the chief executive for settlement; in the second, the chief executive is likely to face conflicts of ideology that are more complex and more intense.

The third general condition important in shaping the responsible chief executive's role is the legislature with which he must work. If strong, it can circumscribe his powers, block or modify his policy proposals, or even initiate policies for him to carry out. But this chapter began by noting the general trend toward diminution of the role of legislatures in relation to executives. The ominous portent of this trend is based on the historical knowledge that in England, "Mother of Parliaments," the *growth* in power of the legislative branch was the means by which the monarchical executive was constitutionalized and through which a free and representative political system slowly evolved. Does the twentieth-century decline of legislatures mean that constitutionalism and political freedom will again give way to executive tyranny?

No certain answer can be given. But our survey of the roles of chief executives, as well as some of the points made in the five preceding chapters, provide us with some of the elements that would have to be taken into account. We can begin by observing that what appeared to work as a causal relationship through one period of time (growing legislative power—increasingly constitutionalized and responsible executive power) does not necessarily hold true in reverse through another period of time (declining role of legislature—decreasing constitutionalization and responsibility of the executive). A number of additional factors have to be considered. One is the development of party and interest-group structures, both those that support chief executives and those that oppose and criticize them. Another is the extension of the suffrage and the dependence of parties and chief executives upon popular electoral support and acceptance. A third is the growth of judicial systems which, in varying ways and to varying degrees, restrain or channel the exercise of executive powers. A fourth is the role of public opinion, supported by the many media of mass communication. And a fifth is the broadly based strength of the values of constitutionalism and democratic responsibility in the ideologies of those political systems under consideration here.

This is not to say that any or all of these factors will necessarily compensate for the changed role of modern legislative bodies in preventing the evolution of responsible chief executives into dictators. But it is necessary to emphasize that factors such as these, intricately related to each other and to legislative bodies, are also strategic factors in relation to executive roles. The chief executive must then weigh them all in his planning and decision-making, sometimes trying to manipulate one or more of them as a means of influencing others. The more powerful the legislative body vis-à-vis the executive, the more his time and efforts have to be directed toward maintaining its confidence and gaining its assent to his proposals. In the United States, where his proposals can be modified or even rejected by Congress, the President's success or failure can depend on how well he manages his relations with that body. Presidents have accordingly developed a wide array of strategies and techniques, both constitutional and extra-constitutional, for leading, influencing, and pressuring Congress; and Congress has available to it a comparable battery of legal and political means, both for self-defense and for influencing the President. In Great Britain, while the government's majority control of Commons assures that its program will be accepted by that body, the prime minister and members of the cabinet have to handle relations with the "back benchers" of their own party so that the latter will not become disaffected. The government must also meet the minority party's questions and criticisms and defend government policies and actions in debate with sufficient skill to maintain its backing among attentive segments of the public, and eventually among the electorate as a whole.

With certain variations, the same requirements and problems face political executives in any political systems that can accurately be called democratic and responsible. In spite of their seemingly great authority, such executives must include persuasion and bargaining as fundamental tools in their political power kit. Therefore, although the trends toward executive predominance have been clear, legislative assemblies should by no means be written off as either obsolete or ineffectual. They continue to be vital factors in the democratic policy-making process and significant aspects of the political environment of responsible chief executives.

The Analysis of Leadership

From a survey of the roles and practices of chief executives in various types of political systems, we turn now to more general and theoretical questions associated with the concept of "leadership." For the executive role requires the exercise of leadership, and few attain executive positions in the modern world without first having demonstrated in one way or another some talent or desire to be leaders.

The distinction between leaders and followers is a familiar one, a first step in political analysis for all concerned with investigating the phenomena of political power. But the meaning of "leadership" as an analytic concept is by no means clear; the word has been used in many different ways and for many different purposes. Most analysts agree that it is unprofitable to think of leadership solely in terms of specific qualities or traits of personality or character (assertiveness, intelligence, articulateness, and so on) possessed by all persons who are "leaders," for the traits of the "good" or "natural" leader in one group of people are qualities which may exclude a person from leadership in another group. Recognition of this shifts the focus of our attention to the *relationships* between leaders and followers in particular group contexts, particularly when we recognize also that the distinction between leaders and followers tends to appear in every human group, whatever its size, purposes, or character. This emphasis on relationships does not mean that we can ignore the personalities of leaders in order to concentrate on their social contexts or situations, for particular groups or situations may consistently require leaders to possess certain skills, talents, or "traits." But it does suggest that the most valid generalizations about leadership may be derived from examining the interaction between leaders and followers.

It is also clear that leadership is not a matter of mere domination by some and submission by others, although what we call dominance and submission may be more or less visible in any group where we can distinguish leaders and followers. Rather than thinking of leadership exclusively in terms of domination, we must think also of distinctions based upon division of labor and specialization of functions. In order for any group, from an informal street corner gang to a highly institutionalized and complicated national political system, to maintain its existence and act with some degree of concert in pursuit of goals or common interests, certain kinds of things must be accomplished. The activities that accomplish these things seem to be associated with "leadership" roles—that is, whoever does them is likely to be considered a "leader," and whoever is considered a "leader" will be expected to get them done. In complex groups, roles are organized to meet these requirements, so that the study of "leadership" involves examining the relationships among a variety of roles in an organizational or institutional setting. In simple groups, leadership functions are usually performed by fewer persons (perhaps only one), not parceled out among a great number of more specialized roles; the role of "leader" may be informal, not attached to any formal office or organizational structure. However, in some groups leadership may shift regularly from one to another according to the type of issue, problem, or activity.

Viewed this way, leadership and followership are interrelated specializations that occur at all echelons of the political system, from the chief executive's cabinet to the road maintenance crew, from Congress to the precinct committee. In other words, wherever a group can be identified, we can expect to find some manifestation of leadership. Thus, since countless subgroups, both formal and informal, can be found within any large-scale organization, it follows that leadership processes and problems extend deep into the hierarchical structure of organizations and are not all concentrated at the top. And this also implies that democratic groups need effective leadership as much as any other kind of group—a point sometimes overlooked by those who too quickly equate executive decision-making with some degree of autocracy, and who limit the use of the term "democracy" to group or collegial decision-making where each member has an equal vote. For even in group decision-making, leadership can usually be found.

To summarize, then, our conception of leadership is quite different from the view that leadership arises from any special traits of character or personality, and in some ways is contradictory to that view. In addition, our conception differs from the view that leadership emerges from group processes without reference to the personalities of those who lead. In analyzing leadership, we think it useful to focus on the relationships between the roles of leaders and those of their followers, with special reference to the tasks performed by leaders.

The Requirements of Leadership. The leadership *roles* referred to above may or may not coincide with formal *offices* in an organizational structure, although they are usually intended to do so. In both simple and complex groups, leadership may be provided by persons holding no formal office, and informal leadership roles may develop no matter what the formal organization of offices may be. Roles can be identified by the general expectations of group members about who will do what, when, and how. Offices, in contrast, are usually identified by an organization's charter or rules that specify rank, duties, obligations, and privileges. The expectations derived from the latter may often be difficult to distinguish—indeed, in some instances may not differ at all—from role expectations. In any event, both have to do with the performance of certain *tasks* or *functions* for the group. Although the relative importance of such tasks may vary among different groups, organizations, and institutions, leaders have to do them, or ensure that they are done, if they are to maintain themselves in leadership roles. What, then, are such tasks?

Thinking primarily of political leaders, but without forgetting the requirements of other types of groups, we can say first that a leader must be able to define or express the goals and demands of his followers, either to them, to outsiders, or to both. In doing so he provides in his words and personality the symbols of group identity and unity that evoke sentiments of belonging and that motivate action to achieve the goals. To varying degrees he may be able to shape and direct such goals and demands himself, even introducing new ones on occasion. But he must remain attuned to the feelings and wishes of his followers; he must be able to sense how far he can go without risking loss of their support, and he must speak and act in ways meaningful to them—he must "talk their language." Sometimes he must even follow their lead.

A different order of skills is called for by the other tasks that leaders perform. These derive from the need to shape and direct organizational structures, devise strategies and policies, and do the many other things needed to satisfy followers that they are making progress toward their goals—or that if they are not, it is not the leader's fault. Shortcomings in this category of tasks may account for the difficulties of leaders of some nationalist groups seeking independence from colonial powers once they have actually become chief executives. The tasks and skills required here involve such things as dividing the work that must be done, making sure that the resulting jobs are assigned to sufficiently capable people, seeing to it that they are supplied with the necessary means (equipment, supplies, money, and so on), coordinating their work by making or approving rules, giving directions, keeping informed of the consequences, and settling conflicts, and dealing with the leaders or representatives of other groups and organizations.

In small groups the activities needed to perform these tasks may not be formally organized or even explicitly recognized, but larger and more complex organizations—particularly governments—must increasingly institutionalize them in offices and roles. Individuals or even entire agencies may be designated to assist in getting these things done. If a leader fails in any of them, the group, organization, institution, or government that he heads will encounter increasingly difficult obstacles and problems in realizing its goals or maintaining its values and norms—and someone else may take over leadership.

The particular style with which a leader performs his role may of course vary not only according to personality, but also according to the type of group or organization, the kind of situation or problems it faces, and the culture in which it functions. These factors may combine with the tone of relationships between a leader and his followers to produce "charismatic" leadership—a style or pattern in which a leader appears to his followers (and perhaps also to himself) to be endowed with extraordinary capacities or powers. This style was true of such contrasting personalities as Hitler and Gandhi. The consequence of strong charisma is to impart an unusual degree of faith, or even fanaticism, to many of the followers of such leaders. But it is also true that the occupant of any exalted office or the performer of any widely revered role is by virtue of that alone endowed with some degree of charisma.

Other styles of leadership result from different combinations of the same factors. They can be characterized in innumerable ways: cautious, aggressive, rational, intuitive, democratic, autocratic, traditional, innovative, energetic, phlegmatic, and so on. The points to remember are that styles of leadership are the products of more than just the personalities of leaders, and that regardless of personalities or styles, leaders must ensure the performance of the kinds of tasks we have indicated, and in some instances of perhaps others as well.

The Bases of Authority. If the preceding section has specified the major tasks or requirements of leadership, it did not deal except tangentially with the primordial question of why people accept, follow, and obey leaders. Until we have some understanding of this central problem, all the rest is likely to remain superfluous.

Ordinarily we say of a person in a position of leadership that he "has" authority. If he is a leader of a formal organization or a government, authority refers to the rules or laws that vest in him the right to direct and command and that impose upon others the duty to obey. Governmental chief executives possess this *formal* authority by virtue of the offices they hold. Yet leadership is more than the exercise of formal authority. We know that leaders do not always operate from positions of formal authority and that sometimes formal authority is not sufficient to bring about obedience. In the final analysis, the degree to which authority exists depends upon the degree to which *others accept* a person's suggestions, proposals, or instructions. When people do, in fact, obey others, we can speak of *effective* authority, as distinguished from merely formal authority.[2]

The compliance or obedience of followers or subordinates presumes in the first place that they understand clearly what is expected of them —that their leaders can communicate clearly their intentions, suggestions, instructions, and orders—and also that followers and subordinates have the means to carry them out.[3] But the question remains: Why do some people accept the suggestions, proposals, or instructions of others? The answer may vary from one situation to another, but there are several general explanations which, singly or in combination, are sufficient to cover most situations.

First, one person may accept the proposal of another because he thinks the proposal is "right." This could be called the "authority of ideas" or the "law of the situation,"[4] although some do not consider it a proper example of authority.[5] Second, he may accept the proposal because he thinks the person making it has the legitimate right to make it, independent of its merits; that is, he accepts the "rules of the game" according to which organizational subordinates "ought" to obey hierarchical superiors, or by which citizens "ought" to obey the laws made by duly elected and constitutionally authorized legislators. This is the "authority of legitimacy." Third, he may accept the proposal because he has confidence in the ability of the person making it to make correct or right decisions, as, for example, we accept the diagnosis of a physician because we think he has the technical medical knowledge to make it. This is the "authority of confidence." When exaggerated, this is a prime ingredient for charismatic leadership. Fourth, he may accept the proposal because it is made by someone who is a member of a group or organization with which he identifies himself; that is, he assumes that the person making the proposal has the same values or goals that he has, so that the proposal is at least not contrary to his interests. This is the "authority of identification." Finally, he may accept the proposal because he expects that he may be rewarded to some degree if he does or punished to some degree if he does not. This, the "authority

---

[2] Some may prefer the words "power" or "influence" to "effective authority." But the terms are unimportant as long as the distinction is clearly understood. This discussion of authority is based upon Chester I. Barnard, *The Functions of the Executive* (Cambridge, Mass.: Harvard University Press, 1938); Herbert A. Simon, Donald W. Smithburg, and Victor A. Thompson, *Public Administration* (New York: Alfred A. Knopf, 1950); and Richard E. Neustadt, *Presidential Power* (New York: John Wiley and Sons, 1960).

[3] That these conditions do not always obtain at the highest level of executive decision-making is demonstrated by Neustadt, *op. cit.*, chap. 2.

[4] Henry C. Metcalf and L. Urwick (eds.), *Dynamic Administration, The Collected Papers of Mary Parker Follett* (New York: Harper & Row, Publishers, n.d.), pp. 58–59.

[5] Simon, Smithburg, and Thompson, *op. cit.*, p. 182.

of sanctions," may be only implicit and in practice rarely resorted to, but the possibility that it may be or can be brought into play may be a persuasive reason for accepting a proposal.

In the performance of his functions, then, the political executive may draw upon and combine several sources of authority. The degree to which one or another of these sources is emphasized or the manner in which they are combined in particular instances reflect the conditions and imperatives of the political system in interaction with the personality and character of the executive, and shape the "style" of his leadership. Failure in any of his major tasks may erode one or more of his bases of authority; weakening of one or more of the latter may result in the leader's inability to perform the necessary functions. If it appears to his followers that a leader is consistently unable to advance them toward their goals, he will lose their support. Success is therefore the result of a highly complex set of interrelationships that can vary widely from one situation to another—and independently of the presumed qualities of a particular leader. The latter must have or must learn the difficult and demanding skills needed to handle or manipulate these interrelationships in the specific group or institutional context in which he is called upon to lead.

A Re-evaluation of Executive Power

Once again we return to the implications of the growth in executive power in democratic political systems. It is hardly to be doubted that modern governments, particularly in the more industrialized nations, must exercise broader responsibilities and must involve themselves in a wider range of socio-economic services and regulations than they did in former times. This in turn requires bureaucracies, and the requirements of rational coordination lead to the vesting of increased authority in the chief executive. Other factors, as we saw in the first section of the chapter, reinforce the trend. But, as we have also observed, all political trends and forces are not moving in that same direction, and the growth in executive powers is significantly offset by the development of other structures and processes in the political systems of modern and democratic industrial countries.

Indeed, we often simplify too much when we consider the political power and governmental authority of chief executives. We often seem to think, for example, that a man in so august an office as the Presidency of the United States has only to make his policy wishes known, or to issue the instructions, for the bureaucracy to go into action, machine-like, and carry them out. But the discussion of administrative behavior in Chapter 11 and of authority in this chapter should make it clear that things are not that simple. As President Truman said, and as Richard E. Neustadt has documented with insight, Presidential power in the United States depends in a basic sense on the President's ability to persuade other powerful people to accept his views.[6] Political power in democratic systems is diffused, fragmented, pluralistic, and shared. In important matters, varying combinations of cabinet members, congressmen, career officials, interest group leaders, and party officials have to be persuaded by the President. In fact, even in a system such as that of the Soviet Union, the topmost leaders cannot command arbitrarily and without some regard to the limits of acceptance of other powerful governmental officials. While power in totalitarian systems is far less pluralistic and diffused than in democratic systems, in no political system can a single man monopolize it all of the time. The discussion of formal and effective authority above, intended to be general enough to apply to any political system, sought to emphasize that authority is a reciprocal relationship. A sophisticated understanding of the conditions and bases of authority requires the recognition that in controversial questions of public policy, enough of such conditions and bases are frequently missing or inoperative to produce real limitations on executive power; thus what a chief executive can actually do is often less than what he is officially authorized to do. Indeed, the argument can be made that chief executives in democratic systems often do not have enough power to accomplish the tasks that twentieth-century politics and crises impose upon them.[7] A very real danger can be seen in the imposition of duties and responsibilities on a chief executive without at the same time providing him with the means necessary to carry them out.

At the same time, it is apparent that present-day governmental institutions and political processes have become so complex, and in some instances so unwieldy, that the maintenance of effective executive accountability is endangered. The legitimate powers of an American President or a British prime minister are already so great that these officials are often in a position to shape the course of events, to structure situations so as to leave legislative bodies or political parties no alternative but to go along with their policies or approve the actions they have taken. Responsibility and accountability are after all not absolutes; an act or a decision considered irresponsible at one time and under one set of circumstances may be acceptable at another time under different circumstances.

Nor should we lose sight of the dangers implicit in the very immensity of the burden imposed on contemporary chief executives. The demands we make upon them for solutions to possibly insoluble problems, the expectations we develop for leadership in a constant stream of crises, the pressures we bring to bear through legislators, interest groups, and public opinion—all of these are of the essence of contemporary politics. But to the chief executive, their weight can be crushing;

[6] Neustadt, *op. cit.*, especially pp. 9–10 and chap. 3.
[7] This argument is made for the United States by Louis Brownlow, *The President and the Presidency* (Chicago: Public Administration Service, 1949).

only an extraordinary man can bear them. Indeed, the only way they can be "borne" is to use them, insofar as possible, in ways chosen to support the most basic policies and to avoid, where possible, the most explosive conflicts and debilitating stalemates. But the task is so great, the responsibilities so awesome, that one can legitimately wonder whether the unavoidable concentration of executive powers may not eventually constitute the Achilles heel of modern political systems. The consequences of a crucial failure of executive leadership or of the system of responsible control are potentially so grave that they have led, in the United States, to serious proposals by responsible citizens and scholars for various reforms of the presidential system—from bridging the gap between President and Congress,[8] through pluralizing the executive,[9] to instituting a system of parliamentary responsibility modeled on the British.[10] Strong political support for these proposals, however, has not materialized, and it consequently goes without saying that, barring the unpredictable effects of major war, the probability of any basic change of the presidential system in the United States is slight.

These remarks can be summarized in several conclusions, not entirely compatible with each other:

1. Executive power has increased greatly in recent decades, for the most part unavoidably, in democratic as well as in other types of political systems.
2. This does not mean, however, that political executives, particularly in democratic systems, are all-powerful; indeed, executives must depend largely upon bargaining and persuasion. They may not always have sufficient power to do effectively what they are supposed to do.
3. It has nevertheless become more difficult to hold political executives responsible.
4. At the same time, the job of chief political executive may have become too big for a single person to handle, particularly in the United States. But no basic changes in the American system at least seem probable in the present period.

All the implications of such conclusions cannot be traced here; some point in directions that seem to contradict others. But they do not necessarily lead to counsels of pessimism and despair. The concentration of powers in the hands of democratic executives is cause for concern, but it is dangerous for political democracies only in certain contingencies. One would be the cessation of such societies to develop political leaders strong enough and skilled enough to handle the job;

8 See Stephen Horn, *The Cabinet and Congress* (New York: Columbia University Press, 1960).
9 Herman Finer, *The Presidency—Crisis and Regeneration* (Chicago: University of Chicago Press, 1960).
10 T. K. Finletter, *Can Representative Government Do the Job?* (New York: Reynal and Hitchcock, 1945).

given their need, however, for leadership in depth for their myriad groups and institutions, this outcome seems unlikely. Another contingency would be a lessening of the ability of the citizens of such societies to discern the best of their leaders and to elevate them to the offices of executive leadership. The dangers of error here are real but are not insurmountable. The maintenance of basic freedoms—of thought and conscience, of speech, of association, of the press, and of opportunities for education and advancement—decreases the likelihood of mistakes in this direction. Also, attention to the effectiveness and integrity of nominating and electoral procedures is important here.

A third contingency would be a breakdown in some of the other institutional means through which executives in office are held accountable for their decisions and actions. The controls exercised by parties, interest groups, legislatures, and courts, while they also could be made more effective in most democracies and while, if abused, they can work much mischief, still are indispensable to responsible executive leadership. Though these institutions bring about much of the great pressure under which executives must labor, a high degree of tension in central arenas of policy-making is unavoidable if democratic responsibility is to survive. The problem is how to provide institutionally for the maintenance of such pressures and tensions without allowing them to become overwhelming, paralyzing, and destructive in their impact.

A final contingency would be a failure of political leaders, scholars, journalists, thinkers, and leaders of all walks of life to continue the endless process of finding or inventing the adaptations necessary for democratic political systems in changed and changing conditions. Special attention is needed to ensure that political executives are supplied with the means, legal and institutional as well as material and technological, to discharge effectively the vast responsibilities that men and circumstances have heaped upon them. No political system is static; Americans have had to do a great deal of inventing and adapting with respect to their Presidency since the Founding Fathers drew up the Constitution. The same, of course, is true of all other peoples who have maintained viable and durable political systems. Sufficient success in past experience gives reason to hope that this contingency also can be avoided.

We may thus conclude that democratic politics probably will not succumb to concentrated executive power in itself. So long as the other major political processes and structures remain vital and so long as the informed and thinking citizenry of democratic societies is both large and disposed to continue the effort, there is no cause for great alarm on this score.

SUGGESTIONS FOR ADDITIONAL READING

BROWNE, C. G., and T. S. COHN (eds.), *The Study of Leadership* (Danville, Ill.: Interstate, 1958).

BURNS, JAMES M., *Roosevelt: The Lion and the Fox* (New York: Harcourt, Brace & World, 1956).

CORWIN, EDWARD S., *The President: Office and Power*, 4th edition (New York: New York University Press, 1957).

DEUTSCHER, ISAAC, *Stalin* (New York and London: Oxford University Press, 1949).

GOULDNER, ALVIN W. (ed.), *Studies in Leadership* (New York: Harper & Row, Publishers, 1950).

HOOVER INSTITUTE STUDIES, *Elites* (Stanford, Calif.: Stanford University Press, 1951–1955), Series B, Nos. 1–5.

JENNINGS, SIR IVOR, *Cabinet Government*, 3rd edition (Cambridge, Eng.: Cambridge University Press, 1959).

KOENIG, LOUIS W., *The Invisible Presidency* (New York: Holt, Rinehart and Winston, 1960).

LASSWELL, HAROLD D., *Politics and Personality* (New York: W. W. Norton & Company, 1948).

NEUSTADT, RICHARD E., *Presidential Power* (New York: John Wiley and Sons, 1960).

ROSSITER, CLINTON, *The American Presidency* (New York: Harcourt, Brace & World, 1956).

Chapter 17

THE POLITICS OF
STABILITY AND CHANGE

So far in this book we have been concerned primarily with questions that ignore the historical and developmental aspects of politics. True, we have noted certain important features of the historical development of government in the countries examined in Chapters 1 through 7. But we did so not in order to discover patterns of historical development or to assess possible lines of future development; instead, we were interested in a better understanding of the workings of each government as an established and relatively stable system.

Similarly, although we have considered the differences between the present-day system of world politics and that of the classic period of the "society of nations," our interest has been in comprehending the structural features of present-day world politics, rather than in examining the process of development and change within that system. In this section, too, we have so far been dealing with the structure, functions, and processes of the major components of governmental systems, with a view to establishing general principles about them rather than to analyzing the dynamics of change in them.

It would be incorrect, however, to say that we have simply taken the static view of politics in government, as contrasted to the dynamic view. Throughout, we have been concerned with understanding how such dynamic forces as interest groups, political parties, opinion groups, and so on, animate the structure of governmental institutions. What we have assumed up to this point is the stability and solidity of political systems as such, and we have therefore concerned ourselves only with those dynamic aspects of the political process that occur *within estab-*

lished systems of one kind or another. We have, so to speak, taken
the system itself as "given" in each case, and have sought to deal with
it quite apart from any dimension of time or historical development.
Although this assumption has proven essential for analyzing some
questions, it is obviously not tenable as an overall description of political
reality. Like the human beings of whose actions and interactions they
are constituted, political systems change, move, and pass through time.
Our general descriptions of any one of them may hold true for a more
or less indefinite future, but we can be sure that they will not hold
true forever. At any given moment, we can gain a great deal of understanding by looking at a system as if it were a sort of "machine." But
just as the mechanic must be concerned with problems of breakdown,
obsolescence, and innovation in dealing with his machines, even more
so must the political scientist be concerned with questions about the
stability and susceptibility to change of political systems.

What are the processes of growth, innovation, obsolescence, "repair," or breakdown in political systems? Why are some systems apparently subject to rapid and frequent change while others appear to
function more or less smoothly and without great change over long
periods of time? At what point should we say that change is something
more than minor modification of the existing model, that in effect the
system we have been examining has gone out of historical existence
and been replaced by another? What are the consequences of different
possible changes, and of different methods of bringing them about, on
the performance of governmental functions, or on the social context
and the world scene within which all governments operate? To what
extent are concepts of "political development" useful? What precisely
do we mean, after all, when we use such deceptively simple-sounding
words as "stability" and "change"?

Political Change and Conflict in the Contemporary World

The twentieth century has seen a bewildering variety of political
changes. Upheavals and conflicts have fundamentally altered the international structure of power, and national political systems in all parts
of the world have undergone far-reaching transformations. Some major
political entities that seemed quite stable at the beginning of the century, such as the Austro-Hungarian Empire, have disintegrated and disappeared forever. Scores of new national states have emerged to independence in Europe, Africa, and Asia. Internal transformations, many
of them violent, have swept ruling groups from power and restructured
social systems. Even where changes have occurred in a relatively orderly
and peaceful manner, political systems have changed in fundamental
respects—in their ideologies and philosophies, in the sources and pro-

cesses of their leadership recruitment, in the extent of popular participation in politics, in the scope of governmental activity, and in their relative power.

Can we view the complex processes of political change in a world seemingly in ferment and arrive at anything more than a despairing impression of senseless and unpredictable flux? Can we come close to some systematic and orderly understanding, some approximation of principles and laws? As a first step, let us attempt to catalogue briefly the major manifestations of political conflict and change over the past fifty or sixty years. Conflict, whether peaceful or violent, is not synonymous with change, but it is symptomatic of it. The appearance of conflict is a signal that political change of some importance has occurred, is occurring, or may be about to occur.

WAR AND CHANGES IN THE SYSTEM OF WORLD POLITICS

The most spectacular conflicts have been international—the two World Wars of the twentieth century. World War I marked the breakup of the international system of power relations that had, for the most part, managed for about a century to prevent general wars among the Western nations. A number of important political changes accompanied or followed in close relation to this war, including the temporary weakening of Germany, the disintegration of Austria-Hungary, and the emergence of the United States as a major world power and its involvement in world politics. The autocratic and militaristic imperial regime of Germany was replaced by a short-lived constitutional democracy. The tsarist monarchy of Russia was overthrown and replaced by a Communist "dictatorship of the proletariat." The latter, while bent on the basic and revolutionary transformation of the Russian (and if possible, the world) political system, had first to fight a long civil war.

Economic and political disturbances in the wake of World War I led to the emergence of the fascist dictatorship in Italy. In Central and Eastern Europe a number of newly independent political systems were created from segments of the old Austro-Hungarian Empire. The moribund Ottoman Empire of the Turks was dismembered, and Britain and France received "mandates" to govern important parts of the Middle East. German colonial possessions in Africa also passed into the control of Britain and France.

The Second World War grew, in part, out of political changes resulting from World War I. The establishment in the early 1930s of the totalitarian Nazi dictatorship in Germany was significantly motivated and facilitated by German resentment of the peace settlement imposed by the Allies. The economic dislocations caused by the great depression of the 1930s also contributed powerfully to the rise of the Nazis—and these same dislocations brought political tensions and greater instability to many other political systems. But this time, Asian involvement in world-wide conflict was much more extensive than it had been earlier. The Japanese Empire, dominated by militaristic expansionists, had been engaged in hostilities with China since 1931. Its alliance with the Rome-Berlin Axis, which went to war with Poland, France, and Britain in 1939, paved the way for Japan's attack on Pearl Harbor in 1941, which brought the United States into the war.

This war, the most extensive and destructive in world history, produced or contributed to yet another series of profound political changes. German, Italian, and Japanese military power was crushed; the totalitarian political systems were restructured along constitutional democratic lines (except, of course, for East Germany, which, being under Soviet control, was recast as a Communist dictatorship). The Soviet Union, its power severely strained by the Nazi onslaught, nevertheless emerged from the war as the dominant force in Eastern Europe. Under Soviet sponsorship and backed by its strength, Communist regimes took power in the Eastern European countries between the USSR on one side, and West Germany, Austria, Italy, and Greece on the other. France and Great Britain, although members of the victorious alliance, were gravely weakened by the war, a circumstance which contributed to their inability to withstand powerful pressures for change in their vast Asian, Middle Eastern, and African colonial territories. Strengthened by the dislocations of the war, nationalist independence movements were able both to press for and to obtain independence in the postwar period— sometimes peacefully, sometimes only after long-drawn-out violence.

Thus World War II, like World War I, helped to bring about extensive changes in the distribution of power throughout the world. The most notable manifestation of this restructuring of world power distribution has been the cold war bipolar tensions which have pitted the United States against the Soviet Union. But the emergence of such world-wide international organizations as the United Nations and its affiliated agencies and such regional organizations as NATO, the Warsaw Pact, and SEATO are equally manifestations of the redistribution of power.

REVOLUTIONS, CIVIL WARS,
AND CHANGES IN DOMESTIC POLITICAL SYSTEMS

Along with recent changes in the international distribution of power and in the structure of the system within which international conflicts take place, similar changes have occurred through violence within many national political systems. Although these revolutionary changes have in almost all cases been associated with war between nations, they all reflect in some degree the operation of forces distinct from those generating world wars. Such modifications of domestic systems are too complex to be explained simply as "results of world wars." The number of revolutions and civil wars that have produced major changes in various countries of the world since 1900 is too great even to list here, but we can perhaps profit from considering three prominent examples—Russia, Spain, and China.

The Russian Revolution. It is ironic in the light of Marxist theory that the first revolution to result in victory for Marxists should have occurred in Russia. While capitalistic industry and finance had made some headway in Russia by the time of World War I, her economic and social structure was at that time closer to feudalism than to the capitalist model that Marx had believed would produce proletarian misery and revolution. As we saw in Chapter 6, the Revolution began as the consequence of popular dissatisfaction with the tsarist regime's handling of the war against the Central Powers, and because of unrest arising out of the privations imposed by the war effort. The Tsar was toppled, not by the Bolsheviks, but by groups that were interested in constitutional reform and in carrying through the war to a successful conclusion. But the Bolsheviks, mainly by virtue of their disciplined organization and their skillful exploitation of popular demands for "peace, land, and bread," gained control of the soviets and seized power. A civil war of several years' duration was necessary before Bolshevik control could be consolidated. But this was accomplished with the support of many peasants, urban workers, and soldiers.

Far more than successful revolutionaries of other countries and earlier times, the Bolsheviks were bent not only upon seizing and holding political power but also upon forcing fundamental changes throughout the entire social system. In the name of Communist ideology and rationalized by it, totalitarian control was extended to all segments of society. Opposition was crushed and consent "engineered" through terror and monopolistic manipulation of all the media of communication. The police and armed forces were used to enforce the decisions of the leadership of the Communist Party, which was of course the only party permitted to exist. The old order was swept away; industry and finance were nationalized and agriculture collectivized. Massive and sustained efforts at planned economic development, involving the allocation of the bulk of resources to heavy industry, transformed the economy. Years of relentless effort have been required to produce these changes, and the process of change still goes on. The cost in human lives and values has been appalling, but the political leadership—from Lenin to the successors of Khrushchev—has not shrunk from the determination to meet whatever cost has been deemed necessary.

The Spanish Civil War. The case of Spain presents interesting parallels —and contrasts. During the 1930s Spain underwent a period of convulsive political change, including a particularly violent civil war. Yet the political system that emerged from this period and has endured to the present bears strong resemblances to that with which Spain entered the 1930s. Until 1931 Spain had been governed by a royalist dictatorship, in which the political elite was a small minority of entrenched army officers, clergy, landowners, and industrialists. Widespread discontent and unrest, stemming both from economic deprivation and from regional resentment of the centralized regime in Madrid, led the monarchist government to concede local elections in April, 1931 and to promise a later election for a constituent assembly. The government, whose thinking had gone no farther than a constitutional monarchy, was staggered by the results of the local elections: a republican, that is anti-monarchical, landslide. The premier resigned, King Alfonso XIII hurriedly left the country, and a junta proclaimed a republic.

With the establishment of the republic, however, irreconcilable forces began to gain momentum, and in 1936 this process culminated in civil war. Various social, economic, and political reforms were initiated, including separation of church and state, secularization of education, state investment in and regulation of industries and enterprises, protection of labor unions, universal suffrage, guaranteed civil liberties, and increased local autonomy. But these and similar changes were unacceptable to various groups who were defending the status quo, including the clergy, royalists, large landowners, and higher army officers. The lines were drawn between these groups on the right, which also included some organizations of a decidedly fascist character, and those on the left, which included republican intellectuals and liberals, workers and peasants, and increasingly active Communists. In 1936, in a context of strikes, public disorders, and violence, several regiments in Spanish Morocco rebelled. When General Francisco Franco, who had previously been exiled, joined them and took over the leadership, the civil war in Spain began.

This civil war, like that in Russia, was particularly important because of its ideological overtones and international implications. Although most nations adopted an official policy of non-intervention, unofficial supplies and volunteers came to both sides from many countries, notably the Nazi and Fascist regimes of Germany and Italy, which aided Franco's "insurgents," and the Soviet Union, which helped the republican "loyalists." A large number of volunteers in support of the republican regime also came from the United States, France, and England. The Spanish civil war became an issue in the domestic politics of many nations of Western Europe and North America.

But the armies of General Franco won in 1939. A regime was established with Franco at its head which, except for its non-monarchist but somewhat more totalitarian character, resembled that of the 1920s. The Franco government was aligned with the church, the landowners, and the industrialists, and sympathetic to the monarchy (as well as, during the 1940s, to Hitler and Mussolini). It has been able, for almost three decades, to quell the comparatively infrequent manifestations of popular discontent—assisted in its efforts, no doubt, by the exhaustion of the Spanish people at the end of the bloody civil war.

Revolution in China. Still another domestic political change with profoundly significant international repercussions was that which occurred in China. After decades of unrest, the moribund Manchu dynasty was overthrown and replaced in 1912 by a nationalist movement under the leadership of Sun Yat-sen, a radical intellectual. But nothing came of the attempt of Sun and his party, the Kuomintang, to establish a reforming, modernizing republic. China was too vast, the forces of traditionalism were too strong, and local military rulers were more interested in their own power and wealth than in the success of a unified republican government. In addition, the Kuomintang was split in the 1920s by the activities of the Communists; later, Japan began to manifest a more aggressive interest in expansion into Chinese territory. These problems degenerated into military conflicts, and during the 1920s and 1930s China was torn both by civil war between the Communists and the Kuomintang and by international war with the Japanese.

The Communists, led by Mao Tse-tung, were more positive and active in their resistance to the Japanese than were the Nationalists, led by Chiang Kai-shek. Furthermore, the Communists appeared to be more interested in the welfare of the vast peasant majority, while Chiang tended to rely more upon the feudalistic warlords who had traditionally controlled most of China. The outcome was inevitable. By the time the Japanese threat had come to an end with Japan's defeat in World War II, Communist armies controlled large areas of China. Chiang's Nationalist forces, although aided militarily by the United States, were unable to prevent the ultimate expansion of Communist control to all of mainland China. By the end of 1949 Chiang, his government, and all his armies had fled to the island of Taiwan, an off-shore province called Formosa by most non-Chinese.

Having achieved control of the mainland, the Communists girded for the transformation of China. The institutions of totalitarian dictatorship—one-party control of all organs of government and especially of the army and police, autocratic control of the party by the leadership. governmental monopoly of all means of communication, incessant indoctrination of the entire population in the dictates and prohibitions of the official (Marxist) ideology, extension of organizational control to all aspects of the social and economic system, and the ready use of terror to evoke compliance and to quell opposition—all these were firmly in place. Mao Tse-tung and the Party elite, unwilling to be mere emulators of their Russian Communist predecessors, decided to try to transform China's backward, peasant-based economy and social structure in one "Great Leap Forward." Human energy was the one abundant resource in China, and massive efforts were made to harness it to the enormous task of rapid industrialization. This entailed radical changes in the ancient Chinese social structure, the violent rejection of many of China's most honored traditional values, and the ruthless suppression of dissent or protest. The Chinese people, most of whom had sympathized with or supported the Communists during the long civil war against the Nationalists, now found themselves in the unshakable grip of the most oppressively totalitarian regime they had ever experienced.

But in spite of the unprecedented mobilization and concentration of labor, results have steadily fallen short of the regime's goals. Overemphasis on industrial growth meant a corresponding underemphasis on agricultural production; as a result, China under the Communists has not been able to solve the perennial problem of feeding a huge and growing population. Also, the planning, management, and implementation of far-flung development programs have been faulty and at times ineffective. Nevertheless, there appears to be little reason to doubt that the Communist regime remains firmly in control. The long period of political instability that accompanied the civil war came to an end when the Communists consolidated their power on the mainland, and such social and economic change as has been undertaken has been kept largely under the control of the political system.

Revolutionary Parallels. While each of these three revolutionary civil wars and changes of regime has its unique characteristics, it is possible to discover some important parallels among them. In all three instances, the preceding monarchical regimes had lost their ability to satisfy the needs of significant elements within the social system. Strikes, demonstrations, and public disorders manifested this incapacity on the part of the existing system. In each instance, a deposed monarch was succeeded by groups whose programs aimed at reforms approximating the model of constitutional democracy found in Western Europe and North America. In all three, however, the original reform groups were unable to establish effective and stabilized control; the changes they introduced seemed to stimulate the appetite of increased numbers of people for still more change. In each case, authoritarian leaders backed by strongly organized followers were able to gain control of or to mobilize sufficient military forces to challenge the first group of revolutionary leaders. The new revolutionaries systematically exploited unrest and the instability of the regime now in power and directed their appeals for support to those groups in the population whose help they deemed essential to success. These groups were different in different countries, particularly when one compares Spain with Russia and China, but in each instance they were the elements without whose consent and support no regime could hope to establish stable political control. In all three instances, the authoritarian leaders and their political followers and armies succeeded in defeating the first post-monarchical regimes and consolidated their power over the national territory. In each a dictatorial system was established, although the Russian and Chinese systems were more completely totalitarian than the Spanish.

At this point, however, the differences are perhaps more obvious than the similarities. The ideology of the winners in Russia and China was Marxist communism; once in power they launched intensive programs to revolutionize their societies thoroughly. In Spain the winners were anti-Communist, intent upon preserving essentially the same social and economic structures that had preceded the period of great instability. But, in all three countries, although the upheavals took different lengths of time to work themselves out, relative stability was finally achieved by restructuring the political systems along much more strongly dictatorial and totalitarian lines than had existed before.

ANTI-COLONIALISM AND THE ESTABLISHMENT OF "NEW NATIONS"

Another variety of political conflict and change is illustrated by the dissolution of the empires of various Western powers and the emergence into independence of numerous former colonial territories. Here the variety of transitional patterns has been great, ranging from the Philippines' peaceful and relatively amicable achievement of independence from the United States to the extremely bitter and bloody insurrections through which Indochina and Algeria broke away from French rule.

Between these extremes, many different degrees of violence and mutual hostility have attended this kind of change. Independence for French and British colonies in Africa south of the Sahara was achieved in a relatively peaceable and cooperative fashion. The break between India and Great Britain, while for years it had been heatedly demanded by Indian nationalist leaders and icily rejected by the British government, was finally carried out in 1947 without undue rancor on either side. Such violence as attended the change derived mainly from the partition of India and Pakistan and the necessity of transferring large numbers of people from one country to the other. In Indonesia, military conflict between the Dutch and the Indonesians preceded and accompanied the transition—although the fighting had neither the scale nor the intensity of that in Indochina or Algeria. In the Belgian Congo, a phase of bloody violence followed the precipitous Belgian withdrawal, and UN intervention was required to quell it. But here interregional and intertribal conflicts complicated the relatively simple question of "nationalism" versus "colonialism."

Whether it was accomplished peaceably or violently, however, the central fact and index of this type of political change is that since World War II the number of political systems with the legal status and attributes of "independence" has almost doubled. During the same period, the geographical extent of the prewar colonial empires of the Western nations has shrunk dramatically. Without attempting to describe the course of events in any specific cases, what generalizations can we make about this category of political change in the contemporary world?

Undoubtedly a major factor in its occurrence, as has been mentioned, was the weakened condition of the colonial powers at the end of World War II. But the ideological commitments and pronouncements of the governments of the victorious coalition—for example, those contained in the Atlantic Charter—were a factor not to be minimized. True, the extent to which their wartime pronouncements about colonial self-government or independence actually motivated or guided the postwar policies of the colonial powers is arguable. But it is less arguable that such slogans bolstered the expectations of leaders among the colonial peoples and played a significant part in helping to shape the policies and programs of many independence movements. Moreover, the British had explicitly promised independence to India during the war, and United States policy in the Philippines had for years been directed toward independence.

In the end, the crucial factor was the development of genuine national independence movements in most of the colonial territories. Although in practically all such territories there had been groups and leaders opposed to colonial rule almost from its beginning, the spread and intensification of nationalist sentiment among these peoples has been one of the fundamentally significant trends of the twentieth century. The process is not difficult to understand. For the colonial power it was necessary, and in varying degrees desirable, to educate at least some of the colonial people in its language and methods of administration and business, and otherwise to impart aspects of Western culture to them. Equally significant aspects of this Western culture, however, have been its political doctrines of democracy and nationalism. And to any colonial people that has been exposed to Western culture, the contradiction between their own dependent status and the political values professed and elaborated in the ruling Western nations has been, to say the least, painfully obvious. The discriminatory practices—economic and social as well as political—of the Westerners in their colonies seemed all the more humiliating and galling precisely when judged by Western ideals, and many a revolutionary has been created in the process of comparing Western colonial practice with Western political dogma.

Thus throughout the colonial world there arose movements, usually led by Western-educated intellectuals and professionals, which sought to mobilize their people for the purpose of opposing and throwing off foreign domination. Colonial administrators reacted to them with varying degrees of suppression and persecution, but they were unable to stamp out the nationalist independence movements. When they killed or jailed nationalists, they created martyrs or merely intensified and helped to spread more widely the determination to drive the foreigners out.

Working largely in the open, as in India, but sometimes clandestinely, as in Indochina, nationalist leaders were able to build sizable followings among their countrymen. The symbols and slogans of nationalism and opposition to colonial domination provided a broad basis for rallying colonial subjects of varying degrees of political awareness and sophistication and a wide range of political orientation. Nationalist independence movements became factors of political significance in most of the colonies; when they were put to the test in insurrectionary wars against the colonial powers, as in Indochina and Algeria, their extent, endurance, and strength proved formidable.

The achievement of independence by new nations, as we have seen above, constituted an important change in the world political system. But in the nations themselves change did not stop there, for independence did not bring stability to most of them. Many of their people had come to believe that the achievement of independence would also usher in major domestic economic, social, and political changes. And the constitutional structures that most of them adopted for their new political systems were largely based on variations or combinations of the formal institutions of the British, the French, and the Americans. But the actual operation of these "new" political systems tended to diverge considerably from the ways implicit in the formal structures they adopted.

As we saw in Chapter 7, levels of national integration were often low, and there were significant discontinuities or "gaps" in the political processes: between rural and urban segments of the population, between "traditional" and "Westernized" communities, between local and central organs of government. Governmental decisions tended to flow more from the charismatic leaders of the nationalist independence movements than from the formally elected legislative bodies. These discrepancies and discontinuities in the body politic, as well as painfully slow rates of economic and social development, made for continued instability. In a number of such situations, those who commanded the ultimate national means of force—the military—stepped in to establish order, to the despair of those who had hoped that national independence—freedom from colonial domination—would herald the birth of vigorous young democracies. Thus, more than any other area of modern politics, the "new nations" have posed and are still posing the problem of internal political stability.

COUPS D'ÉTAT

This brings us to yet another variety of political conflict and change —the *coup d'état*. Here one set of governmental leaders is abruptly replaced by another, usually unexpectedly, and with or without violence and bloodshed—although the threat of superior force, even if that force is not employed violently, is always a crucial factor in carrying out a coup. This form of change differs from those previously considered, chiefly in that there is no prolonged and widespread fighting and popular participation is quite limited. The change is essentially one of leadership, usually from one contending faction to another of the same elite.

Civil disturbances (demonstrations, riots, and so on) may precede or follow a coup, but those who organize it and carry it out are not always directly linked with those who organize or carry through the civil disturbances. And once having seized the offices and instrumentalities of power, the leaders of *coups d'état* are usually interested in the restoration or quick establishment of public order and discipline. In the contemporary world, coups are usually carried out by groups of military or police officers—men who can count on the support of armed forces. Civilian political leaders who resort to this means of political change do so only if they have, or believe they have, the support of military or police commanders, or if they themselves are the agents of such commanders.

Examples of the *coup d'état* are plentiful in the twentieth century. In more recent years, those of some significance include the coup of 1948 in Czechoslovakia, by which the Communists came to power there; that of 1952 in Egypt, which overthrew the monarchy and instituted the regime presently headed by ex-Colonel Nasser; the overthrow of the Argentine dictator Perón by the military in 1955; the bloody seizure of power in Iraq by a military junta headed by Colonel Kassem in 1958; the 1958 coup in Pakistan, in which General Ayub Khan took power in an increasingly unstable parliamentary system, the military overthrow of the dictatorial Ngo Dinh Diem and his family in South Vietnam in 1963; and the practically bloodless ouster of President Goulart of Brazil in 1964. In addition, governmental power has changed hands by *coup d'état* at least once in recent years in Korea, Thailand, Burma, Syria, Lebanon, Turkey, Sudan, Guatemala, Bolivia, Colombia, Venezuela, and the Dominican Republic.

Sometimes the distinction between *coup d'état,* rebellion, and revolution is not easy to draw. Coups may follow prolonged periods of popular dissatisfaction and disturbance and may be greeted by fairly widespread popular acclaim; they may be accompanied by military operations and even by popular uprising; they may be followed by serious attempts by the new leaders to modify or reform the political, social, and economic order. In some of these cases it would therefore be arbitrary to apply a simple label of "revolution," "rebellion," or *coup d'état.* However, a broad distinction, resting on criteria such as those suggested above, is useful for political analysis. Few would deny that the political change that occurred in Russia between 1917 and 1920 differed significantly from the one that took place in Indonesia between 1945 and 1949, or that both of these were quite different from the change in Egypt between 1952 and 1953.

In addition to the numerous successful *coups d'état,* there have of course been many that failed. More than any other sort of political change, the *coup d'état* turns on essentially military factors—on the successful use of power, pure and simple. Thus, the carrying out of a successful coup requires a great deal of careful calculation, planning, and organization. Secrecy is essential, yet strategic wielders of power must be approached in advance, in order to assure their support or at least their benevolent neutrality. Timing is also crucial; the blow must come at a moment when those in power will be least likely to be able to counter it, and during a period when the chances are greatest for gaining popular support or acquiescence, particularly in important urban centers.

Even when plans have been carefully and effectively laid, organization readied, secrecy maintained, and action timed most favorably, unforeseeable events may still cause failure. Take the otherwise masterfully planned and well-timed attempt of a large number of high-ranking German military officers to assassinate Hitler and end the war in 1944. It was thwarted simply because the bomb planted close to Hitler in a briefcase failed to kill him: the Führer had taken a few steps away from the area of fatal impact, and was only injured. In the aftermath, thousands of German officers paid with their lives for their involvement—or suspected involvement—in the plot.

Political considerations usually demand attention soon after an initial military success. Thus, the long-run success of a coup requires coordinated and resolute follow-through, in which all central governmental offices and those of the mass media of communication are seized and all potential centers of resistance are contained or neutralized. Improper coordination or lack of resolution at critical moments can reverse the success of an initial blow, as the leaders of the attempted coup against President Ngo Dinh Diem of the Republic of Vietnam learned to their chagrin in 1960. What a successful junta does after it acquires power will strengthen the political hopes or aggravate the political fears of parties and groups among the population. By its actions the junta may either generate potentially revolutionary new unrest or alleviate already existing dangerous pressures.

The *coup d'état* is both a process or means to power and an index of political stability. While it can occur in political systems that had previously seemed reasonably stable, it is perhaps more frequently found in those systems in which there have already been evidences of instability. A breakdown in the structural integration of a political system or a failure to achieve such integration; inability to arrive at consensus on the broadest political ends and means or the weakening of an established consensus—these are the conditions in which *coups d'état*, as well as insurrections and revolutions, are most likely to occur.

CONSTITUTIONAL BREAKDOWN

A number of important changes in political leadership have occurred in the twentieth century which, although they have taken place in conditions of instability, still do not fall within any of the categories of conflict and change already discussed. For example, Benito Mussolini took power in Italy in 1922 by constitutional means—formally, at least, he was designated by the king to be premier—but the step was preceded and accompanied by violence and threats of violence from Mussolini's black-shirted Fascists. Moreover, his appointment foreshadowed the end of constitutional government in Italy and its replacement by a dictatorial regime. Similarly, Adolf Hitler's assumption of power in Germany in 1933 came about by formally legal, constitutional means—although here too in a context of instability and coercion. And Hitler was careful to base the inauguration of Nazi totalitarianism upon a formally legal "enabling act" by the Nazi-dominated Reichstag. In these cases, while legal formalities could be observed in the process of making the changes, it was apparent that the actual accession to and utilization of political power differed substantially from the patterns prescribed in constitutional law.

The same can be said of the transition from the Fourth to the Fifth Republic in France in 1958, when Charles de Gaulle assumed power for the second time since World War II. Instability deriving from the Algerian war had provoked a crisis that the political system of the Fourth Republic could not surmount. Resolution of the crisis called for not only a change in leadership, but a significant shift in power from the legislative assembly to a more authoritarian executive, and this shift was accomplished by hurried but acceptably legitimate processes of leadership succession and constitutional revision.

A similar shift, but in the opposite direction—from executive to legislative power—occurred in 1961 in Brazil, where the unexpected resignation of President Janio Quadros led to a crisis because his legal successor, Vice President João Goulart, was unacceptable to powerful groups in the country. Rather than abandon or abrogate constitutional processes, remaining members of the political elite revised the constitution so as to weaken the power of the executive. Since it was now assured that he would not have the power feared by his opponents, Goulart was then allowed to succeed Quadros. As in the previously mentioned instances, "stability" was precariously preserved—or rather instability was prevented from breaking down into violent conflict—by following legal processes to modify the formal structure of the political system and to make it more attuned to the demands of the actual holders of power.

Sometimes changes of this sort are brought about, or their outcome is dictated by, the direct intervention of leaders of powerful institutional groups not normally involved in such processes. Such intervention occurred in Argentina in 1962, when military leaders, unable to force the resignation of President Arturo Frondizi, arrested him and installed a successor more amenable to their demands. This event was akin to a *coup d'état* in that there was little pretense of maintaining the niceties of constitutional form and procedure, but other characteristics of a coup were missing. It was also akin to revolution or civil war in that tensions ran high in the political system, yet a violent eruption was avoided.

Yet another example of what might be called "precariously stable" political change should be considered here. This is the struggle for succession that took place in the Soviet Union after Joseph Stalin's death in 1953. In the absence of institutionalized procedures for choosing a successor, Stalin's death precipitated a crisis in which his potential heirs engaged in a long-drawn-out, devious, and for the most part subterranean struggle. For a time it appeared that Malenkov would replace Stalin; then it seemed (to the outside world) that the claims of "collective leadership" would prevent any single individual from assuming Stalin's dictatorial role. Finally, however, and quite possibly because the logic of the political system did demand ultimate decisions and control by one man, Nikita Khrushchev emerged as the dominant figure. The details of maneuver and manipulation, bargaining and coercion, by which this outcome was effected were concealed from the outside world, but there can be little doubt that this transition was fraught throughout with tension and potential violence. Although the long range significance of it is not yet clear, it is important to note that Khrushchev was deposed in 1964 in conditions seemingly less permeated with tension and conflict.

STABLE PEACEFUL CHANGE

Standing in rather clear-cut contrast to all the types of political conflict and change that we have just surveyed are some less spectacular but no less important processes of change during this same period in a number of other political systems. These systems, which can be listed as stable constitutional democracies, include a dozen or so northwest European and North American countries, plus Australia and New Zealand in the Pacific. In these countries during the past fifty or sixty years, and in some of them for many more, political change has occurred under conditions of relative stability, and political conflict has remained for the most part below the threshold of violence. Where violent disorders have occurred, as in some strikes, riots, and so on, they have not been a significant means or concomitant of widespread political change. If we consider only the last decade or so, some other political systems—even though the extent of their democracy might be subject to some qualification—nevertheless appear to have developed relatively stable processes of political change. These would include such nations as India, Malaya, the Philippines, Mexico, Chile, Costa Rica, and Uruguay. In these countries, leadership has changed hands and policies and programs have evolved and changed to meet changing situations and in order to seek new or modified goals. To varying degrees, the structures and processes of the political systems in these countries have undergone evolutionary changes—all without much violence or the expectation of violence and without crises acute enough to call into question the basic legitimacy of the political processes and structures through which the changes have been effected.

One can point, in the more stable countries, to the predominantly honest and peaceful elections in which political leadership has been changed, the deliberative and bargaining legislative and executive processes by which policies have been instituted and modified, and the administrative and judicial procedures through which programs have been implemented and conflicts settled. Structural changes have included the extension of the electorate; the growth and participation of new groups in the political process (and a corresponding diminution of participation by others); modifications in the bases and distribution of wealth, prestige, and power; and changes in the predominant popular conceptions of the roles and responsibilities of government in relation to economic and social affairs.

Dimensions and Categories of Political Change

The first step toward the understanding of complex phenomena in any area is often the precise specification of differences and distinctions between different instances and the classification of these instances into appropriate types or categories for purposes of further analysis. The preceding discussion has utilized a rough classification of sorts. Although the criteria used above are hardly precise enough for any but essentially descriptive purposes, they may serve as the basis for more precise consideration. Thus, although it would be difficult to draw a hard and fast distinction between stable and unstable political change, most readers would probably agree that the examples mentioned in the last section should be characterized as "stable," while those in the preceding sections should be called "unstable."

We are not at this point concerned with the fundamental question of *why* political change is stable in some instances and not so in others. Rather we wish first to note that there are several fairly distinct patterns or types of behavior in accordance with which political change commonly occurs, and second to try to specify more precisely what it is that differentiates one pattern from another. Once we have done this, we can perhaps explore more effectively questions about the causes and consequences of the different patterns.

The reason why we want to determine causes and consequences is above all explained by the nature of the world we live in. It is no exaggeration to state that political change in the twentieth century has overwhelmingly tended to occur under conditions of disorder, violence, and instability. Many citizens of relatively stable political systems may still find it difficult to appreciate how the political climate or men's perspectives in most parts of the world are affected by the resulting uncertainties. But the impact of these less stable processes of change on world politics has made it more than ever important to try to think clearly about them.

STABILITY AND CHANGE AS POLITICAL CONCEPTS

To begin with, the terms "stability" and "change" are altogether relative. Nothing—particularly nothing in political relationships and processes—is static, permanent, and changeless. To be more exact, we
should talk of stable or orderly change and unstable or disorderly
change.

This is not a simple question of the *pace of change*. Although rapid
change is often also unstable, some political systems—for example,
parliamentary democracies—are sometimes able to effect significant
changes of policy or political leadership in a relatively short time without any threat to their stability as viable political systems. Other systems, such as those of some of the Latin American republics, have
endured extended periods of instability without significant changes in
policy or political leadership.

Nor does the question simply concern the *extent of change*. Basic
changes in the structure or framework of some political systems can
occur without seriously endangering their stability, while in others
seemingly small changes in one or another area of public policy may at
times threaten it. If great *structural* change occurs within a short period
of time, however, instability is much more likely to result. Such change
is not to threaten stability, it usually needs a longer time to work itself
out than do changes in leadership or policy.

Perhaps the most usual index of the degree of instability involved
in political change is the extent to which it is accomplished or accompanied by force and violence—or by widespread expectations of
violence. For when violence accompanies political change, that in itself signifies that the government has lost, or is fearful of losing, one of
the basic attributes or conditions of stability: its own monopoly regulation of the means and application of violence.

When the use of violence passes a certain threshold, the political
system is almost by definition unstable. *Almost* by definition, but not
quite. For so-called stable systems often have a surprising tolerance
for violence and disorder. In spite of the civil disorders of the Chartist
agitation in nineteenth-century England, or the widespread violence
in industrial disputes in America during the 1890s and again in the
1930s, most observers still believe that both occurred within basically
stable systems. Much less violence appears (in terms of the number of
contenders or victims) in some Latin American countries, yet those
countries are not therefore judged to be stable.

The words "stable" and "unstable," therefore, cannot be identified
exclusively with either the pace of change, the extent of change, or the
use of violence in the process of change. Stability may mean that change
tends to occur at a "slow" pace, yet the term "slow" is also wholly relative: it may mean that change tends to occur on fewer fronts at any
given moment, and yet an accumulation of changes on a succession of

fronts can transform society. It may mean that a minimum of violence is occurring, but even when violence does occur, change does not necessarily take place. The relative speed, extent, or violence of change may be symptomatic of relative stability or instability, or they may serve as indexes by which we can measure it, but they are not themselves the heart of the matter.

Instead, the concept of "stability" appears to be definable primarily in terms of the expectations, identifications, and attitudes of the people who make up the political system. It relates to the degree of certainty with which they can count on being able to pursue their activities and advance their interests within the existing political system, and to their willingness or desire to do these things in that way. Where the behavior of public officials conforms to established norms more or less embodied in the processes of established institutions; where the channels and the modes of advancing individual and group interests are reasonably clear in the minds of all political participants; where (for whatever reason) almost all citizens and officials expect the structure and the processes of government to continue to conform to these established forms and modes—there we find "political stability." Where (again for whatever reason) men are unclear about the likelihood of success or failure for any of the various methods of pursuing their individual and group interests politically; where they have no reason to count on the continued conformity of public officials' behavior to accepted definitions of official roles; where large numbers of citizens are unclear about their own roles as citizens—there we find "political instability."

Stability or instability of a political system, then, is a reflection of fundamental opinions and attitudes in the minds of participants about the system as a system. The problem of political stability is therefore one of the major problems of scientific political theory.

DIMENSIONS OF POLITICAL CHANGE

Our discussion earlier focused on the different sorts of process by which change has occurred. A review of the many examples of change then given will reveal that change can occur in one or more of several different aspects of a political system. We can readily distinguish three major aspects, or dimensions, of a political system that are subject to changes: personnel, policy, and structure. It is important not only to distinguish these dimensions of change from one another, however, but also to recognize how they are related to each other in particular situations.

The reader should have no difficulty understanding what is meant by each of these dimensions. The personnel of any system are those particular individuals who at the moment occupy the various positions and play the various roles that make up the system. Sooner or later, since all men are mortal, change of personnel is inevitable in every office of every government. In almost all political systems there are presumably established ways of changing personnel and established agreements about when changes in personnel are appropriate, even though in some systems the uncertainties of "succession" may be acute with regard to key positions.

With or without personnel changes, an important function within any political system is the making and implementation of policy—of decisions about how certain problems shall be approached or handled by government officials, about what rules shall be applied in settling certain kinds of disputes among certain classes and groups of citizens, about what rules of behavior shall be enforced among citizens generally, and so on. In modern times, the making and enforcing of policy for the community has become perhaps the most characteristic function of governments everywhere. The politics of almost all modern political systems involve above all contests among groups to have their goals and their conceptions of the public interest made into public policy. Changing policy has therefore become almost as normal in most political systems today as changing government personnel.

The structure of any system includes the established rules and practices for changing the personnel and policies of government, but much more besides. Above all, the term refers to the roles established for public officials, as these are grouped into complex clusters for the performance of the manifold functions of government. Structure refers, then, to the various institutions of government that are described by the innumerable informal and formal rules which channel and shape the official behavior of countless officials, as well as the civic behavior of private citizens. Structure also refers to whatever ways of acting politically are considered "the regular ways" in a given political community. It therefore includes the system of voting (if there is one); the system of electing, appointing, or otherwise choosing the personnel of government, and the organization, conduct, and functioning of parties, legislatures, courts, and administrative bodies. For present purposes we will also include established sequences of action in regular, institutionalized ways of doing things, the "processes" of government.

We should especially note at this point that the structure of any political system usually includes some "regular" ways of changing various features of the institutional structure itself—for example, procedures for constitutional amendment. Finally, as it is used here, the term "structure" refers still more broadly to the particular constellation of forces—the power configuration—that underlies, operates through, and is supported by the institutional structure of government.

While we can distinguish analytically with ease among the personnel, policy, and structural aspects of change, they are all three, of course, often interrelated in actual historical situations. For example, policy changes can occur through decisions of the political leadership (personnel), as that leadership seeks to attain its goals by adapting to new developments. This kind of change is both constant and inevitable in all political systems, because the environments (both human and physical) in which political systems operate are themselves subject to constant change.

Policy changes are also likely to follow changes in the personnel of political leadership, insofar as different people have different goals and values and different approaches to problems. But this is also true in reverse. Policy changes that turn out to be "mistakes," in terms of the requirements and dynamics of a given political system, may themselves lead directly or indirectly to changes in political leadership. In political democracies, for example, unpopular policies can contribute significantly to the defeat of office-holders in subsequent elections. Or, to cite a revolutionary situation, the policy decision of the 1917 Provisional Government in Russia to continue the war against the Central Powers was an important factor in that government's overthrow by the Bolsheviks.

Either policy or personnel changes can result, eventually, in profound changes in the structure and processes of political systems. In the United States, the New Deal policies favoring organized labor made possible the emergence of labor unions as much more important elements in the party, electoral, and interest-group structure of this country. The 1962 Supreme Court decision that the courts could, in effect, require state legislatures to reapportion themselves to represent the urban-rural population distribution more accurately will undoubtedly produce long-run structural changes in the political system of the United States. On the other hand, changes in the processes and structure of a political system inevitably bring new personnel and new policies to the fore. The extension or restriction of the suffrage produces policy-makers different from those who might have held office without such extension or restriction. Changes in media of political communication, such as the development of radio and television, have had far-reaching effects upon the formation of public opinion, the outcome of elections, and the shaping of policy.

A SUMMARY OF POLITICAL CHANGE

Similar examples of the interrelatedness of changes in personnel, policy, and structure could be given from countries around the world, and the reader will be able to think of many more. But at this point let us draw together what we have learned about the dimensions and methods of political change, both stable and unstable.

In the first place, we have distinguished between conditions of stability and instability as two ends of a continuum, rather than as two mutually exclusive types of situation. Next, we have distinguished three important dimensions of political systems along which changes can occur—personnel, policy, and structure. While these do not constitute areas of a continuum comparable to the stability-instability continuum, they do appear to rank in a certain order. In the light of the relative

Table 17.1

Summary of the Methods of Political Change

		Dimension of Change	
Conditions of Change	PERSONNEL (LEADERSHIP)	POLICY	STRUCTURE AND PROCESSES
Stable change	Cooptation Appointment Cabinet "shuffles" Election Inheritance	"Constitutional" legislative, executive, and judicial decision-making processes	Slow evolution of values and behavior patterns, without conscious or formal recognition of change Legitimate legislative, executive, judicial, constitution-amending processes
	Resignation or abdication under pressure, especially threat of violence	Boycotts Passive resistance and civil disobedience Mass demonstrations and riots	Subversion Terrorism Guerrilla warfare
	Assassination Non-violent coup d'état	Extra-constitutional intervention of powerful institutionalized groups (such as the religious or the military)	Insurrection, rebellion
Unstable change	Violent coup d'état		Revolution International war

frequency with which each sort of change is observed in any given system, as well as in the relative ease of accomplishing each sort, and the consequences of each in other areas of political affairs, changes in structure (including process) would appear as a general rule to be the most significant type and changes in personnel and policy less significant. If we now make a table (see Table 17.1) which shows vertically the gradations from stability to instability and horizontally the dimensions of political change, we can characterize degrees of stability or instability by particular methods of change in each of the dimensions we have identified, with the most stable classified in the upper left-hand corner and the most unstable in the lower right-hand corner.

Needless to say, a classification scheme such as this can be only rough and approximate. All of the terms and concepts used are still too imprecise to permit an absolutely clear handling of any particular case. At any given time, a single political system may manifest a combination of several different types; as we have seen, there are relationships among changes in the three dimensions which do not appear clearly merely upon inspection of the table. Although we have indicated the methods of change that seem to be associated empirically with the various conditions of change in the different dimensions, even this association is not directly explained by our figure. Are conditions unstable because many men are ready to resort to violent revolution, or are men inclined to revolution because conditions are unstable? Do military or other cliques intervene because conditions are unstable, or is it they who make a once-stable system unstable by so doing? To such questions neither our table nor political science generally has the answers.

Our table, therefore, is primarily useful for descriptive purposes, as a device to focus attention upon the specific characteristics of any situation that interests us. At best it can serve to raise more general questions about the patterns of change in any system. For example, in a specified period of time, what patterns of change predominate? Or, over a succession of periods, what trends in frequency appear? Answers to the first question can lead to the characterization of a system as stable or unstable, or may even be able to suggest the degree of stability. Answers to the second can clarify whether the system is developing toward greater or lesser instability, and can provide important clues about the kinds of change that may be expected. These matters are not only of great interest to political scientists seeking to understand the workings and development of political systems: they also have obvious import for policy-makers.

The Explanation of Political Change

SOME THEORIES OF POLITICAL CHANGE

Political change in any form cannot be understood without adequate attention to social and economic change as well. The relationship between political and economic change particularly has long attracted the attention of students of politics. Aristotle argued, in effect, that the principal cause of revolution is the separation of economic from political power.[1] In other words, an unstable condition, likely to lead to revolution, is created when the distribution of wealth does not correspond at least roughly to the distribution of power. Aristotle further concluded that the most stable type of political system was that based on a large middle class.[2]

Twenty-two centuries later, the relationship between political and economic change received from Karl Marx its most elaborate and consequential theoretical statement. In Marx's view, all political change is determined by changes in the mode of economic production.[3] Politics is to be understood as at bottom a class struggle; classes are determined by their members' relation to the means of production, and the state is simply the ruling class organized to maintain its control and exploitation of subordinate classes. Marxist theory was an undeniable contribution to the analysis of economic, social, and political change (quite apart from its practical political consequences), but several basic flaws seriously reduce its appeal to those who are interested in genuinely scientific analysis of these phenomena. In particular, its insistence upon economic determinism as the *sole* valid approach to an understanding of human behavior can be regarded as nothing but erroneous oversimplification, even if one grants that there is a special significance to economic motivations and relationships in human affairs. Despite the powerful contributions made by Marxist analysis, social scientists have been impelled to continue the quest for understanding.

One of these social scientists, Vilfredo Pareto, has had sufficient influence to warrant mentioning. While his analysis is too complex to summarize here, we can take note of his concept of "circulation of the elite." This assumes that the distinction between elite and mass is fundamental in all political systems,[4] and that an understanding of access to membership in, as well as the composition of, the elite is crucial to the understanding of political change. The term "circulation" refers to the process through which members of the mass constantly join or are recruited into the elite, at the same time that the elite is losing members who slip back into the governed classes. This process may change the character or temperament of the elite. If that temperament becomes sufficiently different from that of the mass; if it becomes such that the elite is increasingly unfit to govern; or if circulation is choked

[1] Ernest Barker (trans.), *The Politics of Aristotle* (London: Oxford University Press, 1948), Book V. For an interesting formulation that shows the contemporary relevance of Aristotle's thinking, see Fred Kort, "The Quantification of Aristotle's Theory of Revolution," *American Political Science Review*, XLVI (1952), 486–93.
[2] *Ibid.*, Book VI, chap. 11, sec. 10–15.
[3] Marx's writings are available in a number of English translations. For an introduction to his theory of the relation between economics and politics, see the "Manifesto of the Communist Party." A convenient edition can be found in Max Eastman (ed.), *Capital, The Communist Manifesto, and Other Writings* (New York: The Modern Library, 1932).
[4] But we have seen, particularly in Chapter 13 above, that this may also lead to dangerous oversimplification. For another influential analysis based on the same distinction, see Gaetano Mosca, *The Ruling Class*, Arthur Livingston (ed.) (New York: McGraw-Hill Book Company, 1939).

off—then the basis for revolution emerges.[5] Of course, the rate of circulation, as well as the temperament of the people circulating, is directly conditioned by prevailing economic trends and conditions.

But this is not the place to undertake a survey of theories about the causes of political change. Suffice it to say that, although we now have considerable knowledge about political change and its relations to economic and social factors, we still have no theoretical formulation compelling enough to gain general acceptance among social scientists. The most that can be done here is to suggest the broad outlines of a conceptual framework within which political change can be analyzed, and to suggest a few of the factors that may help us to comprehend more fully the politics of stability and change in our own times.

EFFECTIVENESS, LEGITIMACY, AND POLITICAL STABILITY

Whatever we may choose to say about the problem of political change and stability, it is essential to view it in the context of our general conceptions of government and politics. We have already suggested that the concept of "political stability" points to something about the opinions and attitudes of the members of the political system. It is therefore appropriate at this point to consider these opinions and attitudes in more detail, and to make explicit some other concepts that we have employed or implied in preceding discussions.

To begin with, we must acknowledge the universality of those phenomena that we can loosely and generally label "conflicts of interest" —an observation that is thought by some political theorists to be too obvious to require much further thought and on the other hand is resented by other theorists who misinterpret it as a recommendation for human behavior. Very briefly, we recognize that in every society different men put different values on things, interpret events in different ways, and in the process of seeking to accomplish or obtain something, often find that their objectives are incompatible with those sought by other people. Without pausing to describe all the different things that men can and do seek or to consider their relation to ideas about values, we can label the objects of their desire their *interests*.

Of special importance in government and politics is the fact that people's interests are often derived from their belonging to one or another group of people (in a more or less formal and conscious way), or from being associated with some status that they share with other people (even though they themselves may not be fully conscious of belonging to such a "statistical" group). We must be careful to note, however, that the term "interests" is used here in a quite neutral and generic sense, to refer to whatever objects or conditions people may happen to value, regardless of the value we as observers may place upon

5 Vilfredo Pareto, *The Mind and Society* (New York: Harcourt, Brace and Company, 1935), Vol. 4, chap. 12, especially pp. 1515–24, 1636–44.

them.[6] Interests may be economic or material, spiritual, or even fanciful. What they are in any particular society and for any particular persons is a matter for empirical investigation.

The moment when interests become politically significant is when they are formulated as *demands* upon some person or group.[7] More often than not, it is not mere individual wishes that are expressed as demands, but interests that are shared by a group of people and are asserted, therefore, as group demands, usually by group leaders, officials, or spokesmen. In saying this, we must be careful to note that government agencies and government officials have interests not only as individual persons and members of "private" groups but also as officials and members of institutionalized official groups, and that as such they make demands on other officials and on other groups of citizens.

Since not all demands can be satisfied, every society requires some means of deciding who shall get what—which interests shall be protected or advanced at the expense of which others. Whatever else it may be, the political system is an institutionalized pattern of persons, structures and processes by which this is accomplished. In order for it to do so, the political and social system must provide the means by which persons and groups become aware of their interests in a more or less realistic manner, and are able to communicate with one another and formulate their demands. Only in that way can they become aware of the relationship of their own demands to those of other persons and groups, and communicate their demands to the agencies and officials of government, who then attempt to arrive at compromises or other solutions among the interests in conflict.

In other words, how effectively demands are satisfied in any society will depend in the first instance upon the relative effectiveness of the society's processes for "interest articulation," and "interest aggregation" (to use some of the terminology of Gabriel Almond, a political scientist who has been especially concerned with problems of political change).[8] It will depend in the second place upon the effectiveness of governmental institutions, processes, and personnel in devising and applying policies and programs that take into account not only the demands being voiced at any given moment but also the probable impact of future developments, of present and proposed policies, and of other eventualities on the creation of new demands and the emergence of not yet felt interests. In short, it depends upon the relative effectiveness of the governmental processes of legislation, execution, and adjudication in responding to demands over a period of time.

At the same time, we should not forget that political leaders in gov-

[6] For some purposes it is useful to distinguish between "subjective" interests (what people value) and "objective" interests (what turns out to benefit them, even if they did not desire or value them). The distinction is not necessary in the present formulation.

[7] David B. Truman, *The Governmental Process* (New York: Alfred A. Knopf, 1951).

[8] Gabriel A. Almond and James A. Coleman, *The Politics of the Developing Nations* (Princeton, N.J.: Princeton University Press, 1960), chap. 1.

ernment offices seek to influence or to manage the expression of demands. Even in the most democratic systems, government is not simply a passive mechanism responding only to the demands of non-governmental groups. As we noted above, officials make demands themselves. Thus government seeks to stimulate or encourage some demands and to discourage or even suppress others. In addition, some policies, particularly in some areas of foreign affairs, may be almost entirely products of governmental initiative, with relatively little support or opposition from non-governmental groups. But it is important to recognize distinctions of degree in governmental management of demands. A relatively high degree of effort and effectiveness in the manipulation and control of demands generated by groups outside the official orbit, plus the widespread imposition of policies formulated largely by political and administrative leaders, are hallmarks of authoritarian political systems.

However they may have been influenced in their formulation, the expectations of members of a society concerning the likely effectiveness of performance of their government is an important factor determining the degree of stability and the character of change in any society. Many changes can be traced directly to the expectations and demands of particular types of persons, groups, or segments of the society. For some individuals, their "interest" in merely occupying positions of power and influence is sufficient to motivate a demand on their part for a change in the personnel of government. Further, the interests of many groups and classes of people are translated into demands for the particular policies that they believe will serve them best. Policy changes are thus an essential part in most modern governments of the process of accommodating diverse interests; many different groups of citizens expect the government to provide the possibility of satisfying their own demands through changes in public policy.

Expectations of a minimum effectiveness on the part of government do not ordinarily take the form, however, of an insistence that each specific demand find direct satisfaction in some specific change of personnel or policy. There is, rather, a sort of minimum probability, or "sporting chance," which supporters of all interests expect from government, and which is applied as a standard to the government's performance over a period of time. There is, one might say, a general understanding that "you can't win 'em all." When such expectations of minimum effectiveness are not met over a sufficiently long period of time—and let us emphasize that the definitions both of "minimum effectiveness" and of "a sufficiently long period" are relative—then those who feel dissatisfaction with the effectiveness of government tend to develop an interest in change and to demand changes in the structure and processes of government itself. Indeed, even in so-called stable systems, we can always discover some groups of citizens who are dissatisfied and who express such demands; we can also detect the changes that are made from time to time in response to these demands. In such systems, however, it is at least as often true that structural change comes about unnoticed, as the more or less unintended and unde- manded consequence of changes in personnel or policy.

It would be entirely incorrect to suppose that men measure the effectiveness of government wholly or even primarily in the light of its long-run ability to satisfy either the self-interested demands of persons or groups or demands formulated in the light of individual or group conceptions of desirable policy or political structure. For in any society, nearly all groups and persons share at least some values—and con- sequently some interests. Nearly everyone, for example, is interested in the survival of the community of which they all feel themselves part. Most, too, have an interest in the maintenance of conditions conducive to peace and order. And most share (although not always, everywhere, or as fully) notions about how political power should be distributed, organized, and exercised. Expectations based on such general values and interests are often referred to as a "fundamental consensus." It is in the light of these values that men judge the *legitimacy* of the de- cisions and policies of government; of the processes, structures, and institutions through which they are made; and of the particular persons whose actions constitute the acts of government.[9]

The attribution of legitimacy can perhaps be thought of as an ex- pression of a favorable judgment of the appropriateness of persons, processes, and structures from the point of view of achieving this im- portant class of values. The concept is also closely related to the notion of consent. Governments cannot hope to satisfy all the demands of all groups and all persons; nor can they survive on the basis of monopolistic force alone. But they can (and must) win consent—they must be ac- cepted as legitimate by at least the dominant collectivities within the social system. Governmental structures and processes vary widely, in- volving different combinations of representation, negotiation, bargaining, intimidation, fraud, publicity, centralization, domination of some parts by others, and so on. But unless they can maintain their own legitimacy, the policies they adopt and the actions they take as a consequence will not be regarded as legitimate, and one of the key underpinnings of stability will be missing.

If legitimacy, then, is so essential to stability, what determines whether or not a regime, or the structures and processes of a political system, will be regarded as legitimate by the significant collectivities in the political system? The search for an adequate answer to that question would take us far afield, into the realms of psychology and sociology; here we can only note some of the factors that appear to be important.

One factor is the means by which the regime came to power; if

9 On the concepts of effectiveness and legitimacy, see Seymour M. Lipset, *Political Man* (Garden City, N.Y.: Anchor Books, 1963), pp. 64–70.

these means have departed from those sanctioned by established practice or by a written constitution, the legitimacy of the regime may be subject to question. Another factor is the degree to which the preceding regime was regarded as legitimate. If that regime had a high degree of legitimacy, and its successor assumed power through non-legitimate procedures, the latter will surely encounter obstacles in its efforts to acquire the degree of legitimacy needed for stability. A third factor, and in the long run probably the most important, is the one we have emphasized above: the system's effectiveness—the degree to which it is actually successful over a period of time in satisfying the most important demands (those that reflect the most vital interests) of the predominant collectivities of the political system. These demands must, in short, be adequately reflected in policies; programs of governmental action must effectively fulfil the interests that gave rise to them. When effectiveness declines or is lost, legitimacy is likely to erode.

These considerations lead us to criteria differentiating between the conditions that result in stable and unstable change in political systems. Stability, or stable change, we may say, prevails: (1) when institutional channels for communicating demands are able to find room for most of the widespread and persistent demands; (2) when the structures and processes for resolving conflicts among demands and for formulating and implementing acceptable policies are able to operate effectively; (3) when such structures, processes, and policies continue to be recognized as legitimate by the persons and collectivities making these demands. In contrast, instability or unstable change result when conflicting or competing demands cannot be accommodated within existing channels of communication (or when such channels are non-existent or blocked); when the institutional structures and processes for resolving conflicts among demands and for formulating and implementing acceptable policies have lost their effectiveness; or when these structures and processes have lost their legitimacy for important collectivities whose interests have occasioned the demands.

While the categories of stable and unstable change are presented above as a contrasting pair, we should repeat that they are more correctly viewed as the opposite ends of a continuum. Precision requires that, when we analyze a particular political system, we attempt to ascertain *how* stable or unstable it is, rather than simply label it stable or unstable. We are aware that some stable political systems are more so than other stable political systems and that the same thing holds true among unstable political systems. Moreover, developments and shifts within a political system are usually able to move it only part of the way toward one or the other end of the continuum.

This observation recalls the importance of *trends,* referred to at the end of the section above summarizing political change (p. 539). In the same way that economists have been concerned with economic development, political scientists have given increasing attention to processes of "political development." Although as yet there is no general agreement about how political development can most usefully be conceptualized, a number of studies and theoretical analyses can be related to the ideas presented here.[10] Thus, change in the direction of increased effectiveness and legitimacy, particularly when demands are also growing, might be seen as "development." Change in the opposite direction could be termed "decline" or "deterioration."

It should be noted that this is quite distinct from the question of whether a political system seems to be evolving toward or away from "democratic" forms. Some writers prefer to think of political development as involving only those changes that move in the direction of democracy; they see changes in the opposite direction as regressive. This view, while congenial to our values of freedom and progress, nevertheless may imply a teleological or a culture-bound interpretation. In the interest of objectivity, therefore, it seems more useful to apply the criteria of effectiveness and legitimacy, regardless of whether a political system is democratic or autocratic. We might judge it less desirable to the degree that it leans toward the latter pole; but evaluations of this sort would proceed from a different order of assumptions. Similarly, of course, if this viewpoint is accepted for purposes of analysis, we should avoid the implication that more or higher rates of development are either inevitable or more desirable than less or lower rates. We might agree that they are—but again, from different assumptions or criteria.

We must also remember that the concepts outlined above provide only an abstract descriptive framework or schema, which may be useful for organizing our observations of political change. While the framework is built on the idea that political change derives ultimately from conflicting and competing interests, it does not specify the factors that produce changes in interests, or which cause some interests to prevail over others. Some such factors can be identified, but in the present state of political knowledge their interrelations and relative importance cannot be set forth in a precise and systematic way. Nor are we able to say at just what points changes in these factors cause stable processes of change to move toward unstable processes—and vice versa. Nevertheless, this chapter cannot end without specifying such important factors as we can now recognize.

Major Sources of Political Change in the World Today

Technological innovation and change, and the spread of new ways of doing things throughout the world, have always been basically unsettling factors in human affairs. In changing the means through which man attempts to control and exploit his environment, technological in-

10 See particularly the series entitled "Studies in Political Development" published between 1963 and 1966 by Princeton University Press under the sponsorship of the Committee on Comparative Politics of the Social Science Research Council.

novations also change men's values and interests, as well as the membership, structure, and processes of groups and institutions. In addition, they bring new groups and institutions into existence, and undermine the foundations of old ones. The industrial revolution, for example, transformed Western European and North American societies in the eighteenth and nineteenth centuries, and was then extended through trade, colonialism, and war to the far ends of the earth. Wherever its influence is felt, new interests are created and old ones are modified or threatened. Changed patterns of demand consequently confront political systems, which must either adapt themselves to the new patterns or, if they are unable to, must give way to new political structures and processes.

Closely related to technological innovation, and in part deriving from it, is the "revolution of rising expectations," which has been a prominent aspect of the underdeveloped portions of the world during the past few decades. Stimulated by the changes of World War II and moved by a growing awareness of the possibilities of life under conditions of political independence and higher levels of economic development, these "rising expectations" have contributed mightily to nationalist movements in colonial areas—and also to the instability of some of the independent regimes that have supplanted colonial administration. Often, the struggle for independence has created exaggerated expectations of and demands for social and economic well-being, and these demands have survived as a powerful and irreversible ferment in the underdeveloped countries. They do not necessarily emanate from the most numerous or most deprived sectors of the population, but rather from those that have been most exposed to knowledge about the achievements of technology, and about socio-economic and political conditions in those parts of the world where these are thought to be more advanced. Where such hopes and demands are not satisfied, however, this force may be transformed into an equally important "revolution of rising frustrations."[11]

A third factor, which seems sometimes to operate at cross purposes with the first two, is population growth. In most parts of the world, the rate of population growth is greater than that of economic growth—with fairly obvious implications of competition for land, food, and other economic interests. Coupled with the expanded and intensified demands for these things, as indicated by the "revolution of rising expectations," this rate of population growth cannot fail to contribute to political change—and to unstable change, where political systems are unable to satisfy the demands that are thereby intensified.

Lastly, mention must be made of the cold war, as it injects factors for change, particularly ideological change, into the political processes of many countries. Alignment with either the Soviet or the Western blocs

11 Daniel Lerner, "Toward a Communication Theory of Modernization—A Set of Considerations," in Lucian W. Pye (ed.), *Communications and Political Development* (Princeton, N.J.: Princeton University Press, 1963), pp. 330–33.

has implied ideological commitments on the part of many governments, and has resulted in the propagation of either Soviet or Western values through at least parts of their populations. Furthermore, each bloc has attempted to disseminate its values among the peoples aligned with the other, seeking thereby to build the demand for change. Economic and military aid have served to bolster political regimes on each side, but they have also made their contribution to the forces of political change. At the same time, uncommitted or "neutral" nations have been able to draw a certain amount of aid from each side, developing ideological doctrines that justify their positions—and promising more to their people as a consequence. The growing rift between Communist China and the USSR has both complicated and intensified the ideological struggle. Thus the cold war, in varied ways, has added to the forces for political change.

All four of these factors of change are at work in the United States, of course, as they are in other parts of the world. Thus far, however, the American political system has demonstrated a degree of flexibility and resilience that has proved more than adequate to absorb and adjust to powerful trends of change. Only once, in the Civil War of a century ago, has the system been seriously threatened with basic internal change by violence. At present, and for the foreseeable future, there is every indication that the political patterns through which all major interests (and many minor ones) are translated into demands, channeled into institutional structures, converted into governmental policies, and implemented through programs of governmental activity, will retain their effectiveness and legitimacy.

Thus, barring a major international war, the outlook is for continued stability in change processes in the United States. But the predominant instability of change in so many other parts of the world will undoubtedly continue to require much attention and effort and a major share of the resources of the United States. Among the other reasons for it, this degree of involvement in its world environment—illustrating once again the interdependence of foreign and domestic affairs and policies—is an important condition for continuing political stability in this country.

SUGGESTIONS FOR ADDITIONAL READING

ALMOND, GABRIEL A., and JAMES S. COLEMAN (eds.), *The Politics of the Developing Areas* (Princeton, N.J.: Princeton University Press, 1960).

BARKER, ERNEST (trans.), *The Politics of Aristotle* (London: Oxford University Press, 1946).

BRINTON, CRANE, *The Anatomy of Revolution* (Englewood Cliffs, N.J.: Prentice-Hall, Inc., 1952).

DEUTSCH, KARL, *Nationalism and Social Communication* (New York: John Wiley and Sons, 1953).

EISENSTADT, S. N., *The Political Systems of Empires* (New York: The Free Press of Glencoe, 1963).

EMERSON, RUPERT, *From Empire to Nation* (Cambridge, Mass.: Harvard University Press, 1960).

HIRSCHMAN, ALBERT O., *Journeys Toward Progress* (New York: Twentieth Century Fund, 1963).

JOHNSON, JOHN J., *Political Change in Latin America* (Stanford, Calif.: Stanford University Press, 1958).

KAUTSKY, JOHN H., *Political Change in Underdeveloped Countries* (New York: John Wiley and Sons, 1962).

LERNER, DANIEL, *The Passing of Traditional Society* (New York: The Free Press of Glencoe, 1958).

MACIVER, ROBERT M., *The Modern State* (London: Oxford University Press, 1926).

MILLIKAN, MAX F., and DONALD L. M. BLACKMER (eds.), *The Emerging Nations* (Boston: Little, Brown and Company, 1961).

PYE, LUCIAN W. (ed.), *Communications and Political Development* (Princeton, N.J.: Princeton University Press, 1963). See also the other volumes in this series, cited in footnote 10.

Part Four

POLITICAL THEORY
AND
POLITICAL ANALYSIS

Chapter 18

THE LANGUAGE AND METHODS OF POLITICAL SCIENCE

Having completed our survey of government and politics, we return to the problems introduced at the very beginning of this book. We suggested there that one of the most difficult yet most essential parts of the political scientist's job is to be self-conscious about the intellectual status of his knowledge, for full understanding of a subject requires one to understand his understanding itself. In other words, a cardinal rule for political scientists (as for serious students of any subject) is "Know your thoughts and thought processes."

This rule requires both introspection about one's own personal habits and modes of thinking and close examination of those of the reporters, writers, and analysts one believes. Self-conscious examination of the relationship between thinking itself and the substance or content of thoughts expressed should go on before, during, and after further study of the subject matter as such. Our conceptions of knowledge and the proper ways to acquire it determine how we evaluate existing "knowledge," what areas we consider most in need of exploration and research, how we define new problems to be investigated, and what methods we think will most likely produce further knowledge.

The Meaning of Political Terms: The Problem of Language

A most troublesome methodological problem for the political scientist arises from the fact that his subject matter, unlike the natural scientist's, talks to itself and to him about itself. Like other social scientists (and unlike physical scientists), the political scientist must take into account what he sees his subject matter doing, what it *says* it is doing, and what it *thinks* it is doing.

LEVELS OF POLITICAL DISCOURSE

Communication about politics takes place in many different contexts. In complex modern societies everyone probably "talks politics" with his fellows at one time or another, though few may do it as often as some democratic theorists used to think. There is much political talk in clubs, parlors, barber shops, and countless other places we visit in our everyday life. Most of this may appear to be chit-chat among spectators of politics, seemingly affecting political events no more directly and significantly than the comments of "Monday-morning quarterbacks" influence the outcome of last Saturday's football game. More obviously relevant to actual political events are some of the conversations and communications which occur in Senate cloakrooms, political meeting halls, offices of administrative agency heads, and other sites of political activity. "Urge you to vote 'No' on S.B. Number such-and-such," announces a telegram from a local chamber of commerce to a Senator. "I must support the Prime Minister on this motion because my constituents elected me to do so," says a British M.P. In such ways ordinary citizens, spokesmen for groups, public officials and aspirants for public office, judges, administrators, lobbyists, voters, and others verbalize their demands on government, their claims on other people through government, their views on issues, and their conceptions of what politics is all about. Such communications constitute important data for political scientists. From them they discover the interests, values, and orientations that form some of the basic "raw material" of political and governmental situations.

But everyday political discourse does not directly communicate political science knowledge. Only by analyzing it, by treating it as data to be explained, does the political scientist arrive at knowledge either of the specific situations where he hears the talk or of politics generally. That is, he does not study the content of everyday political discourse to learn the truth or falsity of what is there asserted; rather he is concerned with what study and analysis of such assertions can tell him about what people want, how they see the political world, how their perceptions make them act, and the consequences for the political system of their seeing, thinking, wanting, and acting as they do. Words and sentences found in the actual conduct of politics are for him only data, samples of the human behavior it is his job to explain. This applies not only to simple and direct political demands, but also to a more abstract (and often more impassioned) level of everyday political discourse, the kind that is concerned with such matters as "social justice," "equal rights," "the true nature of the state," or "the ultimate ends of government." The political scientist is interested in whether or not, and how far, men engage in this more ideological kind of talk, and what they seem to mean by it; but these usages too he looks on as data about the people who use them. He observes, classifies, and analyzes political doctrines and ideologies in action, as he does more simple interests and attitudes, so that he can generalize about their political function and consequences, not in order to be educated or instructed by the beliefs they convey.

With a closely related level of discourse, "political theories" in the traditional sense, the political analyst must deal somewhat differently. Most treatises on political theory purport to offer the kind of systematic and comprehensive knowledge sought by political inquiry as we have described it above; but they may also become the basis of political action and assume different meanings in actual political life. The ideas and beliefs of "practicing" Communists, for example, which for political scientists are merely data about the attitudes and behavior of those who espouse them, stem directly from the formal writings that Karl Marx and Friedrich Engels offered as genuine knowledge about politics, not simply as evidence of their personal political beliefs. And although it is often said that democracy as an ideology lacks this kind of "authoritative" creed, the beliefs of citizens and statesmen in many democratic political systems are nonetheless similarly related to concepts propounded systematically in the writings of John Locke, Jean-Jacques Rousseau, Jeremy Bentham, and other writers.

Nevertheless, though the political scientist *can* treat ideas found in such sources simply as data about the writers themselves, or even as data about attitudes and behavior generally prevalent in their times, there is good reason for him to do more than that. He is also justified in dealing with them as what they claim to be, justifiable general statements, and in assessing the validity of *what* they assert, regardless of when, how, or by whom they were made. For embedded in all the great traditional political theories are important empirical and "scientifically" theoretical generalizations of the kind that is the nuclear concern of the modern political scientist.

THE AMBIGUITY OF BASIC POLITICAL CONCEPTS

Because political activity consists elementally of the behavior of feeling and thinking human beings, political scientists' conceptual problems are more acute than those of natural scientists. Many key words political scientists use to explain government and politics are used also by people actually engaged in political activity, but generally with quite different meanings. Thus the political analyst is likely to encounter his analytic constructs being used as symbols in the political situations he studies. Conversely, he may pick up words and concepts used in actual politics and invest them with new meaning as analytic constructs—or, what is worse, he may accept them without adequately determining their analytic usefulness. As a result there is serious ambiguity about the meaning of all but the simplest, most descriptive political terms commonly used by both laymen and political scientists.

Most of us are well aware, for example, that the word "democracy" means something altogether different to Soviet spokesmen from what it means to Americans of almost any political persuasion. There is similar disparity of meaning among different users of almost any of the familiar abstractions which sum up political doctrines or ideological disagreements. "Socialism," "liberalism," "conservatism," and similar symbolic words are so commonly used, with such different meanings, that they are practically devoid of all meaning, unless one prefaces each use with explicit definitions.

Many, perhaps most, of the generic terms we use in political science as well as in everyday political discourse suffer from the same kind of ambiguity. The familiar word "state" may refer to one of fifty specific organizational systems in the United States or to the whole American political system; it may also be used as a generic term to refer to the very concept of a political system. The word "law" may mean a particular kind of product of a particular process engaged in by a particular body of men (like the Bundestag); it may mean a supposed absolute rule decreed by God and made known to men by reason or revelation; or it may mean a generalization or principle (like an economic law or the law of gravity). To say "Parliament had the *power* to do thus-and-so" may mean that a specific group of men at a given time controlled an army strong enough to work its will on the king, or it may mean that somebody interpreted precedents to mean that Parliament should be allowed to do certain things even though the king controlled overwhelming armed force against it. Needless to say, these few examples hardly exhaust the common meanings encountered for these terms. Even such apparently unambiguous terms as "interest group" or "political party" may become cloudy when one tries to use them to refer to specific groups in specific situations. Is the Prohibition "party" in America, for example, a "political party" or an "interest group"? Or both? Or neither?

The careful student, therefore, whether conversing with a friend, reading a treatise by some political philosopher, listening to a campaign speech, or studying some report of political science research, must be alert to detect ambiguous words and to discover exactly what meaning is intended by them. To grasp what is asserted by anyone, one must read or hear the words with the meanings intended by their *user,* not with his own preconceived notion about what the word ought to mean. To illustrate the problem, let the reader reflect on the following list of commonly used terms and ask himself what he thinks each one means, how its meaning varies according to the different contexts in which he finds it, and what different meanings are given it by different users in one and the same context. The reader might also ask himself how these terms have been used earlier in this book.

Some Common but Ambiguous Political Concepts

Coercion	Authority	Community
Compulsion	Force	Culture
Consent	Influence	Nation
Constitution	Law	Society
Obligation	Legitimacy	State
Representation	Power	
Revolution	Violence	
Communist	Equality	Citizen
Conservative	Fraternity	Class
Democratic	Freedom	Corporation
Fascist	Justice	Group
Liberal	Liberty	Organization
Radical	Order	Party
Reactionary	Security	Person
Socialist	Welfare	
Totalitarian		

REQUIREMENTS FOR SCIENTIFIC CONCEPTS

The development of clear, unambiguous concepts requires more than mere agreement on acceptable arbitrary verbal definitions. In fact, the attempt to state formal, verbal definitions may cause more trouble than it avoids.

One mistake which often results from a misconception of the problem of defining analytic concepts is known as the error of *reification* (from the Latin *res*, thing)—the assumption that because we have a given word or name, there must be a "thing" to which it points, and the consequent treatment of the word, which is only a symbol, as if it were itself that thing. Most important general terms used by political scientists are not simply "pointer" words, symbols pointing directly to the things which they name, but symbols which single out particular aspects of complex phenomena or which refer to complex relationships among less complicated, more identifiable objects (which themselves may have "pointer" names). They are symbols we make up to refer to abstractions we have invented for talking about and explaining the real political world, not labels which nature or some impersonal force has attached to real objects and obliged us to read verbatim. It is therefore pointless to argue about what words like liberal or democratic "really" mean; it is meaningless to argue about whether or not the American Prohibition party is "really" a political party or not. As one commentator has said, "Words like 'democracy' do not have meanings in the required sense at all; they have uses."[1] Instead of looking for the real object correspond-

[1] T. D. Weldon, *The Vocabulary of Politics* (London: Penguin Books, Ltd., 1953), p. 19.

ing to some word we happen to know or use, we should first be clear about what we want to explain or discuss and *then* affix whatever shorthand symbols seem appropriate to our meaning. The symbols may be adapted from familiar lay or professional usage or invented wholly anew, if that seems necessary to avoid confusion. The task is not to *discover* meanings of words, but to *construct* the concepts needed to grapple with complex reality. For this reason, some philosophers of scientific method refer to the basic concepts used in any scientific discourse as "constructs." At this point the reader might reflect back over the constructs used in the preceding chapters—for example, articulation of demands and charismatic leadership, to name but two—and ask himself whether we have fully avoided the methodological sin of reification.

Not only should political science concepts be untainted by reification. If they are to have any stable meaning, they must also have clear *empirical referents*. That is, all who use a given concept must have no doubt about the kind of real-world phenomena to which it refers. All who use the concept must be directed by it toward the same evidences, signs, and observations; all must be directed to evaluate the relevance of empirical data and observations to the concept in the same way. For example, if in discussing British politics we use so simple a concept as "Conservative," we must be clear whether or not the man who voted Tory in 1945, Labour in 1951, and abstained in a later by-election is referred to by our concept. If we are making generalizations about "underdeveloped nations," our meaning of that concept must be so clear that we know whether or not each one of the more than one hundred countries in the world today is or is not referred to as such. Unless the empirical referents of *all* the concepts and terms used in our generalizations are clear, it becomes hopelessly impossible to investigate their validity. Consider, for example, the difficulties of either proving or disproving the following statements: "All Conservatives are conservative." "No underdeveloped nation achieves political democracy without first undergoing a social revolution." Statements whose terms are so ambiguous and so devoid of clear empirical referents as to be incapable of proof or disproof are not really statements at all; they are meaningless strings of words.

Some methodologists would avoid reification and obtain clarity of empirical referents by what is known as rigorous *operational definition*. That is, instead of saying "what" a concept refers to (thereby already seeming to impute to it too much substantiality), they would specify operations for observing the world and rules for interpreting the observations. An often-used example from physics is the operational definition of "heat" as the results obtained from making readings on an apparatus called a thermometer. The strict operationalist would say not only that he meant something like these operations whenever he used the term "heat," but that that is *all* he means. Similarly, the operationalist political scientist would use the word "liberal," for example, to mean *only* a person who has answered a certain battery of questionnaire items a certain way, and nothing more.

Important as these issues of scientific reasoning are, we need not here take sides nor examine them further. It is sufficient for our purposes to understand the fundamental requirements about which there is little dispute: avoidance of reification and precision of empirical referents. These requirements apply not only to essentially descriptive or denotative concepts (like Conservative, Republican, Democratic, underdeveloped nation, and so on) but also to those more abstract concepts which refer to relationships (power, influence, submission, and so on). Only when our propositions are framed wholly in terms of unambiguous concepts, whatever their level of generality or abstraction, and only when their references to the observable world are unmistakably clear, can we make testable statements about what we see going on. At the same time we must remember that argumentation merely about the "correct" meaning or usage of terms is fruitless. We only *know* something about politics and government when we can make valid general statements. Clarification of language is useful only insofar as it contributes to our ability to do this.

Methods of Investigation

Few laymen or beginning students (and not all political scientists) realize how specialized and complex the process of acquiring political knowledge has become, thanks to the rapid expansion of scientific methods and techniques of research. Many believe that anyone can acquire such knowledge directly and individually by simply reflecting on what he reads in a daily paper and a few library books chosen at random—supplemented perhaps by whatever observations of actual political life chance has afforded him. At another extreme are those who would read one masterwork in the belief that everything is explained there. Actually, of course, there is no single work or series of works by one great interpreter which adequately embodies what we know. Yet at the same time we do know considerably more than any individual could learn alone and unaided through unsystematic, speculative methods.

Most of the political knowledge we have so far accumulated is the product of disciplined and laborious efforts by many investigators past and present; it is also subject to accretion and modification by the continuing and future efforts of countless political researchers. For most political scientists writing textbooks and transmitting knowledge already accumulated is only part of the job. The criticism of existing knowledge, particularly the constant effort to discover the most critical gaps in it and to design and conduct research to fill them or to re-test the validity of what we think we already know, bulk as large in the business activity of political science as does the teaching and communication of existing knowledge. It is not at all uncommon for present-day professors of political science to leave their professing every three years or so for extended study "in the field," systematically observing politicians and statesmen, interviewing voters, or exploring first-hand the political habits of tribesmen in Africa or dons at Oxford.

Because of the complex scientific character of modern political science, and especially in view of its still formative state, today's student must learn more than what political scientists have already learned. He must also understand how that knowledge was acquired and how political science today proceeds to widen and deepen it and make it more reliable. The following sections of this chapter survey the problems and procedures of political research only cursorily, so that the student will be better able to understand and evaluate the fruits of current political investigation. They are obviously not adequate to make him immediately a full-fledged researcher. But there are many excellent handbooks and manuals which will carry him beyond our general discussion and into the practice of research if he wishes to go there.[2]

INDUCTIVE AND DEDUCTIVE APPROACHES

In the Introduction we viewed scientific endeavor as a "theory-data continuum," a logical network linking up statements about the immediately observable facts (data) with highly general and abstract statements (theory). The term "research" refers usually to activities near the data end of the continuum: to collecting, classifying, storing, and analyzing the facts observed by the investigator. But there are two different ways of approaching research, corresponding to two different conceptions of the character and role of theory.

One approach, generally called *empiricist* or *inductive,* we can describe (oversimply) as the effort *first* to collect facts and *then* to see what kind of generalizations we can make about them, that is, to induce from them—"to let the facts speak for themselves," some would say. For example, in studying American elections we might first assemble tables showing how every county in the United States voted over a given period; then by inspection we would discover what kinds of generalizations are inherent or possible in the data. We might perhaps discover that all those counties which invariably went Democratic are in lower income categories than those counties invariably going Republican. Or we might observe that 80 per cent of the Democratic counties are in the

---

2 See, for example, Leon Festinger and Daniel Katz (eds.), *Research Methods in the Behavioral Sciences* (New York: Dryden Press, 1953); William J. Goode and Paul K. Hatt, *Methods in Social Research* (New York: McGraw Hill, Inc., 1952); John Madge, *The Tools of Social Science* (New York: Longmans Green & Co., 1953); Marie Selltiz et al., *Research Methods in Social Relations* (New York: Holt, Rinehart & Winston, 1959); and the series of paperback Handbooks for Research in Political Behavior edited by James A. Robinson and published by Northwestern University Press, Evanston, Illinois.

South, as against 70 per cent of the Republican counties found in the North. By this view of the research process, theory would grow from the bottom up, so to speak, as new researchers throw new empirical generalizations into the pot, and analysts, examining the logical relationships among them, build the generalizations up into higher and higher levels of generality and abstraction.

A different view, sometimes called *deductive* or *hypothetical*, would proceed instead from the top down. Its proponents maintain that the "mere" collection of facts is useless unless it is guided by predictions deduced from some theory. Since the purpose of gathering facts, in this view, is to *test* theoretical propositions, we must *first* make our generalizations and *then* look for the relevant facts—which will either be consistent with them or, by their inconsistency, prove the generalizations (and to that extent, the original theory) false. For example, we would collect election data when some theory led us to predict something about elections, collecting only the data relevant to the prediction in question. From a general theory holding that economic factors largely determine political behavior we might deduce that economic depression would be critical in changing people's political party preferences, and from there deduce the prediction (or research hypothesis) that all those American counties suffering severe economic depression over a certain period ("other things being equal") should show more political realignment than those suffering none. Thus our generalization (the research hypothesis) shows us what kinds of data to look for, in this case data about how certain counties voted in certain elections *and* data about economic conditions in them.

There is little doubt, in principle, that the so-called deductive or hypothetical approach is more consistent with the standards of scientific method than the pure empiricist approach. Even for a simple, finite situation, the number of "facts" is almost infinite; no one can seriously hope to collect "all" of them. Everyone necessarily, whether consciously or not, chooses the facts he collects. What, if not explicitly recognized theory, can properly guide his selection? By the same token, there is no end to what we might discover in the data if we keep examining them long and imaginatively; we cannot begin to exhaust the possible generalizations. Yet without a prior theoretical conception we have little way of knowing which of the innumerable valid generalizations induced from the data are the most fruitful. Furthermore, the influence of the hypothetical approach appears to have been more stimulating for the invention of research procedures and tools. Most of the scales, measures, and modes of analysis we shall look at later in this chapter were devised when theoretical needs led researchers to want particular kinds of data. In contrast, unthinking acceptance of an uncritical empiricist approach has in the past led many researchers to look mainly at collections of data which are readily available because somebody else collected them for some other purpose—such as legislative roll calls collected for legislatures' own record-keeping convenience, or census data originally collected and categorized according to the needs of the American economic community.

Realistically speaking, however, unless these views are held dogmatically, there is perhaps less conflict between them than some disputants seem to feel, at least at the present stage of political science. Theory-builders in political science have not yet developed theoretical propositions that span all the data readily available. Nor have they developed, even for limited sets of data, any single body of "middle-range" theory sufficiently well-established that deductions from it can guide all research in the given area. Moreover, there is fundamental agreement between practitioners of both approaches on several important points. The logical structure of statements—the theory-data continuum—is viewed in essentially the same way by both. Both accept the basic scientific requirement of empirical validation. And both aim at the goal of increasingly general and abstract theoretical propositions. Finally, the generation of hypotheses from theory by deductive methods requires ingenuity and imagination, just as does the induction of generalizations from masses of data. In any case, from the scientific standpoint, it makes little difference where hypotheses come from—what matters most is whether or not they can be substantiated or disproved.

RESEARCH OBJECTIVES

Whether the researcher's or the reader's bent be inductive or deductive, the most important step in research design, after one is clear about the theoretical problem to be investigated, is probably to recognize the kind and level of generalization sought. It is equally important for readers of completed research reports to recognize the kind and level of generalization achieved. In this connection it is common to distinguish first of all between *case* studies and *cross-sectional* or *comparative* studies, the first of which are said to examine only one entity, object, or instance of something, whereas the latter are said to examine a number of similar entities, objects, or instances. A study of the Massachusetts General Court (state legislature) is presumably a case study; a comparison of four or eight American state legislatures is presumably a comparative study.

The distinction is somewhat more complicated than this, however. The term "case study" suggests that, whatever we are studying, we are looking at it as a case or an example *of* something, and that we are interested in it not so much for its own uniquely interesting features as for what it can tell us about the more general class of which it is an example. For instance, a well-known case study of the passage of the Full Employment Bill through the United States Congress[3] is interesting to political science because of what it reveals about the general features

[3] Stephen K. Bailey, *Congress Makes a Law* (New York: Columbia University Press, 1950).

of the legislative process in Congress. A case study of the political activity of a French religious group during the Fourth Republic would be interesting for what it could tell us about the behavior of interest groups in France, about the respective roles of political parties and pressure groups, or about general features of the political process in France at the time.

One could, of course, study the Massachusetts General Court or any other political object or event because he is interested solely and simply in it alone. One could study only one French religious group because he was interested only in it, caring not a whit about American parties, British parliaments, other religious organizations, or anything save his one French group. What can political scientists learn from or contribute by such "case studies," which are not really case studies at all but descriptive journalism or history? The answer is, "Probably not much," *unless* the history or account was prepared with political science problems in mind and presented in terms of political science concepts and categories. But then the supposed account of the single event or object becomes a case study "of" something, even though the larger class of which it is a case remains obscure. Individual political scientists may personally be as fascinated as anyone else by interesting historic events and situations, but they learn from them only insofar as they can interpret them as cases of something more general or incorporate them into generalizations which go beyond the single case at hand.

In this light, the case study as a research method differs less from comparative studies than one might think. Just as the case study is meaningful only when one knows what it is a case of, so the comparative study is meaningful only when one knows what it is that is being compared. Whether one attempts a case study of the Massachusetts General Court or a comparative study of all fifty American state legislatures, he must begin with a theoretical conception of the state legislative institution and process which tells him what kinds of data to collect. Thus one might say that the study of fifty legislatures is essentially fifty case studies instead of one, or that the two studies are essentially the same except that one has a sample numbering fifty, the other a sample numbering one. The theoretical problems and the type of generalizations sought are substantially the same in both instances. The chief difference between them lies in the greater utility of the comparative study (the larger sample) for analysis, since attention to many cases instead of only one usually makes it easier to detect and to investigate relationships among significant variables. In the single case study one can compare his data only with data he guesses he might find in other cases but does not actually have at hand, or with the findings he thinks earlier case studies have produced even though he may not have systematically organized the data of his own case to make such comparisons.

Although the terms "cross-sectional study" and "comparative study" are sometimes used interchangeably, the former term more often refers to a research method which can be differentiated from both the case study and the comparative study as described above. The cases we have so far talked about were all concrete and discrete as cases in the real world. What we most often call "cross-sectional research" does not deal with real-world "cases," with things or entities as such, but rather with complex and abstract concepts and with *analytical* distinctions—not simple *descriptive* distinctions mechanically used to sort out cases. Such studies are called "cross-sectional" because they look not at some total object but at some "slice taken across" the object, as one might examine the cell structure of a slice of apple without any concern for the shape, flavor, or other qualities or characteristics of the whole apple. The difference can be illustrated by comparison of election studies like the "Nuffield Studies," which deal each with a specific election and attempt to describe and account generally for numerous factors thought to enter into that event,[4] and studies which cut across many elections and seek to examine the influence of one or a few specified factors, such as voters' social class status or party identification.[5] What seems in historical or case-study analysis to be the object being studied (for example, the 1955 election) appears to the cross-sectional researcher as no more than a convenient research site (see below, pp. 567–71), a useful source of data about his analytic concepts (one election of many in which voters registered preferences which can be examined in the study of party and social class influences on voting). Where the writer of a case study or the historically inclined researcher is apt to become absorbed in the single event or case, the cross-sectional researcher is necessarily interested in many more events and cases but never really interested in any of them as such.

A further distinction we can make, according to the kind of question research proposes to answer, is that between *static* or *equilibrium* analysis and *developmental* or *longitudinal* analysis. The former seeks to discover normal or relatively permanent and unchanging relationships and conditions; the latter, to explain a process of change over time. Through the accidents of the history of research, developmental studies have frequently been associated with case-study or historical methods of investigation—witness the many attempts to "explain" the Russian or the French Revolutions—whereas cross-sectional and comparative analysis has generally been associated with assumptions about the stability or equilibrium of the system to be studied. But the association is accidental, not logical: for the same reasons that cross-sectional and comparative methods are potentially more fruitful for studying stable situations, they are likely to be more so for studying change. At the same time, a too-easy assumption about the stability over time of the systems being examined by cross-sectional methods can lead to serious errors in inter-

---

[4] See, for example, David E. Butler, *The British General Election of 1951* (London: The Macmillan Company, 1952); *The British General Election of 1955* (London: The Macmillan Company, 1955); and Richard Rose, *The British General Election of 1959* (London: The Macmillan Company, 1960).
[5] A good example is Heinz Eulau, *Class and Party in the Eisenhower Years* (New York: The Free Press of Glencoe, 1962).

preting the results of research: what is best interpreted as the operation of some long-run trend may be erroneously interpreted instead as the short-term interference of supposedly extraneous factors. The other side of the coin is that in the present stage of limited technical sophistication and limited theoretical development cross-sectional study of developmental questions is exceedingly difficult.

RESEARCH SITES

Whether attempting comparative, cross-sectional, or case study, whether examining developmental or equilibrium questions, researchers must make strategic decisions about what data they need, how much of it they can afford to seek, and where they can most easily get it. The theoretical orientation of the research in question will, of course, go a long way toward shaping these decisions, but it will not by any means make them. Whatever his theoretical interests, a researcher may well be able to gather his data in any one of the following ways: by biographical study, by study of institutions or institutional groups, by a community study, or by a regional or area study.

Biographical studies, as the name implies, examine data about the lives and careers of politically important figures. They often take the form of detailed life histories of single personages (Ludwig's life of Napoleon,[6] for example), but may be limited to politically important aspects and events in the career of a single man (Burns' *Roosevelt: The Lion and the Fox*).[7] Still less numerous than the political biographies of individuals, but increasingly important as sources of political knowledge, are investigations of large numbers of political figures, either in primarily narrative form or in the form of comparison of selected features in the careers and backgrounds of a number of men viewed collectively. The most systematic of these efforts have come to be known as "elite studies," following the pioneer ventures into this field by Harold Lasswell and others at the Hoover Institute of War and Peace.[8]

An equally familiar but far more numerous category of studies focuses on the structure and processes of specific political *institutions* or *institutional groups*. Many of these look at one very specific site—the British House of Commons, the American Congress, or the Australian Labor Party, to name only a few obvious examples. Many more attempt to examine more complex sets of institutions, as do, for example, Sir Ivor Jennings' classic studies of British parliamentary government.[9] More and more frequently today political research efforts focus on

6 Emil Ludwig, *Napoleon* (New York: Boni and Liveright, 1926).
7 James M. Burns, *Roosevelt: The Lion and the Fox* (New York: Harcourt, Brace & World, 1956).
8 Harold D. Lasswell, Daniel Lerner, and C. E. Rothwell, *The Comparative Study of Elites* (Stanford, Calif.: Stanford University Press, 1952).
9 Sir Ivor Jennings, *Parliament*, 2nd edition (Cambridge, Eng.: Cambridge University Press, 1957); and *Cabinet Government*, 3rd edition (Cambridge, Eng.: Cambridge University Press, 1959).

analytically defined segments of the political process in some particular institution or system. The Survey Research Center's studies, for example, concentrate on voting in American national elections,[10] and a number of studies concentrate on the decision-making process in various legislative bodies.

Still another common category is often referred to as *community* studies. The earliest of these, like the famous studies of "Middletown" by the Lynds,[11] attempted to survey a great variety of the features of community life and social structure, not merely its politics and government. Studies concentrating on the structure and process of government in various individual American cities are, however, increasingly numerous. Perhaps the best known variety of community study for political scientists is that developed by Professor Floyd Hunter in his study of "Regional City," generally called the community power structure study, which singles out for research one analytically important aspect—in this case, the power structure—of the community's political life.[12]

The name "community study" is ordinarily given to studies of local, city-sized communities, but from our standpoint the term would apply also to studies of larger communities and to different types of communities as well—for example, to anthropologists' investigations of particular tribes and cultures or to such general accounts of political life in particular national communities as Arthur N. Holcombe's studies of American politics.[13] Where research focuses on a total political system, this type of study becomes almost identical with the institutional study of complex systems described above. And whether one chooses to call examples of this type "institutional" or "community" studies is then almost entirely a matter of taste, so long as one recognizes the exact nature of the research site and focus in question.

A fourth type of study that has lately come into prominence is the so-called *area* or *regional* study. Most commonly the term refers to studies of politics and government in regions of the world broader than any single national community yet smaller than the whole world international system itself. Regional studies of Latin America, the earliest of this variety, are now being matched with studies of Africa (sometimes regionally subdivided into North Africa and sub-Saharan Africa); the Middle East; Eastern Europe; and Asia (commonly sorted out regionally still further into Southeast Asia and the individual countries of Asia

10 Angus Campbell, Philip E. Converse, Warren E. Miller, and Donald E. Stokes, *The American Voter* (New York: John Wiley and Sons, 1960); and Angus Campbell, Gerald Gurin, and Warren E. Miller, *The Voter Decides* (New York: Harper & Row, Publishers, 1954).

11 Robert S. Lynd and Helen M. Lynd, *Middletown* (New York: Harcourt, Brace and Company, 1929); *Middletown in Transition* (New York: Harcourt, Brace and Company, 1937).

12 Floyd Hunter, *Community Power Structure* (Chapel Hill, N.C.: University of North Carolina Press, 1953).

13 Arthur N. Holcombe, *The Political Parties of Today* (New York: Harper and Brothers, 1924); *The Middle Classes in American Politics* (Cambridge, Mass.: Harvard University Press, 1940).

proper). The term is sometimes used to refer to studies of areas or regions within a national community (the American South or French Canada, for example); there are, however, almost no examples of studies of areas or regions within local communities.

Viewed in terms of research method, regional or area studies exhibit several interesting characteristics. For one thing, many important political systems are left out of most area studies—the United States, the Soviet Union, and all of Western Europe, in particular. For another, there is little agreement on the exact boundaries of the regions or areas that have been the subjects of these studies. These points suggest that the research sites and focus of many of them are dictated more by convenience and other theoretically irrelevant factors than by theoretical considerations. Until recently, for instance, we have had precious few political studies of any one of the Spanish-speaking countries in Latin America. Therefore it is professionally convenient for a researcher fluent in Spanish to wrap up many national studies in a so-called regional study of Latin America. In much the same way, many regional studies of Africa and Southeast Asia reflect the recent and rapid appearance in these regions of many new nations and the fact that we have hitherto had no political studies of any kind to help us understand what is happening there. Area and regional studies, therefore, even those motivated only by such pragmatic and untheoretical considerations, have been invaluable in helping us expand our knowledge of political leaders, institutions, and communities in the rapidly changing areas of the world. The student of area or regional studies must, however, guard against unwarranted assumptions about the meaning of "regionalism" or the character of political relationships within a purely geographic "area" based only on the merely verbal lumping together of whatever groups and systems some investigator has found it professionally, linguistically, or even touristically convenient to study together.

We should mention here one final type of research site, which we shall encounter again in the next section of this chapter. This is the *contrived* site, as distinguished from the foregoing "natural" sites. Contrived experimental groups, or participants in simulation projects (see below, pp. 574–75), are examples of this type. While experiments as a method of generating data can be performed in real-world contexts like institutional groups, communities, or regions, and must therefore be considered later when we examine varieties and types of data, we should also note here the possibility of manufacturing our own research sites when those in the natural world do not suit our purposes for one reason or another.

The attentive reader may be troubled at this point by a certain ambiguity arising from the discussion of research objectives and research sites. That is, what we have described as research sites in this section may appear to him indistinguishable from what we discussed as research objectives in the preceding section. It is true that a political career, or a specific community, or a region *may* be the object which the researcher wants to investigate by case study or comparative methods. Certainly if he conceives his goals to be understanding of those specific, naturally defined phenomena as such, that conception dictates that those same objects and events be his research sites.

But as we have said, theoretically oriented research is aimed not at exposition of such concrete entities but at discovering abstract relationships. In such research the choice of political careers, communities, or areas as research sites is not governed by the researcher's desire to explain those things but by their utility to him as sources of data about other things which can only be defined analytically. Except insofar as he can contrive research sites to suit his needs, the theoretically oriented researcher is constrained to look for his data in existing, natural research sites. And so he works in the same places, so to speak, as the more factually and historically oriented researcher, who is busy studying the places themselves. For the latter, the distinction between research objectives and research sites may be of little importance; for the former it is crucial, since it directs him to two quite different sets of research-strategy decisions.

A reader's evaluation of the findings from any of these types of study, then, must take into account the same kind of considerations the researcher faced when making his strategic choice of research site. But these considerations may not always be as plain to the reader as to the original researcher. In the first place, the researcher is more likely than the reader to remember that whatever type of study he has accomplished his data are only a sample of all possible similar data he might collect and that his finally chosen research site is only one of many possible sites he might have chosen. Similarly, the researcher is more likely to be aware that whatever his site his data are limited to a particular time period. Readers, in contrast, are less likely to consider fully the problem of sampling raised by the choice of research site, to remember exactly what time period the data cover, to think of historically peculiar features of the period which might warrant restricting generalizations to that particular time and place; conversely, they are more likely to attribute wider validity to striking generalizations than a careful researcher would himself claim for them.

The reader is also more prone than the original researcher to forget how much any given generalization is dependent on the research site selected and how much interpretation of its meaning depends upon understanding the research context in which it was conceived. Once produced, the generalization itself may give no clue to its precise research origins. A finding that political leaders characteristically dodge issues concerning their own succession, for example, might emerge from the political biography of a single leader; it might equally well come out of a study of committee chairmen in the French National Assembly, an investigation of the community power structure in Berlin, or a regional survey of politics in Southeast Asia. But the meaning of key concepts like "political leaders" or "issues concerning succession" depends to a considerable extent upon which research site was used. One can therefore better understand the meaning and significance of a proposition, as well as better evaluate its credibility, if he knows the precise character of its research credentials.

Research Techniques

The problems discussed in the preceding sections of this chapter all relate to the first steps in research design: recognition of a theoretically interesting problem, formulation of the problem in terms that permit research, formulation of research objectives, and choice of a research site. The completion of a research design, however, requires still other technical decisions, and the actual conduct of research according to the design demands further skills on the part of the investigator. In this section we shall do no more than sketch out some of the techniques used in these phases of research. The reader will readily note the great variety of techniques and tools used by the modern political researcher, the ingenuity needed to develop them, and the skills needed to apply them. Although we shall not attempt to illustrate the point in detail as we go along, the reader should also bear in mind that the various techniques for gathering and analyzing data have in most of the cases we shall consider been developed "to order." That is, they have been invented and improved upon because researchers felt impelled to find ways of examining facts and securing data not accessible in existing sources or amenable to existing techniques. At the stage of analysis, therefore, the competent researcher is always alert to the inevitable influence of his research techniques on the data he is analyzing. In particular he guards against premature assertion of what superficially appear to be striking generalizations from the observed facts, lest careful analysis show them to be no more than artifacts of his particular ways of collecting and organizing those facts.

VARIETIES OF DATA

Many of us, particularly those whose principal acquaintance with "research" was gained in high school or early college courses in English, think of data as something found primarily in *documentary* and *library* sources. Although these essentially secondary sources are no longer the political scientist's most important ones, he must be familiar with the principal types of government documents routinely assembled by various agencies, branches, and levels of government in many political systems —and he must know where to find them.

Almost all governments these days publish collections of data

similar to the general decennial and the various special reports of the
U.S. Census Bureau, although not many of these are so extensive, detailed, or reliable as the latter. Most legislatures preserve some sort of
written record of their activities, although few include the extensive reports of floor debate found in the American Congressional Record. Practically all courts and major administrative agencies preserve systematic
records of their decisions, rules, and operating procedures, although none
report debates and votes as systematically as do legislative records. In
addition to basic familiarity with such sources, each political scientist
must also be familiar with specialized records and publications relevant
to his own interests—for example, the collections of voting statistics
published regularly in the United States under the title *America Votes,*
or the translations of articles from Soviet journals published in New
York. The imaginative researcher will automatically make use of whatever data he can find in such sources and will exert himself to discover
as many such sources as possible, since the collection of data is usually
an expensive, time-consuming, and difficult job.

But these data are probably less used in political research today
than are data collected for the first time by specific research projects for
specific research purposes and by methods specifically designed to get
at data that are unavailable in any documentary or library source. One
reason, as we noted earlier, is that library data have been assembled by
other people for other purposes than the research at hand and therefore
usually have serious shortcomings for the researcher's particular purpose. More important, political investigators now need data which would
never be recorded automatically or by anyone else.

An ancient method of data collection which has been extensively
developed by modern political scientists (and others) is that of *direct*
observation, sometimes by observers who are themselves participants in
the activity being studied (*participant* observation). We refer here not
to mere random looking at activity on chance occasions, but to systematic efforts to observe some definite sweep of activity and to record
what is observed in a fashion which can be duplicated in comparable
times and places. An example of such a study is an early effort to record
all the "interactions" of certain types between members of one particular legislative body over a given period of time.[14] Participant observation involves similarly disciplined and systematic observation and record-
ing of pre-selected categories of data, not mere reminiscence about what
happened by someone who happened to take part in some event or
process. A study of the authority structure of a prison by an analyst who
gathered his data "from the inside" as a member of the prison community
and another of the legislative process in a state legislature by a political
scientist who conducted his research while serving as an elected member

14 Garland C. Routt, "Interpersonal Relations and the Legislative Process," *Annals
of the American Academy of Political and Social Science,* XCCV (1938), 129–36.

of the body he studied are examples of the application of this data-collection technique.[15]

The use of public opinion polls by commercial advertisers, political candidates, and political reporting syndicates has given most informed citizens in America and Europe at least casual familiarity with another method of data collection, perhaps the most common one for present-day political scientists: the *sample survey* or *interview*. Laymen, however, are generally less aware than the practicing survey researcher of both the power and the limitations of this technique. Every competent survey researcher knows the importance of selecting the sample of persons to be interviewed so as to minimize bias, and every reputable survey report includes an extensive account of how much probable "sample error" it contains and what kind. Research literature is replete with studies of the influence of the wording of survey questions and related factors on the character and quality of data the questions yield—of "response set," for example, which inclines some people habitually to say "yes" and others to say "no" no matter what the question put to them; of the different results obtained when a key word in a question is replaced by a synonym or a word with slightly altered meaning or connotation. A very important question here concerns the relative utility of "closed" questions, which afford the respondent only a few fixed categories of response from which to choose his answer (for example, "Agree," "Disagree," "Undecided"), as compared with "open-ended" questions, which require the respondent to formulate his answer in such terms and at such length as he himself chooses (for example, "How do you feel about American foreign policy today?"). There are many research manuals on the proper ways to conduct interviews of various kinds with different sorts of respondents and many studies of the influence of the interviewer and the interview process on the data obtained. The preparation and administration of questionnaires for basic political research are therefore much more technical and skilled operations than the preparation of polls on candidates or issues. The technique of *panel* study—successive interviews at selected time intervals with a given set of respondents (panel)—is much more highly developed in political research, where it can help investigate developmental or trend questions, than in the more familiar field of political polls.

Another source of data the utility of which is still to be widely exploited by political scientists is the *experiment* or *prototype* study. Experiments have so far been performed primarily in small, artificially contrived, temporary groups. For example, the influence of different sorts of group authority structure on a group's problem-solving capabilities

15 Mickey McCleery, "Conflict and Accommodation in a Penal Institution," Paper presented at the Annual Meeting of the American Political Science Association, 1958. Wilder W. Crane, Jr., "The Legislative Struggle in Wisconsin: Decision-Making in the 1957 Wisconsin Assembly" (Unpublished Ph.D. dissertation, University of Wisconsin, 1959).

and practices has been studied several times. A number of small experimental groups are formed from persons volunteering to take part in the experiment. Different procedural rules are imposed on each group to approximate different types of authority structure (democratic or authoritarian), and then the way the different groups deal with various problems presented to them for group solution is observed. Experimental methods have occasionally been applied, however, to "natural" situations. The classic example is a study of the reasons for nonvoting in certain American elections. Different types of "propaganda" or stimuli to get out the vote were administered to different groups of voters by the researchers, who then observed the effects of these different stimuli in the ensuing actual election.[16]

Professor Lasswell has given the name "prototype study" to a planned and deliberate "interference" in real-life situations that goes much deeper and wider in its efforts and effects than such small-scale experiments as that on nonvoting. The primary purpose, however, remains the same: to learn something by observing the results. One example Lasswell cites is a large-scale effort by social scientists working at Vicos, Peru, to reshape the village's decision-making processes into a more democratic mold and to learn about the conditions, requirements, and effects of such a change. The other is a study by the Yale Psychiatric Institute to change the decision-making structure in a hospital so as to secure greater participation of patients in hospital policy decisions.[17] Needless to say, such prototype studies and experiments of any great range raise serious ethical questions for the researcher. Do intellectual values ever justify interference with the "normal" values of people who become, even though willingly, manipulated subjects of the experimenter? When is such interference justified? To what extent?

Such ethical problems rarely arise with the use of a closely related research technique, also very recent, known as *simulation*. The familiar mock political convention or model UN Assembly was a precursor of this technique. Simulation for research purposes entails much greater efforts to "build into" the mock situation or "game" the kinds of factors the researcher thinks are critical in the analogous real-world situation. Electronic computers, which can remember and read out an enormous quantity of information at incredible speeds, have greatly facilitated this technique. Using these machines, for example, students of business decision-making have been able to play business games in which sequences of decision can be performed much more rapidly than in the real economic world. The researcher can then observe more directly and immediately the collective effects of different types of decisions on the "market," as well as analyze the decision-making habits of different players. Top-echelon war colleges in the United States and elsewhere

[16] Harold F. Gosnell, *Getting Out the Vote: An Experiment in the Stimulation of Voting* (Chicago: University of Chicago Press, 1927).
[17] Harold D. Lasswell, *The Future of Political Science* (New York: Atherton Press, 1963), pp. 99 ff.

now use "war games" of this kind to investigate problems of strategy as well as to teach prospective commanders the principles of strategic decision-making. And interesting trials of the simulation of diplomatic and foreign-policy decision-making are being conducted at several academic institutions today. Of course any competent practitioner of simulation techniques is well aware of the impossibility of duplicating *all* conditions from real life in his mock situation. A graduate student using a computer and acting the role of the foreign minister of Country X may be given information or definitions of situations which approximate pretty closely those of his real-world counterpart, but he is not likely to duplicate the emotional state of the man who feels his decisions really might mean war. (As anyone who has played "Monopoly" knows, decisions to spend Monopoly-money are not motivated exactly like decisions to spend legal coin of the realm.) But this does not prevent researchers from learning a great deal by simulation of those factors which can be closely approximated by artificial means.

INSTRUMENTS AND ANALYSIS

In no phase of political research has recent technical development been more prolific and rapid than in the invention and use of specialized techniques of analyzing data and of specialized instruments for eliciting, collecting, and organizing data suitable to the new techniques of analysis. A generation ago, the use of elementary statistical techniques, or even the presentation of quantifiable data in simple tabular form, was a rarity, despite the interesting pioneer work of Abbott Lawrence Lowell in the analysis of legislative roll calls,[18] one of the earliest examples of the use of quantitative methods in political science. Until much more recently, few political scientists attempted any statistical analysis more advanced than the simplest forms of correlation.

Although the questions of "quantification" and "measurability" still occasion some polemical controversy among political scientists, there is little doubt that technical development in political analysis has proceeded apace with the development of ways to secure measurable and quantifiable data and to subject hitherto purely "qualitative" data to at least crude forms of measurement. These advances have been made possible primarily by political scientists' becoming more sophisticated about the mathematical meaning of such terms as "number," "measure," and "quantity," as well as by progress in the fields of mathematics and statistics themselves.

The development of such instruments as *attitude scales*, for example, is clearly associated with the effort to make attitudinal phenomena measurable. Most of the commonly used scales of this kind

---

[18] A. Lawrence Lowell, "The Influence of Party upon Legislation in England and America," *Annual Report of the American Historical Association for the Year 1901* (Washington, D.C.: Government Printing Office, 1902), Vol. I, pp. 321–542.

consist of a set of questions (a "battery" of "items") which respondents must answer by selecting one of a few specified response categories (for example, "Agree," "No opinion," or "Disagree"). A given battery of items is devised to discover, that is, measure, a respondent's attitude on some particular point. His degree of political alienation, for example, might be explored by the following questions:[19]

1. The government of a big city like [ours] doesn't take much interest in a person's neighborhood.
2. The government of a big city like [ours] is too costly to the average taxpayer.
3. The average person can't get any satisfaction out of talking to the officials of a big city government like [ours].
4. The government of a big city like [ours] is controlled too much by machine politics.
5. The average person doesn't have much to say about the running of a big city like [ours].

The analyst is not interested in the answers to each specific question but in the overall pattern of response. By assigning values to the different possible answers (say 1 for "Agree," 2 for "No opinion," and 3 for "Disagree") and then adding a respondent's item scores, he can arrive at a total score for each respondent on the attitudinal point in question. In the above example, a person scoring 5 (the minimum, indicating "Agree" to all five items) would be considered politically alienated; one scoring 15 (the maximum, indicating "Disagree" with all items) would not. Scales scored by merely summing arithmetical values in this way, without regard to which items were answered which way, are known as Likert scales, after the man who developed them. A more precise measure, administered in the same way but taking into account which questions are answered which way, is known as the Guttman scale, after its inventor. The number of attitudinal dimensions which can now be assessed by tried and tested scales of these types increases almost daily.

The use of *sociometric* techniques to examine interpersonal relationships within a group is also increasingly common. First used by social psychologists to study small group relationships through such simple "choice" questions as "Whom in this group would you most like to sit next to?" or "Whom are you most friendly with?" this technique has been extended by political scientists to considerably larger groups to explore interesting types of political relationships. Thus a recent study of American state legislators examined the informal friendship and expertise structures of legislatures by asking members to name the col-

[19] Edward L. McDill and Jeanne Claire Ridley, "Status, Anomia, Political Alienation and Political Participation," *American Journal of Sociology*, LXVIII (1962), 208, *n.* 19; 205–13.

leagues they associated with as friends and those they considered most expert in given subject matter fields.[20]

Not all instruments used in political research produce data so readily amenable to mathematical or quantitative analysis. There are, for example, various *projective* techniques, so-called because the subject "projects" into his answers or his conversation his whole way of looking at a problem or even at himself as a person and at life in general. These techniques depend heavily on the subjective interpretation put on the data by the analyst. The Rorschach test, in which the analyst infers a subject's mental state, attitudinal structure, or habits of thinking from the way he describes objectively meaningless ink blots, has been little used in political research, perhaps because its use requires extensive prior training on the analyst's part, as well as because it presumes a psychoanalytical interpretation of the results. But other projective techniques have begun to appear more often in political research. The sentence-completion test, asking subjects to supply their own endings to such incomplete sentences as, "Whenever I think of war, I . . . ." is one example.

As suggested earlier, important factors in the appearance of these and many other new research instruments and techniques of analysis have been the recent rapid advances in the fields of mathematics and statistics and the closely related advances made in data-processing machinery. Many types of analysis which thirty years ago were either wholly impossible or possible only with the most laborious efforts "by hand" have been made comparatively simple and easy by machines. By storing data on Hollerith (IBM) cards in the form of holes punched in rows and columns with assigned (coded) meanings, analysts are able not only to store much more information in much less space than previously but, more important, to retrieve the data at will in almost any form or array they wish. And electronic computers now make it possible literally to accomplish in a few hours statistical manipulations of the data which not many years ago would have required hundreds of thousands of man-hours.

Content analysis is one procedure now possible on a meaningful scale because of these developments. This term refers to the systematic classification of the "content" of a written or verbal record in terms of the frequency with which various words, symbols, themes, topics, and so on appear in it. By content analysis of a given newspaper's political reporting, for example, it is possible to arrive at an "objective" measure (that is, a rating made independently of the analyst's subjective evaluation, by methods which will yield the same measurements for anyone applying them) of the extent to which the paper favors one or another candidate or party. How many column inches does it give to photographs

[20] John C. Wahlke, Heinz Eulau, William Buchanan, and LeRoy C. Ferguson, *The Legislative System* (New York: John Wiley and Sons, 1962), chaps. 9–10.

of each candidate or to news reports about their activities? What proportion of the numbers of times a given candidate's name is printed is that name prefaced by pejorative or by eulogistic adjectives?

The procedure known as *factor* analysis was also impossible, for large-scale purposes at least, until electronic computers became available. This is an almost purely inductive method of analysis which could be applied to political data even by persons possessing only mathematical skills and no acquaintance with political theory. By sophisticated mathematical manipulation of, say, the voting records of a thousand congressmen over a number of years, or the decisions of judges over a great number of cases, it is possible to discover exactly which congressmen have voting records similar to others, or which judges have decision patterns similar to others. Assuming there is some "factor" underlying the similarities constituting each group thus discovered, one proceeds by induction to infer what that factor must have been. At this point, of course, some political knowledge would prove useful, to say the least, to guide the process of inference. But whatever one's opinion about the utility of inductive methods of investigation or his evaluation of the theoretical explanations induced in factor analyses to date, there is no denying that the facts about patterns of behavior which they reveal are essentially new facts; they could not have been discovered in many cases without this technique of data analysis. Nor is there much doubt that further startling new facts will be discovered this way in the future.

Conclusion

Before leaving the subject of research methods and techniques we might well explicitly recognize what some readers have no doubt already noticed. Political science as a discipline is not distinguished from other social sciences by its methods or techniques. Many of the present-day political scientist's tools—sociometric techniques, for example—were invented by workers in other disciplines. Others were first or most fully developed by political scientists but picked up and used widely in other fields—the opinion survey, for example. Although the application of particular research methods and techniques to political subjects may involve difficulties peculiar to the field of political science, the general problems and the fundamental rules of method are the same for political science as for other social sciences. Indeed, we can go further and say (thus coming full circle to our discussion in the Introduction), that the fundamentals of scientific research are the same for the social sciences, including political science, as for the natural sciences.

This suggests that abstract and polemical debate about the merits of this or that research technique is useless to defender and detractor alike. It is easy to maintain as a matter of sublime faith that machine analysis will someday soon answer all our questions for us. And it is just as easy to maintain by faith alone that "you can't measure a human being with a public opinion poll." But it is more difficult to learn enough about research techniques to evaluate properly the knowledge produced by research. And it is still more difficult to acquire the research skills needed to find out whatever one wants to find out. Still, the fact that the advancement of political knowledge depends on the technology of research does not alter the fact that the true test of one's knowledge is the breadth and depth of his understanding of political phenomena, not his sophistication or skill as a research technician.

SUGGESTIONS FOR ADDITIONAL READING

BARZUN, JACQUES, and HENRY F. GRAFF, *The Modern Researcher* (New York: Harcourt, Brace & World, 1957).

BRECHT, ARNOLD, *Political Theory* (Princeton, N.J.: Princeton University Press, 1959).

BROWN, ROBERT, *Explanation in Social Science* (Chicago: Aldine Publishing Company, 1963).

DUVERGER, MAURICE, trans. Malcolm Anderson, *An Introduction to the Social Sciences, with Special Reference to Their Methods* (New York: Frederick A. Praeger, 1964).

KAPLAN, ABRAHAM, *The Conduct of Inquiry* (San Francisco: Chandler Publishing Company, 1964).

MEEHAN, EUGENE J., *The Theory and Method of Political Analysis* (Homewood, Ill.: The Dorsey Press, 1965).

SHILS, EDWARD A., and HENRY A. FINCH (eds. and trans.), *Max Weber on the Methodology of the Social Sciences* (New York: The Free Press of Glencoe, 1949).

WELDON, T. D., *The Vocabulary of Politics* (London: Penguin Books, 1953).

Chapter 19

DOCTRINES, IDEOLOGIES, AND THEORIES OF POLITICS

We come now, in this final chapter, to the ultimate test of this book—really a joint test of the student-reader and the teacher-authors. The test consists of two questions. First, is the student, having been exposed to analyses of several political systems, processes, and methods of research, prepared to think for himself about political values, behavior, and institutions? Second, has he become sensitive enough to the consequences of his choice to pursue one or more of the possible roles by which he is related to his fellow-men and society through politics?

The most inclusive name for the sort of self-conscious, reflective activity that answering these questions would involve is *political theory*. And the first measure of the political theorist is not so much what or how much he knows as the clarity with which he formulates his interest in politics and the relevance and consistency with which he goes about analyzing it.

Political thinking and theorizing, whether of the implicit or the explicit variety, can be differentiated or classified according to the aim or purpose of the theorizer. For example, does the theorist emphasize the goal of *systematically developing and elaborating ideas* about political societies and institutions? Or does he view theory as *a means of acquiring power and influence* in human affairs? Does the theorist emphasize the function of theory as the *specification of preferred views* about the nature, condition and destiny of man? Or does he emphasize the need for *empirically meaningful knowledge of human behavior* in politics, insisting that such knowledge be expressed as general propositions that explain political behavior and institutions in terms of observable, testable concepts and data? The seeker of knowledge in terms of idealized value-systems we call a *philosopher;* the seeker of power in the name of a preferred system of social and economic relations may be labeled an *ideologue;* the sceptical realist who tries to explain political behavior in terms of testable concepts and hypothetical rules by which events observably occur we call a *scientist;* and the man who commits himself to influencing events on the basis of his personal skill in assessing the effective determinants of public action we call a *policy-maker* (see Figure 6). The remainder of this chapter seeks to analyze the kinds of political theorizing typical of these four categories of theorists.

Figure 6

Classification of Political Theorists, By Two Criteria of Theoretical Activity

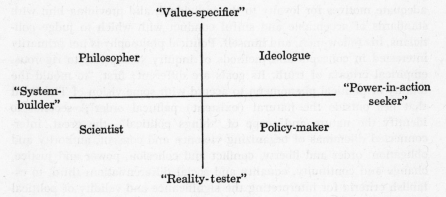

"Value-specifier"

Philosopher   Ideologue

"System-builder"   "Power-in-action seeker"

Scientist   Policy-maker

"Reality-tester"

Systematic Political Philosophy

Political theory—the most inclusive term for political thinking—includes the philosophy, the science, and the art of politics. Political philosophy consists, first, of critical analysis of basic assumptions about political society, institutions, and behavior and, second, of the elaboration of systems of political belief and organization consistent with specified priorities among human ends attainable through government. The philosopher develops criteria for his idealized political system by deriving them logically from a few basic conceptions of the nature, condition, and destiny of man. In modern times, political philosophers have concentrated more upon analysis than on system-building, more upon methodology and textual criticism than on the formulation of new concepts. But the classical tradition of philosophical treatises on human nature, society and the state (such as Plato's *Republic,* Aristotle's *Politics,* Hobbes's *Leviathan,* Rousseau's *Social Contract,* and Hegel's *Philosophy of Right*) has been carried on in such twentieth-century works as Catlin's *Systematic Politics*, Garner's *Political Science and Government*, Merriam's *Political Power*, Barker's *Reflections on Government*, DeJouvenel's *Sovereignty*, and Friedrich's *Man and His Government*.

Relatively few philosophers succeed in writing great works on the theory of politics. What they succeed in doing may be highly important, but their worth is on a different level than that of "scientific" demonstration. Pedagogically, they classify the rich heritage of ideas that have been broached about politics, and provide a kind of cognitive map of the multitude of political vocabularies. Some important works in the history of political doctrines have been written as guides or manuals of political tactics for rulers (Machiavelli's *Prince* and the *Arthasastras* in Hindu political theory); others distill maxims of political "wisdom" or prudence from the experience of great politicians and statesmen. Political philosophies have performed the important function of legitimizing present and potential systems of political organization, furnishing adequate motives for loyalty to the individual, and providing him with standards of acceptable and sinful conduct with which to judge politicians, his fellow-men, and himself. Political philosophy is not primarily interested in concepts and methods of inquiry susceptible to rigorous, empirical criteria of truth. Its goals are different: first, "to mould the totality of political phenomena to accord with some vision of The Good that lies outside the natural (existent) political order";[1] second, to identify the nature and scope of "things political"—the great, interconnected dilemmas of organizing violence and consent, authority and obligation, order and liberty, conflict and cohesion, power and justice, change and continuity, equality and social differentiation; third, to establish criteria for interpreting the significance and validity of political knowledge.

Insofar as the political philosopher tries to express statements of ultimate belief about man and his condition, the political thinker or student is in the position of choosing which one or which combination of philosophical "spectacles" he will wear to look at the political world. In a sense we are *all* Platonists, Aristotelians, Thomists, Machiavellians, and Marxists, to name only a few possibilities. Man seeks justice through social harmony (Plato); he is a member of a political community capable of achieving the Good Life (Aristotle); he wants to know what Divine Revelation requires of him through as much of divine and eternal law as his natural reason and spiritual authority enable him to discern (Aquinas). But man is also a seeker of power and reputation (Machiavelli); security and order (Hobbes); he wants liberty for self-realization and at the same time to protect his privileges and status (Locke); he wants equality and a sense of identification with his fellow-man, but he insists upon promoting his own satisfaction and that of his associates

[1] Sheldon Wolin, *Politics and Vision* (Boston: Little, Brown and Company, 1960), p. 19.

at the expense of outsiders, foreigners, inferiors, and enemies (Rousseau); he needs continuity and stability, yet innovation and change as well (Bentham). And finally, man finds self-mastery and freedom as he learns to adapt himself to necessity and conscientiously to accept the laws and conventions of his political community (Hegel).

Who can deny the "truth" and importance of insights like these? Man is the measure, but man finds himself through belief in something outside and beyond himself. The philosopher asks his question, "What is man?" and seeks his answers in terms of irrefutable statements about ultimate reality—irrefutable, that is, not in the sense that they cannot be denied but that they cannot be objectively judged true or false as a matter of experience.[2]

Ideologies: Philosophy in the Political Arena

No more than philosophies are ideologies concerned primarily with empirical tests of falsification and corroboration. But whereas philosophy is concerned with the status of propositions as coherent, logically related systems of knowledge, the test of ideological truth is whether people can be brought to believe the doctrine. Socialist thought provides an illustration of the difference. Marxist socialism called itself "scientific," and in *Das Kapital* and his other scholarly writings Marx produced a logically coherent, empirically supportable body of propositions about the influence of modes of production, economic institutions, and social stratification upon political power and organization. In other writings, notably the *Communist Manifesto*, Marx and Engels developed the same ideas into a value system, a program and a plea to the workers of the world to unite and to act in accordance with the class struggle, instead of being misled by capitalist propaganda and other non-scientific myths. It was one of the most significant efforts at political persuasion the world has known. Revisionist, Leninist, Stalinist, and Maoist socialism are similarly condensed assertions of preferred fact and belief about desirable forms of society and political organization. Their political significance, however, consists in their audience's "wish to believe," not in their logical coherence or empirical correspondence with objective experience.

It was Lenin who pointed out that the function of a political ideology is to impart belief, to provide a justification for faith, to galvanize followers into accepting the cues to action suggested by leaders invoking its name. In this sense, ideology is essentially similar to propaganda. Ideologies may be analyzed not only for their content, but also by the sociological composition of their mass followings, the survival needs

2 Compare Arnold Brecht, *Political Theory* (Princeton, N.J.: Princeton University Press, 1959) and T. D. Weldon, *The Vocabulary of Politics* (London: Penguin Books, 1953), with John Plamenatz, *Man and Society* (New York: McGraw-Hill, Inc., 1963).

of their leaders, and the psychological needs they satisfy for the per-sonalities of their "true believers."[3] An economist, Anthony Downs, has observed that ideologies enable citizens to "cut their information costs" —another way of saying that political symbols are vehicles for exploit-ing personal ignorance and subconscious mechanisms of non-rational inference.[4] Yet there may be objective elements of truth in different ideological orientations; their significance, however, lies less in their substantive content than in the purposes of their expounders, the needs and composition of their followings, and the psycho-social conditions to which their acceptance is a response.

We have distinguished philosophies of politics from ideologies of politics on the basis of their rationality or non-rationality of approach and method. Nevertheless a confusion remains, since both kinds of dis-ciplines are committed to a "world-view," a desired system of social and political relations with which its adherents identify themselves. The resultant confusion explains, in part, why twentieth-century political thought is often presented in terms of ideological rather than genuinely philosophical categories, with the implication that the individual or student must choose between anarchism, social Darwinism, liberalism, conservatism, syndicalism, socialism, communism, fascism, natural rights, capitalism, or democracy, as if such differentiations represented objective classifications of contemporary political reality. This road leads to the description of political systems in such terms as democratic so-cialism, totalitarian socialism, fascist capitalism, capitalist democracy, and "guided democracy"—analytically not much more enlightening than monarchy, oligarchy, democracy, and dictatorship.[5] If political action and organization boil down to nothing more than ideological warfare, we may well despair for man. Fortunately, political thought is restricted neither in conception nor in methodology to these alternatives.[6] To find the way out of such difficulties, however, we turn at least briefly back to the Greeks, Plato and Aristotle.

[3] B. L. Smith et al., *Propaganda, Communication and Public Opinion* (Princeton, N.J.: Princeton University Press, 1946); Eric Hoffer, *The True Believer* (New York: Harper & Row, Publishers, 1953).
[4] Compare Downs, *An Economic Theory of Democracy* (New York: Harper & Row, Publishers, 1957), with Graham Wallas, *Human Nature in Politics* (London: Mac-millan & Co., 1908) and Robert E. Lane, *Political Life* (New York: The Free Press of Glencoe, 1959).
[5] Compare William Ebenstein, *Today's Isms* (Englewood Cliffs, N.J.: Prentice-Hall, Inc., 1960), with Leslie Lipson, *The Great Issues of Politics* (Englewood Cliffs, N.J.: Prentice-Hall, Inc., 1960); C. Northcote Parkinson, *The Evolution of Po-litical Thought* (New York: The Viking Press, 1960).
[6] H. Eulau et al., "After Thirty Years: Political Science in the New Encyclopedia of Social Sciences," paper presented at the 1963 Annual Meeting of the American Political Science Association, Washington, D.C.

Approaches to Political Science

The attempt to establish systematic general knowledge about politics and government is one of man's oldest intellectual enterprises, established as a distinct discipline as early as the fifth century B.C. in Athens. Plato and Aristotle, and many after them, looked on it as "the queen of the sciences." In almost every succeeding age individual thinkers have set forth systematically and comprehensively what they thought was known about the subject. In the twentieth century the compilation and advancement of such knowledge has become the special concern of the professional academic discipline we now call political science. The term "political science" has until recently been used very broadly as a name for any and all attempts to propound comprehensive political knowledge, whatever kinds of question the seekers tried to answer. But many political scientists today reserve the name "political science" for continuous, collective, disciplined efforts by trained professionals to explain one particular class of the questions which have traditionally occupied inquirers after systematic political knowledge. We refer to the broader field, within which modern "political *science*" singles out one particular class of concerns, as "political theory." And we may understand the character, goals, and methods of "political science"—in the more precise, modern sense—by surveying rapidly the principal kinds of questions historically included in the broader field of political theory.

Political Theory as Ethical Inquiry: What Is the "Good State"? In *The Republic,* undoubtedly one of the most famous treatises on government in human history, the fundamental question Plato sought to answer was, "What is justice?" If men knew the answer, thought Plato, they could deduce from it the answers to such important but essentially derivative questions as, "What is the good state?" Similarly, Aristotle sought to answer the question, "What is the good life?" because he thought the state existed for the sake of "the good life," whereas other social institutions—the family, for example, or the economic arrangements for producing and distributing food and resources—existed simply for the sake of material living, or "mere life." Although Plato and Aristotle gave different answers to the question of what is ultimately or fundamentally good, both agreed that one supremely important task of political inquiry was an ethical one: to tell men what a truly "good" state would look like; and both assumed this could be done only if men knew first what "truly good" meant. This is not to say that these Greek political philosophers were interested in no other political questions. But for both of them, all other questions were interesting and meaningful only if men could find answers to the basic ethical questions.

In all ages there have been political thinkers who, like these earliest political inquirers, considered their primary task to be ethical. Some reached essentially the same conclusions as Plato, others agreed with Aristotle, and still others reached quite different conclusions. A number expressed their views in a form similar to Plato's exposition in *The Republic*, that is, through a description of a kind of political life and government which never actually existed but which corresponded to the author's conception of what a "good" state should be. Such descriptions, when presented in considerable detail with attention to all aspects of political life, have come to be called "utopias," after the title of one famous work of this type written early in the sixteenth century by Sir Thomas More. A number of writers in the late eighteenth and early nineteenth centuries—Robert Owen, Charles Fourier, and Henri de Saint-Simon are probably the best known—offered other pictures of the "good state." Some writers have set forth their conceptions in the form of "anti-utopias," detailed pictures of what they consider the exact opposite of a good state, from which we can infer what they consider to be good. In modern times, Aldous Huxley's *Brave New World* presents such a picture, as does George Orwell's *1984*.

Most political thinkers concerned with the problem of the good state, have not, however, attempted to provide detailed pictures of it. Instead they have sought to set down general ethical criteria by which all political systems should be judged, or to establish ethical goals toward which all governments and all political action should aim. The philosophy of natural rights expounded by John Locke and others represents this kind of attempt. So does the political philosophy of Saint Thomas Aquinas, who sought to interpret human law and government as part of a universe built on four levels of law—eternal, natural, divine, and positive.

As was suggested in the Introduction, an important part of the study of political philosophy is examination of the different conceptions of "good," the different political values espoused by the political philosophers. We cannot deal with such difficult but important questions in the short space here.

Political Theory as Philosophy of History: What Is Man's Historical Destiny? Some men have assumed that human history, and therefore the development of government and politics, follows some hidden law toward some predetermined end. Speculation of this sort, however, is comparatively recent in the history of political inquiry. In Plato's conception, for example, the ideal state might or might not be achieved on earth, and if it were achieved, might or might not endure. Political history for Plato, as for all other writers of his time and of centuries after him, followed no orderly sequence of predetermined steps and moved toward no predetermined end. Only after the eighteenth century, when Condorcet advanced the notion that societies and governments obey a law of inevitable "progress" did such a notion come to occupy a prominent place in political thought. Since then a number of writers, accepting the historicist assumption, as it is called, have sought to discover the predetermined end of mankind, the laws governing development toward it, and the way those laws operate.

Two names in particular are associated with this venture. Georg Friedrich Hegel found the law of historical development to be one of "dialectical" unfolding of a world of ideas,[7] in particular the idea of freedom, and saw the realization of this idea in actual human society as the ultimate end of man's historical course. (Despite the central place in Hegel's theory of what he called the "idea of freedom," however, his judgments and interpretation of actual politics and government in his own day placed him among the political opponents of those who learned about "freedom" from writers like Locke.)

Karl Marx also sought above all to lay bare the mysteries of historical development. For him the law of that development was a material dialectic (as opposed to Hegel's dialectic of ideas), expressed concretely in the constant struggle between exploiting and exploited classes and the great revolutions that periodically resulted from it. The process must inevitably culminate, he said, in a classless, stateless society—the ultimate end of human history. In the light of his understanding of such historical laws, Marx not only claimed to foretell the future of existing societies and governments but to interpret and explain the political events of his own time.

Political Theory as Psychology: How Does Human Nature Shape Government and Politics, or, What Are the Laws of Political Behavior? From the beginning political thinkers have been curious about such questions as how it happens that some men are rulers and others are not. Why do some rulers act one way, others another? Why do people one day happily obey the laws of their government but revolt violently against it the next? Almost never has anyone questioned the assumption that all men are equally human in *some* respects, and that their actions, therefore, reflect laws and principles which in those respects control all men's behavior. The discovery of such laws and principles would obviously tell us much about government and politics. In this sense, "behavioral" concerns have been central to political inquiry from its beginning.

Plato, for example, said that each human person is a compound of soul and body, and each soul a compound of three elements, "reason,"

---

7 "Dialectic" was the method of demonstration or argument used by Socrates—a process of give-and-take of ideas, in which each party to a discussion contributes ideas which are altered in the process of discussion to become part of the presumably truer or more complete idea emerging from the discussion. In Hegel's philosophy (oversimplified), the term "dialectic" refers not to the process of discussion but to the process of logical development. According to Hegel, a given idea (called a "thesis") logically generates its own negation ("antithesis") and out of the logical clash between the two there necessarily results a truer "synthesis." This synthesis becomes in turn a new thesis, starting the cycle over again. Thus Hegel sees the world of ideas unfolding "dialectically" through a succession of such cycles of thesis-antithesis-synthesis.

"spirit," and "appetite." He explained the varieties of political motivation among men, as well as the varieties of governmental form among states, in terms of the predominance of different elements of the soul in individual men, in the classes making up a society, and particularly in the governing group. Machiavelli's pungent and dogmatic assertions about how princes can acquire and keep power, at least as he expounded them in *The Prince* (1513), rest on fairly obvious, if not always explicit, assumptions about the basic, universal character of human beings. The Machiavellian conception of human nature was most effectively expounded by Thomas Hobbes in his *Leviathan* (1651), where it was grounded in a comprehensive materialist philosophy and then used as a starting point from which to deduce all general principles of law and government. According to Hobbes, all human thoughts are at bottom emotions or sentiments which can originate only in sense impressions made by external objects; all human actions are essentially responses (reactions) by the individual organism to these impressions—a response of desire toward those objects giving pleasure, of aversion toward those giving pain. Because there is no objective law to regulate human conduct in the conflicts inevitably arising from all men's pursuit of their self-interests—how could there be, if sense impressions of material objects are the sole ultimate source of all thoughts?—the chief aspiration of all men is for power over others, which alone can promise hope of gratifying their desires. Said Hobbes,

> . . . in the first place, I put for a general inclination of all mankind a perpetual and restless desire of power after power that ceases only in death.

Some modern political scientists, too, have attempted to set down the universal principles of human nature underlying all political behavior. The most notable modern effort to characterize "political man" is Harold Lasswell's, which incorporates concepts and principles from the psychoanalytical theories of Freud. In *Power and Personality* (1948), Lasswell describes the "political man" as one who, for reasons to be sought in his psychic history (especially in infancy and early childhood), has a low estimate of himself and his own worth as a person, who "displaces" his feelings of insecurity onto public objects, and who then rationalizes his activities in terms of "the public interest." He puts a relatively high value on power, as compared to other items on his own scale of values and to the value put on power by other people in his culture.[8] Without pursuing the implications, we might note that Lasswell's "political man," like Hobbes's, desires power; but whereas all people were equally "political" for Hobbes, for Lasswell there are radical and important differences among individuals.

Most modern political scientists are less concerned than either Lass-

[8] Harold Lasswell, *Power and Personality* (New York: W. W. Norton & Company, 1948).

well or the classic philosophers with laws of human nature or simple generalizations about the character of political man. Insofar as they directly utilize psychological insights into human behavior, most of them rely on findings by general psychologists about such particular aspects of individual behavior as perception, cognition, or learning, or on findings by social psychologists about socialization of individuals, role performance, group identification, and so on.

In any case, the study of human behavior is as important to the study of politics and government as it ever was. Our notions about how people act in politics can hardly be taken seriously if they are not consistent with established general psychological principles. Particularly if, on ethical grounds, we think people *should* or *should not* act in a certain way, it must be credible, given what is known about human behavior generally, that they can indeed humanly do what we ask of them.

Political Theory as Sociology: What Principles Govern the Structuring and Processes of Government and Politics? Until modern anthropologists became concerned with thoroughly primitive cultures, political study dealt with only relatively advanced civilizations, where an established, complex system of government—that is, an established set of political and social *institutions*—was taken for granted. No culture was known which was not governed, and government in all known cultures seemed "naturally" to be built of established political institutions and groupings. From the beginning, therefore, political inquirers have sought to answer questions about how various political institutions relate to each other, how the process of government varies as political institutions and processes are shaped by, and in turn shape, other social institutions— education, the family, religion, economic practices.

Aristotle's definition of a constitution as "the organization of political offices," his formidable research to compile descriptions of political institutions and practices in all the Greek city-states of his day, and his extensive discussion in the *Politics* of the consequences of different electoral systems, forms of organization, terms of office, and so on, all testify to the importance he attached to questions about political institutions. In our own day most Americans are aware of, if not familiar with, Montesquieu's ideas about the effects of climate, race, geography, and above all, manners and customs, upon political systems, as well as his analysis of the eighteenth-century British constitutional arrangements called the "separation of powers." Americans generally, like some American political scientists, have often shown a preoccupation with institutional reforms—witness the effort to change the exercise and distribution of power in American cities by adopting some particular form of government, or the attempt to affect the character of state government by redistributing seats in the state legislatures or changing methods of electing members of these bodies. A glance back at the chapters in Part One will reveal that much that is said there concerns the form of political institutions and the character of political processes in each of the systems considered.

Without doubt modern political scientists have devoted far more effort to examining political institutions and to describing and interpreting the way they operate than to any other class of questions. But especially in recent years they have paid increasing attention to the relationship between political and other social institutions and processes. What kind of educational system, religious institutions, or family life, for example, is essential to the effective operation of democratic political institutions? Or *are* there any "social prerequisites" for democratic government? Can the extent of government regulation, ownership, or other action in economic affairs be either reduced or increased indefinitely without noticeably affecting political institutions and political life? If not, what effects do occur, and how are they brought about? Even when they have not systematically sought answers to such questions, political philosophers, political scientists, and ordinary citizens have relied on assumptions about them in their discussions of government and politics.

Applications: Political Theory and Practical Politics. Political inquiry has historically been associated with a wish to resolve some pressing issue. But despite the variety of issues and problems that occasion political inquiry, the linkage of practical political concern to the more general kind of political curiosity has usually resulted in one or another of a few common conceptions of practical political knowledge.

Thus Plato's notion of an appropriate application of political knowledge might be described as the *art of law-giving (constitution-making)*. That is, Plato wished to accomplish long-lasting reforms in the structure of government and the basic legal framework of Athens, much as lawgivers like Solon and Lycurgus had earlier established patterns of government for Athens and Sparta. Many of the American founding fathers entertained a similar conception; indeed, most political philosophers have thought that political knowledge would include answers to the question, "In such and such a specific community, how should government be established and structured?"

Some thinkers have been more concerned than others with the day-to-day conduct of government, the continuing process of recognizing and solving the community's problems through appropriate governmental decisions and actions. Political knowledge thus applied might be called the *art of statesmanship*, or, as some scholars use the term, *public administration*. In the Middle Ages one of the most popular forms of political literature was the so-called "mirror of princes," a handbook of maxims, rules, and homilies for the guidance of rulers in their business of governing. Closely related to this medieval conception in general aim, though far removed in substance, are some modern conceptions of political knowledge as an *art of policy choice*. In this view (more preva-

lent among non-political scientists than among political scientists themselves), political knowledge should enable men to decide expertly and
objectively what policy is called for to meet any given problem, or which
of several proposed alternatives is preferable when a choice must be
made. Although the name is similar, the position espoused by some
contemporary political scientists who recommend that the discipline be
approached as a *policy science* is quite different. In this latter view the
function of political knowledge is not to choose or establish goals for
political action, but, given those goals, to identify areas where policy
decisions may be called for, to clarify the alternatives involved, and to
assess the relative feasibility and probable consequences of the alternatives in the light of relevant general knowledge about institutions, behavior, and processes. Some analysts would select problems and topics
for general, scientific study according to the utility of the prospective
fruits of study for solving the most urgent policy problems.[9]

The relationship between inquiry which attempts to answer specific
practical questions about the organization and operation of government
and that which seeks more general knowledge is the subject of some confusion and considerable disagreement. Some maintain that the kind of
wisdom and insight needed to cope with practical political problems
cannot be obtained from abstract and general political study; at the other
extreme are those who believe that "practical political wisdom" alone is
impossible, but that disciplined political inquiry, by providing answers
to the important general questions, can at the same time answer definitively all questions about the goals of policy and of government itself.
The issues here are closely related to those concerning the relationship
between means and ends and between "pure" and "applied" science (see
the Introduction). Without reopening these questions, it seems clear that
the more general questions described above have at least a certain
logical priority over the more practical ones. Whatever prescriptions we
offer for organizing government, choosing goals, and devising specific
policies, they can hardly be justified unless they are consistent with
whatever general principles we think should govern the behavior of men
and the working of society.

The Goals and Scope of Modern Political Science. Ancient as are its
concerns, political science as a distinctive and autonomous field of study
is a very recent creation, whose character and relation to other disciplines are still in a late stage of development. From the days of its
Greek founders until well into the nineteenth century, the subject
matter of political science was considered a branch of general philosophy; when history and jurisprudence emerged as separate fields of
study during the eighteenth and nineteenth centuries, both took over
many of the important political questions long pondered by philosophers.

[9] Daniel Lerner and Harold D. Lasswell, *The Policy Sciences* (Stanford, Calif.:
Stanford University Press, 1949).

The birth of modern political science, an offshoot of the disciplines philosophy, history, and jurisprudence, took place in the United States in the late nineteenth century; its symbolic (if not precise) birth-date can be fixed no earlier than 1876, when Professor John W. Burgess of Columbia University first began to offer a series of lectures on comparative constitutional law. This led in due time to the creation of Columbia University's Faculty of Political Science (including a separate department of government and public law), to the rapid growth thereafter of separate political science departments in other American universities, and to the appearance of professional political scientists like Woodrow Wilson and Abbott Lawrence Lowell both in the intellectual and on the practical political scenes. The American Political Science Association, founded in 1903 with 214 members, had grown by the mid-1960s to a membership of over 11,000 individuals and institutions. But political science remained a primarily American enterprise for well over a third of the twentieth century. Only in the 1940s, and particularly after World War II, did separate university political science departments and programs appear in numbers elsewhere; in many countries the academic profession of political science is only now beginning. One index of this process is the continuing formation of new national associations, now reported regularly by the International Political Science Association (itself created only in 1947).

Despite its youth, despite variations in outlook and method from one country to another, and despite the fact that for the most part political science is still a peculiarly American discipline, we can nevertheless make several general observations about its contemporary character. In one important respect its objectives are like those of its classical ancestors: they involve the search for answers to *general* questions about politics and government, presented in a systematic, comprehensive, logically coherent framework. That is, the goal of modern political science, as of most earlier political inquiry, is the accumulation of theoretical knowledge.

But in its conception of what such knowledge entails and in its methods of seeking it, modern political science differs in important respects from traditional political inquiry. Although some learned and capable political scientists dissent on this point, modern political science generally seems inclined to leave some of the questions once central to political inquiry to other disciplines. In their philosophical assumptions about the *kinds* of questions they should answer, and the way they should answer them, most (but by no means all) present-day political scientists are much closer to modern physicists and chemists than they are to philosophers of history or to modern metaphysicians.

Similarly, with respect to the specific questions they investigate and the methods they use, modern political scientists on the whole (again, with important individual exceptions) are closer to psychologists, so-

ciologists, and economists than to historians or students of jurisprudence. Indeed, a frequent question for political scientists today is
how does their subject differ significantly from psychology, sociology,
and economics? Is not political science now only a special branch of
sociology or psychology?

Two points are relevant to this query. In the first place, as the preceding discussion suggests, most social scientists today are not looking
for sweeping explanations of broad, philosophically stated problems;
they rather seek answers to limited questions about limited areas of
behavior and definable situations. The few cosmic questions of earlier
inquirers into politics have been superseded by nests of questions not
only more limited in scope but more precise and intricate—part of the
increasingly "scientific" character of modern social science generally.

In the second place, in keeping with this general scientific trend,
political scientists, sociologists, and other social scientists no longer
think of themselves as workers in exclusive compartments, each dealing with a set of objects and events which "belongs" to one discipline
and no other. It is now generally recognized that each discipline is concerned with different *aspects* of the *same* events and phenomena, and
that differentiation of these aspects is an operation performed in the
mind of the analyst, not a property of the events and phenomena themselves. Imagine, for example, the single event of a man's buying votes.
A psychoanalyst might be curious about the man's possible guilt feelings
or his emotional health; an economist might wonder how the price
of votes was determined; a social psychologist might inquire into the
context of groups and social attitudes from which the man acquired
his inclinations to such behavior; and a sociologist might be concerned
with the effects of the man's behavior on the group or community, as
well as about the structural character of the community one might
infer from such behavior. But the political scientist would be concerned
about the kind of government which seemed to result from the man's
behavior. Within this single phenomenon, each social scientist focuses
on those aspects relevant to the central concerns of his discipline.

Social scientists who have accepted this kind of analytical approach
have generally abandoned the notion of studying "the totality" of
human affairs, of developing holistic explanations that account for everything at once. Thus, in the example of vote-buying, we could not claim,
even after the fullest study by all the disciplines concerned, that any one
of them or all of them together enabled us to "know" the "whole man"
or the "total situation" in question. At the same time, modern social
scientists are aware that, because the basic phenomena of human behavior are the common subject matter for all of them, each may learn
much from the others. Thus political science has become decidedly
"inter-disciplinary": students of political science today must be con-

versant with the findings of sociologists, psychologists, and other social scientists, as well as with those of their own discipline.[10]

Scientific or Empirical Political Theory

We have pointed out that modern political scientists relinquish the philosopher's quest for an ultimate answer to questions about the nature of man, society and government in order to ask *limited, refutable,* or *verifiable* questions (stated as hypotheses) about how men behave in political situations, or how human events occur in sequence through time. A problem becomes scientific when it can be formulated in such a way as to test the main proposition asserted about personal or group behavior in a definable political situation. Usually the main proposition does not hold true under all conditions, so the political scientist must set forth subpropositions specifying the variables or factors which affect the degree of conformity to or variation from the general principle. Then his problem is to find relevant data and to organize them into categories and indices which enable him to test his generalizations. Another way of describing the scientist's way of asking questions is: "How much of the problematic behavior I am seeking to explain can be accounted for by the interaction of a minimum number of analytical (conceptualized) variables?" Let us examine several examples of the empirical theorist's approach as compared with that of the philosopher.

The first is taken from the field of voting behavior. The question of whether political preferences were "determined" by a man's social position (status) or his party loyalty (identification) used to be a matter of great debate. On the level of logical argument there was no way of resolving the dispute, and it took many years to demonstrate that if you

[10] It is highly desirable that any modern student of political science understand the breakdown in communication between the "classical tradition" and the "scientific-technological outlook" which was dramatized by C. P. Snow in *The Two Cultures and the Scientific Revolution* (New York: Cambridge University Press, 1959). A common background for comprehending the "classical" viewpoint would include the following titles: R. G. Collingwood, *The New Leviathan* (1942); Bernard Crick, *The American Science of Politics* (1959); Hans J. Morgenthau, *Scientific Man and Power Politics* (1947); Herbert Storing (ed.), *Essays on the Scientific Study of Politics* (1961); Leo Strauss, *Natural Right and History* (1953) and *What Is Political Philosophy?* (1959); Eric Voegelin, *The New Science of Politics* (1952). On the "scientist" side a minimum list would contain: Gabriel Almond and James Coleman, *The Politics of the Developing Areas* (1960; Arnold Brecht, *Political Theory* (1959); Joseph Bronowski, *The Common Sense of Science* (1951) and *Science and Human Values* (1959); R. A. Dahl and E. C. Lindblom, *Politics, Economics and Welfare* (1953), and *Modern Political Analysis* (1963); Heinz Eulau et al., *Political Behavior* (1956); Daniel Lerner (ed.), *The Human Meaning of the Social Sciences* (1959); V. O. Key, *Politics, Parties and Pressure Groups* (1958); Ernest Nagel, *The Structure of Science* (1961); Michael Polanyi, *Personal Knowledge* (1958); Karl Popper, *Logic of Scientific Discovery* (1934, 1957) and *The Open Society and Its Enemies* (1945); Herbert Simon, *Administrative Behavior* (1947); D. B. Truman, *The Governmental Process* (1951) *and* "Current Trends in Political Science," *Liberal Education,* (1961), 280–303; Roland Young (ed.), *Approaches to Political Science* (1958). For efforts to bridge the gap, see the works of Merriam, Catlin, and Friedrich cited above.

could get a man to tell you his party preference and degree of identification with it, it was an empirically better predictor of how he would vote than his occupation, income, religion, and residence (although these also would affect his political attitudes). But how does one account for a situation in which neither social status nor party loyalty explain the results of an election? In the 1952 American Presidential election, a striking shift in the distribution of the two-party vote occurred without any significant change in the demographic distribution of the population (by age, sex, race, occupation, income, or education). Furthermore, the increase in Republican strength occurred not only in every sociologically defined category, but in every shade of party identification (strong and weak Republicans, strong and weak Democrats, independents and indifferents). Political scientists at the University of Michigan's Survey Research Center devised a questionnaire which they administered to a national sample of voters. From the responses they devised measures of the way voters perceived (a) the two candidates, (b) salient issues of foreign and domestic policy, (c) party orientations toward specified groups in the population, and (d) the parties' capacity for managing the government. Without going into a detailed analysis of findings (actually, 85 per cent of the sample did vote in accordance with a prediction based upon the direction and intensity of their scale position with respect to these six variables), what did this study prove? It did not provide a complete explanation of how Americans vote or what the American electorate decided in 1952. But it did demonstrate that *under certain conditions, neither party loyalty nor social condition explains political preference;* and that (a) voter perceptions of the candidates' personalities and (b) voter awareness of broadly stated differences between the parties on specific issues are measurably related to election results.[11] Did anyone say "Obvious!"? Ask him how he would have proved *his* hypothesis on his evidence!

Another example is taken from the field of local government. For more than fifty years, from Lincoln Steffens's "muckraking" studies down through modern "community power structure" surveys, the popular hypothesis has been that effective political control is exercised by the *covert* dominance of influential people of high economic and social status who buy or pay political "bosses" and the *overt*, elected public officials to run things for them, or who in a number of ways (largely financial) exercise an effective veto over leaders occupying formal governmental positions based on popular majorities. A "case study" of the city of New Haven was deliberately designed to investigate the hypothesis that (a) the personnel and patterns of political control in local com-

---

[11] Donald Stokes et al., "Components of Electoral Decision," *American Political Science Review*, LII (June 1958), 367–87; Angus Campbell et al., *The American Voter* (New York: John Wiley and Sons, 1960), chap. 4. For findings of other studies, see S. M. Lipset, *Political Man* (New York: Doubleday & Company, 1960), and V. O. Key, *Public Opinion and American Democracy* (New York: Alfred A. Knopf, 1961).

munities vary by issue, that is, the effective power structure in the field of nominations and elections differs from that in the fields of public education and urban redevelopment and that (*b*) the personnel and patterns of political control vary over time. This study found four different patterns of political control operating in New Haven over a fifteen-year period, some successively, some concurrently; and not one of these conformed to the pattern of the covert, invisible economic oligarchy called for by the old hypothesis.[12] Note that the basic assumption of authority-and-power relationships was not refuted; it was the social categories and the mechanisms of exercising power predicted by the old hypothesis that were found to be absent or inaccurate.

The difference between the philosopher and the scientist may also be illustrated in the field of political representation and the legislative process. The typical starting point of inquiry used to be: "How should the representative act; by what criterion or norm should he guide his decision?" The eighteenth-century English theorist (and politician) Edmund Burke suggested that the representative is faced with the dilemma of voting on the basis of directions from and promises to his constituency, in which case he is a *delegate*, or he may rise to a national, general, or humanitarian conception of the public interest, in which case he is responsible for using his own judgment as a *trustee* of the common good. The German sociologist Max Weber proposed that the politician acts from a personal conception of right public purpose in reaching decisions about what should be done: either he may be guided by an *absolute ethic of moral principle*, or he may consider his duty to pursue that conception of public good which he can discern from anticipation of the consequences of his decision—an *ethic of responsibility*.

Both these distinctions are an aid to thought, and it is no valid criticism of either position to say that a legislator may rationalize his decision on the basis of *both* the narrow and the broad constituency, or of *both* abstract moral principle and responsibility for consequences. What the empirical theorist wants to know is how legislators actually do make up their minds, and what general principles actually explain legislative votes. There are several ways of doing this. One is to make statistical analyses of roll call votes, comparing the votes on different issues with such variables as each legislator's party affiliation, exposure to constituency pressures, alignment with respect to interest group attitudes, position of influence in the legislative structure, and so on. Another is to make case studies of particular bills or particular committees. Some studies interpret legislatures as arenas of conflict between interest groups; others conceive the law-making process as the result of outside pressure from party officials, interest groups, constituencies, administrative agencies, and executives. Recently, there have been efforts to study

[12] R. A. Dahl, *Who Governs?* (New Haven, Conn.: Yale University Press, 1961).

legislatures comparatively as interacting systems of role expectations by the actors themselves, measured by the frequency of occurrence with which legislators (actors) perceive their own roles in relation to operative pressures—parties, the internal power structure of the legislature, constituencies, interest groups, and personal orientations toward politics —and the combinations which are more or less typical of different legislative systems.[13]

For a final example of scientific empirical research we turn to the field of political speculation, which traditionally has exhibited the most suspicion of and disdain for the idea that values can be studied empirically and quantitatively. Two political scientists were intrigued with the proposition that "democracy requires the existence of a large measure of consensus in society," and were impressed with the vagueness and imprecision with which the term "consensus" was used. They administered a questionnaire embodying five statements of general principle on the meaning of democracy and ten specific applications of these principles to a sample of citizens in Ann Arbor, Michigan, and Tallahassee, Florida.[14] They discovered, not very surprisingly, that while there was 94 to 98 per cent agreement with the general principles, there was quantitatively more disagreement than agreement among the respondents about the specific applications, and majorities expressed antidemocratic opinions with respect to half of the suggested "application" statements. Interestingly, the most highly educated respondents expressed the most democratic views, leading the investigators to conclude that democratic opinions are less a function of class or income than of greater familiarity with the logical implications of democratic principles. But the basic significance of the study was that it showed that "consensus on specific principles or policies is *not* a precondition of democracy," and that democracy may depend upon commitment to highly abstract symbols and habitual patterns of behavior rather than upon conscious agreement with specific policies.

To summarize, the empirical or scientific theorist seeks to state principles and generalizations (*a*) in terms that can be objectively and statistically tested by the behavior of human beings in definable situations, rather than in terms of prescriptive norms and alternatives of moral choice, and (*b*) in the form of explicit assumptions and logically derived hypotheses, to the end that empirical investigations can as far as possible be systematically related to established propositions of knowledge.

13 J. C. Wahlke et al., *The Legislative System* (New York: John Wiley and Sons, 1962); Julius Turner, *Party and Constituency* (Baltimore: Johns Hopkins University Press, 1951); D. B. Truman, *The Congressional Party* (New York: John Wiley and Sons, 1959); Duncan McRae, *Dimensions of Congressional Voting* (Berkeley, Calif.: University of California Press, 1958); D. R. Matthews, *U.S. Senators and Their World* (Chapel Hill, N.C.: University of North Carolina Press, 1960).
14 J. W. Prothro and C. M. Grigg, "Fundamental Principles of Democracy: Bases of Agreement and Disagreement," *Journal of Politics*, XXII (May 1960), 276–94.

Political Evaluation and Choice

The last kind of political theorizing we shall discuss may be called "applied theory," or practical political thought. It should first be noted that political thinking in practical policy-making or decision-making situations is not necessarily different from philosophizing, scientific analysis, or ideological thinking. For instance, if a man bases all his political actions upon a particular conception of "the best form of government" or a doctrine of "who is best fitted to rule," he would be engaging in philosophical or ideological thought, and simply (some would say naïvely) trying to make his acts conform to his theories. But the voter, the candidate, the legislator, the administrator, or the judge usually have more immediate, complex considerations in mind when they are called upon to make decisions. Most controversial political questions cannot be decided upon such a simple level of generality; philosophical and ideological criteria are likely to be irrelevant to an appraisal of the problem at hand. For a voter to say, "I believe in democracy; therefore candidate X is preferable to Y" would in most cases be irrelevant or irrational. On the other hand, when "here-and-now" situations call for action, citizens and policy-makers rarely have the time to make a full-fledged research study to define the problem and to identify the possible value choices involved; and even if they did, scientific findings should not necessarily determine what should be done. Facts help to identify, shape, and limit the range of value judgments; they help the policy-maker orient himself more realistically; they give him ideas or grounds for doing something constructive or for rationalizing what he wants to do anyway. But in politics and human affairs, scientific generalizations about what is the case do not determine what decision-makers want or have to do. Law, custom, personal interest, or sense of right—any one of a hundred value premises—may interfere with doing what "the facts" suggest. Philosophical, ideological, or scientific thinking are therefore forms of preparation for qualifying oneself for practical political decision-making, but they do not finally tell one how to make up his mind.

If the philosophical style of thought does not establish a certain automatic guide to decision-making, neither does it produce a typical orientation toward political action. We could, however, predict with a high degree of probability that a person who believes in natural rights, natural law, and the perfectibility of man will have a different political orientation than one who believes in human sinfulness, depravity, and the necessity of an authoritarian ruling elite. The genuine philosopher's quest for "the good" is not easily hitched to the program or leadership of a particular political party; the philosopher is usually committed to larger questions, and his criteria of the best form of government are likely to be too general to be helpful in immediate situations. For example, John Stuart Mill's idea of the best form of government was "that which is best suited to its people"; James Madison's was "that which is least imperfect in terms of the conflict between 'majority tyranny' and 'minority rights'"; Plato's was "that society in which each class and function in society was occupied and performed by those persons best qualified to fill it." These criteria are not very helpful to citizens and public officials occupied with the problems of managing modern governments and making them responsible to the people, although they may furnish justifications for different preferences.

Ideologies pose a different problem. They provide preconceived formulas of belief and organization which predispose people to follow in practice the cues given by leaders in the name of the sacred symbols of the movement. Out of such doctrines and articles of faith the leaders of ideological movements produce answers to every conceivable question of political organization and statecraft. Given complete obedience, organization, and discipline from their supporters, such ideas-in-action become extremely powerful forces in politics; but unfortunately ideologies in real life tend to assume the character of totalitarian absolutes. Leaders of non-totalitarian ideologies, like liberalism, conservatism, and certain forms of socialism, find it difficult to adjust their world-views to the complex facts of technology, economics, and the possibilities of partial adjustments among opposing political views. The people, with rising standards of living and education, begin to turn away from utopian dreams to the difficult enough here-and-now problems of employment, education, housing, urban planning, cultural and recreational development. Insofar as they do this, ideological thinking seems to become less relevant. Political action begins to take the more limited form of discussion within and between political parties, interest groups, and administrative agencies. Politics then becomes a process of coordinating and adjusting conflicting views between organized centers of group initiative, interest, and power *within* the political system, rather than a struggle between rival political systems.

Some extremely interesting future prospects arise in connection with the harnessing of social intelligence and scientific research to politics and public policy-making. Of course, while the world has been assuming that politics is concerned with such matters as wars, diplomacy, elections, and disputes between social and economic classes, a tremendous amount of public policy and administration has evolved— policy dealing with such matters as public health and safety, natural resources, housing, transportation, production, prices, wages and conditions of work, money and credit, and mass communications. All these areas are influenced to a much greater extent than most people realize by technical and scientific knowledge; only since the dramatic discovery of nuclear energy and the inauguration of space exploration has the general public become conscious of the extent to which scientists and engineers provide the data and skills necessary for the resolution of public policy problems. The involvement of scientists has given rise to a great deal of controversy about how to harness scientific intelligence to the political processes of public decision-making. The problem, in brief, is how dependent are we upon technical experts, and how can they be controlled by the institutions of democratic politics?

The person who comes to political science expecting to be told how he does or should make up his mind in politics and public affairs may be disappointed to discover that philosophy is a way of asking questions, not providing final answers, that ideologies offering certainty about "the right attitude toward society and politics" are to be distrusted as guides to political action, and finally that even science is a way of organizing and presenting generalizations about what is rather than an authoritative answer to what ought to be done. Nevertheless, both natural and social-scientific intelligence does offer certain hopeful, helpful ways of approaching problems of political evaluation and judgment, regardless of whether one prefers to take a philosophical or a scientific position. Careful, focused, competent, and brief analysis, presented at appropriate times and levels of policy discussion:[15]

1. Increases awareness of available alternatives of action, including realization of false issues and "phony" alternatives;
2. Enables policy-makers to clarify in advance whether issues as posed can be judged in terms of the required conditions and consequences, and whether such conditions and consequences can be brought about;
3. Makes possible discussion of policy proposals in terms of:
   a. Alternative costs of different means of realizing the conditions necessary to make policies feasible (2, above);
   b. Whether means are compatible with objectives sought;
   c. Clarification of the respective values sought by the participants to the conflict, and the relative weight placed by each on the qualifying factors (costs) of their value-objectives;
4. Permits assessment of probable trends, and the possibility and desirability of modifying objectives in order to achieve limited or partial success in the light of what is likely to happen (rather than insisting upon exclusive realization of personal and group preferences);
5. Facilitates mutual understanding by parties to controversy of vocabularies and objectives sought, and enhances possibility of finding symbolic transformation of terms to permit partial, lim-

---

[15] For statements of the *conditions, uses,* and *limits* of political and scientific research in public policy-making the interested student is referred to such works as Daniel Lerner (ed.), *The Human Meaning of the Social Sciences* (New York: Meridian Books, 1959); Alfred De Grazia, *The Elements of Political Science* (New York: Alfred A. Knopf, 1951); R. A. Dahl, *Modern Political Analysis* (Englewood Cliffs, N.J.: Prentice-Hall, Inc., 1963); H. D. Lasswell, *The Future of Political Science* (New York: Atherton Press, 1963); P. Herring (testimony), Hearings before the U.S. House Subcommittee on Science, Research, and Development, *Government and Science,* 89th Cong. 1st Sess., 1965, pp. 429–46.

ited or substantial achievement of aims in light of evaluated costs and consequences of available alternatives.

Persons who expect complete solutions to political problems and controversies will find little comfort in the painstaking, difficult operations of relating research to realistic policy discussion. "True believers" may scent and scoff "compromise." In a world of democratic politics, however, which assumes the necessity and value of government through free discussion, full and fair presentation of the relevant facts, and access to these facts by opposing political groups—as well as the recognition of universal human interests of justice, freedom, and mutual survival—scientific attitudes and skills are likely to be a requirement. There probably always will be "utopian thinking" and idealized goals of desirable political and social relations. Such styles of political thinking make all the more necessary the trained capacity for assessing political reality and formulating the requirements for making the intervening decisions about how to get from here to there.

SUGGESTIONS FOR ADDITIONAL READING

(See also footnote 10, p. 594)

CASSIRER, E., *The Myth of the State* (New Haven, Conn.: Yale University Press, 1946).

EASTON, D., *A Systems Analysis of Political Life* (New York: John Wiley and Sons, 1965).

EULAU, H., *The Behavioral Persuasion in Politics* (New York: Random House, 1963).

FRIEDRICH, C. J. (ed.), NOMOS V, *The Public Interest,* and NOMOS VII, *Rational Decision* (New York: Atherton Press, 1962, 1964).

LINDBLOM, E. C., *The Intelligence of Democracy* (New York: The Free Press of Glencoe, 1965).

MARCH, J. G., and H. SIMON, *Organizations* (New York: John Wiley and Sons, 1958).

RUNCIMAN, W. G., *Social Science and Political Theory* (Cambridge, Eng.: Cambridge University Press, 1963).

SABINE, G. H., *A History of Political Theory* (New York: Holt, Rinehart & Winston, Inc., 1961).

SORAUF, F. J., *Political Science: An Informal Overview* (Columbus, O.: C. E. Merrill Co., 1965).

STRAUSS, L., and J. CROPSEY, *History of Political Philosophy* (Chicago: Rand McNally Company, 1963).

INDEX

THE AUTHORS

BERNARD E. BROWN, author of Chapters 4 and 7, graduated from City College of the City University of New York and received his doctorate from Columbia University. He has taught at City College, Michigan State University, Vanderbilt University, and the State University of New York at Buffalo, and is presently Professor of Political Science at Brooklyn College of the City University of New York. He has been a Fulbright scholar at the Institut d'Etudes Politiques in Paris and visiting professor at the Universities of Saigon (Vietnam), Delhi (India), and Dakar (Senegal). Professor Brown is the author of AMERICAN CONSERVATIVES *and* NEW DIRECTIONS IN COMPARATIVE POLITICS, *and co-author of* THE DE GAULLE REPUBLIC, COMPARATIVE POLITICS: NOTES AND READINGS *and* CASES IN COMPARATIVE POLITICS.

WILDER CRANE, JR., author of Chapters 5, 8, and 15 and co-author of Chapter 12, received the bachelor's degree from Carleton College, the M.A. from Harvard, and the Ph.D. from the University of Wisconsin-Madison. After study in Australia as a Fulbright scholar, he taught at Vanderbilt University before going in 1962 to the University of Wisconsin-Milwaukee, where he is presently Associate Professor of Political Science and Chairman of the Department of Political Science. He served in the Wisconsin legislature as an Assemblyman from Chippewa County in 1957 and 1958. Professor Crane is the author of THE LEGISLATURE OF LOWER AUSTRIA *and of numerous articles and reviews.*

THE AUTHORS

JOHN T. DORSEY, JR., author of Chapters 11 16 and 17, received his undergraduate and graduate degrees from the University of Alabama and also studied as a Fulbright scholar at the University of Paris. From 1953 to 1961 he taught at Michigan State University, where he was active in the University's Vietnam Advisory Group, serving both in the United States and in Viet Nam. In 1961 he went to Vanderbilt University, where he is now Associate Professor of Political Science. He has been visiting professor at the Fundação Escola de Sociologia e Política de São Paulo in Brazil. Professor Dorsey is the author of articles published in American and foreign journals and in edited collections.

ALEX N. DRAGNICH, co-editor of GOVERNMENT AND POLITICS *and author of Chapters 2 and 6 and co-author of Chapter 12, received the bachelor's degree from the University of Washington and the master's and doctor's degrees from the University of California at Berkeley. He taught at Western Reserve University before going in 1947 to serve as cultural attaché and public affairs officer in the American Embassy in Belgrade. In 1950 he went to Vanderbilt University, where he is now Professor of Political Science and Chairman of the Department of Political Science. He has held the Chester W. Nimitz professorship at the United States Naval War College and has taught summer sessions at the Universities of Montana and Alberta. During World War II Professor Dragnich worked in the Department of Justice and the Office of Strategic Services. He is the author of* TITO'S PROMISED LAND, MAJOR EUROPEAN GOVERNMENTS, *and of numerous articles.*

THE AUTHORS

BERNARD K. GORDON, *author of Chapters 9 and 10, received his bachelor's and master's degrees from New York University and his Ph.D. from the University of Chicago. Now Research Professor of Political Science at The George Washington University, he has also taught at Vanderbilt University and at Harvard. He has on four occasions traveled extensively throughout Southeast Asia, has held Fulbright and Rockefeller Foundation fellowships, and was visiting professor at the University of Singapore. He has been a consultant at the Naval War College and the State Department and a member of the Institute for Defense Analyses. In addition to articles and monographs, including "Civil Defense in Western Europe," Professor Gordon has written two books:* NEW ZEALAND BECOMES A PACIFIC POWER *and* THE DIMENSIONS OF CONFLICT IN SOUTHEAST ASIA.

DANIEL R. GRANT, *author of Chapter 3, received the B.A. from Ouachita College, the M.A. from the University of Alabama, and the Ph.D. from Northwestern University. Since 1948 he has taught at Vanderbilt University, where he is now Professor of Political Science. He has been active in studies of intergovernmental relations and has published numerous articles in this field. He drafted the original plan leading to the 1962 adoption of a single metropolitan government for Nashville and Davidson County. He has also been visiting professor at the Institute of Public Administration of Thammasat University in Thailand. Professor Grant is co-author of* METROPOLITAN SURVEYS: A DIGEST *and* STATE AND LOCAL GOVERNMENT IN AMERICA.

THE AUTHORS

AVERY LEISERSON, author of Chapters 1, 13, and 14 and co-author of Chapter 19, was graduated from the University of Illinois in 1934 and received his Ph.D. from the University of Chicago. He has taught at Princeton and the Universities of Chicago, Michigan, and Washington, and is now Professor of Political Science at Vanderbilt University, where he served as Chairman of the Department from 1952 to 1965. Professor Leiserson has worked for the National Labor Relations Board and the Bureau of the Budget, and was a public member of the Chicago Regional Wage Stabilization Board (1951–1952) and the Secretary of Labor's Advisory Council on Welfare and Pension Plans (1962–1964). He is the author of ADMINISTRATIVE REGULATION *and* PARTIES AND POLITICS. *From 1961 through 1964 he edited the* JOURNAL OF POLITICS, *and in 1965 was President-elect of the Southern Political Science Association.*

JOHN C. WAHLKE, co-editor of GOVERNMENT AND POLITICS *and author of the Introduction and Chapter 18 and co-author of Chapter 19, received his bachelor's, master's, and doctoral degrees from Harvard University. Presently Professor of Political Science at the University of Iowa, he has also taught at Amherst College, the University of Massachusetts, the University of California at Berkeley, at Vanderbilt University from 1953 to 1963, and at the State University of New York at Buffalo from 1963 to 1966. Professor Wahlke is the author of* THE CAUSES OF THE AMERICAN REVOLUTION *and* LOYALTY IN A DEMOCRATIC STATE, *and co-author of* LEGISLATIVE BEHAVIOR *and* THE LEGISLATIVE SYSTEM.

A NOTE ON THE TYPE

The text of this book was set in a typeface called Primer, designed by Rudolph Ruzicka for the Mergenthaler Linotype Company and first made available in 1949. Primer, a modified modern face based on Century broadface, has the virtue of great legibility and was designed especially for today's methods of composition and printing.

Primer is Ruzicka's third typeface. In 1940 he designed Fairfield, and in 1947 Fairfield Medium, both for the Mergenthaler Linotype Company.

Ruzicka was born in Bohemia in 1883 and came to the United States at the age of eleven. He attended public schools in Chicago and later the Chicago Art Institute. During his long career he has been a wood engraver, etcher, cartographer, and book designer. For many years he was associated with Daniel Berkeley Updike and produced the annual keepsakes for The Merrymount Press from 1911 until 1941.

Ruzicka has been honored by many distinguished organizations, and in 1936 he was awarded the gold medal of the American Institute of Graphic Arts. From his home in New Hampshire, Ruzicka continues to be active in the graphic arts.